Secondary Cities and Urban Networking in the Indian Ocean Realm, c. 1400–1800

D1569140

Comparative Urban Studies

Series Editor
Kenneth R. Hall, Ball State University

Associate Editors
James J. Connolly, Ball State University
Stephen Morillo, Wabash College

The Comparative Urban Studies Series encourages innovative studies of urbanism, contemporary and historical, from a multidisciplinary (e.g., architecture, art, anthropology, culture, economics, history, literature, sociology, technological), comparative, and/or global perspective. The series invites submissions by scholars from the fields of American studies, history, sociology, women's studies, ethnic studies, urban planning, material culture, literature, demography, museum studies, historic preservation, architecture, journalism, anthropology, and political science. New studies will consider how particular pre-modern and modern settings shape(d) urban experience and how modern and pre-modern, Western and non-Western cities respond(ed) to broad social and economic changes.

Titles in the series

Secondary Cities in the Indian Ocean Realm, 1400-1800 edited by Kenneth Hall

Secondary Cities and Urban Networking in the Indian Ocean Realm, c. 1400–1800

EDITED BY
KENNETH R. HALL

LEXINGTON BOOKS

A division of
ROWMAN & LITTLEFIELD PUBLISHERS, INC.
Lanham • Boulder • New York • Toronto • Plymouth, UK

LEXINGTON BOOKS

A division of Rowman & Littlefield Publishers, Inc.
A wholly owned subsidiary of The Rowman & Littlefield Publishing Group, Inc.
4501 Forbes Boulevard, Suite 200
Lanham, MD 20706

Estover Road, Plymouth PL6 7PY, United Kingdom

Copyright © 2008 by Lexington Books

All rights reserved. No part of this publication may be reproduced, stored in a retrieval system, or transmitted in any form or by any means, electronic, mechanical, photocopying, recording, or otherwise, without the prior permission of the publisher.

British Library Cataloguing in Publication Information Available

Library of Congress Cataloging-in-Publication Data

Secondary cities and urban networking in the Indian Ocean Realm, c. 1400–1800 / edited by Kenneth R. Hall.
p. cm.
Includes bibliographical references and index.
ISBN-13: 978-0-7391-2834-3 (hardcover : alk. paper)
ISBN-10: 0-7391-2834-5 (cloth : alk. paper)
ISBN-13: 978-0-7391-2835-0 (hardcover : alk. paper)
ISBN-10: 0-7391-2835-3 (cloth : alk. paper)
1. Cities and towns—Indian Ocean Region—History. 2. Indian Ocean Region—Civilization. I. Hall, Kenneth R.
HT147.I53S43 2008
307.76'3091824—dc22 2008022019

eISBN-13: 978-0-7391-3043-8
eISBN-10: 0-7391-3043-9

Printed in the United States of America

™ The paper used in this publication meets the minimum requirements of American National Standard for Information Sciences—Permanence of Paper for Printed Library Materials, ANSI/NISO Z39.48–1992.

Contents

Illustrations

Graphics

Photography Insert (between pages 258 and 259)

Maps

Tables

Illustrations

Graphics

Photography Insert (between pages 258 and 259)

Maps

Tables

Contributors

Charles Argo, Ph. D. Arkansas, Assistant Professor of History at Ball State University, studies the Ottoman-era Balkans and Ottoman ritual tradition. He is completing a book manuscript on the Ottoman *devşirme.*

John Chaffee, Ph. D. Chicago, Professor of History at Binghamton University, specializes in the social and institutional history of the Song Dynasty (960-1279 CE). His publications include *The Branches of Heaven: A History of the Sung Imperial Clan*, *The Thorny Gates of Learning in Sung China: A Social History of Examinations*, and *Neo-Confucian Education: The Formative Stage.* He is currently co-editing the topical Song volume of the *Cambridge History of China*.

Alexandra Green is Research Assistant Professor in the Department of Fine Arts at The University of Hong Kong. Prior to this, Dr. Green was Curator of Asian Art and Museum Director at the Denison Museum, Denison University, Granville, Ohio. She completed a Ph.D. at the School of Oriental and African Studies, University of London. Her catalogue of Burmese art at Denison, entitled *Eclectic Collecting: Art from Burma in the Denison Museum*, is being published in 2008 by the Singapore University Press. Besides researching the Denison collection, she has studied eighteenth-century wall paintings in Burma, and is the author of several articles on the topic. Other publications include *Burma: Art and Archaeology* produced by the British Museum Press. She has also lectured on Southeast Asian Art at the School of Oriental and African Studies, and was Curator of the Museum of East Asian Art, Bath, UK.

Stewart Gordon, Ph. D. Michigan, is currently a research scholar affiliated with the Center for South Asian Studies at the University of Michigan. He is a specialist in the history of India's Maratha confederacy; his publications include *When Asia was the World*, *The Cambridge History of India: Marathas, 1600-1818*, *Marathas, Marauders, and State Formation in Eighteenth-Century India*, *Robes and Honor: The Medieval World of Investiture*, and numbers of professional articles.

Kenneth R. Hall, Ph. D. Michigan, Professor of History at Ball State University, specializes in pre-1500 Southeast Asia and South Indian history. His publications include *An Economic History of Early Southeast Asia* (*Cambridge History of Southeast Asia*), *Maritime Trade and State Development in Early Southeast Asia*, *Trade and Statecraft in the Age of the Colas*; editor of *Structure and Society in Early South India* and *Maritime Diasporas in the Indian Ocean and East and Southeast Asia (960-1775)*; co-editor of *The Origins of Southeast Asian Statecraft,* and author of numerous professional journal and edited volume articles. He is associate editor of the *Journal of the Economic and Social History of the Orient.*

James Heitzman, Ph. D. Pennsylvania, currently divides his time between the University of California, Davis and Bangalore, India, where he is co-founder of *Nagara*, a trust devoted to urban affairs. His books include *The South Asian City, Network City: Planning the Information Society in Bangalore, Gifts of Power: Lordship in and Early Indian State;* he co-edited *The World in the Year 1000*; and has contributed numerous articles dealing with South Asian history, urbanization, and technology to professional journals.

Elizabeth Lambourn, Ph. D. in Islamic Art and Archaeology from the School of Oriental and African Studies, University of London, is a Senior Research Fellow at De Montfort University in Leicester (UK) and a Research Associate of the Centre of South East Asian Studies at SOAS. Her several journal publications are consistent with her research interests in the material culture of Islamic South and Southeast Asia, and the Indian Ocean world. She is completing her book *Coastal Perspectives & Mercantile Cultures: India, Persia and Arabia 500-1500 CE.*

Stephen Morillo, Ph. D. Oxford, June and Frederick M. Hadley Chair in History at Wabash College, is a specialist in pre-modern global and military history, c. 1000-1800. He is the co-author of a world military history textbook, *War in World History. Society, Technology and War from Ancient Times to the Present*, co-author of a world history sourcebook, and author of various articles on English and world history. He is editor of *The Haskins Society Journal.*

Jay Spaulding, Ph. D. Columbia, Professor of History at Kean University, studies the medieval Church in early modern Islamic Nubia, and the legacy of this tradition to the contemporary Arab Sudan. He is the author of *The Heroic Age in Sinnar, Kingdoms of the Sudan* (with R.S. O'Fahey), *Public Documents from Sinnar* (with Muhammad Ibrahim Abu Salim), *After the Millennium: Diplomatic Correspondence from Wadai and Dar Fur* (with Lidwien Kapteijns), *An Islamic Alliance: `Ali Dinar and the Sanusiyya* (with Lidwien Kapteijns), and numerous shorter studies in the pre-colonial history of northeast Africa.

Kenneth M. Swope, Ph. D. Michigan, is Assistant Professor of History at Ball State University and an instructor in the Norwich University Military History Program. He is a specialist in the military history of East Asia in the sixteenth and seventeenth centuries. In addition to several articles on late Ming military and diplomatic issues, he is the editor of *Warfare in China Since 1600* and author of *A Dragon's Head and a Serpent's Tail: Ming China and the First Greater East Asian War, 1592-1598.*

Charles Wheeler, Ph. D. Yale, Assistant Professor of History at the University of California, Irvine, specializes in the history of Vietnam and the South China Sea. He recently completed a book, *The Ecology of Empire: Hoi An Seaport and the Production of Central Vietnam*, on the impact of trans-oceanic networks of commerce, culture, and colonization on the expansion of Vietnamese socio-political norms during the sixteenth through nineteenth centuries, as this laid the foundation for modern-day Vietnam. His journal and collected volume writings address littoral society, political ecology, and piracy in early modern Vietnamese societies; ethnohistory and political identity in Vietnam's Cham regions; and the role of Buddhism in cross-cultural trade.

John K. Whitmore, Ph. D. Cornell, Adjunct Associate Professor of History at the University of Michigan, is a specialist in the history of Vietnam and early Southeast Asia. His publications include *Vietnam, Ho Quy Ly, and the Ming, 1371-1421;* co-editor of *Children of the Boat People*, *Essays on Vietnamese Pasts* and *The Origins of Southeast Asian Statecraft*; and extensive journal and edited collection articles on early Vietnamese history and culture.

Acknowledgements

This book is the end product of a closed conference on "The Secondary City in Global Perspective" hosted by the Center for Middletown Studies at Ball State University, Muncie, Indiana in April 2007. The conference was an outgrowth of several previous conferences organized and hosted by the Center for Middletown Studies, but diverged from those of the past that were largely focused on American cities by purposely addressing comparative global secondary urbanism. This conference was the result of my collaboration with James Connolly, the Middletown Studies Center Director, an American historian who specializes in the study of urbanism in the American Progressive Era, in contrast with my study of the pre-1600 era of south India and Southeast Asia. While Connolly is a legitimate urban historian, whose major publications focus on late nineteenth-century urbanism in America, I am above all a specialist in economic and religious history and write about the Indian Ocean trade routes and the economic and religious networking therein. My publications, however, have periodically addressed urbanism and urban networking inclusive of court-, marketplace-, and temple-centered urban centers. Sharing our knowledge of urban studies in our specialties, Connolly and I wrote a conference prospectus that intentionally challenged Europe and non-West specialists, whose previous scholarship had never directly confronted urban history, by asking them to rethink their sources relative to the issues of secondary urbanism. In part this project was an extension of work I was completing as a contributor to and editor of a collection on Indian Ocean maritime diasporas, a project initiated by John Chaffee of Binghamton University.

Connolly and I solicited our desired participants in the "Secondary Cities" conference from the spring to fall of 2006. Each contributor agreed to complete a paper draft for distribution to all the conference participants a month prior to the Muncie gathering. Each session of the 3-day conference, held at the E. B. and Bertha C. Ball Center mansion, included brief paper introductions by three contributors, detailed commentary by invited discussants from Ball State and neighboring colleges and universities, followed by discussions of the paper drafts. There were lively exchanges among the attending America, Europe, and non-West specialists, who addressed the inclusive "Secondary City" conference topic from their multiple perspectives, and their differing knowledge of applicable primary sources and urban studies, disciplinary, and regional literatures.

Selected conference papers that focused on secondary urbanism in the Americas and Europe are being published, under the editorship of James Connolly, as a special issue of the *Journal of Urban History*, which co-sponsored the conference with the Urban History Association. The papers that shared a common focus on the Indian Ocean and its peripheries were revised for this book during the summer and fall of 2007. Lexington Press, at the initiative of Susan McEachern, Editorial Director of History, International Studies, and Geography, Rowman and Littlefield, agreed to publish this collection. Patrick Dillon, Acquisitions Editor of the Lexington Press supervised the project.

In addition to indebtedness to the editorial and production staff of the Lexington Press, thanks are extended to James Connolly for his administrative leadership as the Middletown Studies Center Director, as well as being an ever-available source for discussions of paper content and clarifications and suggestions relative to urban history scholarship. Special thanks to Stephen Morillo, Kenneth Swope, and Alexandra Green, who agreed to evolve their initial oral presentations as invited discussants at the conference into publishable articles, which contribute world history, military history, and art history perspectives respectively that were not otherwise represented.

Under James Connolly's leadership, the Center for Middletown Studies was the principle source of conference funding, with major supplemental funding secured by James Pyle, Vice-President and Director of Faculty Research and Sponsored Programs at Ball State University. E. Bruce Geelhoed, as the past Director of the Center for Middletown Studies and current Chair, Department of History at Ball State University provided administrative advice and program support. Michael Maggiotto, Dean of the College of Sciences and Humanities, The Department of History, and the Phi Alpha Theta History Honorary Society at Ball State University were contributing conference financial co-sponsors. Thanks to the office staff of the Department of History and the E. B. and Bertha C. Ball Center for their support services. Elizabeth Miller, History Department Graduate Assistant, provided a variety of administrative assistance and coordinated the transportation needs of the participants. Amy Swope and Cynthia Nemser-Hall graciously entertained the conference participants at two evening receptions. Cindy also compiled the book index.

Michael Hradesky, Staff Cartographer at Ball State University prepared most of the maps in this book—and went well beyond expectations in transforming rough sketches and making map revisions requested by the authors. Jason Higgs, Graphics Designer at the Ball State University Teleplex Complex recreated the several graphic displays for this publication, and Don Rogers, Photo Specialist at Ball State University Information Technology and Photo Services transitioned color photographs into black and white masters for the final manuscript. Daniel Goffman of DePaul University and James Heitzman, University of California, Davis, with whom I have collaborated on past south India history projects, provided valuable critique and recommendations.

Kenneth R. Hall, Editor **March 2008**

Introduction

Kenneth R. Hall

Overview

Examinations of large cities predominate in the field of urban studies. Certainly there are finely crafted inquiries into the history, culture, and character of individual small cities. But there are relatively few of them in comparison to the abundant body of work on major urban settings. Most importantly, even those studies that focus on one or more smaller communities generally do not approach them as a significantly different type of community, and none has yet to adequately address diverse communities sharing a common Islamic or Buddhist heritage.[1] All too often models or interpretations that derive from research on the metropolis are applied uncritically to small cities. This book is intended to fill this void, by distinguishing small cities from their metropolitan counterparts as a subject of historical inquiry. This is done through studies of experiences among representative pre-modern non-Western communities sharing in the Indian Ocean trade and cultural networks.

The influence of modernization theories on recent studies of urban history is so pronounced that scholars overlook small cities and neglect pre-modern and non-Western urban settings. This book contends that both today as in the past, not only do small cities have different economic roles to play in comparison to the metropolis, but human experiences within them are markedly different. Their spatial arrangements, power structures, economic opportunities, and degree of cultural diversity distinguish them from major cities. They are different kinds of places—neither small towns nor major cosmopolitan centers. Prior to the rise of Western imperialism and the ascendancy of a global and consumer-driven economy, the people living in small secondary cities in the various regions of the world experienced such broad transformations as the emergence of global religious and trade networks before and during the early modern era, in distinctive ways. These collected studies consider how these particular pre-modern settings shaped human experience and how pre-modern non-Western secondary cities responded to broad social and economic changes. By defining small cities as a distinctive subject of inquiry, this book provides an important new dimension to urban studies.

Urban Studies Theory and the Secondary City

Many urban studies by historians and sociologists explore city life to understand the impact of modernization. Two broad interpretive frameworks for understanding modernization dominated twentieth-century social science. The first was the *gemeinschaft—gesellschaft* transition described by Ferdinand Tonnies in 1887. Modernization was understood in these terms, as the shift from face-to-face community to impersonal urban-industrial society. The loss of community and the search for ways to restore it dominated the agenda of social science from the late nineteenth century on.

One alternative theoretical construct deriving from social scientific research is Marxism. It envisions the transition from feudalism to capitalism and the formation of a working class as inevitable parts of social evolution. Variation from city to city matters less than these broad transformations, leading Marxist-inspired social historians examining individual cities to concentrate on class formation and related issues.[2] In both approaches, the city serves primarily as the site of modernization with relatively little attention paid to the ways that different kinds of cities or individually distinctive cities shape and define social experience in particular ways. Small cities that develop some but not all of the social complexity of the metropolis likely shape the experience of modernization distinctively.

Taking another approach, Western and Western-trained scholars studying contemporary urbanism in the Indian Ocean realm in the post-World War II era focused on the networking between large urban centers and villages, although with the common acknowledgement that intermediate urban centers assumed importance in the development of national cultures. These studies derived from the University of Chicago-based concern for the cultural interactions between the city and the village that shaped the interconnected concepts of Asia's "Great Traditions" and "Little Traditions."[3] In the 1960s, G. William Skinner's *Marketing and Social Structure in Rural China*, initiated a new trend in the study of the Asian urbanism, and what is called "central place theory," by proposing that China's urban centers and villages traditionally networked in a hierarchical relationship to the imperial capital, based more on bureaucratic than economic needs.[4] In a synthesis of these two approaches, the University of Chicago geographer Paul Wheatley defined Chinese, Japanese, Southeast Asian, and Middle Eastern urban space in his studies over the next several decades.[5]

More recent scholarship pays greater attention to cultural formation, to the production of social space, and to the importance of place. A variety of work by literary scholars, architectural historians, sociologists, planners, urban studies scholars, political scientists, and historians commonly address the origin of urban communities relative to movements of commercial commodities, confrontations between alien cultures; formation of plural societies, dual loyalties, and multiple affiliations, and as demonstrations of globalization. Taking their cue from post modernism, they present urban identities and forms as cultural constructions constantly in the process of being refashioned. Once again, these processes are likely to unfolded differently in smaller urban settings, where their scale, timing, and character is different from big cities.

The concept of space gained increasing currency in the last two decades of urban studies scholarship. Following the work of geographers and theorists such as Michele Foucault, Henri Lefebvre, and Edward Soja on the "production of space," urbanists approach space as something more than the background scenery for social activity. They examine urban social spaces such as neighborhoods, streets, parks, or markets as human creations with competing sets of meanings inscribed in them. By closely exploring the process of creating and defining these and other city spaces, scholars hope to better understand the identities, relationships, and experiences of city dwellers. But almost all of this scholarship looks at large cities, with little consideration given to small urban settings, where the process of defining social space may proceed differently.[6]

Geographer Dolores Hayden and others emphasize the importance of place in urban studies.[7] Charles Tilly established the parameters of this work a decade ago, when he argued that urban studies must explore the ways in which factors distinctive to specific times and places mediated the broad social trends associated with the rise of industrial capitalism and other national and international transformations. Cities, he argued, are "prime examples" of historically grounded contexts that contour broader historical patterns. They possess "recognizable street plans, distributions of stores, transport lines, labeled and segregated neighborhoods, configurations of political power, patterns of policing, and much more," all of which powerfully shape human experience. This approach requires "accounting for the creation of the setting's constraining features through interaction of local social relations and those that cut boldly across time and space. It entails tracing ways the constraints shape those local activities people pursue more or less deliberately. It entails following processes—job finding, courting, spending money, and more—in which where and when they happen strongly affects how they happen." In each of these examples, the characteristics of smaller urban settings are likely to differ substantially from their metropolitan counterparts that are the focus of most urban scholarship. Small cities were and are different kinds of places and should be approached as such.[8]

Secondary Cities in Global Context

While this book is certainly grounded in the noted evolution of urban studies literature, it explores secondary center networking, as this networking distinguishes secondary cities from the metropolitan centers. These collective studies explore the history of non-metropolitan urban settings during the late medieval and early-modern eras in the Indian Ocean realm, from the Ottoman realm and the African coastline at the mouth of the Red Sea in the west to China in the east. In that period all these non-metropolitan urban settings were in some way coming to terms with significant political and cultural change that was set in motion by the fifteenth-century globalization of the Indian Ocean world. The book features the research of scholars whose work addresses the representative history of small cities and urban networking in various parts of the Indian Ocean world in an era of change, and allows them the opportunity to compare approaches, methods, and sources in the hopes of discovering common features as well as notable differences.

Despite the differences of time and place, the secondary cities considered in this book do share common ground. They are all communities that responded to economic, cultural, and political developments emanating from metropolitan centers, and while these primary centers in various ways contributed to the secondary centers' potentials, the secondary cities in turn were vital contributors to the development of those primary centers, as the sources of resources, ideas, and/or the earlier foundational communities supporting the rise and sustenance of new metropolitan centers. The point is that networking between primary and secondary cities, within a confined space and in some instances over considerable distance, is by its very nature interactive.

These studies provide a window on the history and culture of an Indian Ocean realm that consisted of well-established and centralizing societies in the era in which Europeans were beginning to establish their trading outposts on their peripheries. This was an age of heightened international commercial exchange that pre-dated the European arrival, which in the Indian Ocean paired Islamic expansionism and political authority, and, alternately, in the case of mainland Southeast Asia, partnered Buddhism with new centralizing monarchies.[9] With the closure of the overland Silk Road in the fourteenth century following the collapse of the Mongol empire, the Indian Ocean provided the remaining vital link for wider cultural, political, and societal integrations prior to the Western colonial presence.

This volume results from a conference held in Muncie, Indiana in April 2007, sponsored by the Center for Middletown Studies at Ball State University. It was appropriate that the Center for Middletown Studies should host this event, and take the lead in internationalizing the study of the small city. Muncie, Indiana is a community synonymous with the study of small cities since the 1920s, when Robert S. and Helen Merrell Lynd came to Muncie as young researchers to study the community and complete what they called a "small city study." Their book, *Middletown: A Study in Modern American Culture*, achieved almost instant success after its publication in 1929 and engendered a large and continuing body of scholarship. Because of the work of the Lynds, Muncie remains a key referential base in studies of American urbanism, and the wider study of global urbanism,[10] and is the focus of three major follow-up studies, the most recent in 1998-1999.

The Conference's title, "The Small City in Global Context," emphasized the need to expand the field of urban studies by encouraging scholars of diverse global interests and specializations to explore the history of non-metropolitan urban settings from roughly 1400 to the present. This volume includes revised working papers purposely solicited from scholars who specialize in the 1300-1800 era, and most of the studies focus on the evidence of urbanism in c. 1400-

1600. The conference organizers charged these scholars, who commonly study regions that were in some way linked to the Indian Ocean, to address the small city experience as a distinctive subject of inquiry within the larger field of urban studies. Although there are remaining questions of whether the studies in this collection are specific to the existing framework of urban history, this is exactly the point. In most cases the studies are contributed by scholars whose previous work is tangential to urban history, who were encouraged to think of their sources in new ways that would provide innovative approaches to the study of historical urbanism. These revisions reflect the significant critical contributions of the several American and European nineteenth- and twentieth-century urban history specialists who attended the 2007 conference and who regularly publish in the *Journal of Urban History*, which was the co-sponsor of the conference.[11]

This volume's authors mutually distinguish small cities from their metropolitan counterparts as subjects of historical inquiry. One premise is that small cities fill an important transitional position between local communities (villages, towns) and major urban centers, as intermediaries in the diverse networking (economic, political, cultural) between the local and the metropolitan. Here, the small city is a creative force in bottom up and top down negotiations. Societal change depends on the small city as the center of transition, where critical localization takes place between the representatives of the traditions and commitments of local populations and the agents of the new economic, political, and cultural options that are being played out in the great cosmopolitan centers. What takes place in these secondary city negations will in turn determine the options of the societal elite in the metropolis. A second premise is that, if one assumes that secondary cities have the potential to become major urban centers, then small cities are important in historical and social science studies that observe the small city's evolution to metropolis stature. But small cities are also the product of failure, as a former metropolis that has devolved to secondary status, or a regional center that never achieved its lofty ambitions. In such cases one may study a small city to understand how populations deal with disappointment after previous success, or had not achieved expected success. Thirdly, secondary cities provide a local view of a society in a time of crisis, and regional windows into the undocumented realm of rural society. Small cities thereby provide a valuable window for understanding social, cultural, political, and economic processes from a distinctive vantage point.

Above all, the studies in this volume demonstrate that there is at present an incomplete understanding of the processes that have and continue to contribute to the successes and failures of urban societies over the centuries. While the overall scope of this volume is historical, the primary sources used in these studies of non-Western urban societies are linguistic, artistic, literary, and a diverse and intriguing selection of cultural artifact. These sources of urban history in the non-West are often at odds with what traditional Western historians are accustomed to using in their investigations, in that they intentionally convey cultural concepts appropriate to local values that are not "political" or "economic" in the Western understanding of these words. For example, traditional Western historians address the origin of cities with emphasis (and consistent with Western documents that place value) on the development of administrative capacity and/or an ability to engender market profits. Alternatively, many non-Western sources are more concerned with expressions of power that are based on an urban society's capacity to define and bestow social rank and sustain ritual performance, which in the local view unifies a society more than any bureaucratic administration or market function. This book's authors demonstrate how to read these non-Western sources accurately to gain better insight and appreciation of ideas concerning the origin and evolution of cities, and how urbanism was central to expressions of identity and interaction.

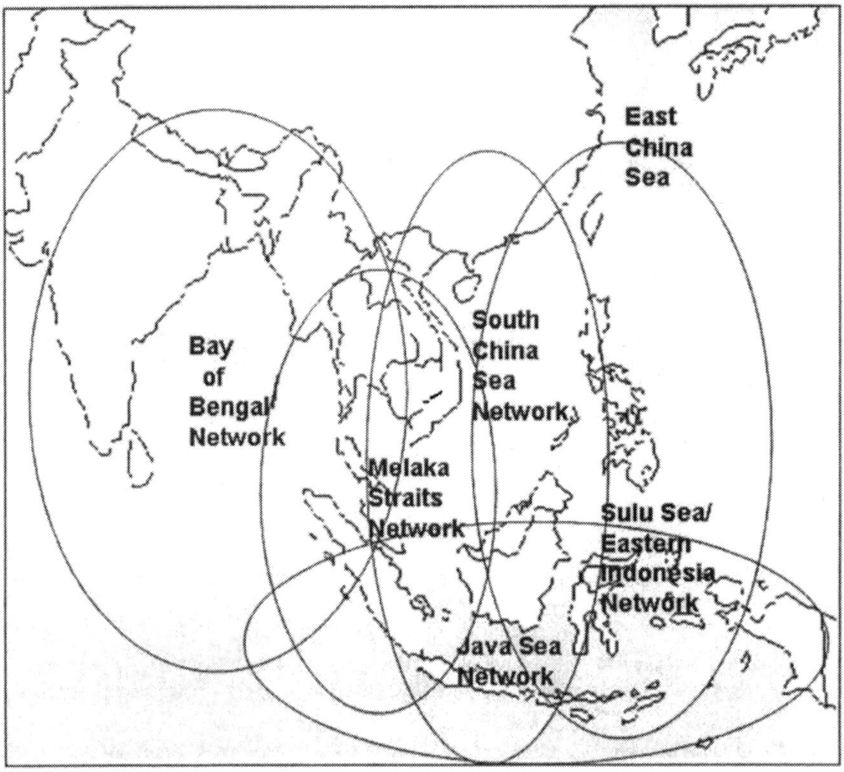

***Map 1.* Eastern Indian Ocean Regional Maritime Networks c. 1400-1800**[12]

This collection purposely focuses on the post-1400 era because the relatively small number of surviving traditional kinds of the historical sources for the previous 1000-1400 era (as discussed in several of the studies) makes it difficult to determine the general patterns or scale of urban networks; even in the 1400-1800 age the available sources still make it difficult to address the sociology of urbanism. These studies, in keeping with the initial Middletown studies by the Lynds, help to understand the sociology of urbanism and to refocus our vision on urbanization away from the fixation on that era's pre-colonial metropolitan centers such as Istanbul, Cairo, Delhi, Vijayanagara, Melaka, and Guangzhou, wherein the reality is that these regional primary centers depended

on a variety of secondary and tertiary urban settlements that were all linked in some way to the Indian Ocean trade (*Maps 1*, *2.1*, *3.1*, *4.1*, *7.1*, and *8.1*).

There is notable omission of statistically based analyses of early-modern era Indian Ocean urbanism, which is demonstrated in the publications of historians who have studied the detailed records of the various European East India trading companies.[13] This is because these statistically based studies center on European metropoles rather than their linked indigenous peripheries, where there are few reliable records available for statistical analysis. The well-developed body of social network theory helps to fill this void.[14] The study of networks avoids the problems of fully defining centers and peripheries. The evidence for linkages is direct, person-to-person, and not inferred; social networks involve actual people and their human connections across space rather than impersonal trends, and can be productively studied in small cities as well as in large cities.

Secondary Cities and Urban Networking in the Indian Ocean Realm

This collection begins with an essay by Stephen Morillo, a specialist in pre-modern global and military history and co-author of a world military history textbook,[15] who was asked to provide his overview reflection on the working papers. Morillo proposes several innovative conceptualizations of primary-secondary urban networking that are based in his understanding of the individual and collective studies. Morillo's thought provoking essay is meant to provide the reader with new insight into how it is possible to understand the experience of these small cities in new ways that provide greater understanding of just how they functioned and how their inhabitants interacted with the larger primary centers in an increasingly global order.

Jay Spaulding, a specialist in the history of the Sudan, follows with his study of Suakin, a small east African port city, as an example of an initially secondary port-of-trade that temporarily became a metropolitan center in the fifteenth century, due to its role as a customs outpost for an Egypt-based imperial regime, only to return to its prior tributary city-state stature in the sixteenth century under new Egypt-based Ottoman rulers. Spaulding's study has much to offer in its commentary on Saukin's role as a strategic market and pilgrimage center, and the importance of linguistic and ethnic distinctions that defined the local societal hierarchy and dictated coastal and port-hinterland networking. He demonstrates how these linguistic and ethnic differences allowed Suakin to remain distinct from the mainland cultures to its own economic and political advantage. As is the case among several of the other studies that follow, Spaulding is able to reconstruct the spatial dimensions of the Saukin port-of-trade from the writings of its early European visitors.

Elizabeth Lambourn, who specializes in the history of Islamic expansion in the Indian Ocean, studies c. 1300-1400 networking between Islamic communities resident in west coast India ports and the Aden metropole. Her study is based in a newly available set of documents that derive from the contemporary Yemen court. These court records list the resident Muslim communities that were provided material stipends in return for their faithful commercial and political linkage to the Yemen court, as specifically demonstrated in their statements of faithful homage to the Yemeni monarchy in the Friday prayers at their city's mosque. Lambourn demonstrates the value of these documents, paired with previously known geographical and travel texts written by Middle Eastern visitors, which allow her to identify and map western and southern South Asia primary and secondary urban centers and their communications networks. The Yemen court records also demonstrate the multidimensional basis for the networking among the urban-based Muslim diaspora residents in South Asia, and their continuing linkage to their Yemeni homeland.[16]

Shifting focus to the opposite end of the Indian Ocean realm, John Chaffee, a China history specialist, like Jay Spaulding makes a case study of the shifting fortunes of a single Chinese port city c. 1000-1500. Quanzhou transitioned from a secondary port-city during the reign of the Song dynasty, to become the primary Chinese port-of-trade under the Yuan, and then returned to being one of several ports-of-trade secondary to Guangzhou (Canton) under the succeeding Ming. While Lambourn's and Spaulding's studies work with fragmentary evidence to suggest the history of their regional networks, Chaffee makes use of the variety of sources available among the Chinese dynastic records to provide valuable details about the Indian Ocean trade, the dynamics of the Chinese port, and supports Lambourn's projections in his study of the fortunes of Quanzhou's resident Muslim trading minority. Here, as in several of the studies that will follow, there was considerable potential for an imperial presence and direct or indirect networking with the imperial court, to the benefit or detriment of the port-of-trade and its residents. Chaffee's study addresses changing dynastic policies relative to the Indian Ocean trade, wherein some rulers promoted China's commercial fortunes and others severely restricted them. Chaffee, like Lambourn, is concerned with diaspora networking, that of the Islamic diaspora and the origins of the Chinese maritime diaspora, and lays the foundation for Charles Wheeler's subsequent paper that considers the then well-established Chinese maritime diaspora in the late Ming era.

Kenneth Swope, a military history specialist, places focus on urban networking and the prominence of secondary cities in China's Ming-era military system. Swope reexamines G. William Skinner's "central place theory" model of early-modern China urban networking, and provides evidence of the military dimension of Chinese urbanism that Skinner omits in his foundational studies. Swope presents two detailed case studies, one on the coastal defenses the Ming implemented against a threatened late sixteenth-century Japanese invasion; the second shifts focus onto China's western frontier. In both case studies Swope finds that the Chinese military system depended on strategic secondary urban centers to provide the foundation for China's defense, whether against a national threat or local banditry and peasant rebellions that might escalate into a national concern. Herein Swope has a good deal to say about the imperial presence in China's cities, and the multiple roles of China's cities as networked bureaucratic, economic, cultural, and military centers. Swope also addresses the importance of cities as agents of Chinese civilization, specifically in China's frontier regions. In these areas previously dominated by semi-nomadic populations, state-encouraged migrations of Han Chinese agriculturalists followed the establishment of paired military colony outposts and new urban centers. These secondary cities and their resident commercial and gentry populations, together with assigned Chinese military and imperial bureaucrats, were the agents of imperial Chinese civilization, and acculturated the local populations into the Chinese mainstream. Swope demonstrates the importance and expectations of local initiative over immediate imperial intervention as foundational to Ming military strategy.

In his study of China's southern neighbor Vietnam, John Whitmore, a Vietnam history scholar, addresses the importance of ritual networking between Hanoi, the continuous imperial capital, and the fluctuating ritual centers of Vietnam's imperial clans from roughly 1400-1600. As Whitmore shows by his analysis of the Vietnamese chronicle and local records, in this age in which there were periodic transitions among several imperial clans, Hanoi's political prominence and functional capacity as an all-dominant metropolitan center was subject to the variable importance of these secondary "capitals," which were the regional clan centers of Vietnam's emperors. Whitmore demonstrates the value of ancestral celebrations in Vietnamese tradition, to explain why Vietnam's emperors were expected to make regular pilgrimage (which Whitmore translates as a "royal progress" accompanied by a considerable court entourage) to the sites of their imperial and ancestral tombs to reconfirm their ancestral commitments. Depending on the length of their stays, these secondary urban centers in their clan homelands temporarily surpassed Hanoi as the functional centers of imperial authority, although Hanoi remained Vietnam's bureaucratic center. As in Elizabeth Lambourn's discussion of Islamic ritual networking between Yemen and India and Charles Argo's address of ritual networking on the Ottoman frontier, John Whitmore's study provides a meaningful example of how rituals and societal artifacts, rather than economic and bureaucratic capacity, were a viable alternative basis for urban networking among pre-modern non-Western societies.

Kenneth Hall, a maritime South and Southeast Asia history specialist, highlights these ritual and cultural variables in his study of the transitional era in the global spice trade. Hall examines the records that document the networking among Southeast Asia's ports-of-trade c. 1400-1600, an age in which, due to increased opportunities in the international maritime trade, previously tertiary ports-of-trade became significant secondary intermediary or even primary metropolitan centers consequential to the Portuguese seizure of Melaka in 1511. Hall's study has much to say about the importance of the emerging Chinese, Malay, and Javanese diaspora communities of Southeast Asia as these relate to urban networking. He begins with a case study of the Melaka metropole prior to the Portuguese seizure, to summarize the details of Melaka's fifteenth-century urbanism. He follows with three case studies of the fluctuating fortunes and networked relationships of the post-1511 Brunei (northwest Borneo), Cebu (in the Philippines), and Banjarmasin (southeast Borneo) port-polities, as these were similar to or different from Melaka. Hall stresses the importance of cultural networking that provided the basis for linkage among regional primary, secondary, and tertiary ports-of-trade. He explores the potential to understand these networked relationships as being based in a hierarchy, heterarchy, or cosmopolis, but concludes with the alternative proposal that one must first understand the importance of human networking among maritime diasporas in this critical 1400-1600 era, which is a shared point also found in the conclusions of Elizabeth Lambourn, John Chaffee, and Charles Wheeler.

Charles Wheeler, a Vietnam history specialist, addresses urban networking in the Cochinchina region of southern Vietnam in the sixteenth- and seventeenth-century era that follows John Whitmore's study of the Vietnam north. Wheeler first addresses the establishment and expansion of the south China maritime diaspora, as a byproduct of the events described in John Chaffee's study of Quanzhou; when in the sixteenth century they became prominent residents of the former Cham settlements in the southern regions of Vietnam. Wheeler shows how the Chinese diaspora of commercial specialists prospered consequent to their ability to link and serve the interests of the expansionist Nguyen branch of the Vietnamese monarchy that was based in Hue. As in Lambourn's study of the western Indian Ocean Islamic diaspora, religious networking assumed a vital role in enabling this linkage between the Chinese maritime diaspora and the Nguyen court, due to the diaspora's role as the dedicated patrons of Chan Buddhism, in addition to their importance as commercial intermediaries dominant in Cochinchina's ports.

Wheeler points out that the Chan Buddhist monk's place in the Cochinchina markets and courts in this era recalls models of religious strategy in merchant diasporas and state formation in the early modern Western world. He considers the mutual benefits to the monarchs, monks, and merchants of establishing new urban centers in the Cochinchina upstream hinterland. In contrast to Kenneth Swope's study, in which military outposts paired with new secondary urban centers as the agents of civilization in the Chinese frontiers, in Cochinchina new urban centers developed around new Buddhist temples and their monastic compounds, which were financed by Chinese diaspora patrons in partnership with newly arrived Vietnamese gentry backed by the Nguyen court. As demonstrated in Lambourn's study, in Islam there was the potential institutional linkage between the elite religious leadership and local clergy. This same potential existed in Buddhism. Particularly in this age in Chan (Zen) Buddhism, there was an inherent institutional linkage between the hierarchy of Chan monastic authority based in south China and local subordinate clergy who tended to the needs of the Chinese diaspora and the diverse populations of Cochinchina. Wheeler asserts that Chan Buddhism provided a common religious doctrine that, when paired with the ambitions of the Nguyen monarchs to acculturate their frontier populations into a localized Vietnamese civilization, established the basis for stable religious, political, and economic communication among the newly networked secondary urban centers that were ultimately linked to the Hue court and its favored coastal ports-of-trade, which were dominated by the Chinese diaspora.

Alexandra Green provides an art historical study representative of small cities issues, and supplies the follow-up details in support of Wheeler in her documentation of the center-periphery Buddhist ritual networking relationship among Buddhist temples in seventeenth- and eighteenth-century Burma (Myanmar). Green illustrates the systemic uniformity of the Buddhist wall murals that are common among the predominantly urban-based Buddhist temples and monastic compounds that date to the era of the then Ava- and Amarapura-centered state. In tracing literary and religious traditions and religious concepts that were foundational to these artistic portrayals, she substantiates how the wall illustrations and accompanying iconography demonstrate commitment to the cosmopolitan linguistic traditions of Burmese Buddhism,[17] through the common portrayal of Burmese Theravada Buddhism's sacred literature in contemporary temple art. Herein primary and secondary urban linkages were documented by the uniformity of ritual expression as represented in the temple murals. These temple murals were integral to the development of a common sense of being Burmese, which centered on the twin concepts of salvationist Theravada Buddhism and the significance of kingship for social and religious well-being.[18] This was the same ambition of Cochinchina's Nguyen monarchs (as portrayed in Charles Wheeler's study), whose patronage of Chan Buddhism had similar expectations of achieving cultural uniformity in Cochinchina, to the benefit of the Nguyen monarchs and their allied elites.

Like Green, Wheeler, and others, Charles Argo, who specializes in the study of the Ottoman-era Balkans, stresses the importance of ritualized urban networking in the Ottoman realm—wherein the Ottoman Empire, as Spaulding documents in his study of Saukin, was a sixteenth-century Indian Ocean power.[19] As a follow-up on the themes of Green's paper, Argo also explores the importance of a secondary center's display of common ritual artifacts. While Green's study focuses on local temple murals that conveyed the periphery's acceptance of center-dictated uniformity, Argo's study highlights similar local acceptance of the center's ritual and its ritual attire in the Ottoman periphery. Argo argues for the symbolic importance of the center as periphery in the Ottoman *devşirme*, the ritualized levy and enslavement of young Christian subjects for palace and military service by the Muslim Turks.

Argo reports the periodic appearance of Ottoman agents sent from Ottoman metropolitan centers to the secondary localities in the Balkans, to receive and take back the local male youth designated for state service. The ritualized act of the transfer, as documented in written records and visual portrayals in contemporary paintings, was executed for all the public to see, and transformed what could have been alienating into a ritual act that renewed the center-periphery relationship. The *devşirme* sacred transfers involved the community's elders, civil officials, Orthodox Church authorities, and the families of the boys, all of whom relinquished their youth to Ottoman service in a ritual act that affirmed their periphery's membership in the Ottoman state. Argo, like many of the other authors in this volume, addresses the relationships between the dominant state lineages and their subordinate local lineages as these were played out in an urban setting. In Argo's study, the Ottoman state bureaucratic and military elite dispatched from the Ottoman metropolitan centers were predominantly urbanized Muslims, who stood in contrast to the populations of the Balkans periphery, where Christian agro-pastoralists were in the majority. Again, the *devşirme* ritualized transfer was the vital means by which an act that could have been alienating was transformed into a celebration of the Christian periphery's confirmation of their rightful place in the Ottoman state, centered in their Istanbul metropole.

Stewart Gordon, a specialist in the era of Muslim rule in north India, follows Jay Spaulding's and John Chaffee's studies of specific urban centers by providing an historical summary of the rise and fall of the north Indian city of Burhanpur from roughly 1400-1800. Gordon's discussion of the military origins of the city is reminiscent of Kenneth Swope's study of the similar importance of military outposts as the source of secondary urbanism in Ming China, and foreshadows James Heitzman's inclusive study of the importance of fortified urban centers in 1000-1800 India that follows. Burhanpur developed on the Delhi Sultanate-era periphery as a service center for the nearby Asir fortress of the breakout Farukhi dynasty. The fifteenth-century Burhanpur urban community consisted of a mixture of local populations and others who entered India from its northwest frontier; its early resident elite spoke mixtures of the Arabic and Persian languages. Burhanpur reached its initial prominence as a secondary administrative and market center under the Farukhi regime, when it was accountable for the taxation of the farming populations of its productive Tapti valley. Because it was also networked with the adjacent Malwa-Gujarat cotton production region, Burhanpur developed into a notable cotton weaving center. Its resident weavers produced high-end cotton textiles for elite consumption and for international export. Burhanpur's emergence as a primary administrative and economic center was also paired with its new role as a secondary religious center, the site of several significant Sufi shrines and a major mosque that were linked to that era's most prominent Islamic ritual centers. Its Sufi shrines were well-known destinations of Muslim pilgrims.

Burhanpur's fortunes soared when it became the Mughal capital in 1630, because of its strategic importance as a regional marketplace (with nine specialty markets) and its role as the staging center for Mughal military expeditions against rebels in the southern Deccan plateau. Gordon uses the accounts of European visitors to the Mughal court to account for life in the city during its prosperous seventeenth century. But Burhanpur's prominence was short-lived. Its fortunes radically changed when it was sacked by rebel Maratha armies in 1685 and 1698, and its stature as a Mughal capital finally ceased at the hands of Maratha warriors in 1750. It was never any more than a tertiary urban center thereafter.

In the concluding study James Heitzman provides his intriguing perspective on the patterns of south Indian urbanization from roughly 1000-1800. Heitzman explains the wider settings for Lambourn's and Gordon's studies, and ends with a view of the future of Indian urbanism, wherein coastal colonial metropoles were superimposed on India's traditional hinterland urban networking system. Heitzman asserts that modern standards of urbanization that are based in the size of an urban community are largely inappropriate to pre-modern India. Until roughly 1400 India's early urban centers were little more than large villages if one applies a population standard, but they can be clearly identified as primary and secondary cities on the basis of their urban function as the focal centers of cultural, political, and ritual networking.

Heitzman reports the recurring importance of fortified urban centers as the basis of "classical age" Indian urbanism, the disappearance of the fortified center as the agent of urbanization by roughly 600 in favor of ritualized urban centers, first Buddhist monasteries (as in Charles Wheeler's study of sixteenth- and seventeenth-century Cochinchina) and subsequently substantial Hindu temple complexes from about 800, and then from 1200 the reemergence of urban networking that was centered in new fortified centers. New technologies first supported the prominence of armies composed of a mounted archer warrior elite and then the spread of gunpowder-based cavalry and infantry competitions, which dictated defenses based in stone-walled and heavily fortified imperial cities. The refocusing of urbanism in fortified urban centers culminated in the building of colonial metropoles on defensible coasts that could be reinforced by colonial navies.

In documenting these evolutions Heitzman presents a series of representative case studies. The first focuses on the transitional fortunes of Kancipuram, still a prominent networked temple and textile weaving urban center near modern Chennai. Vijayanagara follows as the representative transitional imperial "central place," a ritual, commercial, and fortified urban center that at its peak in the 1500s had a population of roughly 500,000. At the end of the sixteenth century Vijayanagara fell to an alliance of Muslim warrior-states based in the neighboring regions of the southern Deccan plateau. Heitzman selects the fortified Bijapur urban center, at its peak in the seventeenth century a city of about 100,000, as representative of this new age. Bijapur assumed multiple regional (rather than Vijayanagara's imperial) "central place" roles. Beyond its military and political function, Bijapur was the regional center of trade, the consumptive center and central marketplace for the production of its linked secondary centers and the recipient of valuable commodities that derived from its overland connections to the ports-of-trade on India's coastline. Like Burhanpur in Gordon's study, Bijapur was also an important ritual center, as the regional center of Sufi/Islamic cults. Heitzman makes the important case that Vijayanagara's dominance as an all-powerful imperial center had discouraged significant development of populous secondary urban centers. In contrast in the Vijayanagara aftermath regional "imperial" primary centers were dependent in numerous ways on their networked secondary cities. Thus, he argues, India's regional patterns of primary and secondary urbanism that would continue until after India's independence developed in seventeenth and eighteenth centuries.

Heitzman uses his concluding study of Pondicherry to assert his view that India's ports-of-trade (as addressed in Lambourn's study) were historically coastal commercial appendages and centers of "foreign" residence rather than having a multidimensional prominence typical of traditional urbanism and urban networking in India's heartland. Thus the traditional Indian multidimensional city, whether under Buddhist, Hindu, or Muslim rulers, served variously as a political, military, and market center, coincident with its function in some way as a ritual center. In Heitzman's view, by the end of the eighteenth century the European rulers of Pondicherry had eliminated any remaining potential of this traditional ritual function. Pondicherry was exclusively a well-fortified urban center, which enabled economic extractions from the preexisting urban networking systems in the Indian hinterland by one or another of the European colonial enterprises that controlled it.

In sum, this collection opens the discussion of both the unique nature of the experiences and roles of small cities and how to use the kinds of historical materials that are available when quantifiable sources are few in number. It does not claim to be definitive, but is intended to encourage others to follow our lead in seeking new ways to understand the importance of secondary urban centers and their variety of networked relationships. This book is our attempt to bring together the existing scholarship on the ways of approaching urban studies, and specifically the small city, as a means to understand how the secondary city experience in the non-West was distinctive and how investigating it can lead to a better grasp of wider social, cultural, political, and economic developments in the pre-modern era.

Notes

1. See, however, Sheldon Pollock, "The Cosmopolitan Vernacular," *Journal of Asian Studies*, 57, 1 (1998), 6-37, for a conceptual model for the study of a "shared vernacular" among networked urban centers in pre-1500 South and Southeast Asia, based in localizations of common Sanskrit religious texts; and, for its broader application, Sheldon Pollack, "Cosmopolitan and the Vernacular in History," in *Cosmopolitanism*, ed. Carol A. Breckenridge, Sheldon Pollock, Homi K. Bhabha, and Dipesh Charabarty (Durham: Duke University Press, 2002), 25-53.

2. John A. Agnew, "The Devaluation of Place in Social Science," in James A. Agnew and James S. Duncan, *The Power of Place: Bringing together Geographical and Sociological Imagination* (London: Unwin-Hyman, 1989), 9-29. See also, Anthony M. Orum, "The Urban Imagination of Sociologists: The Centrality of Place," *Sociological Quarterly*, 39 (Winter 1998), 1-11.

3. Bernard S. Cohen and McKim Marriott, "Networks and Centres in the Integration of Indian Civilization," *Journal of Social Research (Ranchi)*, I (1958), 1-9; see also Burton Stein, "Circulation and the Historical Geography of Tamil Country," *Journal of Asian Studies*, 37 (1977), 7-26.

4. G. William Skinner, *Marketing and Social Structure in Rural China* (Ann Arbor: Association for Asian Studies, 1964). See, for example, Kenneth R. Hall and George W. Spencer, "The Economy of Kancipuram, A Sacred Center in Early South India," *Journal of Urban History*, 6, 2 (1980), 127-151.

5. Paul Wheatley, *The Pivot of the Four Quarters; A Preliminary Enquiry into the Origins and Character of the Ancient Chinese* (Chicago: Aldine, 1971); *From Court to Capital: A Tentative Interpretation of the Origins of the Japanese Urban Tradition* (Chicago: University of Chicago Press, 1978); *Melaka: The Transformation of a Malay Capital c. 1400-1980* (Oxford: Oxford University Press, 1983); *Nagara and Commandery: Origins of the Southeast Asian Urban Traditions* (Chicago: University of Chicago Department of Geography, 1983); *The Places Where Men Pray Together: Cities in Islamic Lands, Seventh through the Tenth Centuries* (Chicago: University of Chicago Press, 2000).

6. Henri Lefebvre, *The Production of Space*, trans. Donald Nicholson-Smith (Oxford, UK: Oxford University Press, 1991). See Janice L. Reiff, "Rethinking Pullman: Urban Space and Working-Class Activism," *Social Science History*, 24 (Spring 2000), 11-13, for a clear and concise summary of Lefebvre's approach. Theoretical work on space is extensive. Valuable works include Edward W. Soja, *Postmodern Geographies: The Reassertion of Space in Critical Social Theory* (London: Verso, 1989); David Harvey, *The Condition of Postmodernity: An Enquiry into the Origins of Cultural*

Change (Oxford: Oxford University Press, 1989); Michel Foucault, "Of Other Spaces," *Diacritics*, (Spring 1986), 22-27; and Gwendolyn Wright and Paul Rabinow, "Spatialization of Power: A Discussion of the Work of Michel Foucault," *Skyline*, (March 1982), 14-20.

7. Dolores Hayden, *The Power of Place: Urban Landscapes as Public History* (Cambridge, MA: MIT Press, 1995); Manuel Castells, *City, Class, and Power* (New York: St. Martins Press, 1978), and *The Rise of the Network Society* (Cambridge, MA: Blackwell, 2000).

8. Charles Tilly, "What Good Is Urban History," *Journal of Urban History*, 22 (1996), 702, 710.

9. Anthony Reid, ed., *Southeast Asia in the Early Modern Era* (Ithaca, NY: Cornell University Press, 1993); Victor Lieberman, *Strange Parallels: Southeast Asia in Global Context, c. 800-1830* (Cambridge: Cambridge University Press, 2003).

10. See Edhem Eldem, Daniel Goffman, and Bruce Masters, *The Ottoman City between East and West: Aleppo, Izmir, and Istanbul.* Cambridge Studies in Islamic Civilization (Cambridge: Cambridge University Press, 2005), which was the product of a previous Center-sponsored conference with specific focus on secondary urbanism in the non-West.

11. Representative papers from the Conference that were contributed by these urban historians, who specialize in the nineteenth century to present, will be published in an upcoming special issue of the *Journal of Urban Studies*, edited by James Connolly, Director of the Center for Middletown Studies.

12. See Kenneth R. Hall, "Local and International Trade and Traders in the Straits of Melaka Region: 600-1500," *Journal of the Economic and Social History of the Orient*, 47, 2 (2004), 213-260.

13. See, for example, Leonard Blusse, *Strange Company: Chinese Settlers, Mestizo Women, and Dutch in VOC Batavia* (Dordrecht/Providence: Foris, KITLV, Verhandelingen 122, 1986); and Gerrit Knaap and Heather Sutherland, *Monsoon Traders; Ships, Skippers and Commodities in Eighteenth-Century Makassar* (Leiden: KITLV Press, Verhandelingen 224, 2004). John Chaffee's study in this volume provides two charts that represent the statistical data available in the pre-1500 Chinese dynastic records. James Heitzman's concluding study, though not based in statistical analysis, demonstrates how the inscriptional, written, and newly discovered archeological records of the evolving seventeenth- and eighteenth-century Indian colonial city of Pondicherry are foundational to the statistical studies derivative of the early-modern era company and colonial records.

14. Like the majority of the urban history studies, contemporary research on social networks is confined to rigid quantitative data based on one-time interviews, as, for example in the journal *Social Network.* The original writings in the field, however, lend themselves to historical data that is not so easily quantifiable. See, for example, Everett M. Rogers and D. Lawrence Kincaid, *Communication Networks: Toward a New Paradigm for Research* (New York: Free Press, 1981) and Mark Granovetter's research on strong and weak ties, plus more recent research on networks of trust, degrees of separation, and dense connections, as in Mark Granovetter and Richard Swedberg, eds. *The Sociology of Economic Life* (Boulder, CO: Westview Press, 2001; Neil J. Smelser and Richard Swedberg, eds., *The Handbook of Economic Sociology* (Princeton: Princeton University Press, 1995); and Frank Dobbin, ed., *The New Economic Sociology: A Reader* (Princeton: Princeton University Press, 2004).

15. Stephen Morillo, Jeremy Black, and Paul Lococo, *War in World History. Society, Technology and War from Ancient Times to the Present* (New York: McGraw-Hill, 2008).

16. Two recent publications address the wider Indian Ocean networking of the Yemeni diaspora: Engseng Ho, *The Graves of Tarim. Genealogy and Mobility across the*

Indian Ocean (Berkeley: University of California Press, 2006); and Roxani Eleni Margariti, *Aden and the Indian Ocean Trade* (Chapel Hill: The University of North Carolina Press, 2007).

17. See Sheldon Pollock, "The Sanskrit Cosmopolis, 300-1300: Transculturation, Vernacularization, and the Question of Ideology," in *Ideology and Status of Sanskrit*, ed. Jan E. M. Houben (Leiden: E. J. Brill, 1996), 197-247.

18. See Lieberman, *Strange Parallels*.

19. Giancarlo Casale, "The Ottoman 'Discovery' of the Indian Ocean in the Sixteenth Century," in *Seascapes. Maritime Histories, Littoral Cultures, and Transoceanic Exchange* (Honolulu: University of Hawai'i Press, 2007), 87-104; Eldem, et al., *The Ottoman City, passim*; Anthony Reid, "Sixteenth Century Turkish Influence in Western Indonesia," *Journal of Southeast Asian Studies*, 10, 3 (1969), 395-414; and Reid, *Southeast Asia in the Age of Commerce 1450-1680*, vol. 2 (New Haven: Yale University Press, 1993), 116, 144, 146-149, 167, 221-222, 230, 285-286. Argo's study provides the potential for follow-up consideration of the Ottoman Empire's networking with Saukin, which, as Spaulding demonstrates, was a notable sixteenth-century commercial outpost on the Ottoman east Africa Indian Ocean periphery.

1

Autonomy and Subordination: The Cultural Dynamics of Small Cities

Stephen Morillo

Introduction

Analyzing the position of small cities in world history raises knotty methodological problems common to many areas of global and comparative history. Much of the uniqueness and individual texture that emerge in the local histories that form the necessary substrate of case studies for larger global analysis must be elided in the course of that analysis. Comparisons within such an analysis can only be productive if the terms and objects of analysis are, in fact, comparable.[1] The fact that "small cities" describes an impressionistic category—that is, that there is no readily agreed on definition of what constitutes a small city, as the range of cities examined in this collection demonstrates—further complicates any attempt to construct a systematic analysis of the historical experience of the specific places populating that category.

The case studies themselves, furthermore, may have very different foci and aims. An example drawn from this collection is that Jay Spaulding's article on Suakin gives us an almost paradigmatic portrait of a very specific and particular small city's world of economic and social connections,[2] while Charles Argo examines a cultural process, *devşirme* (the enslavement of Christian children in the Balkans by the Sultan's government) that operated through a host of small (as well as a few larger) cities.[3] Though the Ottoman periphery encompasses both, the differences between Suakin on the east African coast and the small Balkan cities where the *devşirme* operated are significant, extending from how close they were to the center, through the strength of administrative ties linking these peripheries to the center, to religious, cultural and even geographic and climatic disparities. The Ottoman periphery, in other words, could encompass a number of different sorts of worlds and, clearly, a number of different sorts of small cities. Extending our view across the breadth of the Eurasian world, from the Chinese coast, mainland and maritime southeast Asia, the Indian Ocean ecumene, the Mediterranean, and beyond, simply expands the range of contexts, political, economic and cultural, that small cities existed in, the number of worlds we must compare. Can these different worlds speak to us, through the studies collected in this publication, in a mutually intelligible way?

It is the argument of this overview essay that they can. I will attempt to show how, drawing on the findings of the research that follows. These various studies collectively can supply the elements or the material for an analysis of the cultural dynamics of small cities in world history, or at least the cultural dynamics of small cities in a pre-industrial world that was gone at the latest by 1900, and the death of which was clearly imminent a century earlier. Although I will note a few key questions and issues raised by the great transformation wrought by industrialization on the worlds of small cities, this analysis (and set of subsequent studies) focuses on the era before roughly 1800. But given that temporal limitation, this essay proposes a general analysis of small city cultural dynamics applicable to many pre-modern worlds.

The analysis will proceed in two stages. First, I present a structural analysis of the position of small cities within two intersecting but potentially contradictory webs of connection, one broadly economic and one broadly political. Like much structural analysis, this will view small cities analytically from the outside. But it will ground the second stage, in which I hope to show how these structural contexts shaped and were in turn influenced by the cultural dynamics that gave meaning to (or at times imposed it on) the lives of the inhabitants of small cities enmeshed in these multiple structural webs. It is here, I hope, that we can approach some tentative answers to the questions posed in the call for papers for the conference that generated these studies, in particular, "How did residents of [small cities] define their communities?"

Structural Analysis

Small cities could exist within two different sorts of structures, usually simultaneously, though at times only in one or the other, depending on the geo-political and economic position of the city. The first of these were **networks,** the second I will call **hierarchies.** Understanding the differences between these two sorts of structures and the ways in which they intersected is crucial to analyzing the place of small cities in world history, especially the cultural dynamics at work within them as they defined their own place in the world.

Networks

What I mean by networks are the webs of commercial ties that linked small cities to other small cities, to larger cities, and to the great world cities that formed the centers of gravity of regional and eventually global trade systems. Cities of all sizes formed the nodes of the network; the travels of merchants, facilitated by various means of transportation, created the links between these nodes. Such networks had a number of characteristics that are relevant to the cultural place of small cities within them.[4]

First, they were *horizontal,* or put another way, politically non-hierarchical. There were certainly larger and smaller nodes in the network, but the larger ones tended not to exercise direct political power over the smaller ones, especially

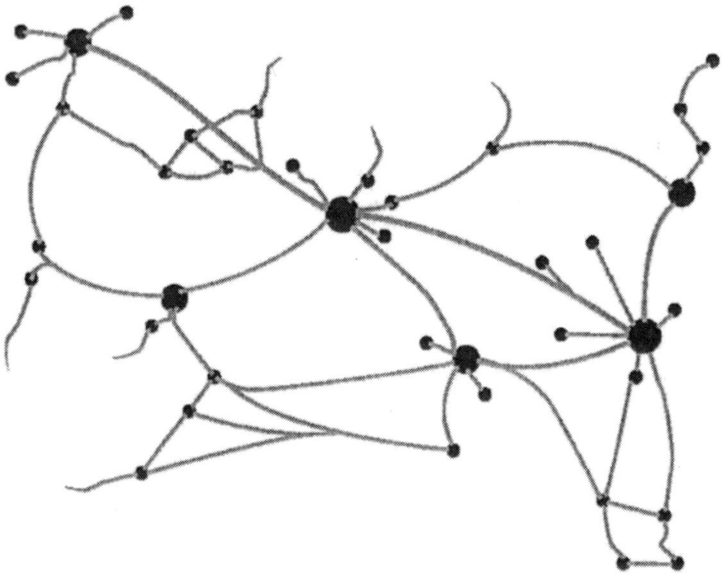

Figure 1.1. **Abstracted Networks**

when considered as network nodes.[5] Larger cities were sometimes also administrative centers for states, empires, or more generally the sorts of structures that can be called hierarchies, and so housed the administrative apparatus by which other, smaller cities might be ruled politically, but as such simply acted as the convenient locus of a function exogenous to their role within a network. Furthermore, no political hierarchy ever controlled all, or even anything like a controlling share, of the major global networks in the period before 1800. Many small cities existed outside the reach of hierarchies—Suakin before the extension of Ottoman rule to its area of the East African coast is a good example, and even when the Ottomans established a presence and created political ties between Suakin and the rest of their Empire, this African urban community was largely self-governing.[6] Larger nodes tended simply to act as commercial centers of gravity within networks. Their influence over smaller nodes was therefore indirect, mediated by market mechanisms, relative wealth, and the global flow of goods. Indeed, the size of the various nodes in these networks generally reflected their proximity to (or distance from) the main flows of the network, though some cities gained economic gravity, attracting a greater volume of trade, because they first grew as political-administrative centers in a hierarchy.[7] But such political boosts to a city's network weight tended to be temporary unless the city were also well-placed geographically in commercial terms, and alternate routes often existed, allowing the merchants whose movements constituted the network to bypass declining or obstructive political centers no longer worth the commercial investment.[8]

Second, networks were *extensive*. Connections between nodes, especially for many small cities, could be to other nodes that were relatively distant. Another way of putting this is that relative proximity conveyed no necessary political relationship, either between nodes of the network itself or between a node and its immediately surrounding hinterland. Here again Suakin provides a paradigmatic example: its dealings with adjacent mainland communities organized on a different socioeconomic basis—that is, as hierarchies rather than as an independent network node—were commercially mediated. Neither side tried to conquer or otherwise rule directly the other.[9] And many of a network node's connections were of necessity indirect; in concrete terms many of the goods and cultural influences arriving in a small city such as Suakin would have passed through one or more intermediate nodes in their journey from point of origin to endpoint in Suakin, and indeed Suakin was a transshipment point for many goods.[10]

Third, and fairly obviously from the previous discussion, networks were *urban*. System connections were between urban nodes. From any particular city's perspective, its connections were to other cities of a sort similar to itself, that is commercially based communities, as well as to the urban commercial markets that served large cities whose focus might be based on political and administrative functions. Conversely, the political connections, in particular, of a small city in a network need not have been to a rural hinterland and its primary production. The physical location of Suakin—on its own island, its settlement deliberately separated from the mainland—was emblematic of this bias towards urban organization and connections, as was Brunei, described by earliest Spanish visitors as a "a city all built on salt water."[11]

Finally, the urban nature of networks was closely connected to the fact that they were *economic*—and specifically commercial—systems. Resources entered these networks via economic processes, not political ones. As Spaulding says of Suakin, "The city-state was committed to the practice of commercial capitalism, supported in a subordinate role by certain forms of craft production and the appropriation of unusual natural resources."[12] Clearly, all of the characteristics of networks are closely tied together: economic commercial ties not only tended to be urban-based, but to reach out extensively to markets wherever they could be profitably found, even across long distances; trade established connections based on the mutually agreed exchange of value in the form of goods and money, which militated against hierarchical relationships within the system. Of course, some actors within networks were free to interpret egalitarian trade networks as hierarchical, as in the Chinese tendency to view incoming trade as "tribute," but such interpretations mattered far more for the internal politics of China than they did for the foreign trade partners of Chinese merchants, whether private or working for the Chinese state. They also highlight the differences in character of networks, on every point, from the other sort of structure that small cities found themselves enmeshed in.

Hierarchies

That second sort of structure is what I am calling hierarchies, and which are more commonly discussed as chiefdoms and states, or more generally complex hierarchical societies. *Figure 1.2* represents the shape of hierarchies as a pyramid. Hierarchies coexisted in varying relationships with commercial networks, and had characteristics that contrast with networks significantly in ways that created potential cultural tensions for small cities that found themselves at the intersection of these two types of structures.

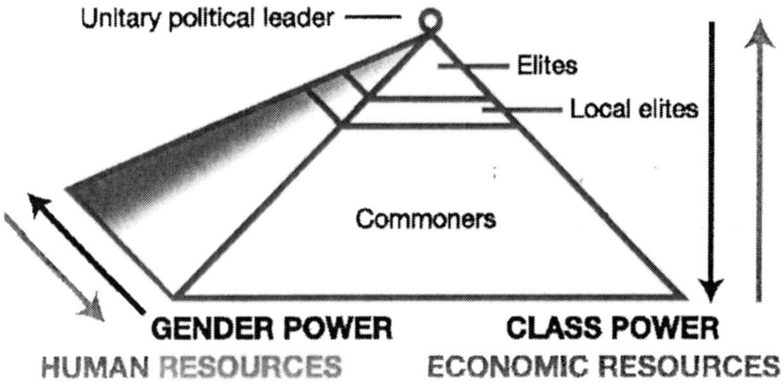

Figure 1.2. **Abstracted Hierarchy**

For starters, as the name of this sort of structure is meant to make clear, hierarchies were *vertical,* not horizontal. They had centers, down from which connections within the structure emanated, and back to which system flows returned, represented in the illustration by the apex of the pyramid. The center was not necessarily a physical place (though of course a center had to be in a physical place at any particular moment), but rather a person (e.g., a king) or more generally the people and institutions that gave the (sometimes symbolic) central person the ability to act as the effective center of the hierarchy. This center was, potentially at least, mobile, and indeed the physical location of hierarchies sometimes changed, with the secondary capitals of Vietnam as an example from the studies in this collection.[13] Measured in terms of political "size"—or influence and prestige within the hierarchy—the largest "node" in the organized system of connections that made up the hierarchy was at the top, or at the elevated and non-geographic center, and node size was indicative, indeed constitutive, of a node's place within the vertical hierarchy. Again, as at the top, "nodes" within a hierarchy, though they had to be in particular places at any one time, could be mobile, and the prestige and actual physical size (in terms of population) of cities or other settlements that housed nodes of the hierarchy was essentially a reflection of the prestige of the node it housed.[14] Thus, unlike the size and wealth of the urban nodes of a hierarchy, which resulted intrinsically from the city's geographic relationship (natural and human) to the flows that constituted the system, the size and wealth of cities generated by their relationship to a hierarchy was more extrinsic and mutable.

Second, hierarchies were *intensive* rather than extensive. Geographic compactness or connectedness was an advantage for the hierarchy as a whole and for any subsection of the hierarchy: proximity was usually the organizing principle for subdivisions of any layer of the hierarchy. That is, empires tended to be divided into provinces, which in turn were divided into districts, and so on, all of which tended to be compact geographic areas.[15] Where different organizing principles were enforced for one reason or another, as for example in Vietnam, in which the estates of the great nobility were scattered across the Vietnam landscape, this simply tended to reinforce the personal rather than geographic nature of the central "node" of the Vietnamese hierarchy, which was constituted in the royal court of sometimes itinerant kings.[16] At lower levels, intensive connections based on compact geography reasserted themselves, whether in great nobles' dealings with particular localities or in the organization of local government.[17] Connections within the system tended to be short-range, and to become concentrated as they rose through the hierarchy.

Third, hierarchies may often have been urban-centric in the sense that the people and institutions that made up the central node of the system tended to settle in what became capital cities, but hierarchies were essentially *rurally based.* This is because the foundation of every hierarchy consisted of the rural production, of both material agricultural wealth and human resources, of peasant communities. The system was designed to draw resources from the bottom up, that is from peasants, slaves, and other subject and dependent forms of labor, to royal courts, noble elites, and their urban entourages. This is represented in the illustration as the exercise of class power downwards, creating a reciprocal flow of economic resources upwards. The system was also designed to draw human resources from what the illustration of the hierarchical system shows as the "back" of the social structure to the "front." What this is meant to represent is the nearly universal gendering of pre-industrial complex societies such that the public sphere (i.e., the front of the pyramid) tended to be constructed as male (whether it was so exclusively being another matter), and the private sphere (i.e., the hidden, back face of the pyramid) as female, with female roles and spheres firmly subordinated to male ones, again at least in terms of the social theories dominant in such societies.

The exercise of gender power, like the exercise of class power, created a reciprocal flow of human resources consisting of both the largely unpaid or unrecognized household production of female labor and the generational reproduction of the workforce (again through female labor). Given the nearly universal tendency for pre-modern cities to be demographic sink-holes, with death rates higher than their intra-urban birthrates,[18] this reproduction of human resources was also, like the vast majority of economic production in agriculturally based societies, rural. Cities, even small cities, therefore existed in the upper tiers of the hierarchy, as the common locations of local and great elites. Indeed, cities, especially small cities, could form important articulation points between urban centers and rural hinterlands. As Charles Argo points out below, we may see the

Balkan city as a setting for the rare linkage between dynastic center and rural periphery.[19]

What this points out is that hierarchies were, finally, *political* systems, with "political" taken in its broadest sense as describing relationships shaped by the exercise of power (formal or informal) rather than the mutual, voluntary, and roughly egalitarian relationships characteristic of commercial exchanges and contracts. Resources often entered and usually flowed through such systems by political (coercive) processes such as taxes, rents, plunder, conscription, enslavement and so forth, and only minimally via purely economic ones. The Ottoman practice of *devşirme* that Argo analyzes stands as an excellent example of this sort of dynamic from a political-economic perspective; similarly, Jay Spaulding points out of Suakin's mainland neighbors that both Ethiopia and Sinnar were autarchic agrarian economies in which trade of any sort played a subordinate role.[20]

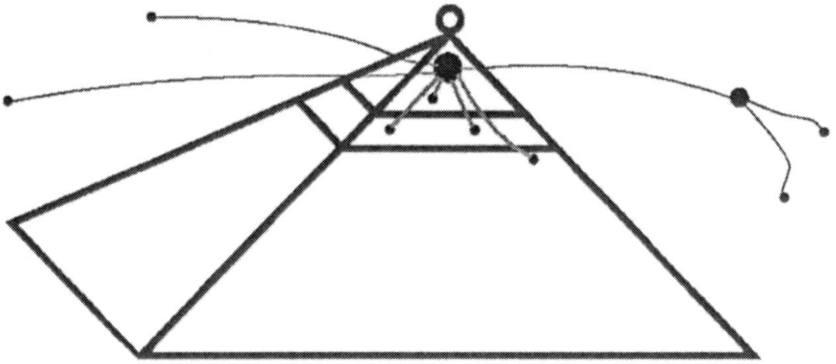

Figure 1.3. **Network-Hierarchy Intersection (1)**

Conflicted Intersections

Thus, networks and hierarchies were two very different types of structures. They could intersect in a variety of ways, from the perspective of the nodes within each type. *Figures 1.3* and *1.4* show, within the limits of two-dimensional representations of what should be visualized as a three-dimensional model, two general views of how the two types of structures intersected. *Figure 1.3* shows the horizontal connections of a section of a network passing through the pyramid of a hierarchy at the level of the elites. *Figure 1.4* shows a number of hierarchies occupying (or more accurately rising up through) a larger network.

Places such as small cities that occupied positions within both sorts of structure were subject to the tension of the conflicting demands of each. Managing and making sense of this tension was one of the key factors affecting the cultural dynamics of small cities in pre-modern world history. Indeed, the tension at the intersection between the two types of structures was potentially most intense at the level of small cities (as well as other sorts of secondary or peripheral nodes in each type of structure). Large cities were likely to be central in both economic and political terms for a number of reasons. Favorable geographic locations for major trade routes were likely to have corresponding strategic advantages from political-administrative and military perspectives.

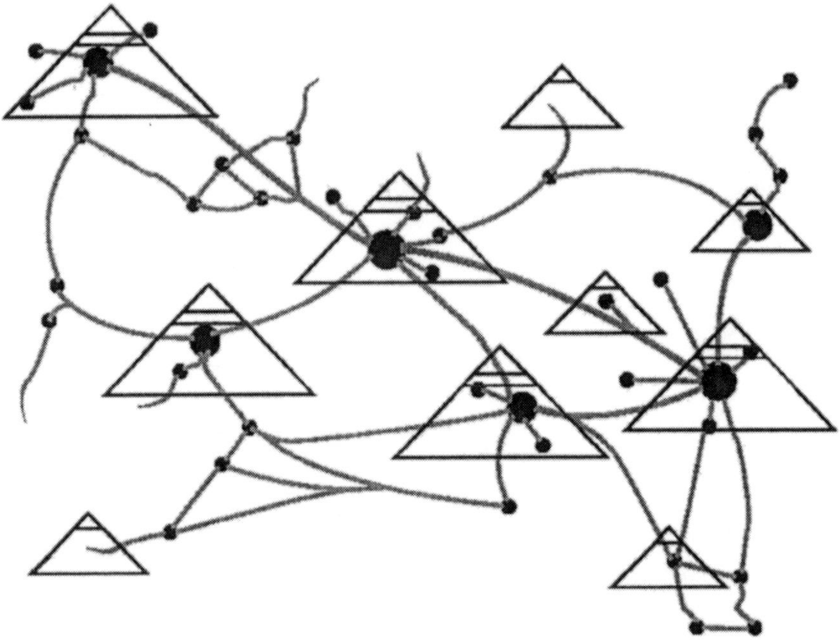

Figure 1.4. Network-Hierarchy Intersection (2)

Any large concentration of wealth and population built on favorable trade connections was likely to attract political attention and occupation; the exceptions, such as steppe-oasis entrepots like Samarkand, lacked the rural agricultural hinterland necessary for the existence of a large hierarchy, and so were not subject to the tensions of the intersection of the two types of structures. Conversely, any political center of significant size automatically attracted trade connections that served the interests of the elites who constituted the city as a political node. It was in large cities, in other words, that the intensive concentration of rural wealth effected by the upward flows of the hierarchy met the extensive distribution of wealth effected by horizontal network flows. Thus, political centrality for a city tended to reinforce rather than conflict with economic gravity. The flourishing of Quanzhou when it was occupied by the Chinese court, transforming it from substantial but secondary commercial city to a major network node, provides a paradigmatic example of this synergy between the central nodes of hierarchies and networks, as does the temporary rise to great Indian city status of Burhanpur under the Mughals.[21]

The commercial population of a large city may have faced somewhat more political regulation and subordination than they felt was ideal, but the compensation in terms of level of business activity and size and scope of market transactions available more than compensated for this in most cases. Where regulation of indigenous merchants was truly restrictive, as for example in eleventh century Constantinople or many Chinese coastal cities under the later Ming, the city as a major network node tended not to decline, but to see its commercial functions shift to the hands of foreign merchants segregated into their own manageable enclaves. Such segregation was an aspect of the tension between the political organization of hierarchies, designed to ensure stability and the continuation in power of established elites, and the economic function of networks, which militated against immobile stability. But it was a tension that, in the vastness and complexity of a large city, was often indirect, factionalized, and otherwise diffused.

Small cities, as secondary or peripheral nodes, by contrast, faced numerous tensions between their roles within networks and hierarchies when they existed at the intersection of both. Or more specifically, the elites, mercantile or traditional, that dominated the social structure of small cities faced these tensions. The key conflict was between their role in maintaining the extensive horizontal connections necessary to their prosperity, on the one hand, and the demands of their localized role in a vertical hierarchy. Put another way, they faced the potential contradiction between their economic and political roles in mediating the flows of resources in each sort of structure; as independent economic middlemen in market transactions and as semi-dependent rent collectors in coercive transactions; in short, between egalitarian participation in a voluntary network and subordinated participation in a hierarchy.[22]

Not all small city communities experienced these conflicts in the same way. Small cities existed at different positions relative to the two types of structures, with each exerting more or less influence on the lives of the cities' communities. Some, such as Suakin, were strongly tied into a network, but fell outside the influence of a hierarchy or were only within a distant periphery of a hierarchy. Small cities could escape the reach of powerful hierarchies by geographic good fortune, existing where conditions militated against large agrarian states. The example of oasis cities such as Samarkand has already been noted. Many of the cities on the margins of Southeast Asia and in the Indonesian archipelago analyzed below by Kenneth Hall also fall into this category, as do some of the small Muslim cities on the west coast of India examined by Elizabeth Lambourn. Some small cities escaped instead by occupying a sort of gravitational neutral ground between large hierarchies, able to play off the influence of one against another in order to escape domination by any.[23] Even the larger city-states and their networked subordinates, however, when viewed through the broader lens of global relationships, are more revealingly seen as highly networked small(ish) cities falling outside the strong influence of a major hierarchy. For example, a number of studies in this collection offer evidence that coastal and port cities were more likely to be networked outside of hierarchical control than inland cities could be.[24] For a city built on trade connections to make the leap to center of a substantial hierarchy necessitated that it be able to leverage trade wealth into the coercive force necessary to subordinate substantial rural hinterlands to itself in political rather than commercial ways.[25] Since most of the productive agrarian land available for hierarchy building in Afro-Eurasia was already controlled by hierarchies of various size, this proved an unlikely path.[26]

The opposite situation for a small city was to be subordinated within a hierarchy, with attenuated or minimal network connections. Many of the small Balkan cities of Charles Argo's analysis seem to fit into this category. They were strongly tied to the Porte, the central administration in Constantinople, their subordination to it ritually emphasized through processes such as *devşirme*, which affected not only the cities themselves but implicated the local elites of the cities in the projection of the image of central power into the surrounding rural communities. None were significant trade centers, and to the extent that economic resources inevitably passed through them, that traffic was dominated by the politically managed provisioning needs of the capital city. The market options and freedom of local merchants who facilitated such traffic were therefore severely circumscribed. In a different way but with similar results, minor administrative centers such as the secondary Viet capitals analyzed by John Whitmore owed their very existence as cities not to trade connections but to the political elites residing in them, and their size and prosperity and thus the strength of their (normally attenuated) network connections tracked closely the political fortunes of the aristocratic clans each housed.

Finally, a small city could be both strongly networked and subordinated within a hierarchy. This was the situation for some of the small Muslim-Indian cities analyzed by Elizabeth Lambourn in this collection, as well as for many of the secondary Indian cities of the type Stewart Gordon and James Heitzman discuss. It also describes the situation of Saukin, as described by Jay Spaulding, and the ports and secondary urban centers of the Cochinchina realm described by Charles Wheeler, where rulers recognized the value of markets and granted to particular cities the privilege of holding them in exchange for lump sum payments to the royal treasury and discounted access to imported luxuries. The self-rule exercised under the umbrella of royal government by the local merchant communities represent one particularly clear institutional instantiation of the complex intersection of network and hierarchy dynamics at work in small cities across the pre-modern world. Networked cities within a hierarchy had the potential to move up and down within the hierarchy based on either the changing fortunes of their mercantile connections or the vagaries of political favor; the rise and fall of Saukin, Quanzhou, Hue, and Kancipuram illustrates this process.[27]

The communities of small cities, especially the elites who dominated them, whether traditional or mercantile, expressed and navigated the complexities and potential conflicts of each of these positions through cultural mechanisms that gave meaning and coherence to their lived experience. Having laid the structural foundations of an analysis of small cities in world history, we may now turn to an examination of the cultural side of this history.

Cultural Experiences

Attempting to look at the experience of small cities culturally, to get at how they experienced life at the intersection of networks and hierarchies, is a more difficult task than building a model of those structures. Structural analysis demands and benefits from generalization and the eliding of difference that comes from standing back and taking an external, social scientific perspective on broad patterns. But cultural analysis is in one sense ultimately about difference and the fine grain of individual detail that emerges from the attempt to capture the internal perspective of particular places. Generalizations are still possible and broad patterns may still be discerned, but one of the first generalizations the cultural historian must make is that no culture is monolithic or static. Every community whether a small pre-modern city or a modern nation-state is a cultural composite, at some level, of smaller sub-cultures, each of which is itself contested and under constant construction.[28] Thus, the "dominant culture" of a community, if there is one, is itself contested, constructed, and lasting only insofar as it gives meaning to the lives of those who participate in the community. It is a widely accepted myth, though no less potentially powerful for being mythic.

Given this starting point, the generalizations we can make about the patterns of cultural history visible in the world of pre-modern small cities must necessarily be somewhat more tentative and subject to local exceptions than those we can make about the broad material and structural patterns outlined in the first part of this analysis. Nevertheless, some conclusions may be drawn, and the mass of cultural details about individual cities, some of which are discussed in the studies in this collection, make more sense when viewed within the context of our structural analysis.

The fundamental starting point, as the previous analysis showed, is the tension between the demands that two very different types of structures placed on small city communities, tensions arising from the different purposes and organizations of networks and hierarchies. One expression of this tension was nearly universal: merchants were everywhere mistrusted to some extent by the elites of traditional hierarchies. This was expressed in various ways, from the classic medieval European "Three Orders" conception of society that leaves merchants entirely out of account to Confucian theory that placed merchants at the bottom of the social order, below even peasants. It was perhaps least strong in some Islamic civilizations, given both the mercantile background of the Prophet, the strong network of mercantile connections that linked the Islamic world and its trade-diaspora satellites,[29] and the somewhat non-traditional social structure of those Islamic polities where slave soldiers formed an important part of the political-military support of states whose relations to their own societies was conflicted,[30] though the Ottomans, for one, maintained very traditional restrictions on their own merchants in a policy descended directly from the Byzantine state. It expressed itself in urban geography: an almost universal model of "foreign" mercantile settlement was to settle communities in separate quarters, sometimes within, sometimes outside, the suburbs of the main city of settlement. In Africa a paired city model existed, one for rule, another for trade.[31] The merchants need not even be foreign, as demonstrated in the example of Saukin, where the local elites resided on its island, and non-elite resided in the market district that lay immediately across the water channel.[32] This pattern is similar to many early medieval European cities that were divided by walls into *bourg* and *ville*, the former for "state and church," the latter for merchants. This was also the case as Kenneth Swope describes the secondary cities on China's periphery, where the local marketplaces were immediately outside the fortified city walls, in contrast to China's cities in the Chinese heartland, where they were within.[33]

This mistrust may be understood as the product of the hostility of those at the top of hierarchies to those such as merchants who had the potential, at least, to escape the control of the hierarchy via their horizontal network connections and whose horizontal ties could weaken their loyalty to the very conception of hierarchy. Hall notes that the royal chronicle of a Borneo coast sultanate, the *Hikayat Banjar*, identified foreign merchants as the ultimate challenge to local stability.[34] It also reflected the traditional elite's hostility to the potentially destabilizing and thus dangerous foreign ideas that network connections could import into a hierarchy. For another truism affecting cultural analysis of the intersection of networks and hierarchies is that trade inevitably moved not just goods but ideas: the concepts of trust and inclusion expressed by the wide distribution, both by trade and gift, of ceremonial robes, originating perhaps in relations between central Asia and China, discussed by Stewart Gordon[35] (and perhaps including the robing ceremony that formed part of Ottoman *devşirme* ritual[36]) is an excellent example of the ideological freight constantly attached to material items. This tendency for networks to spread ideas worked, at times, at cross-purposes to the tendency of hierarchies to generate their own ideologies justifying the unequal social order they embodied. On the other hand, some elites borrowed their ideological justification from others, often in the form of the major salvation religions, a tendency made possible by and reinforcing the emergence of hierarchy-friendly "ideological-religious" components of networks, as John Whitmore, Charles Wheeler, and Alexandra Green explore in their studies below. Nevertheless, at the most general and widespread levels of cultural expression, the tension between networks and hierarchies found common expression throughout the pre-modern world.

These broader cross-currents of culture complicated the efforts of particular small cities to navigate the treacherous structural waters they found themselves in. But they also provided some framework for those efforts, as each small city constructed its cultural response not in isolation, but as part of a network, a hierarchy, or both, each with its own (contested and evolving) cultural matrix; small city cultural responses in turn contributed to the evolution of the larger cultural patterns. Since the structural position of each city—more or less networked, more or less subordinated—contributed to the culture each city developed, we may consider what the broader influences of network and hierarchy cultures each contributed.

Network Culture

For the mercantile elites of networked small cities, identification with the values of the network formed the cultural identity of choice. The basic goal of this cultural construction was to emphasize the autonomy of the city (or, in a large city, the sub-community of networked merchants), and thus to increase the chance of the elite monopolizing local access to the wealth generated by their network connections. This in turn protected their local elite position.[37] The quest for autonomy, expressed via the creation of a unique local identity, formed the context for what may be seen as "rituals of authenticity" in many small city communities. The theme of Elizabeth Lambourn's article is how Muslim cities that existed under the rule of non-Muslim states constructed and emphasized their autonomy from local authority.[38] Law, bi-lingual and geographically or politically differentiated public claims, negotiation with hierarchical powers, public prayer rituals, and even local monumental mosque architecture all contributed to this process. In Brunei and Cebu, elaborate rituals for welcoming foreign merchant guests claimed conceptual space for local autonomy; these included the giving of ceremonial robes, a fascinating appropriation of the widespread robing tradition noted by Gordon, which in mainland contexts signified subordination to a hierarchical center, to the cultural demands of a network.[39] More generally, differing cloth traditions were important in making distinctions among maritime Southeast Asian communities.[40]

The rights and privileges of citizenship in the city, including rules about who was eligible for citizenship, often constituted a major element in the creation of an autonomous local identity by giving the community's cultural norms legally enforceable expression. Thus, at Suakin, the major merchant associations regulated who would be allowed to live on the island as a citizen, a privilege confined to families engaged in specific types of economic activity.[41] Such rituals and rules constituting essentially horizontal local identity could cut across vertical associations connected to larger hierarchies. Muslim and Christian participation in local craftsmen guilds, public parades, and spectacles in Ottoman small cities contributed to complex inter-religious networking among urban merchants in the region that made non-Muslims an integral part of local economies.[42]

Creation of a stable autonomous local identity was not just a matter of creating rules and rituals of inclusion, but also involved conscious stress on separation from the identities of hinterlands or neighboring states and chiefdoms (or indeed from the identity of a hierarchy nominally in control of the city). Suakin again provides a paradigmatic case in its distancing of the island population via linguistic differentiation, practices of endogamy, and so forth from the cultures of the surrounding populations.[43] These even assumed an interesting gendered component, as the male population of Suakin was bilingual, the female population monolingual, a reminder that within cities the public-private and unequal nature of gender relations common to hierarchies was reproduced at a smaller scale: just because a small city's elites created a culture that emphasized the horizontal and distanced ties of network affiliation does not mean that the local community was itself egalitarian. This serves as another reminder of the complexity and contestedness of all constructions of cultural identity, as well as the universal tendency of any concentration of wealth and power in the pre-modern world to generate hierarchy, even at small scales.

It also shows that separation or autonomy as a theme of local identity could be served by elites de-emphasizing short-range vertical connections and emphasizing elements common to distant-network identity webs. This seems to be the use made of a common, mercantile-oriented and popular Islamic legal and political identity, sometimes via voluntary subordination to a distant Islamic polity to balance the influence of a neighboring non-Islamic power, in the small cities studied by Elizabeth Lambourn.[44] Similarly, Suakin accepted immigration not from surrounding populations, but from similar commercial cities connected over much greater distances.[45] In many cases this included the common emphasis on a specifically urban identity designed to separate the city culturally from rural populations that were likely to be characterized by servile status, economic dependence, and tax or rent regimes antithetical to mercantile activity and autonomy.

Construction by a small city's elite of a cultural identity that emphasized the local, the urban, and the separate or autonomous nature of the community was of course easiest for cities that fell outside of or only peripherally under hierarchical control. Such themes are still visible in cities more tightly tied into a hierarchy, but they had to be negotiated against the countervailing demands of hierarchical cultural constructs.

Hierarchy Culture

Cultural identification with a hierarchy, which usually meant identification with the official culture of the center, was the choice of traditional small city elites, that is those dependent not on mercantile activity but on military, religious, or bureaucratic function or office-holding, usually tied to landholding, for their social and political status. It was also the cultural identity the center preferred to impose on the communities of small cities.[46]

From the center's perspective, the goal of fostering a local cultural identity focused on the center was to cement a city's place in the articulated structure of rule. Ottoman rule over Balkan cities, for example, existed not just for the sake of controlling the cities themselves but to create subsidiary administrative centers through which central power (or at least its image) could be projected into the rural districts the cities occupied.[47] Projection of power from the center, as noted in the model of hierarchies above, created a reciprocal flow of resources from the cities themselves and through them from the agrarian production of the countryside. Argo again notes that the *devşirme* was used at times as a "carrot" in negotiations with towns in order to secure economic advantages for Constantinople, with the proposed levy in Christian youth commutable in exchange for payments in cash or kind.[48] This is very comparable to the practice by some medieval European monarchs of granting towns charters of self-rule or other privileges in exchange for annual or lump sum payments to the royal treasury. Hierarchical visual symbolism was also employed, at times quite overtly: in Mughal Burhanpur, the Emperor's palace occupied the top levels of the fort and overlooked the river.[49]

It was, of course, to the advantage of some in small cities to cooperate in this construction of a center-friendly communal identity. This was especially true of the traditional elites noted above, since identification with the center was the surest way of enhancing the benefits of office and landholding, not just by increasing local elites' authority and wealth, but by opening opportunities for them to climb the ladder of the hierarchy. The ritual nature of Chinese exam sittings, one of the most successful mechanisms for co-opting local elites into the ruling culture of an empire, is a notable example of this process at work. But others than just traditional elites might benefit from closer connection to the center. Such connection had the potential to check the power of local elites, especially mercantile ones, but even traditional ones, either through the imposition of accountability to the center or through the center's ability to raise commoners to elite status: *devşirme* again provides an example of the latter, though a typically odd and complicated one characteristic of elite forms of servitude associated with Islamic slave soldier institutions.[50]

Indeed, *devşirme* as Argo presents it is a classic example of the general phenomenon of what we may call "rituals of subordination" for which the goals of hierarchy culture provide the context. Such rituals were the cultural mechanism by which small cities, and through them the rural hinterlands, were tied to the center.[51] The spread of robing ceremonies in Stewart Gordon's analysis of small Indian cities clearly served a similar function.[52]

Culture at the Intersections

The extreme cases—networked cities with little or no subordination to a hierarchy, and subordinated cities with little or no network connection—had relatively straightforward dynamics of cultural construction (as straightforward as communal identity can ever be, given the complexity of the process of identity formation noted above). The key conflicts in networked cities were likely to be between the dominant mercantile elite and the poorer segments of the population of the cities themselves, often over fair distribution of the wealth generated by trade;[53] if local manufacturing played a significant part in that trade, the city could even face something like industrial disputes with their attendant cultural expressions.[54] But such disputes were more likely in larger networked cities (that might still count as small on a global scale) with a more hierarchical internal organization and a more complex economy. The crucial external problem such cities were likely to face involved dramatic changes in the structure and flows of the network, changes that could disrupt or cut off important markets or alter the relative value of goods in ways favorable or detrimental to the city's prosperity. The influx of silver that led Suakin into dependence and eventual decline after the seventeenth century provides an excellent example of this sort of danger,[55] which could play out rapidly or over a century or more. Such external changes tested the cultural flexibility of a city's elites and their sense of identity. Sometimes, the challenges were more direct and immediately catastrophic, as with the Portuguese conquest of Melaka in 1511 analyzed by Hall.[56]

The key conflicts in highly subordinated cities with few network connections could be between traditional local elites and the subject townsmen and peasantry, reflecting the larger dynamics of the hierarchy: peasant revolts are a common feature in world history. Even more, they were likely to reflect the factional political conflicts of the elite politics of the center, played out through local rivalries. These might be culturally significant if center politics were divided by ideology (often expressed via religious sectarianism: one thinks of the way the Iconoclast controversy played out in Byzantine localities[57]), but were more likely to be a form of "intracultural" conflict whose rules were recognized by all sides involved.[58] The crucial external challenge faced by these cities involved disruption at the center of the hierarchical structure. This could involve factional politics gone so wrong as to devolve into civil war. Or it might involve slower transformations characterized by bureaucratic ossification, rising inefficiency, or simply changes in strategic outlook that affected peripheries. The slow transformation of Ottoman rule in the Balkans, attended by the decline of the *devşirme* system, illustrates this possibility.[59] Finally, dramatic changes at the center might come from forces external to the hierarchy as a whole. Quanzhou first became a primary center of trade under the influence of Song initiatives, but began its decline due to changes imposed by subsequent Mongol rulers in Yuan China. In the Ming era, Quanzhou was again a peripheral secondary port-of-trade to Guangzhou (Canton).[60]

But the potential conflicts in small cities that were both networked and subordinated were more complex. The two different structures generated and were articulated through two different sorts of elites: the traditional elites of hierarchical organization, with interests grounded (literally) in domination of agrarian production and reaching upwards to the center of the hierarchy; and mercantile elites with interests reaching broadly across the connections of the network. Each set of elites tended to construct divergent and often opposed cultural identities. In such circumstances, the construction of a coherent cultural identity for a city as a whole became even harder. It was a delicate balancing act involving constant negotiation and redefinition of roles and precedence, negotiations that were usually carried out at the level of symbolism and ritual. When it worked, small cities could become, as Gordon notes, repositories of both high-end craft skills and arts and of courtly custom and knowledge.[61] Where intransigence by one side or the other or too great a divergence of interests caused cohabitation and negotiation to break down, however, the result could be conflicts with significant long-term consequences for the identity and functioning of a city.

Conclusions

These examples and many of the cases examined in the studies that follow in this collection speak to the complex, contested nature of communal identity in small cities at the intersection of networks and hierarchies. Balancing the material and political demands of each type of structure, and making sense of that balancing act through cultural expressions that gave meaning and coherence to the lives of those in small city communities, was a dynamic process engaged in by mercantile and traditional elites, with inputs from other members of the communities and from other cultures outside the cities. The resulting constructions of identity were, especially in small cities, all the more fragile for being subject to outside influences from multiple directions, over which small cities could exert little control.

This model of structural dynamics, experienced by those within them through cultural constructions of identity, aims at framing the studies in this collection, which are drawn from the medieval and early modern worlds of the greater Indian Ocean world extending from East Asia to the eastern Mediterranean. But this introductory essay has introduced comparative material from Western Europe in the same period, and the model is meant to capture the dynamics of small cities' place in global developments from fairly ancient times at least down into the eighteenth century. In other words, this essay makes the claim that the history of these various small cities exposes a set of world historical processes common to the entire pre-modern world.

Transitions to Industrial Modernity

It is beyond the scope of this essay and this collection to attempt a detailed examination of the transformations that characterized the shift from agrarian to industrial modes of production and transportation in the course of the nineteenth century. But I'd like to suggest a few lines along which further research and model-building might proceed by attempting a brief characterization of the major transformations and their cultural implications.

Industrialization and steam power, even when still limited to a few parts of the global system, introduced a major surge in productivity and efficiency of transport that was bound to have significant consequences for the shape of the structures that have formed the basis for this essay's analysis. Most obviously, the power and scope of the global network of trade connections increased dramatically, with major and often fatal implications for small cities such as Suakin that found their products rendered obsolete and themselves bypassed.[62] In many ways, the network became more hierarchical (at least for a time), as a few centers of production, distribution, and finance could exert vastly more influence than previous conditions of production and transport had allowed.

At the same time, the shape of hierarchies changed in ways too complex to go into here even in brief, and their influence expanded. In effect, and somewhat paradoxically, the global network, though becoming vastly more inclusive and powerful, was at the same time increasingly segmented politically and subjected to regulation by hierarchical entities that could tap into the increased resources provided by industry and the expanding global network to exert their will more broadly and deeply. Within both networks and hierarchies, meanwhile, the units of analysis were transformed by massive urbanization and the rise of mass society and politics, often at the expense of traditional elites. Thus, an analysis of the modern analogues of the pre-modern system of networks and hierarchies might best be served by taking small regions as the new small cities, megalopolises as the new large cities, and incorporating multi-national corporations as a key form of node in the modern network.

Such vast material transformations inevitably created greatly changed contexts of identity formation. Any account of the cultural intersection of modern networks and hierarchies will have to take account of the impact of nationalism in assessing the relative attractiveness of networked versus hierarchical identities: the moral dominance of imagined national communities in the last two centuries is a fact of great importance to this topic affecting not just the balance of networked versus nationalized identities, but also shifting the terms and locations of national versus local identity intersections.

But here another paradox emerges, for the increased power of the global network to move not just goods but ideas and people in massive quantity creates countervailing cultural currents that both reinforce and challenge nationalist accounts. Demographic mobility provokes discussion of the notion of "nativeness" and creates multi-cultural communities that make twelfth-century Quanzhou look homogenous. At the same time, global transport and communications in a capitalist dominated system leads to the increasing importance of tourism to local economies and the commodification of local cultures. Small cities in such conditions face a new potential conflict between making themselves accessible to the flows of the modern network while maintaining an "authentic" and unique local identity. Like their pre-modern counterparts, such conflicts are all the more intense for small cities, as their small size gives them less control over the external forces and cultures in which they must find their way and find themselves.

Notes

1. See Stephen Morillo, "Guns and Government: A Comparative Study of Europe and Japan," *Journal of World History*, 6 (1995), 75-106; and "Milites, Knights and Samurai: Military Terminology, Comparative History, and the Problem of Translation," in *The Normans and Their Adversaries at War: Essays in Honour of C. Warren Hollister*, ed. B. Bachrach and R. Abels (Suffolk, UK: Boydell and Brewer, 2001), 167-184, for further discussion of some of the theoretical issues facing global comparative history.

2. Jay Spaulding, "Suakin: A Small East African Port City, 1200-1800."

3. Charles Argo, "The Ottoman Balkan City: The Periphery as Center in Punitive Spectacle."

4. Networks need not be exclusively commercial: see the literature on social network theory cited by Stewart Gordon, "A Tale of Three Indian Cities: Burhanpur, 1400-1800," to which could be added Josiah Ober, *Mass and Elite in Democratic Athens* (Princeton: Princeton University Press, 1991), which uses social network theory to examine the intra-polis politics of classical Athens. Indeed, some networks existed within and between hierarchies: see the articles by Charles Wheeler, "Missionary Buddhism in a Post-Ancient World: Monks, Merchants, and Colonial Expansion in Seventeenth Century Cochinchina (Vietnam)" and Alexandra Green, "Religious Networking and Upstream Buddhist Temple Art in Burma." The networks of this analysis will not be considered strictly from a commercial perspective, but this was their chief character. The two-structure model presented here is an alternative to the theoretical constructions of the heterarchy and the cosmopolis outlined in Kenneth Hall, "Coastal Cities in an Age of Transition: Upstream-Downstream Networking and Societal Developments in Fifteenth- and Sixteenth-Century Maritime Southeast Asia," and critiqued in favor of a diasporic model which may be seen as an aspect of my analysis of networks. By considering small cities in the context of the intersection of two different types of structure, I hope to tease apart some of the contradictions created by trying to fit the entire range of small city experience into a single structural model.

5. Such primacy as certain central trade emporium cities were able to exert tended to be fragile, short-lived, and non-institutional (and thus did not provide foundations for lasting state-building); see Hall, "Coastal Cities."

6. Spaulding, "Suakin."

7. The case of Quanzhou shows how a city's rising political fortunes in a hierarchy could benefit its economic position within a network, as shown in John Chafee, "At the Intersection of Empire and World Trade: The Port City of Quanzhou, 1000-1400." In Hall's study, the rise of Melaka to temporary prominence in the maritime Southeast Asian network, however, resulted largely from its strategic location relative to the international trade route.

8. Note the regular rise and fall commercially of secondary Vietnamese capitals analyzed by John Whitmore, "The Secondary Capitals of Dai Viet: Shifting Elite Power Bases."

9. Spaulding, "Suakin." Compare the non-institutional, largely commercial upstream-downstream connections between Southeast Asian trade centers and their hinterlands in Hall, "Coastal Cities."

10. Spaulding, "Suakin."

11. Spaulding, "Suakin"; Hall, "Coastal Cities," quoting Antonio Pigafetta, *Magellan's Voyage, A Narrative Account of the First Circumnavigation*, ed. and trans. R.A. Skelton (New York: Dover, 1994), 101. See also Elizabeth Lambourn, "Community, *Khuṭba*, Port, and Polity—Reflections on the Political Geography of Muslim Mercantile Communities in Pre-Modern South Asia," wherein the Sultanate of Hinawr was the archetypal port-polity since we are told that it had no agricultural land and depended entirely on the sea for income.

12. Spaulding, "Suakin."

13. Whitmore, "Secondary Capitals."

14. James Heitzmann, "Secondary Cities and Spatial Templates in South India, 1300-1800," below, offers an analysis of urban hierarchy that follows this pattern. Small cities could be the top or central node of not-particularly big or successful kingdoms, as Gordon, "Three Cities," also notes.

15. The organization of Ming military centers analyzed in Kenneth Swope, "Military Networking in Ming-Era China," provides an excellent example of this principle.

16. See, for example, John Whitmore, "Secondary Capitals."

17. John K. Whitmore, "The Development of Le Government in Fifteenth Century Vietnam," Ph.D. dissertation (Ithaca, New York: Cornell University, 1968); Esta Serne Ungar, "Vietnamese Leadership and Order: Dai Viet Under the Le Dynasty, 1428-1459," Ph.D. dissertation (Ithaca, New York: Cornell University, 1983).

18. E.g., Spaulding, "Suakin."

19. Argo, "Ottoman Balkan City." Ming military and administrative centers in the small cities of China clearly served the same purpose: Swope, "Military Networking."

20. Argo, "Ottoman Balkan City" and Spaulding, "Suakin."

21. Chaffee, "Quanzhou" and Gordon "Three Cities."

22. There is an interesting parallel between the liminal position of small city elites at the intersection of two structures and detached but not yet reincorporated devşirme recruits, "suspended between two distinct social strata," as described by Argo, "Ottoman Balkan City."

23. Compare the dynamics of the Farukhi Sultanate and its then small-city capital at Burhanpur, which maintained a relatively weak independence crafted from careful diplomatic and military balancing between powerful neighbors (Gordon, "Three Cities"). Fourteenth-century Melaka, as described by Hall, became prominent in part due to Ming

China's desire to establish a stable emporium in the critical Straits of Melaka maritime passageway.

24. See, for example, Steward Gordon's commentary in "Three Cities," and the studies by Spaulding, "Saukin"; Lambourn, "Community, Port, and Polity"; Chaffee, "Quanzhou"; Hall, "Coastal Cities"; and Charles Wheeler, "Missionary Buddhism."

25. Though see Hall, "Coastal Cities," on moves in this direction in maritime Southeast Asia that were based in networking among ports-of-trade rather than between paramount coastal centers and their upstream hinterlands.

26. "Free land" in the Americas, especially North America and the Caribbean, ended up exploited in a variety of ways, both commercial and coercive, but not by individual cities. The rôle of joint stock companies in this process may be interpreted as foreshadowing one of the characteristics of the shift to modernism discussed below.

27. Spaulding, "Saukin," Chaffee, "Quanzhou," Wheeler, "Missionary Buddhism," and Heitzman, "Spatial Templates in South India."

28. Stephen Morillo, "A General Typology of Transcultural Wars: The Early Middle Ages and Beyond," in *Transcultural Wars from the Middle Ages to the 21st Century*, ed. Hans-Henning Kortüm (Berlin: Akademie Verlag, 2006), 29-42, for further discussion of the dynamics of cultural subdivisions.

29. Lambourn, "Community," notes that the personal rather than geographical conception of Islamic law aided in its adaptation to the mobile activities of merchants and their sometimes far-flung communities.

30. Stephen Morillo, "The Sword of Justice: War and State Formation in Comparative Perspective," *Journal of Medieval Military History*, 4 (2006), 1-17.

31. Lambourn, "Community," with citation to Philip Curtin, *Cross Cultural Trade in World History* (Cambridge: Cambridge University Press, 1984). See also Hall, "Coastal Cities," on the subdivision of Melaka into various neighborhoods of foreign merchant communities, and Spaulding, "Saukin," on the "twin" east African coastal urban center.

32. Spaulding, "Saukin."

33. Kenneth Swope, "Clearing the Fields and Strengthening the Walls: Defending Small Cities in Late Ming China."

34. Hall, "Coastal Cities."

35. Gordon, "Three Cities." As he notes, cotton went out but information came back along the same trade routes.

36. Argo, "Ottoman Balkan City."

37. Hall, "Coastal Cities," notes that the ruler of Cebu's personal administration of his entrepot's trade network was the source of his political power.

38. Lambourn, "Community."

39. Hall, "Coastal Cities," on Brunei; Gordon, "Three Cities," on robing; see below, on rituals of subordination.

40. Hall, "Coastal Cities."

41. Spaulding, "Suakin."

42. Argo, "Ottoman Balkan City." See also Engseng Ho, *The Graves of Tarim: Genealogy and Mobility across the Indian Ocean* (Berkeley: University of California Press, 2006); and Roxani Eleni Margariti, *Aden and the Indian Ocean Trade* (Chapel Hill: University of North Carolina Press, 2007).

43. Spaulding, "Suakin."

44. Lambourne, "Community."

45. Spaulding, "Suakin."

46. The imposition could be imposed through the implied or applied use of force: this must have been the impact of the army garrisons stationed in small Chinese provincial cities discussed by Swope, "Military Networking."

47. See Argo, "Ottoman Balkan City."

48. Argo, "Ottoman Balkan City."

49. Gordon, "Three Cities."

50. Argo, "Ottoman Balkan City."

51. Note the tax structure in Mughal Burhanpur, discussed by Gordon, "Three Cities," where retaining this large a percentage of taxes at the local level connected a local militarized elite's income to damping local feuds and promotion of agriculture. This was similarly the case in the Vijayanagara urban center studied by James Heitzman, "Spatial Templates in South India."

52. Gordon, "Three Cities"; the inclusion of a robing element in the *devşirme* ritual as a possible tie between these two examples has already been noted; as has the appropriation of robing as a ritual of authenticity and thus autonomy by places such as Brunei and Cebu.

53. Note the discussion by Lambourn, "Community," of tensions between Islamic elites and non-elite, perhaps heavily indigenized Muslim groups, and Swope's "Clearing the Fields" and Chaffee's "Quangzhou" discussions of peasant revolts in China. In comparison, see Samuel Kline Cohn, Jr., *Lust for Liberty: The Politics of Social Revolt in Medieval Europe, 1200-1425* (Cambridge, MA: Harvard University Press, 2006).

54. Morillo, "Transcultural Warfare," 36-41, wherein the revolt of the wool weavers of Florence in 1378 illustrates this possibility for what may be seen as "subcultural" conflict. On such labor disputes between textile weavers and community elite in early south India see Kenneth R. Hall and George W. Spencer, "The Economy of Kancipuram: A Sacred Center in Early South India," *Journal of Urban History,* 6, 2 (1980), 127-151; and Kenneth R. Hall, "Merchants, Rulers, and Priests in an Early South Indian Sacred Center: Cidambaram in the Age of the Colas," in *Structure and Society in Early South India*, ed. Kenneth R. Hall (New Delhi: Oxford University Press, 2001), 59-116.

55. Spaulding, "Suakin."

56. Hall, "Coastal Cities."

57. Mark Whittow, *The Making of Orthodox Byzantium, 600-1025* (Berkeley: University of California Press, 1996), 139-164.

58. Morillo, "Transcultural Warfare."

59. Argo, "Ottoman Balkan City."

60. Chafee, "Quanzhou."

61. Gordon, "Three Cities."

62. Spaulding, "Suakin."

2

Suakin: A Port City of the Early Modern Sudan

Jay Spaulding

Introduction

Small cities, typically situated on offshore islands, have long figured prominently in the history of the East African coast. The most ancient had their ultimate origin in the distant Hellenistic age, when Mediterranean mariners in the Red Sea first discovered the regularities of the monsoon winds of the western Indian Ocean. Newer and more southerly city-states then arose during the medieval period under Islamic auspices, and their respective fortunes rose and fell with the passage of centuries.[1] Best known by the dawn of the early modern age were the small cities of the southern coast, where urban culture could be distinguished from its hinterland in terms of Swahili speech and allegiance to Islam.[2] The corresponding cities of the northern coast, however, shared both religion and language with their respective hinterlands, and the distinctive qualities of urban culture are better understood in terms of socioeconomic difference. The present study examines Suakin, a city created by the African ethnic community known from medieval times as the Beja, whose language is To-Badawi.[3] Suakin had modest medieval origins, but became independently prominent only in the fourteenth and fifteenth centuries; it survived as the major Red Sea entrepot of the Sudan until World War I.[4] The study to follow offers a discussion of Suakin's place within the wider northeast African social and political context, followed by an introduction to some specifics concerning the community itself and episodes in its historical experience.

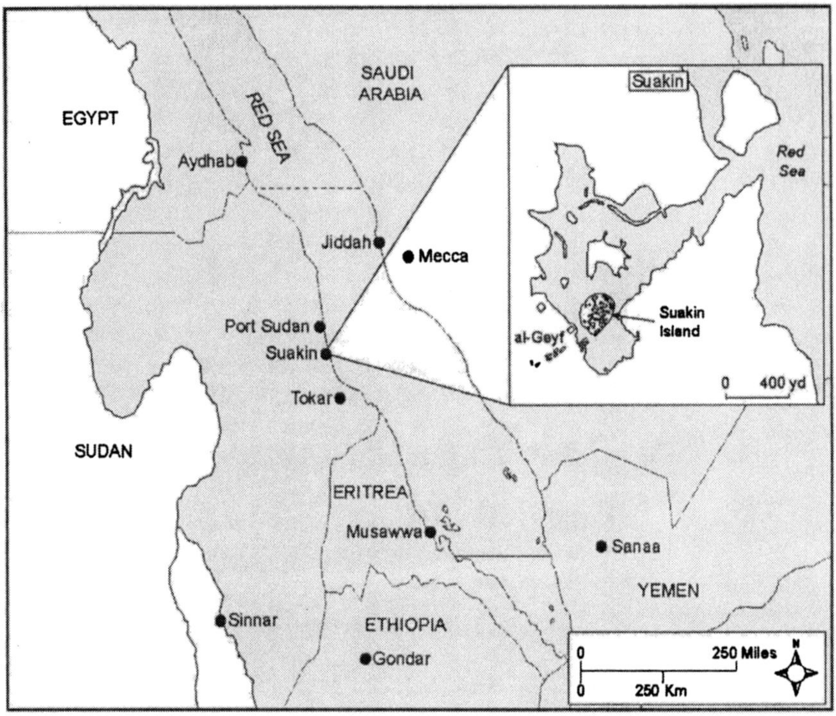

Map 2.1. **Early East African Red Sea Urbanism**

An Urban Society

Suakin, like most of the other East African city-states, was located on an offshore island (*Map 2.1*). The shallow half-mile channel separating it from the mainland was less a fortification or barrier than a statement of cultural difference; the society of island people differed fundamentally from that of the adjoining mainland. The terms of that difference yield to analytical criteria borrowed from the concepts of economic anthropology, a perspective that allows a clear distinction between urban and mainland culture even in cases such as Suakin where linguistic and religious continuities with the mainland prevailed.[5] The city-state was committed to the practice of commercial capitalism, supported in a subordinate role by certain forms of craft production and the appropriation of unusual local natural resources. Time was worth money, and ways were found to circumvent the strictures against the charging of interest imposed by Islamic law.[6] The basic social unit was the extended family, a patriarchal gerontocracy augmented by slave retainers and linked to allied families by arranged marriages. A council of leading family heads held ultimate power within the city, but often governed via a single titled leader with circumscribed powers. Community ethos encouraged competition but also defended a sense of corporate identity that stressed the fundamental differences between city people and others. Citizens normally defined themselves socially through a policy of endogamy. Due to pestilence and other ills of urban overcrowding, however, the city population was probably not demographically self-sustaining, and a certain amount of assimilation had to be tolerated.[7] Acceptable immigrants came most frequently from socially comparable Islamic maritime towns, sometimes geographically remote, rarely from the adjoining mainland however illustrious.[8] Suakin over much of its history interacted primarily with adjacent mainland communities organized on a different socioeconomic basis. In most cases these were lineage communities that practiced various forms of agro-pastoralism whereby the accumulated wealth of farmers was transformed into livestock. They were redistributive chieftainships in which competing big-men struggled for monopoly over the right to gather and dispose of the community's surplus resources.[9] In his dealings with urban merchants such a big-man rarely allowed a transit trade through his tribal territory, though sometimes trade goods themselves passed for considerable distances from one chief's market to that of another via chain commerce. Typically the big-man welcomed an urban merchant as the newcomer's *adhari* (Sudanese and Eritrean) or *abbaan* (Somali). The big-man supplied his guest with food, lodging and protection, in return for which he became the merchant's sole trading partner, disposing of his imports and supplying him with export goods on his own terms.[10] Much of this social and commercial system survived as a regional sphere of exchange when powerful states arose to dominate both the mainland chieftaincies and the island city-states themselves. Sometimes these realms were African, including the successive empires of ancient, medieval and early modern Ethiopia, and the corresponding Nile-valley kingdoms of Meroe, Nubia and Sinnar. On other occasions the city-states fell under the hegemony of more distant seaborne imperial powers. The rise of imperial hegemonies often allowed the urban merchants to pass unhindered among the chiefs of numerous subject communities, sometimes to distant cities where commercial capitalism was practiced, and on other occasions to African courts where the king's representative served as the merchant's host, protector, and partner.[11] These imperial connections also made possible new forms of travel such as diplomacy and pilgrimage, in which city-states such as Suakin were destined to figure prominently.[12]

The Rise and Consolidation of Suakin

The major medieval port on the western shore of the Red Sea was the Egyptian entrepot of ᶜAydhāb, located near the modern Sudanese border.[13] Its virtues included proximity to the Egyptian heartland and a comparatively short and safe caravan route across the desert to the Nile. Unfortunately, however, ᶜAydhāb lay too far north to draw upon the predictable cycle of monsoon winds, which reached their limit at about the latitude of the Arabian port of Jidda. Therefore as early as the twelfth century the Egyptian authorities established a forward customs post, perhaps seasonal, on the Sudanese shore opposite Jidda at the site of Suakin.[14] Significantly, the people sent out to colonize the new southern outpost shared the identity of the citizens of ᶜAydhāb itself; they were Hadaraba, To-Badawi-speaking urbanites who claimed descent from ancient immigrants from the Hadramaut.[15] The town itself emerged over the course of the next century and a half, and in 1266 the Mamluk sultan Baybars formally annexed Suakin to Egypt.[16] This move undercut the hitherto-favored official status of ᶜAydhāb, whose fate suffered another blow on 18 August 1272 when David, king of the northern Christian Nubian realm of Makuria, struck eastward from the Nile to sack the city and massacre its inhabitants, including the governor and a large number of Muslim pilgrims in transit.[17] The dramatic Nubian assault on ᶜAydhāb precipitated a century of massive Egyptian reprisals that pulverized the large medieval kingdoms of the Sudanese Nile valley into a squirearchy of small lordships and facilitated the conversion of the Nubians to Islam.[18] ᶜAydhāb was reconstituted, but during the fourteenth century Suakin inherited much of its commercial pre-eminence, and hostility between the rival Hadaraba cities became intense.[19] The end came for ᶜAydhāb in 1426 when the city was obliterated again, this time by the Mamluk sultan Barsbay in reprisal for a raid against an Egyptian caravan. According to a later account of subsequent events:

> The lord of Suakin, aided by Turks armed with firearms and bows, inflicted on them [the people of ᶜAydhāb] a heavy defeat, so that in one encounter over 4,000 were killed out of these rascals who go naked. One thousand were taken back to Suakin and slaughtered there by [Suakinese] women and children.[20]

Moreover, Mamluk authority along the Red Sea littoral soon gave way to a merely nominal aura of Egyptian hegemony, and the political golden age of the Hadaraba of Suakin was at hand.

During the fourteenth and fifteenth centuries Suakin enjoyed an age of de facto independence, and achieved a brief but interesting regional prominence. Its citizens, in principle merchants, retained "Hadaraba" as the term of self-identification under which they would henceforth be known. Men were bilingual in Arabic, while women normally spoke only To-Badawi; all defined themselves as the descendants of distinguished Arab immigrants, a claim that served both to bestow an identity worthy of respect and one that reinforced the difficulty of assimilating the commercial vocation into mainland culture.[21] Unusual political circumstances in the region opened unprecedented political opportunities to the contemporary Hadaraba leadership. The large medieval kingdoms of the Nile valley had fractured into numerous small polities: "These lordships of the Nobiis are on both sides of the Nile," wrote a contemporary visitor, "and they say that there are as many captains as there are castles; they have no King, but only Captains."[22] The Hadaraba were able to organize an alliance among the erstwhile Nubian subject communities between the Red Sea and the Nile; indeed, Semitic-speaking Eritrean groups from the south, some of them Christian, seem to have joined too.[23] Other local supporters of the Hadaraba included the descendants of Arab immigrants who had flocked to the eastern deserts in a mining boom, brief but intense, several generations before, and who had now intermarried with the Beja and adopted To-Bedawi as a second language. A high point of this expansive period in the history of Suakin was recorded near the middle of the fourteenth century by Ibn Fadl Allah al-`Umari:

> Then there is the Shaykh of the Hadariba Samra b. Malik, who disposes of great numbers and a redoubtable force, with which he makes incursions against the Abyssinians and the peoples of the Sudan, which brings him a rich booty. All the rulers of the interior as well as other Arabs have been commanded in writing [by the Mamluk sultan] to render him aid and assistance and to accompany him on his military expeditions whenever he desires. He has received [from the Mamluks] the investiture of the countries that he has conquered, and has been granted the supreme authority over the Arabs of the interior from al-Qus [the Egyptian border] to the furthermost limits of where he has planted his standard.[24]

The subsequent accounts of visitors to Suakin in 1470 and 1482 testify to the sustained economic prosperity and political vigor of the city throughout the fifteenth century.[25]

Broad political currents of the sixteenth century were destined to strip the Hadaraba of their modestly imperial ambitions and reduce Suakin to the status of a tributary city-state again. Early in the century a community of southern Nubians called the Funj reunited most of the Nile valley under their Islamic sultanate of Sinnar.[26] By the days of Sultan Dakin, who died in 1586 after a long reign, the Funj had extended their authority both northward and eastward to absorb most of the allied clients of the Hadaraba.[27] Meanwhile the Ottoman Turks, having conquered Egypt, gradually extended their authority southward into the Red Sea; their initial concern lay primarily on the Arabian side—conspicuously the Holy Cities of Islam—but shortly after mid-century they also seized Suakin and transformed it into the capital of a new African province of Habeşistan.[28] The Ottomans and the Funj soon reached a compromise agreement by which the customs revenues of Suakin were to be divided between the two newly dominant regional powers.[29] At the end of the century, however, relations soured as the Turks invaded Sinnar unsuccessfully up the Nile from Egypt; in years to follow the Funj were as likely to ally with the Ethiopians as with their intrusive co-religionists at the coast.[30]

The final sixteenth-century imperial contender for Suakin was Portugal. While most of the Lusitanian-Turkish maritime rivalry of the age was fought out in deep water beyond the Bab al-Mandab, in 1541 João de Castro led an expeditionary fleet into the Red Sea; the Portuguese visited Suakin during the first two weeks of March, and their intelligence report or *roteiro* provided an unprecedented written description.[31] The maritime approach led up a shallow reef-infested channel for several miles to the lagoon in which Suakin stood, on a low, flat, oval island about 400 meters in diameter "so dense that there is no corner without a building." "All the city is an island and all the island is a city," observed the newcomers.[32] The prows of merchant vessels protruded over the waterfront streets and their spars brushed the walls of nearby residences as stevedores expeditiously loaded and unloaded them via wooden gangplanks from decks to waterfront warehouses.

The ships came from as far away as India, Burma and Malaya as well as many closer venues, and few cities anywhere could match the range of goods traded or the diversity and sometimes remoteness of origin of the merchants who congregated there. "No other port offers the same advantages to sailors and merchants," the Portuguese concluded. "It is one of the richest cities of the Orient," they said, and could only be compared to Lisbon![33] Having completed their assessment of the city, on the eighth of March the newcomers then undertook to loot, burn, and destroy it; by the end of the week each sailor in the Portuguese fleet would receive four or five ducats worth of booty.[34] The Ottoman authorities who arrived soon thereafter to found a capital for their incipient African Red Sea province thus built upon silent, blood-drenched ashes.

Renaissance

The city that emerged from the ruins of 1541 was destined to survive for four centuries. Early in the nineteenth century Suakin contained several hundred houses, not all in good repair, and a resident elite population of about three thousand; a downscale suburb on the adjoining mainland had another 5,000 inhabitants and a regional market, but no permanent houses or participants in overseas commerce.[35] Building on the island relied upon a native coral material that could be mined and shaped easily underwater, but which hardened into durable stone when exposed to the air. Urban construction exemplified a unique and striking vernacular architectural tradition called "the Red Sea Style," which Suakin shared with Jidda, Masawwa, and other nearby ports.[36]

The fundamental structure was the family residence, a two or three-story edifice designed to house an extended family and retainers, along with the storage and guest facilities vital to the conduct of an international trading enterprise. Carefully designed air shafts, shaded rooftop terraces, and extravagantly elegant *roshans* (large, elaborately decorated bay windows of teak imported from Java that protruded beyond the house walls over the streets) maximized the cooling flow of air in an otherwise very hot, humid climate.[37] The dilapidation of some once-great houses at any given moment in the history of the island testified to the uncertain fortunes of international trade and the insecurity of family status over generations.

Suakin was an Ottoman city, and experienced in a small way the historical vicissitudes of the empire itself. The oldest building on the island, said to be the house of the first pasha, was a modest structure but a potent reminder of the Turkish leadership role in rebuilding the city after 1541.[38] Obviously, early pashas who arrived directly from Istanbul with a garrison of 200 janissaries and proceeded to collect revenue were taken more seriously than later sub-governors sent over from Jidda (after 1701) with a handful of hired Afro-Arab guardsmen who promptly farmed out all sources of revenue to eminent local notables.[39] On the whole, the African urban community was largely self-governing. The Hadaraba remained the urban elite (though some other families had achieved enough wealth and status to reside on the island), and it was the leading Hadaraba families who provided the "patricians" (To-Bedawi, *arteiga*) who comprised the ruling council of the urban republic. The *arteiga* selected a leader or spokesman, entitled *amir*, to represent the citizens of Suakin in their dealings with the Turks and other important matters. The *arteiga* devised and enforced the rules both formal and informal that governed urban society. These ranged from social issues such as the veiling of island women (their mainland cousins wore no veils) and male headgear (only the *amir* was obliged to shave his Afro in order to wear the traditional Islamic skullcap) to the rates of taxation on commerce in every conceivable commodity, and which forms of foreign currency would or would not be accepted, and if so, on what terms.

Perhaps most importantly, the *arteiga* decided the social status of everyone else. They defined which groups would exist, how each would be treated, and whether perhaps in certain cases exceptions should be made.[40] Among the most important of these distinctions was who would be allowed to live on the island as a citizen; this privilege was confined to families engaged in certain forms of economic activity. "All those concerned in the maritime trade, and about the shipping, and those connected with the government, reside upon the island," noted the early nineteenth-century visitor John Lewis Burckhardt, "while the native Arabs and the Soudan traders live in the Geyf [mainland suburb], where the [regional] market is kept."[41] The *arteiga* much preferred to marry among themselves, but over the centuries some individuals of alien origin, largely Turks or Arabs, had been able to establish themselves as citizens—and probably through intermarriage, as they were physically and culturally indistinguishable from the autochthonous To-Bedawi speaking African elite.[42]

The economic logic that governed Suakin defined the islanders as middlemen who exchanged imported luxuries for the traditional African exports of ivory, gold and slaves.[43] To judge by the record of their houses, the islanders enjoyed particular prosperity during the later seventeenth and early eighteenth centuries, perhaps because during this age the sultans of Sinnar organized regular caravans that brought the favored triad of export goods to the city. Later in the eighteenth century, however, Sinnar entered a time of political troubles and the royal caravans ceased.[44]

The Hadaraba commercial establishment embraced the emissaries of Sudanese or Ethiopian kings and exotic deepwater traders from afar, but it rested more fundamentally upon a very elaborate and more predictable regional exchange system mediated by the mainland suburb market at al-Geyf. Indeed some of these regional commodities also found their way into the long-distance commerce in subordinate roles. While a full discussion lies beyond the scope of the present study, some superficial sense of the breadth of activities should be conveyed.

Included in regional exchange were high-quality cotton cloths woven by the city people themselves,[45] salt, local luxury products such as honey and the musk of civet cats, maritime products such as fish, shellfish, coral, and a fragrant shell used in perfumes. Pearl diving was organized by islanders and carried out by their slaves. Also very important were the products of mainland animal husbandry, including live camels or horses, and numerous byproducts such as ghee and leather waterskins; urban entrepreneurs invested extensively in livestock and hired men from the surrounding Beja communities near and far to herd them. In similar fashion, the Hadaraba encouraged the production of surplus grain for export at Tokar, the fertile interior delta of the Ghash river less than a hundred miles inland; by allowing grain into the island duty-free the Hadaraba guaranteed a supply of cheap bread to the city. Shipowners deployed what was not sold locally as ballast on voyages to Arabia, where it could be readily retailed to pilgrims or in the hungry cities of the agriculturally impoverished peninsula.[46]

Only one detailed account of the regulation of business activities at Suakin survives; fortunately, with a few exceptions, there is little in it conspicuously bound by time.[47] The Ottoman authorities in 1814 farmed the taxation of the city to leading Haradaba families; it was said that the governor forwarded 3,200 Spanish silver dollars each year to the Pasha of Jidda and kept 3,000 for himself; no estimate of the amount kept by the tax farmers is at hand.[48] Both imports and exports were taxed; a rate was set for the more familiar commodities (for example, each slave exported was assessed two dollars and each horse three), and the duties upon less familiar cargos were negotiated as the occasion arose. The Hadaraba themselves paid taxes, but only one-half the amount assessed upon all others; the *amir* also paid the Turks 40 ounces of gold each year for the right to assess an additional tax upon goods entering the port from the mainland. He employed spies to accompany incoming caravans and assess the value of the goods carried by each merchant, a task facilitated by the fact that Hadaraba agents served as many or most of the official commanders of caravans bound for the city (and who received a fee for their services from the merchants they led).[49]

A foreign trader, upon arriving at Suakin, was expected to take an *adhari*; a European who did not understand the system put it this way: "it is impossible to carry on business without purchasing the protection of some powerful Hadherebe."[50] Prices in the marketplace at al-Geyf were determined through a process of bargaining; exchange relationships at Suakin, however, were negotiated primarily on the basis of the status of the participants. The value of the commodities involved was less significant because an administratively fixed set of value relationships among all the units of basic commodities prevailed. These served the Hadaraba as "primitive" or "limited-purpose" currencies; for example, a ferry ride to the mainland or a cup of coffee at the island's coffeehouse were fixed in terms of an established number of handsfull of sorghum.[51] Unfortunately for Suakin, there was one value relationship that was destined to prove incapable of permanent fixation—the relation between gold and silver.[52]

The Beginning of the End

The supreme commodity that drew ships from distant lands to Suakin was gold. Gold arrived at the port from sources in the Nuba Mountains of western Sinnar, and primarily from the mountainous borderlands of the Ethiopian massif shared by Sinnar and the highland empire. Both Ethiopia and Sinnar were autarchic agrarian economies in which trade of any sort played a subordinate role; both defined gold via sumptuary laws as something appertaining by right to the hereditary elite, so that although a commoner might well be obliged by tax laws to produce the substance through alluvial placer panning or mining he would not be allowed to keep or sell it.[53] Gold thus normally reached Suakin in the hands of royal agents. It was the fortune of the island city, however, though its ties to the inland monarchies were close, to be a culturally alien bourgeois outpost sensitive to the wider economic currents of the early modern world.

The seventeenth century witnessed the economic consequences of a dramatic influx of silver from the New World, and although the price revolution of western Europe is probably the best-known example, by century's end the silver deluge spilled down the Red Sea toward India and beyond.[54] Virtually all subsequent observers came from the world dominated by silver and assessed the trade of northeastern Africa in those terms; from that perspective the region's exports (gold, ivory and slaves) seemed to be worth considerably more than its imports (luxury goods and weapons to be hoarded or cautiously redistributed by the kings).[55] During the eighteenth century this perceived vacuum of value was filled by an influx of imported silver coinage, which stimulated and facilitated the rise of a new regional social group—an indigenous northeast African mainland middle class.[56] The Hadaraba of that age accommodated their exchanges to imported silver. At century's end the merchants of Suakin preferred the piece of eight of Carlos IV of Spain (reigned 1759-1780) while rejecting most Ottoman coinage; they also came to accept the Austrian dollar of Maria Theresa (reigned 1751-1780; the coin was minted long thereafter).[57]

The rise of silver coinage at Suakin was accompanied by changes in the pattern of trade. By the early nineteenth century the age of long-distance commerce was over; no foreign vessel came to Suakin unless driven to seek refuge by storms, and that happened so rarely that the islanders no longer employed artisans capable of making repairs.[58] The most conspicuous innovation was the rise of an ever-larger private commerce in slaves, a traffic often perceived by contemporary participants to be synonymous with silver itself.[59] By 1814 about 3,000 slaves may have passed through the city annually, but the figure is less than definitive because estimates derive from tax records, and the numerous West African pilgrims in transit to Makka were often obliged to pay the tax on slaves for themselves in addition to the fees required of pilgrims.[60] Since the major markets for slaves lay in nearby Arabia, the activities of the island entrepreneurs were soon confined to the ports of the Red Sea; Hadaraba families posted relatives as commercial agents in Jidda, Hodeida, Mocha and the towns of the Yemen.[61]

In 1820 the Turkish authorities in Cairo began a series of southern conquests that over the decades to follow would bring the mainland Sudan, Eritrea, Harar and the East African island ports as far south as Somalia under Egyptian rule.[62] The age also witnessed rapid changes in technology and modes of governance as European ideas and practices permeated the region. For Suakin this meant an end to the old ways of doing business, conspicuously the slave trade, and often the expulsion of old families as scarce property was requisitioned for new usages; the transition was marked by the rise of a new Egyptian-style architecture that soon dominated the island.[63] For the *arteiga* and other erstwhile Hadaraba citizens of Suakin the radical cultural break caused by disinheritance and exile to the mainland found expression in allegiance to the Majdhubiyya, one of the new Neo-Sufi brotherhoods that provided an intellectual response, in the Islamic idiom, to the sweeping socioeconomic and political transformations of the nineteenth century.[64] The intrusive alien interests that prevailed during the nineteenth century had no loyalty to Suakin itself; with the Anglo-Egyptian reconquest of the Sudan after the Mahdiyya and the coming of the twentieth century they soon relocated north to the superior deep-water harbor of Shaykh Barghut and laid the foundations for modern Port Sudan.[65] Suakin survived for another generation through the passage of pilgrims, who continued to cross the Red Sea in small vessels suitable to the island facilities, but by the 1940s the island was abandoned and its houses well on their way to ruin.[66]

Notes

1. For a general introduction to the historical context see Jay Spaulding, "Precolonial Islam in the Eastern Sudan" in *The History of Islam in Africa,* ed. Nehemia Levtzion and Randall Pouwels (Athens: Ohio University Press, 2000), 117-130, and "An Historical Context for the Study of Islam in Eastern Africa," in *Faces of Islam in African Literature,* ed. Kenneth W. Harrow (Portsmouth, NH: Heinemann, 1991), 23-36.

2. For an introduction see John Middleton, *The World of the Swahili: An African Mercantile Civilization* (Hew Haven: Yale University Press, 1994).

3. For an historical introduction to this African community, see Andrew Paul, *A History of the Beja Tribes of the Sudan* (London: Frank Cass, 1971). For the discovery and exploration of To-Badawi by western linguists, see B.W. Andrzejewski, *The Study of the Bedauye Language: The Present Position and Prospects* (Khartoum: University of Khartoum, Sudan Research Unit, African Studies Seminar paper No. 4. November, 1968).

4. General historical treatments of Suakin include J.W. Crowfoot, "Some Red Sea Ports in the Anglo-Egyptian Sudan," *Geographical Journal,* 37 (1911), 523-550 and J. F. E. Bloss, "The Story of Suakin," *Sudan Notes and Records* [henceforth *SNR*], 19 (1936), 271-300; 20 (1937), 247-280.

5. A useful introduction may be found in Rhoda Halperin, *Cultural Economies Past and Present* (Austin: University of Texas Press, 1994). Valuable treatments of the exchange function in diverse relevant cultural settings may be found in Jonathan Parry and Maurice Bloch, *Money and the Morality of Exchange* (London: Cambridge University Press, 1989) and Caroline Humphrey, *Barter, Exchange and Value: An Anthropological Approach* (London: Cambridge University Press, 1992).

6. In the Islamic sciences the techniques employed to legally circumvent the intent of the law are collectively termed *hiyal* (approximately, "dirty tricks"). While some aspects of *hiyal* are familiar through studies of the Islamic heartlands, very little is specifically known about the practices of the East African city states. The best example available at the moment derives from late nineteenth-century Brava, where very numerous official statements of indebtedness were apparently used to manipulate the value of obligations over time; see Alessandra Vianello, Mohamed M. Kassim, and Lidwien Kapteijns, *Servants of the Sharia: The Civil Register of the Qadis' Court of Brava, 1893-1900* (Leiden: Brill, 2005).

7. Few would argue that East African city-states were more salubrious than the better-documented contemporary European cities upon which this generalization rests. "Over the long run, in most cities of early modern Europe, the number of deaths tended to exceed the number of births . . . only a constant flow of immigration made it possible for cities to grow, or even maintain their existing size" (Christopher R. Friederichs, *The Early Modern City* [London: Longman, 1995], 313).

8. For specific examples from the better-studied Swahili world see the chronicle literature in Arabic and Swahili presented in English by G.S.P. Freeman-Grenville in *The East African Coast: Select Documents from the First to the earlier Nineteenth century* (Oxford: Clarendon Press, 1962), and *The Medieval History of the Coast of Tanganyika* (London: Oxford University Press, 1962). Relevant in this regard is the visit to Suakin by the noted fourteenth-century world traveler Ibn Battuta, who however was apparently not

tempted to settle and join the community. For Ibn Battuta's visit to Suakin see Giovanni Vantini, *Oriental Sources Concerning Nubia* (Heidelberg and Warsaw: Society for Nubian Studies, 1975), 520-522.

9. Basic principles of regional political economy are introduced, with an emphasis upon the state societies that sometimes grew out of redistributive chieftainships, in Jay Spaulding and Lidwien Kapteijns, "The Conceptualization of Land Tenure in the Precolonial Sudan: Evidence and Interpretation," in *Land, Literacy and the State in Sudanic Africa,* ed. Donald Crummey (Asmara: Red Sea Press, 2005), 21-41.

10. For a discussion of the Sudanese *adhari* see Jay Spaulding, *The Heroic Age in Sinnar* (East Lansing, MI: African Studies Center, Michigan State University, 1984), 108-110.

11. Ibid., 112-119. For the system by which northeast African kings facilitated and controlled the import-export trade conducted by outsiders such as men of Suakin see Lidwien Kapteijns and Jay Spaulding, "Precolonial Trade Between States in the Eastern Sudan," *African Economic History* XI (1982), 29-62, and Jay Spaulding, "The Management of Exchange in Sinnar," in *Trade and Traders in the Eastern Sudan,* ed. Leif O. Manger (Bergen, Norway: Institute of Social Anthropology, University of Bergen, 1984), 25-48.

12. Particularly relevant to Suakin were medieval and early modern diplomatic and pilgrimage relations between Ethiopia and the Islamic heartlands. For background and detailed evidence focused primarily upon Jerusalem see Enrico Cerulli, *Etiopi in Palestina,* 2 vols. (Rome: Ministero dell'Africa Italiana, 1943-1947), and O. G. S. Crawford, *Ethiopian Itineraries circa 1400-1524* (Cambridge: Hakluyt Society, 1958).

13. For a thumbnail survey of the port based primarily upon contemporary written sources see A. Paul, "Aidhab: A Medieval Red Sea Port," *SNR,* 36 (1955), 1-7. For the broader context see George F. Hourani and John Carswell, *Arab Seafaring in the Indian Ocean,* revised and expanded edition (Princeton: Princeton University Press, 1995).

14. The earliest presently extant contemporary reference to Suakin may be found in a contract of partnership between Madmun b. Japheth, the leading Jewish merchant of Aden, and his Muslim counterpart there Bilal b. Jarir al-Awhadi, to conduct trade between Aden and ^{c}Aydhāb in 1130. The substance of the partnership included "100 *Qassi* robes for customs in Suwakin and other places" (S. D. Goitein, *Letters of Medieval Jewish Traders* [Princeton: Princeton University Press, 1973], 184). At that time ^{c}Aydhāb was clearly the major northern terminus for the maritime trade of the Red Sea, and Suakin a subordinate administrative outpost.

15. For the Hadaraba of ^{c}Aydhāb see Paul, "Aidhab," 2. For Suakin see A. Paul, "The Hadareb," *SNR,* 39 (1959), 75-78. The most extensive description of the physical appearance of the Hadaraba inhabitants of precolonial Suakin was offered by the early nineteenth-century Swiss explorer John Lewis Burckhardt (*Travels in Nubia,* 2nd ed. [London: Murray, 1822], 395-396), who used an unusual terminology (see note 43 below):

> The Hadherebe, and the Bedouins [urban elite families] of Souakin, have exactly the same features, language and dress, as the Nubian Bedouins [agro-pastoralists]. They are clothed chiefly in the Dammour [cotton homespun cloth] imported from Sennaar; but the better classes of both sexes wear the Nubian shirt, made of Indian cambric; they have, however, one dress, which is seldom seen in other parts of Nubia; it consists of a long piece of cambric, one end of which is wrapped round the loins, while the other, thrown across the breast and left shoulder, hangs loosely down over the back, leaving the legs, and the greater part of the upper body, entirely naked: this is the favourite negligé of

> the Haderebe; and if to it be added a handsome pair of sandals, three or four large amulets hanging over the left elbow, like those worn in the countries of the Nile, a sword and Korbadj [whip] in the hands, the thick and bushy hair white with grease, and a long wooden skewer sticking in it, to scratch the head with, the whole will afford a tolerable picture of a Souakin Bedouin [member of the Hadaraba elite]. In general, they have handsome and expressive features, with thin and very short beards. Their colour is of the darkest brown, approaching to black, but they have nothing of the Negro character of countenance. They are a remarkably stout and muscular race.

Although Burckhardt's description is primary evidence only for his own day, circumstances suggest that in this case considerable continuities may have prevailed across the centuries.

16. Joseph Cuoq, *Islamisation de la Nubia Chretienne, VIIe – XVIe siècles* (Paris: Geuthner, 1986), 70.

17. William Y. Adams, *Nubia: Corridor to Africa* (Princeton: Princeton University Press, 1977), 526. See also Cuoq, *Islamisation*, 72-73.

18. The motive for King David's attack was Baybars' rebuff of the Nubian monarch's official trade initiative; see Jay Spaulding, "Medieval Christian Nubia and the Islamic World: A Reconsideration of the *Baqt* Treaty," *International Journal of African Historical Studies*, 28, 3 (1995), 577-594. For the conversion process within the Nubian-speaking world, see Jay Spaulding, "Classical Medieval Nubian and the Mahas Diaspora," *Islam et Sociétés au Sud du Sahara*, 17-18 (2004), 81-84.

19. Paul, "Aidhab," 4.

20. Leo Africanus in Vantini, *Oriental Sources*, 774.

21. The vocation of "merchant" was not among the job descriptions of mainland society. For the case of the immediate Sudanese hinterland of Suakin after 1500 see Spaulding, *Heroic Age*. For the adjoining Ethiopian hinterland at all times see Donald N. Levine, *Wax and Gold: Tradition and Innovation in Ethiopian Culture* (Chicago: University of Chicago Press, 1965). In Ethiopia males were exclusively farmers, soldiers, or priests; a medieval or early modern merchant (*jabarti*) was by definition a Muslim and a non-assimilable alien.

22. C. F. Beckingham and G. W. B. Huntingford, eds., *The Prester John of the Indies: A True Relation of the Lands of the Prester John, Being the Narrative of the Portuguese Embassy to Ethiopia in 1520 written by Father Francisco Alvares* (Cambridge: Hakluyt Society, 1961), II, 461.

23. Conspicuous were links to the Muslim Beni ᶜAmr, but the Christian Khassa were mentioned by some sources also; see Cuoq, *Islamisation*, 35 and note 5.

24. R. S. O'Fahey and J. L. Spaulding, *Kingdoms of the Sudan* (London: Methuen, 1974), 21.

25. O. G. S. Crawford, *Ethiopian Itineraries circa 1400-1524* (Cambridge: Hakluyt Society, 1958), 127, 143.

26. O'Fahey and Spaulding, *Kingdoms*, 15-24. The conventional foundation date of the sultanate is 910/1504-1505; for sources and a discussion see P. M. Holt, *The Sudan of the Three Niles* (Leiden: E. J. Brill, 1999).

27. O'Fahey and Spaulding, *Kingdoms*, 5-40; Jay Spaulding, "An Incident of Dynastic Succession in Sinnar," *Northeast African Studies* (New Series), 4, 3 (1997), 23-28.

28. Cengiz Orhonlu, *Habeş Eyaleti* (Istanbul: Istanbul Üniversitesi Edebiyat Fakültesi Matbaasi, 1974). Ottoman records from sixteenth-century Suakin emphasize the city's role as a military base and springboard for operations against Ethiopia. They do not greatly elucidate relations between the Ottomans and the Hadaraba themselves. In 1701

Suakin and the remaining Ottoman possessions on the African coast were placed under the authority of the governor in Jidda.

29. O'Fahey and Spaulding, *Kingdoms*, 26.

30. O'Fahey and Spaulding, *Kingdoms*, 35-37. The oldest extant government document from Sinnar is a letter of mid-seventeenth century to the Ethiopian emperor, in which the Funj authorities claimed to have killed a Turkish Pasha of Suakin, and now desired Ethiopian support against Ottoman retaliation; see Jay Spaulding and Muhammad Ibrahim Abu Salim, *Public Documents from Sinnar* (East Lansing: Michigan State University Press, 1989), 3.

31. A. Kammerer, ed. and trans., *Le Routier de Dom Joam de Castro: L'Exploration de la Mer Rouge par les Portugais en 1541* (Paris: Geuthner, 1936), 86-100.

32. Ibid., 86-87, 95.

33. Ibid., 93-94.

34. Ibid., 92.

35. Burckhardt, *Travels*, 390 (number of houses), 404 (population).

36. D. H. Matthews, "The Red Sea Style," *Kush*, 1 (1953), 53-56; Jean-Pierre Greenlaw, *The Coral Buildings of Suakin* (London: Oriel Press, 1976). All students of Suakin are heavily indebted to Greenlaw's gifted drawings and analysis of an abandoned but not yet totally ruined city in the 1940s.

37. For an extended, insightful and appreciative discussion, see Greenlaw, *Coral Buildings*.

38. Greenlaw, *Coral Buildings*, 22.

39. Compare the pre-1701 Pashas of Orhonlu's documents (*Habeş Eyaleti*) with the account of Burckhardt (*Travels*, 393-395). Indirect evidence suggests that although the Ottoman establishment formalized its official adoption of the Hanafi *madhhab* at about the time Suakin was occupied, at least for a time an older Shafi`i regional preference was allowed to prevail. The reason lay in the overall predominance of Shafi`i loyalties throughout much of the western Indian Ocean merchant diaspora (see Lambourn, this volume), as evidenced locally by the survival into the seventeenth century (amidst a land overwhelmingly Maliki) of a Shafi`i *qadi* at Berber, the Nile entrepot most likely to be used by the Suakin transit trade inland toward Egypt, and the fact that the oldest identifiable mosque at (medieval-early modern) Badi`/(nineteenth-century) Massawa is Shafi`i. See J. L. Spaulding, "The Evolution of the Islamic Judiciary in Sinnar," *International Journal of African Historical Studies* X, 3 (1977), 408-426, and Jonathan Miran, *Making Red Sea Citizens: Interregional Connections, Community, and Cultural Change in Massawa, c. 1840 – c. 1920* (Bloomington: Indiana University Press, forthcoming). I am most grateful to Dr. Miran for the opportunity to consult a pre-publication draft of his valuable study.

40. This discussion is based largely upon the account of Burckhardt (*Travels*, 389-413).

41. Ibid., 390.

42. See ibid., 390-392. The insightful visitor noticed that while outsiders called all citizens of Suakin "Hadaraba," insiders were keenly aware of the distinction between "real" Hadaraba and mere "Suakin citizens" (singular, *Sawakini*). It was the latter fraction of the citizenry that was most likely to break the rules of endogamy. Burckhardt's discussion of the issue is complicated by his use of the term "Bedouin." In this context he understands "Bedouin" to mean "member of the To-Bedawi speaking urban elite," and thus the term has a meaning very different from an English-speaker's ordinary expectations, where a "Bedouin" would more likely be a camel-herding nomad from the mainland than a sophisticated urban merchant patrician. Further, at the time of Burckhardt's visit to Suakin bad relations prevailed between the *arteiga* amir and the resident Ottoman gover-

nor, so that the Hadaraba leader preferred to reside much of the time on the mainland rather than in his family's island mansion. He was thus a capital-B Bedouin from al-Geyf, but not just an ordinary small-b Beja bedouin from the hinterland.

43. For ivory and gold in 1541, see Kammerer, *Routier*, 93-94; for gold and slaves in the early nineteenth century, see Burckhardt, *Travels*, 389-413.

44. Greenlaw, *Coral Buildings*, 22-61; Spaulding, *Heroic Age*.

45. Significantly, the superior export cloths of Sawakin are known only from records gathered at the Eritrean port of Musawwa` and the Somali port of Zayla; see E. van Donzel, *Foreign Relations of Ethiopia, 1642-1700* (Istanbul: Nederlands Historisch-Archaeologisch Instituut te Istanbul, 1979), 185 (Appendix IV) and 252, notes 18 and 19. They were described by contemporary Dutch records as "*sjadders*" of Suakin, and understood by modern scholarship to mean "a plain white calico, usually of a superior quality." The production of a limited number of very high-quality cloths for export was characteristic of most East African city-states in this era.

46. Burckhardt, *Travels*, 389-413. For maritime resources see Cyril Crossland, *Desert and Water Gardens of the Red Sea* (Cambridge: Cambridge University Press, 1913); and William Reed, "A Study of Maritime Fisheries in the Sudan," *SNR*, 43 (1962), 1-15.

47. Burckhardt, *Travels*, 389-413.

48. Ibid., 393.

49. Ibid., 392, 394.

50. Ibid., 401. In this case the traveler, who carried secret letters of introduction from Ottoman authorities in Egypt, became a client of the Turkish governor himself.

51. For the system of governmentally-regulated value equivalencies in the precolonial Sudan see Spaulding, *Heroic Age*, 110-111. For the ferry and coffee at Suakin, see Burckhardt, *Travels*, 400, 402.

52. Burckhardt, *Travels*, 400, mentions the fixed relationship between gold and silver at Suakin in his day. However, his previous observations at the northern Sudanese Nile-valley entrepot of Berber reveal that market forces were well on the way to undermining the relationship between gold and silver established by governmental fiat (216-217; see also the situation at Shandi, 258).

53. For Sinnar see Spaulding, *Heroic Age*, 96-99, 112. For Ethiopia, admittedly a more complex situation, see Richard Pankhurst, "The Advent of the Maria Theresa Dollar in Ethiopia, its Effect on Taxation and Wealth Accumulation, and other Economic, Political and Cultural Implications," *Northeast African Studies*, 1, 3 (1979-80), 39. As Pankhurst reports of Ethiopia, "the use of gold was traditionally restricted in many provinces to royalty and was therefore not available for the population at large."

54. For example, see William Foster, ed., "A Narrative by William Daniel of His Journey from London to Mocha and Back, 1700-1701," *The Red Sea and Adjacent Countries at the Close of the Seventeenth Century* (London: Hakluyt Society, 1949), 51-88, and especially 63-64; K. N. Chaudhuri, *Trade and Civilisation in the Indian Ocean: An Economic History from the Rise of Islam to 1750* (Cambridge: Cambridge University Press, 1985).

55. Pankhurst, "Maria Theresa Dollar," 20-22.

56. For the case of Sinnar, see Spaulding, *Heroic Age*, 139-149.

57. Burckhardt, *Travels*, 400. The contemporary Ottoman policy of frequently debasing the coinage produced this result; significantly, quartered silver *paras* of an earlier (and presumably less degraded) issue were still accepted.

58. Ibid., 390, 399.

59. For a discussion see Pankhurst, "Maria Theresa Dollar," 21.

60. Burckhardt, *Travels*, 399, 417.

61. Ibid., 396, 399.

62. Richard Hill, *Egypt in the Sudan, 1820-1881* (London: Oxford University Press, 1959). For Suakin, see Ghada Talhami, *Suakin and Massawa under Egyptian Rule* (Washington, DC: University Press of America, 1979).

63. The demise of Hadaraba society was summarized eloquently by Greenlaw (*Coral Buildings*, 79):

> But the Nineteenth Century was to bring war and revolt to Suakin's very walls, and the restless Western World, seeking further afield for the sale of its merchandise, had cut the Suez Canal which was opened in 1879. This led to the settlement of rich, foreign trading-concerns like the Eastern Telegraph Company, the National Bank of Egypt, Gellatly Hankey, Mitchell Cotts and other private companies, not to mention the G[eneral] H[ead] Q[uarters] of the Anglo-Egyptian Army and enlarged customs and quarantine installations. Private houses were now required for the numerous clerks and other personnel of these establishments.

The Eritrean port of Massawa was in a sense the nineteenth-century regional successor to Suakin, and many distinctive characteristics of this fundamentally different age are discussed in detail by Miran in "Making Red Sea Citizens."

64. For the Majdhubiyya, and particularly its activities among the former citizens of Suakin, see Albrecht Hofheinz, "Internalising Islam. Shaykh Muhammad Majdhub, Scriptural Islam and Local Context in the Early Nineteenth-Century Sudan," 2 vols., Ph.D. dissertation (Bergen, Norway: University of Bergen, 1996). For the Mahdist movement that dominated much of the Sudan during the 1880s and 1890s and threatened Suakin, see P. M. Holt, *The Mahdist State in the Sudan*, 2nd ed. (London: Oxford University Press, 1970).

65. Alastair Mathenson, "Port Sudan and Suakin," *Canadian Geographical Journal*, 57 (1959), 64-67; Kenneth J. Perkins, *Port Sudan: The Evolution of a Colonial City* (Boulder: Westview Press, 1993).

66. D. Rhoden, "The 20th Century Decline of Suakin," *SNR*, 51 (1970), 7-23.

3

India from Aden: *Khuṭba* and Muslim Urban Networks in Late Thirteenth-Century India[1]

Elizabeth Lambourn

Introduction

This study explores the Muslim landscape of western and southern South Asia in the early 1290s, practically on the eve of the Khalji campaigns that permanently changed the extent and character of the Islamic presence in the sub-continent. This focus is possible thanks to the survival of a large group of documents drawn up by the customs house (*furḍa*) at Aden in the Yemen under the Rasulid Sultans and which have recently been edited and published under the title *Nūr al-maᶜārif* or *Light of knowledge.*[2] Among these papers is an extraordinary list of stipends, in effect salaries, awarded to various Islamic judges (*qāḍīs*) and preachers (*khaṭībs*) at over forty different locations along the entire western and south eastern seaboard of the Indian sub-continent.[3]

The Arabic text is still being deciphered and interpreted and this study does not shy away from the important task of analyzing the positivist data it contains. The detailed topography of Muslim settlement at this period is currently extremely poorly understood. The first part of this study, with the Appendix, thus presents a preliminary identification, mapping, and analysis of the locations and networks represented in this list.

The principal focus of this study, however, is on providing a conceptual framework within which to interpret this document. If the topography of Muslim settlement is opaque, we know even less about the identity, internal dynamics, and external relations of these communities. The second part of this study suggests that this list of stipends can only be understood within the context of the important practice of citing the name of the ruler within the Friday sermon or *khuṭba* and on the occasion of *ᶜĪd* prayers, a practice which served as a public sign of that community's wider allegiance. This study demonstrates the currency of this practice among autonomous Muslim communities in the western Indian Ocean, particularly from the thirteenth century onwards; it then initiates the analysis of what exactly this practice signified, what advantages it brought in its new context. My approach highlights the agency of these Muslim communities in translating the *khuṭba* to their particular conditions of existence outside the *Dār al-Islām*. I emphasize its definitive dissociation from ideas of territorial rule and its use as a sign of allegiance (*ṭāᶜa*), in effect a kind of "special relationship," in order to create and maintain a complex network of relations with outside Islamic polities. My analysis suggests that although this relationship may have allowed Muslim rulers to intervene on behalf of these Muslim communities in their dealings with the polities that hosted them, and was certainly exploited by Muslim rulers as a sign of their extensive "rule," the primary benefits were to provide these communities with a way of formalizing their relations with external Islamic polities. This study will also suggest that the *khuṭba* was particularly used to consolidate and formalize trade networks, assigning a kind of "preferred trading partner" status to the two sides.

The identification of this practice adds an important new category of network, tentatively called *khuṭba* or *duᶜā* network, to the many layers of network already identified or imagined for the period. *Khuṭba* networks provide another dimension to the understanding of relations between Islamic center and periphery in the western Indian Ocean, one that carries important implications to our modelling of the idea of Islamic frontier in this area. *Khuṭba* networks also reveal another level at which Muslim identities and belongings were created and negotiated in the Indian Ocean.

The Islamic Landscape of Pre-Conquest South Asia

The fourteenth century marks a watershed in the history of Islam in South Asia. For six centuries Islamic polities remained largely confined to north western India, first to Sind, conquered in 711, subsequently expanding to the Punjab and the Gangetic plain (see *Map 3.1*). Yet in the space of fifty years a series of Khalji and then Tughluq campaigns and conquests pushed throughout western and central India to its southernmost point. In the words of the historian Ibn Faḍl Allāh al-ᶜUmarī, by the reign of Muḥammad ibn Tughluq, "there is not even the space of a span along the coastal region which is outside his rule. He has his *khuṭba* and *sikka* (coinage) in the whole of this country [India] and nobody shares power with him."[4] "Conquest" was in fact an extremely flexible term and in many cases existing South Asian polities simply continued but in a new relationship of clientage to the Delhi Sultanate; in many areas they quickly returned to autonomy. Nevertheless, beneath the bombastic rhetoric of conquest and the reality of its often transient nature, there is no doubt that these campaigns permanently changed the extent and the character of the encounter between Islam and the Indian sub-continent.

The historical narratives and poems of the conquest are framed in a binary mode—Islam conquers the unbelievers of Hind, yet this rhetoric almost completely masks what we know to have been a much more complex encounter, as an essentially Turkish Islam came into contact with the rich and varied social, cultural, linguistic, political, and religious landscapes of South Asia. This landscape also included a large number of Muslim communities of different ethnic origin and occupation, who spoke different languages and followed various branches of Islam, the fruit of seven centuries of trade, missionary activity, even asylum seeking and military campaigns, which led to the settlement and intermarriage of Muslims from across the Islamic world, local conversions, and the gradual genesis of new and distinctive regional Muslim identities and communities.

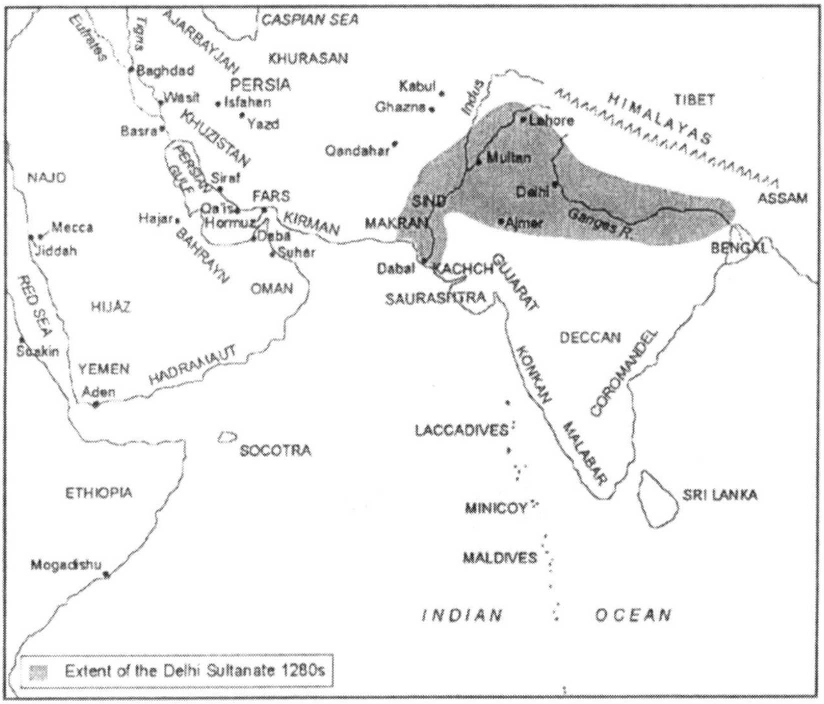

***Map 3.1*. Major Western Indian Ocean Regions and Urban Centers c. 1300**

A passage in Amīr Khusrauw Dihlavī's *Khazā'in al-futūḥ* typifies the problems of incorporating these Muslims into the binary narrative of conquest. After the conquest of the city of Kundūr the Khalji forces encounter a group of Muslims who are described as having "bound themselves to the broken tail-piece of the Hindus," befriended the "infidels" at the expense of other Muslims and are likened to rebels and apostates.[5] With its emphasis on their improper association with Hindus rather than fellow Muslims and rejection of Islam, this account begins by seeing the Muslims of Kundūr as part and parcel of an idolatrous and impure Hindu south. As such it is considered "lawful to shed their blood." However, their ability to recite the *shahāda*, the most basic and yet essential exterior sign of Islam, stalls the rhetoric and prevents their execution.[6] Instead, they are spared and transformed into symbols of the Khalji leader's magnanimity, but remain equally stereotyped—we are given no further information about their identity, origins, and occupations at Kundūr. The location of Kundūr itself remains uncertain and we have no supporting documents or material culture such as inscriptions or archaeological data to add to this mention.

In spite of the heterogeneous and very fragmentary character of the textual and material sources for this period of South Asian Islam, hindered too by a generally dire lack of archeological investigation,[7] something of this Islamic landscape is already apparent in the writings of the Arab geographers of the tenth century. In his *Murūj al-dhahab* (completed in 332/943 but which includes material from his travels along the Konkan coast between 303/915 and 304/916) al-Mas^{c}ūdī estimates the foreign population of Ṣaymūr (Chaul), the principal port of the Rastrakutan kingdom, to have been around 10,000 people, consisting of Basrans, Baghdadis, Sirafis, Omanis, and others, together with Muslims born to Muslim parents in India.[8] This figure can be debated and probably represents a maximum population of both permanent residents, sojourning merchants, and crew waiting for the return sailing season—the round figure of 10,000 likely reflects a convention of estimating large numbers in multiples of 10,000—but nevertheless reinforces the idea of their size. Al-Mas'ūdī and others such as Ibn Ḥawqal also mention Muslim settlements significant enough in size to warrant Friday mosques at the four main ports and cities of the Rastrakutan kingdom during this period. However, it is clear that these settlements are only part of a much wider expansion of Muslim trade communities across the Indian Ocean and through to China, the consequence of the trade boom of the ninth century. From other more fragmentary sources (material and textual) it is clear that by the tenth century Muslim communities, alongside other faith groups of Middle Eastern origin, who should not be overlooked, were settled along the entire western and south eastern seaboard of the sub-continent and in Sri Lanka.

Status and Organization of Muslim Communities Outside the *Dār al-Islām*

This is not the place for an in-depth study of these early Muslim communities,[9] however, in the context of the present study it is important to explore the essentials of their organization and leadership. By their very location outside the strict borders of the *Dār al-Islām* these communities are largely forgotten in the main narratives of Islamic history and are similarly "peripheral" to the history of the South Asian polities that hosted them. However, the surviving sources, including the Abbasid geographical literature itself, suggest that these Muslim communities enjoyed a large degree of autonomy, including responsibility for their own legal administration and organization. Al-Mas[c]ūdī explains how the King (*malik*) of Ṣaymūr (Chaul) known as *Jānij*, apparently a centrally appointed regional governor, "appoints as king over the Muslims a man from among their leaders (*rajulan min rū'asā'ihim*) to whom he delegates the decision of all matters."[10] At the time of his visit the post was held by one Abū Sa[c]īd known as Bin Zakariyya. The Persian sea-captain, Buzūrg ibn Shariyār, also helpfully describes the head of the Muslim community at Ṣaymūr, known as the *hunarmān*, and likens him to a *qāḍī* in a Muslim country, who judges Muslim thieves and sentences them "in accordance with Islamic law."[11]

Undoubtedly the most complete description of Muslim autonomous communities in these territories comes from Ibn Ḥawqal's *Kitāb ṣūrat al-arḍ*, completed in 366/976, which follows but expands on many earlier accounts. Ibn Ḥawqal states that in the kingdom of the Ballahara "Muslims live there and only a Muslim has authority over them, who the ruling Balhara puts in his place over them [the verb used is *istakhlafa [c]alá*]."[12] At the cities of Qamhūl, Sindān, Ṣaymūr and Kinbāya within the Rastrakutan territories "Muslim institutions of law [were practiced] openly" (*wa fīhā aḥkām al-muslimīna ẓāhiratan*).[13] Ibn Ḥawqal's account is the most helpful for the way in which he sets this practice in a pan-Islamic framework, with the observation that "it is a custom (*[c]ādat*) that I have observed in numerous frontier regions where power is in infidel hands, such as the country of the Khazars, the Sarir and the Alains, as well as in Ghana and Kugha. Muslims only accept the judicial authority (possibly "government," the verb is *ḥakama [c]alá*) of a Muslim from among them, and only one of their coreligionists (*man fī da[c]watihim*) can administer legal punishments (*ḥudūd*) and be called as a witness."[14] In effect, Ibn Ḥawqal is suggesting a model of Muslim community autonomy that functioned across the fringes of the *Dār al-Islām*. Unfortunately he does not specify the source of this information, although it is likely to come from a lost or as yet unidentified work of *fiqh*, ("jurisprudential literature"). In spite of this, it is clear that the precedents he cites were designed to operate even at the level of an extremely small, and perhaps transient Muslim community, since he even explains how a non-Muslim can become a witness if the Muslim community is too small to provide one of the same faith.

Together these sources testify both to the large degree of autonomy that prevailed among Muslim communities settled beyond the *Dār al-Islām*, and to the existence text alludes to, but does not make explicit, is the fact that this autonomous status of a consistent model or pattern for this autonomy. What Ibn Ḥawqal's was not the result of exceptional privileges granted to Muslim trading groups, but very certainly a pre-requisite to any settlement. This system is based on the Late Antique idea that law was personal rather than geographical. Muslims carried with them the right to be administered and judged not under the law of the land but according to Islamic law. The system almost certainly predates the tenth century and was by no means exclusive to South Asia, as Ibn Ḥawqal himself underlines. One of the earliest references to this system for Muslim communities pertains to China rather than to South Asia. In the anonymous

Akhbār al-ṣīn wa al-hind, believed to have been completed in 237/851, probably in the Persian Gulf, the author states that in Guangzhou (Khānfū) a Muslim man is given authority by the ruler of China (*ṣāḥib al-ṣīn*) to judge between the Muslims (*al-ḥukm bayna al-muslimīn*).[15] His decisions, the author tells us, are based on the Qur'an and the laws of Islam and are not criticized by the Iraqi merchants. This individual also led the prayers during the main religious festivals. Clearly, although the headship of the community was subject at the very least to approval by local government, and at worse to direct appointment by these powers, Muslim communities nevertheless retained a considerable degree of immediate control over their own affairs and a clear sense of autonomy.

Of course, this model is an ideal that assumes a unified *umma* or Muslim community, whereas in practice we know that well before the tenth century factional divisions had begun to divide it. We do not know at present the extent to which the experience of being Muslim outside the *Dār al-Islām* served to unite a diverse *umma*, or whether these differences were maintained in separate community, administration, or sub-tiers of administration. These early accounts undoubtedly only communicate the topmost tier of what must have been a more complex organizational structure.

In later times, the posts of *qāḍī* (judge) and *ra'īs* (head) were clearly differentiated and held separately, but this headship may also have encompassed other structures allowing for the representation of different ethnic and linguistic, perhaps sectarian, and even occupational groupings. Certainly in later centuries there is growing evidence of council structures that accommodated the diversity of the Muslim *umma*, and there is evidence for this in late fourteenth-century Calicut that will be discussed below. In spite of these caveats, there is evidence that this model of autonomy continued for many centuries in South Asia among Muslim communities that remained subject to non-Muslim polities.

As will be argued later, this long history of autonomy is a fundamental background against which to understand the later actions of these communities in seeking to build networking with Islamic polities. This documentation allows us to impart agency on these India-based Muslim communities, rather than regarding them as passive reactors to the initiatives of Islamic polities.

The *Nūr al-maᶜārif:* Documents from the Customs House of Aden

It is within this context that the newly edited and published evidence from the customs house (*furḍa*) at Aden finds its place. As Eric Vallet explains, the customs house at Aden was much more than its name suggests, and fulfilled a variety of functions from the taxation of incoming and outgoing goods, to welcoming arriving merchants, ensuring that they were treated according to their rank, and granting them gifts of various sorts.[16] Vallet suggests that the documents now grouped together under the title *Nūr al-maᶜārif* or *Light of Knowledge* were probably gathered together and copied for the Rasulid Sultan al-Ashraf ᶜUmar on the occasion of his accession to the throne in 694/1295.[17] Among the many documents in the collection is one of vital importance to the history of India's pre-conquest Muslim communities. As already mentioned in the introduction, it is a detailed record of stipends (*rātib*, pl. *rawātib*), in effect a form of salary, that were awarded out of the Aden customs house to over sixty *qāḍīs* and *khaṭībs*—to Islamic judges and preachers—along the entire western and south east seaboard of the sub-continent. The list itself is not dated but follows a decree awarded in 691/1291-1292 and sits between two lists of gifts made to various Muslim merchants and local administrators in India in 693/1293-1294; our list of stipends is therefore believed to date to sometime in the very early 1290s.

The list provides complete details of the stipends paid. Although this is not the focus of this study, it is worth summarizing what these were. The stipends were not paid in cash, as often occurred within the Islamic world, but in kind. Each individual received a number of white *Sūsiyya* textiles[18] together with turbans. Those *qāḍīs* and *khaṭībs* based in Kachchh and Gujarat also received two *bahār* (equivalent to 240 kilograms) of madder (*fuwwa*), an important dyestuff that is known to have been produced in the Yemen.[19] Those in the Konkan, Malabar, and Ma^cbar each received ten *mithqāl* of gold (equivalent to 42.5 grams). The payment of these in kind rather than cash may reflect the huge range of currencies then in use along the Indian coast[20] and thus the greater simplicity of making a payment in kind. Madder was the source of the deep red dye so prized in Indian textiles; the extensive textile industry in western India would have provided a ready market for this commodity. Gold's value to India needs no explanation and it was clearly in high demand in south India. The quantities of madder and gold involved are obviously significant and represent a substantial payment. It is clear that they belong to the long-established practice of Islamic governments paying stipends to members of court or esteemed figures, and thereby entered into a relationship of clientage with the giver. They differ too from the category of *tashrīf* (pl. *tashārif*), literally honors or gifts, which the *furḍa* also awarded to eminent persons in India around the same time.

The wider economic context to this list is obviously that of Rasulid involvement in Indian Ocean trade. In this period Aden was of vital importance to the Karim trade in spices and textiles from India, through the Red Sea to Cairo.[21] Conversely the Yemen was an important source of madder for Indian textile manufacture, as well as a vital alternative source (besides the area of the Persian Gulf) of cavalry horses for Indian armies. This study emphasizes this document's value in terms of the list of locations and regions to which these stipends were distributed, and the insight this distribution provides into the patterns of Muslim settlement in late thirteenth-century India.

Until now, the *Nūr al-ma^cārif* has principally been exploited by historians working on the medieval Yemen. Foremost among those to work on material relevant to India is Eric Vallet, whose work focuses on the Rasulid dynasty's Indian Ocean policy.[22] However, the list still holds much valuable data on the topography of Muslim communities and regional networks in late thirteenth century South Asia. Part I of this study (together with the Appendix and *Maps 3.2–3.5*) deals with the challenge of identifying and analysing these. The list of stipends also constitutes one of the most detailed and earliest sources on *khuṭba* or *du^cā* networks; Part II of this study focuses on this framework.

Part I. India Viewed from the Yemen: Muslim Communities and Trade Networks along the South Asian Seaboard

The *Nūr al-ma^cārif*: A Rasulid View of India from Aden

At the outset, it must be remembered that the list is by no means a census of Muslim settlements in South Asia in the 1290s, but is one window onto a large and complex Muslim landscape. As Vallet has rightly suggested, the *qāḍīs* and *khaṭībs* mentioned in this list, and thus the Muslim communities they represent, are almost certainly Sunni Muslim, as were the Rasulid Sultans themselves. The rich landscape of Shi^ca South Asia—which in the case of the Isma^cilis also had intense and complex networks linking back to the Yemen—does not feature here. Nor does the list provide a comprehensive view of Sunni Muslim India. That significant places are not mentioned and there were major ports and localities that did not receive stipends is of particular interest, as will be discussed later in this study.

One question that has to be asked is whether the individuals mentioned at the locations receiving stipends were Yemenis and thus whether the list represents networks based upon shared ethnicity, language, and geographical origin. Given the extent of these networks, ranging from western Kachchh to northern Tamil Nadu, this seems highly unlikely. Only fifty years later the travel report of Ibn Baṭṭūṭa, who visited practically the entire western seaboard, testifies to an intensely cosmopolitan Muslim community made up of Indian Muslims of all regional origins, as well as Arabs and Persians of varied degrees of acculturation. Other Rasulid lists of gifts (*tashrīf*, pl. *tashārif*) to personalities in India also suggest a far more strategic rationale behind these networks, with gifts determined by an individual's position as governor or ruler of a particular port or his influence on trade between India and Aden. One of the best known personalities mentioned is Malik Taqī al-Dīn al-Ṭībī (d. 702/1302), the *Marzubān al-Hind*, an ancient title of Sasanian origin designating the Ruler of the Marches. Taqī al-Dīn al-Ṭībī was the brother of Shaykh Jamāl al-Dīn, the influential merchant ruler of the island of Qa'is in the Persian Gulf, and was of Iraqi origin.[23] In 692/1292-1293 he had been appointed governor of the major Pandya ports of Qā'il, Malāyūfatan and Fatan, and he is mentioned as a recipient of presents from the Rasulid court on 11 *Ramaḍān* 693/August 5, 1294.[24] Given this evidence, there is no reason to believe that the *qāḍīs* and *khaṭībs* represents a specifically Yemeni group of networks, though Yemenis may well have been prominent among the Muslim communities, particularly in the Malabar coastal region.

It is equally unclear whether the list represents a Shafi^ci view of India, a network of *qāḍīs* and *khaṭībs* all sharing this particular school of Sunni law or *madhhab*. The Rasulids were themselves Shafi^ci and Ibn Baṭṭūṭa certainly describes the Malabar coast as largely Shafi^ci at the time of his visit there. There is a case that occurred during the reign of al-Muẓaffar Yūsuf (d. 694/1295) in which the people of Tāna wrote to the Rasulid Sultan requesting that a good *faqīh* be sent to serve as their judge. The request was met and the *imām* of one of the mosques in Aden went to fulfill this role.[25] For this to happen, the assumption is that he would have been a Shafiᶜi. However, given the range of immigration to the Indian seaboard, no doubt local communities must have represented a range of *madhhabs*. Immigration in western India was heavily accented by arrivals from Persia and Central Asia where the Hanafi school was dominant, while the Maldives were Maliki until well after 1500. Furthermore, a judge was not restricted to one *madhhab*; Ibn Baṭṭūṭa is a pertinent example, having served as *qāḍī* both in Delhi and in the Maldives. It would therefore be unwise to suggest that these stipends were only awarded to communities that applied the Shafiᶜi school of law.

The *Nūr al-maᶜārif* list thus gives us a specifically Rasulid and Sunni view of Islamic South Asia in this period, an insight into one polity's stipend distribution list during one year in the early 1290s. In spite of this caveat, the list of stipends is undoubtedly one of the most important new sources for our understanding of the pre-conquest Islamic landscape of South Asia. The list considerably expands our knowledge of the pattern of Muslim settlement in India, giving information about over forty different locations and six regional networks—all the way from Kachchh on the north west coast to northern Tamil Nadu on the east coast—on the eve of the Khalji campaigns in western and southern India in the first decades of the fourteenth century, which would irreversibly change the status and identity of these communities.

Regional Networks from a Yemeni Perspective

As already mentioned, the list of stipends provides the names of some forty-two locations, or forty-three depending on whether Dahbatan is included (see discussion in Appendix, no. 32), at which Muslim *khatībs* and *qāḍīs* received stipends. The list provides a level of quantitative data not found in any other source, and allows us to establish a sophisticated mapping of these locations (see *Maps 3.2-3.5* and Appendix). But this list is made even more valuable by of the qualitative data implicit in it. The list groups the stipends by area, in most cases giving a clear heading that includes the name of its principal port or ports, and the name by which the region is known. The areas run sequentially from the west coast down to the Coromandel coast (with the one exception of the area around Tāna, which is placed after Malabar). Thus we have:

I. **al-Qaṣṣ and its districts (*aᶜmāl*), country of Gujarat (*Bilād al-Juzrāt*)** (*Map 3.2*), thirteen stipends to thirteen locations.

II. **Kinbāya and its districts (*aᶜmāl*), country of the *Juzz* (*Bilād al-Juzz*)** (*Map 3.3*), nine stipends to nine locations.

III. **Lamībāsūr and its districts (*aᶜmāl*), country of al-Kamkam (*Bilād al-Kamkam*)** (*Map 3.4*), nine stipends but no locations specified.

IV. **[Country of Malabar]**[26] (*Map 3.5*), eight or nine locations listed,[27] no stipend total given.

V. **al-Kawr, Tāna, country of the Bulgha (*Bilād al-Bulgha*)** (*Map 3.4*), nine stipends to nine individuals at seven locations.

VI. **al-Ṣuliyān (the Colas), [the country of] *Maᶜbar*** *(Map 3.5)*, five stipends to five locations.

Most probably these headings give some indication of the mercantile networks through which the stipends were actually distributed, since it is highly unlikely that the recipients themselves travelled to Aden. They are thus structured from the perspective of maritime trade, giving an insight into the local or regional networks of the South Asian seaboard as seen from Aden. The extent of the Rasulid network is undoubtedly impressive, extending as it does from the frontiers of Sind down to northern Tamil Nadu, covering some 5,000 kilometres (3,000 miles) of coastline, and including both the major ports and inland centers of the day as well as much smaller settlements of a more strategic interest.[28]

The detail of the separation of Gujarat into the two networks of al-Qaṣṣ and Kinbāya (Cambay) (*Maps 3.2* and *3.3*) indicates that these headings are not structured politically. Although Gujarat in this period was split between the Solanki or later Chaulukya dynasty based at Anhilawad Patan (Nahrwāla) and the Vaghelas based at Dholka (Dūlaṣa), both capitals are featured under the country of Gujarat (*Bilād al-Juzrāt*) (*Map 3.2*). The first, second, third, and fifth groupings are clearly arranged under the name of the principal port of the area, thus the port of al-Qaṣṣ, also known as Budlasar (Bhadresvar), for the region of Kachchh; Kinbāya (Cambay) for the central plain of Gujarat; Lamībāsūr (Barcelore) for north Kanara, and al-Kawr (probably Chaul) and Tāna for the Konkan coast.[29] In some cases the mention of these chief ports is extremely significant since places such as Budlasar (Bhadresvar) are not known to have been international trade hubs in this period. These places would appear to act as regional hubs to a network of inland and smaller coastal centers. Among the inland centers there is sometimes the capital of the regional polity, as in the case of Nahrwāla (Anhilawad Patan), the Solanki capital, for Kachchh (see *Map 3.2*) or Duwayjir (Devagiri), the Yadava capital, for al-Kawr and Tāna (see *Map 3.4*), but the overwhelming focus appears to be on ports and towns situated along the main axes of inland trade.

The fourth and sixth groupings, covering in effect the majority of the southern seaboard from Barkur (Fākanūr) around to Mylapore (Ḥaram al-Malībārāt) (*Map 3.5*), appears to be structured quite differently. The fourth grouping, comprising places along the Malabar coast, lacks a heading and so there is no indication of the possible hub or hubs of this network. By contrast, the sixth grouping is headed not by the name of a principal port but by the slightly antiquated term *al-Ṣuliyān*, a clear reference to the earlier Cola rulers of south India.[30]

Khaṭīb, Khuṭba, and Friday Mosque

Another layer of qualitative data implicit in this list provides information about the size of the locations mentioned. *Khaṭībs* are preachers responsible for delivering the sermon (termed *khuṭba*) at Friday noon prayers, the occasion when the entire male Muslim population of a particular settlement was required to gather together in one congregational mosque. Congregational mosques could only exist for settlements of a particular size and importance. The specific details vary according to different *madhhabs* or schools of law, thus for al-Sarakhsī representing the Hanafi view, Friday prayers should only take palace in a town that had acquired "some size and significance." By contrast, under Shafiᶜi law, any settlement with forty or more adult male Muslims was considered large enough to require a Friday mosque, even if it was still only a village.[31] It is difficult to know which definition prevailed in which areas of India. Nevertheless, this information allows the conclusion that the locations mentioned in the lists all had Friday mosques and must have had a minimum Muslim population of at least forty adult males by the Shafiᶜi reckoning, while many may have been much larger. No similarly specific rules exist for the post of *qāḍī* or judge, but it is clear that the post was generally found in larger urban centers.

Nevertheless, from the analysis and identification of the place names (see Appendix and *Maps 3.2-3.5*) it is clear that many places mentioned in the lists were undoubtedly quite modest settlements, secondary cities, places so small as to be absent from the medieval geographical literature and epigraphic record. Some of these smaller settlements, particularly those in coastal Kachchh and around Tāna, might even have been fishing villages or ship-building centers. Unfortunately in many cases there is no supporting archeological survey work for the medieval period, and for the moment these estimations of scale and activity remain to be confirmed.

Regional Networks from a Yemeni Perspective: al-Qaṣṣ and Kinbāya

The lists provide striking confirmation of the penetration of Muslim settlement in inland western India, extending to the principal inland cities and along the trade routes into the very center of the sub-continent. This information is of course not entirely new, but it corroborates existing information derived from geographical sources and epigraphy (see the Appendix entries), as well as adding important new locations to the existing topography of Muslim settlement.

In the Rasulid lists the central plain of Gujarat (see *Maps 3.2* and *3.3*) appears especially thickly settled, with Muslim communities listed at inland sites such as Biṭlāwad (Petlad), Dūlṣa (Dholka), Aṣāwal (the site of the modern Ahmedabad), Bārīj (possibly Bareja), Mandal, Nahrwāla (Patan), Barūda (modern Vadodara), Dhabūhī (Dabhoi), Qadhamān (Ghathaman) and Kūdra (Godhra). The last two locations appear especially important as the first is situated at the southern end of the Palanpur Gap, the main pass through the Aravalli hills into southern Rajasthan, Ajmer, and eventually Delhi, the core territory of the Delhi

Sultanate, and the second on the main trade route into Malwa, then under the Paramara dynasty.

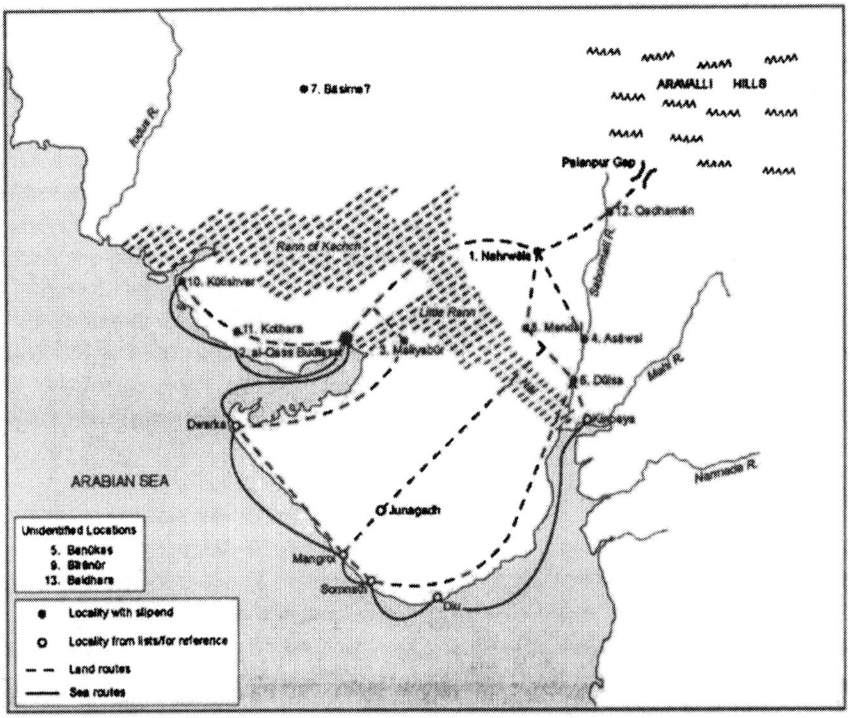

Map 3.2. **Northwest South Asia Coastline c. 1300** (Locations in Kuchchh and Central Gujarat with *Qāḍīs* and *Khaṭībs* in Receipt of Rasulid Stipends)

The division of Gujarat into al-Qaṣṣ (Bhadresvar) and Kinbāya (Cambay) would suggest two separate route systems and networks. As shown in *Map 3.2*, trade networks from coastal Kachchh fed via Maliyabūr (Malia) into trade routes linking Dūlṣa (Dholka), Aṣāwal, Mandal, then Nahrwāla (Patan), and Qadhamān at the south end of the Palapur Gap. As seen in *Map 3.3*, the coastal ports of Gujarat linked to Biṭlāwad (Petlad), Barūda (Vadodara), Dhabūhī (Dabhoi), and then up to Kūdra (Godhra), and the route to Madhya Pradesh and Malwa. Only Ranīr (Rander) and al-Balawdhara (Bulsara, now known as Valsad) appear to lie outside this network, the first communicating very directly with the hinterland via the Narmada river, western India's only navigable river, the second having its own routes up through the northern reaches of the Western Ghats onto the Deccan plateau.

The list of locations for Kachchh is also extremely important for the medieval history of the region and the understanding of the history of the Muslim presence there. Often "lost" among the better documented regions of Sind and Saurashtra, Kachchh rarely appears in the picture of international Indian Ocean trade before the nineteenth century and the well-known Kachchhi migrations to Mumbai and East Africa. The famous Persian scientist al-Bīrūnī, who otherwise provides an extremely detailed geographical description of India in the eleventh century, simply identifies Kachchh with piracy[32] and the *muql* tree, the source of bdellium, a type of gum famous since antiquity for its use in pharmacy, perfumery, and incense.[33] Given this lack of sources it is hardly surprising that all the locations that still remain completely unidentified in the list of stipends—namely Banūkas, Bīrānūr, and Baldhara—belong to Kachchh.

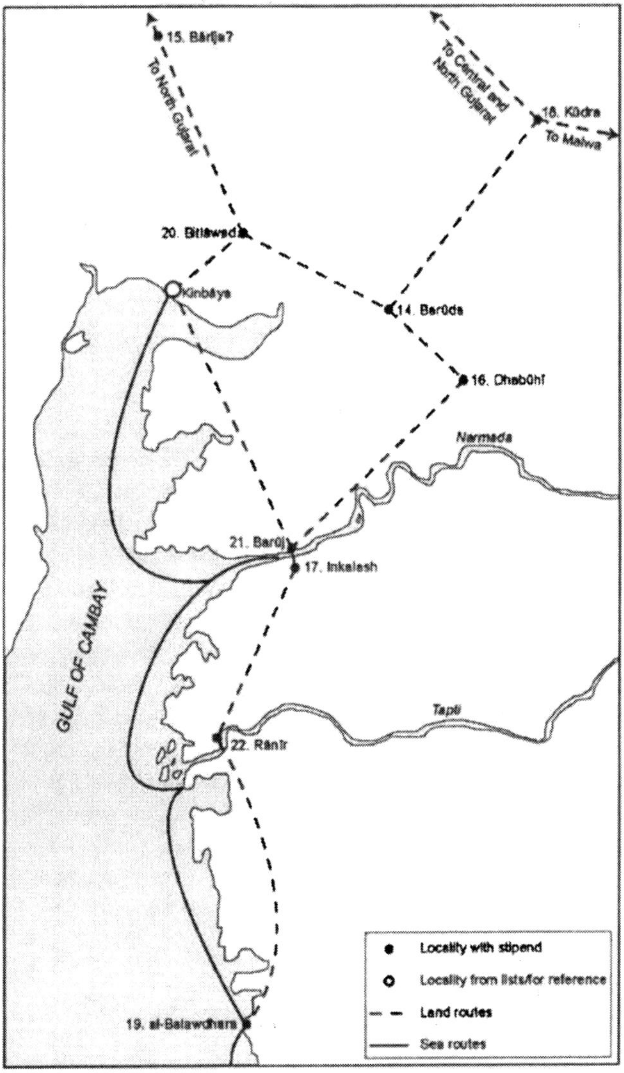

Map 3.3. **Gulf of Cambay Region c. 1300** (Locations in Gujarat with *Qāḍīs* and *Khaṭībs* in Receipt of Rasulid Stipends)

The history of Muslim settlement and conversion in Kachchh is poorly understood at present; however, al-Balādhurī's *Kitāb futūḥ al-buldān*, one of the most famous histories of the early Islamic conquests, lists the region of Qaṣṣa as having been conquered by al-Ḥajjāj, the governor of Iraq.[34] The region is remembered as an early bulwark of Islamization, since the *Futūḥ* records that when the Arab forces withdrew from al-Hind under the Umayyad Caliph Sulaymān (r. 715-717) all the people reverted to their previous religions "with the exception of the inhabitants of Qaṣṣa."[35] Mehrdad Shokoohy's important work at Bhadresvar has suggested the presence of an Isma^c^ili community at the port, active in the late twelfth to early thirteenth century.[36] The Yemeni documents now suggest a Sunni presence alongside this as well as suggesting the continued importance of the port well into the 1290s. The list also provides information about other centers throughout the region.

Perhaps one of the most striking aspects of the *Nūr al-ma^c^ārif*'s list is the extension of Kachchh's trade networks into the very central plain of Gujarat. This definition of Kachchh's territory needs to be understood in the context of the past maritime geography of the area. Until the violent 1819 earthquake which shook western India and raised the Saurashtran peninsula, for six months of the year Saurashtra was an island. Monsoon rains flooded the belt of saltlands between Saurashtra, the central plain and the Little Rann, in effect connecting the Gulf of Cambay and the Little Rann. The phenomenon is mentioned by several reliable authors, namely de Varthema, Baldaeus, and Alexander Hamilton,[37] and is also confirmed by contemporary maps of India.[38] Even more than now, therefore, this part of western India was intimately linked to the sea, the sea reaching far into what we now think of as the landlocked central plain of Gujarat, as far as localities such as Mandal, Aṣāwal (later site of Ahmedabad), and Dūlṣa (Dholka).[39] When the depth of the *Nāl* was measured after the earthquake of 1819, the water was found to be some eight feet deep, but must have been much deeper beforehand; indeed certain accounts suggest that this temporary flooding was exploited by water craft.[40] The structure of the Rasulid lists certainly adds to these suggestions that the Little Rann of Kachchh was far more navigable in the medieval period than it is today. Both Maliyabūr (Malia) and Mandal are situated on the Little Rann and could have been accessible by boat, while Aṣāwal and Dūlṣa (Dholka) are located close to the area of the former *Nāl*. This geographical particularity appears to have had a formative influence on contacts between these areas of western India and the other parts of the Indian Ocean, to the extent that Kachchh and the western areas of the central plain of Gujarat were identified as a common region.

Regional Networks from a Yemeni Perspective: al-Kawr, Tāna

The most compact network listed in the *Nūr al-ma^c^ārif* is that around Tāna (Thane). Tāna was heir to the earlier ports of Sopara and Kalyan and the main Yadava port in the thirteenth century, mentioned by travellers such as Marco Polo and in the Arabic and Persian geographical literature; its appearance here is

Yadava port in the thirteenth century, mentioned by travellers such as Marco Polo and in the Arabic and Persian geographical literature; its appearance here is thus hardly surprising. The list of stipends gives an exceptional level of detail about Muslim communities in and around the port and the distribution of stipends.

The new data for the existence of Muslim settlements and Friday mosques at Māhīm, Vasāhī, Fālī, Ṣubāra and Ajāshī around Tāna is extremely important. Work on the historical geography of the area has indicated that these locations,

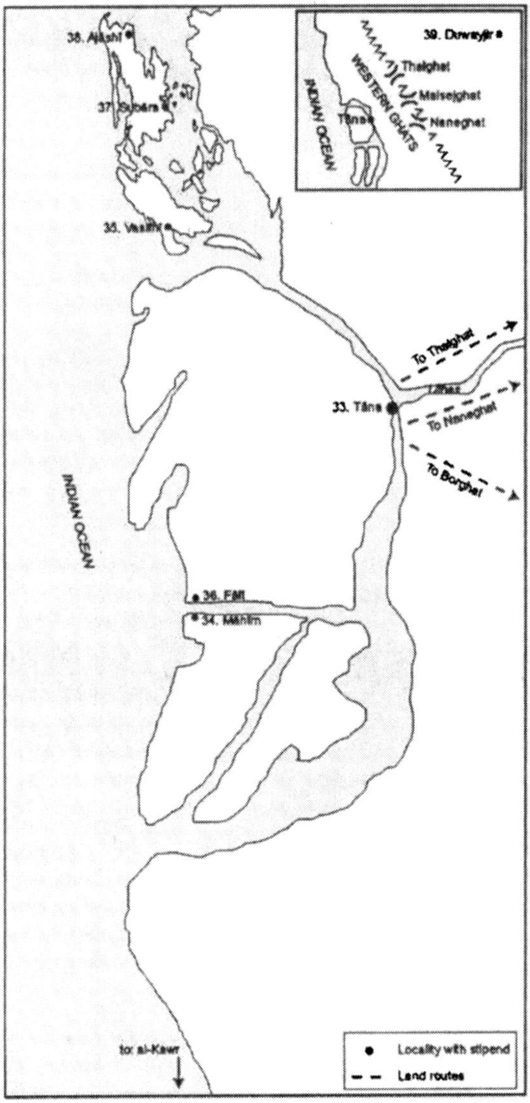

Map 3.4. **Tāna Coastal Region c. 1300** (Locations with *Qāḍīs* and *Khaṭībs* in Receipt of Rasulid Stipends)

now situated inland, were originally small coastal villages and ports located on islands within the Ulhas estuary and off the coast.[41] They thus indicate a dense network of small satellite villages or ports with Muslim communities at the main harbors and river mouths in the area. Their generally small size and locations suggest that they may well have been shipbuilding centers or centers for local trade. Their mention here nevertheless shows the extent of their international connections.

As with the rest of western India, Tāna and its satellite settlements are linked to the main inland centers of the period, here via Kalyani to the main trade route up onto the Deccan plateau and the Yadava capital of Devagiri, the Duwayjir of the list (*Map 3.4*). Devagiri represents an obvious terminus for this network but the information that a Friday mosque existed there before the Khalji conquest is entirely new. Yemen may well have functioned as a source of much-needed horses for the Yadava cavalry and the structure of the network seen here, coupled with evidence in the Yemeni sources for the close contacts between Aden and Tāna, suggests this was the case. The evidence suggests that we should perhaps recast Marco Polo's account of the prevalence of piracy around Tāna and see it less as the desperate act of a polity lacking horses and more as a deliberate spoiling tactic vis-à-vis its rivals.

The list of stipends to this region is also the most detailed; three went to individuals at the network hub of Tāna—to its *qāḍī* and to the *imām* and the *khaṭīb* of its *Jāmiᶜ* or congregational mosque—while another five were distributed to *khaṭībs* located at the satellite settlements of Māhīm, Vasāhī, Fālī, Subāra, and Ajāshī, and the ninth went to the Yadava capital of Duwayjir (Devagiri).[42]

Regional Networks from a Yemeni Perspective: Lamībāsūr, Country of al-Kamkam (*Bilād al-Kamkam*)

One of the most perplexing sections of the list is that for Lamībāsūr, in the country of the Konkan. The list fails to cite the locations where the nine stipends are to be awarded and the place name itself poses problems. As suggested in the Appendix (No. 23), it is probably a variant rendering of Abūsarūr or Basarūr, modern Basrur (colonial Barcelore), located just south of Honavar. Its classification under the Konkan also poses some difficulties since Basrur lies in the area now referred to as the Kanara coast. However, various sources state that the territorial appellation Konkan was extremely vague and originally defined the entire western coast, which was then divided into seven divisions.[43] Nothing is known of a Muslim community at Basrur in this period and the port only emerges in the subsequent Vijayanagara period in a number of local inscriptions,[44] as well as after 1500 in the course of its dealings with the Portuguese.[45] If this identification is confirmed it adds a new chapter to the history of this port.

Regional Networks from a Yemeni Perspective: Malabar

No heading exists for the list of stipends distributed to sites that clearly correspond to the Malabar coast. This absence has generally been interpreted simply as an inconsistency in the document. However, it is also worth considering whether from a Yemeni perspective it actually reflects a qualitative change in the networks along this coast. The very particular geography of the western seaboard is well-known; the high chain of the Western Ghats effectively cuts the coastal areas off from the Deccan Plateau and allowed the area to develop a tradition of independent government, often based around port-polity models. Could the absence and then change in headings for the networks in Malabar reflect the existence of different network models? The suggestion seems to be that in Malabar each small port polity or group of ports had direct links with Aden

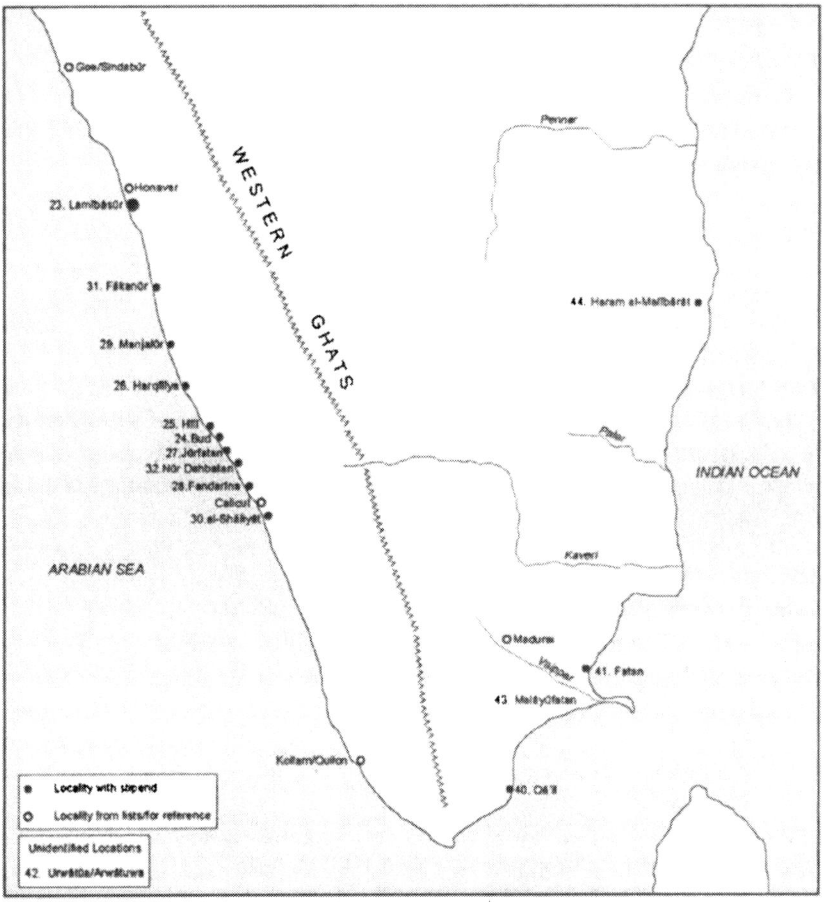

Map 3.5. **South Indian Coastline c. 1300** (Locations with *Qāḍīs* and *Khaṭībs* in Receipt of Rasulid Stipends)

rather than relying on major regional hubs to collect and then ship merchandise, as happened with Kinbāya (Cambay) or Tāna to the north. The Malabar coast certainly had more direct sailing links to Aden then western India or indeed Maᶜbar, though these could not operate all year long due to the monsoon pattern.[46]

A lesser reliance on main hubs emerges clearly from Ibn Baṭṭūṭa's description of trade at Aden in 1331, when he mentions ships arriving directly from major ports such as Mangalore but also the comparatively small ports of Panderani, Shaliyat, and Barkur. By contrast, ships coming from the more northerly part of the west coast appear to come only from the main regional hubs of Cambay and Thane.[47] The *Nūr al-maᶜārif*'s lists of presents to eminent personalities in India also confirms that relations were maintained with numerous port-polities along the Malabar coast.

Whatever the structure of these networks, the list bears unequivocal evidence for the strength of Yemeni contacts with the north Malabar coast, specifically at sites between Fākanūr (Barkur) and al-Shāliyāt (Chaliyam) (*Map 3.5*). The importance of this region in the pepper and spice trade to Aden, which was an intermediary in the maritime trade between India and Cairo, together with Yemen's own direct sailing contacts and commercial interests undoubtedly helps explain this focus.

Regional Networks from a Yemeni Perspective: Maᶜbar

As one would expect the networking with the Maᶜbar is far lighter than that with Malabar with only five locations given, four of them coastal. The small number of listed locations and the quasi-absence of reference to inland centers does not of course mean an absence of trade routes and Muslim settlements. The accounts of the Khalji campaigns suggests that Muslim communities were encountered in these areas and important ports did exist.[48] The Yemeni evidence thus indicates the probable limits of the Rasulid networks in these areas and reinforces the region's natural orientation towards the eastern Indian Ocean. In spite of this, the Rasulid network clearly included the three principal ports of the Pandya kingdom, namely Qā'il, Fatan, and Malāyūfatan (Malīfatan), then under the governorship of Taqī al-Dīn al-Tībī, vizier to the Pandyas and the brother of the ruler of Qa'is. The Pandya capital Madurai is conspicuously absent in the list, but the extension of the network to Ḥaram al-Malībārāt (Mylapore), the center of Christianity in India at that time, is tantalizing.

The Gaps in the Networks

A considerable amount of data remains to be extracted from the list and the maps generated from them; just as fascinating are the areas not listed in the Rasulid list as recipients of stipends. As already mentioned, chief ports named in the "headings" do not necessarily appear as stipend recipients; both Kinbāya (Cambay) and al-Kawr (Chaul) are noticeably absent. However, the lacunae are much bigger than this. A number of important ports on the Kanara and Malabar coasts are not mentioned: notably Sindabūr (Chandore to the south of Goa), Honavar, Calicut, and Kollam (Quilon). Probably the largest "hole" is the entire peninsula of Saurashtra in western India, where Muslim settlement is well attested to for this period at the port of Somnath,[49] as well as inland at Junagadh.[50] The ports of Dwarka and its island Bet Dwarka, Mangrol, and Diu (al-Dīb), as well as the inland center of Vanthali were also active ports and trade centers that were home to Muslim populations at that time. Not one person from any of these localities is listed as receiving a stipend from the Yemen. The second part of this study will attempt to answer the question of whether this is an accidental omission or evidence of a balance of power then operating in the Indian Ocean. To do so we must understand why these stipends were given, the conceptual framework that explains them. Why did *qāḍīs* and *khaṭībs* receive stipends from the Rasulids?

Part II. *Khuṭba* Networks in the Western Indian Ocean

At first glance, the awards of textiles, turbans, and other commodities to *qāḍīs* and *khaṭībs* in India might simply be read as evidence for another layer of gift exchange across the Indian Ocean, one usually omitted from court chronicles or other sources. Present-giving was ubiquitous across the Islamic and medieval worlds, as demonstrated by Stewart Gordon's work on the practice of *khil*ᶜ*a*.[51] This list would seem to be a unique record of Rasulid policy of maintaining relations with all levels of Muslim society in India. As already mentioned, the wider economic context to this list is that of Rasulid involvement in Indian Ocean trade and their consequent need to cultivate good relations with suppliers and societal layers in India. However, a far more specific and complex relationship beyond their economic self-interests appears to lie behind the ritual stipends.

A letter from the *Qāḍī* of Calicut and the Assembly of its Heads

A significant clue to the mechanics and motivations behind the awarding of stipends comes from a later Yemeni chronicle which preserves a unique record of a letter addressed to the Rasulid Sultan al-Ashraf II on 2nd *Rabī*ᶜ II 795 AH/February 15, 1393.[52] The letter came from the *qāḍī* of the port of Calicut in India, on behalf of an assembly or group of its heads (*jamā*ᶜ*at rū'asā'ihā*)[53] made up of "the honored merchants and great leaders" (*al-tujjār al-kirām wa al-budūr al-*ᶜ*uzzām*).[54] The full text of the letter has come down to us in al-Khazrajī's *al-*ᶜ*Uqūd al-lu'lu'iyya* and, in suitably florid language, requests permission to honor the *minbar* with the Rasulid Sultan's titles, that is, to use his titles in the sermon or *khuṭba* delivered from the *minbar* or pulpit of Calicut.[55] His name was to be included among those of the earlier Caliphs and *imāms*. Al-Khazrajī's introduction typically cuts to the chase and states quite simply that the *qāḍī* and merchants tendered allegiance to the sultan and requested permission to perform the *khuṭba* in his name (*waṣala kitābun bi-badhli ṭāᶜatihim li-l-sulṭān wa yasta'dhinūnahu fī iqāmati al-khuṭba lahu bi-hā*).[56] According to al-Khazrajī the offer of allegiance (*ṭāᶜa*) was accepted, with favors duly bestowed, and as part of the formalization of the relationship the *qāḍī* bestowed a robe on Sultan al-Ashraf Ismāᶜīl.[57]

This passage requires decipherment. The *khuṭba* is the sermon traditionally delivered during Friday prayers or on the occasion of *ᶜĪd* prayers. The request concerns one of the components of the *khuṭba* known as *al-duᶜā li-l-sulṭān* or the *daᶜwat al-sulṭān*, a prayer in which most branches of Islam include the name of the reigning sovereign. Countless historical references make clear that the names cited in Friday prayers operated as a very public sign of a sovereign's influence and allegiance, and usually direct rule, in the locality where it was performed. Similarly, after the conquest of a particular area or a transition in control over it, the change in the name of the sovereign mentioned in the *khuṭba* is frequently mentioned by commentators as one of the most public signs of this change. Norman Calder has suggested that the *khuṭba* "may have functioned as a means to symbolize the relationship between the city as a political entity (*miṣr*) and the larger political unit to which it belonged (a local prince whose control extended over more than one city, a local dynasty or the caliphate itself)."[58] There is no doubt that the *khuṭba*, and particularly the *duᶜā*, added to the already political character of Friday prayers, themselves "a symbol of unified political (or social) entity"[59] since they gathered together all male Muslims.

The detailed history of the practice and significance of the *khuṭba*—and even more so of the *duᶜā li-l-sulṭān* or the *daᶜwat al-sulṭān*—is still to be written.[60] Nevertheless, it appears clear that over time the structure of the *duᶜā* evolved to reflect the complex hierarchies of power and contending leaderships in the Islamic world. Whereas early *khuṭba*s simply included the name of the ruling Caliph, as power devolved to independent rulers leaving the Abbasid Caliphs as mere figureheads, or as rival Caliphs emerged as in al-Andalus, so the components changed and expanded in their turn. Hence the Calicuti request to include the Rasulid Sultan's titles alongside those of earlier Caliphs and *imāms*.[61] A somewhat similar phenomenon is observable in coinage, as *sikka* or the right to strike coinage was another important symbol of authority and legitimacy. Here too, hierarchies of power are reflected in the names of Caliphs and rulers given on coins with the Caliph's name accompanied by that of local rulers. Whatever these complexities, the key political message of the *khuṭba* within Muslim polities is in no doubt and it is clear therefore that the request sent to the Rasulid court from Calicut must have been greeted suitably seriously.

Eric Vallet, has emphasized the extent to which the text of this letter is used from a Rasulid angle to emphasize the extent of Rasulid influence in the Indian Ocean, to claim an almost pan-Islamic influence, as part of the Rasulid's self-positioning as Sunni champions in the western Indian Ocean at this period.[62] As we will see later, it is mainly from this perspective, that of the discourse of power emanating from an Islamic polity, that such references to the *khuṭba* among autonomous Muslim communities have been read. From a South Asian vantage point however, there can be no doubt that the request was not simply or only a political act that benefited the Rasulids, but also a political and economic one that benefited the community of merchants at Calicut. In this context, the text of the letter and al-Khazrajī's commentary around it provides an important insight into the agency behind such requests.

The letter takes pain to emphasize to its recipient that all parties at Calicut agreed to this approach; it was presented by the judge on behalf of the *jamā^cat rū'asā'ihā*. The term *jamā^ca* (pl. *jamā^cāt)* can signify not only the congregation of a particular mosque, but also an assembly or group, as well as a community. In the context of the letter the phrase *jamā^cat rū'asā'ihā* seems best translated, not as "Muslim congregation" as suggested in Redhouse's English translation, but as "assembly of its [Calicut's] heads," thus referring to some form of assembly or council of the port's Muslim merchants and notables. Conveniently, the letter gives the names of the six prominent individuals involved in the approach, namely Jamāl al-Dīn Yūsuf al-Ghassanī, Nūr al-Dīn ^cAlī al-Qawwī, Zayn Alī al-Rūmī, Nūr al-Dīn Shaykh Alī al-Ardabīlī, Sa^cd al-Dīn Mas^cūd and Shihāb al-Dīn Aḥmad al-Khūzī. One might ask whether these represent the headships of six distinct groups, just as Duarte Barbosa later broke down the *pardesi* or foreign born Muslims of Calicut into different regional groupings.[63] Thus we have al-Rūmī (a Turk), al-Ardabīlī (a Persian or Khurasani), and al-Ghassanī (an Arab from the tribe of Ghassan), al-Khūzī (from Khuzistan). Might the remaining two, al-Qawwī and Sa^cd al-Dīn Mas^cūd, represent the heads of other influential mercantile groups such as the Deccanis or the Gujarati Muslims mentioned by Duarte Barbosa? Assembly systems are in fact well-attested to among these autonomous communities and the signatures to the letter would appear to confirm that behind this approach lay a collective decision.

This said, the letter is written, and the request fronted, by the port's *qāḍī* who also appears to have played a controlling role in mediating between different interest groups. The letter states that previously other groups (*jamā^ca*) from places such as Bengal, Samutra,[64] or Hormuz had spent vast amounts of money trying to have the names of their Sultans mentioned, but that now the *qāḍī* had agreed to (*ajaba bi*) the request of these particular groups (*al-jamā^ca al-madhkūrūn*). This narration perhaps obviously sets its author, the *qāḍī*, as the main agent of decision in the matter and indeed this would appear to fit with a *qāḍī*'s duties in overseeing the religious affairs of autonomous communities.

Significantly the letter also requests that an order go out to the Rasulid administration (*al-diwān*) that the *qāḍī*'s name be inscribed *fī ṣaḥā'if al-khuṭabā' al-ma^cdūdīna al-mutaqaddimīna.*[65] Redhouse's translation renders this as "on the pages of the enumerated ancient preachers (*al-khuṭabā'*),"[66] and the phrase seems to suggest the existence of some formal ledger recording the names of *qāḍīs* and specifically *khaṭībs* making this request. The letter also cites precedents, since similar requests had been made by eleven *khaṭībs* from eleven towns in India, among them the town of Nalanbūr in Malabar.[67] The date at which these requests were made is not specified but the mention of this clearly establishes local, Malabari, precedents for Calicut's approach.

The letter of 795/1393 highlights several important elements for the interpretation of the earlier list of stipends from the 1290s: firstly the key role of the *qāḍī* in mediating between different local groups and their interests, his role in actually presenting the *khuṭba* request, and the existence of some record of *qāḍīs* and *khaṭībs* who had made such requests. Against this background it seems logical to suggest that the list of stipends sent to Indian *qāḍīs* and *khaṭībs* from the Rasulid court in the early 1290s represents a unique survival of this type of ledger. The letter and al-Khazrajī's comments make clear that this relationship was sealed by a formal exchange of gifts, with the *qāḍī* sending a robe to the Sultan and the Sultan bestowing favors in return, but we can imagine that this relationship was further nurtured and maintained through the payment of a formal stipend. This suggests that the list of stipends awarded to Islamic judges and preachers in India by the customs house (*furḍa*) in Aden in the early 1290s be interpreted as a list of the places where the sermon or *khuṭba* (given at Friday prayers and on the occasion of *ᶜĪd* prayers) included the name of the Rasulid Sultan, a practice known technically as *al-duᶜā li-l-sulṭān* or *daᶜwat al-sulṭān*. The existence of a letter from the judge of Calicut requesting just such a privilege provides immediate support for this interpretation, that behind the list of stipends lay a network of *qāḍīs* and *khaṭībs* who included the name of the Rasulid Sultan in the *khuṭba* of their mosques.

The Pattern and Practice of the *Khuṭba* in the Western Indian Ocean

In fact, the Rasulids were far from alone in accepting these requests. Al-Khazrajī's commentary actually cites precedents, as he notes that earlier that century (*fī awwal al-dahr*), thus, earlier in the fourteenth century, the rulers (the term used is *ṣāḥib*) of Delhi and Hormuz had gained influence over Calicut (*qad ghalaba ᶜalá*) and that Calicuti Muslims had recited the *khuṭba* in their names.[68] The influence of the *ṣāḥib* of Delhi probably refers to the period of Tughluq rule in the Deccan and southern India under Muḥammad ibn Tughluq (c. 1327). This appears to be confirmed by al-ᶜUmarī (cited earlier) and Ibn Baṭṭūṭa, who make reference to various local rulers being subordinate to the Tughluqs.[69] Hormuz refers to the merchant rulers of Hormuz who dominated Gulf trade in that period from their island base; Hormuz's influence in India is confirmed by a number of histories of the thirteenth-century Persian Gulf.

The historian Shabānkāraī records that Maḥmūd Qalhatī, the ruler of Hormuz (r. ca. 641-676/1243-1278), conquered "the islands and the coasts of the sea of Oman such as Qa'is, Bahrayn, Qatif, Tazvin (?), and Zufar,"[70] but most importantly, according to the Persian historian Natanzī, his rule also extended to "certain regions of Hindustan."[71] This statement appears to be corroborated by the recent identification of his name and full titles in the famous bi-lingual Sanskrit-Arabic text from the port of Somnath Patan in Saurashtra in western India, which records various endowments to a mosque built by Fīrūz ibn Abī Ibrāhīm al-ᶜIrāqī in 662/1264.[72] While on the whole the inscriptions produced among autonomous Muslim communities in South Asia studiously avoid any mention of the sovereign authority, Muslim or otherwise, under whom the foundation was made, this inscription is not so shy. The Arabic version formally acknowledges, not Arjunadeva the Vaghela ruler of Gujarat (r. 1318-1331 VS/ 1262-1275), but Maḥmūd Qalhatī, the very ruler of Hormuz said by Natanzī to have "ruled" in India. True to the format of other Islamic inscriptions, the Arabic version begins with the date and the phrase "in the time of" (*fī zamān*), and then gives the full name and grandiloquent titles of al-Sulṭān Maḥmūd ibn Aḥmad.[73] The inclusion of Maḥmūd Qalhatī's full titles preceded by the phrase "*fī zamān*" follows the exact model of royal recognition found in inscriptions or acts of patronage undertaken in other Muslim polities, and suggests that Fīrūz al-ᶜIrāqī regarded his act of patronage as undertaken within Maḥmūd Qalhatī's sphere of authority. The choice of Maḥmūd Qalhatī of Hormuz might simply be linked to the Hormuzi roots of the al-ᶜIrāqī family, since the Sanskrit version of the inscription tells us that Fīruz's father Abū Ibrāhīm had originally come from Hurmuja-desa [Hormuz]. However, it may also indicate a wider allegiance of Somnath's Muslim community.

Other Gulf rulers also partook in this use of the *khuṭba*. According to the Natanzī, the Salghurid ruler of Fars Abū Bakr ibn Saᶜd ibn Zangī (r. 623-658/1226-1260) "conquered the islands and the coasts of the sea of Oman such as Qa'is, Bahrayn, and Qatif, from Kinbaya to Basra,"[74] and, according to the Mongol historian Rashīd al-Dīn, had the *khuṭba* read in his name "in certain parts of Hindustan."[75] These statements are confirmed and indeed clarified in Ibn al-Mujāwir's *Ta'rīkh al-mustabṣir* (completed in the late 1220s), which relates that at Kanbāyat (Cambay), al-Sūmnāt (Somnath), and Budlasar (Bhadresvar) the *khuṭba* was pronounced in the name of the Caliph followed by the name of the king (*malik*) of Qa'is, and no other.[76]

Isolated instances of this practice also continue beyond the thirteenth century. ᶜAbd al-Razzāq Samarqandī noted that in the early fifteenth century the *khuṭba* had been pronounced in certain parts of India in the name of the Malik of Hormuz Sayf al-Dīn (r. 820-840/1417-1436).[77] In 846/1442-1443 ᶜAbd al-Razzāq was himself involved in a diplomatic mission to Calicut engendered in part as a response to an embassy to the court of the Timurid ruler Shāh Rukh from Calicut's Muslims to request the use of the Timurid ruler's name in the *khuṭba* at Calicut.[78] "The *walī* of Calicut," he tells us, "gathered all sorts of gifts and tribute and sent a messenger to say that in his port in the Friday prayer and in the holiday prayer the *khuṭba* of Islam was recited, and if His Majesty [Shahrukh] would allow it, they would recite the *khuṭba* in his royal name."[79] In the sixteenth century the Turkish admiral Seydi ᶜAlī Re'īs recounts, on the authority of two merchants from Surat, that in China "each community (*her ṭāyife*) had wanted to pronounce the *khuṭba* in the name of his own Padishah."[80]

In fact, the oldest reference to the *khuṭba* outside the *Dār al-Islām* dates to the first half of the ninth century and comes from the *Akhbār al-ṣīn wa al-hind*, a compendium of sealore and description of trading conditions on the route to China, believed to have been compiled around 851 CE by a merchant from Siraf (often credited to the merchant Sulaymān). The text is very specific in that the head of the Muslim merchants at the Chinese port of Khanfu (Guangzhou/Canton) performed both the *khuṭba* generally but also the specific sub-element of the *duᶜā' "li-sultān al-muslimīn,"* that is "to the government of the Muslims" (*fī al-ʿīd ṣallá bi-l-muslimīn wa khaṭaba wa daᶜā li-sulṭān al-muslimīn*) on the occasion of *ᶜĪd* prayers.[81] In this period the term *sulṭān* was not yet used as a title but was a noun meaning "government" or "authority." The *duᶜā* was thus to "the authority or government of the Muslims." As the *Akhbār* specifies that these merchants were Iraqis, we can assume that in early ninth-century Khanfu the *sulṭān al-muslimīn* alluded to the Abbasid Caliph in Iraq. This example is especially important evidence that the *duᶜā* travelled outside the *Dār al-Islām* from a very early period.

To date, many of these passages have been either overlooked, directly dismissed as hyperbole, or read as elaborate metaphors for a particular ruler's claim to universal rule. The French historian Jean Aubin, who worked extensively on the Gulf region's history, pronounced these to be "formules reproduites à l'envie et faussées"[82] or "formulae mindlessly repeated and falsified." More recently Sanjay Subrahmanyam and Muzaffar Alam have gently mocked references to this practice in various travelers' accounts.[83] Since the claims are often extremely vague one can understand this skepticism. However, an accumulating body of evidence, of which the Rasulid list of stipends discussed here constitutes a keystone, suggests that these statements reflect actual practices in the Indian Ocean and the real-life initiatives of autonomous Muslim communities. More importantly, these other instances demonstrate that the Rasulids were not the instigators of this practice but followed a well-established system in the western Indian Ocean.[84] The system of autonomous self-government under which these Muslim communities had operated since at least the ninth century allows us to see them as, at the very least, equal partners in the creation of these associations, rather than simply reactors to the actions of Muslim polities.

Many *Khuṭbas* or One?

It is not clear at present whether *khuṭbas* could be read in the name of different sovereigns in a single port and at the same time. From the eleventh century onwards it increasingly became possible to have more than one Friday mosque in any particular location;[85] in the context of autonomous Muslim communities residing outside the *Dār al-Islām* this development offered the possibility of different congregations citing different rulers' names in their *khuṭbas*. This might explain the cacophony of claims during the thirteenth century from the Salghurids of Fars, the rulers of Hormuz, Qa'is and the Rasulids of Yemen for the *khuṭba* being pronounced in their name at certain places in western India. However, the data is currently so imprecise that these parallel claims may simply reflect the rapid shifts in trade and *khuṭba* networks during the course of the century. Certainly, from both the Calicut letter and in Seydi ᶜAlī Re'īs' account, it appears that mentioning different rulers in the *khuṭbas* of different communities at one location was not deemed acceptable. The Calicut letter emphasises the *qāḍī*'s role in mediating between these groups and in finally heading a request to the Rasulids that is backed by an assembly of the great traders and other influential persons at the port. In Seydi ᶜAlī Re'īs' account, by contrast, the Turkish traders gain the upper hand and it is in the name of the Ottoman Sultan alone that the *khuṭba* is performed.[86] This evidence makes it difficult to judge whether the locations given in the list of stipends indicate exclusive allegiance to the Rasulid Sultan or the allegiance of only one mosque congregation or group.

One further argument in favor of exclusive allegiance is the fact that many important ports and the whole of Saurashtra are absent from the Rasulid stipend lists. Saurashtra and its port of Somnath, as well as the port of Cambay are among the locations known to have previously allied themselves with either Hormuz or Qa'is and are notably absent from the Rasulid list of stipends (*Map 3.3*). Possibly the gaps in the Rasulid network reflect the continued association of these places with other Muslim polities. This information is obviously valuable for our understanding of the geography of power in the Indian Ocean in the late thirteenth century, notably the competition between the rulers of Hormuz and Qa'is based in the Persian Gulf and the Rasulids positioned at the entrance to the Red Sea.

However, having established the currency of this system or practice, the question still remains of what exactly the fact of citing the names of particular contemporary Muslim rulers in the *khuṭba* actually meant in this new context. The concluding paragraphs of this study begin the exploration of this problem.

Translating the *Khuṭba* in the Western Indian Ocean

With little research into the *khuṭba* and the *duᶜā* in the Islamic world, understanding their significance in the context of autonomous Muslim communities outside the *Dār al-Islām* is far from straightforward. As already mentioned, the components of the *khuṭba* no doubt evolved to mirror the complexities of power and legitimacy within the Islamic world and particularly the metamorphosis and fracture of Caliphal power. In spite of the territorial focus of the *khuṭba* as mentioned in geographical literature and historical narratives, it seems that the *khuṭba* and the *duᶜā li-l-sulṭān* or *daᶜwat al-sulṭān* allowed for a variety of hierarchical relationships and types of relation to be expressed even within Islamic polities and the *Dār al-Islām*. As Calder states, the *khuṭba* symbolized the city's relationship to a larger political unit which could be "a local prince whose control extended over more than one city, a local dynasty or the caliphate itself but it also allowed for the expression of social belonging."[87] If the *duᶜā* was polysemic to begin with, this can only have increased with its translation to autonomous Muslim communities outside the *Dār al-Islām*. The following discussion attempts to engage with some of these possible meanings and begins by looking at the inclusion of the Caliph's name in the *duᶜā li-l-sulṭān* or *daᶜwat al-sulṭān*.

By the thirteenth century, the period of the majority of our examples, references to the Caliph in the *khuṭba* clearly no longer signified direct territorial rule but communicated a sense of religious, specifically Sunni, belonging and reinforced belief in the ideal of the Caliphate and its ultimate authority.[88] As Eric Vallet has remarked, the juxtaposition of Caliphal authority and that of a Muslim ruler may also have served very usefully to underline the legitimacy of the latter. The practice of including the names of both the Caliph and a contemporary Muslim ruler appears to have continued in *khuṭba*s outside the *Dār al-Islām*. The evidence from South Asia suggests that *duʿā*s acknowledged both the supreme authority of the Abbasid Caliphate and that of a contemporary Muslim ruler. Thus Ibn al-Mujāwir mentions that at some time before the late 1220s, Cambay, Somnath, and Bhadresvar used the name of the ruler of Qa'is alongside that of the Abbasid Caliph. The letter sent to the Rasulid Sultan from Calicut in the late fourteenth century asked to include the names of the Rasulid Sultan and his predecessors alongside those of the Abbasid Caliphs of the past. In all these cases the Abbasid Caliph's name may communicate the same sense of Sunni belonging and belief in the idea of the Caliphate. However, as Eric Vallet rightly points out, our evidence straddles a critical moment in the history of the Abbasid Caliphate, namely the execution of the last Caliph at the hands of the Mongol armies in 656/1258. The ensuing crisis in the Sunni Muslim world was arguably never resolved although the Mamluks re-established the caliphate in Cairo as quickly as 659/1261, and it was to Cairo that Muḥammad ibn Tughluq looked for confirmation of his authority later in the fourteenth century.[89] However, this was by no means a universally accepted solution, as demonstrated by the Calicut Muslim community's apparent preference to cite the names of the past Abbasid Caliphs rather than the new Egyptian Caliph.

The dissociation between *khuṭba* and territorial power seen here in relation to the Abbasid caliphate also appears to have extended to the names of contemporary Muslim rulers when used outside the *Dār al-Islām*. From our examples it is clear that the sheer physical distance between Arabia and the Gulf and the South Asian seaboard, and the ensuing complexities of communication, would have made direct and effective rule a near impossibility. Furthermore, from the perspective of the communities concerned, any perceived challenge to the sovereignty of the (non-Muslim) polities that hosted them could have had disastrous consequences. The Sanskrit portion of the Somnath inscription is careful to acknowledge the reigning Vaghela ruler and inserts the reference to Maḥmūd Qalhatī "governing his chiefdom at the harbor of Hurmuja [Hormuz]" into a short biography of the patron's father.[90] The *qāḍī* of Calicut's letter is similarly careful to avoid any statement that his request implied Rasulid rule at his port. Although court chroniclers and others were all too ready to read such mentions as expression of "rule," "conquest," or as metaphors for the far-reaching influence of Muslim rulers, as these examples show, the inclusion of their names in the *khuṭba*s of autonomous Muslim communities had clearly come to signify quite another type of relationship. But if the mention of the Caliph's name signified Sunni belonging and underlined belief in the ideal of the Caliphate, what kind of relationship did the mention of the name of a contemporary Muslim ruler create?

Al-Khazrajī's commentary, which is contemporary to the Calicuti approach to the Rasulid Sultan at the end of the fourteenth century, is extremely important in offering a more tempered interpretation than the court chroniclers. He describes the letter as a request to pledge allegiance (*ṭāᶜa*) to the Sultan, but gives no details about what this allegiance signified in practice. Vallet's work suggests that the Rasulids positioned themselves as Sunni champions in the western Indian Ocean, a role heightened by the recent demise of the Abbasid caliphate in Baghdad. The list of stipends, he argues, represents a network of Rasulid patronage across South Asia.[91] In practice this patronage may have been expressed, for example, through the dispatch of judges, as exemplified by the case of the Muslims of Thana sending their request for a new judge directly to the Rasulids. Al-Khazrajī also mentions an instance in which a Rasulid Sultan intervened on the behalf of a Muslim in China over the issue of circumcision.[92] However, Vallet's viewpoint perhaps underplays the extent to which these communities had well established systems of autonomous operation and had forged complex systems of representation with the polities that hosted them. Since numerous sources from the ninth century onwards emphasise the extent to which Islam and Muslims were honored and protected among the various South Asian polities, largely because of their trade knowledge and the connections their local presence brought, did the Muslim diaspora actually need the supportive political patronage implied in the Rasulid list?

An element of political strategy may certainly have been at play here. Eric Vallet has suggested that Muslim autonomous communities may have sought to form alliances with external Islamic polities as a protective measure against the new Turkish Islamic polity to their north, principally to indicate to their non-Muslim host polities that they had other allegiances and interests. While this idea may apply to western India, it is not clear how much the Turkish conquest of northern India was felt in southern India prior to the Khalji conquests. It also begs the question of how much host polities knew of an essentially intra-community linkage, one that took place exclusively among Muslims and within the mosque. More importantly, there is no evidence that host polities would automatically have associated these largely Arab, Persian, and Indian Muslim communities with the Muslim Turks empowered to their north. Indeed Chattopadhyaya's research based on epigraphic and linguistic evidence suggests that at that time South Asians did not define "Muslims" as a separate and single grouping, but distinguished them largely on the basis of ethnicity.[93] A far more promising political strategy would have been to cite the name of the Delhi Sultans in their *khuṭbas*, thus pre-empting any potential attack. Al-ᶜUmarī's mention of Muhammad ibn Tughluq's name being cited along the coast of India and al-Khazrajī's specific mention that the name of the ruler of Delhi was included in Calicut prayers appear to reflect reasoning of this type. Later examples of a "strategic defensive" use of the *khuṭba* are also known in relation to the Ottoman Empire.

Some element of common "identity" or "belonging" may well have entered into the decision to forge these allegiances and one can imagine recently arrived groups simply wishing to continue invoking the name of the same ruler they cited "at home." The mention of Maḥmūd Qalhatī in the Somnath inscription might be linked to the Hurmuzi origins of the patron. The merchants at Cambay, Somnath, and Bhadresvar cited by Ibn al-Mujāwir may have called Qa'is home, and thus continued to use the name of its ruler in their *khuṭba*s in India. But this interpretation over-simplifies the human geography and trade systems of South Asia in this period. These were all cosmopolitan places where multiple regional origins and sectarian affiliations not only coexisted but coincided in the interests of trade.

Evidence from the Cairo Geniza documents and other sources points strongly to trade collaboration across faiths and sectarian divides. The documentation available at present does not support the suggestion that these patterns of allegiance were primarily determined by the identity or ancestry of particular trade groups at specific locations. The *qāḍī* of Calicut's letter is especially significant in this respect since the signatures of the merchants and influential men who backed the approach to the Rasulids prove the existence of a multi-ethnic and multi-lingual assembly. Even the earlier competition between groups from Hormuz, Samudra and Bengal mentioned in the letter can be read as a competition between trade networks rather than being based in regional identities. One Calicuti network focused on the eastern Indian Ocean, networking with ports-of-trade in the Bay of Bengal and Samudra in north Sumatra, the other centered on the western Indian Ocean and particularly the Persian Gulf, via Hormuz. Although a common affiliation with Sunni Islam probably underlay the Rasulid *khuṭba* network, it is extremely difficult to prove the importance of a shared Yemeni ethnicity or an Islamic school of law (the Shafiᶜi *madhhab*).

In the present context, there would seem to be far less idealistic motivations behind the forging of these allegiances or the assumption of a greater parity between the two parties. If the continued use of the name of the Abbasid Caliph in the *khuṭba* of autonomous Muslim communities in South Asia appears to have signalled a sense of Sunni belonging, the choices of the rulers' names to be included in the *khuṭba* overwhelmingly point to the determining role of economics. Ibn al-Mujāwir's explanation for the inclusion of the name of the ruler of Qa'is in the *khuṭba* at Cambay, Somnath, and Bhadresvar before the late 1220s is that the people chose this king due to Qa'is' proximity as a trading partner.[94] The direct trade benefits of this relationship are apparent in his explanation that ships coming from Qa'is were treated at these ports with the greatest respect.[95] As the seas between Gujarat and the Gulf were indeed never closed to shipping by the monsoon (in contrast to the more southern seaboard), the Gulf was a natural and important trading partner for this part of the Indian seaboard. The "great respect" shown to the ships of Qa'is suggests the existence of preferential trading conditions, a kind of "special relationship" that benefitted both parties. Further research is needed to confirm this suggestion, perhaps the two parties enjoyed preferential customs and toll rates, or gave precedence to the sale or purchase of commodities belonging to the other party and even acted as agents for each other. Similarly, mercantile lobbying was instrumental in determining which ruler the judge of Calicut would approach with an offer of allegiance (*ṭā^ca*), and the request fits within the context of the importance of the spice trade between Malabar and Egypt via Aden in that era. *Khuṭba* networks were strategic allegiances and changed with changing economic and political conditions, at the micro-level of a single port and at the macro-level of the Indian Ocean. Calicut is the only location for which we have sufficient detail, but it is clear that in the course of the thirteenth though fifteenth centuries Calicut's Muslim community recognized first Hormuz and Delhi, later the Yemen, before finally returning to proclaiming their allegiance to Hormuz. All these shifts correlate with broad changes in the direction of trade across the western Indian Ocean. If we want to talk in terms of personal or even group "identity" and "belonging" in these *khuṭba* networks, one must first and foremost think in terms of trade network relationships.

Conclusion

In sum, the list of Rasulid stipends sent to Islamic judges and clerics in South Asia in the very early 1290s and recorded in the *Nūr al-ma^cārif* or *Light of knowledge* provides invaluable insights into the Islamic landscape of pre-conquest South Asia. This study only begins the work of deciphering and interpreting the topographical and network information it provides.

This study has suggested that the list of stipends awarded to Islamic judges and clerics in India by the customs house (*furḍa*) in Aden in the early 1290s be interpreted as a list of the places where the sermon or *khuṭba* given at Friday prayers and on the occasion of *^cĪd* prayers included the name of the Rasulid Sultan (a practice known technically as *al-du^cā li-l-sulṭān* or *da^cwat al-sulṭān*). This research suggests the existence of an entirely new category of network operating in the Indian Ocean, one we might agree to call the *khuṭba,* or perhaps *du^cā,* network that linked Sunni Muslim communities living outside the *Dār al-Islām* to Islamic polities within the *Dār al-Islām.* Although a common sense of Sunni belonging was frequently expressed via the inclusion of the name of the Abbasid Caliph in these *khuṭba*s, it was the inclusion of the name of a contemporary Muslim ruler alongside this that allowed these communities to construct new and qualitatively different types of networking. Rather than reflecting actual territorial rule, the mention of the name of a contemporary Muslim ruler in the *khuṭba* formalized a relationship of allegiance (*ṭā^ca*) between each Muslim community and a specific Islamic polity. From the evidence available so far these networks appear to have been constituted essentially along politico-economic lines, forging and maintaining favored trading relations between the parties. Research demonstrates that the Rasulids of the Yemen were not alone in maintaining these networks, but followed well-established practice among Middle Eastern polities that were participants in the Indian Ocean maritime trade. "*Khuṭba* networks" bring another dimension to the understanding of the political geographies, economic, and personal networks of the period and encourage us to reshape our models of the relations between the Middle Eastern Islamic center and its western Indian Ocean periphery. [96]

Appendix

The decipherment of this list of locations is not without its difficulties as the orthography of South Asian place names was still far from standardized in Arabic at this period. Particular problems were faced when a wide range of sounds not represented in the Arabic alphabet, notably "ch," "g," "p," and "v" had to be written down. While the letters *wāw* and *bā'* served for the sounds "v" and "p," "ch," and "g" posed particular problems and are rendered by a wide range of Arabic letters. Perhaps one of the more confusing conventions encountered by later translators and geographers was the use of the letter *ṣād* for "ch," seen here in a number of cases.[97] Adding to these difficulties is the fact that the manuscript is believed to be a copy of customs documents, recopied sometime in the mid-1290s. It is apparent that many place names became corrupted in the course of being copied. As many readers will already be aware, many letters of the Arabic alphabet are differentiated only by the number of diacritic marks placed above or below the main body of the letter, similarly even certain letters of different shapes can easily be confused when written hastily or in a cursive script. The manuscript is now in private ownership and not available for consultation or verification, even through photographic reproductions of micro-film, studies of the list are thus entirely reliant on the published edition of the text. The following critical discussions of each place name are an effort to bring some definitive order to a confusion that has endured since the documents first became known in the early 1990s.

I. al-Qaṣṣ[98] and Its Districts (*aᶜmāl*) (*Bilād al-Juzrāt*)

1. Nahrwāla (نهر والة). Jazim's edition reads Bahan Wāla (بهن والة) but it is relatively certain, as Vallet also deduced, that this is a misspelling or misreading of the name of the capital of Gujarat under the Solanki dynasty, Nahrwāla (Anahilavad Patan). The city is mentioned in the eleventh century by al-Bīrūnī (as Anhilwara انهلوره)[99] and by al-Idrīsī in the twelfth century (as Nahrwāra نهروارة) who specifically mentions the large number of Muslim merchants who go there for business.[100] As the capital of the later Chaulukyas, Nahrwāla, or Anahilavad Patana was home to a substantial Muslim community and a number of late thirteenth-century epitaphs belonging to Muslim merchants have been recorded by Z. A. Desai including a tombstone of a Persian merchant dated 681/1282.[101]

2. al-Qaṣṣ (القصّ). The repetition of the regional name among the localities where stipends were awarded suggests that al-Qaṣṣ (القصّ) also designated a specific locality (in many ways the reverse process of the port of Cambay giving its name to an entire region of Gujarat). In the early fourteenth century the geographer al-Dimashqī (d. 727/1327) describes the city of al-Quṣṣ as very large, having a port, great trade, and extensive territories.[102] The clue to the identification of al-Qaṣṣ appears to lie in the list itself, since the heading for this section in fact specifies that al-Qaṣṣ (القصّ) was known as Budlasar (بدلسر).[103] Budlasar would appear to be a later corruption of the place name Bhadreśvar,

Bhadreśvar, itself a corruption of the original name of Bhadravati. Bhadreśvar, is a small but significant port on the coast of Kachchh, active from the eleventh to thirteenth centuries as an independent port state, run by a Jain merchant council; it is now most famous for having preserved the substantial remains of what may have been an Isma^{c}ili mercantile settlement.[104] The letter of a Jewish merchant in India written around 1145 mentions Qaṣṣī robes as exports to the port of Suwākin in the Sudan and other places.[105]

3. Maliyabūr (ماليبور). A number of places in western India have similar names; given that that the site is designated as belonging to Kachchh the most promising candidate may be the modern site of Malia on the north coast of Saurashtra, in effect on the shore of the Little Rann of Kachchh. The addition of the suffix "būr" would simply be an abbreviation of the Sanskrit term *pura* designating a city or town, thus Maliyabūr. The site does not appear to be mentioned in the Arabic and Persian geographical literature but three Islamic inscriptions of the early sixteenth century testify to a Muslim presence at that period and name the town Māliyā. Malia is located at the shortest crossing point over the Little Rann and thus a vital waypoint on internal routes.

4. Aṣāwal (اصاول). This is the name of the settlement that preceded the establishment in the early fifteenth century of the capital of the Sultanate of Gujarat, Ahmedabad. The site of Aṣāwal is mentioned by the geographers al-Bīrūnī and al-Idrīsī as Asāwal (اساول).[106] It is situated in the central plain of Gujarat on numerous trade routes from the coast towards the inland centers of western India. Muslim communities have been attested at Aṣāwal as far back as the eleventh century since a mosque foundation inscription from the Tajpur quarter repeats the text of an earlier foundation inscription dated 445/1035.[107] Other epigraphic records record the foundation of the Mir Hajji mosque in 636/1238 while a gravestone dated 675/1276 is also known.[108]

5. Banūkas (بنوكس). This is an unidentified locality.

6. Dūlṣa (دولصه). This is the town of Dholka, situated between Aṣāwal and the port of Kinbāya (Cambay), also rendered as Dawlqa (دولقه) by al-Idrīsī.[109] In the thirteenth century it was the capital of the Vaghela rulers.

7. Bāsima (باسمة)? No location of this name is recorded; however, a very tentative suggestion is that it may be a heavily corrupted rendering of the place name Bāniya (بانية). Bāniya is mentioned by the geographer Ibn Ḥawqal in the tenth century as a town between the Mihran or Indus river in Sind and the coast of Gujarat; it lay mid-way between the cities of al-Manṣūra in Sind and the town of Qāmuhūl, which represented the furthest limit of the Rastrakutan domains—from here it was four stages to Cambay. Plotting out these stages on a modern map, the site of Bāniya corresponds more or less with the desert city of Umarkot, famous as the birthplace of the Mughal Emperor Akbar.[110]

8. Mandal (مندل). Mandal is almost certainly to be identified with the town of Mandal on the shore of the little Rann of Kachchh. A town named al-Mandal is mentioned by al-Balādhurī as having been attacked by al-Junayd, the governor of the frontier of Sind, under the caliphate of Hishām (r. 724-743), during his battle with a certain Indian ruler named Hullishah. Al-Mandal is mentioned in Ibn Khurdādhbih's famous *Book of Roads and Kingdoms* in the ninth century and later Yaqūt (d. 1229) mentions it as a center for the distribution of Mandali aloes.[111] The historical and territorial context suggests that it was located in western India.[112] Three Islamic inscriptions of the fifteenth century have been recorded at the site.[113]

9. Bīrānūr (بيرانور). No locality of this name has thus far been identified.

10. Kūtishvar (كوتشور). Given as Kawsarar (كوسرر), this is very probably a misspelling of the place name Kūtishvar, a port and important pilgrimage center on the west coast of Kachchh.[114] This was an important Buddhist center in the seventh century and remains a center of Hindu pilgrimage today.

11. Kothara (كثر). Edited as Kanar (كنر), Vallet suggests the town of Kaner or Wankaner in Saurashtra. In the early fourteenth century al-Dimashqī mentions a large city on the coast just near al-Qaṣṣ (Bhadresvar) called Kīr (كير).[115] Is it possible that both are misspellings of the place name Kothara (كثر), a small town in Kachchh.[116]

12. Qadhamān (قذ مان). Given as Qadamān (قدمان) this is probably the small town of Ghathaman, situated at the south end of the Palanpur gap and on the trade route through the Aravalli hills into southern Rajasthan and Gangetic plain.[117]

13. Baldhara (بلذرة). This locality is still unidentified.

II. Kinbāya and Its Districts (*aʿmāl*), Country of Juzz (*Bilād al-Juzz*)[118]

14. Barūda (برودة). Given as Barwa (بروة), as suggested by Vallet it is likely that this is a misspelling of the place name Baroda, the modern Vadodara. Barūda is not referenced in the Arabic and Persian geographical literature but is mentioned as Baḍuda (بضدة) in an Islamic inscription of the mid-fourteenth century.[119]

15. Bārīja (باريج)? The edited text gives Laraiḥ (لرايح) but no location of this name has been identified. Jean Deloche mentions a small site known as Bārejā which lay on the main route between Cambay and Aṣāwal that could be Laraiḥ (لرايح), a corruption of Bārejā to Bārīj (باريج).[120]

16. Dhabūhī (ذ بوهي) Edited by Jazim as Dhayūhī (ذ يوهي) this is without a doubt a misspelling of Dhabūhī, the city of Dabhoi, situated to the east of Baroda and fortified by the Vaghela ruler Vīsaladeva in the mid-thirteenth century. Dhabūhī is not mentioned in the Arabic and Persian geographical literature.

17. Inkalash (إنكلش). Edited by Jazim as Inkalas (إنكلس), this is very probably the small town of Ankleshvar situated on the left bank of the Narmada, opposite Bharuch, and an obvious crossing point on the land route along the coast of south Gujarat.[121] A Qur'nic inscription in characters of the eleventh or twelfth century has been listed at the site.[122]

18. Kūdra (كودرة). Given as Kawdara (كودره) in Jazim's edition a more probable reading would be Kūdra, corresponding to the modern Godhra in the far east of Gujarat. Godhra is situated along a major trade route into central India, specifically the region of Madhya Pradesh and the city of Ujjain,[123] however, it is not mentioned in the Arabic and Persian geographical literature.

19. al-Balawdhara (البلوذرة). Written al-Balawdhara, the only reasonable candidate for this locality would seem to be the town of Bulsara (البلذرة) also known as Valsad, just north of the later site of the port of Daman. It is not clear how the letter *wāw* forms part of this reading unless to differentiate it from the town of Baldhara (بلذرة) mentioned as forming part of the territories of Kachchh.

20. Biṭlāwad (بطلاود). This is very probably the town of Petlad, or Petlawad, located to the north of Cambay, Petlad is mainly remembered in the history of Muslim Gujarat as the site of the shrine to the saint Arjun Shāh al-Akhsī who is believed to have come to

Gujarat from Central Asia, and died at Petlad in 633/1236.[124] The site is not otherwise mentioned in the Arabic and Persian geographical literature but a number of Islamic inscriptions testify to patronage there from the fourteenth century.[125] Another location of the same name, Petlawad, is situated beyond Godhra and Dohad, on the main trade route into Madhya Pradesh and challenges this identification, though no evidence of a Muslim community there is documented.[126]

21. Barūj (بروج). This is without a doubt the port of Bharuch on the Narmada river. Earlier historical and geographical literature gives the name as Barūṣ (بروص), sometimes mistakenly transcribed as Barwaṣ.[127] Al-Bīrūnī references it as Bahrūj (بهروج), and it is described by al-Idrīsī in the twelfth century as a fine city by the name Barūḥ (بروح).[128] The site is also mentioned in the letter of a Mangalore-based Jewish trader written around 1145.[129]

22. Rānīr (رانير). Edited as Rānīz (رانيز) this is more properly read as Rānīr (Rander), the predecessor of Surat on the Tapti river. The site is not otherwise mentioned in the Arabic and Persian geographical literature but an Islamic tombstone dated 633/1236 is recorded there.[130]

III. Lamībāsūr and Its Districts (*a*ᶜ*māl*), Country of al-Kumkam (*Bilād al-Kamkam*)

23. Lamībāsūr (لميباسور). No locality of this name is known, however, it is possibly a variant spelling of the port name Abūsarūr (ابوسرور) or Bāsarūr (باسرور) (the first given by Ibn Baṭṭūṭa, the second by Abū al-Fiḍā') which corresponds to modern Barcelore or Baracelore.[131] The problem is that Barcelore belongs to the Malabar, not the Konkan, coast; however, Ibn Baṭṭūṭa described it as the first town of Malabar which he entered.[132] A district of the Yadava kingdom known as Basavur or Baśura, and corresponding to Dharwar district, is mentioned in an inscription of *Śaka* 1186/1265 and might offer an alternative identification.[133]

IV. [Country of Malabar][134] *(Map 3.5)*

24. Bud (بد). This is possibly a truncated rendering of the port name Buddfattan, mentioned in the early fourteenth century by al-Dimashqī and grouped there with Dahbattan and Fandarayna.[135] Later in the century Budd Fatan is mentioned by Ibn Baṭṭūṭa as belonging to the Muslim ruler of Jūrfatan.[136] It is commonly identified with Pudupattana, between Mount Eli and Cannanore.

25. Hīlī (هيلي). This is the site of Mount Eli, the highest point along this part of the coast which had provided an orientation point for ships since pre-Roman times.[137] It is mentioned along with Jūrfatan by al-Dimashqī in the early fourteenth century.[138] Later that century Ibn Baṭṭūṭa noted its famous Friday mosque that attracted offerings from seafarers as well as the *madrasa* ("school") and soup kitchen attached to the mosque.[139] The site described here probably corresponds to the modern village of Madayi where substantial Islamic inscriptions have survived[140] and which has an elaborate oral history linking it to the Yemen. The gravestone of a certain al-Takrītī (d. 684/1285) suggests links to the famous Takrītī family involved in the Karim trade.

26. Harqīlīya (هرقيلي). Given as Hartīlī (هرتيلي) this is very probably a misspelling of the place name Harqīlīya (هرقيلي) the ancient name of the port of Kasargod.[141] The port of

Hīraqlīya is mentioned by al-Dimashqī in the early fourteenth century as surrounded by 2,000 villages located in the mountains and on the coast.[142]

27. Jūrfatan (جورفتن). Given as Hawrash (حورش), Vallet rightly suggests a misreading of Jurfatan (جورفتن), the name of the early site of Cannanore; certainly no site by the name of Hawrash can be identified at present. A port named Jirbatān (جربتان) is mentioned in the twelfth century by al-Idrīsī.[143] In the early fourteenth century al-Dimashqī identifies Jirabattan or Jūrfattan together with Hīlī as having an infidel population.[144] Later in the century Ibn Baṭṭūṭa talks of Sultan Kuwayl who ruled from Jurfattan over the ports and coast of Dahfatan (Dharmapattam) and Buddfattan (Pudupattana). Described as "one of the most powerful rulers of Malabar," he owned ships going to Oman, Fars, and Yemen, and his ancestors had converted to Islam.[145]

28. Fandarīna (فندرينة). This the town of Pantalayini Kollam, situated to the north of al-Shāliyāt and Calicut. Al-Idrīsī mentions a port of this name, given as Qandarīna or Fandarīna in the twelfth century[146] and it is also mentioned as Fandaraynā in the correspondence of a Jewish merchant based in Aden to a colleague in India around 1139.[147] Al-Dimashqī in the early fourteenth century mentions it as having a mainly Jewish, Indian, and Muslim population with few Christians, and groups it with the ports of Dahbatan and Buddfattan.[148] Later in the century Ibn Baṭṭūṭa describes three Muslim quarters there, each with their own mosque, and a Friday mosque on the seashore.[149]

29. Manjalūr (منجلور). The port of Mangalore is still a major center of trade today; it is mentioned as having trade with Aden in the letters of Jewish merchants in the twelfth century,[150] but only later appears in the subsequent Arabic and Persian geographical literature, as for example in al-Dimashqī as Manjarūr (منجرور) where it is mentioned as a great center of the pepper trade.[151] Ibn Baṭṭūṭa visited later in the century and described it as having a Muslim population of over 4,000.[152]

30. al-Shāliyāt (الشاليات). This is the small port of Chaliyam located just to the south of the present port of Calicut. It is not regularly mentioned under this name in the Arabic and Persian geographical literature but does feature in Abū al-Fiḍā's fourteenth-century *Taqwīm al-buldān*.[153] Two fourteenth-century Islamic tombstones are recorded at the site.[154]

31. Fākanūr (فاكنور). Also listed as Fayakanūr (فياكنور) in the second list of presents to personalities in India in the *Nūr al-maʿārif*, this is the small port of Barkur. Fākanūr is mentioned by al-Dimashqī in the first quarter of the fourteenth century as a large city with a population of Indians, Persians, and Arab Muslims;[155] and is also mentioned by Ibn Baṭṭūṭa.[156]

32. Nūr Dahbatan (نور دهبتن). Dahbattan is usually identified as the small port of Dharmapattam. A letter of 1139 among the Geniza documents records the arrival in Aden of the merchant *nākhūda* Joseph from the port of Dahbattān.[157] Al-Dimashqī mentions Dihfattan along with Buddfattan and Fandarayna,[158] whereas Ibn Baṭṭūṭa refers to a certain port of Dahbatan (دهبتن) as belonging to the territories of the Sultan of Jūrfatan.[159] According to him the port had a magnificent Friday mosque and water tank, as was common in Malabar. The prefix Nūr is not given but might refer to a feature such as a lighthouse; in any case, the identification appears convincing. The problem, however, is with the position of this locality in the edited list. In Jazim's edition (Nūr) Dahbatan is mentioned, along with al-Kawr and Tāna, as one of the localities associated with the country of the *Bulgha* (*Bilād al-Bulgha*), far to the north. As no locality by the name of (Nūr) Dahbatan can be identified in the region of Tāna, it might be possible that (Nūr) Dahbatan was simply added to the end of the last list of gifts and so has been mistakenly grouped with regions to its north and this is how it has been treated here.

V. al-Kawr,[160] Tāna, Country of the Bulgha[161] (*Bilād al-Bulgha*)

33. Tāna (تانة). This is the port of Thane just to the north of the modern city of Mumbai, which is amply mentioned in the Arabic and Persian geographical literature, beginning with al-Masᶜūdī.[162] The site is also mentioned in the letter of a Mangalore-based Jewish trader written around 1145.[163] One of the most interesting later references is in al-Dimashqī's early fourteenth-century geography, which lists it alongside the towns of Vasāhī, Ṣubāra, and Ajāshī.[164] He describes it as having a Friday mosque and thronging with merchants and merchandise.

34. Māhīm (ماهيم). Given in Jazim's edited text as Fahāyim (فهايم), the most likely explanation is that this is a slightly jumbled rendering of the small port name of Māhīm, located on the north of Bombay island and which appears in the early British maps as Mahim or Mayem.[165]

35. Vasāhī (وساهي). This is the small port of Vasai at the mouth of the Ulhas river. This may be the town of Sāhi (ساهي) mentioned by al-Dimashqī in the first quarter of the fourteenth century.[166]

36. Fālī (فالي). This is possibly a rendering of Pali, the name of a group of hills near the port area or Bandra of Mumbai; the name is remembered today in the Palli Hills suburb. No location of this name is mentioned in the Arabic and Persian geographers.

37. Ṣubāra (صبارة). Given in the edited text as Sāra (صارة), this is probably a misspelling of Ṣubāra (صبارة) or Subara (سبارة) , the well-known port mentioned by the Arab geographers beginning with al-Istakhrī. The town is mentioned by al-Dimashqī in the first quarter of the fourteenth century when he describes it as being situated in the land of pirates.[167]

38. Ajāshī (أجاشي). Edited by Jazim as Ajāsī (أجاسي), this is probably a slight misspelling of the place name Ajāshī (أجاشي) or Agashi, a small fishing port north of Vasāhī (Vasai). Ajāshī may be the same as the town of Akānthī (اكانثي) mentioned by al-Dimashqī in the first quarter of the fourteenth century.[168]

39. Duwayjir (دويجر). In the mid-fourteenth century Ibn Baṭṭūṭa refers to the upper citadel of Dawlatabad, the former Yadava capital of Devagiri, as al-Duwayqīr (الدويقير),[169] which appears to be a variation on the more familiar spelling of ديوجير usually rendered Deogir. The identification indicates the terminus of this network from the Tāna area at the Yadava capital via routes through the passes at Borghat and Thalgat.[170]

VI. al-Ṣuliyān[171] [the Country of] Maᶜbar

40. Qā'il (قائل). Edited by Jazim as Qāqil (قاقل), this is undoubtedly a misspelling or misreading of the place name Qā'il (قائل), one of the most famous ports on the Coromandel coast. It is mentioned by Marco Polo as the port of Cail.[172] Recently the object of extensive survey work by Mehrdad Shokoohy, the port preserves a significant number of ancient mosques and graveyards.[173] Muslim settlement is believed to date back to the eleventh or twelfth century though no monuments or inscriptions earlier than the early fourteenth century have survived there.

41. Fatan (فتن). Given as Fanytan (فنيتن) by Jazim, no port of this name is known along the Ma^c^bar coast. A port by the name of Fatan (فتن) is mentioned by both Rashīd al-Dīn and Vassāf. Fatan, the chief harbor of the Pandya kingdom, is believed to have been located north of Deviapatam, near Ramnad, and for the moment this remains the most probable identification.

42. Urwāṭūa or Arwāṭuwa (أرواطوه). Tamil place names appear to have posed particular problems in their transposition to Arabic or Persian and no location of this name is given in the Arabic and Persian literature. Place names beginning with Ūwar or Ūr (اوريهار and اوردبيشو) are mentioned by al-Bīrūnī as lying to the south east of Kanauj, in the Orissa or Andhra Pradesh area.[174] Dimashqī mentions an Abāṭū (أباطو) somewhere in greater Ma^c^bar and Nainar has argued that it might correspond to Adirampattanam in the northwest corner of the Palk Bay.[175] It might also be a corruption of Harkāṭū (هركاطو) as given by Ibn Baṭṭūṭa in the mid-fourteenth century. It is, however, certain that it cannot refer to Madurai, given in Ibn Baṭṭūṭa and other sources as Muthra (مثرة).

43. Malāyūfatan (ملايوفتن). This is probably an alternative spelling of the port name Malīfatan (مليفتن) or Malī Fatan (ملي فتن) mentioned by Rashīd al-Dīn and Vassāf. Abū al-Fiḍā's fourteenth-century *Taqwīm al-buldān* mentions a Manīfattan (منيفتن).[176] Malayufatan (ملايوفتن), Malīfatan, and Manīfattan are believed to be misspellings of Manduri-fattan, a port on the shore of the Palk Bay.

44. Ḥaram al-Malībārāt (حرم المليبارات). Literally the sacred precinct of the Malibars, the place name is not commonly used in the Arabic and Persian geographical literature although the place name Malibārāt occurs in the letter of a Jewish merchant written around 1145, where it appears alongside other locations in Malabar.[177] Jazim's edition vocalizes this Mulaybārāt. Eric Vallet has suggested that this most probably corresponds to the locality of Mylapore, now part of the suburbs of Chennai (Madras), site of the grave of the Apostle Thomas and still the major center of Christianity in India.[178] This appellation might refer to another significant religious center in the Pandya kingdom.

Notes

1. This article could not have been written without the patience and feedback of many scholars. I would especially like to thank Ken Hall for patiently allowing me to write this so close to the final submission deadline, if not beyond it. The audience of the *Seminar for Arabian Studies* provided enthusiastic and helpful feedback on the original Small Cities Conference paper when I presented it in London in July 2007. My thanks also to Eric Vallet for his willingness to share the proofs of his forthcoming article for the *Annales Islamologiques* and for a stimulating discussion of the Yemen lists in the café of the Institut du Monde Arabe in Paris in January 2008.

2. Muhammad ^c^Abd al-Rahim Jazim, ed., *Nūr al-ma^c^ārif. Lumière de la connaissance. Règles, lois et coutumes du Yémen sous le règne de sultan rasoulide al-Muzaffar*, 2 vols. (Sanaa: Centre Français d'Archéologie et de Sciences Sociales de Sanaa, 2003-2005).

3. Jazim ed., *Nūr al-Ma^c^ārif*, I, 516-518.

4. Ibn Faḍl Allāh al-^c^Umarī, *Masālik al-abṣār fī mamālik al-amṣār*, trans. I. H. Siddiqi and Q. M. Ahmad, *A Fourteenth Century Arab Account of India under Sultan Muhammad bin Tughluq* (Aligarh: Siddiqi Publishing House, 1971), 8.

5. Amīr Khusrauw Dihlavī, *Khazā'in al-futūḥ.* Wahid Mirza [English trans.], National Committee for 700th Anniversary of Amir Khusrau (Lahore: United Printers, 1975), 82.

6. Ibid.

7. The happy recent exceptions to this have been the excavations at medieval Chaul undertaken by the Deccan College Pune and work at Sanjan under the auspices of the World Zoroastrian Congress.

8. ᶜAlī ibn Ḥusayn al-Masᶜūdī, *Murūj al-dhahab wa maᶜādin al-jawhar* Arabic text edition edited by B. de Meynard and P. de Courteille, and revised Arabic edition edited by C. Pellat, 7 vols. (Beirut: Publications de l'Universite Libanaise, 1965-1979), I, 20.

9. This will form part of the forthcoming Elizabeth Lambourn *Coastal Perspectives and Mercantile Cultures: India, Persia and Arabia 500-1500 CE.*

10. al-Masᶜūdī *Murūj al-dhahab*, I, 248.

11. Buzūrg ibn Shariyār, *Kitāb ᶜajā'ib al-hind.* G. S. P. Grenville [English trans.], *The Book of the Wonders of India*, (London: East-West, 1981), 83, 94.

12. Muḥammad Abū al-Qāsim ibn Ḥawqal al-Nasībī (known as Ibn Ḥawqal), *Kitāb ṣūrat al-arḍ*, ed. J. H. Kramers, *Opus Geographicum*, 2nd ed. (Leiden: Bibliotheca Geographorum Arabicorum, 1938), 320.

13. Ibn Ḥawqal, *Kitāb ṣūrat al-arḍ*, 324.

14. Ibid., 320.

15. *Akhbār al-ṣīn wa al-hind*, ed. and trans. J. Sauvaget *Relation de la Chine et de l'Inde* (Paris: Société d'Edition Les Belles Lettres, 1948), 7.

16. See Eric Vallet, *Pouvoir, commerce et marchands dans le Yémen rasūlide (626-858/1229-1454)*, Ph.D. dissertation (Paris: Université Paris Panthéon Sorbonne, 2006), ch. 3, "Le Fisc d'Aden, percepteur, acheteur et vendeur."

17. Eric Vallet, "Les sultans rasūlides du Yémen, protecteurs des communautés musulmanes de l'Inde (VIIᵉ-VIIIᵉ/XIIIᵉ-XIVᵉ siècles)," *Annales Islamologiques*, forthcoming.

18. The interpretation of these gifts is as yet far from clear. The term used in the text is *sūsiyya*, plural *sawāsī.* Originally associated with the north African city of Susa where it was exclusively made, the geographer Ibn Ḥawqal describes this linen cloth as "without parallel, and of a startlingly white colour and lustre, not to be found in any other cloth" (R. B. Serjeant, *Islamic Textiles. Materials for the History up to the Mongol Conquest* [Beirut: Librairie du Liban, 1972], 183). However, it appears that the term later came to describe a fabric of similar description though made at other locations; by the time the term appears in twelfth-century Yemeni sources, R. B. Serjeant suggests that it had become a "trade-name for cloth exported from Egypt by this route" (Serjeant, *Islamic Textiles*, 130, n. 66). However, in the same note, Serjeant also suggests that by later periods the term might designate a garment, "the name having been extended from the place to a special piece of clothing." On the other hand, the list does refer to parts of a *sūsiyya* being given, which would tend to support the idea that this was a length of unsewn fabric. It is difficult at present to determine whether the gifts consisted of a set of clothes, robe, and turban, thus belonging to the category of *khilᶜa*, or whether they were stipends, awards of cloth and other merchandise for personal use or resale.

19. See Vallet, "Les sultans rasūlides du Yémen, protecteurs des communautés musulmanes de l'Inde," for this calculation; see Serjeant, *Islamic Textiles*, 131 for information on the madder trade in Yemen at this period as well as new data presented in chapters 3 and 6 of Vallet's Ph.D. dissertation.

20. For a list of these see Jazim ed., *Nūr al-maᶜārif*, I, 260-263. I am grateful to Eric Vallet for pointing this list out to me; he is currently preparing a new article on this topic.

21. See Jay Spaulding's study in this volume.

22. Vallet, "Pouvoir, commerce et marchands dans le Yémen rasūlide (626-858/1229-1454) "; Eric Vallet, "Les communautés musulmanes de la côte indienne face au Yémen (XIIIᵉ siècle-XVIᵉ siècle)," in *Hypothèses. Travaux de l'École doctorale d'histoire de l'Université de Paris I* (2004), 147-156; Vallet, "Yemeni 'Oceanic Policy' at the End of the Thirteenth Century," in *Proceedings of the Seminar for Arabian Studies*, vol. 36, ed.

Lloyd Weeks and St John Simpson (Oxford: Archaeopress, 2007); and Vallet, "Les sultans rasūlides du Yémen, protecteurs des communautés musulmanes de l'Inde."

23. I am grateful to Eric Vallet for clarifying the origins of the Ṭībīs, who are often described as of Omani origin (personal communication).

24. Jazim ed., *Nūr al-maᶜārif*, I, 519.

25. Vallet, "Les sultans rasūlides du Yémen, protecteurs des communautés musulmanes de l'Inde (VIIe-VIIIe/XIIIe-XIVe siècles)."

26. This heading is missing from the text but the locations that follow are all clearly situated along the Malabar coast, consequently no principal city is given.

27. This depends on whether Dahbatan is included in Malabar, as discussed in the Appendix.

28. Another interesting aspect of these lists is that the regional networks and hubs suggested by the headings do not necessarily map directly onto the stipend network, thus, as discussed below, while al-Qaṣṣ and Tāna appear in the heading as regional hubs and as the recipients of a stipend, neither Kinbāya (Cambay) nor al-Kawr are listed as places where a *qāḍī* or a *khaṭīb* receives a stipend.

29. The edited text lists Nūr Dahbatan as part of this group of ports, however, no place of this name is known in this area and the identification appears to correspond to a port in Malabar (see the discussion of this problem in the Appendix).

30. Echoes of earlier territorial histories appear to linger in some other headings with Kinbāya (Cambay) qualified as belonging to the country of the *Juzz* (*Bilād al-Juzz*), and al-Kawr and Tāna as part of the country of the Bulgha (*Bilād al-Bulgha*).

31. Norman Calder, "Friday Prayer and the Juristic Theory of Government," *Bulletin of the School of Oriental and African Studies*, 49 (1986), 35.

32. Muḥammad ibn Aḥmad al-Bīrūnī, *Alberuni's India*, ed. E. Sachau (London: Trübner, 1887), 102.

33. For an excellent resume of the sources on this substance and its role in early Meccan trade see P. Crone, *Meccan Trade and the Rise of Islam* (Piscataway, NJ: Gorgias Press LLC, 2004), 67-70.

34. Al-Balādhurī, *Kitāb futūḥ al-buldān*, trans. F. C. Murgotten, *The Origins of the Islamic State*, 2. Vols. (New York: Columbia University, 1924), II, 220, 228.

35. Ibid.

36. Mehrdad Shokoohy, *Bhadresvar. The Oldest Islamic Monuments in India* (Studies in Islamic Art and Architecture, Supplements to Muqarnas, vol. II, 1988). See also Johanna Blayac, "Bhadresvar: un exemple de la da'wa fâtimide au Gujarat?" in *Les Ismaéliens d'Asie du Sud: gestion des héritages et production identitaire*, ed. Michel Boivin (Paris: L'Harmattan, forthcoming).

37. *Imperial Gazetteer of India: Provincial Series, Bombay Presidency* (Calcutta: Superintendent of Government Printing, 1909), II, 346.

38. For example, a map of Cambaia by Petrus Bertius from the *Caert Thresoor* of 1612 shows Cambay situated on one of the branches of the Indus; another map of India from T. Herbert, *Some Yeares Travels into Divers Parts of Asia and Afrique* of 1665, shows Saurashtra as an island. These maps are reprinted in Susan Gole, *A Series of Early Printed Maps of India in Facsimile, Collected by Susan Gole*, 2nd rev. ed. (New Delhi: Jayprints, 1984), title page and map 11b, respectively.

39. *Imperial Gazetteer of India: Provincial Series, Bombay Presidency*, II, 340–346.

40. See Elizabeth Lambourn, "Brick, Timber and Stone: Building Materials and the Construction of Islamic Architectural History in Gujarat," *Muqarnas. An Annual on the Visual Culture of the Islamic World*, 23 (2006), 191-217.

41. B. Arunachalam, "Use of Imagery in Reconstruction of the Past-A Case Study of Sopara," *Indian Cartographer* (2002), 342-346 (http://www.incaindia.org/technicalpapers/58_CHE01.pdf).

42. Jazim, ed., *Nūr al-maᶜārif*, I, 518.

43. K. V. Ramesh, *A History of South Kanara* (Dharwar: Karnatak University, 1970), 19. Ramesh quotes a passage from the Tamil Sangam literature of the early first millennium in which Mount Eli is referred to as belonging to "the gold-producing Konkana."

44. See Ramesh, *History of South Kanara.*

45. See Sanjay Subrahmanyam, "The Portuguese, the Port of Basrur and the Rice Trade, 1600-50," *Indian Economic and Social History Review*, 21, 4 (1984), 433-462.

46. Ranabir Chakravarti presents some useful information on the variety of routes taken between Mangalore and Aden in the twelfth century by Jewish merchants and others, including voyages that covered smaller ports of the Konkan and Gujarat coast. See his "Nakhudas and Nauvittakas: Ship-Owning Merchants in the West Coast of India , c. A.D. 1000-1500," *Journal of the Economic and Social History of the Orient*, 43, 1, (2000), 44, n. 30; 51-52.

47. Shaykh Abū ᶜAbdallāh Muḥammad ibn Baṭṭūṭa, *Tuḥfat al-nuẓẓār fī gharā'ib al-amṣār wa ᶜajā'ib al-asfār*, ed. and French trans. C. Defrémery and B. R. Sanguinetti, *Voyages d'Ibn Batoutah*, 4. vols. (Paris: 1853-1859), II, 177.

48. For such coast and hinterland commercial networking in contemporary south India, see R. Champakalakshmi, *Trade, Ideology, and Urbanization. South India 300 B.C. to A.D. 1300* (New Delhi: Oxford University Press, 1996).

49. See the famous mosque foundation inscription dated 1264; the Sanskrit portion of the text was first edited by E. Hultzsch, "A Grant of Arjunadèva of Gujarat Dated 1264 A.D.," *Indian Antiquary* (1882), 241-225; a revised edition and edition of the Arabic portion were published in D. C. Sircar, "Veraval Inscription of Chaulukya-Vaghela Arjuna, 1264 A.D.," *Epigraphia Indica*, 34, 4 (1961-1962), 141-150, and Z. A. Desai, "Arabic Inscriptions of the Rajput Period in *Gujarat*," *Epigraphia Indica. Arabic and Persian Supplement* (1961), 1-24. The inscription has since been the object of reinterpretation by many scholars.

50. A twelfth-century mosque survives here; see Mehrdad Shokoohy, *Muslim Architecture in South India: The Sultanate of Ma'bar and the Traditions of Maritime Settlers on the Malabar and Coromandel Coasts.* (London: Routledge Curzon, 2003), 18-20.

51. Stewart Gordon, *Robes of Honour: Khilat In Pre-Colonial and Colonial India* (Oxford: Oxford University Press, 2003); Stewart Gordon, ed., *Robes and Honor. The Medieval World of Investiture* (New York: Palgrave, 2001).

52. ᶜAlī ibn al-Ḥasan al-Khazrajī, *al-ᶜUqūd al-lu'lu'iyya*, ed. Shaykh Muhammad 'Asal and J. W. Redhouse, *The Pearl-Strings; A History of the Resuliyy Dynasty of Yemen*, 5 vols. E. J. W. Gibb Memorial Series vol. III (Leiden and London: E. J. Brill and Luzac and Co, 1907-1918), V, 244-247.

53. al-Khazrajī, *al-ᶜUqūd al-lu'lu'iyya*, V, 245.

54. Ibid.

55. Ibid.

56. al-Khazrajī, *al-ᶜUqūd al-lu'lu'iyya*, V, 244.

57. Ibid. Eric Vallet (personal communication) indicates that the Arabic text is open to interpretation and that a more dialectal reading might suggest that it is the Sultan who awarded a robe to the judge, rather than the other way round.

58. Calder, "Friday Prayer and the Juristic Theory of Government," 36.

59. Ibid.

60. *Fiqh* treatises generally avoid discussing this element of the *khuṭba* in what Norman Calder sees to be "a deliberate abstention" (Calder, "Friday Prayer and the Juristic Theory of Government," 36).

61. Vallet (personal communication) explains that the term *imām* can only refer to the Abbasid Caliphs; indeed this is the term by which they are designated in the Abbasid sources. The mention of Caliphs before this may simply be a florid element of style (in effect a repetition), however, as the Rasulid Sultans designated themselves as Caliphs, this might refer to the practice of including the full sequence of Rasulid Sultans, right

back to the founder of the dynasty, in the *khuṭba*. The suggestion is that in its translation to Calicut the *khuṭba* continued this practice.

62. Vallet, "Yemeni 'oceanic policy' at the end of the thirteenth century," 293.

63. al-Khazrajī, *al-ᶜUqūd al-lu'lu'iyya*, V, 246.

64. This appears to be a clear reference to the port-polity of Samudra-Pasai situated on the north east coast of Sumatra, which then dominated the pepper trade and transit trade through the Straits of Melaka. The reference is important in confirming the early presence of merchants from Samudra in Calicut as a significant group before 1393, but also sheds important new light on the networks of influence that Samudra-Pasai was cultivating in the western Indian Ocean. See Kenneth R. Hall, "Upstream and Downstream Unification in Southeast Asia's First Islamic Polity: The Changing Sense of Community in the Fifteenth-Century *Hikayat Raja-Raja Pasai* Court Chronicle," *Journal of the Economic and Social History of the Orient*, 44, 2 (2001), 198-229.

65. al-Khazrajī, *al-ᶜUqūd al-lu'lu'iyya*, V, 246.

66. al-Khazrajī, *al-ᶜUqūd al-lu'lu'iyya*, II, 219.

67. al-Khazrajī, *al-ᶜUqūd al-lu'lu'iyya*, V, 245. This location can probably be identified as the village of Nilambur in Kerala.

68. al-Khazrajī, *al-ᶜUqūd al-lu'lu'iyya*, V, 244. The text specifies *maᶜāan* suggesting perhaps that this may have taken place simultaneously.

69. Ibn Baṭṭūṭa, *Tuḥfat al-nuẓẓār*.

70. Aubin, "Les princes d'Ormuz," 84.

71. Ibid.

72. See Hultzsch, "A Grant of Arjunadèva of Gujarat dated 1264 A.D."; Sircar, "Veraval Inscription of Chaulukya-Vaghela Arjuna, 1264 A.D."; and Desai, "Arabic Inscriptions of the Rajput Period in Gujarat," 1-24.

73. Desai, "Arabic Inscriptions of the Rajput Period," 13-14.

74. Aubin, "Les princes d'Ormuz," 84.

75. Ibid.

76. Ibn al-Mujāwir, *Ta'rīkh al-mustabṣir*, ed. O. Löfgren, *Descriptio Arabiae Meridionalis* (Leiden: E. J. Brill, 1951), 298. I am grateful to Eric Vallet for making me aware of this reference.

77. Aubin, "Les princes d'Ormuz," 84.

78. Kamāl al-Dīn ᶜAbd al-Razzāq Samarqandī, *Matlaᶜ-i saᶜdayn*, trans. W. M. Thackston, "Kamaluddin Abdul-Razzaq Samarqandi. Mission to Calicut and Vijayanagara," in *A Century of Princes. Sources on Timurid History and Art*, ed. and trans. W. M. Thackston (Cambridge, MA: The Aga Khan Program for Islamic Architecture, 1989), 299-321.

79. Samarqandī, *Matlaᶜ-i saᶜdayn*, 304.

80. Quoted in a new English translation in Muzaffar Alam and Sanjay Subramanyam, *Indo-Persian Travels in the Age of Discoveries, 1400-1800* (Cambridge: Cambridge University Press, 2007), 113.

81. *Akhbār al-ṣīn wa al-hind*, 7, section 12.

82. Aubin, "Les princes d'Ormuz," 84.

83. Alam and Subrahmanyam, *Indo-Persian Travels*, 65.

84. Further research is needed to determine the extent to which this is a practice particular to the Indian Ocean or one that is found around the entire fringes of the Dār al-Islām.

85. Baber Johansen, "The All-Embracing Town and Its Mosques," in Baber Johansen, *Contingency in a Sacred Law. Legal and Ethical Norms in the Muslim Fiqh* (Leiden: Brill, 1999), 100.

86. Quoted in a new English translation in Alam and Subrahmanyam, *Indo-Persian Travels*, 113.

87. Calder "Friday Prayer and the Juristic Theory of Government," 36, cited earlier.

88. It may also have been in this sense that the Abbasid Caliphate was invoked among Iraqi merchants in China during the ninth century.

89. See the account of this in Ibn Baṭṭūṭa. On the re-established caliphate see P. M. Holt, "Some Observations on the 'Abbasid Caliphate of Cairo," *Bulletin of the School of Oriental and African Studies*, 47, 3 (1984), 501-507.

90. Sircar, "Veraval Inscription of Chaulukya-Vaghela Arjuna, 1264 A.D.," 143.

91. Vallet, "Yemeni 'Oceanic Policy' at the end of the thirteenth century," 293; and Vallet, "Les sultans rasūlides du Yémen, protecteurs des communautés musulmanes de l'Inde, " forthcoming.

92. Ibid.

93. See B. Chattopadhyaya, *Representing the Other? Sanskrit Sources and the Muslims (Eighth to Fourteenth Century)* (New Delhi: Manohar, 1998).

94. Ibn al-Mujāwir, *Ta'rīkh al-mustabṣir*, 298.

95. Ibid.

96. See, in comparison, Enseng Ho, *The Graves of Tarim. Genealogy and Mobility across the Indian Ocean* (Berkeley: University of California Press, 2006).

97. The use of the letter *ṣād* to render the sound "ch" is frequent in Arabic loan words and is familiarly seen in the adoption of such loanwords as *ṣīn* (*chīn*) for China. The phenomenon is discussed at some length in Richard C. Steiner, *The Affricated Sade in Semitic Languages* (New York: The American Academy for Jewish Research, Monograph Series No. 3, 1982), see particularly 75-81 for an exhaustive list of examples in Arabic.

98. There seems little doubt that this refers to the region of western India known since at least the mid-second century as Kuchch or Kachchh. In Arabic sources the regional appellation Qaṣṣa (i.e., Kachcha), is encountered as early as al-Balādhurī's *Futūḥ al-buldān* (II, 220, 228) while al-Bīrūnī later renders it as Kach (كچ) (al-Bīrūnī, *Alberuni's India*, 102).

99. al-Bīrūnī, *Alberuni's India*, 100.

100. Abū ᶜAbdallāh Muḥammad al-Idrīsī, *Kitāb nuzhat al-mushtāq fī ikhtirāq al-afāq*, trans. P-A. Jaubert, *La Géographie d'Édrisi* (Amsterdam: Philo Press, 1975), 175-177.

101. Desai, "Inscriptions of the Rajput Period," 15-16.

102. Al-Dimashqī, *Nukhbat al-dahr fī ᶜajā'ib al-birr wa al-baḥr*, trans. M. A. F. Mehren, *Manuel de la Cosmographie du Moyen Age* (Amsterdam: Meridian Publishing Co., 1964), 230.

103. *Nūr al-maᶜārif*, I, 516.

104. See Shokoohy, *Bhadresvar*, 3-11 for a very thorough and up-to-date history of the site.

105. Goitein, *Letters of Medieval Jewish Traders*, 184.

106. al-Bīrūnī, *Alberuni's India*, 102 and al-Idrīsī, *Kitāb nuzhat al-mushtāq*, 176.

107. M. A. Chaghatai, "Muslim Monuments of Ahmadabad through their Inscriptions," *Bulletin of the Deccan College Research Institute*, vol. III, no. 2 (1942), 100-101.

108. Chaghatai, "Muslim Monuments of Ahmadabad," 102-104.

109. al-Idrīsī, *Kitāb nuzhat al-mushtāq*, 175-176.

110. The exact location of Bāniya has long remained unknown in the commentaries on the Arab geographical literature but the equivalence between Bāniya and Umarkot would appear to be confirmed by Ibn Ḥawqal's statement that Bāniya was the home of ᶜUmar ibn ᶜAbdullāh al-ᶜAzīz Habbārī Qurayshī, an ancestor of the then rulers of al-Mansura, hence the later name Umarkot or the fortress of Umar (Ibn Ḥawqal, *Kitāb ṣūrat al-arḍ*, 322).

111. S. Maqbul Ahmad, *Arabic Classical Accounts of India and China* (Shimla: Indian Institute of Advanced Study, 1989), 20.

112. al-Balādhurī, *Futūḥ*, [illegible].

113. *Annual Reports on Indian Epigraphy* (1954-1955), C20-22.

114. *Gazetteer of the Bombay Presidency*, Vol. V, Cutch, Palanpur and Mahi Kantha (Bombay: Government Central Press, 1880), 229-231.

115. Al-Dimashqī, *Nukhbat al-dahr*, 230.

116. *Gazetteer of the Bombay Presidency*, 231-232.

117. Jean Deloche, *La Circulation en Inde avant la Révolution des Transports*, 2 vols. (Paris: École Française d'Extrême Orient, 1980), vol. I, Fig. VIII.

118. Jazim and Vallet edit this section as reading *Bilād al-Juzz* or Country of the Juzz, then begin the list of stipends with the word *rātib* or "stipend." Without access to the original document it is impossible to confirm this reading as it might also be a confusion of the phrase *Bilād al-Juzrāt*.

119. *ARIE* (1963-1964), D85.

120. Deloche, *La Circulation en Inde*, vol. I, 55 and Fig. VIII. The *Ḥudūd al-ᶜālam* mentions a place named Bahrayij (بهرایج) in the section on Sind and Multan but it is not clear how the present location, even if it is a misspelling, could be one and the same. *Ḥudūd al-ᶜālam min al-mashriq ilá al-maghrib*, ed. and trans. V. Minorsky, *Ḥudūd al-ᶜālam 'The Regions of the World' a Persian Geography* (London: Luzac and Co., 1937), 246.

121. Deloche, *La Circulation en Inde*, I, Fig. VIII.

122. *ARIE* (1964-1965), D27.

123. Deloche, *La Circulation en Inde*, I, Fig. VIII.

124. Ghulam Yazdani, "Inscriptions in the Tomb of Baba Arjun Shah, Petlad (Baroda State)," *Epigraphia Indo-Moslamica* (1915-1916), 15-18.

125. *ARIE* (1956-1957), D84-88.

126. Deloche, *La Circulation en Inde*, I, Fig. VIII.

127. See for example al-Balādhurī, *Futūḥ*, II, 209, 227.

128. See al-Bīrūnī, *Alberuni's India*, 102 and al-Idrīsī, *Kitāb nuzhat al-mushtāq*, 175.

129. S. D. Goitein, *Letters of Medieval Jewish Traders in India* (Princeton: Princeton University Press, 1973), 64.

130. *ARIE* (1962-1963), D39.

131. Abū al-Fidā', *Taqwīm al-buldān*. trans. ᶜAbd al-Muḥammad Āyatī (Teheran, 1349 A. H.), 401.

132. Ibn Baṭṭūṭa, *Tuhfat al-nuzzār*, IV, 77.

133. N. N. Bhattacharyya, *The Geographical Dictionary. Ancient and Early Medieval India* (Delhi: Munshiram Manoharlal, 1999), 89.

134. This heading is missing from the text but the locations that follow are all clearly situated along the Malabar coast. Work on the *Nūr al-maᶜārif*'s list highlights the extent to which the historical topography of south India urgently requires attention, Nainar's book is now badly out of date and valuable information is now hidden among a variety of discursive footnotes or lost among new sources such as the Geniza documents.

135. Al-Dimashqī, *Nukhbat al-dahr*, 234.

136. Ibn Baṭṭūṭa, *Tuḥfat al-nuẓẓār*, IV, 83.

137. For an excellent early history of Mount Eli and its region see the early chapters of Geneviève Bouchon, *Regent of the Sea: Cannanore's Response to Portuguese Expansion, 1507-1528*. trans. Louise Shackley (Delhi: Oxford University Press, 1988).

138. Al-Dimashqī, *Nukhbat al-dahr*, 234.

139. Ibn Baṭṭūṭa, *Tuḥfat al-nuẓẓār*, IV, 81-82.

140. *ARIE* 1965-1966, D94-94. Nineteenth-century sources mention an inscription of the early twelfth century but to my knowledge it has not been formally recorded and published. Johanna Blayac reports that during her fieldwork there no such inscription was noted (personal communication).

141. Suggested by Nainar, *Arab Geographers' Knowledge of Southern India*, 39.

142. Al-Dimashqī, *Nukhbat al-dahr*, 234.

143. al-Idrīsī, *Kitāb Nuzhat al-mushtāq*, 175.

144. Al-Dimashqī, *Nukhbat al-dahr*, 234.
145. Ibn Baṭṭūṭa, *Tuḥfat al-nuẓẓār*, IV, 82-85.
146. al-Idrīsī, *Kitāb nuzhat al-mushtāq*, 179.
147. Goitein, *Letters of Medieval Jewish Traders*, 188.
148. Al-Dimashqī, *Nukhbat al-dahr*, 234.
149. Ibn Baṭṭūṭa, *Tuḥfat al-nuẓẓār*, IV, 88.
150. Goitein, *Letters of medieval Jewish Traders*, 62-65.
151. Al-Dimashqī, *Nukhbat al-dahr*, 234.
152. Ibn Baṭṭūṭa, *Tuḥfat al-nuẓẓār*, IV, 80-81.
153. Abū al-Fiḍā', *Taqwīm al-buldān*, 402.
154. *ARIE* (1965-1966), D68-69.
155. Al-Dimashqī, *Nukhbat al-dahr*, 234.
156. Ibn Baṭṭūṭa, *Tuḥfat al-nuẓẓār*, IV, 78-79.
157. Goitein, *Letters of Medieval Jewish Traders*, 188.
158. Al-Dimashqī, *Nukhbat al-dahr*, 234.
159. Ibn Baṭṭūṭa, *Tuḥfat al-nuẓẓār*, IV, 83-87.

160. الكور. No major port of this name is known and Vallet suggests that it may refer to Chaul, the Arab Saymur.

161. This appears to be a corruption of the title Ballahara or Balhara, a rendering of the Indic title Vallabha-rāja, which was borne by a number of Rastrakutan monarchs, and commonly used in the Arabic and Persian literature since the ninth century to refer to the Rastrakuta rulers of the Konkan and southern Gujarat coast (*Ḥudūd al-ᶜālam*, 238).

162. For the history of Tāna see Ranabir Chakravarti, "Horse Trade and Piracy at Tana (Thana, Maharashtra, India): Gleanings from Marco Polo." *Journal of the Economic and Social History of the Orient*, 34, 3 (1991), 159-182.

163. Goitein, *Letters of Medieval Jewish Traders*, 62.

164. Al-Dimashqī, *Nukhbat al-dahr*, 233.

165. *A Statistical Account of the Town and Island of Bombay*, 3 vols. (Bombay: Government Central Press, 1894), III, "Fryer's Map of Bombay 1672" and "Map of the Port and Island of Bombay 1724."

166. Al-Dimashqī, *Nukhbat al-dahr*, 233.
167. Ibid.
168. Ibid.
169. Ibn Baṭṭūṭa, *Tuḥfat al-nuẓẓār*, IV, 46.

170. Deloche, *La Circulation en Inde*, I, Fig. X. A small port by the name Devgarh, of which دويجر might be a rendering, does exist to the south of Tāna, at the mouth of the Savitri river. However, it is located far beyond the group of the main Tāna group and was not a very insignificant port in this period. The identification of Duwayjir (دويجر) as Devagiri thus seems the most likely possibility.

171. This slightly antiquated term, designating the former Cola rulers, is maintained in al-Dimashqī's early fourteenth-century geography: al-Dimashqī, *Nukhbat al-dahr*, 234.

172. Marco Polo, *Le devisement du monde*, II, 459.

173. Shokoohy, *Muslim architecture of South India*, 67-129 for the most comprehensive history and survey of the site to date.

174. Al-Bīrūnī, *Alberuni's India*, 98.
175. Nainar, *Arab Geographers' Knowledge of Southern India*, 25.
176. Abū al-Fiḍā', *Taqwīm al-buldān*, 402.
177. Goitein, *Letters of Medieval Jewish Traders*, 64.

178. Vallet, "Les sultans rasūlides du Yémen, protecteurs des communautés musulmanes de l'Inde."

4

At the Intersection of Empire and World Trade: The Chinese Port City of Quanzhou (Zaitun), Eleventh-Fifteenth Centuries

John Chaffee

> At the end of a five days' journey [from Guangzhou], you arrive at the noble and handsome city of Zai-tun, which has a port on the sea-coast celebrated for the resort of shipping, loaded with merchandise, that is afterwards distributed through every part of the province of Manji [i.e., southern China]. The quantity of pepper imported there is so considerable, that what is carried to Alexandria, to supply the demand of the western parts of the world, is trifling in comparison, perhaps not more than the hundredth part. It is indeed impossible to convey an idea of the concourse of merchants and the accumulation of goods, in this which is held to be one of the largest and most commodious ports in the world.
>
> Marco Polo, late thirteenth century[1]

Introduction

This study is an exploration into the causes and circumstances surrounding the rise and fall of the Chinese port city of Quanzhou between the tenth and late fourteenth centuries. Located in the southeastern periphery of successive dynastic empires in China and close to the easternmost limits of the great medieval trading world of maritime Asia, the medieval history of Quanzhou was remarkable and surprising. Its rise came about through a conjunction of political and economic factors involving both the Chinese empire and the world trade system, and its later decline similarly involved factors largely external to the city itself.

This history of the city of Quanzhou during this eventful period is well-traveled territory. The Museum of Chinese Maritime Trade and its journal, *Maritime Trade Research* (*Haijiaoshi yanjiu*) have accounted for a steady stream of books and articles relating to Quanzhou's history, most notably works by Li Donghua, Li Yukun, and Fu Zongwen.[2] In recent years it has also benefited from major studies by Western scholars, namely Hugh Clark, Billy Kee Long So [Su Jilang], and Angela Schottenhammer, who have greatly contributed to our understanding of Quanzhou's history, as it relates to both the Song and Yuan empires and the world trade system.[3] This study will draw largely on this body of work but it will focus on an issue that these works have dealt with only tangentially: how to explain the rise to maritime preeminence—and subsequent fall—of a city that occupied a very minor position in the Chinese imperial polity.

Asian Maritime Trade

Before turning to Quanzhou, we must first consider the vast system of trade that thrived in maritime Asia during this period and which served as the primary motor in the development of Quanzhou into a major port city. This system has been described and analyzed by many scholars, Jung-pang Lo, Paul Wheatley, Janet Abu-Lughod, K. N. Chaudhuri, and Andre Wink among them.[4] This was a long-lived trade system, dating from at least the eighth century, when Arab and Persian merchants from the Abbassid empire established a trade in luxury items between the Middle East and China, and lasted into the fifteenth century, when the aftereffects of the Crusades, the fall of most of the Mongol empire, and the anti-mercantile policies of the Ming government (after the Chinese expeditions under Zheng He) brought it to a nadir.

For our purposes, there were two turning points in the maritime trade, since they had important implications for Quanzhou. The first occurred around the tenth century, when a major reorientation occurred in the trade. This change had three characteristics. First, whereas the trade had been dominated by Muslim merchants, they were joined by other groups, among them non-Arab Muslims, south Indians, Southeast Asians, and in greatly increasing numbers over the course of the Song dynasty, by Chinese. Second, the Middle Eastern-China trade, which had typically involved shipments going directly between those regions, became segmented, with goods transshipped in India and/or Southeast Asia and with the trade goods themselves diversifying. Third, during the tenth and eleventh centuries the wooden Chinese junk replaced the Arab dhow as the workhorse of maritime trade, with even the Arab merchants typically using them. These changes were triggered by the massacre of foreigners in Guangzhou in 873, which led to the foreign merchants moving their base of operations from that city to Southeast Asia (most likely to the city of Kalāh on the Malay peninsula), thus providing a developmental thrust for the ports and states of Southeast Asia.[5] But whatever the causes, the newly configured trading world was well positioned when the Song economy engaged with it, resulting in the rapid growth of the whole system.

The second turning point occurred in the thirteenth century, when the Mongol conquest of most of Eurasia radically altered the political and economic realities of the entire continent. The opening of the so-called Silk Road thanks to the *pax Mongolica* is most frequently cited in this regard, but as Janet Abu-Lughod has brilliantly demonstrated the maritime trading world thrived as well, reaching perhaps its fullest articulation under the Mongols.[6] But there was an underside to the trade of this period, at least for the Chinese. With the Mongols in control of both the Middle Eastern regions of the Persian Gulf and Iraq and China, there was a politicization of trade that allowed certain merchant families with connections to the Mongol court and their Mongol overlords to benefit enormously, but quite possibly to the detriment of the broader trading community. As we shall see, both of these developments played a role in the history of Quanzhou.

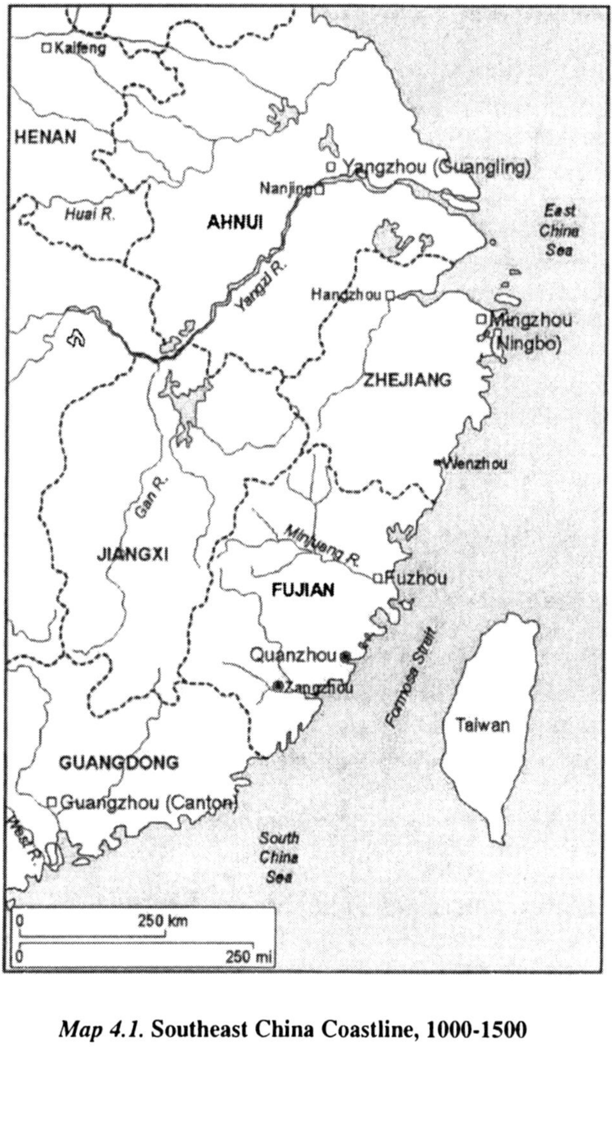

Map 4.1. **Southeast China Coastline, 1000-1500**

Historical Background

Writing in 1154 the Arab geographer Edrīsī described the ports of the southeastern coast of China as a dozen in number: "There are mountains situated in the ocean; between each mountain there is an opening by which one arrives at the maritime cities of China at which people stay."[7] This describes the port of Quanzhou well. Located in the mountainous coastal province of Fujian, Quanzhou lies at the western end of a bay that forms an excellent natural harbor (*Map 4.1*), albeit one of many along the coast, Edrīsī noted.[8] Through the first millennium of the imperial period, Fujian was a frontier region of scant political or economic importance to the government far to the north in Chang'an. Even in the Tang dynasty (618-907), when China maintained a flourishing maritime trade in luxuries with the South Seas (*Nanhai*) through the more southerly port of Guangzhou (Canton), Fujian (and Quanzhou with it) continued as a largely undeveloped frontier, though even then Quanzhou participated modestly in maritime trade.[9] Politically, even though the Tang had an examination system in theory opened to scholars from throughout the empire, Fujian scholars were all channeled through a special "southern selection" (Nanxuan) system, which was less competitive than the regular examinations but also far less prestigious, since its graduates were restricted to the lowest positions, such as assistant county magistrates in the civil service.[10]

By all accounts the period that the Chinese call the Five Dynasties and Ten Kingdoms (907-960) was critical to the development of that frontier. Whereas the Yellow River valley maintained a degree of political unity under a succession of six short-lived dynasties, southern China fragmented into a multitude of states or kingdoms. In Fujian that process actually began in the 880s, when local forces successfully broke away from the Tang. The history of Fujian over the following century is complicated, with the region politically divided through much of it between northern Fujian, centered on the city of Fuzhou, and southern Fujian—or Minnan—with Quanzhou as its center. For most of the tenth century, Quanzhou was independent—in fact and after 944 in name, from the north.[11]

It was during this interregnum between the Tang and Song that Quanzhou rose rapidly in economic importance. Cut off from the supports of the Tang empire, the tenth century rulers of Quanzhou (and Fujian) had to find new ways to maintain themselves, and the most lucrative appears to have been the overseas maritime trade. After the late ninth-century rebellion of Huang Chao, during which the rebels conquered Guangzhou and killed large numbers of foreign merchants, there seems to have been a precipitate drop in the volume of that trade reaching China, but Quanzhou like other of the southeastern states, welcomed the trade and traders. Indeed, Quanzhou sent tribute missions to the fledgling Song dynasty in 963, 964, 966, and 967, and much of his tribute offerings consisted of aromatics and other maritime trade goods.[12] Angela Schottenhammer has argued that the rulers of Quanzhou even sponsored the development of kilns for export-oriented ceramic production, though Billy So disagrees.[13] She also argues, more generally, that the southern rulers during this period used the South Seas trade "not only for their own private consumption needs, but to pay for the political and economic maintenance of the state."[14] We know, moreover, that in 977, just prior to the incorporation of Quanzhou into the Song empire, the Song government attempted to ban private trade in "spices, medicinal ingredients, perfumes, rhinoceros horn and ivory" from "Guangnan, Champa, Srivijaya, Jiaozhou (i.e., Vietnam), Quanzhou, Liangzhe, or foreign countries."[15] Since these were all South Sea commodities, it is clear that Quanzhou's involvement in the trade was already substantial.

The Rise of Quanzhou in the Northern Song

Historians are agreed that the fundamental transformation of Quanzhou from a minor regional city to the primary port for the South Seas trade, and arguably the preeminent port city of maritime Asia, occurred during the Northern Song period (960-1126). The details and causes of that transformation, however, are a matter of ongoing discussion.

Song policy towards the lucrative South Seas trade took a while to develop. Although the dynasty consistently encouraged the trade and was generally the most pro-trade of any major Chinese dynasty, initially the Song emperors attempted to follow the Tang example of having the inner palace monopolize the most lucrative part of it—the trade in aromatics—and of channeling it through Guangzhou. To this end they employed two institutions. The tribute system, in which envoys from states near and far brought tribute to the Song court in return for reciprocating gifts, flourished most notably during the first sixty years of the dynasty, attracting fifty-seven missions from the South Seas states during that period (virtually all of them stopping in Guangzhou on their way to the capital). Maritime trade offices (*shibosi*) were responsible for overseeing the coming and going of ships, inventorying their cargoes when they arrived, collecting taxes and certain other goods for mandatory government purchase, and guaranteeing the welfare of the foreign merchants and seamen. The first of these was established in Guangzhou in 971, a year after the Song conquest of the Southern Han kingdom where that city was located, and this was followed by a second office in the Zhejiang city of Mingzhou in 992, but no others followed.

This arrangement posed a serious obstacle for Quanzhou and other port cities that had been engaged in the South Seas trade. Foreign traders were not barred from visiting them and trading, but by law they could only do so after stopping at Guangzhou or Mingzhou and paying their import taxes. In Quanzhou this situation was remedied in 1087, when a third trade office—in this case termed a maritime trade superintendency (*Shibo tiju si*) because it was headed by a supervisor or superintendent but with the same functions as the *shibosi*—was established there. From then until the end of the Northern Song the Quanzhou trade superintendency flourished, becoming the largest source of income. But lest we assume that the success of Quanzhou was a simple result of receiving a superintendency, there are compelling reasons to think that the city's spectacular rise was well underway by 1087.

Table 4.1 presents the available population data for Quanzhou from the eighth to the mid-thirteenth century. Because of the notorious unreliability of Song population data for individuals (*kou*), the household (*hu*) figures are used here, with the widely accepted understanding that households, on average, had five individuals.[16] These figures are, of course, for the entire prefecture of Quanzhou and not the city itself. Nevertheless, the table's findings are striking. While the prefecture experienced apparently continuous growth over this five-century period, by far the greatest growth occurred between 980 and 1080, increasing from around 380,000 to just over one million.

***Table 4.1.* Quanzhou Prefecture Population Figures (in Households), Tang-Song[17]**

	Population, in households (*hu*)	Landlord or "host" households (*zhuhu*)	Tenant or "guest" households (*kehu*)
713-42	31,600		
980	76,581	32,056 (41.90)	44,525 (58.1)
1080	201,406	141,199 (70.1)	60,207 (29.9)
1241-52	255,758	197,279 (77.1)	58,479 (22.9)

Second is the striking rise in the landlord households and corresponding decline in tenant households, through the Song generally but most particularly between 980 and 1080. Hugh Clark, citing the argument of Yanagida Setsuko that tenants could change status as soon as they had acquired (or opened up) land and registered as landowners, has argued persuasively that these figures reflect a large-scale immigration and a successful settlement process that transformed tenants (*kehu*) into landlords (*zhuhu*): "In Quanzhou and Xinghua [located immediately north of Quanzhou] … the immigrant society of the late tenth century had apparently been replaced by a society of independent landholders whose status had been reclassified as *zhuhu* by the late eleventh."[18] In his book on southern Fujian, Clark demonstrates how this growth was accompanied by the development of the rural economy, as seen in increased acreage under cultivation, the establishment of numerous townships, and widespread bridge-building which facilitated communication and commerce.

If demography offers one broad measure of accomplishment, the civil service examinations offer another. This was an institution in which Quanzhou natives demonstrated remarkable success; the prefecture's 344 *jinshi* ("advanced scholars"—examination graduates) in the Northern Song and 582 in the Southern Song made it the sixth most successful prefecture in the empire in each period.[19] Although this success was almost certainly related to the city's flourishing maritime economy, the connection was complicated. For one, Quanzhou shared success with other Fujian prefectures, most dramatically Fuzhou to the north, but also the neighboring Xinghuajun and the inland Jianzhou during the Northern Song, which indicates that the maritime trade could not have been the sole factor behind its success.[20] However, Quanzhou stood out from its Fujian neighbors by the precocity of its examination success. Its first *jinshi* actually received his degree in 977, a year before the prefecture's formal incorporation into the Song, and as we can see from *Table 4.2*, its record was especially remarkable through the first half of the Northern Song, with an average of ten *jinshi* per examination through the middle decades of the eleventh century. I have remarked elsewhere that this success reflects high levels of economic and cultural development that must have had their origins during the Tang-Song interregnum.[21] And that development would have been unthinkable had it not been for Quanzhou's growing presence in the overseas maritime trade.

***Table 4.2*. Quanzhou in the Song Examinations[22]**

Year (# of exams)	Quanzhou *jinshi* (% of all *js*)	Quanzhou *jinshi* per exam	Fujian *jinshi* (% of all *js*)	Fujian *jinshi* per exam	Empire *jinshi*	Empire *jinshi* per exam
960-997 (23)	21 1.3%	0.9	67 4.2%	2.9	1,587	
998-1020 (10)	48 3.0%	4.8	183 11.3%	18.3	1,615	162
1021-1063 (13)	128 3.0%	9.8	623 14.6%	47.9	4,255	327
1064-1085 (8)	50 1.8%	6.3	497 17.5%	62.1	2,845	356
1086-1100 (5)	36 1.5%	7.2	370 15.5%	74.0	2,379	476
1101-1126 (8)	64 1.1%	8.0	860 14.7%	107.5	5,831	729
1127-1162 (11)	84 1.9%	7.6	743 17.5%	67.5	4,238	385
1163-1189 (10)	96 2.7%	9.6	869 24.7%	86.9	3,525	353
1190-1224 (12)	204 3.6%	17.0	1,367 24.1%	113.9	5,680	473
1225-1259 (10)	165 2.3%	16.5	1,360 17.0%	110.4	9,102	650
1260-1274 (4)	25 1.1%	6.3	186 8.1%	46.5	2,303	561

Unlike these measures of population growth and academic success, the evidence concerning that trade is scanty and qualitative. For example, according to a Yuan source the oldest mosque in Quanzhou was the Ashab or Shengyou Mosque, which was built in 400 AH (1009-1010 CE).[23] We also have the following account from the thirteenth-century *Zhufan zhi*, a compendium of geographical information about the countries of the world by Zhao Rukua, an imperial clansman who served as superintendent of maritime trade in Quanzhou in 1224-1225:

> In the Yongxi period (984-988), a priest by the name of Lohuna arrived (in Quanzhou) by sea. He called himself a native of Tianzhu (India). The foreign traders, considering that he was a foreign priest, vied with each other in presenting him gold, silks, jewels and precious stones, but the priest had no use for them himself. He bought a piece of ground and built a Buddhist shrine in the southern suburb of Quanzhou; it is the Baolinyuan of the present day.[24]

That foreign merchants were participating in the construction of religious structures—either directly as in the case of the mosque or indirectly through the support given Lohuna—suggests a settled rather than purely itinerant foreign community in Quanzhou in the early Northern Song. Moreover, since one was Muslim and probably Arabic and the other Buddhist and Indian, we can probably infer that there was more than one foreign community in the city, something that was demonstrably the case in later periods.

Another measure of Quanzhou's maritime trade activities can be seen in records of Quanzhou merchants traveling abroad. Hugh Clark has compiled five examples of merchants from Quanzhou or Fujian venturing into Hainan, Vietnam and Southeast Asia in pursuit of trade.[25] Similarly, Billy So has documented the close commercial link between Quanzhou and the Korean kingdom of Koryŏ in the early eleventh century, with Quanzhou merchants outnumbering all others who are recorded as having visited Korea.[26] Quanzhou's maritime merchants, who were to become a very visible group in the Southern Song, were already established at this time.

There are, finally, government documents relating to the illegal maritime trade in Quanzhou and other Fujian ports. A complaint from 1025 took aim at the city of Fuzhou:

> Year after year two or three ships come to the harbor of Fuzhou where the local prefectural and county officials direct the people to bring specie and goods to trade for the pearls, ivory and spices [which the ships bring] and which they then sell among the people.[27]

During the 1060s, the official Du Chun described the harbor of Quanzhou as being:

> ...clogged with foreign ships and their goods were piled like mountains. At that time the local officials traded privately with the merchants, collecting [as their share] less than a tenth of the value (i.e., considerably less than the fifteen per cent levied by the official monopoly in the superintendency ports.[28]

Du's epitaph further states that foreign merchant captains came to Quanzhou every year, each bringing "as many as twenty ships carrying exotic goods and controlled items."[29] Then in 1075 there was a complaint by Zhang Fangping that "Ship captains today go anywhere in Guangnan, Fujian, Liangzhe, and Shandong where local public officials give them protection and privately trade in the prohibited goods."[30] Finally, at some point in the late 1070s or 1080, the government dictated that Quanzhou merchants traveling abroad had to stop and register at Guangzhou both on their way out and their way back.[31]

These documents reveal a growing consciousness of a maritime trade problem along the southeastern coast, where a burgeoning trade could not be accommodated by an antiquated system of official supervision. But exactly what that problem was has been a matter of scholarly dispute. Billy So believes that the system basically functioned as intentioned. Concerning the Du Chun quotation about local officials trading privately with the merchants, he argues that this constituted an added, even extortionate, demand by the officials, since the merchants would already have paid their taxes at one of the maritime trade offices elsewhere.[32] He further believes that the maritime trade of Quanzhou prior to 1087 was conducted primarily by local merchants, with foreign merchants constituting only a small role.[33] How then does one explain Quanzhou's economic dynamism during this period? So argues that it was due to the city's success at serving as a transshipment center for South Sea goods, not only to the rest of China but to Korea and Japan as well. The unwieldy system imposed by the Song government undoubtedly created frustration among the merchants involved, but according to So they were held in check until after 1087.

Although So's interpretation more or less fits the historical facts as we have them, it does not adequately explain why merchants would have chosen to make Quanzhou a transshipment center, especially when Mingzhou had a long history of ties with Japan and Korea and was ideally located for the shipment of goods to the Yangze Delta and further north to the capital. It is far more plausible to argue, following Clark and Schottenhammer, that the Song bureaucracy was sufficiently loose—or corrupt—to allow an illegal trade to flourish in Quanzhou. By avoiding the official tariffs, moreover, the South Sea merchants—Chinese and foreign—would have increased their profit margins, thus giving them an added incentive to use Quanzhou. Given the paucity of the evidence, this theory must remain conjectural, but it is further supported by the circumstances behind the establishment of the Quanzhou's maritime trade superintendency in 1087.

In 1072 the transport commissioner Xue Xiang proposed the establishment of a maritime trade office in Quanzhou on the grounds that maritime merchants were the most profitable group in the southeast.[34] Nothing resulted from this, in part because the issue became embroiled in the factional politics surrounding the New Policies (*Xinfa*) of Wang Anshi. As described by Hugh Clark, the reformers under Wang were determined to enforce the South Sea trade regulations, and in fact put through the very restrictive requirement, described earlier, that Quanzhou merchants involved in South Sea trade stop at Guangzhou on their way out and also on their return. In the first half of the1080s this was protested by the Quanzhou prefect Chen Cheng, even as the Fujian assistant fiscal commissioner Li Zijing was actively prosecuting merchants who were violating the regulations. Then in 1087, following the death of the emperor Shenzong in 1085 and the coming to power of the anti-reform faction, a proposal by the president of the Board of Revenue, Li Chang, was accepted and the Quanzhou maritime trade superintendency was established. Clark argues that while the reformers' policies created a difficult if not intolerable situation for the Quanzhou merchants, the anti-reformers—who were opposed to "state management of the economy and regulation of individual economic activity—nevertheless recognized the need for the collection of tariffs and therefore backed the creation of a trade office rather than reverting to the earlier free-trade practices of the Quanzhou merchants."[35]

In his discussion of the success of Quanzhou in the examinations, Billy So argues that it does not appear to have translated into political power for Quanzhou during the Northern Song. Although one might expect the Quanzhou *jinshi* to constitute a lobby for Quanzhou interests at the capital, So argues that "most seem to have devoted more energy to national politics than to their home region."[36] But So himself points to an exception concerning the establishment of the maritime trade superintendency in Quanzhou, for Li Chang was closely connected to the prominent Quanzhou official Su Song, and So concludes that "we can be certain that all involved in the campaign did have direct or indirect connections with the region."[37] Thus it appears that politics may well have played a role in the establishment of the maritime trade superintendency, which was crucial for Quanzhou's rise to preeminence as a port city.

Quanzhou at Its Height: Twelfth and Thirteenth Centuries

The two centuries following the legitimizing of Quanzhou's maritime trade witnessed the growth and apex of the city's prosperity, a prosperity that we observed—well after its prime—in the quotation by Marco Polo that began this study. The dynasty's maritime tariff revenues, which had hovered around half a million strings of cash through most of the eleventh century, increased to an average of 1.1 million in the years 1102-1110, and then swelled to around two million in the mid-twelfth century.[38] Although these figures include income from all of the maritime trade offices, it is clear that most of this income, and almost all of the increases over the eleventh-century figures, were generated in Quanzhou.[39]

A far more long-term but nevertheless impressive indication of the growth of Quanzhou city can be seen in its morphological development, which has been meticulously mapped by Billy So (as redrawn in *Map 4.2*). Some years ago Arthur Wright observed that, whereas in Tang and earlier times, Chinese cities were almost always administrative centers first and foremost, characterized by a rectangular layout mirroring that of the capital, during the Song cities were more "natural" in form, with urban sprawl in response to commercial development.[40] In So's map we can see how the city grew out from the rectangular walled city of Tang times with a predominant northwest to southeast orientation paralleling the riverbank, and he explains how this was determined by military and economic considerations (the former during the tenth century).[41] We know, more-

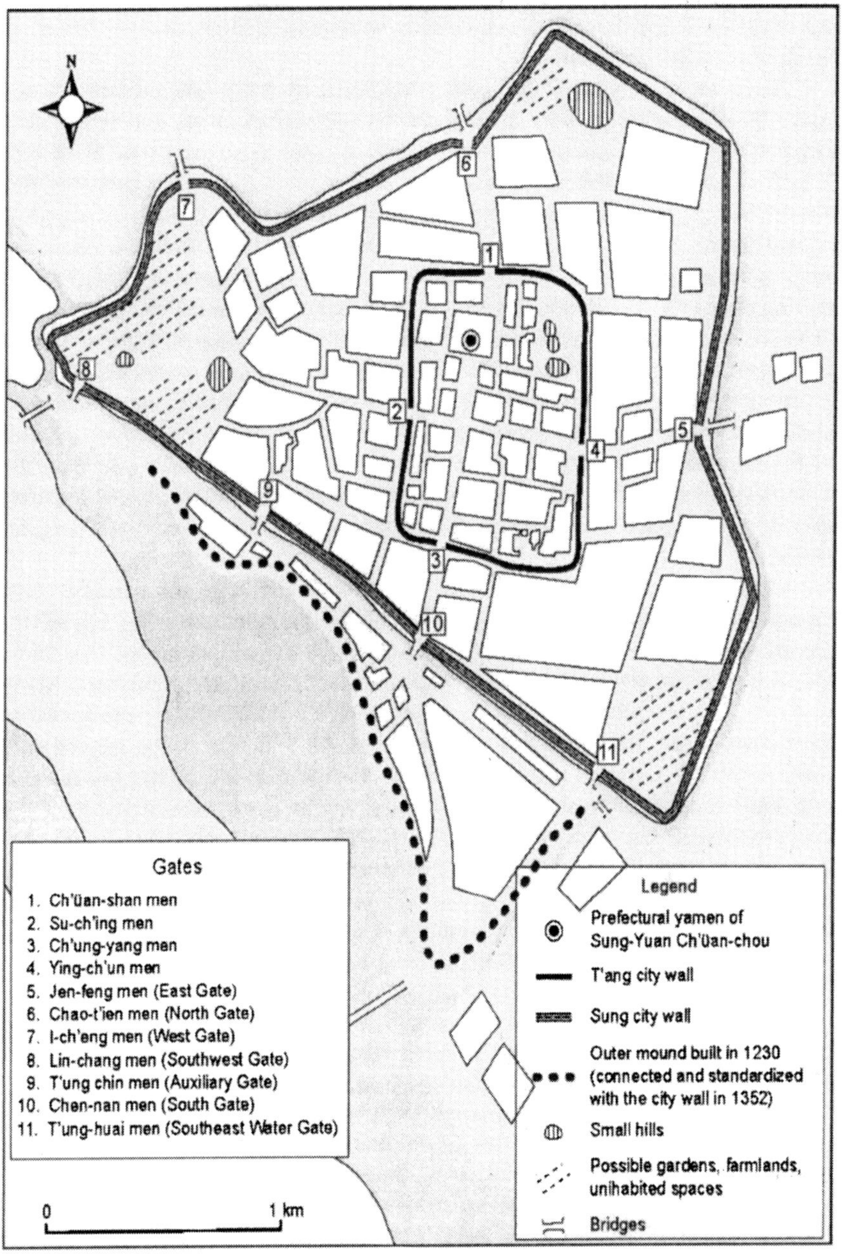

Map 4.2. **Quanzhou City Map c. 1400**[42]

over, that much of the Song city lay outside of its city walls; in particular, the triangular stretch of land to the south, which was walled in during the Yuan era, was the crowded harbor district containing warehouses, shops, and the homes of much of the foreign community.

As for the population of Quanzhou city (as distinct from the prefecture), because the demographic units in imperial China were counties and prefectures rather than walled cities, we have only estimates, and these have been quite varied. Using two twelfth-century texts, one that refer to 500,000 inhabitants and the other to 100,000 households, living within the walls of the city; some have argued for an urban population as high as half a million. Given the relatively small size of the city and a considerable literature by historical demographers casting doubt on excessively large urban population claims, the careful analyses of Clark and So are persuasive, as they both estimate Quanzhou's population to have been around 200,000-250,000.[43] Of course, even this is extremely large for a pre-modern city, putting enormous demands on the surrounding hinterland, and it is noteworthy in this regard that Quanzhou's population growth—and that of Fujian generally—had by the twelfth century outstripped the capacity of the countryside to support it, resulting in frequent famines and the regular importation of grains from Guangnan and Liangzhe to the south and north respectively.[44]

One of the fascinating aspects of Quanzhou is the large and varied foreign community that had gathered and settled there by the Southern Song. For example, the official Zheng Xie (1044-1119) had this to say of Quanzhou: "Maritime merchants crowd the place. Mixing together are Chinese and foreigners. Many find rich and powerful neighbors."[45] Although most of these foreigners appear to have lived in the commercial district south of the wall and in the eastern suburbs, as the quotation suggests there was no designated foreign ward or quarter. The most prominent, and perhaps largest, group of foreigners consisted of the Muslim Arabs,[46] but there was also a Tamil Hindu community, which has been documented by John Guy,[47] as well as what were probably multiple groups from Southeast Asia.[48] Although this group was not as large or diverse as it was to become in the Yuan, when, for example, there were Christians with their own bishop, the foreign communities in the Song era were characterized by their very considerable integration into local society.

Early in the twelfth century, Guangzhou and Quanzhou were asked by the central government to establish foreign schools (*fanxue*) at which non-Chinese boys could receive a Chinese classical education.[49] In the late twelfth century, foreign merchants in Quanzhou contributed to the construction of coast guard ships for local waters, and in 1211, the foreign merchant Pulu was publicly acknowledged for his contributions to the rebuilding of the walls of Quanzhou.[50] Most remarkable in this regard was the family of Pu Kaizong, an Arab merchant who migrated to Quanzhou in the thirteenth century (probably via Southeast Asia), obtained an official rank, and established his family. Two if not three of his sons served as local officials and the most famous of them, Pu Shougeng (d. 1296), served concurrently in Quanzhou as Superintendent of Maritime Trade and "master of pacification" (a local military commander).[51]

Maritime commerce was by no means the exclusive preserve of the foreign merchants. As noted early in this study, Chinese merchants were increasingly active, not only trading in Chinese port cities but venturing abroad. For example, the Quanzhou merchant Wang Yuanmao grew up in a Buddhist monastery doing odd jobs, but managed to study with monks and learn about foreign countries. Later he went on a merchant ship to Champa (Zhancheng), and because of his proficiency in writing both Chinese and foreign languages (i.e., Annamese), he gained the affection of the king of Annam, married a princess, and lived there for ten years. After this he returned to Quanzhou and became an established maritime merchant.[52] Foreign and Chinese merchants alike shared far-flung networks of business associates and contacts, and must have interacted with each other as rivals and partners. There was, however, an important restriction on Chinese maritime merchants during the Song, namely an 1164 requirement that Chinese merchant vessels venturing overseas return within a year of their departure.[53] This did not prevent individual sojourners like Wang Yuanmao from extended stays abroad, nor did it prevent a lucrative trade between Chinese and Southeast Asian ports. As Derek Heng has noted, it impeded the entry of Chinese ships into the Indian Ocean because those roundtrips generally required over a year, and made it difficult for them to make multiple stops while in Southeast Asian waters.[54]

As important as they were, the maritime merchants of Quanzhou were far from the most prominent or important inhabitants of the city. For one, the merchants' activities were shaped in considerable part by the maritime trade superintendency, whose functions included the inspection of cargoes on arriving and departing ships, the collection of tariffs, compulsory purchases, and insuring the welfare of the foreign merchants.[55] It, with the superintendencies in other Chinese ports, was also unique in the Asian maritime world, for while virtually every port had political authorities concerned with protecting trade while also taxing it (or otherwise profiting from it), the wide-ranging functions and institutional complexity of the Chinese superintendencies were unique.

Beyond the realm of trade, we can see an elite society that was far more consequential, politically, than its Northern Song predecessor. We earlier discussed Quanzhou's success in the examinations during the Northern Song (*Table 4.2*). In the Southern Song the prefecture fared even better, both numerically and in terms of its proportion of all degree recipients. Noting "the remarkable parallel between the patterns of the transshipment trade and the pattern of examination success," Hugh Clark argued that maritime trade was the motor force behind a remarkable process of social mobility in Quanzhou, while also asserting that a decline in that trade in the late decades of the dynasty—a decline accepted by most economic historians of Song Fujian—was also mirrored by a decline in the examinations.[56] The prefecture's examination success also translated into added importance within the central government. According to Fu Zongwen, Quanzhou in the Southern Song produced four vice councilors (*zhizheng*), three of whom went on to be chief councilors (*zaixiang*).[57]

For an individual prefecture to have produced this number of chief councilors and vice councilors (the highest positions within the bureaucracy) was an impressive accomplishment, since it suggests that many more Quanzhou officials occupied other important positions. But what most distinguished Quanzhou in the Southern Song polity was the role as the largest center for the imperial clan in the empire. When northern China fell to the Jurchen from Manchuria in the late 1120s, most of the imperial clan—all descended from the first two emperors and their younger brother—were taken from their palatial residences in Kaifeng into captivity in the north, never to be seen again. However, hundreds of clan members who had been living in two satellite centers outside of the capital made their way south, and by the late 1120s most reached Fujian, where two new centers had been established. Fuzhou hosted those from the former Western Clan Office in Luoyang (the western capital of the Northern Song), while Quanzhou became home to the Southern Clan Office and those from Yingtianfu (the southern capital; Kaifeng was the eastern capital), and they were by far the largest group. For the entire Southern Song, these clansmen (and women) were housed in a large complex to the west of the city, provided with stipends for their living expenses, and given special examination and recruitment privileges.[58]

The political implications of this development were significant. Whereas in the Northern Song clansmen had been given sumptuous support and high official rank but barred from substantive office, in the Southern Song clansmen participated fully in government and, in fact, could be found throughout the bureaucracy. Some sense of the impact that they had on Quanzhou may be gleaned from the fact that from 1190 to the end of the dynasty, over twenty percent of Quanzhou *jinshi* were imperial clansmen, and in the period 1225-1247 that figure reached a startling thirty-nine percent.[59]

Within Quanzhou clan members were active players in the maritime trade from almost as soon as they arrived in the city, though the most notable evidence for this comes from the Song ship dating from the 1270s that was excavated in 1973 in the bay leading to the city. The ship, which measured twenty by nine meters in length and beam, carried 2,300 kilograms of pepper, betel nut, cowries, tortoise shell, cinnabar, Somalian ambergris, and Southeast Asian fragrant wood.[60] Since many of the containers bore the label, "Southern Family" (*Nanjia*), it would appear that the ship was either owned by the clan, or at least that the clan was one of the principal investors in the voyage.[61] Because clan members received government stipends in addition to whatever official salaries officials in their ranks might have drawn, the clan also accounted for significant consumption of the luxuries that were imported through the maritime trade.

Politically, Quanzhou appears to have enjoyed greater autonomy than its neighbor and rival to the south, Guangzhou. Angela Schottenhammer has observed that whereas in Guangzhou the superintendent of maritime trade was generally dispatched directly by the court, in thirteenth century Quanzhou most superintendents served concurrently as prefect, thus suggesting more local control over the activities of the maritime trade superintendency.[62] Moreover, the role of the imperial clansmen-officials in that control was also considerable, for they accounted for nine to ten (ten to eleven percent) of the eighty-seven superintendents of maritime trade in Quanzhou during the Southern Song.[63]

In short, between the maritime trade, whose importance to the Southern Song government was unmatched in any other period of Chinese history, and the imperial clan, Quanzhou had achieved an importance—economically and politically—very much at odds with its modest bureaucratic status.

Decline and Collapse: Yuan to Early Ming

Quanzhou's transition to rule by the Mongols was a traumatic one. By late 1276 the Mongol conquest of the Song was largely complete. Early that year the imperial capital at Lin'an (Hangzhou) had surrendered and with it much of the Song political apparatus came under Mongol control, but prior to this the infant emperor and his brother had been sent out of the capital under the protection of a loyalist general, and this contingent made its way down the southeastern coast, eventually settling in Guangzhou, where they held out until 1276. The Mongol forces followed in pursuit of them, which would undoubtedly have involved Quanzhou in a protracted battle had not Pu Shougeng, the Arab-Chinese official mentioned earlier who was superintendent of trade, together with the prefect secretly surrendered, and in the process massacred some 3,000 imperial clan members.[64] Bloody as that even was, the surrender resulted in both the city and hinterland of Quanzhou surviving the Song-Yuan transition virtually unscathed.

The designation of the Yuan period as part of Quanzhou's decline might strike the reader as odd, for this is the period of the city's greatest fame in the Asian maritime world. The quotation from Marco Polo that began this paper is based upon his visit there in the late thirteenth century, and to this might be added the comments of Ibn Battuta from the mid-fourteenth century: "The harbour of Zaitun is one of the greatest in the world, – I am wrong: it is *the* greatest! I have seen there about one hundred first-class junks together; as for small ones they were past counting. The harbour is formed by a great estuary which runs inland from the sea until it joins the Great River."[65]

By all accounts maritime trade flourished through most of the Yuan, encouraged by the Mongols who were mindful of the riches that it brought. The city also witnessed an influx of foreigners. There was for the first time a documented Christian presence, with a Catholic bishopric centered in Quanzhou—Andrew of Perugia served as its third bishop—with a cathedral endowed by an Armenian woman.[66] Most dramatically, large numbers of Muslims came and settled there. During the fourteenth century they numbered in the thousands—perhaps tens of thousands—and supported five mosques, including the rebuilt—and still standing—Ashab Mosque, possibly modeled on fourteenth-century mosques in Cairo that it resembles.[67]

This foreign presence was not limited to Quanzhou, nor was it a simple result of the maritime trade. One important difference between the Song and Yuan was the Mongols permitted foreign merchants to participate in domestic commerce. Upon their arrival from abroad they were required to convert their precious metals into paper currency, but they were then given full access to the domestic markets[68] with a result that foreign—especially Muslim—merchants were found in cities throughout the empire. This presumably allowed the Quanzhou merchants to develop a level of integration between their foreign and domestic trade that would have been impossible in the Song. In addition, throughout their Chinese domains the Mongols encouraged outsiders to come and used them preferentially in official posts. The result for Quanzhou, in any case, was a level of political power for the Muslims, in particular, that was truly unprecedented. Pu Shougeng and his family were immediate beneficiaries of these policies. Until his death in 1296, he held a variety of high provincial posts in Guangdong, Jiangxi and Fujian, while a son and grandson likewise held important official positions in Fujian.[69] The Pus were far from unique; according to Billy So, Muslims and other foreigners held most of the local government positions in southern Fujian during the Yuan.[70]

Yet the apparent prosperity of Quanzhou during the Yuan masked signs of decline problems that were to lead to the collapse of the city by the dynasty's end. One was demographic; whereas its prefectural population was 255,758 households in 1241-52 (see *Table 4.1*), according to the census of 1290 it had declined to just 89,060. These figures are complicated by the fact that the count of individuals (as opposed to households) actually registered a slight increase between these two years, from 358,874 to 455,545. But demographic historians have long discounted Song individual figures as systematically undercounted, so the conclusion that the prefecture suffered a real population loss is inescapable, even if some of the apparent loss is discounted as rural landowners evading the tax collectors.[71] The decline probably began in the late Song, for as Billy So has demonstrated there was a downturn in Quanzhou's maritime trade and the southern Fujian economy in the thirteenth century.[72] So argues that the Mongols' promotion of the maritime trade led to a recovery in the trade and the Quanzhou economy, but offers no explanation for the population loss, which he does not question.[73] Fu Zongwen is more persuasive, arguing that the loss of population reflects a crisis in the rural economy in Quanzhou and its neighboring prefectures during the early Yuan.[74]

As for Quanzhou's maritime trade, it indeed flourished during the Yuan, but the structure of the trade was very different from that of the Song. In 1284-1294 and again, on three occasions in the fourteenth century (1303-1307, 1311-1314, 1320-1322), the government actually banned all private foreign trade.[75] Following their conquest, the Mongols re-established the maritime trade offices and they additionally organized the Muslim merchants into merchant associations called *ortoy* (Chinese *wotuo*), which allowed them monopolistic privileges but also restricted them in various ways.[76] In practice, however, control of the trade was exercised by powerful patronage networks header by Mongol royalty and generals at the court and extending down through powerful Muslim officials and then to local families, the Pus among them.[77] These networks worked through the *ortoy* but they, and not the *ortoy*, controlled the trade.

Another difference from the Song was that the Yuan trade was more focused direct commerce between China and the Persian Gulf. This trade had actually been curtailed in the eleventh and twelfth centuries, thanks to the decline of the Abbasids in Mesopotamia and the growing power of the Seljuk Turks in Persia.[78] By the late thirteenth century, however, not only were both the Persian Gulf and China under Mongol control (the former within the Il-Khanate), but fighting in the late thirteenth century between Qaidu and Qubilai made the sea passage preferable to the land route.[79] This provided the opportunity for enormous fortunes to be made, and we have two examples of what may have been a brief era of shipping magnates. One was the son-in-law of Pu Shougeng, a native of Bahrain named Fo Lian, who at the time of his death had a fleet of eighty merchant ships.[80] From the western end of this trade, we have Jamal al-din Ibrahim Tibi (d. 1306) from Qais, a merchant who claimed the title of "Superintendent of Taxes for Persia and the Island" and the father of an envoy to China in 1297-1305. Jamal was described by the Arab historian Wassaf: "He enriched himself on trade with China, which he himself had visited and controlled in an exclusive manner the trade from India to the oceans and seas of the Far East...He had almost a hundred boats always in motion."[81]

This high profile maritime trade in the Yuan—monopolistic and under the control of patronage networks—left few opportunities for the Song trading elite of Chinese and foreigners to benefit as they had in the Song. Related to this is the lack of evidence for the sinicization of Quanzhou's foreign merchant elite, as there is for the Song.[82] The Muslim officials and merchants who thrived in the Yuan were largely divorced from the population at large and therefore more vulnerable once their Mongol masters departed. At the same time, we know that Quanzhou also maintained a thriving trade with Southeast Asia throughout the Yuan,[83] so it seems quite possible that this less visible and prestigious arena became the primary venue for the Song trading elite.

The collapse of Quanzhou as a world city came quickly, though in two stages. First, as rebellions were spreading throughout central China in the 1357, a group of soldiers under the command of the Persian merchants Saifuding (Saif un-Dīn) and Amiliding (Amīn un-Dīn) seized power in the prefecture. In 1362 they were assassinated by another Persian official, Yawuna, who also was related by marriage to the Pu family. Between them, these Persians dominated southern Fujian for most of the following decade. Known as the Persian Garrison, their rule was characterized by plunder and exploitation (of the maritime trade in particular). In 1366 provincial forces captured Yawuna and his followers by surprise, thus sparing Quanzhou the destructiveness of a conquest, and two years later the city was incorporated into the new Ming empire.[84]

The Ming dynasty, for its part, took steps to resurrect the maritime trade apparatus, but in a very different configuration and with far less concern for the benefits of that trade. Although a maritime trade office was established in Quanzhou (and also Guangzhou and Ningbo), it was restricted to trading with the Ryukyu Islands (modern Okinawa), thus cutting it off from the South Sea trade.[85] Within Quanzhou, popular anger was directed against the Muslim community. According to a Chinese Muslim genealogical account, large numbers of Muslim (and other "big nosed" Western people) were butchered in the streets.[86] Although imperial edicts proclaiming toleration for Islam were issued in 1368 and 1407 and posted in mosques around the empire, surviving genealogies from Muslim lineages in Quanzhou portray the descendents of those who had flourished as officials in the Yuan as trying to lie low in the face of local persecution.[87] Others fled, by land or especially by sea, never to return. Without question, the vital role that the Quanzhou Muslims had played as a trade diaspora had disappeared, as had Quanzhou's role as a great port city of maritime Asia.

Conclusion

Since this is a volume devoted to the historical role of small (or in this case, secondary) cities, the question must be asked: what, if anything, about Quanzhou's history from the tenth through fourteenth centuries might be instructive for this book's broader purposes? Let me propose a distinction between what I would call natural versus accidental secondary cities. The former are characterized by a location that gives them an enduring claim to commercial—if not political—importance. East Asian examples include Yangzhou at the juncture between the Yangzi River and Grand Canal, Guangzhou with its accessibility to all shipping coming from the south, and Nagasaki on the Japanese island of Kyushu.

Quanzhou, by contrast, is the quintessential accidental secondary city. Except for its general location on the southeast coast and its possession of a good harbor, there was little to set it off from its neighbors on the coast, and there was little in the millennium of imperial history prior to the Song to suggest the enormous importance that maritime commerce would come to play. What were the accidents that propelled Quanzhou to its position of maritime preeminence? The maritime trade system itself was the driving force, aided by a Song empire boxed in by powerful states to the north and west. For the city itself, its period of semi-independence during the tenth century was instrumental for its initial involvement in the South Sea trade, while its ability to circumvent the legal restrictions on its trade through much of the Northern Song followed by the establishment of its maritime trade office in 1087 enabled it to challenge and eventually surpass the supremacy of Guangzhou in the trade. The prefecture's academic successes—gradually translated into bureaucratic influence—followed by the arrival of the imperial clan in the early Southern Song, then gave it a remarkable degree of political influence. Even in the Yuan, when the political equation had completely changed, the importance of the maritime trade insured the continued success of the city, if not of its hinterland.

By the same token, the fall of Quanzhou in the early Ming can be seen as a stripping away of the accidental advantages that the city had accrued. Excepting the great imperial—rather than commercial—undertaking of the Zheng He expeditions in the early fifteenth century, the Ming proved fundamentally uninterested in Asian maritime commerce, thus feeding a decline of the trade system itself. Ming Quanzhou had none of the political advantages that had benefited it during the Song and the Yuan, but instead confronted conflicts stemming from the multiethnic society that maritime trade and the Mongols had bequeathed to it.

Finally, the accident was never repeated. Although it has gone through cycles of success and decline, for the past six hundred years Quanzhou has never been more than a minor provincial city, albeit one that today, at least, has a vivid memory of past greatness.

Notes

1. Marco Polo, *The Travels of Marco Polo the Venetian*, ed. John Masefield (London: J. M. Dent & Sons, 1911), 317-318.

2. Li Donghua李東華, *Quanzhou yu woguo zhonggu de haishang jiaotong* 泉州與我國中古的海上交通 (Taibei: Xuesheng shuju, 1985); Li Yukun 李玉昆, *Quanzhou haiwai jiaotong she lüe* 泉州海外交通史略 (Xiamen: Xiamen daxue chuban-

she, 1995); Fu Zongwen 傅宗文, "Houzhu guchuan: Song ji nanwai zongshi haiwai jingshang di wuzheng," *Haijiaoshi yanjiu* 2 (1989), 77-83. See also, "Citong gang shi chutan" 刺桐港史初探, Pt. 1, *Haijiaoshi yanjiu* 海交史研究 19, (1991), 76-165 and "Citong gang shi chutan," Pt. 2, *Haijiaoshi yanjiu* 20 (1991), 105-151.

3. Hugh Clark, "Quanzhou (Fujian) During the Tang-Song Interregnum, 879-978," *T'oung Pao* 68 (1982), 132-149; *Community, Trade, and Networks. Southern Fujian Province from the Third to the Thirteenth Centuries* (Cambridge, MA: Cambridge University Press, 1991); "The Politics of Trade and the Establishment of the Quanzhou Trade Superintendency," in *Zhongguo yu haishang sichou zhi lu* 中國與海上絲綢之路 (*China and the Maritime Silk Route*), edited by Lianheguo jiaokewen zuzhi haishang sichou zhilu zonghe kaocha Quanzhou guoji xueshu taolunhui zuzhi weiyuanhui 聯合國教科文組織海上絲綢之路綜合考察泉州國際學術討論會組織委員會 (Fuzhou: Fujian renmin chubanshe, 1991), 375-393; "Muslims and Hindus in the Culture and Morphology of Quanzhou from the Tenth to the Thirteenth Century," *Journal of World History* 6, 1 (1995), 49-74; and "Overseas Trade and Social Change in Quanzhou Through the Sung," in *The Emporium of the World: Maritime Quanzhou, 1000-1400,* ed. Angela Schottenhammer (Leiden: E. J. Brill, 2001), 47-94; Billy Kee Long So [Su Jilang 蘇基朗], *Tang Song shidai Minnan Quanzhou shidi lungao* 唐宋時代閩南泉州史地論稿 (Taibei: Shangwu yinshuguan, 1990); "Financial Crisis and Local Economy: Quanzhou in the Thirteenth Century," *T'oung Pao* 77 (1991), 119-37; and *Prosperity, Region, and Institutions in Maritime China. The South Fukien Pattern, 946-1368* (Cambridge, MA: Harvard University Press, 2000); Angela Schottenhammer, "The Maritime Trade of Quanzhou (Zaitun) from the Ninth through the Thirteenth Centuries," in *Der Indische Ozean I historischer Perspektive* (Hamburg: E. B. Verlag, 1999), 89-108; "Local Politico-Economic Particulars of Quanzhou during the Tenth Century," *Journal of Sung-Yüan Studies*, 29 (1999), 1-41; *The Emporium of the World: Maritime Quanzhou, 1000-1400* (Leiden: E. J. Brill, 2001); *Das Songzeitliche Quanzhou im Spannungsfeld Zwischen Zentralregierung und Maritimem Handel* (Stuttgart: Franz Steiner Verlag, 2002); "China's Emergence as a Maritime Power," *The Cambridge History of China, Vol. 5B, The Sung* (Cambridge: Cambridge University Press, forthcoming).

4. Jung-pang Lo. "China as a Sea Power During the Late Sung and Early Yuan Periods," *Far Eastern Quarterly,* 11, 2 (1952), reprinted in *China: Enduring Scholarship from the Far Eastern Quarterly–The Journal of Asian Studies 1941-1971,* ed. John A Harrison (Tucson: University of Arizona Press, 1972), 91-105, and "Chinese Shipping and East-West Trade from the Xth to the XIVth Century," in *Sociétés et companies de commerce en Orient et dans l'Océan Indien. Actes du Huitième Colloque International d'Histoire Maritime,* ed. Michel Mollat (Paris: S.E.V.P.E.N., 1970), 167-78; Paul Wheatley. "Geographical Notes on Some Commodities Involved in the Sung Maritime Trade," *Journal of the Malaysian Branch of the Royal Asiatic Society,* 32, 2 (1959), 1-140; Janet L. Abu-Lughod, *Before European Hegemony: The World System A.D. 1250-1350* (Oxford: Oxford University Press, 1989); K. N. Chaudhuri, *Trade and Civilization in the Indian Ocean. An Economic History from the Rise of Islam to 1750* (Cambridge: Cambridge University Press, 1985); and Andre Wink, *Al-Hind. The Making of the Indo-*

Islamic World. Vol. I. Early Medieval India and the Expansion of Islam 7th to 11th Centuries, 3rd ed. (Leiden: E. J. Brill, 1996).

5. G. R. Tibbetts, "Early Muslim Traders in Southeast Asia," *Journal of the Malayan Branch of the Royal Asiatic Society*, 30 (1957), 19-22.

6. Abu Lughod, *Before European Hegemony.*

7. Gabriel Ferrand, *Relations de voyages et textes géographiques arabes, persans et turks relatifs a l'Extrême-Orient du VIIIe au XVIIIe siecles*, 2 vols. (Paris: Enest Leroux, 1913-14), 192.

8. So, *Prosperity, Region, and Institutions*, 134-135, argues that Quanzhou had the best natural harbor in all of southern Fujian.

9. Schottenhammer, "Maritime Trade of Quanzhou," 92-93.

10. Clark, *Community, Trade, and Networks*, 43-44.

11. Ibid., 38-43.

12. Lin Tianwei 林天蔚, *Songdai xiangyao maoyi shi* 宋代香藥貿易史 (Taibei: Zhongguo Wenhua Daxue chubanshe, 1986), 169-173.

13. Schottenhammer, "Local Politico-Economic Particulars," 24-25; So, *Prosperity, Region, and Institutions*, 38-39.

14. See Schottenhammer, "China's Emergence as a Maritime Power."

15. *Shihuo*, 36/1b-2b in *Song huiyao jigao* 宋會要輯稿 (Taipei: Shijie shuju, 1964) as cited by Robert Hartwell, *Tribute Missions to China, 960-1126* (Philadelphia: Hartwell, 1983), 34.

16. Ping-ti Ho, "An Estimate of the Total Population of Sung-Chin China," in *Études Song/Démographie* (Paris: Mouton & Co., 1970), 33-53.

17. Clark, *Community, Trade, and Networks*, 20, 77. The figures for 713-742 and 980 are from *Taiping huanyu ji* 102, that for 1080 from *Yuanfeng jiuyu zhi* 9, and that for 1241 from *Puyang bishi* 1.

18. Clark, *Community, Trqde*, 76-77.

19. John W. Chaffee, *The Thorny Gates of Learning in Sung China: A Social History of Examinations. New Edition.* (Albany: State University of New York Press, 1995), 196-202.

20. The top six prefectures for the two periods were as follows: N. Song—Kaifeng (in the thousands), Jianzhou, Fujian (809), Fuzhou, Fujian (550), Changzhou, Liangzhe (498), and Xinghuajun, Fujian (468), and Quanzhou (344). S. Song—Fuzhou, Fujian (2,249), Wenzhou, Liangzhe (1,125), Mingzhou, Liangzhe (746), Jizhou, Jiangnanxi (643), and Raozhou, Jiangnandong (621), and Quanzhou (582). Chaffee, *Thorny Gates*, 196-202.

21. Chaffee, *Thorny Gates*, 150.

22. See the research records for Chaffee, *The Thorny Gates of Learning*.

23. Chen Dasheng 陳達生, *Quanzhou Yisilan jiao shike* 泉州伊斯蘭教石刻 (Fu-chou: Ningxia renmin chubanshe, Fujian renmin chubanshe, 1984), 4. The source for this is an Arabic inscription on one of the north walls of the Ashab Mosque in Quanzhou. The building dates to the middle of the fourteenth century.

24. Frederick Hirth and W.W. Rockhill, *Chau Ju-kua: His Work on the Chinese and Arab Trade in the Twelfth and Thirteenth Centuries, Entitled Chu-fan-chi* (St. Petersburg:

Imperial Academy of Sciences, 1911/translation reprinted, Taipei: Ch'eng-wen Publishing Company, 1971), 109, with adaptations of the translation.

25. Clark, *Community, Trade*, 123-124.

26. So, *Prosperity, Region, and Institutions*, 36, 38.

27. Clark, "Politics of Trade," 379.

28. Ibid., 380.

29. Ibid.

30. Clark, *Community, Trade*, 125, and *ibid.*, 379.

31. WXTK. Ma Duanlin 馬端臨, *Wenxian tongkao* 文獻統考 (Song; Taibei: Xinxing shuju, 1984), 62, 563. This is the source cited by Clark, "Politics of Trade," 125, and it dates the regulation to the Xining reign era (1068-1077). So, ibid., 48, citing a Chinese article on Song trade with Korea, dates it as 1080.

32. So, *Prosperity, Region*, 39-40.

33. Ibid., 36-37.

34. Tuo Tuo 脫脫, *Song shi* 宋史 (Beijing: Zhonghua shuju, 1977), 186: 4560.

35. Clark, "Politics of Trade," 384-386.

36. So, *Prosperity, Region*, 101.

37. Ibid., 48. So acknowledges the work of Fu Zongwen, whose article on the establishment of the maritime trade superintendency spells out the political connections of those who were involved. Although I have not been able to obtain the Fu's article used by So , much of the same material is covered in Fu, "Citong gang shi chutan," 90-92.

38. Clark, *Community, Trade*, 132.

39. Ibid., 133-135.

40. Arthur F. Wright, "The Cosmology of the Chinese City," in *The City in Late Imperial China*, ed. in G. William Skinner (Palo Alto: Stanford University Press, 1977), 33-74.

41. So, *Prosperity, Region*, 165-166.

42. Based on So, *Prosperity, Region and Institutions*,163.

43. Clark, *Community, Trade, and Networks*, 138-139, 183-184.

44. Ibid, 141-148.

45. Zheng Xia 鄭俠, *Xitang ji* 西塘集 Song; Siku quanshu, ed., 8: 20b.

46. See John W. Chaffee, "Diasporic Identities in the Historical Development of the Maritime Muslim Communities of Song-Yuan China," *Journal of the Economic and Social History of the Orient*, 49, 4 (2006), 395-420.

47. John Guy, "The Lost Temples of Nagapattinam and Quanzhou: a Study in Sino-Indian Relations," *Silk Road and Archaeology*, 3 (1993-94), 291-310; and in *Zhongguo yu haishang sichou zhi lu* 中國與海上絲綢之路 (*China and the Maritime Silk Route*), edited by Lianheguo jiaokewen zuzhi haishang sichou zhilu zonghe kaocha Quanzhou guoji xueshu taolunhui zuzhi weiyuanhui 聯合國教科文組織海上絲綢之路綜合考察泉州國際學術討論會組織委員會, Vol. 2. (Fuzhou: Fujian renmin chubanshe, 1991), 294-295.

48. Mention should be made, at least in these notes, of the purported account of Quanzhou in the 1270s by the Italian Jewish merchant Jacob d'Ancona, for if it is accepted as genuine then the multitude of information that it provides will serve as an in-

valuable source for Quanzhou and the late Southern Song. However, its translation by David Selbourne as *The City of Light: The Hidden Journal of the Man Who Entered China Four Years Before Marco Polo* (New York: Kensington Publishing Corporation, 1997, 2000), has been the focus of great controversy because, according to Selbourne, the original manuscript's Italian owner has refused permission to anyone besides him to examine it. Western reviews of the book have been overwhelmingly negative, but the book has its defenders, most notably the respected Quanzhou historian Wang Lianmao. In my opinion, neither the criticisms nor the defenses are conclusive, but until the original manuscript is made available to scholars and properly evaluated, it will remain suspect and unreliable as a source.

49. Cai Tao 蔡絛, *Tieweishan congtan* 鐵圍山叢談, zh. 2; cited by Jitsuzo Kuwabara, "On P'u Shou-keng, a Man of the Western Regions, who was the Superintendent of the Trading Ships' Office in Ch'üan-chou towards the End of the Sung dynasty, together with a General Sketch of Trade of the Arabs in China during the T'ang and Sung Eras, Part 1," *Memoirs of the Research Department of the Tōyō Bunko,* 2 (1928), 59.

50. Kuwabara, 52.

51. So, *Prosperity, Region*, 107-110.

52. Li Yukun, 45-46.

53. *SHY*, Zhiguan, 44:27a-28a.

54. Derek Heng Thiam Soon, "Economic Interaction between China and the Malacca Straits Region, Tenth to Fourteenth Centuries A.D.," Ph.D. dissertation (Hull: University of Hull, 2005), chapter 5; "The Trade in Lakawood Products between South China and the Malay World form the 12th to 15th C. A.D.," *Journal of Southeast Asian Studies,* 32, 2 (2001), 133-149.

55. Ma Huan, *Ying-yai Sheng-lan: The Overall Survey of the Oceans Shores,* trans. J. V. G. Mills (London: Cambridge University Press, 1970), 37-38.

56. Clark, "Overseas Trade," 60-62. That examination decline to which Clark is refereeing is visible in the 1260-1274 row of *Table 4.2*, but in fact began with the 1250 examination, at which Quanzhou had only six *jinshi*, in contrast to nineteen in 1247.

57. Fu, "Citong gang shi chutan," 128. The three who served in both positions were Liang Kejia, Zeng Huai, and Liu Zheng. Zeng Conglong served as vice councilor only. In addition to these individuals, Fu points out that the neighboring prefecture of Xinghua, which was very much in the economic orbit of Quanzhou, produced six vice councilors and two chief councilors, one of whom served in both positions.

58. John W. Chaffee, *Branches of Heaven: A History of the Imperial Clan of Sung China* (Cambridge: Harvard University Asia Center, 1999), 227-234.

59. Ibid., and John W. Chaffee, "The Impact of the Song Imperial Clan on the Overseas Trade of Quanzhou," in Angela Schottenhammer, ed., *The Emporium of the World: Maritime Quanzhou, 1000-1400* (Leiden: E. J. Brill, 2001), 27.

60. Jeremy Green, "The Song Dynasty Shipwreck at Quanzhou, Fujian Province, People's Republic of China," *International Journal of Nautical Archaeology and Underwater Exploration*, 12, 2 (1983), 253-261.

61. Fu, 77-83; and Chaffee, "Overseas Trade of Quanzhou," 33-35.

62. Schottenhammer, *Das Songzeitliche Quanzhou*, 125-150, and "China's Emergence as a Maritime Power," 74.

63. Chaffee, *Branches of Heaven*, 238.

64. Ibid., 252-253.

65. Ibn Battuta, *Travels in Asia and Africa 1325-1354*, trans., H. A. R. Gibbs (London: Routledge & Kegan Paul, Ltd., 1929), 287-288.

66. Hugh Moffett Samuel, *A History of Christianity in Asia. Volume 1, Beginnings to 1500* (New York: HarperCollins Publishers, 1992), 458.

67. Chen Dasheng 陳達生, *Quanzhou Yisilan jiao shike* 泉州伊斯蘭教石刻 (Fu-chou: Ningxia renmin chubanshe, Fujian renmin chubanshe), 10.

68. Morris Rossabi, *Khubilai Khan: His Life and Times* (Berkeley: University of California Press, 1988), 122-123.

69. Li Yukin, *Quanzhou haiwai jiaotong she lüe*, 50-51; So, ibid., 114-116.

70. So, *Prosperity, Region*, 115-116.

71. Fu, "Citong gang shi chutan," Pt. 2, 131-132.

72. See So, "Financial Crisis"; and *Prosperity, Region and Institutions*, 88-95.

73. So, *Prosperity, Region, and Institutions*, 117-122.

74. Fu, 132.

75. Franz Schurmann, *Economic Structure of the Yuan Dynasty* (Cambridge, MA: Harvard-Yenching Institute, 1956); So, *Prosperity, Region*, 119.

76. Elizabeth Endicott-West, "Merchant Associations in Yüan China: The *Ortoy*," *Asia Major*, 3rd Ser., 2, 2 (1989), 139.

77. Yokkaichi Yasuhiro 四日市康博, "Gencho kyūtei ni okeru kōeki to teishin shūdan," *Bulletin of the Graduate Division of Literature of Waseda University* 早稲田大學大學院文學研究科紀要, 45, 4 (2000), 3-15, and "The Structure of Political Power and the *Nanhai* Trade: from the Perspective of Local Elites in Zhejiang in the Yuan Period," paper presented to the annual meeting of the Association for Asian Studies, San Francisco, 2006.

78. Tibbetts, "Early Muslim Traders in Southeast Asia," 23.

79. Thomas T. Allsen, *Culture and Conquest in Mongol Eurasia* (*Cambridge:* Cambridge University Press, 2001), chapters 4-5.

80. Li Yukun, 50-51.

81. Monik Kervran, "Famous Merchants of the Arabian Gulf in the Middle Ages," *Dilmun: Journal of the Bahrain Historical and Archaeological Society*, 11 (1983), 21-24; Moira Tampoe, *Maritime Trade between China and the West: An Archaeological Study of the Ceramics from Siraf (Persian Gulf), 8th to 15th Centuries A.D., BAR International Series* 555 (1989), 124-125.

82. Chaffee, "Diasporic Identities," 414-416.

83. See Heng, *Interaction between China and the Malacca Straits Region.*

84. Maejima Shinji, "The Muslims in Ch'üan-chou at the End of the Yuan Dynasty," Pt. 2. *Memoirs of the Research Department of the Tōyō Bunko* 31 (1974), 47-71; So, ibid., 122-125.

85. So, *Prosperity, Region*, 125.

86. "Li shi shixi tu 李氏世系圖," in *Quanzhou Huizu pudie ziliao xuanbian* 泉州回族　牒　料选 (1980), 78b.

87. Donald Leslie, *Islam in Traditional China* (Canberra: Canberra College of Advanced Education, 1986); Chen Dasheng, 11-13.

5

Clearing the Fields and Strengthening the Walls: Defending Small Cities in Late Ming China

Kenneth M. Swope

Theoretical Overview

More than thirty years ago G. William Skinner suggested that studying the urban history of China was best approached not in terms of a single integrated urban system for the empire as a whole, but rather from the standpoint of macroregions, which he classified according to physiography. These macroregions did not conform to the empire's traditional provincial boundaries, but were intended to aid scholars in understanding how cities actually functioned in terms of collecting, processing, and dispersing resources of all kinds as well as mediating relationships to the state. Skinner further suggested that studying China according to macroregions would facilitate the consideration of China's "internested hierarchy of local and regional histories."[1] The eight macroregions identified by Skinner consisted of: 1. North China; 2. Northwest China; 3. The Upper Yangzi; 4. The Middle Yangzi; 5. The Lower Yangzi; 6. Southwest China; 7. Lingnan (Guangxi and Guangdong); and 8. The Southeast Coast (*Map 5.1*).

In Skinner's conceptualization, each of these regions engendered their own system of cities that collected, multiplied, and dispersed regional resources along their own transportation nodes.[2] In keeping with his emphasis on trade and other governmental functions, all Skinner's regional boundaries followed watersheds, and most of them were also divided along the crests of mountain ranges.

***Map 5.1.* Skinner's Ming-Era China Macroregions**

Skinner's major breakthrough in terms of analysis was to highlight the importance of functional or nodal regions, as opposed to studying formal or uniform regions, the latter being the favored method of studying China prior to Skinner's work. Essentially, scholars prior to Skinner tended to look for similarities such as climate, agricultural practices, ethnic concentrations, or lineage structures within areas of China and then study the development of cities within these.

While useful for providing basic insights about urban life in traditional China, such an approach often illuminated little about how cities actually functioned vis-à-vis either the subjects of the empire or the interests of the imperial state. Skinner's functional mode of analysis, however, recognized that "functional regions are internally differentiated and constitute systems in which activities of many kinds are functionally interrelated."[3] Within Skinner's system, cities serve as the nodes or command posts that articulated and integrated human activity within time and space. While Skinner's focus was on cities' political and economic function, they were frequently "command posts" of China's military as well. This study will address this military function of China's small cities. As will be discussed below, even if cities served primarily as administrative or commercial centers, since most Chinese cities were walled they were natural defense posts in times of strife or invasion. The Chinese empire's defense hierarchy was thus intimately connected with its urban systems. Even isolated garrisons were located in or adjacent to small cities, where local resources were concentrated for potential local defense. Defensive centers on the Chinese periphery operated as the first line of the imperial realm's defense, as also the agents of imperial power and legitimacy.

In Skinner's model, each of China's major physiographic regions developed their own relatively discrete urban system and each system had its own core area where regional resources naturally concentrated. The transportation network of each region climaxed in lowland urban centers. Most of the transportation nodes were situated in the less rugged areas of the cores, where the construction of roads and canals complemented riverine transport.[4] The Chinese defense network, on the other hand, tended to go in the opposite direction, as defensive installations and military personnel were more concentrated along the hinterlands of the macroregions. In terms of demographics, most Chinese tended to live the majority of their lives within a specific macroregion and their interests and interactions tended to be focused on that region. The military was again the exception, since imperial soldiers were required to travel all over the empire, minimally in their rotational training and command-center postings, and on campaigns against regional and national-level threats. Historically, nevertheless, even major events or catastrophes such as floods or peasant rebellions tended to be confined to one or two macroregions, again highlighting the regional unit of analysis as the focal node for understanding urban networking in imperial China.[5]

Though criticized by some scholars for, among other things, slighting the importance of interregional activity, Skinner's mode of analysis has become so pervasive in studies of late imperial China that nearly every subsequent study of Chinese local or regional history published in English has made at least some reference to Skinner and how the work in question positioned itself with respect to the macroregional framework of analysis.[6] Despite the fact that some of these studies have focused on peasant rebellions and social disturbances, little scholarly attention has been devoted to the relationship between the location of cities and the placement of military garrisons, or to the implications of defending secondary cities within discrete regional hierarchies.

Indeed, neither Skinner nor any of the subsequent writers influenced by his theories have seriously considered the military and defense implications of the macroregional model, though Skinner himself noted that it was an area demanding further investigation. The military apparatus of the late imperial state also had its functional and nodal regions. Troops, supplies, and equipment needed to be transported to battlefields and frontiers. Defense posts needed to be scattered around the empire in appreciation of the state's defense requirements. In practice, with the exception of the capital cities of Nanjing and Beijing, which boasted an awesome array of defense posts and personnel for obvious reasons, normally secondary cities on the outskirts of the macroregions assumed greater importance than their position in the regional political and economic hierarchy or their relative size or location might otherwise suggest.[7] This was because the majority of major military threats tended to arise far from the centers of political authority and economic activity, often engendered by the precarious environment in which they emerged.[8] As these threats expanded, they tended to travel along the same transportation nodes as "regular" political and economic activities; that is to say they moved along trade routes, generally moving ever closer to the productive centers of macroregions, where invaders or rebels could access material resources. On the other hand, rebels or invaders who restricted their activities to the macroregional hinterlands could extend their operations by seeking refuge in forests, mountains, or similarly isolated terrain. From the perspective of the state, this threat from the periphery was a perpetual threat, but one that could be managed. Keeping the major lines of transportation and communication open was paramount. This is reflected in the ways that authorities responded to the different types of military challenges that will be discussed below. Extremely large uprisings or invasions could encompass multiple macroregions, but most disturbances never reached this level, as they were adequately contained by local or regional authorities.

This study will consider strategies of defending small or secondary cities in Ming dynasty (1368-1644) China, drawing attention to the relationship between military networks and the urban and commercial systems that comprise Skinner's macroregions. Consequently, this study will present a modified version of Skinner's model that will allow better understanding of how military and urban networking intersected at various levels of the Ming imperial hierarchy, with specific focus on two exemplary case studies of national and regional level threats, in which small cities assumed a vital role in the defense of the Chinese state. This study will consider how late Ming defense networks related to urban and commercial networks and hierarchies, and how local areas envisioned and articulated their own defensive needs and interests with respect to those of the imperial state. Indeed, it is essential that we consider the relationship between military networks and the political hierarchy, by examining local, regional, and national intersections of networks and hierarchies as they pertained to defense matters. In doing so, this study provides a local view, from the bottom up, of the increased threats to the late Ming state. In a nutshell, looking from the top down, it seems that the management and coordination of defense efforts varied according to official perception of the threat. Threats that were confined to one macroregion or locality were expected to be handled and contained by local civil and military officials in their capacity as agents of the imperial state. Major threats, those which encompassed more than one macroregion, elicited a broader official response that generally included a top-down approach, in directing or superceding local initiatives, and featured significant efforts to amass and redistribute local and national resources.

An examination of the actions of mid-level local officials in carrying out varied defense responses to different types of military threats sheds light on the role and importance of small cities in Ming China in the successful defense of the empire, as well as the critical role of local officials in taking responsibility for the considered and deliberate application of imperial decrees in a manner consistent with imperial assertions of concern for the wellbeing of all the peoples of a region. It can also yield insights about the relationship between military and commercial activity, in ways that suggest how Skinner's model can be applied to the study of Chinese society beyond the urban setting. Of most salience for the purposes of this study are government responses to military threats along the fringes of Skinner's macroregions, which, as noted above, were the areas where military authority was most often concentrated. When a military threat emerged in these hinterlands, it was essential that the local government officials literally hold down the fort until the cavalry, or, more typically, regional infantry arrived.

One must keep in mind, as noted above, that the Ming empire's military power was distributed along lines that differed from the urban networks considered by Skinner, because military installations were of necessity located in distant areas that were perceived as potential trouble spots. In keeping with their vital role as the last bastions of Ming civilization, they prominently appear on Ming maps as urban centers of note.

In addition to their military importance in the Ming defensive scheme, the establishment of military commands in the Ming periphery was often the first step in the colonization and acculturation of a frontier. Markets and urban centers soon followed in the wake of new army command posts. In essence, military garrisons served as the first step in extending Ming urban and market networks. Conversely, when Han settled agriculturalists began opening up new lands along the empire's frontier, a military presence always accompanied them. Normally it took a long time for such areas to be effectively incorporated into the regular administrative structure of the empire. During this transition, unsurprisingly, the newly settled periphery where the reach of the state was limited was the most vulnerable to peasant uprisings, invasions, sectarian revolts and even troop mutinies.[9] The common state response to such challenges was inherently defensive, but local officials, as will be seen below, were very cognizant of their vital role in regional and national defense, often pointing out to their superiors the dangers of allowing local disturbances mushroom and threaten the core areas of their macroregions.

Principles of City Defense in the Ming Period

As indicated above, Ming cities were more than just sites for economic exchange and political activity. They were also symbols of imperial military power and defense nodes. Virtually all Chinese cities were walled and therefore expected to be able to serve as foci for sheltering and rallying the local populace in times of strife. Urban defense was integral to the maintenance of imperial authority and prestige on the local level; the ability of a state official to defend or for a rebel to capture even a small city could have fairly serious implications for local and regional stability and order. To this end, virtually all city magistrates and local gentry were reasonably expected to be prepared to assume a prominent military role in the case of rebellion or invasion. This would be especially true of officials stationed in frontier posts or in small towns on the peripheries of macroregions. In fact, assignment to such posts was often a way of testing junior officials to determine their potential for more prominent positions later in their careers and many officials gained good reputations from their management of local military problems. Moreover, this was but one manifestation of their more general Confucian charge to "nourish the people" as articulated in both Confucian philosophical and more purely military strategy texts. Thus, military defense was a dynastic priority (including the reconstruction and maintenance of the Great Wall as a barrier against attacks from the Central Asian steppes) not only because of its functional importance in guarding against armed threats, but also because of its symbolic merit in maintaining local commitment to the state's interests.[10]

The military strategy widely used during the Ming (1368-1644) period was known as "clearing the fields and strengthening the walls" (*qing ye jian cheng*), which characterized the type of response that might be expected in a massive empire that was severely under-governed by modern standards. Essentially, this entailed relocating the entire local populace into a walled city and arming them with whatever weapons were at hand. In many cases, this would also involve burning crops or other resources that could not be brought into the city and thus deny them to military opponents. In extreme cases along the Chinese coastline this included burning large swathes of arable land or even removing fishermen from coastal villages, to escape the depredations of pirates or would-be invaders. Both were used against the so-called "Japanese pirates" of the 1550s and a century later in Qing efforts to deny resources to the Ming loyalist pirate Koxinga (d. 1662). Because such measures often harmed the very populations they were ostensibly designed to protect, modern scholars have often interpreted Ming defense of their coastline as a manifestation of imperial lassitude, weakness, or callousness. But in fact such a strategy had its roots in the complex hierarchical consolidation of Chinese governmental units that developed through the long course of imperial history. As Skinner has shown, the only way that the imperial government could continue to function at a reasonable level of effectiveness without over burdening its people with taxes was to reduce the government presence in the localities, by keeping the number of government functionaries reasonably stable even as populations and territorial responsibilities increased, and cede bureaucratic initiative to local representatives.[11] Although Skinner did not consider the military policies of the Ming government, this included defensive accountabilities.

Sensitivity to the implications of the practice of clearing the fields and strengthening the walls is crucial to understanding the networking among the military, the state, and the populace in late Ming China. Because the Ming state was founded by a peasant rebel, much was made by early Ming emperors of their state's responsibility towards its people, particularly with respect to not overburdening the people with taxes. The Ming also made a concentrated effort to reverse the policy of their Yuan (1279-1368) forebears, who had actively discouraged or even forbidden the construction of city walls in order to limit the potential of local resistance, to demonstrate their authority over their Han Chinese subjects, and to emphasize their spatially "open" steppe roots.[12] For the Ming, the construction of city walls was both a return to traditional Chinese practice and a fairly economical defense measure that could serve the long-term interests of the state. Cities were considered the foremost targets of rebels, raiders, and invaders, and thus the defense of cities constituted the first line of defense for the imperial state.

Ming Military Networks, Hierarchies, and *qing ye jian cheng*

Emperor Hongwu (r. 1368-1398), the founder of the Ming dynasty, who had suffered through natural disasters, warfare, and famine during his youth, determined that military exactions should never become a source of hardship for his own people. Therefore he endeavored to create a military system that would be both cost effective and suitable to fulfill the defensive needs of the idealized agrarian state he desired. The result was a hereditary military system whereby certain families were categorized as "military households" (*jun hu*) and were thereby responsible for supplying one able-bodied male per generation for military service.[13] These conscripted soldiers were expected to provide their own sustenance by their own physical labor in a network of military farms (*tun tian*), among which they were rotated periodically. Their tactical rotations of service included assignments to the training garrisons at the capital and in the field, where they would receive specialized instruction, including the use of firearms.

The Ming military was, like the state, a systemic hierarchy. Each prefecture had three guards (c. 5,600 men), each guard command had five battalions under it and every battalion command (c. 1,120 men) consisted of two full battalions and ten companies (112 men each).[14] The prefecture guards and battalions had three basic functions: 1) to defend imperial lands; 2) to act as the state's support forces in times of war; and 3) to rotate to the imperial capital and regional field camps for training and to border garrisons to assist in basic defense and patrols in times of peace.[15]

With respect to this study's analysis of networks and hierarchies, the Ming military system served to reinforce the relationship between the center and the periphery, since provincial soldiers rotated to the imperial metropole as well as to distant frontier regions. On the positive side, training rotations ideally created a skilled, but cost efficient military apparatus that could readily respond to military challenges throughout the empire. The practice of rotating troops for training and field operations also created conditions for extended informal personal networking, which would have positive and negative ramifications for the state. In theory commanders and their loyal subordinates might conspire to foment rebellion, but various structural measures were in place to prevent such actions, and on the whole it seems that the Ming state did a good job of ensuring a confluence of interest between the goals of the empire and those of its military commanders.

For our purposes, the most important aspect of this system was that it placed a disproprtionate share of the empire's military power along the northern frontier and in the environs of the capital, particularly after the creation of permanent frontier defense commands in the fifteenth century. There were specific reasons for these measures, as the Mongols constituted an ongoing threat in the north and defending the capital, which was shifted to Beijing in 1420, took precedence. But as a consequence of these priority northern border troop concentrations, the interior regions had small garrisons and local militia performed the bulk of ordinary defense duties. The records of troop counts for this middle dynastic era are misleading. While the regular guards and battalions experienced a serious decline in their real numbers, the troop counts were not always valid, since commanders regularly falsified their rosters and exagerated the number of men under their authority in order to collect the pay due to those men who in fact had deserted, been lost to official peculation, or had died. As a consequence of the systemic reduction in the number of imperial troops, local officials and commanders were forced to recruit peasant militia and turn to other irregular expedients to maintain local order, a state of affairs that encouraged local defensive strategies, like clearing the fields around and strengthening the defensive walls of urban centers (*qing ye jian cheng*).

Additionally, over time the prestige of the hereditary officer corps declined, as indicated by the fact that numbers of the sons of military officers increasingly chose to pursue non-military careers rather than following in their fathers' footsteps. At the same time, the power and prestige of the civilian bureaucracy waxed and civilian officials often assumed military responsibilities. On the local level this resulted in county magistrates and other local civil officials assuming the responsibilities for the defense of their towns in times of military distress. A simple policy like clearing the fields and strengthening the walls was easy enough for even the least martially inclined to implement, provided a city was properly constructed and outfitted with the materials needed to sustain a siege. Civil bureaucrats were also well-suited for such a task because of their familiarity with the vagaries of Ming bureaucratic practice and procedures. They knew local productive capacities and were able to estimate rates of consumption in besieged cities. Furthermore, since they had extensive networks of friends and associates, they could rely on their personal relationships to secure aid in times of need from former classmates or ministerial co-workers.

Almost all Chinese towns of any significance were walled. The Chinese character for city, *cheng* (城), literally translates as "walled town." Like walled cities elsewhere, Chinese cities were built to protect palaces, residences, temples, granaries, resources, and people against the depredations of bandits, tribal menaces, and foreign invaders, among others. Towers typically stood at wall corners and over entry gates: corner towers were usually fashioned of stone and those over gates were usually made of wood, and housed the town's garrison. In this respect Chinese walled cities differed from Japanese castle towns, which more closely resembled their contemporary European counterparts with central *donjon* structures. A Chinese city's number of gates seems to have been consistent with the city's relative place in the empire's administrative hierarchy. Most Ming cities had a gate opening in each of the four cardinal directions; larger cities had more gates, and the imperial capital cities Beijing and Nanjing each had twelve gates. Most county-level seats had four gates, and smaller secondary cities usually had just one or two gates.[16] Chinese cities were usually built on the lowlands near water,[17] in contrast to Korean *sansŏng,* or mountain fortresses, which made extensive use of Korea's mountainous terrain, but served the same functions as China's walled cities.[18] Indeed, one of the striking characteristics of walled Chinese cities is how infrequently they made use of the natural terrain to augment their defenses.[19] This may have been because of local preferences for simpler designs, which were easier to construct and maintain with conscripted labor, or it might have been due to desire to facilitate commercial activities. Primarily military frontier or coastal cities made use of natural features such as cliffs to augment their defense works. They frequently had moats for defense and were often pierced by small water gates as well. Moat widths and depths varied by region and typically depended upon the availability of water in a particular locale. Moats were usually broader near the main gates. The bridge spanning the moat was usually not constructed in a straight line for both *feng shui* and practical defense purposes.[20] Larger cities might have multiple walls and zigzag defense structures, not unlike those found at Japanese and European castles; smaller cities were unlikely to have such arrangements.

City walls themselves were almost always square or rectangular. They were usually very thick, sometimes fifteen meters (50 feet) or more in thickness, and fairly tall, ranging in height from five to fifteen meters (16 to 50 feet) on average. Ming cities were typically surmounted with cannon and were nearly impregnable to bombardment by cannon until the modern era. Likewise, their thickness made sapping or mining an equally daunting task for would-be besiegers. Most towns had a drum tower where hourly watches were sounded and a bell tower, where alarms or calls to assembly were raised. The former would often be near the center of town, while the latter would most likely be near the outer gates. The most prominent features of any town such as major temples, markets, or official offices were usually located near the town's center. Typically the city governor's residence was expected to be the last bastion of defense, where the seals of office were supposed to be guarded at all costs. Rebels who captured these seals often displayed them at their first opportunity in conjunction with their occupation of the symbolic center of authority within a town. Officials who abandoned their seals of office could expect serious punishment from their superiors, even if the town in question was later recaptured.

As in other empires, walled cities in Ming China also served as markers of the advance of "civilization" and were poignant reminders of the march of settled agrarian Han civilization into Ming China's frontiers. Moreover, the Ming government stepped up the pace of assimilation in its frontier regions, creating even more districts and prefectures out of territories that had formerly been independent and outside the regular administrative structure of the Chinese state.[21]

Maps and gazetteers from the Ming period often depict Chinese walled towns on the Chinese frontiers amidst curious tents or rude stilt houses that represent the "barbarian" menace lurking just beyond the pale. It was standard Ming imperial practice to establish garrisons and walled towns in frontier regions and gradually assimilate these lands by setting up regular government offices and building post houses, bridges, schools, and the like.[22] Such activities often brought local resentment or even rebellion. If the latter occurred the government would engage in the clearance of the surrounding fields and strengthening the walls until sufficient force could be brought to bear to crush the threat. Far from being symbolic of Ming fear in the face of aboriginal or Mongol threats, construction and maintenance of a city wall was a potent symbol of the power and reach of the imperial state.

One thing that jumps out at the modern historian reading the Ming-era records is the underlying tension between central directives and local interests. Figures such as county magistrates and censorial circuit civil servants were indisputably agents of the imperial administration. Because of the law of avoidance whereby state bureaucrats could normally not serve in their home provinces, they were often rightly perceived as outsiders by the local populace they governed. So these officials had to be sensitive to local interests and conditions. In forming relationships with local elites who assisted them in matters of public works, defense, and judicial matters, among other things, the state's bureaucrats often came to identify more with their local constituents than with the imperial government. A prominent example was the Zhejiang provincial government's response to pirate attacks in the 1550s.[23] Such times of crisis often lead to the obfuscation or even disregard of central directives. In this particular case local elites and officials assumed that the central government was simply too distant to really know what was going on in the locality and assumed the burden of local defense themselves, believing that they were infinitely better suited to handle such matters.

Yet, on other occasions and in other places there was a fair degree of central-local coordination of defensive efforts. This seems particularly to have been the case when military threats were deemed national rather than local or regional. Peasant rebellions and outbreaks of banditry were usually viewed, at least initially, as local matters and best left to the discretion of local officials to handle. From their own perspective, local officials generally preferred to deal with such threats on their own, perhaps because the penalties for failure could be harsh—whether at the hands of the victors or, subsequently, those of the imperial government, but also because if they were situated on the outskirts of the empire's major transportation and communication nodes, help would not be speedily forthcoming anyway. Since state officials were evaluated periodically as the basis for their promotions or demotions, their ability to successfully defend a small city or quell a local disturbance could be useful in advancing their bureaucratic careers.

This brings us back to Skinner's notion of macroregions. As we have seen, defense networks tended to be distributed along the peripheral areas of the macroregions, away from centers of population and commerce because this was where military emergencies were most likely to arise. But officials stationed in these posts were cognizant of the very real dangers they faced and often went to great lengths to point out to their colleagues and superiors how their seemingly distant frontier regions were vital to the security and stability of the empire as a whole. That is to say, they recognized that the prosperity enjoyed by the heart of the empire, in other words the core areas of the macroregions, was contingent upon the efforts of those living in the peripheral areas. So it was in everyone's interest for the frontiers to be reasonably secure if for no other reason than the fact that there was a significant amount of interregional trade and interaction that crossed provincial and jurisdictional lines. It was therefore incumbent upon local authorities to maintain order in their own jurisdictions, but when military threats encompassed broader areas, provincial and eventually national authorities might get involved.

For their part, it seems that Ming officials at all levels of the administrative hierarchy also recognized this basic fact when approaching matters of defense. As noted, when a military threat was confined to a single macroregion, it was more likely that locals would be left to their own devices to handle the problem, with minimal assistance from other networked urban centers or the central government. But when a threat encompassed a broader area and crossed both jurisdictional and macroregional boundaries, it was more likely that serious efforts would be made to coordinate national and local defense activities. Of course it must be remembered that these are broad generalizations and categories such as local, regional, and national are malleable. An attack on a strategically important garrison town that guarded the approaches to Beijing, such as the seizure of Ningxia by Chinese troops allied with the Mongols in 1592, would provoke a national response.[24] But even a fairly large aboriginal uprising in distant Yunnan might be considered only a regional threat, preferably handled by local authorities.

Even in such cases of a national threat, it was important for local officials to recognize the important link they constituted in the imperial chain of command. In the case of the 1592 military mutiny in Ningxia, after seizing the imperial seals of authority and forcing the local governor to hang himself, the Mongol-allied mutineers quickly seized some forty-seven outlying border fortresses, putting Ming control over the entire province of Shaanxi in jeopardy. The only small city to hold out was the town of Pinglu, located some 200 kilometers south of Ningxia. Pinglu was defended by a young official named Xiao Ruxun, who was a hereditary military officer. Xiao found himself encircled by the rebels, but vowed to defend the city until his death. He was assisted by his wife, surnamed Yang, who was descended from an illustrious Ming official family.[25] As Xiao rallied the city's populace to drive the rebels back, his wife gave the defenders food and wine, and even pawned her earrings and hairpins to provide them with rewards for their valor. After several assaults on the town were bloodily repulsed, the attackers gave up. This helped prevent the eastern part of the province from falling into rebel hands and provided the government with an important symbolic victory at a crucial moment.[26] Xiao would later be honored by the emperor for his efforts and would go on to a distinguished career before running afoul of a eunuch faction at the court in the 1620s.

Secondary Networking in Responding to a National Threat: The Japanese Menace of the 1590s

One of the more notable examples of attempting to coordinate national and local defenses based in secondary city networking can be found in the Ming response to the threat of invasion from Japan in the 1590s. After being rebuffed in their efforts to solicit assistance from the Koreans in attacking the Ming empire, the Japanese decided to invade Korea and use it as a base from which they would strike at China. But rumors were rampant that they were also going to launch a direct naval invasion of China, most likely by landing on the southeast coast, where pirate depredations from the 1550s and 1560s were a vivid memory.[27] As the Ming had only recently lifted a long legal ban on Chinese overseas maritime trade, this threat had serious implications for commerce as well as national security.[28] Official communications concerning the threat are quite revealing in this regard and demonstrate the sensitivity of Ming officials to both national interests and local concerns. They also show how peripheral urban centers were crucial to national defense, and the ways in which local areas could be integrated into larger national defense networks.

When concrete news of an all-out Japanese invasion of the Korean Peninsula reached Ming ears in the spring of 1592, the court acted quickly to gird itself for a possible invasion. The Ministry of War immediately put Liaodong, Shandong, and all other coastal provinces on alert and ordered them to step up training and repair existing defenses.[29] These repairs were in the hands of local officials, who, as was typical of the Ming system, were expected to find and allocate their own resources for such efforts. The Ming Supreme Commander of Jiliao, Jian Da, asked that another commander be transferred to Tianjin, which guarded access to Beijing from the sea, so that their forces could be combined.[30] In the sixth month of 1592 requests were made for the shipment of 60,000-70,000 *shi* of grain to Tianjin to support the additional troops there.[31] Although an initial request for the dispatch of a high-ranking military censor from the capital to inspect local defenses in Shandong was turned down, local touring censors were dispatched to coastal areas to "soothe the hearts of the people."[32] This was also fairly standard practice and demonstrates how the Ming state attempted to show its concern for its subjects and underscore the gravity of the situation. The symbolic importance of sending out agents of the imperial metropole to the localities should not be overlooked when considering the relationship between the center and its peripheries.[33] Sending an official censor with his retinue of guards and imperial banners and seals of office was intended to awe his local subjects and convince them of the emperor's concern for his subjects.

This general overview is foundational to understanding the specific directives and memorials pertaining to the plans to bolster coastal defenses against the Japanese. Because maritime trade had been actively discouraged by the Ming state for more than a hundred years, most of the towns discussed in these plans would still be considered secondary cities in terms of their relative size and perceived economic importance to the empire, though they were growing rapidly with Ming China's increased participation in the global silver trade.[34] In fact, as it stimulated the development of secondary cities along all of China's frontiers, China's increased direct participation in the international trade allowed for the speedier monetization of the economy, which allowed the Ming to transition from a hereditary to a mercenary-based army in the seventeenth century.

Indeed when reading the primary sources from this era, one is struck by the vast material and monetary resources of the empire even as one appreciates the thriftiness of Ming officials, especially at the local level. Most local officials were very sensitive to the potential economic impact of any defensive measures and they continually sought to maximize and accumulate resources for local needs. But there was also a curious mix of technology and simplicity in programs for local defense, as, for example, the state's attempt to deploy the latest cannon technology along the frontiers where it was most needed to buttress the state's otherwise simple "burn the earth and build city walls" defensive strategy. In response, local officials expressed their concerns about having the proper training or supplies to even use such weapons. How much gunpowder, for example, might a small county seat expect to have on hand? Spears and bows and arrows, on the other hand, might more reasonably be procured and would be more familiar to most peasant militiamen, who would constitute the bulk of a secondary city's defenders.

Historical scholarship on coastal defense in the 1590s benefits from Song Yingchang's impressive collection of primary sources, the *Jinglue fuguo yaobian* ("*Important Documents from the Military Commissioner's Restoration of the Country [Korea]*"). Song Yingchang (1536-1606) was appointed Military Commissioner for Korean Affairs (*jinglue*) in the late summer of 1592 by Emperor Wanli.[35] Song Yingchang's compilation includes hundreds of official letters, imperial commands, directives to colleagues and subordinates, battle reports, censorial reports, and official communications among the Chinese, Japanese, and Koreans. The collection is especially valuable for this study as documentation of the ways various officials connected local and national interests in their plans for defending China's coast.

For example, a typical memorial on coastal defense including commentary on the repair of local walls and towers would begin with a depiction of the Japanese overlord Toyotomi Hideyoshi's (1536-1598) overly arrogant ambitions in the course of the first months of the war in Korea. Given the consequence of events to that point (the Korean king had already fled towards the Chinese border), and the strategic implications should the Japanese control the sea lanes, Censor Peng Haogu of Shanxi argued that the best course of action was to stop the Japanese at sea, before they reached China. In his mind, defending the coasts was second best, and waiting for the invaders to disembark before fighting them on land was equivalent to no plan at all.[36] Another memorialist from the Ministry of War warned that the Japanese were after the lucrative southeast coast of China and that, if Korea fell, China would be forced to spread its military forces thin. But simply recruiting mercenaries and bravos and deploying them along the coast would not be sufficient, because many officials were unversed in warfare and, more importantly, would not know their own troops or their abilities.[37] While in some memorials officials championed the recruitment of stalwart mercenaries, people's militia being insufficient for the task of resisting the Japanese, others argued against bringing in outsiders, because they believed that locals tended to be superior because they really had something to fight for.[38]

Concerns such as these over local capacity prompted most, in contrast to the official cited above who argued that the best defense was a preemptive offense, to stress local defensive tactics.[39] As noted above, the strategy of clearing the fields and strengthening the walls (*qing ye jian cheng*) often made sense because sieges inherently favored the defender. Confronted with a military foe whose capabilities generally exceeded those of the average peasant conscript, creating a strong defense in the hope of slowing down the enemy while the regular troops moved into position was in line with conventional wisdom.

Military Storehouse Commissioner Liu Huangshang, who was in charge of coordinating defensive efforts along the northeast coast, went beyond this simplicity in his proposal that watchtowers should be erected every three *li* along the seacoast to guard against Japanese incursions.[40] In the event that an enemy was spotted, smoke signals were to be used to communicate between towers. As most of these local towers were to be constructed of wood, he argued that local communities could assume the costs, which would be fairly low.[41] Each watchtower should have a platform capable of holding twenty men on top. Ten volunteers were to be recruited from the localities and put on regular patrol duty around the watchtowers. Two thundering cannons (*hong lei pao*) were to be deployed per *li,* with a company of men to use and guard each. Six men per a squad of fifty were to be assigned cannon responsibilities; others were to be tasked with maintaining equipment, signal fires, and the like. He stressed that firearms training and distribution were critical. Ideally, up to fifty percent of the defense forces were to be equipped with guns.[42] He also paid attention to the placement of guns, by recognizing that while heavier firearms were not very mobile, they were more effective when positioned in stoneworks that afforded them elevated positions.[43]

Liu Huangshang's suggestions are interesting in that they speak to both the sophistication of the Ming military apparatus and its resources and to the desire to keep costs manageable. Rather than use stone, local towers were more often built of wood, but they were still outfitted with cannon. In addition to the cost issue, wooden towers were quicker to erect than stone towers. He argued in favor of training defenders in the use of the sophisticated weaponry. As noted above, Ming armies were supposed to have training rotations. Earlier in the Ming period it was standard practice for soldiers to spend time training in the capital firearms divisions. But, as noted above, by the late Ming era the hereditary military system had declined, the quality of mercenary troops was significantly uneven, and there was little uniformity of troop training and supply. Thus, Liu Huangshang expressed his realistic concern that steps needed to be taken to ensure that local troops could operate the strategically placed sophisticated equipment they were provided. This necessitated the dispatch of training officers, to save expense as also due to the noted systemic decline, because in the late Ming system training officers were most often dispatched rather than rotating troops through the capital or periodically reassigning them to field training camps. It is unclear how much training troops received locally, though the assumption that half of any force was equipped with firearms suggests that at least some rudimentary training was offered to most. Again, however, the fact that the threat in this instance was a national one explains why greater resources were to be allocated to these vital defensive sites. As will be seen below, lesser threats would not typically garner the same kind of attention, meaning that local officials would expect less (if any) help or major weaponry from the central government.

Another memorial on coastal defense stipulated that every circuit (roughly equivalent to a province) was to construct 1670 large cannon, 60 military carts, 10,000 one character small cannon (*yi zi xiao pao*), 333 small reliable cannon (*xiao xin pao*), 12,000 crossbows, 333 felt and 333 bamboo shields, 60,000 crossbow bolts, and an undetermined number of bullets for emergency use.[44] All these items were to be made to specific standards and using specific materials.

The memorialist concludes with the observation that if all his suggestions were followed, the Japanese would not dare invade because they would be cowed by China's superior coastal defenses. This memorial serves as a testament to the strengths of and confidence in the Chinese bureaucratic system, in its penchant for minor details and assumption that local officials would fulfill the minutest demands of the center. In reality the memorials contain an interesting mixture of pragmatic strategy and sound advice mixed with wishful thinking.

The city of Tianjin was considered the linchpin in China's coastal defenses because of its proximity to the capital. Therefore, the needs of officials in charge of defensive matters in this region were given priority. Yang Hao, who would later earn notoriety for his mishandling of the Siege of Ulsan in Korea in 1597-1598,[45] pledged to repair northeastern coastal defenses by early 1593, but emphasized the need for more horses to facilitate faster communications between defense locales. Yang requested a total of 2,000 additional mounts: 600 were to be stationed in Jizhen and Tianjin respectively and another 800 were to be allocated between mobile corps commanders (100 each times 2) and commandants (100 each times 4).[46] Yang also recommended fortifying offshore islands and arming peasant stalwarts with long spears. Again, the key, according to Yang, was for the Chinese to create an interlocking defense network which would thereby present a much more formidable defense than had been the case during the *wokou* troubles of the mid-sixteenth century. This involved greater integration between larger and smaller cities and the appointment of officials to act as coordinators and liaisons between such units. This included the neighboring islands, where the islanders were supposed to keep watch, and extra boats that would allow them to carry messages to warn the mainland should a Japanese fleet attack, as well as to allow a Chinese naval defense.[47]

All the islands within a 500 *li* radius north and south of Tianjin and Dagu were to erect defenses and keep watches. The commoners of the islands were supposed to till their fields during the day and keep watch by night. Each house was also to be furnished with a drum so that anyone in any village could call his compatriots to arms.[48] Each locale was entrusted with the task of selecting the most upright, brave, and trustworthy to act as squad commanders and lead the assembled stalwarts of the region.[49] As of late 1592, one estimate projected an assemblage of 7,000 marines and 200 boats from various locales and 950 sailors and 80 flat-bottomed (*shahu chuan*) boats from the Nanjing area.[50]

In another memorial on naval warfare dating from mid-December 1592, Song Yingchang stressed that because the Japanese were not particularly adept at naval warfare, the Chinese should focus on building large warships and smashing the enemy at sea. Boats from Fujian were deemed superior, followed by *cang chuan* and then *sha chuan,* which were flat-bottomed vessels. He asserted that the Ministry of War should bring all these kinds of vessels, as well as various other types, north at once; if they lacked sufficient ships, the Ministry of Works was to construct them in due haste.[51] Twenty *sha chuan* were to come from Zhejiang and another twenty from Nanzhili.[52] Various other locales were to furnish fifty to sixty more ordinary boats for conversion into war vessels. Song also called for Tianjin and other northern areas to supply one hundred salt transportation and fishing boats for government use.[53] Song argued that both these kinds of vessels and their crews could go about their normal business most days but serve as spy ships when needed. Between them Zhejiang and Nanzhili could supply one hundred more mid-sized galleys (*hu chuan*) while the Ministry of Works should open its vaults to finance the construction of five-and eight-oared galleys (*ba la hu chuan*) to defend key points around Jizhen in the north.[54]

The proposed conversion of ordinary boats for military purposes and the use of fishermen as spies are noteworthy. For one, it illustrates that despite Chinese resources and technological capabilities, the Ming had not yet developed a very impressive naval capacity. That shortcoming would be rectified over the next several years during the course of the war with Japan. In doing so, the Ming military command had to be creative. The empire's traditionalist military organization had never had a formal navy per se,[55] so fishermen and traders made the most likely candidates for incorporation into naval units when they were needed.[56] Recruitment of fishermen to spy while carrying out their normal business reflected the state's sensitivity to the economic plight of its coastal subjects. Above all, consistent with the other memorials discussed above, this memorial again makes it clear that is was the responsibility of the localities to provide the state with the needed ships and manpower in a time of crisis.

Some 1,535 troops were to be posted on various islands and furnished with small cannon.[57] Each such station was to possess several dozen torches to cast great light at night. He reasoned that "once the Japanese realize how well-prepared we are, they won't dare to advance."[58] At the end of this report, Song Yingchang again reiterated the importance of defending Tianjin and its environs and argued that successful naval preparations were essential to the positive and speedy resolution of the Eastern Expedition as the Chinese called their intervention in Korea.

Song Yingchang also recognized the possibility that China's initial defenses might still be breached. Although some officials advocated a frequently used strategy of moving coastal inhabitants forty to fifty *li* inland, that was deemed both potentially too harmful to the people, possibly even provoking them to help would-be invaders, and dangerous from a military standpoint, particularly if defeating a Japanese fleet out at sea was considered the preferred strategy. In the event the Japanese scaled the coastal stockade walls, iron caltrops and rows of wooden stakes were to be placed behind them. In fact, Song notes that he had already placed orders for caltrops, stakes, and saltpeter. Pit traps were to be set and ambushes prepared.[59] Song envisioned Ming defenses coordinating like the spokes of a wheel, funneling the invaders to a central location where they could be wiped out. In the north, both regular and peasant auxiliary units were to be deployed in both passive defense and active patrols. This striking power was deemed sufficient to deter nighttime Japanese raids. In Jiangnan and areas to the south, the primary preparation was to be the erection of watchtowers. Signal fires were to be kept burning at all times at these posts. Additionally, throughout China wherever possible, bamboo palisades were to be erected and existing walls and moats repaired.[60]

The most elaborate plan called for the construction of a wooden wall, two *zhang* high, stretching 180 *li* from Dagu to Zhengjiagou.[61] Building a wall this size would require a force of 30,000 men and take just one month to build.[62] It was envisioned that this structure could even augment the existing Great Wall in the northeast and would be a good plan for bolstering overall defenses in the long term. Again stressing the importance of active as well as passive defense, Song ordered the Military Commissioner of Shandong to station an assistant regional commander at the central location of Tangtou with 3,000-4,000 troops so they could respond quickly to an alert. Likewise, those in Liaodong were to be on constant watch for plunderers from Tsushima. The ultimate plan was to have 40,000-50,000 troops guarding the port cities of the northeast alone, though it is highly unlikely that this number was ever attained.[63]

In terms of equipment, fire carts and defensive weapons were to be distributed amongst the common folk. It seems that the localities were supposed to provide at least some of the materials for these weapons, though there are documents indicating that materials were procured and distributed from central locations as well. Villagers were told to store extra firewood and water within the safety of city walls. In case of trouble, villagers were to adopt the classic "clear the wilds and defend the city" (*qing ye jian cheng*) strategy.[64] The Ministry of Works was to dispatch officials to tour and inspect defenses. This ministry was instructed to work closely with all relevant government agencies in assuring that supplies and defense preparations were adequate.

All these memorials placed emphasis on the necessary incorporation of irregular expedients to meet China's defense needs. Given the decentralized nature of the imperial Chinese system, Ming officials fully expected that the locals would take an active interest in their own defense and respond to central directives. The state would provide some weapons and other supplies to local militia, but the Ming officials placed the responsibility for selecting local militia leaders in the hands of the locals themselves, assuming they would appoint those best suited for the task, and these local militia leaders would adequately prepare their troops for combat. These late sixteenth-century expectations were based in the systems of local defense set up in the early days of the dynasty, known as *bao jia* or *li jia*, or "mutual security" or "mutual accountability" organizations. Under this system households were grouped into units of ten, each of which had a head (*li zhang*) who reported to a larger grouping of one hundred. Ten groups of one hundred were organized into a group of one thousand.[65]

During the Ming era, the *li jia* practice was never fully discontinued, but was revived periodically by Ming officials entrusted with local defense against bandits or rebels. This was the case during the Yang Yinglong tribal uprising in the western Sichuan borderland province in the 1590s, a rebellion of highland tribal populations that was provoked in part by increasing Han transmigration into an aboriginal region.[66] The establishment of *li jia* in this region was seen as part of the "civilizing" process by Ming bureaucrats, as it created hierarchical order and control in an otherwise hostile and dangerous borderland territory. When Miao tribal rebels under Yang threatened newly established frontier towns populated largely by Han Chinese, the initial response was to invoke the *qing ye jian cheng* strategy of clearing the fields, strengthening the walls, and organizing mutual defense organizations. These actions in the Ming frontier, in the same decade as the Ming defense of their coastline and Korean borderlands against a Japanese threat, demonstrates the Ming proclivity for defensive measures and their belief in the universal applicability of Han Chinese practices and institutions. This conclusion is also born out by later Ming acculturation initiatives in the southwest and similar strategies along their Vietnam borderland in the southeast.[67]

So what was the end result of all these Ming defensive efforts in the 1590s? It is difficult to determine the degree to which these measures were implemented. Scholars have suggested that much of the Ming bureaucracy's work, like that of bureaucracies everywhere, consisted of little more than filing memorials, making reports, and otherwise shuffling papers, with few actual results. Contemporary observers did report that fears of invasion ran high along the coast and that there was a heightened distrust of foreigners even in more cosmopolitan port cities, but there is not definitive evidence that all the anticipated local preparations for war along the Chinese coastline ever took place.[68] It is clear that during the 1590s it was even more difficult than normal for foreigners to move about the empire due to the widespread fear of Japanese spies. Despite the prevailing concern in the noted memorials advocating a Japanese invasion of China rather than Korea, Hideyoshi sent his troops to the Korean Peninsula, to facilitate an overland assault on China that never took place. So the Ming defenses against Japan were never tested. It is unlikely that the Japanese refrained from attacking the Chinese mainland because they received word of China's extensive defensive preparations. It was simply much easier for Hideyoshi to ferry troops and supplies across the Tsushima Straits to Korea than hazard the perilous waters of the East China Sea, particularly given the mediocre quality of most Japanese ships. And given the problems the Japanese encountered even maintaining supply lines to Korea, extending them all the way to China was out of the question.

The variety of Ming defensive measures in the 1590s show how vital secondary areas were conceived to be in their expected contributions to the imperial realm's defense, and how the empire's central and local officials could act in concert to devise defensive measures that benefited the whole. Small cities, in particular, were to serve as integral spokes in the wheel of defense and as shelters for the populace should the invaders manage to land. The initiative for erecting and maintaining urban defenses was ceded to local officials, but the central government issued directives to these local defenders with the full expectation that local officials would implement the center's demands. But this was not a one-way street. The center did solicit advice from local officials, recognizing that they had a better idea of their own defensive capabilities. In overview, this case study of the 1590s defensive preparations against a threatened Japanese invasion illustrates how the Ming defense system functioned, under the watch of a concerned monarch and competent officials, when confronted with a national threat, and as it might similarly against a local crisis.

By the last decades of the sixteenth century the vigor of the imperial state was being sapped by factionalism and power struggles among the emperor, his officials, and court eunuchs. That this was widely understood is reflected in the events of the next few decades, when the Ming state was confronted by both internal rebels and external invaders, and proved unable to meet the challenge.

Responding to Local Challenges: Defending Small Cities Against Peasant Rebels in the Late Ming Era Peripheries

The final phase of Ming history is instructive in that it shows the continued viability of the "clear the fields, strengthen the walls" (*qing ye jian cheng*) defensive strategy in the minds of Ming officials. Late Ming era local officials continually found themselves isolated and short of resources. With little hope of rescue, they resorted to the time honored defensive strategy, and often acquitted themselves quite well against domestic peasant rebels. The historian Harry Miller sees the 1572-1644 era as the age in which state versus local society tensions reached their apex. He uses the successful defense of the town of Neijiang, which will be considered below, as a prime example of how local gentry leadership was supposed to operate: sanctioned, but unfettered by the central government.[69] Given the widespread scope and nature of the military threats faced by the Ming from the late 1630s, in Miller's mind the Ming state really had little choice in the matter. That the reliance on the secondary city defensive strategy remained fairly effective in enabling outnumbered local officials to maintain control over their small cities, with little hope of assistance from the Ming court, demonstrates the efficacy of the policy, which insured the continuity of Ming control over their provinces until their ultimate fall to Manchu invaders in 1644.

The social unrest and peasant rebellions of the late Ming period had many causes.[70] Natural disasters such as drought, flooding, earthquakes, and locust plagues destroyed crops. The state's ongoing war with the Jin (later the Manchus), from 1616, further compromised its capacity to distribute famine relief. The power vacuum in the countryside provided fertile ground for bandits and sectarian leaders, who found ready audiences for their anti-Ming messages. The earliest uprisings came from starving peasants, who were easily quelled by governmental forces.[71] But a subsequent policy of leniency towards former rebels backfired, and the grass roots movements mushroomed, albeit in a rather haphazard and disorganized fashion, through the 1630s. After another five-year (1636-1641) period of government successes again reversed, the two most prominent peasant rebel leaders, Zhang Xianzhong (1605-1647) and Li Zicheng (1605-1645) became serious contenders for dynastic authority.[72] Both realized that rebellions that simply raided and plundered were not enough. They had to take and hold cities. Naturally, they launched their rebellions by taking smaller cities that had symbolic importance for the Ming state, and were also fairly easy to take. To defend their cities, Ming officials typically relied on the longstanding "strong walls and empty fields" defense. Though such relatively passive measures did little to roll back the tide of rebellion, they proved remarkably successful in enabling cities of all sizes to hold out against the rebels.

In contrast, several attempts at more aggressive defenses of small towns ended in failure. The town of Shangqiu in Henan province was attacked by the rebel leader Gao Yingxiang (d. 1636) in 1635, but its defenders lacked coordination in their response; military officers allegedly rode around on their horses while civil officials debated defense plans, leaving the commoners to defend themselves. They erected earthen ramparts and filled city alleys with obstacles, but in the end the local defenders were easily defeated by the rebels. Numbers of commoners who resided outside the city walls met their death after government officials closed the city gates to protect themselves, with little consideration for the suburban dwellers facing the rebels on their own. After looting Shangqiu's suburbs, the rebels moved against the nearby garrison of Suizhou, where they routed a government defense force stationed just outside the city. There they killed a hapless drummer who had kept the defenders' morale up as they fought, by stringing him up on a flagpole![73] The victorious rebels finally entered the now undefended town, which by this time had been abandoned by the local magistrate, who fled to a monastery and disguised himself as a monk. In this instance, deviating from the normal defensive practice of clearing the fields and strengthening the walls had cost the defenders of Suizhou dearly.[74]

The Henanese provincial capital of Kaifeng, on the other hand, withstood two major sieges and nearly survived a third in 1641-42, by virtue of its defenders adopting the clearing the fields and strengthening the walls defensive stance. Prominent local civil and military officials stationed themselves at each major gateway. Their city had impressive walls that hearkened back to its earlier status as the capital of the entire empire. During the first siege, the defenders drove the armies of Li Zicheng back with arrows, rocks, and stone tiles, hurled from atop the walls. After this first siege was lifted, a local official adopted the *bao jia* strategy of dividing the city into defense wards, headed by students who became militiamen for the city's defense. The wealthiest families in the city selected, equipped, and trained the militia. Regular civil and military officials took charge of these irregular units, consistent with Ming preference for some vestige of governmental authority rather than allowing any pretence of non-elite empowerment. The city's magistrate ordered that the countryside around the city be cleared. While this afforded the locals some measure of protection, it also hampered efforts to take the fight to the rebels. In the end, the city held against this siege for nearly a month.[75] This passive defense strategy again served the people of Kaifeng well during another siege by Li Zicheng that lasted from May-October 1642, and ended when broken dikes flooded and destroyed most of the city.[76] The third siege featured a number of daring actions and stratagems by both sides, and even though it concluded unfavorably for the defenders, it proved that the strategy of clearing the fields and strengthening the walls was still sound.

The siege of Neijiang, a small city in Sichuan province not far from Chengdu, provides another especially useful example of successful secondary city defense. Attacked by the peasant rebel Zhang Xianzhong in late 1640, the defenders of this small city left a remarkable record of their successful response to this raid, in a military manual called the *Dengpi jilue,* "Record From Atop the Battlements." Written by the local official Miao Yuan, this work offers a fascinating glimpse into how local defenses could be coordinated and organized independent of the central government.[77] Indeed, Harry Miller argues that the work demonstrates that local gentry leadership is "the only essential to military defense, and it is not even considered for a moment that the central government had any competent authority over such matters."[78] Organized into topical chapters, the work is a "how to" guide for organizing the defense of a small city. Above all, according to the 1640s book, the successful local defense depended on active local gentry who acted in partnership with local officials, which was not always the case elsewhere. In essence the imperial *bao jia* system was ideally supposed to operate this same way, with local officials and gentry in partnership taking the initiative to maintain local order and security, and to thereby perpetuate imperial rule with minimal imperial intervention.

Neijiang was located approximately 155 kilometers (93 miles) southeast of the Sichuanese provincial capital of Chengdu, in the Upper Yangzi macroregion. Like most Chinese secondary urban centers, it was situated along a river, in this case the Luo River, which emptied into the mighty Yangzi some 75 kilometers (45 miles) to the southeast at the prefectural capital city of Luzhou. Neijiang's location was strategically important in that it lay along the riverine and overland communication channels that connected Sichuan's two most important urban centers: Chengdu and Chongqing.[79] Neijiang was a county center of trade, religious activity, and education even though it was not the county seat. The hills and mountains that surrounded the city were dotted with temples, shrines, schools, and Confucian academies. This is significant, because there were sufficient numbers of local gentry and minor officials locally resident to lead the town's defense against a bandit army. The city had four major gates situated in each of the major compass directions, and five minor gateways. It also had a moat that could only be crossed via a bridge that accessed the Great West Gate. A few towers and minor defensive structures were outside the town's main walls.[80]

In 1640, the major peasant rebel leaders transitioned between what James Parsons calls their "disorganized raiding" and "dynastic ambitions" phases.[81] After temporarily surrendering to government authorities and being released following his pledge to change his ways, Zhang Xianzhong recommenced his raiding activities in central and southwest China. Following a series of major defeats in Hubei province, Zhang Xianzhong and his diminished following took refuge in the remote Sichuan province mountains, where they bided their time and rebuilt their troop strength.[82] Mountainous and located on the empire's periphery, Sichuan was ideally suited for such activities since there was little official presence. But it also had enough resources to make it attractive as a base of operations for bandits and rebel bands, where they could plunder the newly settled agricultural communities on the Ming periphery.

The plans for defending Neijiang were not hatched overnight. In fact, the successful defense of the city resulted from three years of work. Repairs to the city walls commenced in 1638, using rock harvested from the surrounding Yankaishan hills. Altogether 130 people excavated some 39,490 stones and transported these using some 30 boats to bring them downriver. Once in Neijiang, these rocks were broken up and mixed with lime to augment the existing walls.[83] The cityfolk extended the height of the city walls by some two *zhang* (approximately six feet), and the thickness of the walls by about three feet. They also extended the radius of the walls, and modified the towers that surmounted the city's nine gates, including the construction and placement of wooden catapults atop these gates.[84] These initiatives forced would-be attackers further back from the city's walls, where they could not look into the urban community or attack from portable siege towers. The likes of a local censor, the city magistrate, a former capital official, an ex-prefect, local civil and military officials, and government students all made private contributions to finance these repairs and innovations.[85]

In addition to repairing the town's physical defenses, locals belonged to militia units that were based in local societal affiliations. Hence there were "street militia," "monk soldiers," and the like. According to Miao Yuan, the principles of local militia organization derived from the Ming *baojia* system described above. Local residents were members of militia units lead by local gentry leaders (*xiangshen*), many of whom were students or petty officials with bureaucratic or military ranks. Miao stressed the need to assign the young and vigorous to the militia, not old and weak men who could not fight. According to his estimates, the city had just over 3,000 potential defenders.[86] He emphasized that training was of the utmost importance in preparing each unit to defend the urban community, noting that, even with innate courage, those who were not properly trained would not be able to win one battle out of a hundred.[87] Training activities emphasized ground combat, archery, and horsemanship. Punishments and rewards for soldiers followed standard military regulations.

In the event of an attack, each militia unit, led by local gentry, defended one of the city's nine gates. If one gate came under heavy attack or was breached, units from other gates would rush to its defense. Some militia members would fight while others acted in supporting roles. Units returned to their original posts once they had driven off the bandits. No one was to leave their post (in an attempt to gain personal glory) without their commander's directive. Different cannon signals assembled and deployed units, consistent with the standards said to have been introduced by the Ming general Qi Jiguang in the 1560s. Catapults were the first line of defense when an enemy approached the city, with the hope that a threat could be easily deterred. Following this, defenders employed both active and passive measures. Torches lit the wall tops all night, to prevent bandits from spying on the town's defenses and thus gaining valuable information. Miao estimates that 110 catties of lamp oil were necessary to light the town walls each night.[88]

As he also reports, "even though our walls might be strong and our moats deep, without sufficient food our troops cannot defend the city."[89] Thus militia provided some of their own food, which they grew on designated military farms (*tuntian*) just outside the city walls.[90] The local gentry also set aside supplies or funds for army provisions. According to Miao's accounting, local notables provided some 542 piculs of grain to the city's defense, which he considered to be a fair sum. With respect to the procurement of weapons, there was once again local accountability. Local materials were used wherever possible; the surrounding county was responsible for supplying saltpeter and gunpowder.[91] Thunder carts and gunpowder and fire weapons were essential because bandits especially feared them. Carts and weapon construction used local woods; most weapons were forged locally.[92] Each of the nine gates/units received some two hundred taels of cash for the purchase of weapons, but the origin of these funds is not revealed and it is unclear how they were used by the town's defenders. Miao Yuan provides a list of recently manufactured weapons, which included muskets, three-eyed (triple barreled) guns, fire lances, great swords, pikes, bows, crossbows, ammunition and some 2,500 catties of gunpowder.[93] Such figures are a testament to both the wealth of local society and the bureaucratic efficiency of local officials, and provide insight into how local order could be maintained throughout the Ming period without an overwhelming official imperial bureaucratic or military presence in the countryside.

Owing to the absence of foreign or regional threats through most of the Ming period, the allocation of defensive responsibilities to individual counties and their cities was functionally possible. Thus Harry Miller has declared that during the Ming period, "counties waged wars, not countries."[94] While such an assertion has a certain degree of validity with respect to local banditry and everyday defense, the imperial state did take an interest in local defense when national interests were at stake, as seen in the example of the Ming defensive initiatives along their coastline as discussed above. Major problems in the system could be exposed during longer, more protracted conflicts, as local resources would not have been sufficient to handle prolonged challenges.

Of special interest in the account of Neijiang's defense are the chapters on espionage and the ferreting out of traitors. Noting that the local people were the "eyes and ears of defense," Miao Yuan devoted a significant portion of his account to discussing how the city's residents gathered intelligence concerning the movements of the bandit armies through western Sichuan, and provided brief battle narratives and information about the bandits' tactics. A major point he repeatedly makes in his battle accounts is that bandits preferred to attack places that were not well defended and were therefore easy to take. Constantly harried by government pursuit, bandits were seldom willing to engage in protracted sieges. To avoid a long engagement, they sent scouts who pumped locals for information concerning their city's defenses. In the case of Neijiang, the city benefited from the purposeful spread of false counter-intelligence. In Miao's account, when the bandits first entered Neijiang county they captured a local resident and plied him for information about the city's defenses. He cleverly told them that the city was defended by some 20,000 soldiers, including local militia units, Han Chinese soldiers, aboriginals, and even monks. He told them about the great catapults (or did he mean cannon?), which could shoot so powerfully that a single stone could kill several people at once.[95] The bandits were reportedly shaken up by these tales and decided to avoid Neijiang for the time being. With respect to such internal intelligence gathering, the *Dengpi jilue* also contains a chapter on the discovery of spies and traitors, detailing the backgrounds and aliases of several rebel spies captured in the city.[96]

The work then turns to what might be termed "psychological defenses." The resolve of the populace to defend the city was steeled by gathering them together in the center of Neijiang to swear a solemn oath to hold out until the end. Officials and commoners alike took their oath as a whole, in the midst of burning incense, to reinforcing their sense of mutual dependence.[97] The people of Neijiang also sent letters to nearby settlements, keeping them apprised of their defense efforts. A public proclamation listed all the measures the city had implemented and boasted of their successes. These accounts praised the local gentry leadership, as the author observed that confidence stemmed from the skillful leadership of local gentry and the people's faith in their leadership, in continuity with the local past.[98] The literati of Neijiang county responded to a circular call to arms to fulfill their duty to protect the common folk. A subsequent chapter on raising troops again repeated that only by acting in concert under the capable leadership of local gentry could the people attain victory.

It was noted earlier how it is difficult to ascertain how widely coastal defense programs were implemented or what effects they had in discouraging the would-be Japanese invaders. After all, they were never really tested. While the truth of the 1590s China-Japan conflict may never be known, in the case of Neijiang we have a definitive account of the efficacy of local Ming era defense strategies. The defense of Neijiang is noteworthy in its combination of the classic defensive "clear the fields and strengthen the walls" policy with a more activist defense, one that was not necessarily sketched out before the battle took place, at least judging from the evidence presented by Miao Yuan.

In any event, in late 1640 the forces of Zhang Xianzhong once again began to raid widely in southern and western Sichuan province. Though frequently bested by government forces and sometimes suffering hundreds or even thousands of casualties, the bandit forces would coalesce once more and recommence raiding and plundering.[99] They initially approached Neijiang from the southeast, sending out spies in advance of their main columns. The city's defenders caught one of these scouts and learned of the potential threat. Worried that a requested Ming relief column would not arrive in time, the defenders of Neijiang circulated a false story that 30,000 Ming troops were en route.[100] As the bandit army approached, they sent their scouts out again. Seeing the fields cleared and the walls stoutly guarded, they were leery of coming too close.

The Great East and Small South gates of Neijiang had recently been augmented with stockades and the troops were positioned in their units all around the city. The local military censor was strict in his enforcement of discipline and commoners were used as informants, shouting out information about bandit troop movements outside the city walls. Food and wine were distributed freely amongst the defenders, to boost morale, and mushrooms were distributed to alleviate hunger.[101] Commanders took their place atop the walls alongside the commoner defenders. The gentry went to the north tower and rallied the people of Neijiang, shouting, "The bandits will never be able to determine our strengths and weaknesses. Before, we set up these [defense] measures. And now we can take solace in our security and hold out!" They asserted that the bandit cavalry were disadvantaged in this terrain. Even if they dismounted and tried to cross the moat with boats, their boats would be torched. Censor Wei exhorted the people to place their trust in their gentry leaders. He asserted that the bandits could only take isolated, undefended cities, not ones that were prepared and protected. In fact, some bandits had already fled east after seeing the city's defenses. Wei then suggested laying an ambush at a bridge ten *li* outside the city and trapping the bandits against the river.[102]

The bandits entered the county on the twenty-third day of the eleventh month of 1640 (January 4, 1641). Zhang Xianzhong's primary target was actually Luzhou to the south, but he sent a wing of his army to secure Neijiang so that his rear would be protected.[103] At their approach, Neijiang's local leaders stationed all the militia at their respective posts and waited. Some thought the mountains would protect their city, but as the bandits advanced they seized other neighboring cities and towns. The gentry assembled and agreed to create a left wing vanguard of 500 troops under Mao Wen, a military official, and to hold the approach along the small road leading into city. Another 500 made up the right wing under one Li Yingrong, and 600 aboriginal troops made up the center army.[104] Others were sent to hold the bridge and 500 were detailed as a rear guard. 300 more troops took defensive positions on the walls with orders to help the left and right wings if necessary. Another 500 stood at standby to assist in enveloping attacks, and another 300 to their places in boats with the charge of defending the moat.[105] Local centurions led another mobile corps of 300 men.

Rather than wait for a full-scale assault, the city's defenders sallied forth and skirmished with bandit scouts. The bandits pulled back and tried to lure the Neijiang units into an ambush, but they did not take the bait. Seeing the bandits' rather meager defenses, the Neijiang units asked the town's defenders to send another 500 troops out to take the offensive against their attackers. They first engaged the bandits with cannons and then lured them into an ambush of their own. They recovered weapons, supplies and horses, and, in sum, quickly crushed the morale of the bandit forces. As they withdrew, the bandits fell into another ambush, where they lost 300 men and significant numbers of their weapons and military supplies.[106] They eventually pulled back some twenty *li*. Fearful they would be caught with their backs against the river, they soon withdrew even further.

Meanwhile, the defenders poised for another assault on the city. The bandits approached, but when cannon fired from atop the walls the bandits scattered, and were then vulnerable to the defenders who mounted a sortie to engage them. Some bandits then climbed the nearby mountains to inspect the town's defenses. They were impressed by what they saw and decided not to further press their attack. The bandits decided to strike camp that night and pull back, but, as they did so, the defenders of Neijiang came forth again, pursuing the bandits for some 40 *li* before heading back to the city rather than falling into an ambush. Though they were beaten badly at Neijiang, Zhang's forces did manage to capture Luzhou, albeit only holding the city for a brief time before a larger Ming relief army put them to the run.[107] The residents of Neijiang were jubilant, crowing that the bandits had taken them lightly and had thus paid the price.[108]

The defense of Neijiang should be considered an archetypal example of the creative application of the *qing ye jian cheng* defense policy. In summing up the successful defense of the city, Miao Yuan talked about how the measures implemented in Neijiang might be adopted by other small cities in Sichuan. He also laid out a plan of sorts for the defense of southern Sichuan as a whole.[109] Unfortunately for the residents of the region, the success of Neijiang would be an isolated case. Within three years the Ming dynasty fell, following which Zhang Xianzhong established his own short-lived kingdom in the province. Zhang's reign devastated the region and retarded its economic development for decades. Secondary cities like Neijiang simply lacked the resources to resist his depredations after the collapse of the central government and the creation of several Ming courts-in-exile, where the remaining central authorities were concerned with their mere survival rather than protecting local interests.

The defense of Neijiang illustrates the importance of local officials as mediators between the state and society in late imperial China. While it is true that there were often tensions between state and local interests, the local officials in this case clearly recognized the congruence between their own and broader regional, if not necessarily national interests. They also had a clear sense of how Neijiang fit into the commercial and defense hierarchy of Sichuan province. This is illustrated in the book's final chapter, which articulates the program for the mutual defense of the whole region. Indeed, the author is explicit in discussing the importance of secondary cities in the defense hierarchy and in recognizing that if these smaller urban settlements were not held, then the communication arteries of the province would be severed and the entire area would be lost.

In sum, the importance of the relationship between the officials and gentry and the common people is an important theme of this battle account. Time and again the book's author promotes the vital accountability of local gentry in maintaining order and the public good. Likely this theme responded to so many gentry and officials shirking their responsibilities in this late era of Ming rule. But it also reflects the author's continued appreciation that the people were the roots of the state. Since so many commoners had already joined the roving bandit forces, officials had to realize that they needed to take drastic measures to ensure that other elite and commoners remained loyal, lest the state itself crumble, which is of course what ultimately happened.

Conclusion

Humans have always been China's greatest resource. Bringing them into cities for protection in times of strife recognized this fact, and was a manifestation of the traditional Confucian concern for the welfare of the people. It is also interesting to note that similar strategies were pursued in neighboring Chosŏn Korea, which was, if anything, an even more staunchly Confucian society than Ming China. As related in the *Analects* of Confucius, which every Chinese official was expected to have memorized:

> Zigong asked about government. Confucius said, "Sufficient food, sufficient armament, and sufficient confidence of the people." Zigong said, "Forced to give up one of these, which would you abandon first?" Confucius said, "I would abandon the armament." Zigong said, "Forced to give up one of the remaining two, which would you abandon first?" Confucius said, "I would abandon food. There have been deaths from time immemorial, but no state can exist without the confidence of its people."[110]

The Ming defensive strategy of clearing the fields and strengthening the city walls tacitly acknowledged the importance of human resources as integral to maintaining state authority. This chapter's case studies illustrate how military defense networks and political and administrative hierarchies functioned in times of crisis. National and inter-regional threats received attention from all levels of the administrative hierarchy. Considerable efforts initiated the collection and disbursement of resources, supplies, equipment, and military personnel. These could even involve the dispatch of specialized training officers to local areas. Local threats, on the other hand, were expected to be handled by local officials, regardless of whether or not they had military training. Local officials were also expected to facilitate interaction and communication with higher levels of the administrative hierarchy, even if they were conditioned to expect little assistance from the upper levels of the imperial system.

What is particularly striking in this context is how the accounts of local officials were sensitive to their own relative positions within the administrative and commercial hierarchy. The officials associated with the defense of Neijiang emphasized their town's importance to the defense of Sichuan province as a whole, as well as Neijiang's commercial significance regionally, a self-realization that suggests how we might usefully modify Skinner's macroregional theory of development to include defense matters. Although defense installations and frontier towns such as Neijiang were located on the peripheries of the macroregions, their importance in maintaining the economic vitality and political stability of the core areas was readily acknowledged. Lest officials in the core areas or capital seem inclined to forget this point, as we have seen, local officials were keen to remind them of the strategic importance of the secondary cities under their purview.

In terms of urban defense, it is interesting to see how the constellation of Ming defense posts either inhibited or facilitated rebellion. The state's defense posts tended to be clustered in distant frontier regions where trouble was most likely. They often presaged later colonization efforts by Han Chinese in previously peripheral regions, to the state's political and economic benefit. Such expansionism brought order to what was potentially threatening, in promoting the spread of hierarchical Han civilization. With the gradual settlement, cultural integration, and administrative incorporation of such frontier regions, new urban and commercial networking developed. More work remains to be done on these complex processes, but it seems that modifying Skinner's macroregional model of urban and commercial development by including an analysis of defense installations and procedures as they related to local, regional, and national threats can offer intriguing possibilities for researchers. Given that secondary cities were usually both the first line of defense and the first link in any commercial chain leading to the macroregional hub, it seems logical that their significance be highlighted in future studies.

This study has attempted to initiate this process by suggesting that Ming responses to military threats to secondary cities were contingent upon the scope and nature of the threat in question. National-level threats that crossed macroregions, such as the danger posed by the Japanese in the 1590s, necessitated the mobilization and assembly of resources from all over the empire. They also typically involved extensive coordination at all levels of the Ming administrative hierarchy. Supplies and manpower would be dispatched from outside the imperiled regions, but significant pressure would be exerted upon the locals to aid in their own defense. Lesser threats that were confined to one macroreigon were expected to be handled by local officials, who were then wont to emphasize the importance of their actions for the security of the empire as a whole. Yet in both cases officials tended to initially rely upon the fairly simple defensive strategy of "clearing the fields and strengthening the walls." While on the surface it might seem that such a policy had the potential for atomizing Ming society, in actuality the emphasis upon self-sufficiency as it pertained to the stability of the whole was deeply rooted in Chinese tradition, and was a serviceable means of defending the vast Chinese landscape in an age in which government resources and communication infrastructures could not support higher levels of political, economic, and military centralization.

Both the central government and the local authorities recognized the importance of secondary cities in the empire's defenses as seen in the examples given herein, as also the implications of local urban defense relative to the empire's political and economic well-being. The economic role of cities would assume greater primacy in the late Ming period, when the empire became increasingly involved in the global economy. As in the earlier Ming era, secondary cities continued as vital agents of imperial authority in a variety of ways, including the extension of imperial authority and commerce to and from the Ming realm's vulnerable peripheries.

Notes

1. G. William Skinner, "Presidential Address: The Structure of Chinese History," *Journal of Asian Studies* 44, 2 (1985), 288.

2. See G. William Skinner, "Regional Urbanization in Nineteenth-Century China," in *The City In Late Imperial China*, ed. Skinner (Stanford: Stanford University Press, 1977), 212-215.

3. Skinner, "Regional Urbanization," 216.

4. Ibid., 216-217.

5. Ibid., 219.

6. See, for example, Joseph W. Esherick, *The Origins of the Boxer Uprising* (Berkeley: University of California Press, 1987); Robert J. Antony, *Like Froth Floating on the Sea: The World of Pirates and Seafarers in Late Imperial South China* (Berkeley: University of California Press, 2003). For a modification of the macroregional model and a treatment of its implications for studying Qing social history, see Susan Naquin and Evelyn Rawski, *Chinese Society in the Eighteenth-Century* (Princeton: Princeton University Press, 1987), 138-216.

7. On the spatial distribution of Ming military garrisons, see David Robinson, *Bandits, Eunuchs, and the Son of Heaven: Rebellion and the Economy of Violence in Mid-Ming China* (Honolulu: University of Hawai'i Press, 2001), 38-43.

8. On the tendency for rebellions to emerge in peripheral regions, see James Tong, *Disorder Under Heaven: Collective Violence in the Ming Dynasty* (Stanford: Stanford University Press, 1991).

9. See Tong, *Disorder Under Heaven*. For a more recent treatment that challenges Tong's characterizations, see David Robinson, *Bandits, Eunuchs, and the Son of Heaven*, 45-46; 164-168.

10. For more on the economy of wall construction as it pertained to the Great Wall, see Arthur Waldron, *The Great Wall of China: From History to Myth* (Cambridge: Cambridge University Press, 1990), 157-164. The debates surrounding the maintenance of the Great Wall were less concerned with these broader implications, but were focused instead on the more specific immediate threats, as detailed by Waldron.

11. G. William Skinner, "Urban Development in Imperial China," in *The City in Late Imperial China*, ed. Skinner, 19-21.

12. Sen-dou Chang, "The Morphology of Walled Capitals," in ibid., 75.

13. Virtually the entire population was divided into hereditary occupational classes, the two largest being civilian and military households.

14. *MS,* 2194. The locations of the guards and battalions are listed in *MS,* 2222-2228.

15. He Zhiqing and Wang Xiaowei, *Zhongguo bing zhi shi* (Taibei: Zhongguo wenhua shi congshu, 1997), 239.

16. Sen-dou Chang, 96.

17. Sen-dou Chang suggests that water was the most important factor behind site selection since these cities served primarily agrarian populations (ibid., 85).

18. For more on Korean walled fortresses, see Yu Jae-chun, "Mountain Fortresses: The Front Line of National Defense," *Koreana,* 19, 1 (2005), 18-23; Hur Kyoung-jin, "Town Walls Create a Safe Haven for the Populace," *Koreana,* 19, 1 (2005), 24-31. For a comparison of Chinese and Korean defensive responses to the Mongols, see Huang K'uan-chung, "Mountain Fortress Defence: The Experience of the Southern Song and Korea in Resisting the Mongol Invasions," in *Warfare in Chinese History,* ed. Hans van de Ven (Leiden: E. J. Brill, 2000), 222-251.

19. Sen-dou Chang, 83-85.

20. It was considered bad fortune for a road to provide direct access to any structure via a straight line because malicious spirits could only travel in a straight line. Therefore, most cities and buildings often had irregular approaches, perhaps augmented by natural features like water, hills, and mountains. On the broader application of *feng shui* principles in city construction in East Asia, particularly Vietnam, see John Whitmore's study in the present volume.

21. See, for example, Mao Ruizheng, *Wanli san da zheng kao* (Taibei: Wenhai chubanshe, 1971), 83.

22. See Leo K. Shin, *The Making of the Chinese State: Ethnicity and Expansion on the Ming Borderlands* (Cambridge: Cambridge University Press, 2006), 29-36.

23. See Merrilyn Fitzpatrick, "Local Interests and the Anti-Pirate Administration in China's South-east, 1555-1565," *Ch'ing shih wen-t'i,* 4 (1979), 1-50.

24. The Ningxia mutiny of 1592 is treated in Kenneth M. Swope, "All Men Are Not Brothers: Ethnic Identity and Dynastic Loyalty in the Ningxia Mutiny of 1592," *Late Imperial China,* 24, 1 (2003), 79-129.

25. Zhuge Yuansheng, *Liang chao ping rang lu* (Taibei: Xuesheng shuju, 1969), 131.

26. See *MS,* 6221.

27. On popular fears of the Japanese in Ming China, see Wang Yong, "Realistic and Fantastic Images of 'Dwarf Pirates': The Evolution of Ming Dynasty Perceptions of the Japanese," in *Sagacious Monks and Bloodthirsty Warriors: Chinese Views of Japan in the Ming-Qing Period,* ed. Joshua A. Fogel (Norwalk, CT: Eastbridge, 2002), 17-41.

28. See Charles Wheeler's study in this volume.

29. Qian Yiben, comp. *Wanli dichao* 3 vols. [hereafter cited as *WLDC*] (Taibei: Zhengzhong shuju, 1982), 674. Also see Tan Qian, *Guoque,* 10 vols. (Taibei: Dingwen shuju, 1978), 4681. Hereafter cited as *GQ.*

30. See Zheng Liangsheng, comp., *Mingdai wokou shiliao* 5 vols. [hereafter cited as *WKSL*] (Taibei: Wenshizhe chubanshe, 1987), 475. The passages from this particular volume (2) are all taken from the *Veritable Records of the Ming Dynasty.*

31. *WKSL,* 476.

32. *WKSL,* 477.

33. See, in comparison, Charles Argo's study in this volume.

34. There are far too many studies of the international silver trade and its connections to China to enumerate here. For an overview, see Richard von Glahn, *Fountain of Fortune: Money and Monetary Policy in China, 1000-1700* (Berkeley: University of California Press, 1996), 113-206, dealing with the late Ming period. Also see Dennis O. Flynn and Arturo Giraldez, "Born With a Silver Spoon: The Origin of World Trade in 1571," *Journal of World History*, 6, 2 (1995), 201-221.

35. See Song Yingchang, comp., *Jinglue fuguo yaobian* 2 vols. [hereafter cited as *FGYB*] (Taibei: Xuesheng shuju, 1986), 1. Also see *WLDC*, 695.

36. *FGYB*, 15.

37. *FGYB*, 16.

38. See the arguments in *FGYB*, 66, 74. In terms of cost, mercenaries were paid six *liang* a month, with an additional one *liang*, eight *qian* provided for food. See *FGYB*, 77.

39. *WKSL*, 479.

40. On the twenty-seventh day of the ninth month of 1592.

41. *FGYB*, 49.

42. By contrast, a recent estimate suggests that perhaps thirty percent of Japanese fighters in Korea were equipped with firearms. See Samuel Hawley, *The Imjin War* (Seoul: Royal Asiatic Society, 2005), 102.

43. *FGYB*, 48.

44. *FGYB*, 52.

45. On the siege of Ulsan, see Kenneth M. Swope, "War and Remembrance: Yang Hao and the Siege of Ulsan of 1598," forthcoming in *The Journal of Asian History*.

46. *FGYB*, 94-95.

47. A letter from Song Yingchang to Shi Xing concerned a request for boats to be assembled at Lushun, across the Yellow Sea from Korea and the surrounding islands. *FGYB*, dated the 13th day of the 11th month (December 16), 167.

48. *FGYB*, 171.

49. This was actually an avenue for social mobility during the Ming. In fact the famed late Ming commander Chen Lin, the most highly decorated veteran of the Ming intervention in Korea, had entered military service in just this fashion, answering a call to battle pirates in his native Guangdong. See *MS*, 6404.

50. *FGYB*, 171. It is not clear if those from Nanjing are included in the estimate of 7000 troops.

51. *FGYB*, 174.

52. The *sha chuan* was a sailed vessel favored in rough northern waters. See Mao Yuanyi, comp. *Wubei zhi*. 22 vols. [hereafter cited as *WBZ*] (Taibei: Huashi chubanshe, 1987), 4806-4807.

53. *FGYB*, 174.

54. *FGYB*, 175.

55. After the ambitious Ming armada voyages of Zheng He in the early fifteenth century, Ming emperors concentrated their military expenditures in their army, to provide a noted concentration of imperial forces to defend their northwest border against an inevitable invasion from the Central Asian steppes.

56. This was not a situation unique to the Ming. Prior to the late sixteenth century, few states anywhere had regular standing navies.

57. *FGYB*, 172.

58. Ibid.

59. *FGYB*, 178.

60. *FGYB*, 179. These efforts had the added benefit of providing protection against common marauders and mountain bandits.

61. A *zhang* is approximately three feet.

62. *FGYB,* 185.

63. *FGYB,* 186-187.

64. *FGYB,* 179.

65. In sum, the *bao jia/li jia* system was foundational to Skinner's hierarchical macroregional model in his discussions of late imperial China.

66. For details on this uprising, see Swope, "Three Great Campaigns," chapter seven.

67. In contrast to these Ming initiatives on their Vietnam border, see Charles Wheeler's study in this volume, which places focus on the role of Fujianese merchants, in partnership with Cham Buddhist monks, as agents in the spread of Han civilization in the Cochinchina regions of southern Vietnam.

68. See Timothy Brook, "Japan in the Late Ming: The View From Shanghai," in Fogel, ed., 42-61.

69. Harrison S. Miller, "State Versus Society in Late Imperial China, 1572-1644," Ph.D. dissertation (New York: Columbia University, 2001), 508-509.

70. The standard English language monograph on the late Ming rebellions is James B. Parsons, *Peasant Rebellions of the Late Ming Dynasty* repr. (Ann Arbor: Association for Asian Studies, 1993).

71. See Gu Yingtai, *Mingshi jishi benmo*, repr. in *Lidai jishi benmo*, 2 vols. (Beijing: Zhonghua shuju, 1997), 2448-2489; Dai Li and Wu Jiang, *Liukou changbian*, 2 vols. (Beijing: Shumu wenxian chubanshe, 1991), 29-34; and Parsons, 1-8.

72. For their official biographies, see *MS,* 7948-7977.

73. See Roger V. Des Forges, *Cultural Centrality and Political Change in Chinese History: Northeast Henan in the Fall of the Ming* (Stanford: Stanford University Press, 2003), 189-191.

74. Shangqiu, however, would not actually fall until the following year after a brutal siege. Its new defender also fled the scene and abandoned his seals of office when the city walls were breached.

75. See Des Forges, 213-216, 222-226.

76. For a narrative of the third siege, see Des Forges, 254-267.

77. Miao Yuan, *Dengpi jilue* (Taibei: Taiwan xuesheng shuju, 1986).

78. Miller, "State Versus Society," 507.

79. Miao notes the strategic importance of Neijiang and other secondary cities in Sichuan, calling these cities "the throat of the province," thereby underscoring their importance within the broader administrative hierarchy, a point which is downplayed by Harry Miller in his treatment of the town's defense.

80. See the image in *Dengpi jilue,* 601-602.

81. See Parsons, 63-89.

82. For an overview of peasant rebel activities in Sichuan in 1640, see *Liukou changbian,* 673-720.

83. *Dengpi jilue,* 604.

84. *Dengpi jilue,* 604-605.

85. *Dengpi jilue,* 605-607, which includes a list of who gave how much money.

86. *Dengpi jilue,* 610-611.

87. *Dengpi jilue,* 609.

88. *Dengpi jilue,* 620.

89. *Dengpi jilue,* 629.

90. *Dengpi jilue,* 615-617.

91. *Dengpi jilue,* 617, 631.

92. *Dengpi jilue,* 631.
93. *Dengpi jilue,* 632-633.
94. Miller, "State Versus Society," 510.
95. *Dengpi jilue,* 642-643.
96. See *Dengpi jilue,* 651-661.
97. See *Dengpi jilue,* 664-665 for the oath itself.
98. *Dengpi jilue,* 671-672.
99. See *Liukou changbian,* 714-719.
100. *Dengpi jilue,* 687.
101. *Dengpi jilue,* 687-688.
102. *Dengpi jilue,* 688-690.
103. *Liukou changbian,* 720-721.
104. *Dengpi jilue,* 694. Aboriginals often made up the bulk of local military forces in southwestern provinces. See Shin, 91-95, Kenneth M. Swope, "Civil-Military Coordination in the Bozhou Campaign of the Wanli Era," *War and Society* 18, 2 (2000), 54-66; and Geoff Wade, "Engaging the South: Ming China and Southeast Asia in the 15th Century," *Journal of the Economic and Social History of the Orient*, forthcoming.
105. *Dengpi jilue,* 695.
106. *Dengpi jilue,* 696.
107. Parsons, 78.
108. *Dengpi jilue,* 704.
109. See *Dengpi jilue,* 707-716.
110. Translation excerpted from Wing-Tsit Chan, *A Source Book in Chinese Philosophy* (Princeton: Princeton University Press, 1963), 39. I have rendered the original Wade-Giles into pinyin Romanization.

6

Secondary Capitals of Dai Viet: Shifting Elite Power Bases

John K. Whitmore

In Dai Viet (covering northern Vietnam from the eleventh century to the end of the eighteenth), there existed one primary city, the capital of Thang-long (now Hanoi), and a number of lesser urban areas. Generally, the latter consisted of economic intersections, that is, market areas, and, especially in the early modern era, administrative seats for provincial, prefectural, and district offices, often coinciding with the former. What I am examining here were aggregations of population formed by local political power that had risen to the level of the realm. This political power then drew economic and administrative concentration to itself as it developed its own aristocratic and ritual center.

Dai Viet formed in the tenth and eleventh centuries out of a number of localities that became linked to the primary city, the capital, through alliances, intermarriages, and power struggles. As increasingly the political, ritual, and economic center of the realm, the capital at first bound together these localities as essentially the first among competitive rivals, then established the monarchy of the Ly dynasty (itself a Chinese-style innovation) more strongly over the localities. As the central power grew, the localities themselves did not remain static. Over the coming centuries, shifting political and economic circumstances led to the emergence of different localities and their elites as central powers. The bases of these elite localities became the secondary capitals of Dai Viet as each new power retained Thang-long as the primary capital and used its own home as their personal center.

This study describes the consecutive emergence of the home base of each Vietnamese dynasty as the subsidiary capital during that particular age. It discusses the apparent nature of these secondary capitals in relation to Thang-long and how this nature depended on both location and the circumstances of that age.

All such secondary capitals arose in different parts of the country, as power shifted among the localities, and were different distances from the capital (*Map 6.1*). The population sizes of these sites are difficult to determine, but they were certainly much smaller than that of the capital and probably varied significantly by region. Self-confident in their own power, these sites would have had varying relations with the capital and its population. Certainly, each such secondary capital had its own distinct character. The different locations would have had

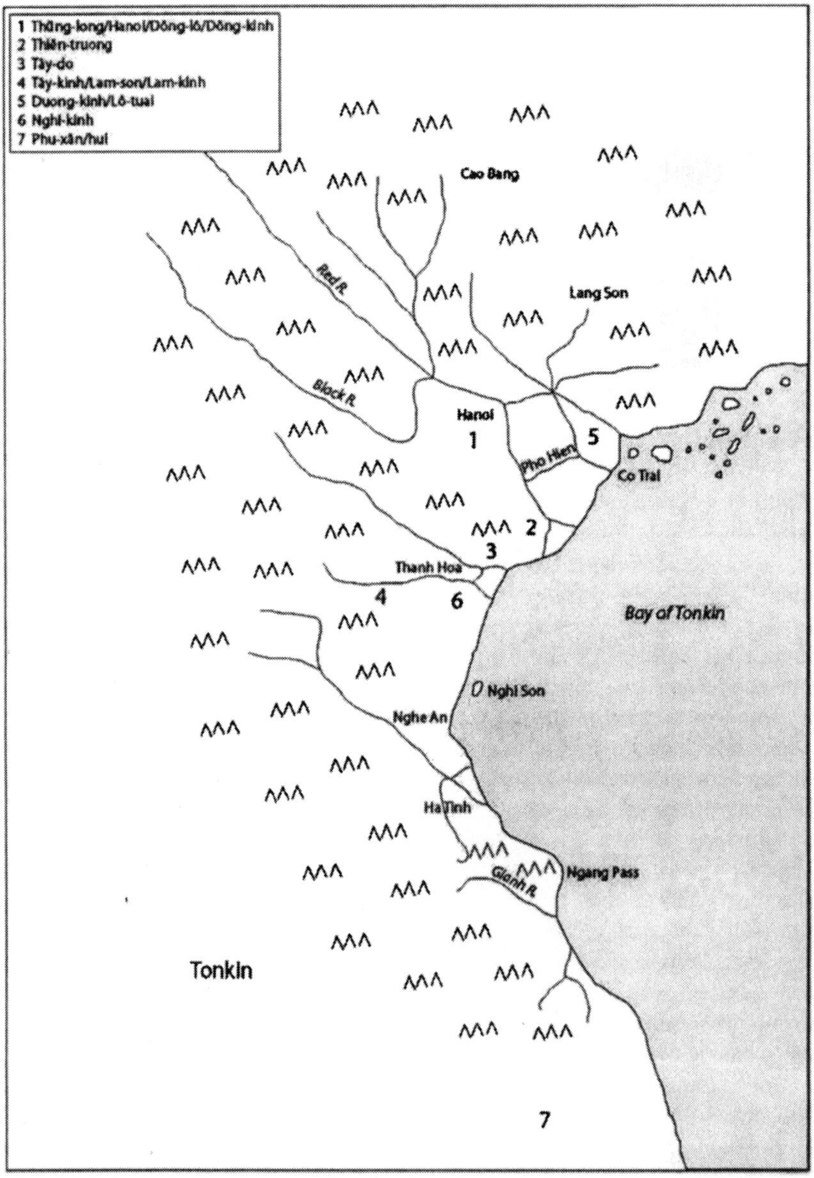

Map 6.1. **Ly Era Vietnam Urban Centers**

differing spatial relations within themselves, been embedded in their specific local social patterns, existed in different economic relations, and developed their own cultural ways. As the power shifted through the centuries, the former power centers faded back into the countryside as the new ones emerged. Hence, as urban sites, these centers lasted only as long as did their power. Ritual centers of former dynasties were all that remained of the prior special situations existing there.

The Primary Capital

As the recent, and extraordinary, archaeological excavations in Hanoi make clear,[1] the history of the primary capital of Dai Viet goes back over a thousand years, deep into the great age of the Tang dynasty in China. First known as La-Thanh (Chinese: *Lo Cheng*, "Walled City"), then as Dai-la (Chinese: *Da Lo*, "Great Walled [City]"), the Chinese administration of what was then a southern border province of the cosmopolitan empire established its local capital here originally in 768. For the next century, this location suffered numerous vicissitudes until, after the Nanzhao wars, the Chinese general Gao Pien in the 860s rebuilt Dai-la as the provincial center.[2]

One hundred fifty years later, the Tang dynasty had fallen and the localities in the area had fought for dominance. The capital of the dominant chieftain first lay at Hoa-lu in the hills to the south of the Red River delta. In 1010, the new dominant chief, Ly Cong Uan, allied with the Buddhist establishment of the central delta and brought his capital back to the old site of Dai-la, renaming it Thang-long ("Emergent Dragon"). He and his successors developed the city as the royal capital during the time they strengthened the monarchy. Located not far south of their home village, Dinh-bang (referred to as the Northern Capital Bac-kinh), Thang-long sat in the midst of the thriving Buddhist community and its lands. The Ly thus came to rule from Thang-long over an increasingly strong realm in the midriver section of the Red River system. Like Angkor in Cambodia and Bagan in Myanmar, Thang-long ruled over rich agricultural territory upriver from the coast.[3] This site would remain the central capital for almost eight centuries[4] until, in an expanded Vietnam, the new southern dynasty of the Nguyen shifted the capital to its own site of Hue in what had become the center of the new land. Only with the French colonial organization of Indochina at the end of the nineteenth century would the main administrative center return to what had become Ha-noi.

Over the eight centuries of Dai Viet, the eleventh through the eighteenth, while the center of the government almost always remained at Thang-long, shifting power relations around the realm meant that different localities served as the home bases of new dynastic families.[5] The beginning of these shifts away from the midriver core of Dai Viet took place through the twelfth century and into the thirteenth. The strong economic development of the core region around the capital drew in international trade and joined with the major surge in Chinese trade of those years to bring wealth and population, many of Chinese coastal origin, to the eastern coastal zone of the lower Red River delta. Here there developed the power of the Tran family, which allied with and then displaced the Ly in the capital. Unlike elsewhere in Southeast Asia (Angkor, Bagan, and Mataram in Java), the classical capital of Dai Viet was not displaced and abandoned by the growth of coastal power. The new Tran dynasty (itself of Chinese coastal descent) kept the old capital and maintained many of its established rituals, while also building up their home base to the east as the secondary capital and calling it Thien-truong ("The Heavenly Capital").

This remained the situation in Dai Viet for a century and a half until a new regional power base emerged further south, in Thanh-hoa province. Also part of the coastal zone and led by another family of Chinese coastal origin, the new group for the first time brought southerners into the capital in significant numbers. The group's leader, Ho Quy Ly, established a new political center, the first Western Capital (Tay-do) in his home territory, making Thang-long the Eastern Capital (Dong-do). Though the Ho regime was short lived, the citadel it built to the south would remain. The Ho defeat by the Ming dynasty of China led to the capital becoming a provincial center called Dong-quan for two decades. A multiethnic group from the western mountains of Thanh-hoa province in turn defeated the Ming in 1428, took control of the capital, and began a new dynasty, the Le. Its home base in the mountains to the west was Lam-son, and it in turn became the Western Capital (Tay-kinh), or Lam-kinh as an alternative name. Thang-long thus became the Eastern Capital (Dong-kinh, or as the Westerners would later say, Tonkin).

Lam-kinh would stay the ritual center and burial place for the Le dynasty during its 360 year existence. This existence was, however, broken into three parts. The first, that of the dynasty's rule, lasted almost a century (1428-1527). In the second period (1528-1592), the Mac dynasty from the coastal east of the Red River delta ousted the Le and set up their own home base as Duong-kinh to be their secondary capital. The Le and their supporters, the Nguyen and Trinh lords, took refuge in Lam-son and its hinterland (for the duration known as Tay-do, the Western Capital) where they based their war against the Mac. Succeeding in 1592, the Le forces led by the Trinh lord retook the capital, once again making it Dong-kinh and restoring Lam-son as Tay-kinh/Lam-kinh. Thus would it stay for the remaining two centuries of Le reign and Trinh rule until 1789, though the Trinh Lords set up their own home base in Thanh-hoa (Nghi-kinh) and their rivals the Nguyen built a base for themselves in Phu-xuan to the south.

Having sketched out the shifting bases of the changing dynastic powers of Dai Viet from the center to the east, to the south, to the west, back east again, and finally returning to the west and the far south, our focus shifts to the limited sources available that allow description and analysis of each of these secondary capitals. What was the topography in which each of these towns existed? How did this topography relate to the power of that particular dynasty? How similar were the situations of these towns? In what ways did their situations differ?

Thien-Truong

The new Tran dynasty in the early thirteenth century had established its base in the southern part of the eastern (lower) delta of the Red River. When the state of Dai Viet with its capital at Thang-long had first developed in the upper midriver zone of the Red River valley, the coastal portion had remained underpopulated with little economic development. It may even have had a different ethnicity and was seen as separate from the core region upriver. The parallel twelfth-century rise of the great port of Quanzhou in southern Fujian along the south China coast and the upsurge of maritime commerce along the Indian Ocean trade network had local consequence. Through the twelfth century, the combination of inland agricultural expansionism and downstream connection to the international trade brought generalized prosperity to the Red River delta region. The flow of goods and men down the southeast coast of China, through the coastal zone of Dai Viet, and on into its upstream core led to the rise of a new port, Van-don, in the islands off the northeast edge of the delta. Increasingly, the international goods, their handling, and the manufacture of other goods locally led to growing wealth and population in this eastern delta zone. Quanzhou sat at the apex of the regional trading system that tied together Champa to the south, Hainan Island to the east, and the coast of Dai Viet and its port of Van-don.[6]

On the southern edge of the Vietnamese coastal zone, southeast of the capital, the Tran clan (Chinese: Chen, originally from Fujian province in China, like many others who settled in this coastal zone) developed their base of Tuc-mac in the watery domain of the lower delta. Lying just north of the present Nam-dinh, this base in the flatlands near the coast, not far above sea level, sat amidst the twisting water courses of the complex river system there where fishing was plentiful. At this time, unlike now, the lands around it were being domesticated and converted from their natural state. Highly fertile, once turned into rice paddies, they sustained an ever increasing population. Initially, the importance of this location was its access to and strategic location at the intersection of the numerous lower delta waterways. In that riverine and tidal world, the Tran had an expansive agricultural base that supported their maritime interests, whether enhancing their trade opportunities or allowing them to move their troops quickly and easily by boat in all directions.[7]

Originally fishermen, by 1200 the Tran had gained local power with their naval forces and began to challenge the Ly dynasty in Thang-long. Through the first quarter of the thirteenth century, the two alternately competed and allied to keep the profitable upstream/downstream flow of goods going, and to engage in combat against other regional powers. Eventually, the Tran took advantage of the Ly pattern of forging marriage alliances with their regional opponents by marrying one of their sons to a Ly princess, which legitimized their seizure of the throne and the capital for themselves. Unlike elsewhere in Southeast Asia at about this time, where the center of royal power regularly shifted consequent to the rise and fall dynasties,[8] the coastal Tran kept the Dai Viet capital in its classical Thang-long location, to reinforce their claim to be the legitimate heirs to the Ly dynasty by maintaining the Ly dynasty's ritual center.

The Tran promptly joined upper and lower Dai Viet, integrating their territory of the eastern delta into the core region of the realm. As their dynastic chronicle stated, "The kingdom became one." The new dynasty also renamed its local base southeast of the capital Thien-truong ("The Heavenly Capital") and rebuilt it as an aristocratic center appropriate to their clan's new political stature. Their rebuilt clan center became politically vital in 1258, when the dynasty began its new pattern of having the reigning monarch abdicate and become the

Senior Ruler (*Thuong Hoang*), allowing his eldest son to ascend the throne as the junior sovereign. This resolved the succession problems that had plagued the Ly dynasty before them (and had allowed the Tran themselves to seize the throne). Thereafter, the father resided in Thien-truong, elevated to become the new royal seat, while his son reigned from the capital of Thang-long.[9]

Another aspect of the Thien-truong court's legacy was its role as keystone in the development of landed estates in the previously underpopulated lower delta. Multicultural, literate, and powerful Tran clan princes each had their own base of operations at strategic locations across the lower delta. Through the middle of the thirteenth century, the Tran constructed their estate system, centered at riverine crossroads and anchored by Buddhist temples. Princely estates were constructed of reclaimed deltaic lands that were populated by the resettlements of transient populations, war captives, and military. These strategically situated and garrisoned estates controlled the waterways and served as a defense network that protected the Dai Viet upstream hinterland, and above all the routes to and between the dynasty's primary and secondary capitals. They were economically self-sufficient, with agricultural, fishing, commercial, and artisanal resources, and became local social, political, economic, cultural, and religious centers where these princes, their families, and retainers spent much of their time.[10]

The Tran kings built their palaces in Thien-truong where, to quote a Vietnamese literati witness of the scene, it "was surrounded by tidewater, and the coast there was full of fragrant trees and flowers. Gaily painted pleasure boats went back and forth—[the place] was like a fairyland."[11] This royal site was well stationed with troops and well staffed with officials.[12] After the first royal succession in 1258, when the position of Senior Ruler emerged, the reigning monarch essentially retired to his clan's home village of Tuc-mac, now Thien-truong, where in 1262 he held a grand banquet, honoring the elderly (those fifty-nine and over) of the realm. He used the main palace and had a new palace compound built there where the reigning (junior) monarch could reside during the course of the festivities. The Senior Ruler also had a new Buddhist temple constructed west of his palace. In the words of the Chronicle, "Hereafter the abdicated (senior) rulers all lived in this palace. And so they established two palaces for the palace women as well as officials for supervision."[13] A later ruler composed a poem entitled "At the Royal Palace of Thien-truong," which describes the court setting:

> In this solitude, beings and things exist in a gentle infinity.
> 'Tis here that is the most beautiful of the twelve regions
>   of the realm.
> The birds sing in a hundred voices: a true concert!
> And such thousands of guards, the orange trees rank on rank.
> A serene moon shines on men at peace,
> And the autumn sky sees itself in the autumn waters.
> The four seas are calmed, the turmoil of dust settled.
> This stay, more than those of years past, delights me.[14]

With the wealth of the royal family and the entourage of the Senior Ruler situated there, Thien-truong must have created quite a sight in the midst of the delta lowlands. Though sacked twice by wars, in the 1280s with the Mongols and a hundred years later with Champa to the south, it remained the vital royal base of the Tran clan until the dynasty's end late in the fourteenth century.

Tay-Do

As the Tran clan collapsed over the final third of the fourteenth century, afflicted both by internal weakness and by the attacks of Champa, a new regional power emerged to displace it. This power, also coastal in orientation, situated further south in the modern-day Thanh-hoa and Nghe-an provinces, centered on Mt. Dai-lai, was again based in a clan of Chinese origin that had moved into the area in the thirteenth century from the southeast coast of China (Zhejiang province).[15] To consolidate their defensive position against Champa in these southern borderlands, the Tran rulers recruited members of the provincial elite, who had previously had rare occasion to visit the Dai Viet court. Against royal protocol, two clan women married into the Tran royal clan. Consequently, two of the princes sired by these ladies became, in the 1370s, the king (then Senior Ruler) and his half-brother, the subsequent Junior Ruler until the latter's death in an attack on Champa.[16]

Through his clan's marriage links to the Tran throne, Quy Ly (whose own wife was a Tran princess) rose to power following the devastating attack by Champa on Thang-long in 1371.[17] As he and others of his southern clan became integrated into the Tran aristocracy and served in increasingly important roles in the government, he began to draw in more of his southern clansmen for support. Increasingly through the 1380s and into the 1390s, Quy Ly developed both his power in the center and his base in the south. In the mid-1390s, Ho Quy Ly began to think of establishing his southern base as an alternate capital. In 1397, against opposition, he initiated his shift of the capital from Thang-long to a location in northern Thanh-hoa province. The Tran delta-based opposition complained of leaving the land of the Dragon's Belly (Long-do) around Thang-long for an area of

> borderlands ... closed in and miserable, at the end of the rivers and the beginning of the mountains. It is a rebellious area, unable to be ruled, whose men may be trusted to be dangerous. There is an old saying, "Live in virtue, not in danger!"[18]

This plea did not persuade Quy Ly and he proceeded with his plans.

Quy Ly sent a top minister to lay out the plan for the new capital. In a time of potential threats from both the south and the north, from Champa and Ming China, this site differed considerably from the openness of the Tran seat of Thien-truong. Where the latter lay at a riverine crossroads with social, economic, cultural, and religious communities and no major fortifications, Quy Ly's new location would be out of the way and well fortified, with little in the way of the other amenities, it would appear. As the quotation stated, the new site lay on the edge of civilization and the beginning of the wilds. Quy Ly's minister was to examine the chosen site of the new capital at An-ton, design and build a citadel, and prepare the new city for the court's occupation. This meant building the necessary infrastructure of access roads, digging a surrounding moat, and establishing a shrine and altar to the local spirits. While Thien-truong had existed in the

Tran territory (and so would already have been integrated with its spirit world and that of the longstanding Thang-long capital city), Quy Ly was moving into rather strange territory that required efforts at such spiritual considerations.[19]

Archaeological remains allow us to have a fairly specific idea of Quy Ly's citadel and its surroundings. It was square, 1640 feet on each side, and essentially north-south in orientation. Its walls were thick earthen ramparts, covered with stone, and surrounded by a moat. An irregular outer defense wall encircled the citadel at a distance of about a half mile. The massiveness of the citadel would have been meant both for protection and to impress the local populace with its might. Each wall had a great stone gate, with the primary southern one containing three entrances.[20] The great stone slabs weighed as much as sixteen tons being over twenty feet long and three-fourths feet thick. Chinese-style pavilions sat atop the gates. Behind the citadel, to the north, was a range of hills; to the south and east lay open plain, and here, about ten miles directly south, was a 450 foot hill standing as an advance guard, militarily and geomantically. There was also a smaller fort with rock faced walls and another triple gate here. A huge undertaking (it was the only Vietnamese citadel before the nineteenth century to make such use of stone), An-ton was constructed so rapidly, in only three months, that within four years it would require repair.[21]

An-ton now became Tay-do, the Western Capital, and consequently Thang-long was renamed Dong-do, the Eastern Capital. Though more northwest/southeast in relation to each other, it seems likely that Quy Ly picked up on the Chinese classical scholarship then growing strongly in Dai Viet and made an explicit reference to the *Book of History* (Chinese: *Shu Jing*; Vietnamese: *Kinh Thu*). In the antiquity of the Duke of Zhou, an iconic figure in Dai Viet at that time, there were a Tay-do and a Dong-do, and it is quite possible that Quy Ly exploited this connection. Its classical justification would have overlain the strategic necessity. Quy Ly brought the young Tran ruler and his court to this new capital, along with court buildings dismantled in Dong-do and reassembled in Tay-do. The new southern court's layout was standard sinic-style: the triple gate on the south, a rectangular pattern of east-west and north-south paved streets, and the palace on the north end of the central north/south axis, with dragon balustrades at its entrances.[22]

With his new capital in place, Quy Ly changed the provincial nomenclature to match, as Thanh-hoa became Thanh-do. Basing himself in Tay-do, Quy Ly placed a son in the old capital with a title recalling the Chinese Tang empire at the same location over five hundred years before. Control of the delta and the Tran territory from his southern base was his central aim in his attempt to re-strengthen Dai Viet. He undercut the economic base of the delta elite, limiting the amount of land and manpower they might control. In 1398, as he placed a very young Tran king (his own grandson) on the throne, Quy Ly officially completed the royal palace in the new capital. He sponsored the performance of the proper investiture rites, followed by a great banquet to celebrate and commemorate the event. The annual blood oath of loyalty to the throne was then held here instead of in Thang-long—shortly thereafter Quy Ly would replace this long-standing dynastic ritual with the contemporary Ming ceremony of the Nam-giao, the great suburban sacrifice to Heaven.[23]

When resistance broke out against Quy Ly's increasing grasp on power at Tay-do, he mercilessly shattered the opposition and, with the help of a group of Confucian literati, consolidated his new government and then took the throne, proclaiming himself Senior Ruler and his son the junior sovereign, the king. To strengthen his new capital's position, he resettled a colony of prisoners from Dong-do in the Tay-do area, who constructed a wall of sharpened bamboo to complete the west side of the outer wall and to clear forests and settle new farmlands. He had resthouses built along new roadways to facilitate travel to the new capital, as well as a new fortified river station for security along a network of rivers and canals that connected Thanh-hoa to Tay-do.[24]

The new Ho dynasty, father and son, now ruled together from Tay-do, with Dong-do controlled by a major minister as Prefect there. They re-organized this territory into the Four Pillars of the Capital (*Kinh Ky Tu Phu*), protected by the Three Pillars Army (*Tam Phu Quan*). The Tay-do region became the royal territory, settled by a new resident aristocracy. They constructed the altar for the great Sacrifice to Heaven (Nam-giao) south of Tay-do on the hill there and adopted the general sinic pattern of royal ritual. The king (Quy Ly's son) performed these ceremonies after moving in grand procession from the Great Southern Gate in his royal palanquin with his grand entourage. Temples went up at the tombs of the Ho ancestors, male and female, throughout the south. In Dong-do, they built Eastern and Western Ancestral Temples (*Dong Thai Mieu* for the Ho male line and *Tay Minh De* for the Tran rulers, ancestors of the Ho king's mother).[25]

By this time, tensions had begun to rise with the Ming dynasty in China to the north. A variety of issues, not least of which was the Ho seizure of the Tran throne, increasingly aggravated relations between the two realms. Soon after Chinese envoys who came south went first to the old capital (now Dong-do) before proceeding on to Tay-do, the Ho regime began to prepare for conflict with their northern neighbor. They planned to dismantle the remaining palaces in Dong-do and stash them safely in caves as defenses went up north and west of the old capital. Plotting their campaign with local officials called to Tay-do, the Ho decided on an aggressive resistance to the expected Ming invasion. The Vietnamese attacked and wiped out the Chinese force escorting a Tran pretender back to his throne. Infuriated, the Ming Yongle Emperor sent a massive invasion force south. Dong-do anchored the main defense line, commanded by Quy Ly's eldest son. Tay-do with the two resident rulers served as the command post. But the Ming armies swiftly shattered the defense line, taking Dong-do and receiving support from many Vietnamese there. Quy Ly then torched Tay-do and moved his forces further south before the Ming caught up with him.[26] With the Ming conquest and two-decade occupation, the Ho dynasty and their Tay-do capital city lost their significance.

Tay-Kinh/Lam-Kinh

In their twenty year domination of Vietnam, the Ming turned Dai Viet into their province of Jiao-zhi and crushed all resistance within the reach of their forces.[27] Where remnants of the Tran dynasty revolted and were defeated, as were a variety of others from both the lowlands and highlands, a local group in a multiethnic region deep in the mountains to the southwest, near Lao territory, was able to survive, just barely, and launch a successful strike. Far to the west in Thanh-hoa province, this group, led by their local chief Le Loi, rose in the region of Lam-son (Mt. Lam), one river valley to the south of Tay-do and further upriver. This region, with a mix of Vietnamese, Muong, and Tai, as well as some Cham influences, was far enough up the river valley in the mountain ranges to be relatively protected from the lowland forces. Nevertheless, Ming troops, joined with Lao forces, twice chased the rebels deeper into the mountains where they suffered dire straits. Yet these rebels, through various ruses and tactics, managed to break out of their mountain redoubt, recruit lowland supporters and supplies in the south, and, after a decade long struggle, drive the Chinese out, capturing the Ming garrison at Tay-do in the process.[28]

These victorious armed forces became, in 1428, the new Le dynasty and the new aristocracy of Dai Viet, roughhewn though they were. In the process, a new elite power base emerged with another secondary capital, this time to the west. The Le kept Thang-long as their primary capital and took their home base of Lam-son as the new Western Capital. At first, the Ho names of Tay-do and Dong-do were applied, but two years later, in 1430, the Le changed them to Dong-kinh and Tay-kinh,[29] undoubtedly to distinguish the Le system from that of the Ho. Hence Thang-long became Dong-kinh, the Eastern Capital (and the source of the Europeans' varied versions of Tonkin). Where the Tay-do of the Ho had been the point where lowlands and highlands met, Tay-kinh (also known as Lam-kinh) was deeper in the mountains. Emile Gaspardone, seventy-five years ago, saw the region then as multiethnic (Vietnamese, Muong, Tai) and on the Chu River:

> All the hinterlands have remained good hunting territory, and the countryside of Lam-son, whose territory has changed (through the centuries), at the limit of the padi fields and in the middle region, is yet more Muong in appearance than Vietnamese. The land has rounded hillocks and is embossed with small hills. The ends of the padi fields insinuate themselves poorly there, in the low lying bottomlands, often left as pasture for the waterbuffalo. The monotone hedge of green along the south bank of the Chu River masks it from the road . . . dominated by the silhouette of a limestone block . . .[30]

In among the forests extending around the hills and Mt. Dau, rising 190 feet, would be the tombs of the future kings.[31]

Vietnamese historians, several decades later, described Lam-son as having been accessible both by the river from the east and by a land route running north-south to other villages. To the west, it reached the mountainous edge of Thanh-hoa, its wilds, ridge on ridge, and the headwaters of the east flowing streams. Dangerous peaks and jungles stretched toward the Lao territory. Le Loi had drawn men from the villages of the stream valleys, of a variety of ethnicities. The community that formed in this frontier region under the leadership of the Le clan (Le Loi's father and grandfather before him) lived in a world distant from that of the delta, of the Tran, and of the Ho, geographically, socially, culturally, and religiously.[32] To quote Esta Ungar, "Awesome geomantic powers were believed to emanate from the steep mountains and narrow defiles that were prominent features of the landscape."[33] Lam-son (Mt. Lam) sheltered a dragon spirit.

The sturdy yeomen of this region were rural and little educated, very different from the urbane residents of Thang-long and Thien-truong, and even Tay-do. These westerners were more egalitarian, prizing able leadership over bloodline and status. Forming a familial group (a brotherhood rather than a hierarchical clan), they supported their leader, called the *phu-dao*, a title perhaps derived from the *putao* title of Champa, whose forces had gone through this area in the 1380s. Using guerrilla tactics and well-known terrain, these local forces had survived and then pushed back the strong Ming incursion.[34]

With their victory over the Ming and the rise of the new dynasty in 1428, Lam-son became Tay-do, then Tay-kinh and Lam-kinh. It would continue as the ancestral home of the Le dynasty and its western supporters until their ultimate fall in 1789. During these three and a half centuries, Lam-son would function as the ritual center of the Le family and its lieutenants, the site of the Le royal tombs, which were marked with large stone inscriptions that honored past kings and queens.

During the resistance Le Loi had lost his wife and buried her in Lam-son, among the prior burials of his honored kinsmen. Declaring, "(She) was worthy of being lord of the spirits of our land," he had a shrine built for her spirit and ceremonies performed to present offerings to her.[35] At the end of 1429, he returned to Lam-son as king. On the mountain there, he visited and performed ancestral rituals at the tombs of his male kin. These included his older brother Hoc who, when their father had died young, had raised and taught his younger siblings. Hoc too died before the resistance, and his and his wife's tombs lay to the northwest of Lam-son. The king then bestowed higher ranks on his followers as well as on their descendants, many of whom had come from this region.[36] He visited again in 1433, staying for several months before returning to Dong-kinh. There Le Loi died and at the end of the year his remains were returned to Lam-son for burial. His comrade in arms, the great scholar and minister Nguyen Trai, composed the inscription for his tomb.[37]

Hereafter, when they were old enough and the times were safe, new rulers of the Le dynasty traveled to Tay-kinh, their ancestral home, to renew symbolically their commitment to their ancestral predecessors. Thai-tong, the young successor to Le Loi, does not appear to have returned to Tay-kinh due to his youth and constant turmoil at the royal court in Dong-kinh.[38] Nevertheless, proper rituals were performed on his behalf at the Royal Ancestral Temple (*Thai-mieu*) in Tay-kinh. Court officials had supervised the construction of a new shrine there to honor Le Loi's late wife, now posthumously recognized as the Queen Mother.[39] In 1438, the king responded to strange occurrences at the Royal Ancestral Temple in Tay-kinh by proclaiming in an edict, the first of its kind in Vietnamese history, that Heaven was showing its displeasure and that he, as ruler, bore full moral responsibility for it. Four years later, the young king was dead and buried to the left of his father's tomb.[40]

These first two royal tombs of the Le dynasty, in the far reaches of the southwestern mountains, show the pattern of Ming Chinese influence that was beginning to enter Dai Viet at the time. The direct contact of the Vietnamese with the Ming during the two-decade era of Ming occupation meant that much contemporary knowledge came south into Dai Viet. New elements of Vietnamese society began to advocate for Ming modernist solutions to their own problems. Court ritual and music took on a distinctive Ming character, as did court architecture.[41] Within a decade of the death of the Ming Yongle Emperor, and the construction of the new northern capital at Beijing and its nearby tombs, the Le consecrated the tomb of their founder, Le Loi, which mimicked that of the Yongle Emperor. Built within a powerful geomantic field among the hills and streams of Lam-son, the Le tombs were oriented north/south and had their spirit walks lined with sculpted figures (pairs of tigers, lions, elephants, horses, and officials as one approaches the tombs) and their inscribed stone stelae sitting on large stone turtles, just like those of the Ming.[42]

Thai-tong's successor, an infant, would not leave Dong-kinh or visit Tay-kinh for six years, until 1448. The six-year-old ruler was accompanied by his mother (the Regent), the three young princes (his half brothers), and numbers of courtiers and their attendants. Two veteran generals were left to maintain Dong-kinh. On this royal tour there was interaction between the growing Confucian thought that was becoming dominant at the Dong-kinh court and the celebratory customs of the countryside, notably those of the mountainous west. At one stop-over local boys and girls entertained the royal party by performing their songs and dances. With the boys in one line and the girls in another, they held hands and sang, at times crossing their ankles and then their necks. This was too much, too lascivious for one official. He complained to the top lord, Trinh Kha, who put a stop to it and banned such inappropriate conduct completely. The royal party proceeded to visit the tombs, celebrating the appropriate rites, and to hold a banquet to honor the young ruler's first visit to his ancestral land. At the latter, the king honored his officials, civil and military, those on the tour as well as the local ones.[43]

Eight years later, the now teenage king again visited Tay-kinh and personally directed his officials in their visits and conduct of rituals at his ancestral tombs. He instructed them on how to care for the graves: "Each task at the shrines must be done with much respect and purity (whether it is) cutting wood, chopping bamboo, (or) choosing the (right) fuel for the fires." He also called on the lords to discuss and establish correct names for the shrines at these royal tombs, and they did so. Local soldiers were sent to build new shrines for the queens west of the kings' tombs. The officials sacrificed four buffalo at the tombs and the shrines, striking bronze drums, with the soldiers shouting responses. The martial music was "Destroying the Wu (the Chinese)," and the civil music "The Lords Come to Court." They also sacrificed three buffalo at the shrine of the lineage of the king's elder great uncle and one at that of his younger great uncle (that is, Le Loi's two elder brothers). A banquet followed honoring the officials in the royal entourage as well as the local ones, each receiving an appropriate material reward. The royal progress out of Tay-kinh back to the capital was said to have taken place under a rainbow of green, gold, red, and white arching over the sky, thought to be symbolic of the future good fortune of the king's reign.[44]

Four years later, after a coup that killed the young king and two counter-coups, the king's younger brother took the throne at age eighteen and reigned for 37 years. Once matters had settled down and he and his court literati supporters had control, the new ruler, Le Thanh-tong, visited his ancestral home and its tombs on a regular basis. In this, as in other matters like the examinations, he set the standard to be followed by subsequent Le rulers. After formally burying his predecessor in 1460, the new king traveled upriver to Tay-kinh every three years, beginning in 1461. These visits usually took place near the beginning of the year (in the second lunar month after the ritual of the sacrifice to Heaven Nam-giao and the royal plowing ceremony in Dong-kinh). In Tay-kinh, Thanh-tong visited the royal tombs of his ancestors, reported events to them, and performed the appropriate ancestral rites. He began at the "Original Shrine" in Lam-son, then traveled by the Thuan Mau ("In Accord With Mother") Road along the river bank to the home village of his beloved mother. Next the king performed rituals at the royal tombs of his lineage. At this time, he stressed the significance of the capital Thang-long (Dong-kinh), stating, "The Primary Capital (Thuong Kinh) is (our) foundation, so it is essential for you to know (this)!"[45]

At times, Thanh-tong had other than ritual concerns in Tay-kinh and its surroundings. In 1467, when he had just finished his great reform of the government, he declared his sentiments about private power and powerful families (*the-gia*), and their seizing and usurping of regional resources that belonged in the public sphere. He sent officials to check the public lands of Lam-son and its environs, and to bestow misappropriated property rights on the Meritorious Subjects (*Cong-than*), those who had served his grandfather against the Chinese, and their descendants. As the king declared,

> Lam-kinh is the root and homeland of (Our) kings (and) cannot be compared with other capitals. Now, powerful families (*the-gia*) have gone against (this), considering the common laws (yet) seizing land as their own (so that) the princes and princesses have not enough land to plant a stick! (We) wish to use the law to punish (such) crimes, to apply the ritual and righteousness previously proclaimed, and to allow the royal family to thrive and have a place to support themselves. Now (We) have determined the boundaries, (so) any who dare to transgress (them) will be punished according to the law.[46]

Another activity of this king's on these trips was to compose poetry, proposing lines of his own and drawing them out of his companion literati officials. As they moved through the countryside to and from Tay-kinh, they would respond to each other's verses and, in the process, compile poetic collections proclaiming Confucian virtues while admiring the scenery. In what is called "capping" (*hoa*), the poets matched each other's rhyme schemes and themes, with the king setting the lead lines. In 1468, the court Chronicle stated, "There were many lines that rang like gold!" One such came twenty-three years later on one of the king's last trips to Lam-kinh, when an accompanying Han-lam official capped Thanh-tong's line with his own:

> Lam-son is renowned throughout the South of Heaven.
> For 10,000 ages, it has been awesome in its bright achievements!

Thereby this literati-official tied together Thanh-tong's placement of Dai Viet within the sinic domain as well as the geomantic power of his ancestral homeland.

On his progress to the ancestral shrines in 1470, the king composed a poem declaring how wonderful it was that the water level that year was so much better for the padi fields than in earlier years. In Confucian cosmic terms, good agriculture meant good rule, and the king and his companions celebrated this fact. In all, they admired the beauty of the landscape through which they passed: "Along the shore, all is green mountains and great heights, the peaks rising out of the river mouths, very strange looking!" At one point, the king went ashore and climbed one such peak on foot, jotting a poem on the spot:

> Round Mount Duc-thuy the river twists and twines.
> Who carved this tower of jade—cold, proud, aloof?
> Toward the old shrine I climb against the wind.
> Till sundown I decipher epitaphs.
> I fumble through dark caves—a dwindling world?
> I reach high peaks—how vast, the clouds and waves!
> The hills have stood intact since they were built.
> Look back on heroes—phantoms in some dream.[47]

Throughout Thanh-tong's reign, from 1461 on, these visits to his ancestral home regularly occurred in three year cycles, except late in his reign, when his advanced age must have posed a problem. An additional trip in 1468 lacks a specific explanation and no ceremony was mentioned—perhaps the king simply felt that it was a good time for such a trip. That in 1471 was to report and celebrate Dai Viet's great victory over Champa at the royal shrines. This destroyed his realm's foremost opponent and thus removed a great worry from the land. He skipped the trip in 1479, perhaps because of preparations for the great Lao campaign later that year. A trip in 1485, too, was missed, perhaps because the king, now in his forties, was beginning to be slowed by his age. He went in 1488 and 1491, but then not until 1496, which would be his last. On that trip he called to mind lineages that went back to the resistance against the Ming decades earlier and had loyally served the country since then. He wrote poetry in his own hand and presented it to the local clans and sponsored banquets for their members. The following year, Thanh-tong was dead and buried with his ancestors, to the left of Le Loi, as was his beloved mother.[48]

Thanh-tong's pattern of visits to Tay-kinh every three years was continued by his successors. His son Hien-tong (1498-1504) went in 1501 on the lunar New Year, three years after burying his father, and again in 1504. He died that same year and was returned to Tay-kinh with the "old ceremonies." His successor as well as his mother, Thanh-tong's queen, followed him to their tombs the next year.[49] The following kings continued their visits to their ancestral home (1507, 1511, 1514) until increasing turmoil interrupted the practice. 1526 would mark the last visit to Tay-kinh by a Le king before the dynasty fell to the Mac the following year. By this time the Le kings were being buried elsewhere, up and down the valley of the Chu, occasionally up in the Red River delta.[50]

Duong-Kinh

As turmoil among the great families tore Dai Viet apart over two decades, a new political power with a new base appeared. This was that of the general (or perhaps admiral) Mac Dang Dung, whose literati lineage perhaps went back two hundred years. He came from the east, deep in the Red River delta, a village called Co-trai, north of the Tran base at Thien-truong. Taking the throne from the Le in 1528, he renamed the now well populated eastern delta (including the province of Hai-duong and parts of King-bac and Son-nam) Duong-kinh, with his palaces at Co-trai, and celebrated his purported seven generations of literati ancestors dating back two centuries to Mac Dinh Chi. He built a palace in Dinh Chi's old village and proclaimed him a Literary Emperor (*Van Hoang De*). Dang Dung also upgraded his own father's tomb. He had a large mound ritual site constructed on the river bank north of his palace. More palaces, shrines, and a school for the royal clan were built there as well. A Western source one hundred fifty years later would note how Dang Dung had fortified his home village, though a Chinese source stated that it was surrounded not by a great wall, but merely by a wooden stockade.[51]

After two years on the throne, Mac Dang Dung did as his Tran predecessors had done and relinquished his throne to his adult son. Declaring himself Great Senior Ruler (*Thai Thuong Hoang*), he returned from Thang-long to his Co-trai roots, where he lived and controlled his home base. While the contemporary royal Chronicle declared that Dang Dung was going to do some fishing there, an eighteenth-century retrospective by the scholar Le Quy Don asserted that, like the Tran Senior Rulers before him, Dang Dung continued to determine the key issues of the realm. When he visited the capital, his reigning son would visit him on the eighth and twenty-second days of each lunar month.[52]

Mac Dang Dung continued to reside in Duong-kinh, east of the capital. When his son, the king, died in 1540, Dang Dung returned to the capital to place his grandson on the throne. The following year, Dang Dung fell ill in Co-trai and his grandson, the king, came back from the capital to attend to him. But, as his illness worsened, Dang Dung ordered his grandson to return to the capital to control the situation there and to calm the people's hearts. Dang Dung's last words were said to have been, "Do not construct an altar, fast, (or) make offerings to the Buddha!" He was buried on a nearby hill (Dragon Mountain Long-son).[53]

Thereafter, for the next fifty years, a series of single Mac kings (with no Senior Rulers) ruled their territory from the Thang-long capital. The region of Duong-kinh and the village of Co-trai remained the Mac home base, but we do not have chronicle evidence of the royal comings and goings, as we do for the Le. At one point, in 1581, there was mention of a Mac prince "often" going to Duong-kinh when he should have been in the capital. A few surviving stone inscriptions make mention of the area. In 1583, a scholar from Duong-kinh composed an inscribed text at a local Buddhist temple. Six years later, another Duong-kinh-based scholar prepared another inscription at a nearby Buddhist temple, which spoke of "the victorious land of Duong-kinh." A poem on the stone also described this famous temple of Duong-kinh. Another inscription of the same year at a hall in the region told of Kinh-dong City (East of the Capital) as also being "a victorious land, the one and only."[54] Presumably, like Lam-kinh, Duong-kinh continued as the familial and ritual center of the ruling Mac clan. Certainly, when the victorious Le/Trinh forces reached this eastern region in the early 1590s, they took great pains to destroy what they saw as the rebels' nest. After taking the capital, the eighteenth-century scholar Le Quy Don tells us that:

> They killed the entire bandit gang (and) brought troops to destroy completely the palace at Co-trai, to shatter the stone inscriptions at (their) graves, (and) to chop down all the trees planted at (their) tombs. This was to declare the true punishment (of the Mac)![55]

Lam-Kinh (Again)

Where Duong-kinh lay within reach of the enemies of the Mac, Lam-kinh had remained outside the Mac realm. Just as Lam-son and its Lao hinterland had preserved the Le forces from the Ming conquerors in the early fifteenth century, so had that location and its isolation and distance kept the rebel forces striving to restore the Le to Thang-long safe from Mac Dang Dung and his descendants. Fleeing to this remote Lao land, lords of Lam-son established a Le pretender and began to work their way back to the capital. As the Chronicle declared, "From this time, it was mainly the bravos of the west (who) would bring (the monarchy) back!" By 1539, working out of the south (Thanh-hoa and Nghe-an provinces), the Le forces had enough strength to return to Tay-kinh, where they would bury their next two kings. For the next fifty years this was their base for attacks on the Mac.[56] From the 1540s through the 1580s, the Le, based in Tay-kinh, fought the Mac, based in Dong-kinh, in a war between the southwestern upstream and the northeastern downstream delta. Tay-do, the old Ho fortress, was a major point of contention between them. Finally, in the 1580s, the restoration forces began to gain the upper hand, and in 1592 they were able to chase the Mac upstream into the northern mountain redoubt of Cao-bang and to destroy their base in Duong-kinh.[57] The Le and their lords returned to Dong-kinh, and Tay-kinh was, now again, the secondary royal center.

Once matters had settled down throughout the realm, the restoration forces gave priority to repairing the buildings in Thang-long and brought the Le ruler back from Tay-kinh in 1593. Two years later, they repaired the structures in Tay-kinh. Through the 1590s, unstable events appear to have kept the Le king from returning to his ancestral land, and it is unclear how often royal visits were made thereafter. The Chronicles continue to place emphasis on Thang-long with more reconstruction and the official move of the ancestral tablets of Le Loi and his royal successors into the Royal Ancestral Temple (*Thai-mieu*) there for ceremonies throughout the year.[58]

Yet the Le monarchy was being downgraded as the Trinh clan developed its power throughout Dai Viet. They had chased the Mac up into Cao-bang and their rivals, the Nguyen lords, down to the southern border. It is no surprise, then, that the Trinh home of Thuy-nguyen, though also in Thanh-hoa not far from Lam-son, began to gain attention. Lam-kinh was too narrow a space, while Thuy-nguyen had many mountains and a broad river and was much more pleasant. This became the favorite site of royal progresses. In any time of danger, the king would retreat here, not to Tay-kinh. Thuy-nguyen was where the Trinh lord preferred to be, his ancestral home with palaces and shrines. And so this area came to be called Nghi-kinh. As the early nineteenth-century scholar Phan Huy Chu declared, "For over two hundred years," it (and two other locations) were "most important."[59]

At the same time, the other aristocratic clan, the Nguyen, established its own theoretically secondary capital, Phu Xuan, at the site of the present Hue in modern-day central Vietnam. In a situation rather similar to that of the Tran some four centuries earlier, the Nguyen drew their strength from the coast (here southern) and its port of Hoi-an across the Hai-van Pass, while proclaiming their status as administrators of the twelfth and thirteenth provinces of the Le ruler in Thang-long to the north. Yet this competing secondary capital aspired to greater things by seeking a higher form of legitimacy, by their patronage of the visiting Buddhist monk Da Shan.[60] In time, at the beginning of the nineteenth century, this site would become Hue, the primary capital of a much larger Vietnam.

The Secondary Capitals of Dai Viet

This examination of these regional power bases that served as secondary capitals through the history of Dai Viet demonstrates a variety of differences among them as urban centers. They had formed, not because of economic or administrative circumstances, but due to power relationships. They were temporary royal and aristocratic gathering points and when their time had passed (i.e., their political power had ebbed) they continued only as ritual centers for the past dynasties. Meanwhile Thang-long remained the primary capital and major city of the realm through almost all these centuries.

The differences among these four sites are striking. Thien-truong was a royal lowland estate among other such estates of the royal clan. Tay-do was a fortress meant to protect and awe. Tay-kinh was a family (and regional) ancestral shrine, with its royal tombs, in the upstream highlands. Duong-kinh, in the eastern deltaic lowlands, was not the center of a clan estate, but was the center from which another family network dominated the adjacent prosperous agricultural and commercial region, and was the site of their family's ancestral tombs. Thien-truong, Tay-do, and (at least at the beginning) Duong-kinh were all homes of the Senior Ruler, whose residence was secondary to the Thang-long capital. Tay-do was alone in ever having both rulers dwelling there, while the Tran and Mac reigning kings lived exclusively in Thang-long. Tay-kinh was a place to visit, every three years at the most, though for half a century it served as the base of resistance while the Le forces sought to restore their king and oust the Mac.

Each of these sites presented the ruling king(s) the opportunity for royal progresses through the countryside to and from Thang-long on what was probably a fairly consistent basis. Thus, royal glory and power tied the primary and secondary regions of the realm together and strengthened the royal presence throughout this most important dynastic territory. At the same time, the presence of the king and his entourage in and around the secondary capital heightened the patronage of religion and its temples there. In the coastal areas of Thien-truong and Duong-kinh, the Tran and the Mac respectively were deeply involved with and supported Buddhist temples, the former on their estates, the latter in their immediate vicinity. For the Ho and the Le, not Buddhism, but what would loosely be called Confucianism, that is, Chinese state ideology, was what they patronized in and around Tay-do and Tay-kinh. Ho Quy Ly established a combination of classical Chinese thought emphasizing the Duke of Zhou and contemporary Ming ritual, as in the Nam Giao sacrifice to Heaven. The Le, as seen in their tombs and rituals, brought modern Ming thought and procedures to their mountain home and from there to the Thang-long capital.

And what did this royal and aristocratic presence mean for the locality itself? Following Stewart Gordon's discussion of Burhanpur in central India in this volume, we can speak of the possible implications of this presence in these otherwise unexceptional locations. First, wealth flowed into them from the main capital region, as resources of the realm were diverted toward these favored home areas. Palaces for the royal clan, large homes for the accompanying aristocracy and the supporting officials, and, where necessary, notably at Tay-do, fortifications—all these were built there. Administration, troops, and their supplies drew more money in. The development of service industries and craft luxuries responded to the growing local aristocratic market for such skills. Artisans and merchants were needed, and local agriculture also responded, not to mention the subsequent demands for leisure activities and entertainment, as well as new temple establishments. Each of these secondary capitals would have grown significantly, in varying degrees, while its dynasty held power.

Once power had shifted to another dynasty, these former royal bases were generally respected and left alone, to retain only familial and regional significance. The Ho, the early Le, and the Mac appear to have honored their predecessor's accomplishments as signs of royal glory past. Only the restoration Le acted against their predecessors the Mac—the latter had defeated the former and now suffered for it (as the Tay-son dynasty of the 1790s would against the rival Nguyen in 1802).

These fairly temporary secondary capitals contrast with the other towns of the world discussed in this volume. The Vietnamese secondary royal cities were generally not part of the regular economic and political structure of the land of Dai Viet. While Thien-truong and Duong-kinh were both located in the increasingly rich agricultural and commercial environment of the lower Red River delta, Tay-do and Lam-kinh sat on the edge of or in the mountainous fringe, away from the usual economic and administrative situation of the land. The first two existed in the midst of the watery communication systems of the delta, the latter two among the more restricted networks in the upstream uplands. None of them was a major port or an economic center, nor were they natural and dominating points within the Dai Viet administrative structure. Rather they were incidental centers of family and regional power that rose and fell with that power, royal and aristocratic bases dependent on human power relations. Elsewhere in this volume perhaps only Burhanpur in central India comes close as such a passing phenomenon, yet it too had a more consequential regional existence, due to its rise to prominence as a focal economic and administrative center during the era of Mughal rule. In contrast, these four secondary capitals of Dai Viet were above all and almost exclusively structurally and functionally important because of their role as ancestral ritual centers.

Notes

1. Tran Quoc Vuong, "*Nhung Vet Tich cua Hoang Thanh Thang Long Tran Mat va Duoi Long Dat* [Vestiges of the Imperial City of Thang-long on the Surface and Underground]," in *Hoang Thanh Thang Long*, Phat Hien Khao Co Hoc [The Imperial City of Thang-long, Archaeological Developments] (Hanoi: Dac San Xua va Nay, 2004), 41-49; Iain Finley and Trish Clark, *Good Morning, Hanoi* (Pymble, NSW: Simon and Schuster, 2006), 213-15, 253-57.

2. Keith W. Taylor, *The Birth of Vietnam* (Berkeley: University of California Press, 1983), 199, 223, 226, 233-34, 237, 241, 243, 247, 250; Tran Quoc Vuong, "Hanoi de la prehistoire au 19e siecle," *Etudes Vietnamiennes*, 48 (1977), 17-19.

3. Taylor, *Birth of Vietnam*, 251-254, 257, 270, 279-80, 296; "The Rise of Dai Viet and the Establishment of Thang-long," in *Explorations in Early Southeast Asian History*, ed. Kenneth R. Hall and John K. Whitmore (Ann Arbor, MI: Center for South and Southeast Asian Studies, University of Michigan, 1976), 149-91; John K. Whitmore, "Rise of the Coast: Trade, State, and Culture in Early Dai Viet," *Journal of Southeast Asian Studies (JSEAS)*, 37, 1 (2006), 104-08. For Dinh-bang, see Katrin Jellema, " 'When You Drink From the Stream, Remember the Source': Moral Landscapes of Memory in a Northern Vietnamese Village," Ph.D. dissertation (Ann Arbor: University of Michigan, 2007); *Dai Nam Nhat Thong Chi* [Unified Record of the Great South], trans. (Hue: NXB Thuan Hoa, 1997), IV, 104, 106.

4. Do Van Ninh, *Thanh Co Viet Nam* [Old Cities of Vietnam] (Hanoi: NXB Khoa Hoc Xa Hoi, 1983), 64-78, 93-104.

5. Phan Huy Chu, *Lich Trieu Hien Chuong Loai Chi* [Institutes of the Successive Dynasties], trans. (Hanoi: NXB Khoa Hoc Xa Hoi, 1992), I, 36-40; Diep Dinh Hoa and Nguyen Van Son, "*Lang Thu Do: Duong Kinh Nhan Xet Dan Toc-Khao Co Hoc* [Capital Village: Duong-kinh as Seen through Anthropology and Archaeology]," in *Nhung Phat Hien Moi ve Khao Co Hoc Nam 1996* [New Developments in Archaeology 1996] (Hanoi: NXB Khoa Hoc Xa Hoi, 1997), 492.

6. Whitmore, "Rise of the Coast," 108-14; Li Tana, "A View From the Sea: Perspectives on the Northern and Central Vietnamese Coast," *JSEAS*, 37, 1 (2006), 83-102; John Chaffee in this volume.

7. Phan Huy Chu, *Lich Trieu Hien Chuong Loai Chi*, I, 96; Pierre Gourou, *Les Paysans du Delta Tonkinois* (Paris: Mouton, 1985), 559, maps 1, 4; Sakurai Yumio, "Land, Water, Rice, and Man in Early Vietnam: Agrarian Adaptation and Socio-Political Organization," ms., ch. 3, pt. IV, sec. 6, "My Loc," 176-80.

8. See Victor Lieberman, *Strange Parallels. Southeast Asia in Global Context, c. 800-1830* (Cambridge: Cambridge University Press, 2003).

9. Whitmore, "Rise of the Coast," 114-119; John K. Whitmore, *Vietnam, Ho Quy Ly, and the Ming, 1371-1421* (New Haven: Council on Southeast Asia Studies, Yale University, 1985), 1-8; Phan Huy Chu, *Lich Trieu Hien Chuong Loai Chi*, I, 57, 89, 105; *Dai Nam Nhat Thong Chi* (1997), III, 324, 343, 353, 357. The name Thien-truong appears to have been a reference to the great Tang dynasty capital of Chang-an (V. Truong-yen).

10. Whitmore, "Rise of the Coast," 118; Nguyen Thi Phuong Chi, *Thai Ap Dien Trang Thoi Tran* [Fiefs and Estates of the Tran Period] (Hanoi: NXB Khoa Hoc Xa Hoi, 2002). See, in comparison, Kenneth Swope's study of networked Ming military garrison centers in this volume.

11. Le Tac, *An Nam Chi Luoc* (1333); translated in Li, "A View From the Sea," 99.

12. *Dai Viet Su Ky Toan Thu* (*TT*) (Hanoi: NXB Khoa Hoc Xa Hoi, 1998), 5, 30a.

13. *TT*, 5, 24a, 27b (quotation).

14. *Anthologie de Litterature Vietnamienne* (Hanoi: Editions en Langue Etrangere, 1972), I, 82.

15. The reasons contributing to their migration are discussed in Chaffee's study in this volume.

16. Whitmore, *Vietnam, Ho Quy Ly, and the Ming*, chs. 2-3.

17. John K. Whitmore, "The Last Great King of Classical Southeast Asia: Che Bong Nga and Fourteenth Century Champa," paper presented at the "Symposium on New Scholarship on Champa," Singapore, August, 2004.

18. Whitmore, *Vietnam, Ho Quy Ly, and the Ming*, 44-45 (quotation); Phan Huy Chu, *Lich Trieu Hien Chuong Loai Chi*, I, 43.

19. Whitmore, *loc. cit.*, 45; Do Van Ninh, *Thanh Co Viet Nam*, 79-90; *Dai Nam Nhat Thong Chi* (1997), II, 269-70.

20. See the cover of Whitmore, *loc. cit.*

21. Whitmore, *loc. cit.*, 45-46.

22. Whitmore, *Vietnam, Ho Quy Ly, and the Ming*, 46-48; Le Quy Don, *Kinh Thu Dien Nghia* [Commentary on the Book of History], trans. (Ho Chi Minh City: NXB Thanh Pho Ho Chi Minh, 1993), 270-74 (n. 6). This region (Ai-chau) had also been called Tay-do in the late tenth century; *TT*, 1, 7b.

23. Whitmore, *loc. cit.*, 47-54; Phan Huy Chu, *Lich Trieu Hien Chuong Loai Chi*, I, 29.

24. Whitmore, *loc. cit.*, 52-57, 73.

25. Whitmore, *Vietnam, Ho Quy Ly, and the Ming*, 58-64; Phan Huy Chu, *Lich Trieu Hien Chuong Loai Chi*, I, 42.

26. Whitmore, *loc. cit.*, ch. 5.

27. Whitmore, *loc. cit.*, ch. 6.

28. Phan Huy Le and Phan Dai Doan, *Khoi Nghia Lam Son, 1418-1427* [The Lam-son Resistance], 4th ed. (Hanoi: NXB Quan Doi Nhan Dan, 2005).

29. *TT*, 10, 72b; Le Quy Don, *Dai Viet Thong Su* [Complete History of Dai Viet], trans. (Hanoi: NXB Khoa Hoc Xa Hoi, 1978), 85; *Dai Nam Nhat Thong Chi* (1997), II, 254-55, 270-71.

30. Emile Gaspardone, "Avant Propos," *Les Steles Royales de Lam Son* (Hanoi: Ecole Francaise d'Extreme Orient, 1935).

31. Phan Huy Chu, *Lich Trieu Hien Chuong Loai Chi*, I, 91-93.

32. Phan Huy Le and Phan Dai Doan, *Khoi Nghia Lam Son*, 114-18.

33. Esta Serne Ungar, "Vietnamese Leadership and Order: Dai Viet Under the Le Dynasty, 1428-1459," Ph.D. dissertation (Ithaca, NY: Cornell University, 1983), 52.

34. Ibid., ch. 2. The *putao* suggestion is from Tran Ky Phuong, personal communication, central Vietnam, August 2004.

35. Le Quy Don, *Dai Viet Thong Su*, 119.

36. Le Quy Don, *loc. cit.*, 85; *TT*, 10, 71b-72b.

37. *TT*, 10, 74b, 76a-b; Le Quy Don, *loc. cit.*, 95-96; Gaspardone, *Les Steles Royales de Lam Son*, plates 1-2, 4.

38. John. K. Whitmore, "The Development of Le Government in Fifteenth Century Vietnam," Ph.D. dissertation (Ithaca, NY: Cornell University, 1968), ch. 2; Ungar, "Dai Viet Under the Le Dynasty," chs. 5-6.

39. Le Quy Don, *Dai Viet Thong Su*, 120.

40. *TT*, 11, 50b-51a.

41. John K. Whitmore, "The Fate of Ming Ritual Music in Dai Viet: Changing Regimes, Changing Musics?" paper presented at a conference on "Musiking Ming China," University of Michigan, Ann Arbor, May, 2006.

42. Louis Bezacier, "Les Sepultures Royales de la Dynastie des Le Posterieurs (Hau-Le)," *Bulletin de l'Ecole Francaise d'Extreme Orient*, 44, 1 (1951), 21-33, 2 tables, 22 plates; *Dai Nam Nhat Thong Chi* (1997), II, 282-84; Anne Paludan, *The Imperial Ming Tombs* (New Haven: Yale University Press, 1981).

43. Later in that year, during a drought, the throne sent Trinh Kha back to oversee the workers repairing and constructing new shrines and palace buildings there. *TT*, 11, 64a-b, 72a; Le Quy Don, *Dai Viet Thong Su*, 123, 212, 222; Whitmore, "Fifteenth Century Vietnam," 46.

44. *TT*, 11, 91a-b; Whitmore, *loc. cit.*, 72-73.

45. *TT*, 12, 6b, 7a, 26a, 27b, 48a; 13, 1a-b, 8a-b (quotation), 32b, 57a, 65b; Whitmore, *loc. cit.*, chs. 3-5; "Queen Mother: The Origin of Family Politics in Early Modern Vietnam," in *Le Viet Nam au Feminin*, ed. G. Bousquet and N.Taylor (Paris: Les Indes Savantes, 2005), 43-49.

46. *TT*, 12, 27b-28a.

47. By his own hand, he also wrote poetry for prayerful appeals when rain did not come. *TT*, 12, 48a (1st quotation), 53a-b; 13, 8a-b (2nd quotation), 71b; John K. Whitmore, "The Tao-Dan Group: Poetry, Cosmology, and the State in the Hong-Duc Period (1470-1497)," *Crossroads*, 7, 2 (1992), 56-62; *Dai Nam Nhat Thong Chi* (1997), II, 255 (1st poem); Huynh Sanh Thong, trans., *The Heritage of Vietnamese Poetry* (New Haven: Yale University Press, 1979), 124 (#301) (2nd poem).

48. *TT*, 12, 48a, 65a; 13, 71b-72b, 77a-b; 14, 2b-3a, 9a; Gaspardone, *Les Steles Royales de Lam Son*, plates 2-3, 6-9.

49. *TT*, 14, 23b, 34b, 36b-37a, 40a-b; Gaspardone, *Les Steles Royales de Lam Son*, plates 2-3, 10-12.

50. *TT*, 14, 44a; 15, 8a, 23b, 65a, 65b, 68a-b; Whitmore, "The Tao-Dan Group," 117-22; Phan Huy Chu, *Lich Trieu Hien Chuong Loai Chi*, I, 44; Bezacier, "Les Sepultures Royales," 21, 33-41, table 1, pl. 9.

51. *TT*, 15, 66a-67b, 69b; Le Quy Don, *Dai Viet Thong Su*, 253-54, 264-66; Phan Huy Chu, *Lich Trieu Hien Chuong Loai Chi* , I, 120, 136; *Dai Nam Nhat Thong Chi* (1997), III, 375, 385, 411, 439; Diep Dinh Hoa & Nguyen Van Son (1997), 493-494; Dinh Khac Thuan, *Lich Su Trieu Mac* [History of the Mac Dynasty] (Hanoi: NXB Khoc Hoc Xa Hoi, 2001), 170-75; J. K. Whitmore, "Chung-Hsing and Cheng-T'ung in Texts of and on Sixteenth-Century Vietnam," in *Essays on Vietnamese Pasts*, ed. Keith W. Taylor and John K. Whitmore (Ithaca, NY: Southeast Asia Program, Cornell University, 1995), 122-30; Samuel Baron, "A Description of the Kingdom of Tonqueen," in *Views of Seventeenth Century Vietnam*, ed. O. Dror and K.W. Taylor (Ithaca, NY: Southeast Asia Program, Cornell University, 2006), 239-240.

52. *TT*, 15, 74a; Le Quy Don, *Dai Viet Thong Su*, 269 (quotation).

53. Le Quy Don, *Dai Viet Thong Su*, 271-73 (quotation, 272), 280.

54. Le Quy Don, *Dai Viet Thong Su*, 328; *Van Bia Thoi Mac* [Stelae of the Mac Era], trans. (Hanoi: NXB Khoa Hoc Xa Hoi, 1996), 235-36, 287-89, 283-87.

55. Le Quy Don, *Dai Viet Thong Su.*, 273.

56. *TT*, 15, 77b (quotation), 78a; 16, 1a-b, 2b-3a; Le Quy Don, *Dai Viet Thong Su*, 270; Bezacier, "Les Sepultures Royales," table 1.

57. *TT*, 15, 3b, 5b, 6b, 7b-8a; Le Quy Don, *Dai Viet Thong Su*, 275-363.

58. *TT*, 17, 41a, 52b, 57a-b.

59. Phan Huy Chu, *Lich Trieu Hien Chuong Loai Chi*, I, 45; on the Trinh and the Nguyen, see Nola Cooke, "Regionalism and the Nature of Nguyen Rule in Seventeenth Century Dang Trong (Cochinchina)," *JSEAS*, 29, 1 (1998), 122-61.

60. John K. Whitmore, "The Thirteenth Province," in *Asian Expansions*, ed. Geoff Wade (forthcoming); Charles Wheeler in this volume.

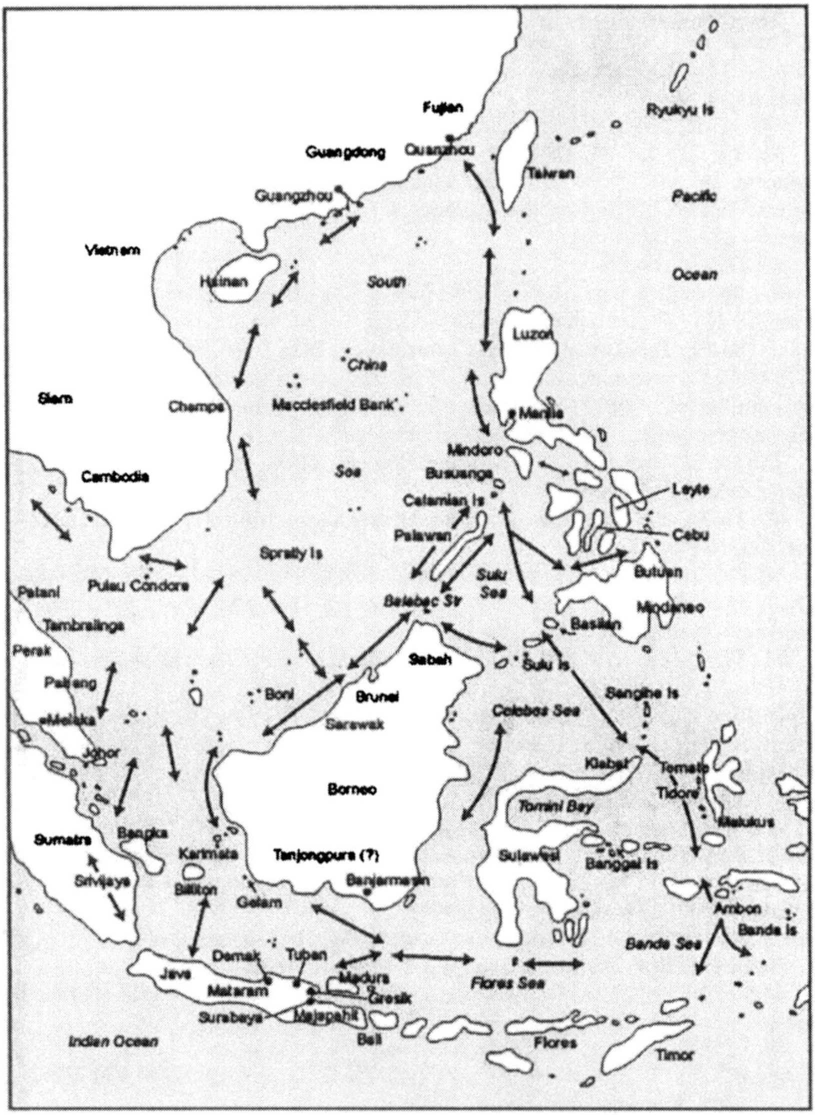

Map 7.1. **Maritime Trade Networking in Eastern Southeast Asia c. 1000-1600**

7

Coastal Cities in an Age of Transition: Upstream-Downstream Networking and Societal Development in Fifteenth- and Sixteenth-Century Maritime Southeast Asia

Kenneth R. Hall

Heterarchy and Cosmopolis in Early Southeast Asia

Southeast Asian urbanism in the pre-1500 era offers marked contrast to the longstanding hierarchical traditions of its Indian and Chinese neighbors. It has been argued that maritime Southeast Asia lacked an urban tradition in the pre-1500 age, because its cities had limited and often fluctuating populations.[1] Unlike its counterparts in other regions of the world, the archeological evidence of early maritime Southeast Asia's larger settlements does not include elaborate fortifications, despite the long history of piracy throughout the region. This lack of permanent structures is consistent with other archeological remains that suggest that the early centers were mobile, regularly shifting rather than demonstrating societal commitment to a single place. Only the elite and their immediate servants populated the region's differentiated centers of political (royal courts) and religious authority (temples), which were insulated in the agrarian hinterlands. The major marketplaces were at river mouths on the coast at the societal periphery rather than in the upstream heartland. These emporia served as points of contact with the outside world, networked with other regional ports of relatively equal stature.[2]

Sensitive to these characteristics, historians have introduced several alternative approaches in their attempts to conceptualize early Southeast Asia urban development. Victor Lieberman's *Strange Parallels* explores the patterns of urban hierarchy that he believes developed in mainland Southeast Asia (Myanmar, Thailand, Cambodia, and Vietnam) from roughly 1100 to 1800.[3] He addresses the rise of conceptual cities that were the focal centers in the development of emerging nation-states, in the tradition of G. William Skinner's and Paul Wheatley's seminal studies of early East Asia.[4] Believing that early maritime Southeast Asian cities were different than those of continental Southeast Asia, scholars who research the history of the Southeast Asian archipelago have explored different approaches. Instead of addressing the development of institutionalized hierarchies that are comparable to the characteristics of pre-modern cities in other regions of the world, several have found it fruitful to consider the networked *heterarchy* and *cosmopolis* as meaningful alternatives.

O. W. Wolters initially explored the conceptual early Southeast Asian *heterarchy*, which he defined as including horizontally linked regionally semi-autonomous urban-like centers that shared in common goals, acknowledged the political independence of its "members," included multiple networked concentrations of power that had different levels of connectivity, and were based in some degree of acknowledged cultural homogeneity (Indic, Islamic, Chinese).[5] Heterarchies might have multiple organizational patterns (monarchies, chieftainships, sultanates), types of knowledge (written, oral), and means of acknowledgement (ritualized gifting; assignments of title and privilege). A heterarchy distributed privilege and decision making, in contrast to a hierarchy in which power and privilege was concentrated in its higher members. Wolters argued that the heterarchy network was ideal in an age of rapid change, as its horizontal linkages allowed a good deal of flexibility and encouraged cooperation among its members rather than submission. The heterarchy was a means to encourage linkage of extended communities across some substantial space or isolating geography, especially maritime space. In his mind early maritime Southeast Asia was defined by the movements of goods and religious (e.g., Hindu-Buddhist and Islamic) and cultural (e.g., Indic, Chinese, Malay, or Javanese) ideas. The conceptual early maritime Southeast Asian heterarchy was a religious, ideological, and commercial world that spanned space and overcame isolation, by linking communities with common interests—especially their mutual participation in the international maritime trade.

In contrast, Anthony Reid and Eric Tagliacozzo have more recently addressed the conceptual *cosmopolis*, which in their minds is also a multi-centered linked community based in the pluralism among its members.[6] Their model Southeast Asian cosmopolis is a network of coastal entrepots that share in their international orientation, their dual functionality as port and political center, their flexible capacity to rapidly adapt to new circumstances, their centrifugal and centripetal roles in relation to uplands, jungles, and outlying regions away from the metropolis, and as the collection points for the forest and agricultural products of their dependent regions. In contrast to Wolters' view that heterarchies prevailed in the pre-1500 era and that hierarchical patterns of urbanism developed later, coincident to the heightened commercialism that began to prevail after 1500, Reid and Tagliacozzo make the case that there is a continuity of the earlier patterns of urbanism in maritime Southeast Asia into the present, as in the notable case of Singapore. The principle difference between their notion of a cosmopolis and Wolters' depiction of pre-modern heterarchies is their stress on the hierarchical elements of cosmopolis urban networking. In their view the cosmopolis was linked horizontally, but networked secondary centers were less semi-autonomous than in Wolter's heterarchy model. In their conception the cosmopolis primary or paramount center's economic prominence gave it considerable degree of hegemony over other members of its commercial network, which in turn dictated a degree of political and cultural leadership over its secondary centers. Since the cosmopolis fell short of fully institutionalizing its networked relationships, there was always opportunity for a secondary center to challenge the primacy of the prevailing center if it fell short in its economic capacity—due to internal decay, conquest by a rival, or the ever-changing nature of the Indian Ocean trade network.

Map 7.2. **Maritime Trade in the Eastern Indian Ocean c. 1200-1600**

Urbanism in maritime Southeast Asia in the fifteenth and sixteenth centuries, an age that Anthony Reid characterizes as maritime Southeast Asia's "Age of Commerce," when international trade was the motor for widespread societal change, is the topic of this study.[7] It will examine several exemplary cases of 1400-1600 regional secondary centers, in representing these early port-polities based on the limited archeological and textual sources, to allow a concluding evaluation of the appropriateness of the networked *heterarchy* and *cosmopolis* interpretive options.

This study begins with Melaka, which became the region's preeminent emporia in the fifteenth century, and remained a major factor in regional trade after it fell to the Portuguese in 1511. The best documented of the early Southeast Asian ports-of-trade, Melaka provides a point of reference in making comparisons with its contemporary regional secondary centers and in providing greater clarity to the incomplete records of the lesser ports-of-trade. The northwest Borneo coastline networked port-polities the Chinese knew as *Boni*, by the fifteenth century based in the modern Brunei river estuary, were initially secondary centers to Melaka, the Vietnam coast port-polity network (*Maps 7.1* and *7.2*), and to south China's ports-of-trade (*Map 4.1*). Following the Portuguese seizure of Melaka in 1511, Brunei would claim to be Melaka's successor as the paramount intermediary in South China Sea regional trade—in part due to Ming China's severe restrictions on China-based traders' activities in the region from the 1430s until the late sixteenth century. Sixteenth-century Brunei was minimally the primary center to networked north Borneo coast and Sulu Sea/Philippines secondary emporia. This study highlights the existing documentation of Brunei and Cebu, one of Brunei's networked Sulu Sea secondary centers, as the remaining archeological remains coincide with these centers' portrayals in Antonio Pigafetta's account of Magellan's 1521 voyage.

The final example of the Banjarmasin port-polity on Borneo's southeast coast provides useful contrast to the examples of Brunei and Cebu, in that the most important record of fifteenth- and sixteenth-century Banjarmasin is not an external source, but instead the sixteenth- and seventeenth-century Banjarmasin court chronicle, which provides a local retrospective portrait of Banjarmasin's rise to prominence. The southeast Borneo port-polity in the vicinity of modern Banjarmasin was a fifteenth-century minor secondary emporium networked with Java's primary ports-of-trade. But in the post-1511 era, it became a key intermediary in the eastern Indonesian archipelago spice trade network, and an alternative source of pepper for the eastern Asia marketplace after the Portuguese restricted the Indian Ocean trading community's access to Sumatra's pepper.

The Melaka Straits Passageway c. 600 to the 1430s

From 1300-1500, prior to any significant European presence in the Indian Ocean, maritime Southeast Asia was the transitional commercial center where the goods of India and the Middle East such as cotton cloth, pepper, and glassware were exchanged for the silk and porcelain of China. Here, too, international traders acquired maritime Southeast Asia's spices and exotic jungle products: sandalwood, rhinoceros horns, colorful birds, and medicinals (notably Borneo's camphor). By the fifteenth century this commerce centered on the port-polity of Melaka on the southwest Malay Peninsula, which lay adjacent to the strategic Straits of Melaka maritime passageway. Maritime sojourners made stopovers in Straits of Melaka ports. One group arrived on the northeast winter monsoon winds from China and other eastern locales, and waited there for the reversal of the winds for their return on the southwest summer monsoon winds. In their absence other maritime sojourners arrived on the southwest summer monsoon winds from India, the Middle East, and the ports-of-trade in the Bay of Bengal region, and remained in Melaka until the northeast winter monsoons allowed their return voyages.

From roughly 600 to 1300, a polity that the Chinese knew as *Srivijaya* dominated the Straits passageway. Srivijaya used its navy to limit regional piracy as also to coerce shipping passing through the Straits to use its ports and to pay its port fees. From 1300 to 1400, the east Java-based Majapahit Hindu-Buddhist polity superceded Srivijaya, by sending its navy to force the submission of competing Straits of Melaka port-polities to its indirect sovereignty. Samudra-Pasai, which had become the first major Straits sultanate around 1300, acknowledged its place in Majapahit's archipelago network, but remained the most prominent among the east coast Sumatra port-polities through the fourteenth century, because it had become a source of Sumatra pepper as also an important stopover for sojourning merchants.[8] With the initial backing of Ming China naval fleets, Melaka became the paramount emporium among other networked Straits port-polities in the early fifteenth century.[9] After their Chinese supporters withdrew from the region in the 1430s, Melaka's rulers stepped back from aggressive militancy, lowered their port's duties, and facilitated a functional and open marketplace.

Melaka's fifteenth-century monarchs based their legitimacy in their succession to the royal lineage of Srivijaya, but by the late 1430s had shifted their religious patronage from a prior eclectic Hindu-Buddhist tradition to Islam, in part because the majority of the merchants who were using their uniquely open crossroads were Muslims. It must have seemed logical to Melaka's rulers that their conversion to Islam would gain them economic advantage among Muslim merchants—and distinguish them from Majapahit Java, where Muslim merchants of largely Chinese ethnicity were in control of Java's north coast ports. Melaka's elite took Muslim names, accepted circumcision, worshipped in mosques, and promoted conversion to Islam among the elite of their networked Malay Peninsula port-polities that supplied Melaka with the assortment of local produce necessary to provision Melaka's residential commercial communities.

Herein Islam also became the basis for political alliance that linked the loosely allied Melaka "hinterland," which was a network of ports and their upstreams that were not immediately adjacent to the Melaka port.[10] Though Islam had been promoted earlier by Samudra-Pasai, the new religion became so closely identified with Malay society in Melaka that to become Muslim, it was said, was to *masuk Melayu*, "to enter [the fold of the] *Melayu* [Melaka]."[11]

The Melaka Primary Center

Hybridized Malay-speaking elite ruled over the fifteenth-century Melaka cosmopolitan emporia. Most of Melaka's residents derived their incomes from its trade or from their provision of services to those involved in the international shipping that passed through the Melaka port.[12] The Portuguese scribe Tomé Pires, writing around 1512, just after Melaka's conquest by the Portuguese, offers this description of Melaka's cosmopolitanism:

> Moors from Cairo, Mecca, Aden, Abyssinians, men of Kilwa, Malindi, Ormuz, Parsees, Rumes, Turks, Turkomans, Christian Armenians, Gujaratees, men of Chaul, Dabhol, Goa, of the kingdom of Deccan, Malabars and Klings, merchants from Orissa, Ceylon, Bengal, Arakan, Pegu, Siamese, men of Kedah, Malays, men of Pahang, Patani, Cambodia, Champa, Cochin China, Chinese, Lequeos, men of Brunei, Lucoes, men of Tamjompura, Laue, Banka, Linga, Moluccas, Banda, Bima, Timor, Madura, Java, Sunda, Palembang, Jambi, Tongkal, Indragiri, Kappatta, Menangkabau, Siak, Arqua (Arcat?), Aru, Bata, country of the Tomjano, Pase, Pedir, Maldives . . . The above-mentioned peoples come to Malacca with junks, pangajavas and ships . . . Finally, in the port of Malacca very often eighty-four languages have been found spoken, every one distinct, as the inhabitants of Malacca affirm.[13]

The majority of Melaka's population consisted of permanent and semi-permanent residential communities of foreigners, among whom the Gujarati and Tamil (Keling) from India, Javanese from the archipelago, and the Chinese were the most prominent. The foreign communities were assigned their own "suburban" neighborhood. Each of the major foreign communities also had its own "chief-of-port" (*shahbandar/syahbandar*) who received merchants on their arrival, presented them to the civilian head-of-state (*bendhahara*), found them lodging, storage, and shops to sell their goods, and, according to the Portuguese sources, up to the late fifteenth century acted as their trade broker in return for one percent of the value of their sales. The *shahbandar* also provided visiting merchants with small boats and elephants for local transport, and in time of war he might also gather, arm, and command his community, along with its slaves and other dependents, to fight on Melaka's behalf, as Melaka did not have a large standing army of its own.

Melaka was in theory an open marketplace free of royal monopolies, yet it imposed certain royal regulations and taxes. Resident merchants and visiting sojourners who had resident families paid a three percent tax on imports, while other sojourners were subject to other regimes. Those who came from countries to the east (*negeri di-bawah angin*), including island Southeast Asia, were exempt from direct customs duties but were required to participate in the local "reciprocal buying" (*beli-belian*) system. Specifically, they were required to supply twenty-five percent of their goods directly to the Sultan's trade representatives (*hamba raja*, the "king's servitors" who managed the Sultan's business) at twenty percent less than the current market price, and to buy commodities from the Sultan's shops at twenty percent higher than the market price.[14] In contrast, ships arriving from countries to the west (*negeri di-atas angin*) including India, the Bay of Bengal, and the Middle East were charged a flat six percent fee on their imports, probably because they brought the most desired products: India's cotton textiles. There is no evidence that Melaka's taxation system discriminated between Muslims and non-Muslims, as was common in India's ports during this era. Rather, the goal was to manage the foreign trade communities and promote trade. It was only in the next century, after the arrival of Europeans, when it became common in Straits of Melaka Muslim ports to base taxes on the Islamic rules (*fiqh*) enjoining the rightful supplemental taxation of non-Muslims. In the fifteenth century, Melaka law, *Undang-undang Melaka,* was based in local custom, but in extreme cases the "Law of Allah" (*Shari'ah,* or *Itulah adatnya negeri, tetapi pada hikum Allah*—"*Customary Local Law and the Laws of Allah*" in Malay) was applied when harsher punishment seemed appropriate.[15]

Despite the diverse array of ethnic groups discussed, merchants were loyal to their families or to personal contracts rather than to any sense of a shared corporate commercial community. Rich merchants maintained residences in Melaka, where they transacted their business, and they sent trade representatives outward with their ships. Not all the wealthy merchants owned ships, as most overseas trade was conducted as silent partnerships in which a ship owner contracted with other merchant-financiers to share a voyage's expenses at a rate dependent on the destination, with all investors sharing in the profits on a ship's return. In other cases, small-scale merchant/sojourners could lease a "compartment" (*petak*) in a ship, which might go for a freight charge equivalent to twenty percent of the merchandise value. If a ship was lost, all investors lost, but if a ship was successful, it would normally return profits of thirty-five to fifty percent on voyages to Southeast Asia, eighty to ninety percent on India missions, and up to two hundred percent on China ventures.[16] Trade profits were reinvested in merchandise, or in the purchase of slaves (*belati*), who worked in the shipyards, served on ship crews, transported merchandise, hauled ships onto the beach, and performed various other labor tasks. Funds could also be spent on "slaves of debt" (*ulur, orang berhutang*), who were "household" or personal slaves. Common to the Malay tradition, and in competition with local Malay elite, those of the greatest social and political status in Melaka regardless of their ethnicity had the largest number of dependents of this type. There was also a substantial amount of conspicuous consumption. Tomé Pires comments:

> And true it is that this part of the world is richer and more prized than the world of the Indies, because the smallest merchandise here is gold, which is least prized, and in Melaka they consider it merchandise . . . in Melaka they prize garlic and onions more than musk, benzoin, and other precious things.[17]

This pattern of consumption also reflects the fifteenth-century development of a high regional standard-of-living that depended on an intra-Southeast Asian trade in basic commodities.

Portuguese Conquest of Melaka in Regional Context

After the fall of Melaka to the Portuguese in 1511, numbers of Melaka's Muslim merchants of mixed Malay and Chinese ethnicity migrated to other regional ports, which, paired with substantial new international demand for their products, benefited from their presence.[18] The refugee Melaka dynasty relocated in

Johor on the southern tip of the Malay Peninsula; the Johor court claimed succession to the Srivijaya/Melaka legacy, but could only exercise leadership over Melaka's networked east coast Malay Peninsula ports-of-trade.[19] Java's north coast ports remained prominent, and in 1527 a coalition of these ports, led by Demak, defeated the remnants of the Majapahit court, and followed by asserting its control over Palembang in southeast Sumatra and Banjarmasin on the southeast Borneo coast. Demak could initially dominate exchanges between the north Java coast and its hinterland, which supplied its networked ports with the rice and Javanese cloth (e.g., batik) that were vital in their sojourning trade with linked eastern Indonesian archipelago ports. But Demak was unable to institutionalize this network, and by the late 1550s the north coast alliance could not resist the successful reunification of Java under the central Java based Mataram polity.[20]

The new wealth derived from the international trade route enhanced the prospects of other enterprising sixteenth-century ports that had previously been secondary to Melaka, Java, and Vietnam coast ports-of-trade. New port-polities also emerged where the international trade provided access to luxury goods, notably cloth, ceramics, and precious metals, which became marks of status that raised the prestige of assertive port-connected local notables and allowed them to control the ritualized redistributions of these to those who acknowledged their sovereignty.

Antonio Pigafetta's account of Ferdinand Magellan's 1521 voyage among the Philippine Islands, Borneo, and the eastern Indonesian archipelago provides a vital outsider's view of the early sixteenth-century transitions. When Magellan's ships visited most of the ports in the eastern Indonesian archipelago and Sulu Sea region they were appalled by the nakedness and primitive lifestyles of the local populations. Only chiefs and their allied elite wore cotton clothing and displayed a "civilized" behavior. Ordinary people wore bark cloth coverings at most. In contrast, the Spaniards were highly impressed when they visited the port-polity of Brunei on Borneo's northwest coast, where even the servants wore gold and silk. Brunei's elite were recreating the splendor and ritual of Melaka's court, if not that of China's imperial court where Brunei's ambassadors were regular visitors.[21] The Brunei court's conspicuous ritualized display of wealth certainly reinforced its claim to be Melaka's successor as the dominating port-of-trade in the eastern South China Sea regions.[22]

The Brunei Secondary/Primary Port-of-Trade

The northwest Borneo coast port-polity that the Chinese knew as *Boni* was one among five Southeast Asian polities recognized by China's fifteenth-century Ming rulers as an independent maritime political entity worthy of ambassadorial exchanges—Melaka, Samudra-Pasai, Majapahit Java, and Champa were the others, and invested Brunei's monarchs with an imperial seal and commission. In doing so the Chinese court acknowledged that the Brunei coastline was a strategic stopover for ships traveling to China from Melaka or Java on the southwest monsoon, and for a return voyage on the seasonal northeast monsoon.

According to Chinese dynastic records, west coast Borneo was a prominent product source as well as intermediary port. The *Boni* coast was the source of rhinoceros horns, benzoin, camphor, tortoise shells, beeswax, and lakawood (known for its fragrance); its imports were porcelain, jewelry, cosmetics, silks, Middle Eastern glass, gold, silver, and tin. The first four exports were used in antipyretics, diuretics, analgesics, and tonics.[23] By the fifteenth century the *Boni* coast had become a gateway to the "East Sea Route" (*Jiaoguang*). Sojourning merchants left Champa by the northeast monsoon and crossed to *Boni*, where they might travel on to the Philippines, to southwest Luzon, Mindoro, or Batuan, or were satisfied to acquire Philippine and eastern Indonesian archipelago products in *Boni*'s port. Historians and archeologists debate whether any China-based traders ever went to *Boni* and beyond, or if they were content to acquire "Eastern Sea" products at the noted Champa, Melaka Straits, or north coast Java mainline ports, where Southeast Asia-based sojourners of mixed Chinese ethnic heritage acted as their intermediaries.[24]

Scholars also speculate on the site of *Boni*. Based on the analysis of local deposits of Chinese ceramics and other accompanying archeological evidence, current consensus is that the *Boni* polity identified in the eleventh- through mid-fourteenth-century Song and Yuan records periodically shifted. There is general agreement that during the Song era Sarawak coast port-polities were dominant, and Brunei river mouths, notably at and around Kota Batu, were the *Boni* base in the Yuan era and following.[25] The *Songshi* account, consistent with the other cited Chinese records that purposely provide information useful for navigation, reported that *Boni* was separated from Java by forty-five days journey, from the Srivijaya realm in the Straits of Melaka by forty days, and thirty days voyage from Champa. The point was that *Boni* goods were arriving in China's marketplace via these three primary port centers. The role of linked intermediaries that supported the primary centers is demonstrated in the *Songshi* account of an 1156 Srivijaya tributary presentation at the Chinese court that included nine pieces of plum flower shaped "Borneo camphor," 200 taels of "Borneo camphor planks," as also 117 *katis* of cloves (from the Malukus), 127 *katis* of nutmeg (from Banda), and 10,750 *katis* of sandalwood (also an eastern archipelago product, likely from Timor). In a following 1178 Srivijaya mission the Chinese court received four pieces of "plum-flower shaped Borneo camphor planks weighing 14 *katis*," 210 *katis* of nutmeg, 210 *katis* of benzoin, 150 *katis* of turtle-shell, and 1570 *katis* of sandalwood.[26]

The Chinese port commissioner Zhao Rugua (1225) asserted that the *Boni* port had a population of 10,000, who populated a "city" surrounded by timber walls, and was also defended by a "defense force of 150 ships." Its king wore Chinese silks on special occasions; he and his elite regularly wore gold jewelry and imported cloth from Java (batik?) that contained gold threads.[27] Zhao Rugua enumerates the local riverine systems subordinate to *Boni*, with the note that the populations among these places traded with *Boni* in small boats and dressed and had diets similar to *Boni*'s. Among these were *Xifenggong* (River Serudong?), *Shimiao* (Sibu?), *Hulumandou* (Martapura?), and *Suwuli* (Matan?), all sub-regional ports of the west and south coast of Borneo.

While the list of locally networked *Boni* ports remained the same, the wider Borneo realm reported in the 1304 *Nanhai zhi* had changed, due to the new prominence of an as yet unidentified polity on the southwest Borneo coast that the Yuan era sources knew as *Tanjongpura.*[28] In the early fourteenth-century account *Boni*'s trade realm was now focused northward, on the Philippines-Sulu Sea region. *Boni*'s domain included southwest Luzon (*Maleiluo*), Mindaro (*Mayi*), Batuan (*Butuan*), Sabah (*Shahuzhong*), Sarawak (*Yazhen*), and the Sarawak pirate liar of *Manaluonu.* In the Yuan sources Tanjongpura, not *Boni*, was preeminent over the southern route to the eastern archipelago. Tanjongpura's networked realm consisted of *Lundu* and *Shaluogou* in western Kalimantan, Banjarmasin (*Biennuxin*), Sulawesi (*Bindixien*), Makassar (*Mengjiajien*), Maluku (*Weilugu*), and Banda (*Bandan*).[29]

A Chinese tombstone inscription dated 1264, discovered in the Brunei estuary, which commemorated "Master Pu" ("Abu"), provides a vital local window on *Boni*'s early links. The tombstone was recovered in a Muslim cemetery at Jalan Tutong in the Kota Baru area, near the Kedayan tributary river of the Brunei River. Since the tombstone is not consistent with other tombstones in this cemetery, archeologists assume that the tombstone was moved from its original site in the Kota Baru area (associated with earlier archeological remains of the China trade) to its recovery site, which is not.[30] This tombstone takes on special significance, because its beneficiary was a Chinese official from Quanzhou, an emissary to the *Boni* court, descended from the powerful Bu merchant clan that dominated south China commerce under the Yuan.[31]

The tombstone provides definitive evidence of early thirteenth-century diplomatic and commercial networking between *Boni* (Brunei) and China, and it also raises issues relative to the level of interaction between *Boni* and Quanzhou, and how this relationship might have supported the development of Islam in Brunei. The tombstone's "Master Pu," who would seem to have been a member of the Muslim community of Quanzhou, implies the transmission of Islam from China to Brunei, as opposed to earlier suggestions of Arab merchants visiting Brunei or Muslim merchants of Middle Eastern heritage from Champa as the source.[32] Another local tombstone dated 1301, discovered in 1984, reinforces the Quanzhou connection since it is similar to contemporary Quanzhou tombstones, and was apparently shipped to Brunei from China.[33] In addition to providing further evidence of *Boni*'s role in the contemporary China trade, this tombstone takes on added significance in that it is believed to mark the grave of the *Boni* monarch, possibly the first Brunei sultan.[34] In local tradition, as reported by a Spaniard who visited around 1590, Sultan Yusuf, Borneo's legendary first sultan, was of Malay (Muslim) heritage, but had lived in China for some time, where he married a Chinese noblewoman.[35] Chinese dynastic records relate that a fifteenth-century Brunei monarch made an embassy to China, where he died. The Chinese monarch subsequently endowed his burial in a tomb near modern Nanjing and provided support for future ancestral rites there.[36] Certainly Brunei was able to exploit its favorable China relationship in asserting its rightful leadership over its networked ports-of-trade, as also to attract sojourning maritime diaspora to its marketplace.

Pigafetta's account of his 1521 visit to Brunei speaks of approaching it by sailing along the west coast Borneo coastline with stopovers to secure provisions at several small coastal villages, where the residents "have their houses on boats, and dwell nowhere else." Finally they reached Brunei, which was an imposing urban center:

> . . . [a] city all built on salt water, except the king's house, and the houses of certain chief men. And it has twenty or twenty-five thousand hearths. All their homes are of wood, and built on great beams ["stilts"] raised from the ground. And when the tide is high, the women go ashore in boats to sell and buy the things necessary for their food [in the local marketplaces]. In front of the king's house is a thick wall of brick, with towers in the manner of fortress, and in it were fifty-six large, brass cannon, and six of iron.[37]

Pigafetta provides commentary on the Spanish expedition's ritualized welcome. Their ship was first approached by a lead vessel (*prao*, which was larger than a *tunguli*, and smaller than a *junces*/junk), a ceremonial craft that had gold ornaments at its head and stern, and was decorated with cloth banners and peacock feathers. Drummers announced the arrival of eight senior officials, who seated themselves on a carpet, and then presented a jar of betel leaves and areca nuts (which when chewed leave the teeth with a red stain) as a sign of friendship, as also food supplies (meats, sugarcane, and rice wine), before they began their negotiations.

Being satisfied, a group of local elite returned six days later with six ceremonial vessels to escort a representative Spanish delegation to the court. They made their way to the port "governor's" residence escorted by an elephant procession. There they stayed overnight, sleeping on luxurious cotton mattresses. The next day they proceeded to the royal court along a street lined with people carrying spears, swords, and shields. They entered a large hall filled with court elite, who sat on carpets amid halls that were covered with crimson silk draperies.

Their court visit consisted of ritualized gift exchanges. The Spaniards presented:

> . . . a green velvet robe after the Turkish fashion, a chair of violet velvet, five cubits of red cloth, a red cap, three cubits of paper, a pair of silver shoes, and a silver needlecase full of [metal] needles. To the governor three cubits of red cloth, a cap, and a gilt cup. To the [head among the eight senior officials] a robe of red and green cloth after the Turkish fashion . . . and to the seven other chief men [other pieces of cloth].[38]

In return, the king gave "to each of us cloths of crimson and gold and silk, which they put on our shoulders. And they forthwith gave us a collation of cloves and cinnamon [among other food items]."[39] They were subsequently allowed to acquire the provisions they needed, and to have a delegation trade in the local marketplace.

Shortly after setting sail from Brunei, the Spanish ships were attacked by "a hundred praos, divided into three or four squadrons, and larger junks."[40] Successfully defending themselves, the Spanish crew took as their prisoner the son of the king of *Lozzon* (Luzon, the northernmost island of the Philippines), who was the "captain general" of a fleet of ships sent by the Brunei monarch's rival, the "heathen" king of another port-polity (*Burne*).[41] Based on the captain's account Pigafetta reports this rival port to have been "a city of heathen, larger than that of the Moors [i.e., Brunei], also built on salt water." According to Pigafetta, the captive captain told them that he had just returned from destroying a "large" port-polity called Laoe (perhaps Laut, an island off Borneo's southeast coastline), because they had been disloyal and allied with the king of Brunei instead of the king of *Burne*. The Spaniards freed the captain, because he "was highly esteemed in those parts, but more by the heathen because they are great enemies of the Moorish king [of Brunei]." As a consequence of their releasing the enemy captain, Brunei's enraged monarch refused to return three Spaniards who had remained at his port. Consequently the Spaniards kept the sixteen notables and three accompanying women who had been sent to the Spanish ship to negotiate. The Spaniards had intended to take them back to Spain, but the ship's Moro pilot (who had guided the Spaniards from the Sulu Sea region) kept them himself, as his rightful due because his son was one of the captives retained by the Brunei monarch.

The Emerging Secondary Downstream Center at Cebu in the Sulu Sea Region Circa 1500

International trade played a key role in stimulating major changes among Sulu Sea regional societies in the pre-European age. Archeologists assume that Chinese traders had established their initial bases in the Philippines as early as the eleventh and twelfth centuries.[42] Chinese traders had early settlements in Laguna and on Mindoro, where there are substantial remains of that era's Chinese ceramics; when the Spanish arrived in Manila in the early sixteenth century they found some twenty Chinese traders residing there with their wives.[43] This was likely the norm in other early Philippines regional ports, and archeologists assume that an intensive and extensive network of native trade existed to distribute imports and to gather the forest products desired by sojourning Chinese traders based in south China, Vietnam, or in the Brunei region of northwest Borneo.[44] These trade activities necessitated formal regulation, and this encouraged the rise of local chiefs *(datu)* who controlled and protected networks of *barangay* (villages).[45] Archaeological excavations document urban settlements of over five hundred households in the Laguna (Manila) area, as well as sites on the Mindoro, Mindanao, and Cebu coasts.[46] The Laguna, Mindoro, and Cebu sites especially demonstrate the rapid growth of trade centers—in response to the opportunities and demands afforded by foreign trade—as populations from the interior and other islands congregated around ports whose locally made brass artillery protected them against the piracy rampant in this region's sea channels.[47] Each of these early urban sites is associated with significant deposits of Chinese porcelain dating to the late Song and early Ming eras (twelfth through sixteenth century).[48] Excavations in the Cebu City region, for example, revealed multiple levels of Chinese porcelains predating the Spanish incursions, including large quantities of early Ming blue and white ceramics dating at least one century prior to the arrival of the Spanish.[49]

Magellan's ships anchored at Cebu in 1521 to take on provisions. According to Pigafetta's account, Magellan's crew had asked the ruler of Limasawa, a small island off the southern tip of Leyte, to direct them to a port where they could obtain food, and the ruler named three ports, adding that Cebu was the largest and the one with the most trade.[50] At Cebu the Spanish encountered a population of almost 2,000 and an extensive entrepot trade based on the exchange of Chinese articles for Southeast Asian products. Humabon, the ruler of Cebu, initially informed the Spanish that it was the custom of all ships that entered the port to pay him tribute, and that it was also customary for the ruler of the port to exchange presents with the captains of all ships that came to trade.[51]

This practice of ritualized exchange between ruler and commercial populations was similar to that described in Pigafetta's more detailed account of the Spaniard's visit to the luxurious Brunei court. Such gift-giving created a symbolic bond of friendship, in an attempt to mitigate the potential for conflict during the subsequent commercial transactions.[52] Not only had the Cebuanos adopted this practice, but they were also excellent hosts to the Spanish, well accustomed to offer ritualized hospitality to foreign dignitaries. Humabon and his nephew repeatedly provided Magellan and his men with food, invited them to meals, and entertained them with examples of local music and dance. The ruler's collection and redistribution of tribute, as well as his mediation and facilitation of trade exchanges, reinforced his position, and he applied these roles to the Spanish. Humabon's brother, reportedly called a *bendara* ("minister of trade"),[53] facilitated their exchanges. In addition, Humabon took Spanish goods under his personal care along with the four Spaniards assigned to trade the goods. In the local marketplace the Cebuanos traded rice, pigs, and other food provisions for small Spanish articles, but they especially wanted Spanish iron.[54] In these exchanges the Cebuanos impressed the Spanish with their use of a sophisticated system of weights and measures; local merchants carried about small wooden balances marked off into units equivalent to roughly one-fourth pound, one-third pound, and one pound.[55]

Chinese porcelain was one of Cebu's principal import items. Pigafetta was impressed by the frequent use of Chinese porcelains by prominent members of Cebu society, both in common household activities, and as a means of displaying their wealth and social status. For example, Humabon ate turtle eggs from Chinese porcelain dishes and served the Spanish explorers meat on Chinese porcelain platters. Porcelains were also used in local religious ceremonies as storage containers for myrrh, stoax, and benzoin, and these containers were prominently displayed in the funeral services of wealthy Cebuanos.[56] Other imports noted by the Spanish explorers included three Ming Buddha images made of greyish white jades; variously sized brass gongs said to have been manufactured in China (these were played by local musicians to entertain Magellan's crew and were also used in religious ceremonies); and cotton and silk clothing, imported from China, that was worn by Cebu elite. Pigafetta recorded the arrival of a Muslim merchant from Thailand with a cargo of gold and slaves for trade.[57] Pigefetta makes special note that this sojourning merchant was "more intelligent than the others,"[58] perhaps because he was literate, or because he was so well versed in the diverse etiquette of the international trade routes, in contrast to the locals who were not.

Cebu's regular trade connection to Ayutthya ("Siam") is demonstrated by the presence of the Thai porcelain that accounts for roughly one-third of the ceramics recovered at Cebu.[59] This is consistent with the patterns of the ceramic trade in Southeast Asia from roughly 1430 to 1580, when the Ming restriction on the export of Chinese Blue and White porcelains provided a market opportunity for Thai and Vietnamese manufacturers. Since there are few corresponding examples of native pottery, and that which has been found is of such poor quality compared to that of the earlier levels of habitation, it would seem, then, that Cebu's local pottery production largely ceased as imported ceramics became readily available.[60]

Cebu's exports included gold, slaves, and food supplies. Cebu's gold likely came from other parts of the Sulu Sea region, or from farther away, since Cebu itself was not known to have produced gold. At this time gold was a standard medium of international exchange (as also copper cash), which would account for its availability at Cebu. Pigs were raised locally, and Pigafetta's list of the indigenous products normally exchanged at Cebu's port also included rice, millet, sugar cane, palm wine, and various fruits that grew in Cebu's hinterland. Cinnamon, ginger, and silk articles, all reportedly from the Malukus, were marketed at Cebu, although it is not clear whether they were brought by Cebuanos or others.[61]

Adornments obtained through international trade marked personal status. Humabon's retainers wore only a short piece of palm tree cloth, while Humabon wore an embroidered scarf on his head, a necklace of great value, and two large gold earrings inlaid with precious gems. His wife dressed in a black and white cotton cloth, covered her shoulders with a large silk scarf crossed with gold stripes, and "wore a large hat of palm leaves in the manner of a parasol, with a crown about it of the same leaves, like the tiara of the Pope."[62] Humabon promised Magellan two large gold earrings, two armlets, two anklets, and gems to wear in his ears, as appropriate to someone of Magellan's rank.

Cebu's foreign trade brought Humabon status and wealth. Pigafetta's commentary characterized Humabon to be at the apex of a sequence of *datu* relationships, that is, personal alliances among chiefs who led *barangay* upstream-downstream networks and were therefore responsible for the flow of local agricultural goods to Humabon's port for the entrepot trade. Pigafetta specifically references two *barangay* settlements along the Cebu coast, Mandaui and Lalutan (Liloan), which were subordinate to Humabon. Subsequent early Spanish visitors to the area reported that such alliances were subject to flux, and that populations often moved from place to place according to the current hierarchy of a region. Thus, Humabon was competing with a rival chief, Lapulapu, who ruled the Maton and Bulaia *barangay* on the neighboring island of Mactan, and commanded a force of 1,500 fighting men. Whichever of these two chiefs controlled the strait separating the two islands would dominate regional commerce and the wealth associated with the international trade. Humabon enlisted the support of

Magellan's crew to establish his supremacy over Lapulapu's competing alliance network, and Magellan died in the ensuing battle.[63]

Pigafetta's account implies that loyalties to Humabon were based on the chief's personal strength, itself a product of the wealth he had achieved in his role as the principal facilitator of trade. Humabon made great displays of his trade-derived wealth in his use of Chinese ceramics, in his wearing of foreign clothing and jewelry, and in his association with visiting foreigners, including Chinese, Thai, and Europeans. The Spanish were amazed by the extent of Humabon's understanding of international trade as well as by his expectations of traders who participated in his marketplace. Yet such awareness is not surprising, since Humabon's personal administration of Cebu's entrepot trade was the source of his political power. Humabon mediated and monopolized the outward flow of locally produced foods as well as those spices acquired in the Molukus that found their way into Cebu's marketplace. He also dominated the internal redistribution of foreign goods—for instance the Chinese and Thai ceramics, Indian cloth, and Chinese and European metals—from his port to those dwelling in his subordinate upstream, whose production of local foodstuffs made possible the flow of Maluku spices to his port. While Humabon's direct authority would appear to have been confined to the coast, he was able to exercise his hegemony over the Cebu upstream via the strategic position of his court center relative to the indigenous and external networks of exchange. It is the movement beyond such a localized system based on personal alliance to a more structured and less personal state system involving a more direct integration of the upstream hinterlands and coastal populations, especially a more formal subordination of the hinterland to the coastal populations, and formalized linkage to other regional ports of trade, which is characteristic of the emerging "states" in maritime Southeast Asia in the fifteenth and sixteenth centuries.[64]

The Upstream-Downstream and Java Sea Networking of the Banjarmasin Intermediary Port-Polity

As was the case elsewhere in the region, the dominant early southeast Borneo coast port-polity periodically transitioned among a series of river mouth sites. During the mid-sixteenth century the new Banjarmasin Islamic court at the downstream intersection of the Barito and Martapura river systems succeeded two previous Hindu-Buddhist courts that had been located further upstream on the Barito River. The local record of the shifting port-polity is contained in the oldest and most complete remaining chronicle text from the eastern Indonesian archipelago, the sixteenth- and seventeenth-century *Hikayat Banjar*. This accounting provides a local perspective that contrasts to the historical observations of outsiders cited above relative to the early Brunei and Cebu secondary centers. The Banjar chronicle is unique; it consists of two surviving and overlapping textual traditions. The earliest written text incorporates previous oral tradition, and is the product of a sixteenth-century Hindu court that had limited contact with the international trade;[65] the second is a seventeenth-century retrospective that reports the new Banjarmasin port-polity's transition into a major secondary emporia.[66]

Surviving oral tradition asserts that the founder of the Barito river system's first court (*kraton*), Nagara-Dipa, was a merchant who initially came from India (a *Keling*), but was previously a Java-based sojourner who settled in the local river system during the late thirteenth century.[67] The sixteenth-century chronicle text confirms the local intervention by a Java-based outsider, but personifies the founding sojourner from Java as the semi-divine son (male) of the mythical ruler of the world (based on a sacred volcanic mountaintop in the Javanese tradition), sent by his divine father to marry a Borneo foam/*naga* (a guardian animistic spirit) princess (female), associated with the sea. This sacred union initiated the mystical connection (sea and land; female and male) between the Borneo coastal port-polity and the regionally powerful Majapahit court. The seventeenth-century Islamic court's retrospective text stresses local initiative (female/maternal) over external intervention (male/paternal): the Heavenly Father in the Islamic tradition instructed the semi-divine Borneo foam princess to send an embassy to Java's Majapahit court, to secure a Javanese prince as her suitable mate, and thus to initiate Banjar's royal bloodline.

In the mid-fourteenth century, according to the sixteenth-century chronicle account, a usurper of uncertain descent overpowered the previous Nagara-Dipa court with Majapahit's support, to restore the Javanese Hindu-Buddhist cultural tradition and influence that the initial court had betrayed by patronizing a local synthesis of traditional animism, Buddhism, and Shi'a Islam. After establishing his new Nagara-Daha court, the usurper voyaged to the Majapahit realm to receive its recognition of his authority, and no doubt to reaffirm his port-polity's networking with Java's prosperous ports-of-trade. The seventeenth-century Muslim court's retrospective enhanced the Java connections of the second Hindu-Buddhist court, asserting that it was founded by a Borneo prince who had been raised by a wealthy Surabaya merchant, and had returned to his Borneo homeland where he reestablish stable civil authority. Consistent with the earlier text's account, after the prince's military victories, he sent envoys to the Majapahit court, where Majapahit's chief minister acknowledged his realm's rightful place as the Majapahit court's subordinate.[68] The initial chronicle text characterized the sovereign (*daulat*) as a magically endowed person, whose existing ritual powers were further enhanced by this Majapahit contact. The monarch could release power on his faithful followers and thus bring them peace and prosperity. The sovereign (*daulat*) was the common representative of the community. There were times when the subject population would have disassociated themselves from a particular ruler, but not from the institution of sovereignty itself.[69]

Chinese sources report that the Nagara-Dipa thirteenth-century court [*Bien-nu-hsin*] had limited appeal to international traders; it was primarily a secondary stopover where sojourning merchants traveling to the Spice Islands might secure local rice and sago that they could exchange for eastern archipelago spices. In return Java- and China-based merchants supplied the Borneo court elite with Chinese and Indian luxuries.[70] By the fifteenth century, the second court's port had become a secondary intermediate marketplace servicing Java- and Makassar-based sojourners, and was especially known as a marketplace for the acquisition of slaves.[71] The nature of the port-polity changed significantly following the fall of Melaka to the Portuguese in 1511, as the Portuguese restricted access to north coast Sumatra's pepper. Consequently, numbers of Melaka Straits-based Muslim traders of Chinese ethnicity relocated to the Nagara-Daha port-polity, which became the base for their networking with the local upstream as well as with the Spice Islands to its east. They and Java-based sojourning traders, who were also of Chinese ethnicity, encouraged local pepper production and even began to organize and run local pepper plantations in cooperation with court elite (*pengeran*). Around 1550, the new Banjar court was the end result of this transition; it came into being with the support of Demak, then the dominant port on the Java coast. The new Banjarmasin court, ruled by a largely Malay-ethnic elite supported by Muslim sojourners of mixed Chinese and Javanese ethnicity, consolidated its control over the export and import trade of the Negara-Barito river system. The result was similar to the administered tributary trade described in Pigafetta's accounts of Brunei and Cebu. The king and his *pengeran* court elite had the exclusive right to negotiate the terms by which foreign merchants conducted trade with Banjarmasin and its upriver hinterland.

The *Hikayat Banjar*'s seventeenth-century narrative places the conversion of Banjarmasin to Islam around 1550, and explains acceptance of Islam as the price Banjarmasin agreed to pay for military assistance from Demak in establishing the new court. There followed neither the request for, nor the influx of Islamic scholars or administrators from Java. There was no royal patronage of mystical teachers; there were no miraculous conversions of Banjar's rulers; and although specialists in Islamic law were consulted in certain legal cases, their advice could be superceded by Banjar's ruler. The seventeenth-century *Hikayat*'s authors focused on the formality of the state and its new institutions that were then conceived as necessary to insure Banjarmasin's future rather than highlighting the magical qualities of its rulers, as had been the focal theme in the earlier chronicle text. The seventeenth-century text redirected the earlier chronicle text's concern for the ruler's ritual intervention, in asserting his secular responsibility to maintain the traditional cultural practices that had been inspired by Majapahit Java. The following *Hikayat Banjar* passage addresses the rightful concerns of the new Banjarmasin polity:

> . . . [the new state was successful because of the] excellent way it was organized, and that was because it was conducted in conformity with the arrangements and procedure followed by the king of Majapahit and in agreement with the Javanese usage. In the way they dressed, too, people followed the Javanese fashion. Everyone in the land . . . had given up dressing in the old style. Young and old, male and female alike, dressed in the Javanese way. The king . . . once said, when all the dignitaries with their subordinates were sitting before him . . . "let none of you dress like the Malays or the Hollanders or the Chinese or the Siamese or the Acehnese or the Makassarese or the Buginese. Do not imitate any of them. You should not even follow the old customs of dress . . . we have . . . set up a country of our own following the ways and manners of Majapahit. Therefore we should all dress like the Javanese." According to the stories of olden times handed down by the elders, whenever the inhabitants of a country imitated the clothing of people from elsewhere, misery inevitably fell upon the country that had turned to foreign ways of dressing. . . . The king's instructions are not carried out because the common people do exactly as

> they themselves like . . . Let not our country plant pepper as an export-crop, for the sake of making money, like Palembang and Jambi. Whenever a country cultivates pepper all food-stuffs will become expensive . . . [and this will] cause malice all over the country and even the government will fall into disorder. The rural people will become pretentious towards the townsfolk if pepper is grown for commercial purposes, for the sake of money . . . During the reign of the founder of our country many foreigners settled down in the land . . . but the people . . . did not imitate their clothing. For the people . . . it became the tradition to dress in the manner of Majapahit and to follow the Javanese fashion.[72]

The chronicle acknowledged Banjarmasin's relationship as a self-perceived secondary urban center to Java. The "Javanese" ideal was the legendary fourteenth- and fifteenth-century Majapahit court, where sanctioned status-based distinctions induced security and prosperity.[73] But the Banjar chronicler's emphasis on dressing Javanese went beyond this symbolic tie to the past, by acknowledging the importance of practical adherence to the Javanese cloth tradition rather than that of India and China.

In this era Banjarmasin and other participants in the eastern Indonesian archipelago trading network were linked to various north Java ports-of-trade, which provided ample access to regional textiles; chief among these were Java's batiks. Resident and sojourning Chinese and Javanese Muslim trade communities based in Banjarmasin opened trade contacts with Thailand, Cambodia, and southern Vietnam to the west and the Melukus to the east.[74] Bugis and Makaserrese based in the eastern archipelago had become competitors to these multiethnic Muslim traders based in Java's ports. The seventeenth-century *Hikayat Banjar* characterizes Banjarmasin's marketplace as being populated by an assortment of residential and sojourning Bugis and Makaserrese, as well as Chinese, Malays, and Javanese, among others. Sojourning merchants who arrived from Melaka, Brunei, Siam, and Aceh (in north Sumatra), who collectively followed the Malay code of dress, supplied more expensive Indian cotton textiles, in contrast to those who came from Java and its linked ports-of-trade who traded a variety of regional textiles, among which "Javanese batiks" (which were also woven in Bali and other eastern archipelago locales) chief among these.[75]

In the above citation, the *Hikayat* author warned against behaving like the Bugis, the Makaserrese, and the other market-based communities of sojourning merchants, as also the "Malays," who in this instance would have been linked to Melaka, Johor, or Brunei rather than the local ethnically Malay *pengeran* elite. These foreign Malays were likely to have dressed in cotton and silk sarongs instead of the Javanese cotton wrap-around that Banjar's court preferred. The chronicler's repeated use of cloth references to reinforce his points reflected the universal importance of cloth as a standard of exchange in maritime Southeast Asia during this era, and how differing cloth traditions were important qualifiers in making distinctions among these communities. Citations of Palembang and Jambi were well-known examples of societal chaos that resulted when previously stable ports-of-trade became overly vulnerable to the international marketplace.[76] But to return to the "old manners of dress" (i.e., to the wearing of bark cloth) and to withdraw from the international marketplace was equally undesirable. The local standard of dressing in the Javanese manner and thereby accepting "cultured" Javanese standards of orderly conduct provided a necessary symbolic means by which otherwise autonomous upstream tribesmen (as in the case study of Cebu cited above) might be drawn into a more centralized Java-like polity.[77]

In both *Hikayat* texts the symbolic marriage of a Borneo princess to a Majapahit prince not only initiated the Nagara-Dipa *kraton*'s dynastic line, but also forged a lasting bond between the southern Borneo coast emporium and Java. The transitions from the first to the succeeding *kratons* of Nagara-Daha and Banjarmasin demonstrated the continuity of certain mystical/magical elements associated with the Borneo royal family that it had acquired from the divinely-ordained Javanese royal bloodline. Continuing ties to Java, symbolized by the retention of Javanese-style administration, dress, and repeated diplomatic exchanges with Java polities, validated local authority, by reinforcing Banjarmasin's monarchs' claimed bloodline superiority over his subjects, as also substantiating Banjarmasin's rightful membership in the post-Majapahit community that was dominated by Java's north coast ports such as Demak, which also claimed its roots in the legendary Majapahit polity as partial justification for its superior stature over other linked north Java coast port-polities.[78]

Heterarchy, Cosmopolis, and Diasporic Communities

The case studies cited above are representative of the expansive urban networking common to the maritime Southeast Asia region in the 1400-1600 era, when the region was a vital source of products that were heavily in demand by international traders. While Melaka was the focal regional emporia in the fifteenth century, when it fell to the Portuguese in 1511 its functional primacy diffused to its previously networked secondary centers, which absorbed numbers of its past resident traders. This study has highlighted the subsequent consequences in the Java Sea and eastern South China Sea regions, where Demak and its networked north coast Java ports-of-trade became the new focal centers linked to secondary trading partners in the eastern Indonesian archipelago, as in the case of Banjarmasin, and Brunei on Borneo's northwest coast assumed a similar primary role relative to its networked secondary port-polities such as Cebu in the Sulu Sea region.

Consistent with both the heterarchy and cosmopolis models introduced at the beginning of this study, these fifteenth- and sixteenth-century port-polity networks may be thought of as extended communities that commonly accepted subordination to a primary port-of-trade. The primacy of the focal port in the network was in part due to its strategic location relative to the international trade route. North coast Java was at the intersection of the Java Sea connection to the eastern Indonesian archipelago Spice Islands and the main East-West maritime route that connected India and China. Java was also the critical source of rice and batik, which were the staple commodities in that era's exchanges for eastern Indonesian archipelago spices.

Brunei was likewise at a strategic point relative to the international trade route, where the international sojourners traveling between the Melaka Straits and Java Sea region could make stopovers on their way to and from China's marketplaces. Brunei was also the collection center for Borneo's camphor and other noted jungle and sea products that were much in demand in the China marketplace.[79] It was as well the recipient of a variety of products (including spices from the eastern Indonesian archipelago) that arrived from the Sulu Sea region and beyond.

Both the Java and Brunei networks were extremely fragile. Demak's hegemony over its networked Java Sea port-polities was short lived, ending when the new central Java-based Mataram state came into existence in the second half of the sixteenth century. Similarly Brunei's leadership over its networked ports-of-trade ended when the Spanish took control of its port in 1578. Although the Spanish remained there for only a short time, it was long enough for Brunei's former secondary ports in the Sulu Sea region to link with a new Sulu Sea based sultanate.[80]

In common with both the heterarchy and cosmopolis models, none of the described fifteenth- and sixteenth-century maritime Southeast Asia port-polity networks developed into elaborate institutionalized "states." In each case, the focal primary center held its prominence because it was a major international trade emporium that linked a number of secondary port-polities across substantial maritime space. Demak's sixteenth-century military leadership among its networked Java coast ports-of-trade reinforced its previous stature as the acknowledged sacred center of Javanese Islam. Demak led its port-polity network to victory over the remnants of the Majapahit state in 1527, and, according to the *Hikayat Banjar*, later sent its forces to assist in the establishment of the new Banjarmasin sultanate in the 1550s. The *Hikayat Banjar* asserts that Demak's intervention was not for its economic self-interests, but to restore orderly Javanese culture in the new sultanate. Demak was, in the mind of the *Hikayat*'s authors, the regional center of Islam, the legitimate successor to Majapahit Java's royal authority, and its predecessor's heir as the rightful guardian of Java's long-standing cultural traditions. Thus in the *Hikayat Banjar*'s account, only Demak's sultan could confirm the cultural if not mystical connection between Banjarmasin and Java.[81]

The *Hikayat Banjar* and Pigafetta's accounts of Brunei and Cebu suggest that a greater degree of economic, political, and cultural hierarchy was operative in sixteenth-century maritime Southeast Asia than O. W. Wolters allows in his definition of a networked heterarchy. But the evidence cited does not lend itself to confirming the alternative: that there was sufficient economic and political leadership exercised by Demak or Brunei over their secondary port-polities to conclude that the networked cosmopolis model applies instead. What can be said is that the sixteenth-century port-polity networks fell short of fully institutionalizing their extended relationships, with the consequence that network leadership was constantly vulnerable to internal or external challenges that resulted in the shift of the paramount center to a new location, whether as the result of a rival port-polity usurping power or as one in a series of periodic transfers of royal authority to a new court/port site because of a variety of internal and external causes.

A key ingredient that is overlooked in both the heterarchy and cosmopolis models is the vital role that maritime diaspora assumed in the creation of the networked communities. Herein the integrity of the early maritime Southeast Asia port-polity networks may be less the product of the political, economic, or cultural initiatives of local elite, and due more to their successful networking with the sojourning merchants who traded in their ports. As noted in the cited Melaka evidence, maritime sojourners of this era held networked loyalties to their families and/or to personal contacts rather than to any sense of a shared corporate community based in any single port-polity or network. The *Hikayat Banjar* identified foreign merchants as the ultimate challenge to local stability as symbolized by their foreign style of dress, which the authors of the *Hikayat* perceived as evidence of their threatening cultural practices and self-interest as these might destabilize the existing social order. Against this pessimistic view, and without promoting local withdrawal from the international trade, the *Hikayat* authors assert that local participation in the international trade might be locally productive only if the transactions of the marketplace were properly managed by those with continuing residential commitment to local society. Those who had only external loyalties, as symbolized by their foreign dress, should not gain control. Herein the *Hikayat* is not concerned with racial identities, but with cultural standards and the visible expressions of community membership. The seventeenth-century *Hikayat* text emphasizes that as long as local residents abided by the behavior appropriate to Javanese culture, whatever one's ethnicity, then surely a just moral order would prevail.

Rather than focus on the structure and function of political institutions that might define early urbanism in maritime Southeast Asia, the alternative proposed here is that focus on networked maritime diasporas might lead to a better understanding of the early patterns of urbanism in maritime Southeast Asia. Southeast Asia's maritime diasporas were the product of movements of commercial commodities, confrontations between alien cultures, formations of plural societies, dual loyalties, and multiple affiliations, and demonstration of early globalization. Well-documented fifteenth- and sixteenth-century Indian Ocean maritime diasporas are identified by their spatiality, distances traveled, itineraries, temporality, fixity, rootedness, and sedentary qualities.

Today's multidisciplinary studies of diasporas commonly accentuate the process of a population's dispersion in space, place, and time. Therein, "place" is an anchor point, a settlement spot where a number of people have gathered "temporarily" or "permanently"—with the implication that "permanently" is really temporary, and subject to better opportunities elsewhere, or an ultimate return to the ethnic homeland. Like the application of the heterarchy and cosmpolis models, diasporic studies address original cores ("homelands") and "secondary cores," where a number of migrants stay, but are likely candidates for subsequent dispersal and re-migration. Thus this study has been place centered, depicting network-based spaces with porous boundaries that are changeable in association with intra-diasporic contexts and events. The evolving diasporas active in Southeast Asia populated conceptual activity spaces in which individuals, families, and varieties of political and socioeconomic networks derived from places of origin as well as destinations.[82]

This study has addressed the importance of those of mixed Chinese ethnicity, most of whom had converted to Islam, who by the fifteenth century were committing to a Southeast Asian residence (e.g., Java and Borneo), as demonstrated by some form of local allegiance, whether by permanent settlement, taking local names, intermarriage with locals and the engendering of mixed-blood families, religious conversions, and/or long-term integration and incorporation into an indigenous society. Most early Chinese in Southeast Asia were maritime sojourners, inclusive of pirate bands, who may or may not have had a single permanent base of operation/residency, but spent most of their time traveling from place-to-place according to the seasonality of the Asian monsoons. Such a sojourner or sojourning community might live in one place for a period of time, as for example waiting for the change in the monsoon winds, and thus have a network of residencies and loyalties (wives, families) among several "homes," as for example in Champa, Melaka, north Java, or Borneo. These sojourners regularly networked with their extended family members in the major regional ports-of-trade, as in the above example of the Pu family that was based in Quanzhou, but networked throughout the Indonesian archipelago, in Vietnam, Champa, and Brunei.[83] Indeed, historians assert that from the fifteenth century China-based sojourners rarely went to the eastern Indonesian archipelago themselves, but instead depended on Chinese who had settled on the Borneo coast to act as their intermediaries.[84]

In light of the cited new archeological evidence and inquiry, scholars debate how and when the concept of assimilation by those of non-Southeast Asian bloodlines applies to those living in these and similar communities. Revisionists challenge the prior commonplace assumption that diaspora members maintained some degree of loyalty to their homeland, ethnicity, family roots, etc., rather than being fully integrated into their new place of residence, and that overseas Chinese in particular might temporarily settle regionally, but inclusively desired to repatriate to China if the opportunity afforded itself. On the contrary, the evidence of regional networking in 1400-1600 maritime Southeast Asia cited in this study suggests that overseas Chinese acculturating into Southeast Asian societies, or negotiating relationships with their neighboring communities, were the source of subsequently stable pluralistic communities that contributed to the Indian Ocean trade boom that was coincident to substantial European presence in the post-1600 era.

Notes

1. Paul Wheatley, *Nagara and Commandery, Origins of the Southeast Asian Urban Traditions* (Chicago: University of Chicago Department of Geography Research Papers nos. 207-208, 1983).

2. Kenneth R. Hall *Maritime Trade and State Development in Early Southeast Asia* (Honolulu: University of Hawaii Press, 1985), 1-25.

3. Victor Lieberman, *Strange Parallels. Southeast Asia in Global Context, c. 800-1830* (Cambridge: Cambridge University Press, 2003).

4. G. William Skinner, *Marketing and Social Structure in Rural China* (Ann Arbor, MI: University of Michigan Center for Chinese Studies, 1974); Paul Wheatley, *The Pivot of the Four Quarters: A Preliminary Enquiry into the Origins and Character of the Ancient Chinese City* (Chicago: Aldine, 1971); and Paul Wheatley, *From Court to Capital:*

A Tentative Interpretation of the Origins of the Japanese Urban Tradition (Chicago: University of Chicago Press, 1978).

5. O. W. Wolters, *History, Culture, and Region in Southeast Asian Perspectives* (Singapore: Institute of Southeast Asian Studies, 1982; revised edition Ithaca, NY: Cornell University Southeast Asia Program, 1999). Wolters' conception of heterarchy represented his opposition to historians "who detect . . . change in the form of centralizing tendencies" (Wolters 1999, 152). Other heterarchy-like options were Stanley Tambiah's "galatic polity" (Stanley J. Tambiah, *World Conqueror and World Renouncer: A Study of Buddhism and Polity in Thailand Against a Historical Background* [Cambridge: Cambridge University Press, 1976]); Clifford Geertz's conceptual "Negara" (Clifford Geertz, *Negara: The Theatre State in 19th Century Bali* [Princeton: Princeton University Press, 1980]); Leonard Andaya's exploration of the "cultural state" (Leonard Andaya, "Cultural State Formation in Eastern Indonesia," in *Southeast Asia in the Early Modern Era,* ed. Anthony Reid [Ithaca, NY: Cornell University Press, 1993], 23-41); and Paul Wheatley's "Commandery" (Wheatley, *Negara and Commandery*).

6. Anthony Reid, "Cosmopolis and Nation in Central Southeast Asia," Asian Research Institute, National University of Singapore, *Working Paper Series #22* (Singapore: 2004); Eric Tagliacozzo, "An Urban Ocean: Notes on the Historical Evolution of Coastal Cities in Greater Southeast Asia," *Journal of Urban History,* 33, 9 (2007), 911-932. See also Sheldon Pollack, "The Sanskrit Cosmopolis, 300-1300: Transculturation, Vernacularization, and the Question of Ideology," in *Ideology and Status of Sanskrit,* Brill Indology Library #13, ed. Jan. E. M. Houben (Leiden: E. J. Brill, 1996); and "The Cosmopolitan Vernacular," *Journal of Asian Studies,* 57, 1 (1998), 6-37.

7. Anthony Reid, *Southeast Asia in the Age of Commerce, 1450-1680; I, The Lands Below the Winds; II, Expansion and Crisis* (New Haven: Yale University Press, 1988, 1993).

8. Kenneth R. Hall, "Upstream and Downstream Unification in Southeast Asia's First Islamic Polity: The Changing Sense of Community in the Fifteenth Century *Hikayat Raja-Raja Pasai* Court Chronicle," *Journal of the Economic and Social History of the Orient* (henceforth *JESHO*), 44, 2 (2001), 198-229.

9. Geoff Wade, "Ming China and Southeast Asia in the 15th Century: A Reappraisal," Asia Research Institute *Working Paper Series #28* (Singapore: 2004).

10. A. C. Milner, "Islam and Malay Kingship," *Journal of the Royal Asiatic Society,* 6 (1981), 46-70; Milner, *Kerajaan: Malay Political Culture on the Eve of Colonial Rule* (Tucson: Association for Asian Studies by the University of Arizona Press, 1982), 20-28; Nordin Hussin, *Trade and Society in the Straits of Melaka, Dutch Melaka and English Penang, 1780-1830* (Singapore: NUS Press, 2007), traces the flow of assorted commodities to Melaka's from its regional hinterland in the eighteenth century, which he suggests was a continuation of earlier networking.

11. Barbara Watson Andaya and Leonard Y. Andaya, *A History of Malaysia* (London: Macmillan, 1982), 55.

12. Luis Filipe Ferreira Reis Thomaz, "Malaka et ses communautes marchandes au tournant du 16e siecle," in *Marchands et homes d'affaires asiatiques dans l'Ocean Indien et la Mer de Chine 13e-20e siecles,* ed. Denys Lombard and Jean Aubin (Paris: Editions de l'Ecole des hautes etudes en sciences socials, 1988), 31-48; trans., "Melaka and Its Merchant Communities at the Turn of the Sixteenth Century," in *Asia Merchants and Businessmen in the Indian Ocean and the China Sea,* ed. Denys Lombard and Jean Aubin (New Delhi: Oxford University Press, 2000), 25-39.

13. Armando Cortesao, trans. and ed., *The Suma Oriental of Tome Pires* (London: The Hakluyt Society, 1944), 118-119, 268.

14. Barbara Andaya, "The Indian Saudagar Raja (The King's Merchant) in traditional Malay courts," *Journal of the Malay Branch of the Royal Asiatic Society* (henceforth *JMBRAS*), 51, 1 (1978), 13-36.

15. Christopher Wake, "Melaka in the Fifteenth Century: Malay Historical Traditions and the Politics of Islamization," in *Melaka: The Transformation of a Malay Capital c. 1400-1980,* ed. Kernial Singh Sandhu and Paul Wheatly (Kuala Lumpur: Oxford University Press, 1983), vol. I, 128-161; R. O. Winstedt and de Josselin de Jong, "The Maritime Laws of Malacca," *JMBRAS,* 29, 3 (1956), 22-59; and Cheah Boon Kheng, "The Rise and Fall of the Great Melakan Empire: Moral Judgment in Tun Bambang's *Sejarah Melayu,*" *JMBRAS*, 71 (1998), 104-121.

16. Thomaz, "Melaka and Its Merchant Communities," 33.

17. Cortesao, trans., 286-287.

18. Nicholas Tarling, ed. *The Cambridge History of Southeast Asia.* 2 vols. (Cambridge: Cambridge University Press, 1992), I, 481.

19. Leonard Y. Andaya, *The Kingdom of Johor, 1641-1728* (Kuala Lumpur: Oxford University Press, 1975); Barbara Watson Andaya, *Perak, The Abode of Grace* (Kuala Lumpur: Oxford University Press, 1979).

20. Denys Lombard, *Le carrefour javanais: essai d'histoire globale* (Paris: Editions de l'Ecole des hautes etudes en sciences socials, 1990).

21. Geoff Wade, *Southeast Asia in the Ming Shi-lu, An Open Access Resource* (http://www.nus.edu.sg/msl) (Singapore: 2005).

22. Melaka's *Hikayat Hang Tuah*, composed during the sixteenth century, cited Brunei as an "alien country," in contrast to ports-of-trade that had remained loyal members of the Melaka association then centered in Johor (Barbara Andaya in *Cambridge History,* I. 412). By the end of the sixteenth century regional ports-of-trade were citing their linkage to Brunei as validation of their legitimacy, as in the case of Manila, where by 1570 two allied Muslim chiefs *(datu)* claimed themselves rightful monarchs because of their marriage alliance with the Brunei court (ibid., 411); this polity was short lived, as the Spanish seized Manila in 1571. In 1578, when the Spanish took temporary control over Brunei this allowed a new sultanate to develop in the Sulu Sea, which claimed to be Brunei's rightful successor. When Brunei regained its independence from the Spanish, it was unable to reassert its dominance over Sulu Sea port-polities, which continued to favor the Sulu sultanate's leadership.

23. Daniel Reid, *Chinese Herbal Medicine* (Hong Kong: Chinese Medicinal Materials Research Center, Chinese University of Hong Kong, 1987), 118, 184.

24. Kenneth R. Hall, ed., *Maritime Diasporas in the Indian Ocean and East and Southeast Asia (960-1775)*, Special Issue of *JESHO*, 49, 4 (2006).

25. Pengiran Karim bin Pengiran Haji Osman, "The Evidence of Oriental Ceramic and Earthenware Distribution in Brunei Darussalam as an Aid in Understanding Protohistoric Brunei," Ph.D. dissertation (Southampton: University of Southampton, UK, 1997); Jan Wisseman Christie, "On Po-ni: The Santubong Sites of Sarawak," *Sarawak Museum Journal*, 34 (1985), 77-89.

26. Grace Wong, "A Comment on the Tributary Trade between China and Southeast Asia, and the Place of Porcelain in This Trade, During the Period of the Song Dynasty in China," in *Chinese Celadons, and Other Related Wares in Southeast Asia*, ed. Lu Yaw (Singapore: Southeast Asian Ceramics Society, *Arts Orientalis*, 1979), 80-83.

27. Frederick Hirth and W. W. Rockhill, *Chao Ju-kua, His Work on the Chinese and Arab Trade in the 12th and 13th Centuries Entitled Chu-fan-chi* (New York: Paragon Reprint of St. Petersburg, 1911 original, 1966), 155-158.

28. F. Andrew Smith, "Pre-17th Century States in Borneo: Tanjungpura Is Still a Mystery; Lawei Less So," in *Borneo 2000: Proceedings of the Sixth Biennial Borneo*

Research Conference, Politics, History, and Development, ed. Michael Leigh (Kota Samarahan: Universiti Malaysia Sarawak, 2000), 149-178.

29. Wong, "Commentary on the Tributary Trade."

30. W. Franke and T. F. Chen, "A Chinese Tomb Inscription of A.D. 1264, Discovered Recently in Brunei—A Preliminary report," *Brunei Museum Journal* (henceforth *BMJ*), 3, 1 (1973), 91-99; Pengiran Karim bin Pengiran Haji Osman, "Further Notes on a Chinese Tombstone Inscription of A.D. 1264," *BMJ* , 18, 1 (1993), 1-10.

31. Billy Kee Long So, *Prosperity, Region and Institutions in Maritime China, The South Fukian Pattern, 946-1368* (Cambridge, MA: Harvard University Press, 2000), 107-110; also see John Chaffee's study in this volume.

32. Roderich Ptak, "From Quanzhou to the Sulu Zone and Beyond: Questions Related to the Early Fourteenth Century," *Journal of Southeast Asian Studies* (henceforth *JSEAS*), 29 (1998), 269-294; Hirth and Rockhill, 159, note 13; Geoff Wade, "Arab Traders, Song Mercantilism and an Earlier Age of Commerce in Southeast Asia, 10th-13th Centuries," paper presented at the International Economic History Association Conference, Helsinki, August 2006; John Chaffee, "Muslim Merchants and Quanzhou in the Late Yuan-Early Ming: Conjectures on the Ending of the Medieval Muslim Trade Diaspora," paper presented to the conference on "The East Asian Mediterranean-Maritime Crossroads of Culture, Commerce, and Human Migration," Munich, November 2007.

33. Metassim bin Haji Jibah and Suhaili bin Haji Hassan, "Tomb of Maharaja Brunei," *BMJ*, 6, 3 (1987), 10-15.

34. Chen Da-sheng, "A Brunei Sultan in the Early 14th Century: Study of an Arabic Gravestone," *JSEAS*, 23, 1 (1992), 1-13. See Robert Nicholl, "Some Problems in Brunei Chronology," *JSEAS*, 20, 2 (1989), 175-195, for an argument this was not the grave of the first sultan, but that of an earlier monarch.

35. John S. Carroll, "Berunai in the Boxer Codex," *JMBRAS*, 55, 2 (1982), 4.

36. MSL 116.4ab, September 8, 1530; from Geoff Wade, *Southeast Asia in the Ming Shi-lu* (http://epress.nus.edu.sg/msl/entry/1875).

37. Antonio Pigafetta, *Magellan's Voyage. A Narrative Account of the First Circumnavigation*. trans. and edited by R. A. Skelton (New York: Dover, 1994), 101.

38. Ibid., 100.

39. Relative to the importance of such ritualized presentations of "robes of honor" by outsiders, as the means of initiating a favorable local relationship throughout the Eurasian realm during this era, see Stewart Gordon, ed., *Robes and Honor. The Medieval World of Investiture* (New York: Palgrave, 2001).

40. Pigafetta, 102.

41. *Burne* was perhaps, as Robert Nicholl suggested, the previous *Boni* center on the Sarawak coastline (Robert Nicholl, "Notes on Some Controversial Issues in Brunei History," *Archipel*, 19 [1980], 25-41), or others have suggested it to be *Tanjongpura* in the Chinese records as noted above; the Spanish visited neither of these. Nicholl clarifies that Pigafetta's reference to "Java Major" is to Borneo, while his references to "Java Minor" are to Java, as was the common distinction among the earliest European voyagers, and is consistent with their earliest maps of the region.

42. Roderich Ptak, "The Northern Trade Route to the Spice Islands: South China Sea-Sulu Zone-North Moluccas (14th to early 16th century)," *Archipel*, 43 (1992), 27-56; and "From Quanzhou to the Sulu Zone and Beyond."

43. Karl L. Hutterer, "The Evolution of Philippine Lowland Societies," *Mankind*, 9 (1974), 287-299.

44. Ptak, loc. cit.

45. Gordon Thomasson, "Beyond the Barangay: Rethinking the Question of Social Organization in the Pre-Hispanic Philippines," *Cornell Journal of Social Relations*, 5, 2 (1980), 171-192.

46. Laura Lee Junker, *Raiding, Trading, and Feasting: The Political Economy of Philippine Chiefdoms* (Honolulu: University of Hawaii Press, 1999).

47. Hutterer, "Philippine Lowland Societies."

48. Junker, *Raiding, Trading, and Feasting.*

49. Karl L. Hutterer, *An Archaeological Picture of a Pre-Spanish Cebuano Community* (Cebu City, Philippines: University of San Carlos, 1973).

50. Pigafetta, 71-91.

51. His demand for tribute was quickly dropped after a Muslim merchant based in a Thai Ayudhya port, mistaking the Spanish for the Portuguese, informed Humabon that his visitors had recently conquered the great entrepot of Melaka and part of India (Pigafetta, 75).

52. Gordon, *Robes of Honor*; Junker, *Raiding, Trading, and Feasting.*

53. Pigafetta probably meant *bendahara* or a local form of the word, a "treasury" official commonly found in contemporary Malay ports-of-trade. For references to *bendahara* in the Malay world, see for example Tomé Pires' references in Cortesao, 167, 193-194, and *passim.*

54. According to Paul Wheatley, "Geographical Notes on Some Commodities Involved in Sung Maritime Trade," *JMBRAS*, 32, 2 (1959), 117, due to the absence of local deposits, iron was commonly traded by Chinese merchants in the Southern Seas during Song times, and was said to have been used as a unit of barter. See also Bennet Bronson, "Patterns of the Early Southeast Asian Metals Trade," in *Early Metallurgy, Trade and Urban Centres in Thailand and Southeast Asia*, ed. Ian Glover, Pornchai Suchitta, and John Villiers (Bangkok: White Lotus, 1992), 64-96. One would assume that Gujarat textiles were another important market product. The specific Spanish goods exchanged in Cebu are not listed in Pigafetta's report, but an idea of them can be gathered from his account of trade with the king of Ternate, where a bahar of cloves was acquired for two cubits of a fairly good red cloth, thirty-five glasses, fifteen axes, twenty-five pieces of linen, one hundred fifty knives, fifty pairs of scissors, forty caps and ten ells of Gujarat cloth (Pigafetta, 118).

55. Ibid., 80.

56. Death rites were focal in local religious practice. As in other archipelago areas of his age, local elite, including Humabon, would have derived a degree of legitimacy by their personal involvement in the elaborate performance of these rites. Pigafetta's report stressed the conversion of a number of non-Muslim elite to Christianity. In Cebu, for instance, Pigafetta claims that Humabon and some eight hundred of his followers converted (Pigafetta, 82). Pigafetta noted that such conversions took place after the local populations witnessed the impressive Christian rituals performed by Magellan's crew. Perhaps the elite decided that the new rituals were another kind of magical ceremony that could further substantiate their legitimacy, similar to the motives of other archipelago rulers who were converting to Islam in that same age. See Thomas Gibson, *Islamic Narrative and Authority in Southeast Asia From the 16th to the 21st Century* (London: Palgrave-Macmillan, 2007), chapter 1. However, it could also be supposed that Humabon and his elite saw conversion as the necessary foundation for their continuing commercial and political exchanges with the Spanish, including Spanish military support against their regional rivals.

57. Pigafetta, 75. It was this merchant who advised Humabon to treat the Spanish visitors with care. The sojourning merchant intervened on the Spaniards' behalf while he was making the tribute payment Humabon demanded of the international merchants who

traded in his port.

58. Ibid., 76.

59. Hutterer, "Pre-Spanish Cebuano Community."

60. Ibid., 43.

61. Cebuanos likely visited many islands to plunder and trade, voyaging in canoes. However, it is not known how far they went. See Junker, *Raiding, Trading, and Feasting*, and Leonard Andaya, "Cultural State Formation." Pigafetta is not the only sixteenth-century Spaniard reporting Cebu as a center of commerce. Father Urdaneta (1525-1526) notes: "North of Benenao (Mindanao) is Cebu, and according to the natives it also contains gold, for which Chinese come to trade each year." Alvaro de Saavedra (1527-1528) writes that "there are many fine hogs in the island (Cebu), and it has gold. They say that people from China come hither, and that they trade among these islands." See Emma Helen Blair and James Alexander Robertson, eds., *The Philippine Islands, 1493-1898* (Cleveland: A. H. Clark, II, 1903-1909), II, 35, 42.

62. Pigafetta, 82.

63. Filipino historians characterize these events as the first act of European aggression in the Philippines, and Lapulapu is honored as the first Filipino to have repulsed this aggression; colonial-era Spanish historians, on the other hand, viewed these events as the first attempt to bring civilization to the Filipino population, stressing Magellan's conversion of some eight hundred Cebuanos in the name of God and to the glory of Spain (David Joel Steinberg, *In Search of Southeast Asia* [New York: Praeger, 1971], xi). Whatever the case, by the late sixteenth century Cebu had become eminent without Spanish help, as Spanish records fail to recognize a sizeable Mactan community. See Bruce L. Fenner, "Colonial Cebu: An Economic-Social History, 1521-1896," Ph.D. dissertation, (Ithaca, NY: Cornell University, 1976).

64. L. Andaya, "Cultural State," for a similar depiction of the neighboring Maluku region; and Thomas Gibson, *And the Sun Pursued the Moon: Symbolic Knowledge and Traditional Authority among the Makassar* (Honolulu: University of Hawaii Press, 2005), relative to the transition to Islam in neighboring Makassar.

65. A. A. Cense, *De Kronick van Banjarmasin* (Santpoort: C. A. Mees, 1928), summary and commentary on Leiden Codex Or. 6664—the earliest recension of the *Hikayat Banjar*, considered to be the written version of a previous oral tradition.

66. J. J. Ras, *Hikayat Bandjar: A Study in Malay Historiography* (The Hague: Martinus Nijhoff, 1968).

67. Ras, 181-182

68. Ras, 57-68.

69. Milner, *Kerajaan*.

70. W. P. Groeneveldt, *Historical Notes on Indonesia and Malaya Compiled from Chinese Sources* (Jakarta: Bhratara Publishers, 1960 [reprint of 1880 original, *Notes on the Malay Archipelago*]), 107.

71. Cense, 92.

72. Ras, 264-265.

73. Kenneth R. Hall, "Personal Status and Ritualized Exchange in Majapahit Java," *Archipel*, 59 (2000), 51-96.

74. Kenneth R. Hall, "Upstream and Downstream Networking in 17th Century Banjarmasin," in *From Buckfast to Borneo: Essays Presented to Father Robert Nicholl on the 85th Anniversary of His Birth 27 March 1995*, ed. A. V. M. Horton and V. T. King (Hull: Centre for South East Asian Studies, special issue of *Indonesia Circle* [1995]), 489-504.

75. Kenneth R. Hall, "The Textile Industry in Southeast Asia 1400-1800," *JESHO* 39 (1996), 2: 87-135.

76. Barbara Watson Andaya, "The Cloth Trade in Jambi and Palembang during the Seventeenth and Eighteenth Centuries," *Indonesia* 48 (1989): 27-46; "Cash Cropping and Upstream-Downstream Tensions: The Case of Jambi in the Seventeenth and Eighteenth Centuries," in Reid, ed., *Southeast Asia in the Early Modern Era*, 91-122.

77. The value of Javanese textiles as the source of ideational linkage is substantiated by scholars of textile design, who argue that the heightened consumption of Java's batik was especially important as a source of integrating upstream and downstream in the eastern archipelago, in that batik designs represented a resurgence of animistic traditions. In wearing Javanese batik the lower body was wrapped in layers of cloth that contained powerful symbolic images, as opposed to the designs of Indian textiles that had little local meaning. As such, Java cloth was not unlike local cloth in that it could *bestow* power, in contrast to other imported cloth that was less likely to be spiritually possessed. See Hall, "Textile Trade."

78. Demak's origin myth focuses on the personal history of Raden Patah, known as "the visitor," a member of Southeast Asia's multi-ethnic maritime diaspora who was born at Palembang in Sumatra to a Chinese woman with bloodlines that bound him to the Majapahit royal lineage. Raden Patah was thus not only descended from the Majapahit court, but also from the Chinese Muslim sojourning communities who were based in the Sunda Straits and north coast Java region's ports. Raden Patah temporarily settled in the north Java coast port of Gresik, which was largely populated by Chinese merchants, and then moved to Demak in the first quarter of the fifteenth century. He became immeasurably wealthy, and as acknowledgement of his commercial and personal prowess, and because he had royal blood, the Majapahit monarch appointed him Demak's governor in the second half of the fifteenth century. See Anthony Reid, *Charting the Shape of Early Modern South East Asia* (Chiang Mai, Thailand: Silkworm Books, 1999), 56-84.

79. Robert Nicholl, "Brunei and Camphor," *BMJ*, 4, 2 (1979), 52-74.

80. L. Andaya, "Culture State"; Ellen, *On the Edge of the Banda Zone.*

81. In the seventeenth-century *Hikayat* account, as noted, the Demak sultan was said to have directly intervened to assist in the establishment of the new Banjarmasin sultanate. Local appreciation for the memory of Majapahit was no doubt a factor in the seventeenth-century text since there had recently been an influx of Javanese emigrants to Banjarmasin when the commercial centers of Java's north coast fell to the expansion of the revivalist hinterland-based Mataram polity, especially after Mataram's victory over the Surabaya port-polity in 1625. These migrations of largely Muslim commercial specialists to Banjar further enhanced the noted economic and political transitions that were coincident with the new Banjarmasin sultanate in the mid-sixteenth century (Hall, "17th-Century Banjarmasin").

82. Kenneth R. Hall, "Multi-Dimensional Networking: Fifteenth-Century Indian Ocean Maritime Diaspora in Southeast Asian Perspective," *JESHO*, 49, 4 (2006), 454-481.

83. Chaffee, "Muslim Merchants and Quanzhou."

84. Ptak, "From Quanzhou to the Sulu Zone and Beyond."

8

Missionary Buddhism in a Post-Ancient World: Monks, Merchants, and Colonial Expansion in Seventeenth-Century Cochinchina (Vietnam)[1]

Charles Wheeler

Overview

The following essay represents an ongoing effort to understand what produced the changes that transformed the socio-political culture of a place and its people, to render a Vietnamese landscape peopled by Vietnamese faces. This event happened in a place now associated with the southern half of today's Vietnam—a place called *Cochinchina* herein for practical purposes—and in a time associated with the early modern era.[2] So transformative an event owes its outcome to Vietnamese conquerors and migrants, a fact long celebrated in Vietnamese historiography as the "March South," when Vietnamese conquest and colonial policies transformed the face of historically Cham and Khmer territories along the southeastern coastal plains of mainland Southeast Asia.[3] Non-Vietnamese were critical to this outcome as well, too, as recent work has shown. However, in looking at the contributions of these non-Vietnamese catalysts to the creation of Vietnamese frontier societies, scholarly attention has been limited to overseas commerce.[4] Yet sea-trading merchants were only one of several important facets to the maritime factor that shaped the Vietnamization of Cochinchina. Onshore, merchants relied on a host of local, "subaltern" agents to make their commerce possible.[5] At sea, ships plying Vietnamese ports carried more than just merchants and their commercial wares. They transported people of other social groups as well, and with them exogenous behaviors, objects, and ideas. Their cultural cargo left imprints of their own upon host societies like Cochinchina, and in doing so shaped the potentialities of future Vietnamese societies and states in the long run.

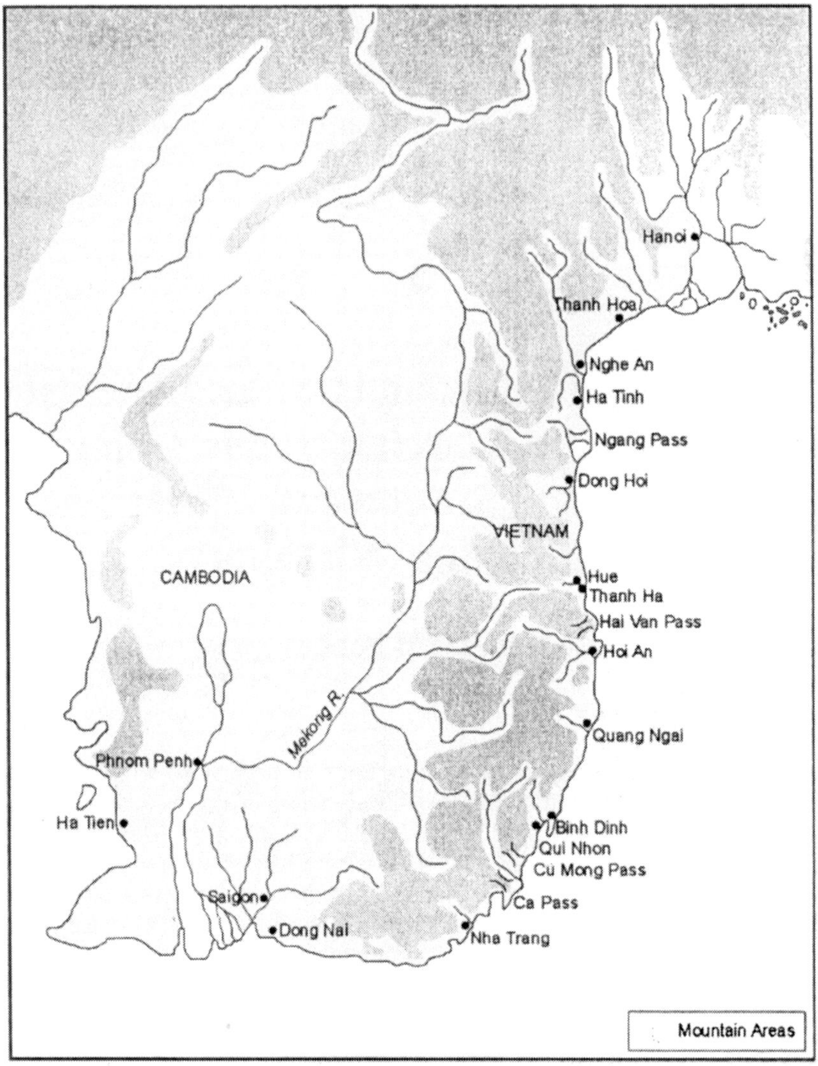

***Map 8.1.* Vietnam Coastline c. 1700**

Chinese monks, for example, traveled in significant numbers to Cochinchina during the late seventeenth century. Their circulation through the polyglot society of Cochinchina, and the institutions and practices they established there, decisively shaped the religious, economic and political character of Vietnamese colonial societies as they formed among historically non-Vietnamese populations during the seventeenth and eighteenth centuries. Without understanding these foreign monks, then, we cannot fully comprehend the social processes that empowered Chinese to build sea-trading merchant colonies along Cochinchina's seaboard, colonies dominated and defined by Vietnamese norms to take shape in new regions, and a Vietnamese state to successfully expand its domain.

In his recent dissertation, Wu Jiang asserts that the tendency "to perpetuate a sinicized form of Buddhism as static and ultimate" defies all evidence of a living religion, dynamic and contingent long after its reputed post-Tang fossilization. At times, it even became expansive.[6] The same could be said for Vietnamese forms of Buddhism. In the seventeenth century, Chan Buddhism experienced a revival that became "increasingly missionary" in practice.[7] As a consequence, Chan monks from monasteries in southern China traveled overseas in order to evangelize, or to put it another way, to "transmit the [authentic] *Dharma*." The actions of these missionary monks led to a renaissance of Chan Buddhism in Japan, and produced some of Japan's largest schools of Buddhist practice today.[8]

Wu does not prove such missionary activity actually happened in Cochinchina (though he does prove so in Japan), but this study will demonstrate that it did. During the late seventeenth century, monastic communities in south-coastal China organized missions to port cities in the Asian maritime zone, in an atmosphere of weak state authority, where they built temples and monasteries with the material wealth and political sanction of Chinese merchant colonists and local elites in host societies. They were inspired by the same renewal of Chan Buddhism that induced missions to Japan, and relied upon the very same patrons—shipping merchants from China's seafaring province of Fujian—who sponsored evangelizing missions to Japan.

These missions exemplify facets of Buddhism thought to have vanished with the Silk Road: a missionary religion propagating branch temples through long-distance networks of merchant colonies; forming satellite monastic communities within host societies; weaving its institutions into the social fabric of the social groups it encountered; and influencing economic, cultural, and political behavior there.[9] The monk's place in markets and courts also recalls models of religious strategy in merchant "diasporas" and state formation that has revolutionized historical research on the origins of the modern world, even though Buddhism remains absent from this general literature.[10] Unlike Japan, however, these missions strengthened a process of frontier expansion in Cochinchina, by contributing to the development of commercial centers, social integration, and state formation thanks to its networked temples and syncretic ideology.

In their missionary capacity these monks resembled their European contemporaries, who were deeply implicated in the causes of commerce, colonies, and empire as a means to support their evangelical cause. These missionary monks differed from their European counterparts, however, by their lack of an imperial sponsor at home. In this sense, they resembled Chinese merchants overseas, whom Wang Gungwu described as "merchants without empire."[11] Just like their merchant counterparts, these Chinese missionaries hardly sat helpless in their host societies. Nor were they loathe combining their agenda with the commercial, colonial, or imperial interests of other cultural groups when it suited their desired ends. In this sense, their activities seem comparable to those of Christian clerics in the post-1500 era, for the actions of these missionaries contributed to a bond of inter-patronage among monk, merchant, and monarch that defined a new set of ethno-historical potentials wherever they sailed.

Buddhist Missions and the Institutional Anchoring of the Fujianese-Ming Loyalist Trading World

In order to understand the evolution of Chinese monastic expansion overseas, one simply follows the merchants and their ships. The first Chinese missions to Cochinchina began with the backing of shipping merchants based in the South China Sea who captained the large deep sea merchant ships that sailed north from the Taiwan Straits region to Nagasaki and south to Hoi An during the seventeenth century, trading in China's southern coastal ports in between (*Maps 4.1, 7.1, 7.2, and 8.1*). This merchant society developed from a longer evolution of private syndicated sea trade that culminated in the 1640s with the commercial empire of the Zheng clan, whose armed merchant fleets, based in south China, Taiwan, or on the islands that lay between, dominated the stream of Chinese carrier trade that flowed between Cochinchina and Japan, centering on the strategic Taiwan Straits off Fujian. Commercial power translated into military power after 1644, when the Manchus toppled the Ming imperial house and declared a new Qing Dynasty for China. The Zheng clan took up the banner of "Ming Loyalism" to resist the Qing from China's southeastern littoral and the island of Taiwan, until the last Zheng overlord surrendered to the Qing in 1683. Their power rested on control of the Taiwan Straits and Chinese merchant colonies overseas, and on the Fujianese trading world that had its origin in the ports of Fujian province, but was inclusive of places like Japan, Southeast Asia, and other locales where Fujianese conducted business. The geographical logic of this Fujianese, Ming Loyalist trading world of the late 1600s is not hard to see: draw a straight line on any modern map between Nagasaki and Hoi An and it forms a tangent with the province's curved coastline.[12]

The Fujian merchants had good reasons for recruiting monks to Nagasaki. Monks were important to merchants, not only for the religious rites they provided and the prestige they lent, but also for the cultural conformity and social integrity they could promote, important to the efficacy of diasporic trade communities. In the long run these Buddhist institutions would migrate into their host societies, sometimes with important long-term consequences. In the short term, however, they developed in order to strengthen socio-cultural bonds among the Fujianese merchants and seafarers themselves. How they did so can be seen in two ports, Nagasaki in Japan and Hoi An in Cochinchina.

Nagasaki (Japan)

Between the 1620s and 1680s merchants invested in the construction of three out of Nagasaki's "Four Chinese Temples." Zhen Dan, a Jiangsu monk who originally had been a wealthy merchant, founded the first temple, Kofuku-ji, in the 1620s.[13] Anointed disciples raised money, appropriated land, recruited monks, supervised the construction of temples and other religious structures, and reaffirmed traditions, the sum of which bestowed legitimacy and status upon merchant and monastic communities within Nagasaki's Chinese quarter.

Beginning in the 1650s, patricians of the Chinese merchant community in Nagasaki recruited monks from China. They did so in order to expand monastic networks or maintain sectarian links with affiliate monasteries in China. The merchant community recruited monks from Jiangsu and Fujian provinces in China to oversee the design, construction and maintenance of temples, and to lead monasteries once temple construction was completed.[14] Given the renewed importance of Dharma lineage in seventeenth-century Chan Buddhism in South China, the patrons of these monasteries sought masters who objectively demonstrated genealogical ties to reputable masters in China.[15] One famous example of this process is a monk of the Huangbo Linji school of Southern Chan named Yinyuan Longqi, known to Japanese as Ingen Ryuki, the founder of a popular Obaku Rinzai (that is, Huangbo Linji) branch of Zen (Chan) Buddhism.[16] Like most of his merchant patrons, Yinyuan hailed from Fuqing Prefecture in Fujian. In 1654 he and thirty of his disciples boarded a merchant ship bound for Nagasaki at the invitation of patrons of Kofuku Temple and at the behest of another Fujianese, the powerful merchant-adventurer Zheng Chenggong (aka Koxinga), who asked Yinyuan to deliver a message to the Tokugawa shogun asking support for the Zheng clan's Ming Loyalist cause.[17] As was the case among many of the Chinese religious, artistic, and other specialists who merchant leaders recruited to serve their maritime colonies, Yinyuan elected to remain in Japan. By 1661, the master had founded a new monastery, *Mampuku-ji.* He did so with the support of Japanese patrons, including the Tokugawa shoguns, who provided funds as well as a land grant. Not long after his arrival, Yinyuan began accepting Japanese disciples. Obaku grew quickly. By the time the Manpuku-ji's abbotage passed from Chinese to Japanese hands in 1736, it had firmly established itself within Japanese society. Today it is one of Japan's largest sects.[18]

There are other examples of Chinese monks like Yinyuan. Some came in response to political developments in China, some at the invitation of Japanese, many in response to invitations by the Tokugawa court, often mediated by Chinese or Sino-Japanese living in Nagasaki. All of these Chinese monks came to Japan through Nagasaki, on merchant ships. Some monks sojourned, while others settled or even migrated further into Japanese territory and society. For example, Mu'an Xingtao, who traveled to Nagasaki in 1655 at his master's behest, helped to popularize Obaku by founding monasteries and recruiting Japanese novices. In addition to leading Mampuku-ji, Mu'an founded twenty-four temples throughout Japan, including Zuisho-ji in Edo, the capital. Through these temples, he held ordination rituals that established Obaku's long-term presence. Mu'an and other Obaku masters traveled to Edo as guests of the Japanese court, as did monks from Linji and Caodong branches of Chan. They welcomed Japanese disciples soon after their establishment in Japan, devotees like Tetsugen Doko, Tetsugyo Doki and others who helped lay Obaku foundations outside the walls of the Nagasaki's Chinese merchant quarter. Within a century Japanese held all Obaku abbacies and the sect had fully integrated into Japanese society.[19]

Chinese merchants were important to the Tokugawa shoguns not only as a revenue resource, but also as a cultural channel, as they recruited a host of skilled workers besides monks to Japan. Just as the Confucian thought that changed Japan in the eighteenth century could be traced to seventeenth-century Chinese migrants like Zhu Shunshui, Japanese Buddhism developed new schools like that of Yinyuan in response to a new brand of "missionary Buddhism" that informed many Southern Chan sects. Moreover, sources suggest that the hard line between Confucians like Zhu, Nagasaki merchants, and Buddhist monks wasn't so firm. For example, Zhu Shunshui corresponded with the merchant Wei Jiushi, a prominent shipping merchant in the Vietnamese-Japanese carrier trade, who in turn patronized Yinyuan's religious community and his temple building enterprises.[20] Within Chan missionary society, many Southern Chan lineages that sent monks to Japan long embraced the concept of a trinity synthesizing the "Three Teachings," called *sanjiaoyi*, that grew especially popular among Fujianese in the sixteenth century. It did not take Fujianese mariners long, therefore, to carry their hybrid practices overseas, and thereby help transmit a variety of beliefs and practices normally associated with Daoism or Neo-Confucianism to Japan.[21] Because of this, Chan monks acted as a medium for transmitting a host of nominally non-Buddhist religious ideas—not to mention a wide variety of cultural practices—to Japan, as they would to Cochinchina.

In addition to temples dedicated to Buddha, Chan missionaries and their Chinese patrons in Nagasaki sponsored the construction of three Chinese deity temples: one to the warrior god Guandi; a second to the goddess/Bodhisattva of Compassion, Guanyin, and a third to the sea goddess Mazu, also known as Tianhou Shengmu, the Empress of Heaven. Guandi and Guanyin were generally supported by merchants, while sailors patronized Mazu. These subordinate deity temples were a regular feature of all monasteries that seafaring Fujianese patronized, in port cities or offshore island enclaves.[22] Not surprisingly, all the monasteries involved in this story housed Guanyin Goddess of Mercy temples, while many Buddhist monastic networks sponsored Mazu temples as well. The temples grew even more popular after 1684, when the Qing court strengthened its patronage of the Boddhisattva Guanyin and began to sponsor the Mazu sea goddess as the "Empress of Heaven," in an effort to gain control over Chinese maritime society.[23]

Hoi An (Cochinchina)

The same process developed in Cochinchina during the seventeenth century. Wherever they settled, Chinese merchants funded the building of Buddhist temples, as well as altars dedicated to Guandi, Guanyin, and Mazu. Monasteries provided a vital institutional complement to kin and other associations that Fujianese merchants utilized in order to create a lasting diasporic network across maritime Asia. Capable of broader social ties than family or native-place institutions, monasteries provided Chinese overseas with a complimentary institutional interface among merchant, monarch, and monk. In this way monasticism helped Fujian merchants collectively secure their controlling share of Cochinchinese commercial enterprises, maritime trade, and maritime shipping, which in turn enhanced their mercantile power vis-à-vis the Cochinchinese state.

The Fujianese, Ming Loyalist merchants of Cochinchina prayed to the same gods as their Nagasaki counterparts. The Chinese monk Dashan, who journeyed to Cochinchina in 1695 and 1696, describes two temples in the port town of Hoi An: the Guandi or Chinese God of War temple, "where the Fujianese merchants' guild [*huiguan*] met" and, next to that, inside Di Da (or Maitreya) Monastery, a Guanyin or Goddess of Mercy temple, where merchants came to pray. Both sat directly across from Hoi An's main market.[24] The Guandi temple is the oldest temple in Hoi An's Chinese quarter, built in 1653, but the god's presence is much older: the structure replaced an earlier Guandi hall built years earlier. Guanyin and earlier incarnations of the *Avalokitesvara* sea goddess had been part of the fabric of local society in the region for centuries, and enjoyed the patronage of Vietnamese and Chinese alike. Local inscriptions also verify that a Mazu temple stood along the riverside street of the "Tang" or southern Chinese during Dashan's time, in a "hut of waddle and thatch."[25] Numerous other deities populated the Chinese quarter, neighboring communities, the hinterland, and the offshore islands to serve Chinese merchants and mariners, but none were as important as this trinity in serving the social functions of Fujian's merchant society in Cochinchina. Together, Guandi, Guanyin, and Mazu formed the primary patron deities in Hoi An, and in all Cochinchina's Chinese enclaves.[26]

A principle center of sea trade long before the first Vietnamese arrived, Cochinchina could boast Buddhist temples and Chinese masters whose presence predated the kingdom's founders by a millennium.[27] These temples and their monastic communities played an important role in promoting the patron saints of Chinese merchant society in Cochinchina. Set among coastal sands, merchants supported a number of ancient grottoes, temples, and monasteries in the religiously important Marble Mountains [*Ngu Hanh Son*, literally "Mountains of the Five Elements"] north of Hoi An, Cochinchina's principle port of trade for deep sea carriers in this era. Back in Hoi An, the town's Chinese merchants, probably Ming Loyalists, sponsored two monasteries during the mid-1600s: Long An, built in the old Guandi temple sometime after 1653, and Quang Yen, established before 1680.[28] However, Hoi An's elders built the city's other important monasteries within a window of only ten years, between 1688 and 1698, at a time when the kingdom's longtime permanent Chinese residents were busy renegotiating their relationship with the Cochinchinese state by formalizing their political identity as "Ming Loyalists" or *Minh Huong* (literally "Ming incense" to indicate fealty), in order to distinguish themselves from their Qing subject compatriots who began to descend on Cochinchinese shores after the Zheng defeat.[29]

Across from the Guandi hall, merchants sponsored a monastery dedicated to a bodhisattva popular among merchants, Maitreya—commonly known as the Laughing or Future Buddha—whom Vietnamese call *Di Da*. It is not clear when patrons constructed Di Da Monastery, though local lore credits the widow of a wealthy Ming Loyalist merchant who donated lands around the Guandi hall in 1688, and whom the town still venerates as its principle benefactor.[30] Nor is it clear who oversaw the development of the temple and its grounds, though sources suggest that it may have been a master from Guangzhou named Xinglian Guohong, who began the restoration of Tam Thai, an ancient monastery in the Marble Mountains, soon after.[31] The patricians of Hoi An also raised funds for three more new monasteries in the 1690s: Chuc Thanh in 1694-1695, Kim Son in 1696-1697, and Phuoc Lam in 1698.[32] With the foundation of Van Duc several years later, the principle monasteries associated with Hoi An were completed.[33]

This wave of Buddhist temple building was not confined to Hoi An, of course. At the same time that the Fujian merchants sponsored temple-building enterprises in Hoi An, their compatriots funded building activities in Cochinchina's other port towns, wherever Ming Loyalist villages formed: in Thanh Ha, Hoi An, Quang Nghia, Qui Nhon, Nha Trang, Dong Nai, and Ha Tien (*Map 8.1*).[34]

In each case, Chinese masters or first-generation Vietnamese disciples of Chinese masters oversaw the construction or renovation of Buddhist temples and monasteries. The best known example may be the monk Yuanzhao, better known to Vietnamese as Nguyen Thieu. According to his biographers, Yuanzhao and several disciples left China in 1677, and "traveled by Chinese commercial freighter to Binh Dinh," a port city in Cochinchina where Ming Loyalist Chinese were settling in large numbers. In 1679, Yuanzhao founded a monastery with a temple popular with sea traders, which he named Thap Thap Di Da, "Ten Stupa Maitreya Monastery," named for the ten Cham stupas that sat behind the walls of the complex. Called into the service of the court, Yuanzhao traveled to the royal capital Phu Xuan (in modern-day Hue) in 1683, and he soon rose to prominence among the monks residing there. During his years as court favorite, he founded two important monasteries, Quoc Am and Ha Trung, and restored the capital's oldest and most prestigious monastery, Thien Mu. Allegedly, he also sailed to China in 1688 on behalf of the Nguyen court in order to gather Buddhist images, sutras, records of the Chan patriarchs, and perhaps most importantly, other Chan masters. For reasons that remain unclear, Yuanzhao left the capital in 1694 and sailed south, resettling among Ming Loyalists in the frontier region of the Mekong Delta, where he founded more temples, most importantly Kim Cang. Some speculate he fled there in disgrace, but have offered unconvincing circumstantial evidence to prove this.[35] The master died there in 1729, and was thereafter acclaimed by the Nguyen court as one of the country's most venerable masters. Today, Yuanzhao's school of Chan, called the Nguyen Thieu school, is the largest Chan school in Vietnam today.[36]

As with the case of Yinyuan, dharma heirs who migrated with their masters from China to Cochinchina established their own religious communities, and worked to popularize their master's teachings among Cochinchina's local inhabitants.[37] They also tutored numerous Vietnamese disciples, who themselves established a number of temples throughout the country. For example, the Caodong Chan monk Shilian Dashan (better known as *Thach Liem* in Vietnam) sailed to Cochinchina in 1695-1696 by invitation of Cochinchina's reigning lord, Nguyen Phuc Chu, allegedly in order to "correct the Dharma" there.[38] Once there, the Nguyen ruler asked Dashan to remain in Vietnam as the abbot of Thien Mu, the primary monastery of the realm. While there, a seventeen-year-old Vietnamese boy named Lieu Quan came to the monastery and asked to become a novice of Dashan. Allegedly, "Lieu Quan was influenced considerably by Dashan as he practiced ... the precepts of a novice, under his guidance."[39] In the years after Dashan returned to China, Lieu studied with a number of Yuanzhao's dharma heirs of the Linji branch of Chan, and then went on to found a second school of Chan in Vietnam, which soon grew to become the largest Buddhist school in southern Vietnam (and the first founded by a Vietnamese).

It is likely that, as monastic networks expanded, building new temples and increasing the number of clergy, their administrators looked to merchant networks to supply their material needs. The technological complexity of building temples made a variety of demands on those who wished to build them. Monks who traveled afar in order to renovate a monastery's buildings and grounds, organize an estate's structure, or build sangha and patronage anew, faced a complex set of organizational, fiscal, technological, and, all too often, political challenges that demanded the diverse kinds of specialized skills that overseeing any large scale enterprise or institution might require. Masters often possessed a variety of artistic and technical skills important to the missionary enterprise. But the demands of temple building enterprises also required a host of skilled lay workers who could only come from China, sometimes only Fujian. Chinese temples in Japan like Mampuku-ji, for example, included not only monks but carpenters, sculptors, painters, cooks, tailors, and shoemakers. Some of them sojourned, while others stayed.[40]

Moreover, monks and patrons placed a high premium on the reproduction of Chinese cultural forms, making it necessary to import expertise from home monasteries overseas.[41] Yuanzhao's disciples chanted sutras in Fuqing dialect, chanted to Fujianese style music, prayed in Fujianese style halls, and wore robes and shoes reminiscent of the Huangbo monks of their principle monastery in the Fujianese district of Fuqing.[42] The sect governed itself by a monastic code "that reflected Chinese practices of the day, and which sought to preserve the character of the group." Tones of cultural chauvinism often took on a missionary zeal during the late seventeenth century; patrons of Dashan celebrated the overseas mission of their master, whose enterprise promised to "spread the moralizing influence of the Son of Heaven [the emperor of China]" through his travels.[43] Missionary masters and their disciples—whether monk, merchant or artisan—therefore traveled as a kind of cultural junket aboard the merchant ships who carried them, bringing a complete package of Chinese (in this case mainly Fujianese) high culture.

An abbot may have benefited enormously from local patronage and gifts, but even if his monastery were well endowed he would have relied in some way on regular forms of trade in order to supply his monastery's ritual needs or architectural development. The likelihood of such a monastic-driven commerce becomes all the more plausible when we consider the fact that a lucrative portion of the maritime trade between China and places like Hoi An had been in the raw materials of ritual—precious woods, gems, stones, etc.—in exchange for finished ritual goods like incense, sutras, and statuary. In other words, monasteries generated their own exchange economy.[44] The heartland of Cochinchina, once the domain of the pre-1500 Champa realm, had a long history of long distance trafficking of items, including exotic commodities that came from the Cham upstream highlands, the source of the premium aromatic known to Chinese merchants as the "floating incense" (C: *chenxiang*; V: *tram huong*). Here other Southeast Asian and multi-ethnic Muslim, Hindu, and Buddhist seafarers and sojourning merchants had long ago assimilated into the local coastal society.[45] Under Vietnamese rule, the region exported the same raw materials.[46] At the same time, locally based Chinese merchants provided the wider Mahayanist world with a variety of devotional objects, religious art, and classical literature produced in China and other religious items, as well as ritual raw materials like the Cochinchinese incense wood *ky nam huong* that Japanese burned inside and outside their temples.[47]

Functions of Missionary Buddhism Among the Merchants of Cochinchina

Monasteries have long served a variety of social and economic functions. A close physical and social proximity between merchants and monks was a common feature among maritime Fujianese society. Hoi An temples were central to the cause of community social integration and cultural continuity. In Cochinchina, as in other Fujian mercantile communities from the late Ming era, temples served as a meeting space for merchants. They were often, though not always, housed in or adjacent to monasteries, and were typically under the care of resident monks. Temples were central to the organizational success of smuggling and trade networks that defied imperial bans. Temples housed the compacts regulating trade and societal norms, property, customs revenues, as well as the important archive of the community's government and commerce. Monasteries served important social welfare functions, by serving the indigent and the ill.[48]

Buddhist masters offered religious authority that helped to legitimize institutional arrangements within merchant society as a whole, and between individual merchant colonies and their local sponsors. Sometimes, Chinese missions and their merchant patrons looked to Buddhism's trans-cultural authority to enhance their prestige across cultural or political lines. In Guanyin merchants found a useful medium. In the Buddhist Goddess of Mercy merchants found a deity amenable to all Buddhists, and thus able to legitimize trans-cultural agreements made across social, cultural, and political boundaries. In Hoi An, signs of cross-cultural patronage of the bodhisattva among Chinese merchants and Vietnamese elites appear as early as 1640.[49] The Vietnamese had used Guanyin to legitimize their claims to holy sites of the Chams who had long before held dominion over Cochinchinese territory, and whose cultural descendents still populated much of it.[50] The goddess provided a logical bridge between the two locally prominent cultural groups. In Vietnam as elsewhere, Chinese merchants looked to monks to protect popular non-Buddhist deities by sanctifying them, thanks to the trans-cultural authority they enjoyed among Chan host societies. Chan syncretic doctrine permitted the integration of new forms of religiosity. In Nagasaki, for example, the leaders of the Chinese quarter patronized the construction of Buddhist monasteries around existing Guandi and Mazu temples in order to protect them from suspicious Tokugawa officials.[51]

This protection also provided opportunities for new relationships between merchants and deities to evolve. To illustrate, reports of Mazu altars in monasteries and monastic worship of the sea goddess grew increasingly regular as the seventeenth century progressed.[52] As abbot of Changshou Monastery in Guangzhou, Dashan supervised one of the most important Mazu temples in the regions of Chinese sea trade, the A Ma Temple of Macau, and likely played a role in the ceremonies elevating the sea goddess to Chinese imperial status in 1684.[53] When China instituted a new trade system, sea traders responded by organizing a new institution, the guild or *huiguan*, and adopted Mazu as its patron deity.[54] Dashan was the first to notice the new sea merchants' guild overseas when he traveled to Hoi An in 1695; the Fujian merchant group had established themselves in the town's Guandi Hall.[55] Two years later, however, they helped found a new monastery, named Kim Son, and installed the guild's first Mazu temple there.[56] Within a decade or so, Hoi An's merchants built a separate guild hall and began to venerate the goddess there, outside the monastery.[57] Until then, however, Buddhism had a role to play in legitimizing a new deity and a new institution in Chinese merchant society overseas.

At the same time they created the new guilds, patricians in Chinese merchant colonies like Hoi An and Nagasaki also promoted the construction of public cemeteries, and looked to Chan monks like Dashan to ensure their orthodox construction. The construction of standardized graveyard architecture typically accompanied the creation of the post-1683 merchant guild or *huiguan*, according to Kwangching Liu.[58] The construction of graveyards, and with them the institution of a Chinese orthopraxy in death ritual, contributed to the evolution of more permanent Chinese identity in diasporic merchant communities overseas. Buddhist monks played an important role in this development.

During his sojourn in Hoi An during 1695-1696, the Chinese monk Dashan performed a number of services to the merchant community of Hoi An. He administered precepts to new devotees who couldn't make it to the previous ordination at the Cochinchinese capital of Phu Xuan (Hue). He wrote a tract on behalf of his disciple Xinglian, now Cochinchina's royal preceptor, in order to help raise funds for the renovation of the Di Da Monastery. The head of the Fujian merchants' guild asked Dashan to draft an inscription to dedicate their hall, and he complied. He was also asked to inscribe a message to monks repairing a key road linking Hoi An with the Nguyen capital.[59]

Most significant among his many services to Hoi An, however, was the impassioned plea that Dashan wrote to the community, asking them to contribute to the construction of an "orthodox" Chinese graveyard. The piece reveals the role that monks like Dashan sought to play in the task of promoting the institutional structures of cultural cohesion that successfully kept Fujianese sojourners and migrants culturally oriented towards a normative ideal represented by China in general and Fujian in particular. Indeed, it is more a warning of the terrible cultural, even mortal, consequences awaiting the sea trading community should they abandon the cultural institutions of kin, native place, and faith. It is worth quoting at length from Dashan's memoir:

... Everywhere there are bones [of Chinese] left to the sun and dew by those [abandoned souls] who left their families without returning. Learning this I flushed with emotion, and I enjoined the preceptor [his disciple, Xinglian] to speak to the leaders of the Fujian guest [i.e., merchant] quarter to levy for land for a public cemetery to receive orphaned bones. This is the impression I made [for the cemetery]:

[Whenever] someone among the celebrated living suffers death, relatives and friends are typically moved to inter their bones and bury their flesh, as a testimony to their humanity. Look closely at the bones left to the elements, [and] listen to the indigent itinerant, who turned [his] back on his [ancestral] fields and left home, leading himself who-knows-where, without reason or purpose, and no one [that is, a relative] able to accompany them.

In the inscription's prose, the indigent itinerant merchant who abandoned his moral obligations to his Chinese kinsmen lost his very sense of place, purpose, identity, and the welfare security that cultural institutions like family provided. Such uprootedness in the mortal world, however, only raised the specter of a soul condemned to endless wandering in the afterlife:

A day dawns [when you] kneel before death, and only then recall that day when your family bonds were broken, as distant as the heavens the seas . . . Orphaned spirit, weep. [You] dream of following your family . . . [Yet your] bones just scorch in a smoldering lot, entrusted to some "expert" from the [Cochinchinese] countryside.[60]

Of all the possible consequences that could rate as frightening as eternal abandonment, Dashan chose to focus on the Vietnamese ritual specialist. By implication, cemetery architecture and funerary rite might not be "properly" done without the appropriate religious specialist—that is, someone *not* from the "Chinese countryside." Following the logic of this inscription, the individual dangers of leaving China's physical boundaries—with its daily risks of shipwreck, violence, and disease—were nothing compared to the supernatural consequences that awaited merchants and seafarers who left its social or cultural boundaries and "entrusted" their fate to host societies. Cemeteries thus served a vital function to every colony within the Fujianese merchant diaspora, as important reminders of cultural ancestry and thus as markers of identity, as part of a larger cultural strategy that relied upon institutions of kin, culture, native place, and faith.[61] Buddhist monasteries provided the appropriate ritual specialists, who enforced normative practice and identity. They imparted a uniform Fujian cultural logic across vast distances, as this was vital to the survival of the diasporic mercantile community. In this way, Buddhist death ritual helped give "representational shape" to Chinese merchant society overseas as it begin to assume a more durable form.[62] But, once established, it was inevitable that communities of monks would transcend the merchant communities that first sponsored them, and settle into host societies, to pursue their own religious agendas.

Missionaries and the Agendas of an Expansionist State

Understanding the role of Buddhist temples in proliferating trade networks also touches upon their function as a means to state building in host societies. The early Nguyen rulers, forced into unfamiliar terrain and engaged in a heated feud with a rival Vietnamese overlord to the north,[63] strengthened themselves in their still ethnically diverse fief and sought ways to survive, and then to flourish. Reliable trade was crucial to their establishment as a separate state. During the early seventeenth century they successfully competed against Macao and Manila for a position within the clandestine trade between China and Japan (China had lifted its ban on trade in 1683, with the exception of Japan), a trade originally operated by Japanese, but after 1639 mostly by Chinese from Fujian.

Two events brought the Nguyen Lords and Chinese merchants together. First, Fujianese shipping merchants all but monopolized Japan's overseas carrier trade almost immediately after the Tokugawa shogunate severed Japanese links abroad between 1635 and 1639. Foremost among them was Zheng Zhilong, who secured a monopoly over Nagasaki's shipping in 1641.[64] Then, a decade later, the Manchus conquered China—an event that for South China really only ended in 1683 with the defeat of the Ming Loyalist's maritime regime. Zheng Chenggong's Ming Loyalist resistance survived largely as long as it dominated commercial traffic through the Taiwan Strait and fielded a large merchant fleet to maintain commercial links with Japan and Southeast Asia. An important trade partner to the Zheng clan was "Jiaozhi," that is, Cochinchina.[65] The Zheng clan could then invest profits from trade overseas and their smuggling enterprises into Fujian military and state development. As the Ming cause disintegrated in the 1670s and 1680s, the Zheng overlord and his government made plans to evacuate their longtime base on Taiwan for the Mekong Delta, then on the eastern periphery of a very weak and fragmented Cambodian kingdom.[66] Most supporters abandoned the plan when the Zheng patriarch instead surrendered to Qing forces in 1683, but two remnant fleets settled in the great river delta between 1679 and 1682, allegedly with the blessing of the Nguyen overlord.[67] Sources suggest that a struggle for control of the region ensued into the 1690s, but ended with the establishment of Vietnamese supremacy no later than 1698, when the Nguyen created their first formal government presence there with the creation of Gia Dinh Garrison in 1698.[68]

By this time Ming Loyalist Chinese settled in the Mekong region were willing to lend their political allegiance to the Nguyen. The Nguyen in turn incorporated the Ming Loyalists settled throughout their realm into a new and distinct set of enclaves, the Ming Loyalist or Minh Huong villages. This allowed the Ming Loyalists to maintain their sociological and cultural ties to China, while beginning to acculturate into Vietnamese society, by simultaneously restricting their political loyalties to the Nguyen overlord. In return, Ming Loyalists received a host of formal privileges. They staffed the Nguyen court, oversaw foreign trade out of Nguyen ports, and handled all the business of control and transactions with Qing-loyal Chinese expatriates (called *Thanh nhan* or "Qing people") who returned to overseas trade after the maritime ban was lifted in 1684. So effective were these Ming Loyalists that both community leaders and the Nguyen court had to insert special provisions regulating membership, as many sojourning Chinese endlessly sought entrée into the community. The Ming Loyalists had metamorphosed into a "minority elite" within Cochinchina.[69]

Temple building, and the structural implications of networking between primary and new secondary temples helped the Nguyen court to harness the Ming Loyalists' commercial, military, and other forms of power to their own agenda of political expansion. Wherever the Nguyen and their minority elite established military offices, state offices, and markets, they engaged in temple building. At times these endeavors were initiated by the Nguyen court. More often these enterprises were the endeavors of village elders in Ming Loyalist villages, leaders of Fujian merchant guild halls, and other local Chinese and Vietnamese wealthy benefactors. Still, royal patronage mattered as well, if only for the legitimacy that a dedicatory plaque or celebratory inscription might lend to a newly built or restored temple. Even still, Buddhist monks and Ming Loyalists who spearheaded these temple building projects required the approval of Lord Nguyen and local Vietnamese officials in order to purchase land, build temples, and most of all, to appoint abbots.[70]

The Nguyen lords could have turned such a situation into an opportunity to insert their royal presence among Ming Loyalist communities, by having loyal Buddhist abbots appoint and approve the assignments of loyalist monks to serve local temples, the better to local clergy agendas consistent with those of the Vietnamese court. This would have helped the court, in agency with the Buddhist sects they patronized, facilitate better control over Ming Loyalists and, through them, expatriate Chinese. Controlling religious institutions by heavily patronizing Southern Chan schools provided an opportunity to transform these autonomous, potentially subversive communities with substantial external links, notably the militarized Chinese merchant colonists, into a colonial vanguard for the Nguyen state. In this way, the Nguyen state brought new territories and populations into the Cochinchinese fold "due to the agency of what we would now call 'overseas Chinese' who were already [settled in the Mekong] before them."[71] This Buddhist cultural initiative, based in temple patronage, co-opted settled Chinese agriculturalists in the Mekong delta region as subordinates to the Ming Loyalist minority elite, whose power was based in their control over Cochinchina's ports-of-trade.

This seventeenth-century patronage of Buddhist temples and monasteries and local deity temples served the Nguyen lords' primary need to control the wider demographic shifts underway in their frontier regions. It is important to remember here that local friction derived from the immigration of Vietnamese and Chinese into coastal and lowland territories long cultivated by Cham and Khmer speakers. By 1708, when Mac Cuu, the ruler of Ha Tien, declared his loyalty to the Nguyen, Vietnamese dynastic rule for the first time extended to the Gulf of Siam, consuming the southern half of historical Cambodia. By the 1690s tensions peaked among Cochinchina's indigenous inhabitants.[72] The Nguyen court preempted this volatile combination that could have produced rebellion along cultural, religious, or political lines. Buddhist monks offered Lord Nguyen greater legitimacy, since Buddhism provided one of the few common bonds within this diverse, hybridizing society, especially among Vietnamese and Ming Loyalist colonists. The Nguyen lord's preface to Dashan's travelogue suggest that the Cochinchinese monarch submitted to the Chan master in order to establish lineage authority over all the monks of his realm, and to present himself as a *cakravartan*, an "enlightened monarch." The lord who presided over the most critical phase of these transformations, Nguyen Phuc Chu, used the posthumous royal title *Minh Vuong* or "Enlightened King," an allusion to Buddhist kings of antiquity and a reflection of the commitment that he and his forefathers made to Buddhism as something close to a religion.[73] There are indications, too, that the syncretic practices of the Chan missionaries offered the Nguyen the opportunity to appeal to diverse constituencies through Confucianist, Daoist and various other local modes as well, which broadened their appealed to other targeted ethnic or social groups. Chan monks had effectively incorporated one sea goddess, Mazu, and they incorporated others just as easily, as in the case of Thien Y A Nha, the sea goddess of Vietnamese who had settled in the former Cham regions.[74]

In promoting this orthodoxy among merchants, commoners, and rural elite, the Nguyen court created another problem, that of controlling the monks, including those who were the local agents of the court-sponsored sects. As was repeatedly the case in neighboring Myanmar, where the hierarchical networking between central and secondary temples regularly challenged the authority of secular authority, similarly monks and monastic communities could potentially challenge Nguyen political authority.[75] The Nguyen apparently sought to resolve this potential for conflict by selective cooptation. Early efforts by the Nguyen court to establish an enduring court-centered orthodoxy failed. Royal patronage of the Zhulin school that began in the 1670s met with failure, when the state preceptor departed for the Trinh north in 1683. The reigning lord, Nguyen Phuc Tan, recruited Yuanzhao, leader of the rival Linji sect, and a Chinese presided as court master for the first time. Within a decade Nguyen Phuc Tan's grandson, Nguyen Phuc Chu, faced a number of political crises that threatened the stability of his realm. Almost immediately after he ascended to power in 1691, in 1692, Lord Nguyen suppressed a rebellion in Champa. Less than two years later, during the lunar New Year of 1694, two of the lord's cousins tried to overthrow him. The lord prevailed, arrested the cousins and their conspirators, and executed them. Then in 1695 a Chinese merchant named *Linh* and a reported follower of Yuanzhao named Quang Phu led a failed revolt against Nguyen rule that spread to the region south of Hoi An where Dashan was visiting.[76] In each case, monks and/or merchants were implicated.

Some have argued that Yuanzhao himself may have been involved in two of these plots, and to avoid punishment fled south to the Mekong delta. In these accounts, with the Linji sect in disgrace, the Nguyen court replaced Yuanzhao with a master from a rival sect, the Caodong master Shilian Dashan.[77] More likely, however, Yuanzhao traveled to the southern frontier in service to his Nguyen lord rather than in defiance. After the transfer of royal patronage to the Caodong sect, Lord Nguyen did not purge any of Yuanzhao's disciples from their abbacies, keeping them in positions of both important religious and political importance in some of the most volatile regions of the kingdom. This included Quang Nghai, where Yuanzhao's powerful disciple Minghai presided, and where in 1695 another alleged Yuanzhao disciple led a failed revolt against the Nguyen court.[78] In fact, as Yuanzhao migrated south to the Mekong, his disciples built new temples in troubled places with the blessings of the court.

In the meantime, Lord Nguyen used the monk Dashan to implement greater central authority over the monks of his realm. Dashan presided over the conversion of thousands of monks, officials, and other important subjects to the precepts of his peculiar brand of Caodong Chan, which contained within it many elements of Linji thought. Lord Nguyen offered himself as the master's first dharma disciple.[79] In effect, Dashan conferred supreme dharma authority over his royal disciple, because the master claimed to be a twenty-ninth generation dharma disciple, placing Lord Nguyen as thirtieth generation disciple a full four generations ahead of leading monks in the kingdom, including Yuanzhao, who could only claim status as a thirty-fourth generation dharma master. It appears that the Chinese masters may have been part of a larger, more sophisticated scheme hatched by their Vietnamese benefactor and disciple.

Thus, by compounding dharma authority with more regular means of control like patronage, Lord Nguyen secured control over his kingdom's fast growing, fast changing monastic community. Religious strategies like these helped the Nguyen lord reinforce his efforts to grasp effective, legitimate authority over a society in a moment of tremendous flux. The establishment of a new monastic order in Cochinchina offered the Nguyen a religious means by which they could first reconfirm their legitimacy over their multi-ethnic realm, and to pursue greater social regulation and cultural uniformity in agency with select Buddhist sects. In this way, the Nguyen encouraged native, non-Vietnamese subjects to adopt Sino-Vietnamese socio-political norms. The Nguyen rulers utilized temples as logical means of institutional accommodation and control over a variety of mixed ethnic and expatriate communities. The resulting wider and more inclusive cultural uniformity helped him to dictate court authority over institutional Buddhism in Cochinchina as well.

Monks, Diplomacy and Regional Legitimacy

These missionary monks of the late seventeenth century also helped the Nguyen court attempt to negotiate new relationships with the outside world. Monks had previously functioned as prominent mediators and diplomats in the interstate relations between the Chinese and Vietnamese kingdoms initially during the Silk Road era.[80] In the seventeenth century, monks occasionally assumed an informal, meditative role. One reason the monk Yinyuan traveled to Japan in 1654 was to act on the behalf of Ming Loyalists under the maritime privateer Zheng Chenggong, in an unsuccessful appeal to Japan's Tokugawa shogun for help. Dashan appears to have played an indirect role in a similar failed effort, when Nguyen Phuc Chu sent an embassy to Guangzhou in hopes of launching an initiative to overturn Cochinchina's outsider status in China's interstate relations. This move would have helped the Nguyen realm to adapt to the new realities that set in after the Qing Dynasty consolidated its rule over South China in 1683, and subsequently regularized overseas trade based in China's ports. The changed international and domestic climate forced the Nguyen to seek diplomatic recognition from China, both to negate a potential Qing military incursion as also to promote the Nguyen realm's commercial interests. The king sought diplomatic contact with the Qing government through the reestablishment of monastic connections with the assistance of Dashan, who had intimate ties to China's gentry and officialdom within the society of Guangzhou, China's most important port city in the south. Nguyen Phuc Chu was already considering this during Dashan's 1695 visit.[81]

Evidence to support this hypothesis can be found in a collection of reports by a northern Vietnamese official dated 1776, which contains material that document a diplomatic mission the Nguyen court sent to Guangzhou in 1702. The embassy appears to have been conceived originally by Dashan, after he had anointed Lord Nguyen dharma master in 1695.[82] The mission was led by Huang Zhen, a Fujianese lay disciple of Dashan and a former student of the Chinese National Academy (*Guo Zijian*), and Xingche, a monastic disciple. The entourage allegedly included "some of Dashan's old friends from Vietnam" as well. They had arrived aboard a merchant ship en route from Siam to Guangzhou, in order to ask Guangzhou authorities to forward a letter to the Qing Emperor requesting a formal embassy as a precursor to China's formal diplomatic recognition.[83] The letter began:

> Our ancestors prayed to the Buddha, and practiced the Dharma. I received the Sacred Books from Shilian [Dashan] of Changshou monastery in Guangdong, and chanted its liturgies, so that I may prepare to submit [myself] to His Majesty [the Kangxi Emperor], sagely and divine in peace and at war, heavenly in His humanity.

Their attempt failed, apparently because the Qing court feared it would upset relations between China and the Le monarchy of the north.[84]

Regardless of the outcome, the event carries significance for a number of reasons. First, it demonstrates the mediation potentials that monastic communities could provide among diverse social groups and over long distances. Had the embassy visited the previous governor, Wu Xingzuo, perhaps the outcome might have been different. Wu knew Dashan through both religious and literary circles in Guangzhou.[85] These personal contacts were not unusual, since the Nguyen lords maintained diplomatic and personal contacts with officials in China, as well as other countries overseas.[86] Secondly, the mission provides solid evidence that monks inserted themselves regularly into the mundane affairs of monarchs as well as merchants. In Yinyuan and Dashan we find two examples of monks attempting to assume the diplomatic role monks had regularly played in Silk Road times. These examples suggest that monastic leaders in the early modern era continued to play important long-distance intermediary roles across state, cultural, and even commercial lines beyond the purview of central authorities.[87] Third, the mission underscores the continued importance of Buddhist rhetoric in diplomatic discourse. The intended recipient of this letter, the Kangxi Emperor, was a strong supporter of the Linji school of Chan, and had worked to present himself as a bodhisattva as well as a Confucian sage, and was thus likely to listen to these appeals.[88]

Conclusion

Buddhism was important to the formation of Chinese merchant colonies overseas during the seventeenth century. Chan institutions provided maritime merchants with a cosmological map of a centered political-economic order that helped them solve many of the basic problems of the world of trade, by encouraging flexible, adaptive, and "multilateral" responses to different regional circumstances.[89] In the world at sea, the Chinese diaspora were able to bind their inchoate social geography into a durable, integrated whole, at a critical, mercantile-driven stage in the development of transoceanic Chinese society during the seventeenth century.[90] Monastic power increased whenever their mercantile disciples settled in areas where Chan Buddhism already held sway. There, monks wielded a religious authority that transcended cultural boundaries and harmonized common and competing interests between their local patrons and the Chinese merchant quarter, which in turn divided into an expatriate "guest merchant" class of expatriate Chinese and a "minority elite" of "creolized" Sino-indigenous middlemen, namely Ming Loyalists.[91] In return, Chan missionaries won the patronage of seafaring merchant communities. This provided the material, social, and political capital that the merchants needed to undertake their own overseas expansion. Once settled, they could leave their merchants' quarters, and better integrate into local societies on their own.

For the Cochinchinese ruling elite, Chinese Chan missionaries addressed the pressing domestic and international political problems that were vital to their state's success. The Nguyen state faced the consequences of their expansionist policies at home and the volatile world of overseas commerce. Chan Buddhist institutions and the syncretic concepts of the Chan Revival in China offered the Vietnamese court in Cochinchina a means to strengthen the legitimacy of their rule over their increasingly plural, mobile, and migrant society through religious means. This ranged from the patronage of local gods to the gradual introduction of Confucianist ideas of statecraft. Strengthened state patronage of Buddhism also provided the monarch with an institutional means to secure better control over frontier and other social groups that potentially threatened the state's stability. Ironically this included better control over monks, as well as merchants, both of whom were major partners and agents in the state's expansionism. Looking abroad, the court sought to enlist monks to establish Nguyen connections with Chinese and other officials abroad, and to especially pursue a diplomatic strategy bent on shedding Cochinchina's outsider status in Chinese foreign relations, in hopes of adapting to the new international realities that Qing consolidation of the China's southern shores in 1683 had produced. Looking ahead, their agenda was not unlike that pursued by the Nguyen clan in the early nineteenth century, as they sought to stabilize their even larger empire, where again political expansionism involved significant religious patronage by the court.[92]

Notes

1. My thanks go to the National University of Singapore's Asia Research Institute, especially its director Anthony Reid, for a Visiting Research Fellowship in 2004-2005 which gave me time to develop parts of this study. Gratitude also goes to Danielle McClellan, Steven Miles, Ken Pomeranz, Wensheng Wang, Michael Wert, John Whitmore, Jack Wills, Chi-hong Yim, and Small Cities conference participants, for help and advice.

2. There are several names for the Nguyen domain, even within a single language. While Vietnam specialists today prefer the name *Dang Trong*, most English readers today are familiar with the European term *Cochinchina*. The Nguyen domain grew from humble origins as a regional upstart in the late sixteenth century to become a powerful state, which expanded Vietnamese rule south to roughly the extent of the nation-state today (see John Whitmore's study in this volume as it provides discussion of the immediately previous era in the Vietnam north, which was foundational to the establishment of the Nguyen regime). Rebellion destroyed it in 1775, but a member of the Nguyen house survived and returned to conquer all Vietnamese territories, and unite them under a single Vietnamese empire in 1802, which lasted until 1945.

3. For the best overall study of Cochinchina to date, and a summary of the March South (*Nam tien*) thesis, see Tana Li, *Nguyen Cochinchina: Southern Vietnam in the Seventeenth and Eighteenth Centuries* (Ithaca, NY: Southeast Asia Program Publications, Cornell University, 1998).

4. Examples include Do Bang, *Pho cang vung Thuan-Quang the XVII-XVIII* [The harbors of Thuan-Quang, seventeenth-eighteenth centuries] (Hanoi: Nxb. Thuan Hoa, 1996); Li, *Nguyen Cochinchina*; Li Tana, "A View from the Sea: Perspectives on the Northern and Central Vietnamese Coast," *Journal of Southeast Asian Studies*, 17, 1 (2006), 83-102; Victor Lieberman, *Strange Parallels: Southeast Asia in Global Context, c. 800-1830* (Cambridge: Cambridge University Press, 2003), 394-419; Shiro Momoki, "Dai Viet the South China Sea Trade: From the 10th to the 15th Century," *Crossroads*, 13, 2 (1999), 1-34; Charles Wheeler, "Cross-Cultural Trade and Trans-Regional Networks in the Port of Hoi An: Maritime Vietnam in the Early Modern Era," Ph.D. dissertation (New Haven: Yale University, 2001); John K. Whitmore, "The Rise of the Coast: Trade, State, and Culture in Early Dai Viet," *Journal of Southeast Asian Studies*, 17, 1 (2006): 103-122.

5. Charles Wheeler, "Re-Thinking the Sea in Vietnamese History: The Littoral Integration of Thuan-Quang, Seventeenth-Eighteenth Centuries," *Journal of Southeast Asian Studies*, 17, 1 (2006), 124-125, 142-152.

6. Wu Jiang, "Orthodoxy, Controversy and the Transformation of Chan Buddhism in Seventeenth-Century China," Ph.D. dissertation (Cambridge, MA: Harvard University, 2002), for an important dissertation that coined the term "missionary Buddhism" for Japan.

7. *Chan* is the Mandarin pronunciation of the character pronounced as *Zen* in Japanese, and *Thien* in Vietnamese. Since we are discussing Chinese monks, Mandarin pronunciations of Chan religious terms are used for consistency, while characters for persons or places are transliterated according to their origin or geographical context. Chan constitutes one of the principle schools of Mahayana Buddhism practiced in eastern Asia. Both its teaching that anyone can attain sudden enlightenment—albeit through the guidance of a reputable master—and its syncretic capacities found popularity in Fujianese maritime society.

8. Although historians of Mahayana Buddhism have generally ignored post-antiquity missionaries, students of Theravada Buddhism have addressed their activities; see Melvin Spiro, *Buddhism and Society: A Great Tradition and Its Burmese Vicissitudes* (Berkeley: University of California Press, 1982); Stanley Tambiah, *World Conqueror and World Renouncer: A Study of Buddhism and Polity in Thailand against Its Historical Background* (Cambridge: Cambridge University Press, 1976); Michael Charney, "Beyond State-Centered Histories in Western Burma: Missionizing Monks and Intra-Regional Migrants in the Arakan Littoral, c. 1784-1860," in *The Maritime Frontier of Burma*, ed. Jos Gommans and Jacques Leider (Leiden: KITLV Press, 2002), 213-224.

9. This study was influenced greatly by two important "Silk Road" studies: Liu Xinru, *Silk and Religion: an Exploration of Material Life and the Thought of the People, AD 600-1200* (Delhi: Oxford University Press, 1996); and Himanshu Ray, *The Winds of Change: Buddhism and the Maritime Links of Early South Asia* (Delhi: Oxford University Press, 1994). Works on ancient China that were vital to my understanding of Buddhism's interactive relationship with post-ancient trade and politics include Kenneth Ch'en, *The Chinese Transformation of Buddhism* (Princeton: Princeton University Press, 1973); Jacques Gernet, *Buddhism in Chinese Society: An Economic History from the Fifth to the Tenth Centuries*, trans. Franciscus Verellen (New York: Columbia University Press, 1985); Tansen Sen, *Buddhism, Diplomacy, and Trade: The Realignment of Sino-Indian Relations, 600-1400* (Honolulu: University of Hawai'i Press, 2003); and Liansheng Yang, "Buddhist Monasteries and the Four Money-Raising Institutions in Chinese History," in *Studies in Chinese Institutional History* (Cambridge, MA: Harvard University Press, 1961), 174-191. All of these works envision an eclipse of Buddhism's evangelical facet before early modern times.

10. Abner Cohen's omission of Buddhism from his influential thesis on merchant diasporas is typical of literature on cross-cultural trade. Abner Cohen, "Cultural Strategies in the Organization of Trading Diasporas," in *The Development of Indigenous Trade and Markets in West Africa*, ed. Claude Meillassoux (London, 1971), 277. Revisionist interests in Indian Ocean maritime diasporas is represented in two recent issues of the *Journal of the Economic and Social History of the Orient*, 49, 2 (2006), and 50, 2/3 (2007).

11. Wang Gungwu, "Merchants Without Empire: The Hokkien Sojourning Communities," in *The Rise of Merchant Empires: Long-Distance Trade in the Early Modern World, 1350–1750*, ed. James Tracy (New York: Cambridge University Press, 1990), 400–421.

12. For a big picture thesis of maritime Fujian's rise and fall as an autonomous region, see John E. Wills, Jr., "Contingent Connections: Fujian, the Empire, and the Early Modern World," in *Qing Formation in World Historical Time*, ed. Lynn A. Struve (Cambridge, MA: Harvard University Press, 2004), 167-203 (on the Zheng see 172, 174-176). The most important study of the development of privately operated, armed Fujianese trade syndicates is Lin Renchuan, *Mingmo Qingchu siren haishang maoyi* (Private sea merchant trade during the late Ming and early Qing [dynasties]) (Shanghai: Huadong shifan daxue chubanshe, 1987), see esp. 131-175. On the political economy of sea trade in the Zheng-led Ming Loyalist regime on Taiwan see Patrizia Carioti, "The Zheng's Maritime Power in the International Context of the Seventeenth Century Far Eastern Seas: The Rise of a 'Centralized Piratical Organization' and Its Gradual Development into an Informal State," *Ming Qing Yanjiu* (Napoli), 5 (1996), 29-67; and Cheng K'o-ch'eng, "Cheng Ch'eng-kung's Maritime Expansion and Early Ch'ing Coastal Prohibition," in *Development and Decline of Fukien Province in the 17th and 18th Centuries*, ed. E. B. Vermeer (Leiden: E. J. Brill, 1990), 222-241. Other important works that help shed light on Ming Loyalist commercial strategy includes Nan You, "Taiwan Zheng shi

wushang shi yanjiu [A study of the five merchant firms established by the Zhengs on Taiwan]," in *Taiwan Zheng Chenggong yanjiu lunwen xuan* (Fuzhou: Fujian renmin chubanshe, 1982), 194-227; and articles by Lin Renchuan, Han Zhenhua, and Yang Yanjie in *Zheng Chenggong lunwen ji* [Collected essays on Zheng Chenggong] (Fuzhou: Fujian renmin chubanshe, 1984), 190-241.

13. Aloysius Chang, "The Chinese Community of Nagasaki in the First Century of the Tokugawa Period (1603-1688)," Ph.D. dissertation (New York: St. John's University, 1970), 113-37.

14. Louis Jacques Bergere IV, "The Overseas Chinese Community in Seventeenth-Century Nagasaki," Ph.D. dissertation (Cambridge, MA: Harvard University, 2004), 103-26; Wang, "Merchants," 410; and Wu, "Orthodoxy," 269-280.

15. Wu, "Orthodoxy," 20, 55, 110; Holmes Welch, "Dharma Scrolls and the Succession of Abbots in Chinese Monasteries," *T'oung Pao* 50 (1963), 93-149, esp. 142. In fact, the first Japanese monk to lead a Nagasaki temple did not emerge until the mid-eighteenth century. This form of legitimizing master-disciple lineages was politically significant to monastic communities because it constituted the basis for appointing abbots. For the "various Chan Buddhist lines" competing for adherents overseas, this "provided them an opportunity to privilege their respective schools." Michel Mohr, "Zen Buddhism during the Tokugawa Period: The Challenge to Go beyond Sectarian Consciousness," *Japanese Journal of Religious Studies*, 21, 4 (1994), 347. See also William M. Bodiford, "Dharma Transmission in Soto Zen: Manzan Dohaku's Reform Movement," *Monumenta Nipponica*, 46, 4 (1991), 423-451.

16. *Obaku* is used for convenience. In fact, the lineage only began to refer to itself by that name in 1876. Yinyuan preferred to call his school "the true Linji" (Mohr, "Zen Buddhism," 345). "Southern Chan" refers to the branch of Chan practices in South China, including Fujian.

17. Hu Chuanzong, "Zheng Chenggong yu Yinyuan chanshi guanxi luelun [A sketch of the connections between Zheng Chenggong and Chan Master Yinyuan]," *Fujian shifan daxue xuebao (zhexue shehui kexue ban)*, 4 (1997), 96-101; Wu, "Orthodoxy," 256.

18. The literature on Yinyuan is quite large. This paragraph draws mainly from Helen J. Baroni, *Obaku Zen: The Emergence of the Third Sect of Zen in Tokugawa Japan* (Honolulu: University of Hawai'i Press, 2000), 35-57, 82-83; Baroni, *Iron Eyes: the Life and Teachings of the Obaku Zen Master Tetsugen Doko* (Albany: State University Press of New York, 2006), 15-17, 26-28; *Zhong-Ri wenhua jiaoliu shidaxi* [Compilation on Sino-Japanese cultural exchange], 10: *Renwu juan* [Biographies volume], comp. Wang Yong (Hangzhou: Zhejiang renmin chubanshe, 1996); and Wu, "Orthodoxy," 254-304.

19. Baroni, *Obaku*, 58-63, 67-84, 165-92; Baroni, *Iron Eyes*, 6-7; Berger, "Chinese Community," 92; *Jinjiang xianzhi* [Jinjiang gazetteer] (Jinjiang, 1990), 1522-1523; Marius Jansen, *The Making of Modern Japan* (Cambridge, MA: Harvard University Press, 2000), 88-89; Mohr, 341-372. For a longer list of Chinese monks see Berger, "Chinese Community," 92, 109, 113-115, 120, 121-130.

20. *Lu Ri gaoseng Yinyuan zhi Zhongtu laiwang shuxin ji* [Collected letters to and from China by the Japanese sojourning master Yinyuan], ed. Chen Qichao, et al. (Beijing: Zhonghua quanguo tushuguan wenxian suowei fuzhi zhongxin, 1995), 284.

21. On the *sanjiaoyi* see Kenneth Dean, *Lord of the Three in One: The Spread of a Cult in Southeast China* (Princeton: Princeton University Press, 1998), 16-27, 44-55, 58-60, 125-36; Timothy Brook, "Rethinking Syncretism: The Unity of Their Joint Worship in Late Imperial China," *Journal of Chinese Religions*, 21 (Fall 1993), 13-26. On Chinese practices in Obaku culture see Baroni, *Obaku Zen*, 85-105; and Wu Jiang, "Orthodoxy," 256, 294-297. Yinyuan was said to consult with a Taoist spirit medium (Wu, 300-302). For Southeast Asia see Wolfgang Franke, "Some Remarks on the 'Three in One Doc-

trine' and Its Manifestations in Singapore and Malaysia," in *Sino-Malaysiana: Selected Papers on Ming and Qing History and on the Overseas Chinese in Southeast Asia, 1942-1988* (Singapore: South Seas Society, 1989), 343-377.

22. Kwang-ching Liu, "Chinese Merchants Guilds: A Historical Inquiry," *Pacific Historical Review*, 57, 1 (1988), 10; Ng, *Amoy Network*, 89-93; Tan Chee Beng, "The Study of Chinese Religion in Southeast Asia: Some Views," in *Southeast Asian Chinese: The Socio-Cultural Dimension*, ed., Leo Suryadinata (Singapore: Times Academic Press, 1995), 146. On the development of Mazu temples in merchant society see Jiang Weitan, "Qingdai shang huiguan yu Tianhou gong [The commercial guilds and the Tianhou temple]," *Haijiao shi yanjiu* (Quanzhou), 27, 1 (1997), 45-63; Wang Rongguo, *Haiyang shenling: Zhongguo haishen xinyang yu shehui jingji* [Spirits of the seas: The development of Chinese sea deities and socio-economy in China] (Nanchang: Jiangxi gaoxiao chubanshe, 2003), 121-58, 162, 178-94. This generalization weakens outside the Chan ecumene. See, for example, Claudine Salmon and Denys Lombard, *Les chinois de Jakarta: Temples et vie collective* (Paris, 1977), 14-15, 18, 21, 238-245; and Tan, "Chinese Religion," 146-151. For examples of Buddhist patronage of Mazu temples in Chinese diasporic communities in Japan see Wu, "Orthodoxy," 276-277.

23. *Li Shizhen, Li Xu fuzi nianpu* [Annual chronology of Li Shizhen, Li Xu's father], comp. Wang Liqi (Wenhai chubanshe, 1983), 184-186.

24. Shilian Dashan, *Haiwai jishi* [Overseas journal], 1699, ed. Ch'en Ching-ho (Taibei: Guangwen shuju, 1969), 83, 107.

25. Ch'en, *Notes on Hoi-an*, 17.

26. Professor Tran Quoc Vuong, personal correspondence, May 1999.

27. Pierre-Yves Manguin alleges that Mahayana Buddhism gradually disappeared among the Cham of the Hoi An region in the thirteenth century in "The Introduction of Islam into Campa," *Journal of the Malaysian Branch of the Royal Asiatic Society*, 58 (1985), 6. At precisely this point in history, however, Chan-practicing Vietnamese began to settle this part of former Champa; see Huynh Cong Ba, "*Tim hieu cuoc khai khan vung bac Quang Nam duoi thoi Tran (qua tai lieu dia phuong)* [Investigation into the task of opening the northern Quang Nam region during Tran times (through local sources)]," *Nghien cuu lich su*, 2 (1998), 46-49. Their Tran monarchs endeavored to establish ties "with the Chams and their Buddhist sites" (Whitmore, "Rise of the Coast," 118-119). So Mahayana did not vanish, but rather survived through the fusion of various local elements.

28. Ch'en, *Notes*, 48, 92, 136.

29. On the foundation of Ming Loyalist colonies in Cochinchina see Ch'en. *Notes*, 40; and Salmon, "Refugies," 181. On the evolution of Minh Huong identity, see Charles Wheeler, "Interests, Institutions, and Identities: The Minh Huong Villages of Vietnam, Sixteenth to Twentieth Centuries," in *When Past and Present Collide: The Chinese in Vietnam* (Bangkok: l'Institut de Recherche sur l'Asie du Sud-Est Contemporaine, forthcoming).

30. The widow donated land; Ch'en Ching-ho believed that she also donated funds to build the temple (Ch'en, *Notes*, 55). Dashan claimed that the temple was originally built during the Tang (Dashan, *Haiwai jishi*, 108). Many today support the monk's claim, but there is no documentary evidence to support it.

31. Nguyen, *Phat giao Dang Trong*, 200-201.

32. Ch'en, *Notes*, 39; Nguyen, *Phat giao Dang Trong*, 2: 8, 48. Scholars have claimed that Chuc Thanh Monastery was founded in the fifteenth century, based on inscriptions at the site, but the elder monks residing there assured me that it actually dates only to the seventeenth century based on the monastery's Dharma lineage (conversation

with Thich Hanh Hoa, May 1999). Minhhai Fabao, the founder, was a disciple of Yuanzhao (see below), so this is impossible.

33. Nguyen, *Phat giao Dang Trong*, 2: 53. The town may have given Di Da Monastery another face lift after Dashan's visit there in 1695-1696. In his travelogue, he reports his discussion with Xinglian, who was the monastery's abbot at the time and reprints the appeal he wrote asking residents to support the renovation of Di Da. Dashan, *Haiwai jishi*, 108.

34. Nguyen, *Phat giao Dang Trong*, 1: 126-146, 167-170, 183, 200-206, 256-257, 181-189; 2: 64-386; *Dai Nam nhat thong chi* [Unified gazetteer of Dai Nam] (Hue: Nxb. Thuan Hoa, 1992), 1: 81-84, 199-202; 7: 385-387; 8: 441-442; 9: 49-51; 26: 29-30; 27: 79; 31: 236-237.

35. Nguyen, *Phat giao Dang Trong*, 1: 29.

36. On Yuanzhao (Nguyen Thieu) and his school, see *Dai Nam liet truyen* [Biographies of the Eminent in Dai Nam], 19th century, translated into Vietnamese vernacular by Do Mong Khuong et al. (Hue: Nxb. Thuan Hoa, 1997), 1: 204-206; Leopold Cadiere, "La pagode Quac-an: le fondateur," *Bulletin des amis a vieux Hue* 2 (1914), 147-162; Gaspardonne, "Bonzes des Ming réfugiés," *Sinologica* (Basel) 2 (1950), 14-17; Nguyen, *Lich su Phat giao Dang Trong*, 1: 26, 91-163; and Thich Thien An, *Chan and Buddhism in Vietnam* (Rutland, VT: Charles E. Tuttle, 1971), 148-161, esp. 149-150. Wu Jiang discusses Yuanzhao briefly in the context of Huangbo missions overseas; Wu, "Orthodoxy," 318-319. There is some confusion over dates. Some have suggested that Yuanzhao migrated in 1655, however, Gaspardonne shows the more likely date to be much later, based on Yuanshou's age and other factors. For more on Yuanzhao's impact in the Mekong frontier, see Tran Hong Lien, *Phat giao Nam bo tu the ky 17 den 1975* [Buddhism in the South from the 17th Century to 1975] (Saigon: Nxb. Thanh pho Ho Chi Minh, 1996), 17-20.

37. For example, Yuanzhao's disciple Minghai Fabao presided over the creation of Chuc Thanh monastery in 1682 (Ch'en, *Notes*, 39), though others claim a later date for the temple's founding (Nguyen, *Phat giao Dang Trong*, 2: 8). Minghai also assumed the position of first abbot of Thien Lam Monastery in Quang Nghia south of Hoi An in 1695. (*Phat giao*, 2: 5-63.) Minghai's Vietnamese dharma disciple Au Trieu later migrated to Hoi An, where he founded Phuoc Lam Monastery in 1698 (Nguyen, *Phat giao Dang Trong*, 2: 48).

38. On Dashan AKA Thach Liem, his voyage to Cochinchina, and his legacy in Vietnamese Buddhism, see Nguyen, *Phat giao Dang Trong*, 1: 166-211.

39. Thien An, *Zen Buddhism*, 163; 262, n. 2. For more on Lieu Quan, see ibid., 162-187; and Nguyen, *Lich su Phat giao Dang Trong*, 1: 290-385.

40. For examples of temple-mediated Chinese cultural transmission to Japan see Joan Stanley Baker, *The Transmission of Chinese Idealist Painting to Japan: Notes on the Early Phase (1661-1799)* (Ann Arbor: Center for Japanese Studies, University of Michigan, 1992); Bergere, "Nagasaki," 112-120; James Cahill, "Phases and Modes of Transmission of Ming-Ch'ing Painting Styles to Edo Period Japan," in *Sino-Japanese Cultural Interchange: Aspects of Archaeology and Art History*, ed. Yue-him Tam (Hong Kong: Institute of Chinese Studies, The Chinese University of Hong Kong, 1985), 68-70, 73-74; Wu, "Orthodoxy," 254-304; Zhou Yiliang, et al., eds., *Zhong-Ri wenhua jiaoliu shidaxi* [Compilation on Sino-Japanese cultural exchange] (Hangzhou: Zhejiang renmin chubanshe, 1996), 7, 232-240.

41. See, for example, the process of transferring and implementing ritual, organizational, technological, and other cultural knowledge necessary to create "the full Zen monastic life" in Japan during the thirteenth century as discussed in Martin Collcutt, *Five*

Mountains: The Rinzai Zen Monastic Institution in Medieval Japan (Cambridge, MA: Council on East Asian Studies, Harvard University, 1981), 171-220.

42. Baroni, *Iron Eyes*, 6; Baroni, *Obaku*, 98-101.

43. Preface by Chou Zhao'ao in Dashan, *Haiwai jishi*, 3.

44. Again, the close relationship between the development of Buddhism and the development of trade has been much studied in the field of pre-modern Asian history. See, for example, Liu Xinru, *Ancient India and Ancient China: Trade and Religious Exchanges, A.D. 1-600* (Dehli: Oxford University Press, 1988).

45. For a history of trade in the Hoi An region before 1600, see Wheeler, "Cross-Cultural Trade," 72-131. Europeans recognized *Aquilaria agallocha* most commonly by the names *eagleswood* or *aloeswood*. See also Kenneth Hall's study in this volume.

46. See Le Quy Don's 1776 inventory of the region's goods; *Phu bien tap luc* 1: 63-64, 219-20, 369; 2: 45-54, 73-74, 369, 401-404. See also Robert L. Innes, "Trade between Japan and Central Vietnam in the Seventeenth Century: The Domestic Impact," manuscript, Ann Arbor, MI, 1988), 10.

47. Baker, "Obaku Connection," 99; Oba Osamu, et al., *Jianghu shidai Zhongguo dianji liubo Riben zhi yanjiu* [Research on the diffusion of Chinese books to Japan during the Edo period] (Hangzhou: Hangzhou Daxue chubanshe, 1998), 403-408; Oba, *Jianghu shidai Ri-Zhong mihua* [Sino-Japanese underground communication during the Edo period], trans. Xu Shihong (Beijing: Zhonghua shuju, 1997), 31-59, 99-114, 179.

48. See, for example, the study of a guild hall inscription in Ch'en Ching-ho, "On the Rules and Regulations of the Duong-Thuong Hoi-Quan at Faifo (Hoi-an), Central Vietnam," *Southeast Asian Archives* (Kuala Lumpur) 2 (1969), 148–156.

49. "Pho Da Son Linh Trung Phat," Han-Nom Institute, Hanoi, no. 12623. See also Albert Sallet, "Le montagnes de marbre," *Bulletin des Amis a Vieux Hue*, 24, 1 (1924), 131-133.

50. The Nguyen typically placed their new monasteries over ancient Cham religious sites. Charles Wheeler, "One Region, Two Histories: Cham Precedents in the Hoi An Region," in *Viet Nam: Borderless Histories*, ed. Nhung Tuyet Tran, et. al. (Madison: University of Wisconsin Press, 2006), 163-193; Nguyen The Anh, "The Vietnamization of the Cham Deity Po Nagar," in *Essays on Vietnamese* Pasts, ed. Keith W. Taylor and John K. Whitmore (Ithaca: Southeast Asia Program, Cornell University, 1995), 49. On syncretism in Cochinchina, see Ta Chi Tai Truong, *Than, nguoi va dat Viet* [Spirits, people, and the land of the Vietnamese] (California: Van Nghe, 1989), 217-244.

51. Baroni, *Obaku*, 32. The nineteenth and twentieth centuries offer numerous examples of non-Buddhis. societies that similarly "pushed" Chinese devotees of syncretic sects "to label themselves as Buddhist." Tan, "Chinese Religion," 154.

52. Baroni, *Obaku*, 32-3; Jiang Boqin, *Shilian Dashan yũ Aomen Chan shi* [Shilian Dashan in the history of Macau Buddhism] (Shanghai: Xuelin chubanshe, 1999), 446-468; Wu, "Orthodoxy," 275-277.

53. Jiang, *Shilian Dashan*, 463-468. Even in China, monks played a role in the order of commerce. After their defeat of anti-Qing forces like the Ming Loyalists in 1683, the Qing court sent officials like Li Shizhen to China's southeastern seaboard in order to construct political order. Sent to Guangdong, Li ordered the reconstruction of Guanyin and Guandi temples at strategic transportation sites, and "the recruitment of monks for their upkeep," as part of his plan for securing the province. Li Shizhen, *Li Xu fuzi nianpu* [Annual of Li Xu's father], ed. Wang Liqi (Taibei: Wenai cchubanshe, 1985), 178-179.

54. On the development of Mazu temples in merchant society see Jiang Weitan, "Qingdai shang huiguan yu Tianhou gong [The commercial guilds and the Tianhou temple]" *Haijiao shi yanjiu* (Quanzhou), 27, 1 (1997), 45-63; Wang Rongguo, *Haiyang shenling: Zhongguo haishen xinyang yu shehui jingji* [Spirits of the seas: The develop-

ment of Chinese sea deities and socio-economy in China] (Nanchang: Jiangxi gaoxiao chubanshe, 2003), 121-58, 162, 178-194.

55. *Haiwai jishi*, 109.

56. Ch'en, *Notes*, 65.

57. Sometime during the early eighteenth century, a separate *Yanghang* or Ocean Guild hall was built, complete with a Mazu altar. "Duong thuong Hoi quan quy le [The covenant and regulations of the Ocean Merchants Guild Hall]," Han-Nom Institute, no. M.180. See also Ch'en, *Notes*, 95-98, 138-141; "Duong-Thuong Hoi-Quan," 148-156.

58. Kwang-ching Lie, "Chinese Merchant Guilds: An Historical Inquiry," *Pacific Historical Review*, 57, 1 (1988), 11. See also, for comparison, Elizabeth Lambourn's study in this volume, which considers earlier overseas Muslim merchant communities and their religious patronage on west-coast India.

59. On the ordination, see Dashan, *Haiwai jishi*, 109; on temple renovations, 108-110; on the huiguan, 110-111; and on the roadworks, 138-139.

60. Dashan, *Haiwai jishi*, 109-110.

61. Liu, 'Chinese Merchant Guilds," 11.

62. *Haiwai jishi*, 109-110. On Nagasaki see Chin, "Merchants," 117; Engseng Ho, *The Graves of Tarim: Genealogy and Mobility across the Indian Ocean* (Berkeley: University of California Press, 2006), 14. Ho notes that graves offer the potential "to create powerful dynamics of signification with the potential to create communities based not on revelation but on something authochthonous and incipient in the grave complex," 25.

63. See John Whitmore's study in this volume.

64. Ronald Toby, *State and Diplomacy in Early Modern Japan: Asia in the Development of the Tokugawa Bakufu* (Princeton: Princeton University Press, 1984), 139. In the 1630s, the Tokugawa government issued a series of edicts that effectively ended Japanese-run carrier trade overseas until the nineteenth century. Isolated enclaves like Nagasaki were allowed to conduct trade with Chinese or Dutch carriers under strict supervision.

65. See, for example, Cheng K'o-ch'eng, "Cheng Ch'eng-kung's Maritime Expansion and Early Ch'ing Coastal Prohibition," in *Development and Decline of Fukien Province in the 17th and 18th Centuries*, ed. Edouard Vermeer (Leiden: E. J. Brill, 1990), 231-237. This historically referred to the Red River Delta; however, some late-sixteenth and early seventeenth-century Chinese works apply the name to Cochinchina. See, for example, Zhang Xie, *Dong Xi yangkao* [A study of the Eastern and Western seas] (1617, repr. Beijing: Zhongguo shudian, 1981), *juan* 1. The same is true for Japanese geographers; see Ch'en, *Notes*, 1.

66. Ch'en Ching-ho, "Qingchu Zheng Chenggong zhibu zhi yizhi [The migration of the Zheng partisans to southern borders (of Vietnam)]," *Xinya xuebao* (New Asia Journal), 5, 1 (1960), 436-450; Ch'en, "Mac Thien Tu and Phraya Taksin: a Survey of Their Political Stand, Conflicts, and Background," in *Proceedings, Seventh IAHA Conference, 22-26 August 1977* (Bangkok: Chulalongkorn University Press, 1979), 1534-1539.

67. *Dai Nam thuc luc tien bien* [Veritable record of Dai Nam, ancestral edition] (Hanoi, 1962), 125; Trinh Hoai Duc, *Gia Dinh thanh thong chi* [Unified gazetteer of Gia Dinh Citadel] (1820, repr. T.p. Ho Chi Minh: Nxb. Giao Duc, 1998), 3: 77. Sources confirm that one of the fleet captains, Yang Yangdi, had been admiral of the Zheng regime's *Longmen* fleet responsible for patrolling the coast between Guangdong and Cambodia, a stretch that included Cochinchina (*Gia Dinh thanh thong chi*, 76).

68. See the summary of events as described by Yumio Sakurai, "Eighteenth-Century Chinese Pioneers on the Water Frontier of Indochina," in *Water Frontier: Commerce and the Chinese in the Lower Mekong Region, 1750-1880*, ed. Tana Li and Nola Cooke (Lanham, MD: Rowman & Littlefield, 2004), 40.

69. The term comes from John Middleton, "Merchants: An Essay in Historical Ethnography," *Journal of the Royal Anthropological Institute*. 9 (2003), esp. 510-517.

70. Ming Loyalists (aka Minh Huong) possessed the right to own land; expatriate Chinese merchants did not. This is just one example of how the blanket term "Chinese" can grossly mislead our understanding of Chinese merchant society and power in Vietnamese history.

71. Paul Boudet, "La Conquête de la Cochinchine par les Nguyen et le rôle des émigrés Chinois," *Bulletin de l'Ecole Française d'Extrême-Orient*, 42 (1942), 115-131 and *passim*. The court pursued the same strategy to secure the clientage of another self-declared Ming Loyalist Chinese, Mac Cuu, who controlled the trading outpost of Ha Tien on the Gulf of Thailand.

72. Cham revolts were frequent. Chinese revolts were just as potentially troublesome. For example, a Chinese merchant ignited a revolt in the south in 1692, while in 1695, a Chinese merchant at Qui Nhơn, named "A Ban," or "Quang Phu," together with Chinese "Linh," revolted across the Qui Nhon-Quang Nghai region. All were successfully repressed. See *Thuc luc*, 148-149.

73. *Minh vuong*, pronounced *Mingwang* in Chinese, refers to the Sanskrit name *vidya raja*, who were "fierce spirits" who represent or embody the wrath of Vairocana or Sakyamuni, "the Sun-Buddha," "against evil spirits." W. E. Soothill, *A Dictionary of Chinese Buddhist Terms* (Delhi: Motilal Banarsidass, 1987), 263, 281. On this aspect of Nguyen religious strategy see Li, *Nguyen Cochinchina*, 107-109; and Nguyen *Lich su phat giao Dang Trong*, 13-40. On this strategy in Southeast Asian environments, see O. W. Wolters, *History, Culture, and Region in Southeast Asian Perspectives* (rev. ed., Ithaca: Southeast Asia Program, Cornell University, 1999), 19-20, 23, and *passim*. The Nguyen may even have been taking a cue from the early Qing emperors. See David M. Farquhar, "Emperor as Boddhisattva in the Governance of the Ch'ing Empire," *Harvard Journal of Asiatic Studies*, 38, 1 (1978), 5-34; and Wu, "Orthodoxy," 88-108.

74. On the Nguyen appropriation of the Cham sea goddess Po Nagar, see Nguyen The Anh, "The Vietnamization of the Cham Deity Po Nagar," in *Essays into Vietnamese Pasts*, 42-50; and Li Tana, *Nguyen Cochinchina*, 99-116. On state patronage of local deities as a strategy of rule in the nineteenth-century Vietnamese South, see Alexander Woodside, "Vietnamese Buddhism, the Vietnamese Court, and China in the 1800's," in *Historical Interactions of China and Vietnam: Institutional and Cultural Themes*, ed. Edgar Wickberg (Lawrence: Center for East Asian Studies, University of Kansas, 1969), 11-24, esp. 15-16; Choi Byung Wook, *Southern Vietnam under the Reign of Minh Mang (1820-1841): Central Policies and Local Responses* (Ithaca: Southeast Asia Program, Cornell University, 2004).

75. Lieberman, *Strange Parallels*.

76. *Thuc luc*, 148.

77. Nguyen, *Lich su Phat giao Dang Trong*, 1: 29-30.

78. Nguyen, *Lich su Phat giao Dang Trong*, 2: 6; *Dai Nam nhat thong chi*, 8: 441.

79. *Haiwai jishi*, 11-12, 56-57.

80. Sen, *Buddhism, Diplomacy and Trade*.

81. Dashan, *Haiwai jishi*, 84-85.

82. *Haiwai jishi*, 35.

83. *Thuc luc*, 158-159. For the earliest record see Le, *Phu bien tap luc*, 2: 217-223. Le Quy Don transcribed letters from Nguyen Quang Tien, a high official in Nguyen Phuc Chu's court, that claim the king offered fifty million taels to the governor of Guangdong for this investiture. Ibid., 2: 218-223.

84. See also Whitmore, this volume.

85. Dashan enjoyed many connections to Guangzhou's political elite like Wu Xingzuo. Xie Guozhen, *Ming-Qing biji xiaoshuo congtan* [Collected discussions of prose and short stories during the Ming and Qing] (Shanghai: Zhonghua shuju, 1962), 49.

86. For example, when the Liang Guang Governor-General died, Nguyen Phuc Chu sent condolences gold to his family. Le, *Phu bien tap luc*, 2: 29-30. Le Quy Don commented that the Cochinchinese capital maintained regular correspondence with the governor of Guangdong, despite no further attempts to seek diplomatic recognition from Beijing. Ibid., 2: 27.

87. Jiang Boqin has already mapped out Dashan's connections to sea trading merchants and Guangzhou officials as well. Jiang, *Shilian Dashan*, 445-463.

88. Farquhar, "Emperor as Boddhisattva," 22-24.

89. Cohen, "Cultural Strategies," 226-228. See also Avner Greif, et al., "Coordination, Commitment, and Enforcement: the Case of the Merchant Guild," *Journal of Political Economy* 102, 4 (1994), 751, 758-762.

90. For the historical phases of this diaspora, see Wang Gungwu, *China and the Chinese Overseas* (Singapore: Eastern Universities Press, 2003), 4-13.

91. G. William Skinner, "Creolized Chinese Societies in Southeast Asia," in *Sojourners and Settlers: Histories of Southeast Asia and the Chinese*, ed. Anthony Reid (Honolulu: University of Hawai'i Press, 2001), 52-59. More widely, see John Middleton, "Merchants," 510-517.

92. Woodside, "Vietnamese Buddhism," esp. 15-16.

9

Religious Networking and Upstream Buddhist Wall Paintings in Seventeenth- and Eighteenth-Century Burma[1]

Alexandra Green

Victor Lieberman in his books *Burmese Administrative Cycles* and *Strange Parallels: Southeast Asia in Global Context* argues that Burma experienced a long integrative trend, particularly in the sixteenth through eighteenth centuries, and that by the beginning of the nineteenth century had a high level of cultural uniformity.[2] This in part resulted from the political, social, and religious initiatives of assertive Burmese rulers and their courts.

A variety of artistic productions in the seventeenth and eighteenth centuries reflects this trend of homogenization. Particularly exemplary of the new cultural orthodoxy are the seventeenth- and eighteenth-century murals painted on the walls of numerous temples and religious complexes located in the core regions of political authority in the Burmese dry zone around the confluence of the Irrawaddy, Mu, and Chindwin Rivers and along the central reaches of the Irrawaddy.[3] The standardization evident in painting styles and narrative structures and themes of seventeenth- and eighteenth-century wall paintings marks a cultural intersection of the court, the *sangha*, and outlying areas, with changes demonstrating continuing artistic and cultural negotiations between primary and secondary centers.

Longstanding core beliefs on which Burmese society rested, including faith in the merit path to enlightenment and the importance of kingship itself, ensured the maintenance of a high level of uniformity in the murals' narrative subject matter and the manner in which it was portrayed through a series of political and religious crises of the seventeenth and eighteenth centuries, when Burmese kings had varying levels of control over the central zone. The court was an exemplary model that people aspired to and attempted to emulate. Thus, even though subordinate areas of power grew stronger in Burma in the first half of the eighteenth century and a new dynasty came to power in the middle of the century, the new leaders followed already established precedents of religious and social behaviour.[4] These beliefs were reinforced by the consistency of temple murals, which in turn reflected fundamental ideas embedded in Burmese thought.

In this study, Burmese wall paintings of the seventeenth and eighteenth centuries are examined to establish this consistency by identifying what stories were represented, which scenes were selected, and the manner in which particular events or images were portrayed. The high level of uniformity found in the murals and the paintings' distribution across the central dry zone of Burma indicate that during this time period an artistic and narrative canon was established that supported centralizing social, religious, and political trends, exemplified regional connections, and illustrated the strong link between secondary centers and the court.

The Regional and Political Setting of the Wall Paintings

The central area of Burma is a semi-arid zone because of the lay of the mountainous regions to the east and west of the Irrawaddy River valley. The agricultural areas of Minbu, the Mu River valley north of Ava, the Kyaukse area southeast of Ava, and the lower Chindwin River valley were prominent centers of regional political authority, because these were the areas of the greatest agricultural productivity, each able to produce large quantities of rice paddy. Other areas were too dry to sustain wet rice agriculture and primarily grew dry rice, millet, and sesamum.[5] Networking between the court and its secondary centers is documented in written records that report the assignment of regions and towns as appanages to those favored by the king.[6] Beginning in the seventeenth century princes were required to live at the court, and local administration of the delegated landed estates was assigned to headmen and other locally resident agents.[7] While the court's provincial authority diminished in the late seventeenth and early eighteenth centuries,[8] by the mid-eighteenth century the new Konbaung dynasty, established in 1752 by King Alaungpaya after the defeat of the Mon uprising, re-established the supremacy of an Ava-based monarchy.

As Lieberman demonstrates, the seventeenth and eighteenth centuries in Burma were a period of important economic growth, administrative integration, and "centrally determined orthodox acculturation," notwithstanding the mid-eighteenth century dynastic change.[9] The re-establishment of the Burmese capital at Ava in the central zone in 1635 contributed to the development of the region politically, agriculturally, and demographically. Deportees from conquered territories lying outside the core augmented local labor.[10] Lieberman identifies three elements of integration that are tied to this study of the development of Burmese art: economic growth that produced the funds necessary to produce the paintings, administrative consolidation that focused significant political control on the dry zone where the paintings were located, and orthodox acculturation that ensured the murals' common depictions.

The sites of extant seventeenth- and eighteenth-century wall paintings are concentrated in the central dry zone along the Irrawaddy, the lower Chindwin, and the lower Mu River valleys.[11] Most of the seventeenth- and eighteenth-century towns and villages with temples and murals were located in close proximity to rivers and water networks that increased their trade potential, contributing to the wealth of the area and thereby the ability of the inhabitants to make

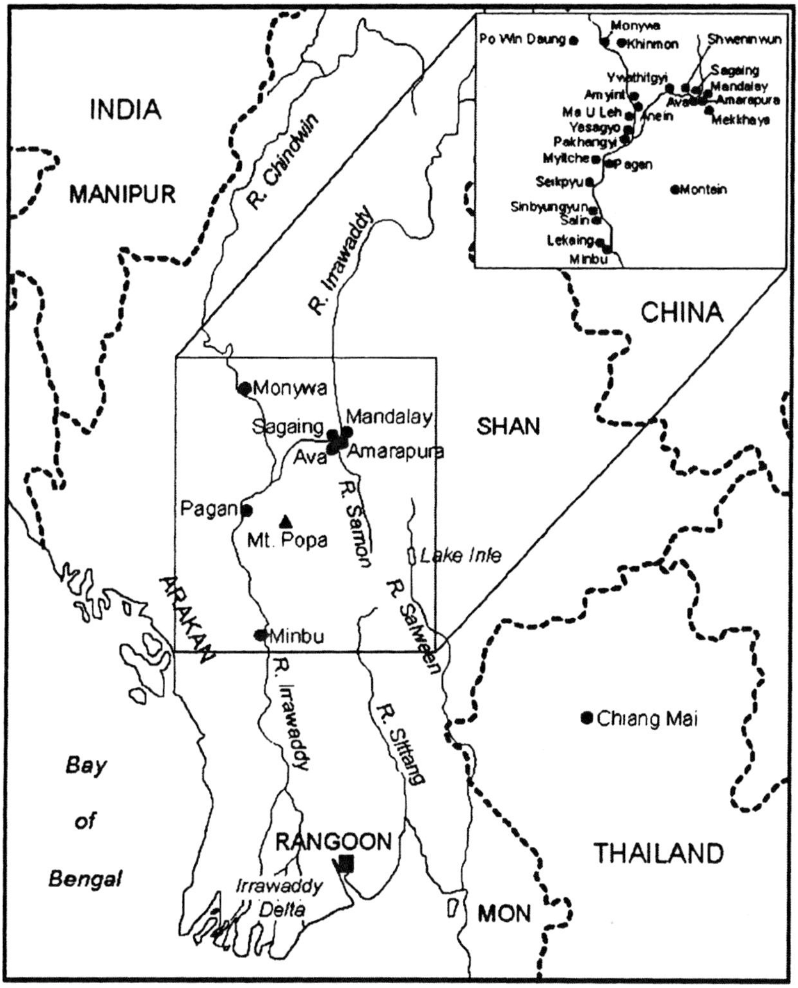

Map 9.1. **Distribution of Burmese Temple Murals**

religious donations in the form of temples and wall paintings. Most of the remaining murals survive in clusters of small-scale temples and stupas. These buildings have a standardized appearance in contrast to the unusual forms produced in the nineteenth century, and are conspicuously smaller when compared with the massive religious buildings constructed during the Pagan period

duced in the nineteenth century, and are conspicuously smaller when compared with the massive religious buildings constructed during the Pagan period (c. 1044-1287).[12] The stupas consist of low terraces, a squat *anda* (bell), and an extended series of *chattravalis* (umbrellas marked by grooves or discs) that culminates in a *hti* (metal umbrella placed at the top of the stupa) or in a lotus bud form. Temples are either rectangular or square in form with one, three, or four entrances and concentric, receding roof layers. Sometimes the temple and stupa forms are combined with temples having stupa superstructures or stupas having entrances and a shrine room (*Fig. 9.1*). Murals were painted in the interiors of many of these buildings and also in man-made cave-temples. Compared with the number of architectural remains, the complete or nearly complete remains of paintings are relatively limited in number, and most sites have fragmentary images or none at all. Extant wall paintings are located in the following towns and areas (*Map 9.1*):

- The towns of Salin, Lekaing, Sinbyugyun, and Myitche on the west bank of the Irrawaddy River and Pagan on the east bank in the mid-Irrawaddy region.
- The villages of Ma U Leh, Pakhangyi, and Yesagyo around the confluence of the Chindwin and Irrawaddy Rivers.
- The cave site of Po Win Daung west of the Chindwin River.
- The villages of Amyint, Anein, and Khinmon on or near the Chindwin River.
- The village of Ywathitgyi along the Irrawaddy River east of the Mu River.
- Shweminwun village and Sagaing Hill west of the Irrawaddy River.
- The villages of Mekkhaya and Montain south of the capital area of Ava, Amarapura, and Mandalay.
- Amarapura in the capital area.

Based on the distribution of extant murals, it is possible to state that wall paintings appear to have been largely produced and maintained within the core zone of the country in the seventeenth and eighteenth centuries. Most of the wall painting sites are close to the capital area of Ava, Amarapura, and Sagaing, and, from the mid-nineteenth century, Mandalay. Salin, Lekaing, and Sinbyugyun, close to the significant agricultural area of Minbu, are the furthest from the capital.

Contemporary Religious and Political Orthodoxies Reflected in the Murals

During the seventeenth and eighteenth centuries the monarchy enhanced religious standardization in its core region significantly, in part by increasing the centralization of the kingdom but also through proselytizing work. The king encouraged orthodox practices within the *sangha* by emphasizing Sri Lanka as a source of authoritative texts. The court managed the interpretation of texts and religious communication within its realm by controlling local access to spiritual authorities who were authorized to teach the Buddhist canon and perform its rituals. Monks had to prove that they were textually knowledgeable and morally fit by passing mandated tests before they were sent to serve surrounding areas and outlying provinces.[13]

Despite this emphasis on a textually-based religious orthodoxy, the contemporary Burmese belief system was a mix of Theravada Buddhism, spirit propitiation, astrology, alchemy, black and white magic, and the use of cabbalistic signs and letter combinations, and other local practices. Two significant practitioners of such arts were wizards (*weikza*) and alchemists (*zawgyi*). Wizards acquired magical powers through trances, which allowed them to gain greater control over nature and the supernatural.[14] Alchemists sought a supernaturally youthful body that would last thousands of years.[15] Both of these figures are connected with Buddhism through practices that accord with the religion's soteriological goals. For example, the alchemist is said to prolong life until the time of Maitreya, the future Buddha, with the implication that he can achieve nirvana through this route, while the wizard is connected with meditation, *iddhi* (power), and world-conquerors (*cakravartin*) implying that he is a *bodhisattva* or future Buddha.[16] Functioning more closely within mainstream society than either the *weikza* or the *zawgyi*, astrologers and soothsayers satisfy the need to determine auspicious courses of action, for the neutralization of malevolent influences, and to warn of possible catastrophes. At the court level men practiced in these arts were influential in determining how to conduct state affairs and deciding courses of action.[17]

Besides such activities as fortune-telling and the interpretation of omens, a wide range of non-canonical beliefs were in practice at court.[18] This is corroborated by several royal orders. One dating to the seventh of May 1635 orders two monks, Maha Dhamma Zayya Thura and Maha Baya Thura, to supervise the drawing of magical squares and figures for protection against enemies, that only known squares and figures were to be used, that proper procedures were to be followed, and that spelling and punctuation were to be checked. Another order followed on the ninth of May 1635, when two lords mandated that magic figures, magic squares, circles, and triangles, verses, and mantras were to be copied on cloth and attached to the ceilings of gate towers in a variety of towns and on the drums of the palace and clock tower. The specific locations and the particular magic circles, squares, and triangles to be utilized were also detailed, as were the size of the cloth pieces, the ink, the quality of the product, and the level of supervision.

Nearly 150 years later on the tenth of March 1784, the use of magic squares on the city walls, gates, and turrets was again authorized in order to make the city invulnerable to both human and supernatural enemies.[19] Although these concepts seem antithetical to orthodox Buddhism, the fact that many were a standard part of daily life or were manipulated to fit within the Theravada framework indicates the extent to which local tradition was an integral part of Burmese religious beliefs. As such, it is not surprising that non-canonical imagery can be seen in the era's wall paintings.

Despite this major strand of local belief and practice, Theravada Buddhism formed the major religious focus with the acquisition of charity-derived merit the primary form of religious practice.[20] At the apex of secular society, the Burmese king had the largest store of merit.[21] He stood as an exemplary model of the benefits of meritorious giving for the rest of the country and represented a state of virtue and material wealth to strive for. Kingship was thus an important concept in Burma, and despite problematic kings occupying the throne periodically, it was a concept that provided continuity in Burmese society. As Michael Aung-Thwin has shown, Burmese rebellions, the consequence of poor leadership, did not advocate the transformation of social institutions, but attempted to place more able custodians of traditional values in power.[22]

Two influential texts that reiterated the importance of kingship and merit generation, the *Lokaniti* and the *Rajaniti*, are compendia of didactic stories and sayings intended to act as a guide to personal behavior (morality) and the rules of social interactions. The *Lokaniti* was intended for people generally and the *Rajaniti* instructed kings and princes in appropriate actions and beliefs.[23] These texts taught the need for self-protection, the value of learning and wisdom, wealth as a personal goal, and the absolute supremacy of royal authority; they also indicated the foundations of royal power, including wealth, military strength, conquest, and control of subjects and officials.[24] By reinforcing the idea that those of royal and high status were close to perfecting the ten virtues necessary for the attainment of enlightenment, the last ten *Jataka* tales, collectively known as the *Mahanipata,* inspired numerous seventeenth-century wall paintings.

Consistent with the themes of Theravada Buddhism, the murals illustrate the samsaric path to enlightenment through their overall organization, as can be seen at the Zedi Daw Daik complex in Anein village (*Fig. 9.2*). The twenty-eight previous Buddhas were portrayed along the top of temple walls as a band of single scenes with each Buddha seated in *bhumisparsha mudra* under his specific tree of enlightenment, representing the escape from the cycles of rebirth, *samsara*. Below this were painted extended narrative scenes of the life of Gotama Buddha, which primarily showed events leading up to or occurring shortly after the Enlightenment. The remainder of the walls were filled with extended narrative representations of the *Mahanipata*, the last ten Jataka stories, where the *bodhisattva* perfected the ten virtues necessary for attaining enlightenment.[25] Thus, the organization of the murals suggests that there is a movement from the bottom of the walls, associated with the earthly world, towards the top, which is linked with the release from the cycles of rebirth. Painted in strips around the temple walls with the stories spiraling upwards in a mimesis of the circumambulatory path that worshippers take and the round of rebirths to which every being is subjected, the murals reflect religious practices and beliefs and physically mimic the path to enlightenment. The hierarchical organization from floor to ceiling also stratifies beings based on their proximity to enlightenment, and can be linked with the hierarchical nature of Burmese society with the king considered to be the layperson closest to enlightenment and therefore a *bodhisattva* at a similar stage in the samsaric cycle as Gotama was in the last ten Jataka tales.[26]

The greatest portion of the walls was usually utilized to represent the focal ten Jataka stories. This practice may derive from the functional fact that the ten tales are more extensive than the life of the Buddha and the single scenes of the previous Buddhas, but it is also evidence that a being goes through innumerable rebirths. The extensive depictions of the Jataka stories may further reflect the Burmese desire to remain in the cycle of rebirths in order to experience pleasurable existences. Because the last ten Jataka stories are largely set among royalty, they provide ample opportunity to show the lifestyles of the wealthy, the interiors of palaces, and the drama of pomp and circumstance, advantages that are conferred upon recipients because of their good karma gained from appropriate behavior.[27] Palace scenes, processions, celebrations, and battle scenes were depicted frequently and occupy extensive portions of the narrative space in seventeenth- and eighteenth-century murals. When portraying the *Mahanipata* and often also the life of Gotama Buddha, the wall paintings, by illustrating scenes of luxury and the benefits of good karma, thus present the viewer with incentives to participate in the main religious practice of Burmese society—ritualized giving.[28]

The Standardization of the Wall Paintings and its Origins

The standardization of the seventeenth- and eighteenth-century wall paintings resulted in part from the supervision of the painters by monks. Primary source documentation from the seventeenth century includes a royal order issued on the seventh of April 1633, which stated that seven monks were to supervise a group of 500 artists assigned to paint the enclosure walls of the Maha Myat Muni pagoda.[29] These paintings were to comprise illustrations of the 547 Jataka stories, an inscription of the Buddha's teachings, the story of the spread of Buddhism to Burma, and the event where the Buddha gave eight of his hairs to Tapussa and Bhallika. Donations from the officer of the Royal Granary and five wealthy men named in the order supported the monks and the painters' production.[30]

The consistency of mural representations also resulted from the employment of illustrated manuscripts as copy books, which would have guided mural artists in their use of certain painting styles when portraying particular stories, as well as indicated the way in which scenes were to be represented. The earliest surviving illustrated Burmese manuscripts date from the end of the eighteenth century, but their compositional similarities with murals, including the organization and demarcation of space within stories, the strip format, and the use and placement of captions, strongly suggests that the two were stylistically coincidental in their development during the seventeenth and eighteenth centuries.[31]

During this time period considerable changes occurred in literary production in Burma. In the seventeenth century, an increasing number of religious texts were re-written or elucidated in Burmese prose.[32] This made written material available to a wide audience, including monks and artists who were involved in mural production, but were not well versed in Pali.[33] The efflorescence of literary activity in the second half of the eighteenth century, which was part of a growing interest in story-telling that led to the rise of narrative verse forms, such as the *yagan*, and drama, included the translation of all the Jataka stories and the life of Gotama Buddha into Burmese prose.[34] Eight tales from the *Mahanipata* were translated by the monk U Aw Ba Tha, and the remainder of the 547 stories was translated by a monk named Nyaung-gan Saya-daw. An account of the life of the Buddha, called *Malalingarawutthu*, was also translated into the vernacular at the end of the eighteenth century by the monk titled Dutiya Medi Saya-daw.

The wall paintings can be linked with these literary trends in several ways. First, the prose writing in the murals can be considered a form of vernacular narrative. The tendency for prose to be a method of elucidation is evident in the written sections of the murals, which are specifically identified as captions because each sentence ends with the Burmese word "*han*" meaning "a representation of."[35] Secondly, the extensive details found in the vernacular prose texts from the eighteenth century are reflected in the murals through the increase of visual details and the length of the captions, which were expanded from one to several sentences during the second half of the eighteenth century.[36] Third, the extended representation of the narratives connects with the social interest in telling tales for the moral, ethical, and religious instruction of the population. While much of the written evidence—manuscripts and the extant translations of the life of Gotama and the Jataka stories—for this trend dates to the second half of the eighteenth century, the earlier production of standardized murals illustrating these themes suggests that it dated back to at least the seventeenth century. Fourth, the use of standardized religious texts that were emphasized by the court would in turn have ensured the consistency of narrative representation in the murals.

The visual and textual standardization seen in the wall paintings thus reflects the cultural homogenization of the central zone, influenced by the circulation of newly translated texts and the production of manuscripts. The employment of the vernacular, the near-exclusive use of the last ten Jataka stories, the life of Gotama Buddha, and the twenty-eight previous Buddhas, and the extended way in which the narratives were portrayed connected the murals with contemporary literary and social trends, while the supervision of artistic production by monks and the use of manuscripts as copy books assisted with the establishment of an artistic narrative canon that lasted for nearly two centuries.

Painting Styles

Although there are local variations in the colors used and in the level of care with which the temple paintings were produced, the standardized patterns and stylistic usage reveals an artistic network that extended across the central zone of Burma. Four main mural painting formats were utilized, sometimes simultaneously, during the seventeenth and eighteenth centuries in the central region. The first two were used during the seventeenth and eighteenth centuries. A third style emerged in the late eighteenth century, but was not used in the nineteenth century. The fourth style originated in the late eighteenth century, and was used well into the nineteenth century.

In the first painting format, seen in *Figure 9.4*, the narrative portions are laid out in multiple narrow registers with the stories winding up the walls. The colourful ornamental ceilings and borders are covered in repetitive interlocking floral and geometric designs, which may derive from textile patterns.[37] Scenes are divided by wavy lines and decorated panels, as well as vegetal forms, landscape features, and architectural structures. The landscape is flat with the action occurring along a single ground line formed by the base of the register. Scenes usually fill the entire height of the register, though occasionally small-scale scenes are inset along the top of the register. Most stories progress from left to right, although sometimes they are illustrated from right to left. If two separate actions occur in the same location, they are often shown together to conserve space, and since many of these conflations occur in scenes that are located in palace complexes, there is an emphasis on the wealth and status of the king and his court.[38] This type of spatio-temporal relationship is also extant in illustrated Burmese manuscripts.[39]

Buildings, which occupy the full height of the registers, are shown frontally and in a stereotypical fashion. Realistic proportions are not maintained, with people and animals almost the same size as the landscape and buildings they inhabit. Except for images of Buddhas, which are shown frontally, people are mostly illustrated in three-quarters profile and are characterized by broad faces, large ears with plug earrings, and three lines on their necks. They are clothed in textiles elegantly decorated with geometric patterns. Men are portrayed with a large lump in their cheeks, possibly representing a betel quid. The mural colors are bright and usually include a red background and an extensive use of deep green; less bold colors include yellow, white, and light brown. These basic elements, produced with greater or lesser skill, are widely distributed around the dry zone, and can be seen at Sagaing, Shweminwun, Pagan, Po Win Daung, Lekaing, Salin, and Pakhangyi.

The second painting format contains many elements of the first style, but with a few significant alterations (*Fig. 9.6*), suggesting that the two were related styles that perhaps derived from different workshops following similar templates or were temporal variations. The second style is seemingly later because more people are included in group scenes and images are arranged to provide a modicum of depth perspective, all of which are characteristics of later paintings influenced by contemporaneous Thai art.

In this style, ceilings are elaborately decorated with geometric and floral designs, of which the latter can assume a naturalistic appearance. The narrative registers are still narrow and numerous, and scenes are divided by double green and white wavy lines, solid black lines, changes in the hue of the background, as well as the standard landscape and architectural features. Scenes do not necessarily fill the entire height of a register, and the use of insets within the register or a horizontal line to create an additional space for narrative action is common. Unlike in the first painting format, a bird's-eye perspective was used on occasion. People are now shown in groups, rather than in straight lines, and the sense of depth and space is generated by figures standing in front of each other or stacked above and behind one another. In this way larger numbers of people can be shown, giving the paintings a more populated feel. The representation of people and architecture remains formulaic, however. Men have largely lost the bulge in the cheek, though a broadness of face, especially around the cheek area silhouetted against the background, is sometimes still evident. The color palette varies from the first style in that a buff-pink color has been added to the repertoire, and the green, while still present, is significantly reduced in quantity. Beige, white, and varying shades of blue were also used.

This second style is found in a variety of towns including Amarapura, Ywathitgyi, Anein, Amyint, Po Win Daung, Yesagyo, and Pakhangyi. The strong similarities of the two styles described suggest that they are variations on a theme. The location of many of the second style's sites around the upper reaches of the Irrawaddy River and the lower Chindwin River, rather than following the broad distribution of the first style, may indicate that the former was more of a regional style.

In the second half of the eighteenth century, there were radical stylistic changes, particularly noticeable in the coloration of the murals and in the extensive use of multiple perspectives allowing the viewer to see simultaneously different areas in a palace compound (*Fig. 9.7*). This was due in part to the resettlement of Thai artists into the central zone after the Burmese military campaign against neighboring Ayutthaya in the 1760s.[40] These murals are characterized by a bright red and a brilliant turquoise coloration. Ceilings, borders, and panel dividers are highly ornamental with complex, repetitive, and interlocking floral and geometric designs, which, as with earlier paintings, may have been based upon textile patterns. Greater emphasis upon external landscapes makes the pictures more naturalistic, and figures are more to scale with the environment than in the first two styles. The base of the register is no longer necessarily the only ground line used, as a bird's eye view into palace compounds and landscape scenes is common, differing greatly from the first style where frontal views of buildings were the norm. The use of multiple perspectives enables more than one row of people to be represented without having to place one person above the other or separate the levels of people with line dividers. In general, figures are integrated into the landscape more naturally than before.

Insets are less frequently employed, as the use of differing ground lines has reduced the need for them, but the scene located along the base of the register is the largest in size and is usually the main one in a narrative episode. Scene divisions are now indicated by a change of background color, which produces a more subtle and continuous effect than the use of buildings, trees, lines, and rocks. Greater amounts of contextual, and often non-religious, material are included in the depictions, and this additional imagery is accommodated in wide registers, up to three feet high, of which there can be as few as two in a building. The change in register size and the addition of contextual material are also a result of Thai influences.[41] This style of painting is distributed widely across the central zone, ranging from Mekkhaya, Amyint, Khinmon, and Ma U Leh to Myitche, Pagan, and Sinbyugyun.

A final style of painting that emerged in Burma during the late eighteenth century is similar to the third format in terms of perspective, but has a much duller palette of colors, usually a dark red and a deep green, as well as black, which is now used for more than outlining images (*Fig. 9.3*). Clothing, architecture, and landscape are not articulated as finely as in some of the other styles, but the murals are not without details. Scenes of everyday life are interspersed with the religious imagery and palace scenes or groups of people occupy considerable space in each band. In this style, the apparent combination of the coloration of the first and second styles with the spatial organization of the third suggests that the first three styles were conflated, an indication of the continuity prevalent in Burmese art.[42] While most of the remaining sites painted in this manner date to the early nineteenth century, the villages of Khinmon near Monwya on the Chindwin River and Montain near the city of Meiktila, located between the Samon and Irrawaddy Rivers, have temples dating to the eighteenth century that contain examples of this style.[43]

Commonly, all four mural styles are composed of two main parts: narrative material that is found on the walls and non-narrative material composed of floral and geometric motifs, magical signs, and protective figures that is found on ceilings, in doorways, and sometimes around the narrative imagery on the walls. Most temples and caves with wall paintings from the seventeenth and eighteenth century contain both narrative and non-narrative imagery, although a few sites scattered across the dry zone contain only non-narrative material composed of kneeling devotees. The narrative material, usually comprising the last ten Jataka stories, the life of Gotama Buddha, and the twenty-eight previous Buddhas, is highly consistent in terms of the stories chosen for representation, the scenes used to portray the tales, and the manner in which particular scenes are presented.[44]

The Twenty-Eight Previous Buddhas

The twenty-eight previous Buddhas were most often painted in a linear sequence along the top of temple or cave walls and against the ceiling with its floral and geometric decoration. Not differentiated visually except for occasional minor variations in the style of the trees, the images are shown seated in *bhumisparsha mudra* under their respective trees of enlightenment (*Figs. 9.4* and *9.5*). Sometimes they are flanked by kneeling disciples and devotees holding flowers, pennants, or umbrellas. Captions under the figures name each Buddha reaching enlightenment and his tree. Most temples and caves at all mural locations throughout the central zone contain this imagery.

Exceptions to this standard method of organization and portrayal do exist. At a few sites, including the Tilokaguru cave-temple on Sagaing Hill and the Mipaya cave-temple at Po Win Daung, the previous Buddhas are represented by a short sequence of four life events, comprising living in luxury, the *bodhisattva* being stopped by Mara while making the departure from the palace, the hair-cutting event which finalized his renunciation of worldly life, and the Enlightenment. The images are differentiated primarily by the manner in which the Buddha-to-be leaves the palace—riding on an elephant or horse, or in a carriage or palanquin. The way this expanded material was presented is the same at all sites. Sometimes the standard monoscenic representation of the previous Buddhas was presented along the top of the walls above the expanded, narrative version, such as can be found at the Tilokaguru cave-temple.

A further variation to the presentation of the previous Buddhas can be seen at Anein village, Po Win Daung, and two early nineteenth-century sites, the Shwezayan Pokala and the Pitakadaik located east of Mandalay and at Pagan respectively. Images of the previous Buddhas were sculpted and placed in painted niches or along a ledge around the walls at a height easily reached by worshippers. Often the surrounds, trees, and devotees were painted around the niches or on the wall above the ledge on which the images sit. At the Anein temple there are two rows of painted Buddhas, one in the normal location and the second above a ledge that runs around the center of the walls. The ledges and niches provide worshippers with an area to place offerings, which people continue to do today. A desire to be able to make offerings to the Buddhas reaching enlightenment may account for the reorganization of the traditional hierarchical order of the murals.[45]

The three main ways of portraying the twenty-eight previous Buddhas can be found at a variety of sites, with the first format the most evident one. Interestingly, however, even the variations are virtually identically portrayed at the sites where they are found. No site illustrates the previous Buddhas in a unique manner. The method and consistency in the depictions of the previous Buddhas can in part be attributed to the homogenous way in which they are described textually. As I. B. Horner writes, "The precision of the sequences of their [the Buddha-Chronicles] statements . . . is of almost mathematical beauty in its unvarying regularity. The features are constant, the content varies."[46] In keeping with the *Buddhavamsa*, the murals illustrate the same pattern for each life, altering only the details.

The Life of Gotama Buddha

Located below the monoscenic portraits of the previous Buddhas and portrayed in long strips that wind around temple walls, scenes from the life of the Buddha are usually composed of events that occurred prior to and surrounding the Buddha's Enlightenment, with a few sites continuing the narrative into the Buddha's life after that major event and even showing the Parinirvana and the distribution of relics. The most commonly portrayed episodes include the Buddha's birth, the departure and renunciation, Sujata offering food to the future Buddha, and Gotama's Enlightenment. Each of these is further broken down into a sequence of scenes. As with the illustrations of the previous Buddhas, the scenes of the Buddha's life are highly standardized.

Found at the sites of Amyint, Myitche, Anein, Po Win Daung, Yesagyo, Amarapura, Ywathitgyi, and Pagan,[47] the birth sequence includes the birth itself; the Buddha-to-be taking his first seven steps; being held up in a cloth with *devas* pouring water over him; being transported to his parents' palace in a palanquin; and placing his feet on the head of the *rishi*, Asita, who weeps because he realizes that he will not be alive when the *bodhisattva* reaches Enlightenment. These events are expanded or contracted by adding (or removing) additional scenes of the future Buddha being held and lustrated in a cloth, enlarging the size of the procession following the palanquin taking him home, and the inclusion or exclusion of Brahmins, who make predictions about whether he will become a Buddha or a *cakravartin*, in the scene with Asita.[48] Only rarely are the events of his life after his birth but prior to the Great Departure illustrated in the murals. At Yokson temple in Myitche, a scene of music and dance has a caption describing it as the marriage of Prince Siddhartha to Yasodhara, and the same temple appears to contain the only seventeenth- or eighteenth-century illustration of the prince's father performing the annual plowing ceremony and making an obeisance to his son because of the miraculous events that occurred around the latter.

The Departure and Renunciation scenes are among the most popular of the life of the Buddha sequence, being illustrated at most temples. They include Prince Siddhartha encountering the four sights that cause him to decide to renounce his life of luxury, viewing his wife and child for the last time while Channa the charioteer and Kanthaka the horse wait behind him, leaving the palace with the horse's hooves held up by *devas*, Mara obstructing this retreat from worldly life and promising the prince *cakravartin* status within seven days, Channa weeping over the dead body of Kanthaka, and Siddhartha cutting off his hair, which is caught by Sakka, on the far bank of the Anoma River.

At some locations, including Anein, Pagan, Myitche, Pakhangyi, Khinmon, Yesagyo, Ywathitgyi, Shweminwun, and Po Win Daung, images of Gotama's initial attempts to reach enlightenment are shown. These scenes include Bimbisara's wife living in luxury and donating to the Buddha-to-be in Rajagaha, the future Buddha in Anupiya forest, studying the meditational methods of Alara and Uttaka, and lying down surrounded by the *Pancavaggi* while the god Sakka plays the lute to indicate the middle way. After renouncing extreme austerities, Gotama's first meal is served by Sujata, a popular sequence that is also found in most temples. The scenes associated with this episode include the gods cooking the milk-rice, Sujata offering the bowl of food to the Buddha, and the Buddha setting the bowl afloat on the Neranjara River, where it rouses the *naga* who in the past gathered the bowls of the previous Buddhas. A less common scene connected with Sujata's offering is of her father living in luxury, which indicates the wealth and high status that enabled Sujata to make her significant offering (Lay Htat Kyaung U at Pagan).

After eating Sujata's offering and setting the bowl afloat, the future Gotama is often shown reclining in a grove of trees and then taking grass from a grass cutter to build a throne on which to meditate (Pakhangyi, Khinmon, Yesagyo, Po Win Daung, Anein, and Ywathitgyi). The Enlightenment itself is not focal, but is shown simply as part of the entire sequence, if it is shown at all. The Buddha reaches Enlightenment seated under the Bodhi tree, sometimes with the Earth Goddess wringing out her hair at his feet and occasionally with Mara's army to one side (Pakhangyi, Yesagyo, Po Win Daung, Anein, and Pagan).

The Seven Stations that the Buddha occupied during the seven weeks after his Enlightenment are fairly commonly illustrated (Pakhangyi, Myitche, Po Win Daung, Pagan, Anein, Ywathitgyi), and images of Tapussa and Bhallika paying homage to the Buddha can also be seen at a few sites (Pagan and Anein). Other post-Enlightenment scenes include being asked to teach by Sahampati Brahma (Anein and Pagan) and the Parinirvana. Events associated with the Parinirvana of the Buddha, such as his cremation and the distribution of the relics, are seen in only a few temples, including temple number 195 and the Shwe U Min temple at Pakhangyi, the Sunsagandalidaik temple at Shweminwun village near Sagaing, and at a temple in Ma U Leh near the confluence of the Irrawaddy and Chindwin Rivers. Illustrations of events associated with the activities of King Ajatasattu, Shin Ananda, and Shin Mogallana, as well as the Buddha bathing are very rare. Such scenes are primarily found at the Taung-bi Ok-kyaung and the

Upali Thein at Pagan and at temples in Amyint village. In general, the vast majority of post-Enlightenment events, usually shown as single scenes, focus upon the Buddha engaged in teaching at different monasteries during the rainy season, and repetitive, often identical, images of the Buddha seated in a generic monastery surrounded by monks are the standard method of portrayal of this activity at Anein, Pagan, Po Win Daung, Yesagyo, Myitche, and Amyint.

While the above list may appear extensive, the pictures of the life of the Buddha coalesce around a few main events, primarily the birth, Departure and Renunciation, Sujata's gift, the Enlightenment, and the Seven Stations. Each section is expanded or contracted through the addition of scenes with less action, such as people paying homage to the Buddha, palace scenes, and the Buddha walking. The illustrations in general reflect a fairly narrow body of material that is standardized across the region. This is due to the fact that the stories closely follow versions derived from Pali literature, particularly the *Jataka-nidana* or *The Story of Gotama Buddha*, of which the intermediate epoch section narrates the majority of the events shown in the murals.[49] The distribution of the relics is detailed in the *Buddhavamsa*.[50]

Similar to the selection of scenes, the way in which events were illustrated is quite uniform across the region, with a visual code of gestures and positions in place. For example, as Prince Siddhartha was about to depart from his life of luxury he took a last look at his sleeping wife and son (*Figs. 9 6* and *9.7*). This incident is represented by the prince standing to one side of a palace building that housed the bed on which Yasodhara and Rahula were reclining. Siddhartha lifts the curtain at the foot of the bed to view his family, while Channa the charioteer kneels and Kanthaka the horse stands behind him. This pictorial format can be seen at Loka Aung Mye temple in Khinmon, at temples in Anein, Amyint, Myitche, Ma U Leh, Yesagyo, and Pakhangyi villages, and at Lay Htat Kyaung U at Pagan. Another highly standardized image found at most locations is the death of Kanthaka from grief at being parted from the prince (*Figs. 9.8* and *9.9*). Occurring on a bank of the Anoma River, the horse lies curled up on the ground and Channa kneels behind the body with his hand over his eyes, a general gesture indicating grief that occurs in other relevant contexts. Other aspects of the life of the Buddha narrative are also virtually identical from site to site, and some of these devices for representing specific actions were used through the nineteenth and early twentieth centuries in a variety of visual media.

Jataka Stories

Primarily located below the scenes of the life of Gotama Buddha, the Jataka stories were usually organized, like the life events, in strips that wrapped around the temple walls. Enough episodes of each story were selected to provide a clear, if sometimes truncated, narrative. Most sites display a number of the last ten Jataka stories, the *Mahanipata*, but the murals in many temples are not sufficiently intact to determine whether all ten were once present. While some locations clearly do not have the space for all ten, based on the extent and composition of the remaining murals it is possible to suggest that many locations once did portray the entire group of stories, with the comprehensiveness with which the stories were illustrated often relating to the size of the temple or cave. Generally, the first tale was shown closest to the floor, and the Vessantara Jataka, the last of the 547 previous lives of the Buddha, was portrayed directly beneath the scenes of the life of the Buddha—an element of the hierarchical organization discussed above.

Some of the stories were shown in greater detail than the others, with the Mahanaradakassapa (no. 544) and the Khandahala (no. 542) Jatakas, for example, given the least amount of space,[51] while the representation of the Vessantara Jataka (no. 547), where the *bodhisattva* perfects the virtue of generosity, is the most extensive.[52] A full discussion of the scenes selected to depict the *Mahanipata* is beyond the scope of this study, instead, the focus of this section will be on the Vessantara Jataka as an example of how the other stories were consistently portrayed in the political core of seventeenth- and eighteenth-century Burma.

The Vessantara Jataka, which represents the virtue of perfect generosity, was illustrated in the greatest number of scenes and at the largest number of sites—two temples at Amyint; one temple at Ma U Leh; Yokson and Kyaung U temples at Myitche; Shwe U Min and Payani temples at Pakhangyi; Shwe Tha Lyaung cave-temple and cave numbers 284, 378, and 480 at Po Win Daung; Taung-bi Ok-kyaung and Shwe Kyaung U at Pagan; Chinthe, Shwe Gu Twin, two temples in the village, and two temples at the Zedi Daw Daik complex at Anein village; and Laung U Hmaw at Ywathitgyi.

The primary illustrated episodes are those associated with giving away the elephant, the horses, the carriage, and the children, but other scenes such as Vessantara and his family living in luxury, Vessantara giving away the 700 things, the family walking and receiving directions from a monk, Jujaka, over eating, sickening, dying, and being buried, and the family being reunited can also be found. The least frequently portrayed episodes were those where Vessantara donates a variety of things and the reunion of the family; Vessantara giving away his wife, Maddi, was never shown. All other events exist at most sites with variation almost exclusively occurring in the number of sub-scenes. Vessantara giving away his children to the Brahmin Jujaka appears to be the most significant episode of the story, as it is represented in the largest number of sub-scenes, which illustrate the action in detail. Thus the viewer can see Vessantara donating his children to Jujaka, the children asking not to be sent away, the children hiding in a lotus pond, the children being driven forward by Jujaka, Jujaka stumbling on the path, the escape of the children, the children being given away again, Jujaka driving the children on again, Jujaka sleeping in a tree while the children are being comforted at its foot by *devas* disguised as Vessantara and Maddi, Maddi picking fruit, Maddi being hindered from returning to the monastery by three *devas* disguised as felines, and Jujaka and the children arriving at the palace of the children's grandfather.

For example, at Laung U Hmaw in Ywathitgyi village the scenes chosen for representation include a palace scene (the family living in luxury); Vessantara giving the elephant to the Brahmins; the Brahmins departing on the elephant; Vessantara and his family riding in a carriage with a Brahmin asking for the horses; the family in a carriage drawn by deer with a Brahmin asking for the carriage; the family walking and getting directions from a monk; Vessantara giving the children to Jujaka; the children hiding in the lotus pond; the children asking not to be sent away; the children driven by Jujaka; the children escaping when Jujaka falls down; the children running; the children being given to Jujaka again; Maddi blocked by three wild animals; Jujaka driving the children; Jujaka asleep in the tree with the children tied at the bottom; devas comforting the children; Jujaka driving the children; Jujaka begging; a palace scene; and Jujaka presented with food. The remainder of the representation is unclear, but is not extensive.[53] The scenes of Vessantara giving away his children, with the three animals blocking Maddi's return just visible in the upper right corner, are illustrated in *Figure 9.10.* As with the illustrations of this story at other sites, the episodes on giving have been chosen to emphasize beneficence, and the scenes depicting this giving are allocated the largest amount of space to reinforce the importance of the virtue being perfected.[54]

Gestural codification also occurs in depictions of the Jataka stories with specific scenes portrayed in set ways. For example, in the Bhuridatta Jataka (no. 543), representations of the *naga* being forced to perform by the snake charmer always show the serpent draped over his captor's shoulders with Bhuridatta's brother standing to the side about to rescue his hapless sibling (*Figs. 9.11* and *9.12*). The use of specific gestures for particular scenes or certain events of a story makes the identification of the visual tale easy among the repetitive illustrations. Thus, as with the representations of the twenty-eight previous Buddhas and the life of Gotama Buddha, the Jataka stories are illustrated highly consistently in seventeenth- and eighteenth-century Burma.

Non-Canonical Features

While the majority of the imagery painted on the walls of seventeenth- and eighteenth-century Burmese temples is illustration of canonical material, there are a few examples of non-canonical material. The three themes of these latter images include the depiction of the fruit maidens favored by alchemists, the use of twisted *naga* forms as a central panel on ceilings and as a surround for footprints and other motifs, and the inclusion of two magic diagrams, the so-called magic square and the representation of the Buddha seated in the center of a circle surrounded by a number of other figures. These elements occupy little space in the mural paintings as they were usually placed in doorways or window alcoves, on ceilings, or were formed into thin bands around the edges of the narratives. As with the canonical material, this imagery is highly standardized, and although it is not found in many temples, it is distributed around the central zone, rather than concentrated in one particular area. The sites with these illustrations include Lekaing, Sinbyugyun, Amyint, Anein, Po Win Daung, Ywathitgyi, Ma U Leh, and Yesagyo. As discussed earlier, these non-canonical features were a wide-spread cultural phenomenon found at all levels of Burmese society, with even the kings participating in occultist practices, despite efforts to establish orthodox Theravada Buddhism.

Nagas

The *nagas* portrayed on the ceilings of a number of temples from the central zone are enlarged versions of those portrayed in the Jataka stories and in the life of Gotama Buddha, usually with a green scaly body, a buff-colored face, and a red crest. In the non-narrative format they are intertwined to create a generally circular or oval, centered pattern on ceilings where lotus flowers and geometric shapes were traditionally placed (*Fig. 9.13*). Alternatively, twined *nagas* were painted around footprints and other ceiling motifs. *Nagas* in the center of the ceilings are found only in the lower Chindwin region, though the limited extent of such imagery may be due to whitewashing and decay, as the *nagas* surrounding footprints and other ceiling motifs can be found south of Pagan in the Minbu region. *Nagas* are a feature of some stucco work in the Shan State, and were also carved as supports for the raised platform of certain wooden structures, especially palaces and monasteries. *Naga-lein* is an interlocking snake pattern found on lacquer, and while this imagery is abstract, unlike the snakes in the murals, it appears that this was a popular form of decoration in Burma.

Associated with the earth, water, and fertility, *nagas* are also often credited with an understanding of the Buddhist law, as can be seen in the Bhuridatta Jataka (no. 543), where the *bodhisattva* is a *naga*, and in the Vidhurapandita Jataka (no. 545), when the *nagas* listen to the preaching of the *bodhisattva*, Vidhura.[55] They are also recorded as honoring the Buddha in Pali texts.[56] Furthermore, *nagas* are believed to have a protective function since the Buddha was shielded from rain by Muchalinda Naga during meditation in the sixth week after Enlightenment. The *naga* also physically forms a bridge between the human world and the subterranean world when they are carved on the pillars supporting a building.[57] Less positively, the chapter on King Duttabaung in the early nineteenth-century *Glass Palace Chronicle* records that the king was abducted because he insulted the *nagas* by spitting into the sea.[58] The place where he was abducted was in the whirlpool of *Naga-yit* ("where *nagas* twist and turn").[59] Because of their proximity to images of the Buddha, the intertwined *nagas* and the *naga* surrounds can be considered protective images.

Magic Imagery

Instructions to draw magic figures, sometimes called *in,* on buildings and walls to protect a space, such as a city, and lists of different named magic squares, circles, and triangles are found in royal orders from the seventeenth and eighteenth centuries.[60] One form of magic square draws on the Jataka stories for its significance. In Gotama Buddha's former lives, called *apyit-daw-paun*, he died a natural death as an animal 136 times. In sixteen of these lives he was a crane, in fifteen a yak, in fourteen a bull, in thirteen a duck, in twelve a cock, in eleven an elephant, in ten a monkey, in nine a duck, in eight a water buffalo, in seven a mynah bird, in six a pigeon, in five a *karaweik* (goose or *hamsa*), in four a *kinnara* (a mythical bird), in three a parrot, in two a peacock, and in one a horse. Magic squares are usually represented as a box with sixteen squares in which the number of each of these groups of animal lives is written numerically (e.g., 16,

15, etc.). The numbers are arranged in such a way that when adding together the numbers of four boxes in a row (vertical, horizontal, or diagonal) or the four corner boxes, the sum will always be thirty-four. In this form, the squares are believed to provide protection against evil.

The magic square associated with the Jataka stories can be identified in the wall paintings at two sites: Laung U Hmaw at Ywathitgyi village and the Mi-paya cave at Po Win Daung.[61] In the murals, each of the animals was enclosed in a circle, all 136 of which were arranged in a line along or around the edges of the visual narratives.[62] In *Figure 9.14*, the animal second from the left is identified in the caption as a horse, literally "horse one life," and the buffalos seen here are labeled "water buffalo eight lives."[63] Although the linear organization of these images negates the function of the magic square technically, the importance of the natural death in each of these lives transcends a specific method of portrayal,[64] as the position of these images along the edges of the narrative protects the canonical scenes inside and demarcates the particularly sacred portions of the illustrations.

A second form of magical protection seen in the paintings is the representation of a Buddha image on the ceiling of a cave or temple. This imagery is characterized by a Buddha image in *bhumisparsha mudra* at the center of a series of concentric circles, which have been divided into sections (*Fig. 9.15*). Sometimes the Buddha is flanked by kneeling devotees or monks, while at other times the image is the sole one in the innermost circle. In the second ring ten kneeling monks in individual sections, one of whom is seated in a building, a lone king or wealthy personage, and a group of five monks can usually be seen. A horse and elephant, *chinthes*, *nagas*, ogres, gods, a person on horseback, and more monks are usually depicted in the outer ring. This imagery is found in a virtually identical format in temples and caves at Amyint, Ma U Leh, and Po Win Daung. The one significant exception occurs in cave number 472 at Po Win Daung where the center is occupied by a standard representation of a lotus flower, rather than a Buddha image, but the imagery in the surrounding circles remains the same.

A reference to this magic circle is found in the *Upper Burma Gazetteer*, where it is illustrated with the explanation that it was a magic device inscribed on the turban of a military officer for protection in times of war. Scott and Hardiman described the image as follows, "In this charm the placid and peaceful Buddha is incongruously placed as the central figure; an army of *nats* followed by contingents of lions [*chinthe*] and dragons [*naga*] is led by a celestial ogre; the dwellers in the sky are headed by the sun and moon; and lastly, as if to cast oil on troubled waters, a band of monks is requisitioned."[65] A second possible reference can be found in a royal order from the ninth of May 1635 in a list of drawings ordered to be fixed to the ceilings of gate towers. The image to be reproduced is described as, "[t]he Sitting Buddha on the Jewelled Pedestal flanked by the disciples Kondanna and Bhattiya with their hands in the Prayer Attitude, Vappa holding a begging bowl, Mahananda holding a pitcher."[66] Additional material to be illustrated was the story where the *bodhisattva* as a quail performs an act of truth (Vattaka Jataka, no. 35), the rabbit *bodhisattava* donating his body (Sasa Jataka, no. 316), monks at the house of Ghatikara (Ghatikara Sutta, no. 81, Majjhima Nikaya), the *bodhisattva* as a monkey king protecting his troop from the ogre (Nalapana Jataka, no. 20), the *nat* spirits of the sun and the moon (peacock and rabbit respectively), and the jackal, otter, and monkey *bodhisattvas* practicing *silas* (precepts), all of which, except for the sun and the moon, refer to the four miracles of this era that endure for the entire period.[67]

The information in the order does not correspond identically with the images painted on the ceilings of the temples and caves, but the fact that the requisitioned image consisted of a seated Buddha in a circle format depicted on a ceiling suggests that it represented a form of magic circle. The order also lists named magic circles, squares, and triangles thereby indicating that specific images were produced for particular functions. The imagery as painted on the ceilings of the temples and cave-temples was thus included to protect the Buddha and the ritual space.

Alchemy

Depictions of the Thuyaung (literally, "fake person") tree can be found primarily at temples in Amyint village and at Sinbyugyun just north of Minbu, but an example in glass mosaic also exists near Inle Lake in Shan State. These images, which are virtually identical in format at the different locations, consist of a large central tree with young women dangling from the branches and men flying through the air towards the tree and/or fighting at the base (*Fig. 9.16*). These images are of successful alchemists who have managed to attain a permanently youthful body.

According to Burmese beliefs, alchemists do not eat meat because of the smell and are unable to have regular contact with normal humans because they smell as a result of consuming animal flesh. However, alchemists are not ascetics and are subject to normal bodily desires. The result is that alchemists make love to a type of fruit in the form of a young human woman that grows in the Himalayas. The fruit women get easily crushed, however, and therefore do not last long. Furthermore, this type of fruit is not particularly common, so alchemists fight and quarrel over access to it, as seen in the visual representations.[68] In the instances where this painted scene can clearly be identified, it is located over an entrance into the building or in a window alcove, and thus is somewhat separated from the canonical material in the main area. Such scenes may denote the transition from profane to sacred space or indicate the desire to live as a human until the arrival of Maitreya, the next and last Buddha of this era, whereupon the individual will reach enlightenment.[69] The organization of the murals places canonical material closer to the central Buddha image in the temple than the non-canonical, revealing a hierarchy of belief systems.[70]

Discussion

In summary, improving economic conditions and political and administrative reorganization in the central dry zone of Burma during the seventeenth and eighteenth centuries contributed to the expansion of agricultural land and an increase in population numbers, the latter also augmented by the arrival of war-time deportees. These trends in turn provided the social organization and the funds necessary to construct and decorate numerous temples complexes around the lower reaches of the Mu and Chindwin Rivers and along the central reaches of the Irrawaddy River. In the murals that embellish these religious structures, narrative elements of the lives of the Buddhas and the previous lives of Gotama Buddha were represented in highly similar patterns, ranging from the overall organization through the level of gestural detail. These illustrations were of accepted stories and reflected fundamental religious and social beliefs. The close connection between kingship and merit is reflected in the wall paintings through a combination of images of enlightenment and the benefits of wealth and status, and these concepts were influential in institutionalizing the subject matter of the wall paintings.[71]

Regional development of a strong canon of imagery relates to the probable use of manuscripts with illustrations as guides and the fact that monks also supervised the production of wall paintings, as well as the standardization of textual use. The emergence of vernacular religious literature during the seventeenth and eighteenth centuries, along with the materialization of a variety of vernacular and prose story-telling methods, as well as drama forms, reveals a predilection for stories among the Burmese that textual material evidence suggests was highly prevalent in the eighteenth century, but which the murals indicate was already in existence in the seventeenth.

The fact that a canon of artistic representation was established during the seventeenth and eighteenth centuries indicates that a network allowing for the transmission of visual material existed between villages and towns in the dry zone. Furthermore, the standardization of religious and social concepts, particularly the merit path to enlightenment and the desirability of wealth and status as exemplified by the king suggests that there was a strong network in existence between the court and the central zone, which corroborates Lieberman's theory of increasing centrality and the consolidation of the Burmese state during the seventeenth and eighteenth centuries.[72] The similarities in the wall paintings testify to the cultural homogeneity, which as Lieberman states was both a symptom and a cause of political cohesion,[73] found in the dry zone in Burma during this time period.

Further corroboration that fundamental cultural concepts had been established in Burma by the late seventeenth century is the fact that the illustrations of the twenty-eight previous Buddhas, the life of Gotama Buddha, and the *Mahanipata* maintain their consistency through stylistic alterations that occurred in the middle of the eighteenth century. They do not appear to have been significantly affected by the crises and loss of crown control over the central zone during the first half of the century. Michael Aung-Thwin has argued that the continuity seen in Burmese history is a result of the strength of Burmese institutions and that this cultural system can be viewed as a spiral where the same institutions are expanded and contracted rather than eliminated to make way for new ones.[74] Specifically in the case of the wall paintings of the Jataka stories and the life of the Buddha, the Burmese court created exemplary models for Burma's citizens, and these continued to be used even during a time of crisis for a king, precisely because it was an individual king who was problematic, not the institution of kingship, and the Buddhist belief system of the merit path to enlightenment was never in question.[75] The desire of the periphery to generate good karma and to emulate an idealized king was therefore able to survive political changes and upheavals, and as a result the imagery in the murals was unaffected.

In conclusion, seventeenth- and eighteenth-century wall paintings suggest that both orthodox and unorthodox ideas were widespread, indicating a significant level of homogenization religiously and culturally, with the standardization of the wall paintings both defining cultural concepts and legitimizing them. The Burmese state's unity can be considered in part to emerge from the adherence of the population to core beliefs that "establish the physical and spiritual parameters of their world."[76] The location of the wall paintings across the central zone can be viewed as a cultural map of a unified area that consisted of networked secondary centers under the central administration's control, with the subject matter of the murals providing a spiritual rationale for the relationships thus established.[77]

Notes

1. The author wishes to thank Ken Hall for his support and encouragement on this project. Thanks are also due to William Pruitt for his editorial assistance.

2. Victor Lieberman, *Burmese Administrative Cycles: Anarchy and Conquest, c. 1580-1760* (Princeton, NJ: Princeton University Press, 1984). Victor Lieberman, *Strange Parallels: Southeast Asia in Global Context, c. 800-1830* (Cambridge: Cambridge University Press, 2003).

3. The wall paintings in this study are drawn from the seventeenth and eighteenth centuries for several reasons. Extant Pagan period (1044-1287) murals are highly concentrated at Pagan and a few surrounding towns, such as Sale and Pakhangyi. There are numerous buildings from the Pagan period scattered around the central zone, which once contained wall paintings. Few murals of the fourteenth- to seventeenth-century period remain, and most likely shifting political centers and multiple capitals, as well as significant warfare, contributed to this dearth of material. The merit-making activity of whitewashing temples to make them appear clean and new has also taken its toll on artistic material through the centuries. Similarly, extant murals from the nineteenth century are very limited, and, interestingly, they are quite disparate in style; the reasons for this are unexplored and go beyond the scope of this study. The cohesive nature of the seventeenth- and eighteenth-century material coupled with a large number of existing sites, however, provides the scholar with a significant body of material to explore. It should be noted that few sites from this latter period are located within the capital cities; most of them are in secondary centers within the central dry zone of Burma.

4. Lieberman, *Burmese Administrative Cycles*, 80.

5. William J. Koenig, *The Burmese Polity, 1752-1819: Politics, Administration, and Social Organization in the Early Konbaung Period.* Papers on South and Southeast Asia, no. 34 (Ann Arbor, MI: University of Michigan, Center for South and Southeast Asian Studies, 1990), 54, 105.

6. In the early seventeenth century, after a change in the system by which appanages were granted, most were located close to the capital (within 140 miles) and few were further south than Minbu. Frank N. Trager and William J. Koenig, *Burmese Sit-tans, 1764-1826: Records of Rural Life and Administration* (Tuscon: University of Arizona Press, 1979), 17. See also, Koenig, *Burmese Polity*, chapter 4 for additional information on Burmese administrative organization. There are numerous references to specific areas relating to the appanage system in the *Royal Orders of Burma* (*ROB*), the *Royal Admini-*

stration of Burma, and the *Glass Palace Chronicle*, among others. Than Tun, ed. *Royal Orders of Burma*, AD 1598-1885, vols. 1-10 (Kyoto: Center for Southeast Asian Studies, Kyoto University, 1986-1990). Pe Maung Tin and G.H. Luce, trans., *The Glass Palace Chronicle of the Kings of Burma* (Rangoon: Rangoon University Press, 1960); U Tin, *The Royal Administration of Burma* (Bangkok: Ava Publishing House, 2001). For example, in 1801 Princess Shwegu was given Pakhangyi to hold in fief (*ROB*, 19 July 1801, vol. 5, 177).

7. Victor Lieberman, "Was the Seventeenth Century a Watershed in Burmese History?" in *Southeast Asia in the Early Modern Period: Trade, Power, and Belief*, ed. Anthony Reid (Ithaca, NY: Cornell University Press, 1993), 238.

8. Lieberman, *Burmese Administrative Cycles*, 152, 182, 183, 192, and 194.

9. Victor Lieberman, "Secular Trends in Burmese Economic History, c. 1350-1830, and their Implications for State Formation," *Modern Asian Studies*, 25, 1 (1991), 29-30; Lieberman, *Burmese Administrative Cycles*, ch. 3.

10. After military campaigns in the seventeenth century, the political strength of the nuclear zone in Burma was further augmented by large numbers of deportees being forcibly relocated into the Burmese heartland, particularly around Kyaukse, the Mu River, and the lower Chindwin River valley. These people were given land to cultivate within a seventy mile radius of the capital. A further demographic resurgence of the central area came in the 1760s with deportees arriving from Manipur and the Shan, Lao, and Thai regions. See Trager and Koenig, *Burmese Sit-tans*, 17; Koenig, *Burmese Polity*, 7, 31; Lieberman, "Was the Seventeenth Century a Watershed," 235; and Lieberman, "Secular Trends," 5.

11. Murals are preserved in part because of the dry climactic conditions in the central zone. It should not be assumed that other areas of the country lacked such an art form simply because nothing has survived to the present. It must also be borne in mind that the conclusions of this research are most likely skewed because of their reliance on material remains. Contemporaneous literature provides little information about the existence of mural sites outside the dry zone.

12. Pagan period buildings at Pagan have been the subject of considerable research, but there are few studies of nineteenth-century structures. The minor temples with seventeenth- and eighteenth-century wall paintings have not been studied, nor have Pagan-period buildings located outside Pagan. For further information on architecture in Burma, see Paul Strachan, *Pagan: Art and Architecture of Old Burma* (Whiting Bay, Arran: Kiscadale Publications, 1989) and Pierre Pichard, *Inventory of Monuments at Pagan*, vols. 1-8 (Gartmore, Stirling, Scotland: Kiscadale, 1992-2001). For later monuments see Aung Thaw, *Historical Sites in Burma* (Rangoon: Sarpay Beikman Press, 1972), 125-150; and. Sylvia Fraser-Lu, *Burmese Crafts: Past and Present* (Kuala Lumpur: Oxford University Press, 1994), 63-65 and 71-74.

13. Lieberman, "Secular Trends," 26; Lieberman, "Was the Seventeenth Century a Watershed," 242-243.

14. E. Michael Mendelson, "Observations on a Tour in the Region of Mount Popa, Central Burma," *France-Asie*, 19 (1963), 797. See also, E. Michael Mendelson, "A Messianic Association in Upper Burma," *Bulletin of the School of Oriental and African Studies*, 24 (1961), 560-580 for further information on the role of *weikzas* in Burmese society.

15. Maung Htin Aung, *Folk Elements in Burmese Buddhism* (London: Oxford University Press, 1962), ch. 4.

16. Mendelson, "Observations on a Tour," 797-798.

17. Koenig, *Burmese Polity*, 44-45. For the role of Brahmins in Burma and their use of occult techniques as part of the rituals and ceremonies of the court, see Jacques P.

Leider, "Specialists for Ritual, Magic, and Devotion: The Court Brahmins (*Punna*) of the Konbaung Kings (1752-1885)," *Journal of Burma Research*, 10 (2006), 169-178.

18. For a discussion of how prophecies and omens were viewed and utilized in Burma, see Michael Aung-Thwin, "Prophecies, Omens, and Dialogue: Tools of the Trade in Burmese Historiography," in *Historical Essays in Honor of Kenneth R. Rossman*, ed. Kent Newmyer (Lincoln: University of Nebraska Press, 1980), 171-185. Than Tun, "The Influence of Occultism in Burmese History with Special Reference to Bodawpaya's Reign 1782-1819," *Bulletin of the Burma Historical Commission*, 1, 2 (1960), 117-145.

19. *ROB*, 1, 44-47, and 4, 43.

20. See Koenig, *Burmese Polity*, 41-45 for a summary of the Burmese system of belief. Melford E. Spiro, *Buddhism and Society: A Great Tradition and Its Burmese Vicissitudes* (Berkeley: University of California Press, 1982). Michael Aung-Thwin, *Pagan: The Origins of Modern Burma* (Honolulu: University of Hawai'i Press, 1985), 39-46.

21. Michael Aung-Thwin, "Divinity, Spirit, and Human: Conceptions of Classical Burmese Kingship," in *Centers, Symbols, and Hierarchies: Essays on the Classical States of Southeast Asia*, ed. Lorraine Gesick (New Haven: Yale University Southeast Asia monograph series, no. 26, 1983), 51. For further information on kingship in Burma, see the following: Michael Aung-Thwin, "Jambudipa: Classical Burma's Camelot," *Contributions to Asian Studies*, 16 (1981), 38-61; Aung-Thwin, *Pagan*, 47-68; Michael Aung-Thwin, "Heaven, Earth, and the Supernatural World: Dimensions of the Exemplary Center in Burmese History," in *The City as a Sacred Center: Essays on Six Asian Contexts*, ed. Bardwell Smith and Holly Baker Reynolds (Leiden: E.J. Brill, 1987), 88-102.

22. Aung-Thwin, "Conceptions of Classical Burmese Kingship," 74.

23. James Grey, *Ancient Proverbs and Maxims from Burmese Sources, or The Nîti Literature of Burma* (London: Routledge, 2000 [reprint]), introduction.

24. Ibid. Koenig, *Burmese Polity*, 90.

25. The Jataka tales demonstrate the law of cause and effect and illustrate the perfection of the ten virtues necessary for reaching enlightenment. The last ten Jataka stories are, as Reynolds phrases it, ". . . popular and effective vehicles for the inculcation of specifically Buddhist virtues." Frank Reynolds, "The Many Lives of the Buddha: A Study of Sacred Biography and Theravada Tradition," in *Biographical Process: Studies in the History and Psychology of Religion*, ed. Frank E. Reynolds and Donald Capps (The Hague: Mouton, 1976), 43. See also, A.L. Basham, "The Pali Jatakas," *Literature East and West*, 12 (Dec. 1968), 114-128; and John Garrett Jones, *Tales and Teachings of the Buddha* (London: George Allen and Unwin, 1979). The narratives influenced popular culture by explaining Buddhist ethical teachings to lay people, and numerous examples of how the stories were used in Burmese society exist (Lu Pe Win, "The Jatakas in Burma," in *Essays Offered to G.H. Luce by His Colleagues and Friends in Honour of His Seventy-fifth Birthday*, vol. 2 (Switzerland: Artibus Asiae Publishers, 1966), 94-108. Instances where the Jatakas play a political and influential role are found in the royal orders of the kings of Burma and in Shin Sandalinka's *Maniyadanabon*, which was completed in 1781 (*The Maniyadanabon of Shin Sandalinka*. L.E. Bagshawe, trans. [Ithaca, NY: Cornell University Press, Data Paper no. 115, Southeast Asia Program, 1981]). The tales presented in the *Maniyadanabon* relate to actual problems and are cited so as to reveal precedent and custom. In the royal orders, stories are cited as cues to appropriate behavior. For instance, Alaungpaya sent a message to the king of Hanthawaddy on the 28th of September 1756, stating "Firstly, he should know that he is fighting a losing battle. Secondly, he failed to take the cue of [the] Bhuridatta Jataka" (*ROB*, vol. 3, 33.) The use of these stories as exemplars and precedents indicates that the Jataka tales were well-known throughout Burmese society.

26. The regulation of the overall layout of the paintings is further suggested by a royal order pronounced on the eighth of April 1649, which stated that the Rajamanicula pagoda was to be painted from bottom to top with scenes of hell, the abode of men, the abode of *devas*, the abode of *brahmas*, one on top of the other, all 547 Jataka stories, and finally the life of the Buddha (*ROB*, 1, 139). See also, Alexandra Green, "Buddhist Narrative in Burmese Murals," Ph.D. dissertation (London: University of London School of Oriental and African Studies, 2001), 208-212.

27. In the last ten stories the future Buddha is born a prince or king in six of the tales, a king's main minister in two (Vidhurapandita and Mahosadha), a god in one (Mahanaradakassapa), and the child of parents born to village chiefs in one (Sama).

28. Green, "Buddhist Narrative," 37-8, 277-293. Alexandra Green, "Deep Change? Burmese Wall Paintings from the 11th to 19th Centuries," *Journal of Burma Studies*, 10 (2006), 1-50.

29. The number 500 merely indicates a large group of people, a standard method of aggrandizement, rather than a specific numeral.

30. *ROB*, 1, 35-36.

31. Patricia M. Herbert, *The Life of the Buddha* (London: British Library, 1993), 9-15. Nineteenth-century murals of the twenty-eight previous Buddhas, the life of Gotama Buddha, and the Vessantara Jataka at the Shwe Gu Nyi in Kyaukka near Monywa on the Chindwin River follow the format of the late eighteenth-century illustrated manuscripts identically down to the use of a yellow ground for the extended captions.

32. Prose had previously been considered a strictly functional form of communication reserved for the clarification of the Pali texts.

33. Mabel Haynes Bode, *Pali Literature of Burma* (London: Royal Asiatic Society of Great Britain and Ireland, 1966), 48. These translations were part of a movement that made story collections more accessible to a general audience, which built on the earlier popularity of story-telling. Other literary forms, such as the new verse form, the *yagan*, and drama, also were used as narrative vehicles. Anna Allott, *Burmese Literature*, English manuscript; published copy in Italian in Hla Pe, Anna Allott, and John Okell, "Letteratura Birmana," *Storia Delle Letterature D'Orient*, vol. 4, ed. O. Botto (Milano: Vaillardi, 1969) 19, 26-27, 30. Herbert, *Life of the Buddha*, 9-10.

34. These stories remain in print today. Other, possibly earlier, translations may not have survived. Allott, "Letteratura Birmana," 19, 26-27 and 30. Bode, *Pali Literature*, 63.

35. Green, "Buddhist Narrative," 122-127.

36. Herbert, "Letteratura Birmana," 9-10. Patricia Herbert, "Burmese Court Manuscripts," in *The Art of Burma: New Studies*, ed. Donald Stadtner (Bombay: Marg Publications, 1999), 92. See the description of style three in this study.

37. John Guy, *Woven Cargoes: Indian Textiles in the East* (London: Thames and Hudson, 1998), 56-58.

38. Green, "Buddhist Narrative," 253-256.

39. Herbert, *Life of the Buddha*, 11. For similar spatio-temporal relationships in other Asian visual narratives, see Vidya Dehejia, "India's Visual Narratives: The Dominance of Space over Time," in *Paradigms of Indian Architecture: Space and Time in Representation and Design*, Collected Papers on South Asia no. 13, ed. Giles Tillotson (Richmond, Surrey: Curzon, 1998), 80-106.

40. The full impact of the Thai deportees on Burmese art has yet to be studied. See Allott, "Letteratura Birmana," 27. Herbert, *Life of the Buddha*, 10.

41. Thai manuscript and wall paintings exhibit these same characteristics. The connections between Thai and Burmese painting of the eighteenth and nineteenth centuries is part of a research project, currently in very early stages, comparing and contrasting Burmese, Thai, and Sri Lankan wall paintings.

42. The limited number of sites with murals painted in this style and the fact that very few sites have paintings from the nineteenth century precludes further analysis.

43. It is conceivable that the buildings were constructed first and the paintings were added later or are examples of re-painting.

44. A few sites, most significantly Tilokaguru Cave-temple on Sagaing Hill and Ananda Ok-kyaung at Pagan, contain depictions of Jatakas that are not among the last ten.

45. Green, "Buddhist Narrative," 210-211.

46. I. B. Horner, trans., *The Minor Anthologies of the Pali Canon, part III, Chronicle of Buddhas (Buddhavamsa) and Basket of Conduct (Cariyapitaka)* (London: Pali Text Society, 1975), xx.

47. As noted above, the poor condition of many temples makes the pool of sites with this imagery smaller than it once was.

48. Expansion or contraction may have to do with practical considerations, such as the size of the temple. Stories tend to be longer in larger temples, most likely because more space is available. In small temples such as the Kamma Kyaung U at Pagan, the Jatakas are shown in a small number of scenes because of space constraints.

49. N.A. Jayawickrama, trans., *The Story of Gotama Buddha (Jātaka-nidāna)* (Oxford: Pali Text Society, 2000). There are three parts to the text: the distant epoch, the intermediate epoch, and the recent epoch. The first relates Sumedha's decision to become a Buddha and gives an account of previous Buddhas making a prophecy about Gotama Buddha. The intermediate epoch tells of the life of the Buddha from his descent from Tusita Heaven to be born as Prince Siddhartha through his Enlightenment, and the third section describes post-enlightenment events through the donation of the Jetavana monastery. It concludes with praise for the dedication of monasteries. The murals illustrate the story presented in this text closely.

50. Horner, *The Minor Anthologies*, 98-99.

51. The Khandahala Jataka is usually represented by a palace scene and a flaming cauldron by which a series of animals stands either waiting to be executed or being freed. The Mahanaradakassapa Jataka is commonly depicted as a palace scene with the *bodhisattva* Narada admonishing King Angati. The more discursive nature of these stories may account for the small amount of space devoted to portraying them visually.

52. The focus on this tale is due to the fact that Burmese society emphasizes the generation of merit through gift-giving.

53. The next Jataka story begins at the corner of the wall, and the identifiable sections of the Vessantara ends just shortly before the edge.

54. For a discussion of the use of space in Burmese wall paintings, see Green, "Buddhist Narrative," 280-284.

55. E.B. Cowell, ed., *The Jataka or Stories of the Buddha's Former Births*, vol. 6 (Cambridge: Cambridge University Press, 1897), 80-113, 126-156.

56. Horner, *The Minor Anthologies*, 4.

57. Sylvia Fraser-Lu, *Splendour in Wood: The Buddhist Monasteries of Burma* (Bangkok: Orchid Press, 2001), 75-77, 87-89.

58. Pe Maung Tin, *Glass Palace Chronicles*, 14-18.

59. Maung Htin Aung, *Burmese Folk-Tales* (London: Oxford University Press, 1948), xix and xxi.

60. *ROB*, 10 March 1784 (vol. 4, 43), 7 and 9 May 1635 (vol. 1, 44-47). In these contexts the space being protected is the city or urban area, palace, and clock tower. The fact that they are painted in temples and caves indicates that they were used in other contexts as well. Jacques Leider discusses the role of Brahmins in the production of magic squares in Burma in Leider, "Specialists for Ritual, Magic, and Devotion," 176-177.

61. Elizabeth Moore notes that the magic square became popular before the middle of the eighteenth century; and other sites that illustrate the magic square include the Mahamuni temple in Mandalay, the Yadanamyitsu temple at Pagan, the Pyinnya Zegon pagoda, and on ceramic tiles at the U Htaung Bopaya in Salingyi near Monywa. Elizabeth Moore, "The Royal Cities of Myanmar 14th-19th Centuries with Reference to China," in *South East Asia & China: Art, Interaction & Commerce*, ed. Rosemary Scott and John Guy (London: University of London, 1995), 110-111. The references to such magic devices in royal orders from the seventeenth century indicate an early date for their popular use on structures.

62. Magic imagery has not been extensively studied, and therefore the specific name of the magic diagram shown in the paintings is not known.

63. "Myin ta pyit" and "kywe shiq pyit."

64. Patricia Herbert, personal communication, 2000.

65. James G. Scott and J. P. Hardiman, *Gazetteer of Upper Burma and the Shan States*, pt. 1, vol. 2 (Rangoon: Superintendent of Government Printing, 1900-1901), 80. Some of these cloths are currently held in the British Library and museum collections.

66. *ROB*, vol. 1, 45.

67. Ibid. Cowell, 1897: vol. 1, 56. These last three animals are the friends of the rabbit *bodhisattva* in the Sasa Jataka, no. 316.

68. Maung Htin Aung, *Folk Elements in Burmese Buddhism*, 45. See also Maung Htin Aung, "Alchemy and Alchemists in Burma," *Folk-Lore*, 44, 4 (1933), 346-354.

69. The desire of alchemists for eternally youthful bodies is often normalized within mainstream Burmese Buddhist thought b attributing it to the desire to be alive as a human during the future Buddha Maitreya's lifetime in order to be assured of reaching enlightenment.

70. At Sinbyugyun this illustration is in a window alcove with hell scenes, and may imply the problematic nature of the alchemical path for reaching enlightenment. At one temple in Amyint village, the Thuyaung tree is found over an entrance into the building. Another doorway into the same structure illustrates Dipankara's prophecy to Sumedha, which was Gotama's embarkation point on the path to becoming a Buddha. Perhaps the use of these images in the doorways of this temple refers to different paths to the same goals.

71. Green, "Buddhist Narratives," 294-299; and Green, "Deep Change."

72. For a survey of the integrative trend in Burma, see Lieberman, *Strange Parallels*, ch. 2.

73. Lieberman, "Secular Trends," 21.

74. Michael Aung-Thwin, "Spirals in Early Southeast Asian and Burmese History," *Journal of Interdisciplinary History*, 21, 4 (1991), 592.

75. See Green, "Deep Change," where it is argued that there is significant continuity between Pagan period paintings and seventeenth- and eighteenth-century ones due to the fact that underlying cultural and religious beliefs had not fundamentally changed over the centuries. See also Aung-Thwin, *loc. cit.*, 597; Leonard Y. Andaya, "Cultural State Formation in Eastern Indonesia," in *Southeast Asia in the Early Modern Era: Trade, Power, and Belief*, 31, 41.

76. "Attention to these cultural perceptions of unity, rather than to events, may be useful in helping us understand the process of later political state formation in certain parts of Southeast Asia. . . . unity is forged through a common adherence by these different groups to legitimizing myths that establish the physical and spiritual parameters of their world." Andaya, "Cultural State Formation," 25.

77. Ibid., 32, 39.

Figure 9.1. General View of Temples at Anein Village

Figure 9.2. General Wall View at Zedi Daw Daik Complex (Anein Village, late-seventeenth to eighteenth century)

Figure 9.3. Style 4. The Four Sights, Loka Aung Mye (an old man, a sick man, a dead man in coffin, and a monk—and a palace. Khinmon village, mid- to late-eighteenth century)

Figure 9.4. Style 1. Detail of the Twenty-Eight Previous Buddhas, Po Win Daung (Cave 109–10, seventeenth to eighteenth century)

Figure 9.5. Detail of the Twenty-Eight Previous Buddhas, Ma U Leh (second village temple, mid- to late-eighteenth century)

Figure 9.6. Style 2. Prince Siddhartha, Zedi Daw Daik Complex (taking a final look at his wife and child with Channa the charioteer and Kanthaka the horse waiting behind him. Anein village, late seventeenth to eighteenth century)

Figure 9.7. Style 3. Prince Siddhartha, Ming Ye Gyi Complex (taking a final look at his wife and child with Channa the charioteer and Kanthaka the horse waiting behind him. Temple 1, Amyint village, mid- to late-eighteenth century)

Figure 9.8. Death of Kanthaka the Horse, Po Win Daung (cave 242, seventeenth to eighteenth centuries)

Figure 9.9. Death of Kanthaka the Horse, Loka Aung Mye (Khinmon village, mid- to late-eighteenth century)

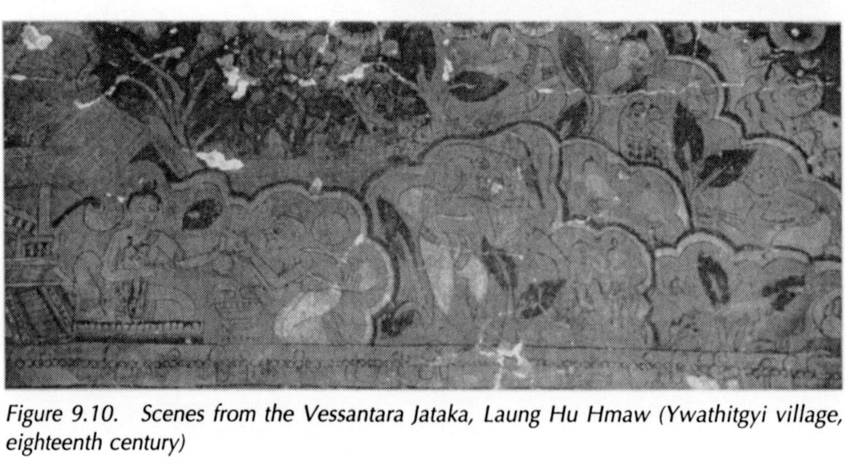

Figure 9.10. Scenes from the Vessantara Jataka, Laung Hu Hmaw (Ywathitgyi village, eighteenth century)

Figure 9.11. *Naga Bhuridatta. Zedi Daw Daik Complex (being forced to perform by the snake charmer. Anein village, late seventeenth- to eighteenth-century)*

Figure 9.12. *Naga Bhuridatta, Min Ye Gyi Complex (being forced to perform by a snake charmer. Temple 1, Myint village, mid- to late-eighteenth century)*

Figure 9.13. Naga Pool on the Ceiling, Po Win Daung (over the reclining Buddha image. Mipaya cave-temple [no. 480], eighteenth century)

Figure 9.14. Animals from a Magic Square (in), Laung U Hmaw (Ywathitgyi village, eighteenth century)

Figure 9.15. Magic Circle, Min Ye Gyi Complex (Temple 3, Amyint village, mid- to late-eighteenth century)

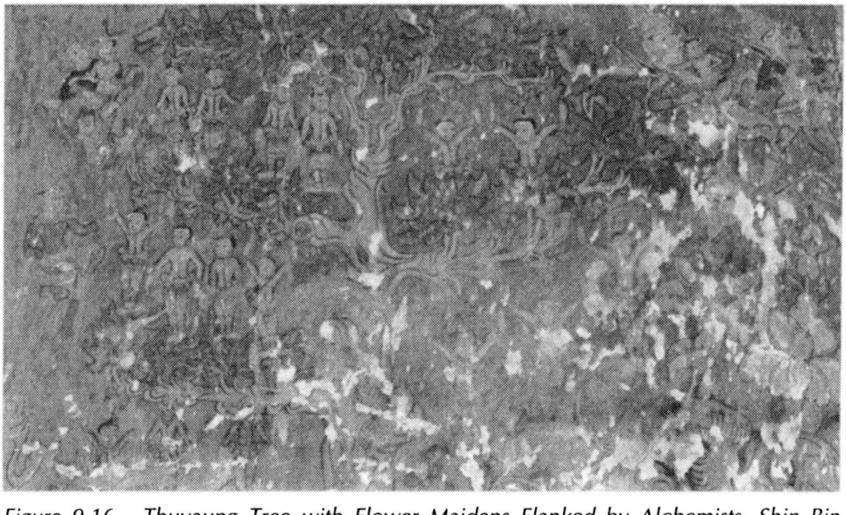

Figure 9.16. Thuyaung Tree with Flower Maidens Flanked by Alchemists. Shin Bin Popayone Hpaya (Sinbyugyun village, mid- to late-eighteenth century)

Figure 10.1. Folio 31b from the Süleymanname*, 965 AH/1558 CE*

10

The Ottoman Balkan City: The Periphery as Center in Punitive Spectacle

Charles Argo

Земята отнемем,
Децата откупим,
Шените избавим,
Бащите поменем,
За майките отменем . . .
[Save our land,
buy back our children,
save the wives,
honor the fathers,
and avenge the mothers.][1]

Introduction

This study investigates the Ottoman *devşirme*, the infamous levy and enslavement of young Christian subjects for palace and military service by the Muslim Turks. The *devşirme* is somewhat of a historical anomaly in Islamic history, and has long fascinated scholars. Scholars have traditionally viewed its execution and function as a vehicle of elite recruitment. The most glaring deficiency among previous studies has been their silence regarding the most obvious element of the *devşirme*—it was enacted as a public spectacle. More specifically, this was a punitive spectacle, expressing the arbitrary power of the Ottoman sultan to physically appropriate Christian (and theoretically protected) subjects at his discretion. From this position, the *devşirme* becomes something altogether different: it transforms into a snapshot of sultan/subject interaction that helped shape the political reality of Balkan Christians under Ottoman rule.

From an urban historical perspective what is interesting here is—if we assume the *devşirme*'s spectacle form in this instance—the Balkan city as setting for the rare linkage between dynastic center and rural periphery. Court ceremonies and the public processions of Istanbul have been well-researched, yet virtually nothing is known about Ottoman spectacle or ceremony in the provinces. This study will discuss why the *devşirme* should be considered a punitive spectacle, and how it was one of the few instances in which the ritual dramas acted out daily in the Istanbul court found expression in provincial towns and cities of the Ottoman realm.

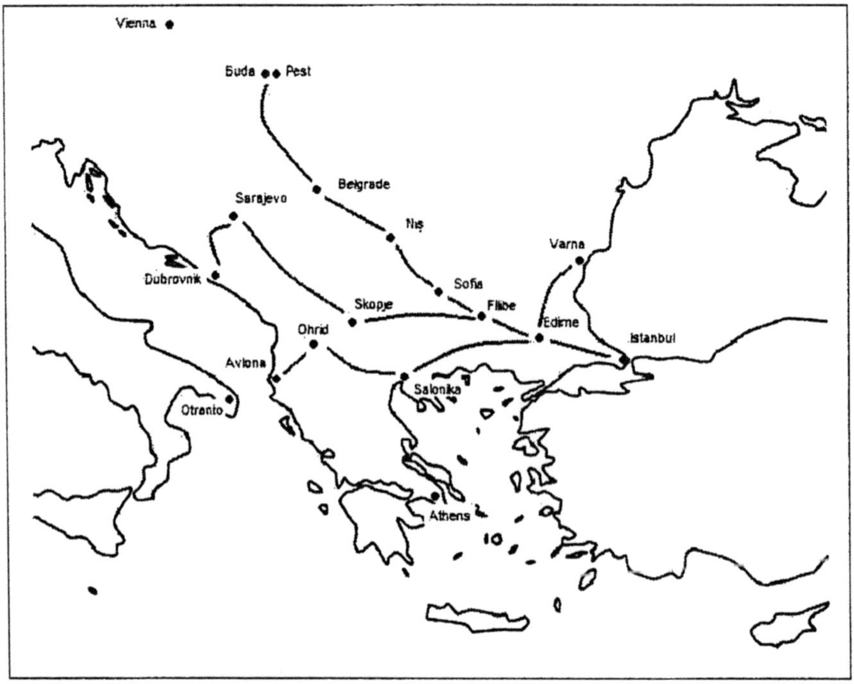

Map 10.1. **Primary Overland Routes in the Ottoman Balkans**

Brief Overview of the *Devşirme*

The *devşirme* was typically a rural collection (although urban hinterlands were often included) because the Ottomans valued physically rugged peasant children as recruits. Cities were directly levied on occasion, and there is evidence of multiple recruitments in Sofya and Üsküp (Skopje) for instance, which were important secondary administrative centers under the Ottomans. Merchants and artisans were considered too valuable in the local economy to dispense with; high birthrates among the Balkan peasantry could more readily absorb losses in the male labor pool.[2] The final selection and transport of recruits typically took place in district centers (*sancaks*) or the cities that lined the important campaign and trade routes, particularly the important Istanbul-Sofya-Niš-Belgrade artery (see *Map 10.1*). "Small cities" in this context varied widely from towns of several hundred inhabitants to cities of several thousand. Population densities in the Balkans were the highest in the empire and corresponded roughly to those of central Europe. Despite the mountainous topography, urban settlements were closely linked along major roads.

The origins of the *devşirme* ("to collect" or "gather" in Turkish), or "child levy" as it is commonly called, remain murky, but it appears to have been in place by the late eighth century AH/fourteenth century CE under the sultan Murad I. Sustained, regular levies ordered by the palace took place largely in the ninth/fifteenth and tenth/sixteenth centuries. The last known levy occurred in Greece in 1116 AH/1705 CE, after a century of declining use.[3] Provincial officials and other Ottoman grandees may have mimicked the sultan by performing their own local palace recruitments, but these unofficial levies are difficult to document, and were not officially sanctioned by the state.

While in reality there were significant deviations, Ottoman sources note the ideal *devşirme* recruit was a rural peasant child, aged fifteen to twenty, of good physical and mental health, who was neither married or an only child. Christian populations in Anatolia were subject to the levy, and on occasion Jews, Armenians, and even Bosnian Muslims (who petitioned successfully to be included) were taken as well, but the levy was localized predominantly within the Orthodox communities of the Balkans. Selected youths were subjected to a complete reshaping of their social and religious identities. They were educated in Turkish (some learned Arabic and Persian as well), converted to Islam, and eventually joined the ranks of the Ottoman military and administrative elite.

Most boys recruited through the levy were assigned to the Ottoman infantry corps—the famous *yeniçeri* or "Janissaries"—or, if exceptionally talented, educated within one of the palace schools for a lucrative career as a page to the sultan, a provincial governor, or even the office of *vezir-i a'zam* (grand vezir), the second-most powerful office in the Ottoman state. Despite forming powerful factions within palace politics, all of these young men were considered *kapukullar*, or "slaves of the gate." They would remain, regardless of subsequent status, the personal slaves of the sultan. In principle, the sultan maintained all rights over their lives and their property, and could revoke either without cause.[4]

It should be noted that there was no legal justification for the *devşirme* under Islamic law, and the systematic conscription of supposedly protected minorities, Christian *zimmis* (Arabic, *dhimmi*), was unique to the Ottoman world as a method of recruitment. Some allusion was made to the sultan's traditional right of *pencik*, or claims to one-fifth of war booty; it appears the Ottomans simply regularized this gift well after the initial conquest of Christian lands. Not surprisingly, Ottoman jurists rarely discussed the matter.

The *Devşirme* in Ottoman Historiography

Ottoman historians have been chided for their methodological conservatism. This is partially unfair, partially deserved. The Ottoman archives may be to blame—their vast reserves guarantee a perpetual stream of monograph production. One Ottomanist has labeled this the "fetish of the *defter* [register]," which implies the discipline has settled into overly specialized studies, lacking synthetic works or grand narrative histories.[5] Not surprisingly, some historical interpretations enjoy remarkable longevity since they are not challenged unless new documents surface. This seems to be the case with the *devşirme*.

In Ottoman historiography there are two widely-held assumptions about the child levy. First, most historians agree the primary rationale for the *devşirme* was for the selective recruitment of able soldiers and administrators. Handpicking manpower from their own backyard so-to-speak guaranteed quality and proved more stable than relying on prisoners-of-war and expensive slave markets. Second, the levy served the political needs of the sultan by securing loyal servants for his palace staff and infantry that was removed from the ties of patronage so endemic to Turkish (and Arab) tribal society, thus assuring himself and the ruling dynasty an independent power base. Slave soldiers had been a fixture of Islamic polities since the ninth/thirteenth century for this very reason.

Virtually all Ottomanists reiterate these two points. Both are true enough. This becomes problematic, however, because the *devşirme* has generated tremendous editorial response from historians. The *devşirme* acts much like a lightening rod within the field, and is easily the most emotive and controversial topic in Ottoman history. As a result, competing interpretations of the child levy often center around historians' own moral attitudes about the institution (and the Turks, more broadly) rather than investigating alternative perspectives on its function and purpose. Some go as far as to include damning invectives against the Ottomans for such an immoral act. For these authors, there is far more consideration of the human impact of the *devşirme* on Christian communities. Other historians take the polar extreme of this position, avoiding any discussion whatsoever of its human resonance.

These divergences follow a predictable geographic pattern. For example, in Western Europe the invention and diffusion of the printing press roughly paralleled the Ottoman conquest of Constantinople and further inroads into southeastern Europe.[6] In due course, the *devşirme*, which naturally aroused powerful reactions from neighboring European Christians, became a popular signifier of Turkish barbarity in the press and pamphleteer media. The horror of abducting children for conversion to the infidel faith was an easy target for Europeans warning of the Turkish menace.

Ironically, other European contemporaries offered a muted appreciation for the system, assuming that the use of slaves in positions of power was a form of meritocracy where advancement was achieved on talent alone rather than position of birth. In such cases theorists' (Hobbes and Machiavelli in particular) praise was less about admiring the Turks as it was offering critique of their own hierarchy-conscious societies. Nonetheless, the *devşirme* gradually became seen as a source of Ottoman strength; it represented an oddly modern form of social mobility that allowed an otherwise barbarous civilization the leadership needed to challenge Christian Europe. It goes without saying that implicit in this analysis was the belief that Muslims administered by former Christians was more formidable than a state ruled by native Muslims alone. By drawing on the human resources of Christian lands, the Turks were able to bridge the civilizational divide.

As Ottoman power relative to Europe began to wane, historians of the Ottoman Empire began to highlight the dissolution of the *devşirme* system in the eleventh/seventeenth century as one of the primary catalyst for Ottoman decline. In the modern era, this theme has been taken to its logical extreme. The *devşirme* during the twentieth century was viewed almost exclusively in light of Ottoman political success and failure. A common theme was the correlation between state centralization and the so-called "classical age" (roughly 853-1008/1450-1600) which represented the apogee of Ottoman power. Seen as a critical component of state centralization (an effective cadre of elite manpower loyal to the sultan alone), interpretation of the child levy was buried within the larger schema of Ottoman state-building analysis. For European scholars, the *devşirme* became a static pillar of a lost age; one that signified success when implemented and failure when discontinued.

In modern Turkey the *devşirme* has aroused little controversy among scholars, who by and large focus on its pragmatic function. As the first group to routinely utilize Ottoman records, whose bureaucratic jargon and formulaic style leave much to the imagination, Turkish historians interpreted the child levy just as it reads—as one of the many extraordinary taxes (*avarız-ı divaniye*) levied upon Ottoman tax paying subjects, the *re'aya*. In fact, Turkish historians tend to argue that the levy had a unique and potentially positive impact on Christian communities by opening the ranks of the elite to non-Muslims. It was a path of opportunity, not a point of cultural conflict. In Turkish historiography, rarely does the disclaimer that many Balkan subjects actively pursued collection of their children go unsaid. For their part, ignoring or minimizing the effects of the *devşirme* fits within the broader narrative of Ottoman history in Turkey that emphasizes Ottoman rule over Balkan peoples as a positive era that brought peace and prosperity to a region that historically lacked either.

For Balkan scholars, however, the emotive response that early Western observers of the Ottoman state attached to the levy remained intact. Though lessened somewhat since the fall of Communism, Balkan historians speak of the *devşirme* in terms of "lost generations," of "demographic catastrophes," and of a "systematic blood drain" of their most intelligent and able Christian youth. Others point to the child levy as proof the Turks wished to systematically eradicate Christianity from Europe, or that the *devşirme* constituted a perpetual state of war against Balkan Christians. Unlike European or Turkish historiography, the images of wailing mothers, peasants fleeing into the hills with children in tow, weddings for ten-year-old children, and barbarous, inhumane Turks wresting away young boys are much more commonplace here.

Obviously these attitudes reflect the interplay of modern political agendas and nationalists narrative constructions. It is no coincidence that the Balkan literature most critical of the *devşirme* emanates from societies once subject to the levy, and/or states where the legacy of Ottoman rule includes unresolved tensions over national and ethnic identities. The construction of politically useful history explains much regarding the various interpretations of the *devşirme*.

Bulgarian historiography is a good case in point. Here, the child levy remains iconic, the one institution that succinctly encapsulates nearly 500 years of religious, political, and cultural oppression at the hands of the Turks. The Ottomans did not simply rule *our* lands, they took *our children*—our best children—turned them from the true faith, and unleashed them back upon their own people like rabid dogs.[7] Indeed, the *devşirme* has even been blamed for the relative backwardness of the modern Balkans, associating its use to a demographic catastrophe little different than an outbreak of the plague or pandemic. Emblematic of this perceived historical injustice, most people in Bulgaria are wholly unfamiliar with the term "*devşirme*," opting instead to use the Slavic phrase "blood tribute," or *kruvnia danuk*. "*Devşirme*" is not even used among Balkan scholars despite the consistent borrowing of Ottoman terminology otherwise.

The construction of competing historical narratives cannot be addressed here. They do however suggest that perhaps a more nuanced view of the *devşirme* might now be in order, one that embraces all of the characteristics of the child levy—not only the utilitarian and pragmatic, but one that attempts to understand the real resonance such an act might have had on affected communities. To recreate the feelings and attitudes the child levy generated is to stand on somewhat shaky ground. Any singular emphasis on "forests filled with fleeing Bulgarians" has little to offer, but in many respects, neither does the view that the child levy was simply a tax. The *devşirme* in many ways represented—even in the early-modern period when slavery was a ubiquitous feature in most societies—a remarkably coercive act of political force that resonated in profoundly personal ways for those involved. It simply is not possible to discount the emotional ramifications of such an event if we wish to recreate this shared world of two distinct religious communities.

Therefore, this study is focused on the actual act of collecting children. What was occurring on the ground at that moment of interaction between the Islamic Ottoman state and the Orthodox Christian peasant when children were selected? This question seems to be of the utmost importance, because here, in the provincial districts of the Balkans, where young boys and their families gathered under the order of official decree, which likely marked the first and last encounter between many rural Christian peasants and what might be loosely consider the central government proper. Those entrusted with the levy were not the local and familiar *sipahi* cavalry commanders who collected rents and taxes; nor were they the village *kadi*s that enforced sultanic laws. These men were present, but the primary actors were agents of the sultan himself, acting on his behalf as an extension of his household, executing a sultanic decree to take these children. How could this brief contact not serve as the most powerful and effective confirmation of one's political subordination? Therein may lie the *devşirme*'s greatest and lasting significance—the additional manpower merely served the short-sighted needs of the state.

Ottoman Centralization and the *Devşirme*—The Role of Provincial Structures

There were significant structural (i.e., hierarchical systems of land owning, urban authority, and revenue collection that comprised local or regional government under Ottoman rule) reasons why Balkan populations were subject to the *devşirme* as opposed to Christian populations in Arab domains that held sizeable non-Muslim communities. Of course, the critical difference was religious. Former Christian European lands populated by infidels (*küffar*) were subject to more punitive and transformative policies than Muslim lands. Beyond this point, however, certain conditions existed in the Balkans that favored the use of the child levy here, while rendering it less advantageous elsewhere.

With a few notable exceptions, studies of Ottoman urban history have been confined to Istanbul, Anatolian port cities, and the Arab-speaking lands of the empire. Utilizing the enormous documentary wealth of the Ottoman archives, micro-studies of specific industries (e.g., wool and silk manufactures, mining), regional and global trade connections, and European penetration of native markets have proliferated. Also, the Ottoman *sicills*, or court registers, have allowed historians to situate the legal and economic limits of the empire's ethnic and religious minorities, delineating the static (or fluid) conditions that regulated their participation in the economic life of Ottoman cities.[8]

This population concentration is partly a result of the sources, since the availability of Arabic language primary sources in these regions opens the ranks of Ottoman history to a broader field of Middle Eastern scholars. Additionally, intensified European activity in the eastern Mediterranean (especially Anatolia and the Levant) from the eleventh/seventeenth century produced document collections that have drawn the attention of Europeanists. Naturally, the opposite has been true of the Balkans, where native historians working under Communism and writing in Slavic languages have been subject to the double effect of having the legitimacy of their work undermined on ideological grounds, as well as being almost entirely inaccessible to Western scholars. While this is gradually changing, there still exists a real divide between Ottoman Balkan and Ottoman Arab scholarship that has impeded production of synthetic and comparative histories.

Weberian notions of Islamic patrimonialism or Marxist models of "Oriental despotism" framed Ottoman urban analyses for much of the twentieth century. Ottoman cities were generally considered parasitical entities that consumed rural surpluses for the specie and goods needed to provision Istanbul and the military complex, and whose markets were ultimately limited by severe protectionist policies, state price controls, and unsophisticated credit/finance systems. Recently, more nuanced perspectives have emerged. Repeated reference to a "command" or "tributary" economy has been muted in favor of highlighting the innovative merchant entrepreneur or manufacturer, or the effective diffusion of modern technologies. Researchers seek to uncover proto-capitalist (or outright capitalist) exceptions at the local level to counter models that peripheralize the Ottoman state in "world systems" paradigms. Ottomanists today are increasingly engaged in combating the persistent decline motif that has dogged Ottoman historiography for two centuries.[9]

Revisionist scholars have as well challenged the traditional formulation of Ottoman urban centers as a vertical matrix of religious/ethnic classes (*millets*) composed of distinct, semi-autonomous communities (*mahalles*) under the sultan's rule. While Muslim social and economic dominance was considered the natural state of affairs in Ottoman cities, the reality was certainly more complex. Muslim and Christian mutual participation in local craftsmen guilds, and public parades and spectacles have undercut the perspective of rigid urban segregation. Court records show Christians eschewing their own confessional courts in favor of *sheri'at* courts to exploit leniencies in Muslim law regarding marriage, divorce, and property settlement. Sumptuary laws issued periodically reasserted Muslim distinctiveness in public dress and behavior; these distinctions were generally blurred without occasional enforcement. Even in the twelfth/eighteenth century, when the Ottoman state had adopted a more rigidly orthodox Sunni attitude towards law and society, one could still find officially sanctioned public prayers performed in times of famine or plague by Orthodox priests for the safety of Istanbul and the sultan himself.

Much work has been done by Ottoman historians to disassemble the enduring and totalizing assumptions of past Orientalist scholarship. The Ottoman Empire could not have existed for six centuries without a measure of flexibility and institutional fluidity. For our purposes at least, one could certainly argue that cities in the Ottoman world differed considerably across time and space, and that the divide between European and Islamic cities is perhaps not as acute as once thought. These points were all raised at a previous conference held at Ball State University in 1995 that specifically addressed Ottoman urbanism.[10]

Significant Divergences Between Ottoman Arab and Ottoman Balkan Cities

During Ottoman expansion, the mechanisms of integration were necessarily different for Arab cities than Balkan ones. While appointed Ottoman officials exercised nominal authority in Arab cities, daily patterns of life were not reconstituted along "Ottoman" lines. These were, after all, Islamic communities of significant antiquity. The great diversity of Arab cities that existed prior to the Ottomans would survive into the modern era. In traditional Muslim lands, the indigenous elites often remained intact, as did their local expressions of Islamic corporate identities—guild arrangements (*esnaf*), Sufi brotherhoods (*tarikats*), merchant and trading communities, and *medreses*.

For revenue collection, the Ottomans did not reorganize Arab societies towards greater centralization; generally, tax farms (*iltizam*) were awarded to local agents and officials to provide lump sum annual payments to the state. There was no liquidation (though reshuffling was not uncommon) of the landed nobility, and newly assigned Ottoman military and administration officials often merged into, rather than supplanted, the local power brokers. As a result of this continuity, Arab urban centers constructed legacies of civic pride—or at least sense of communal *patria*—centered around the genealogies of local notable families. The existence of extensive biographies and prosopographical histories of Arab cities attests to this, and have no equivalent in other Ottoman lands. These sources are virtually nonexistent for the Balkans, which not only hinders recreation of the urban political landscape, but hints at the lack of political continuity in these cities.[11]

The Ottoman conquest of the Balkans unfolded much differently. Balkan historians, in the spirit of nationalist sentiment, have often exaggerated the violence of the Turkish invasion of Europe and the destruction of Christian cities. Fighting did secure significant territories. However, the Ottomans were keen diplomats. Treaties with petty dynasts were forged against common enemies; daughters of the local nobility were married into the Ottoman dynasty (including, for the only period in the empire's history, to sultans), and gradually the Ottomans reduced Christian kings and princes to vassalage. After a fashion these elites were assimilated into the Ottoman administrative machine, and eventually replaced with outsiders appointed from the center to rule their lands (including *devşirme* recruits). Recalcitrant or wavering vassals were dealt with quickly and their land appropriated under the flimsiest of justification. This transitory process did not take long; within a few generations the Ottomans typically had engineered a radical transformation over the political landscape of conquered lands.[12]

Conquests in southeastern Europe therefore proceeded more securely and successfully for the Ottomans than, for instance, in Anatolia, where rival Turkish emirates chafed under Ottoman rule. In fact, after Bayezid I's disastrous defeat in 804 AH/1402 CE to the armies of Temür, the lone remnants of the Ottoman state to remain loyal to the dynasty were located in the Balkans. During a decade long interregnum and the subsequent rebuilding of the state, Balkans territories provided the resources and manpower for revival. For some perspective, the Ottomans were still attempting to subdue the neighboring southern Anatolian emirate of Karaman in 865/1461—more than sixty years after the capture of Bulgaria and twenty years since Serbia was annexed. Simply put, the Balkans became the bedrock foundation on which the Ottoman Empire was ultimately constructed.

The process was not easy of course. A series of four pan-Balkan "crusades" had to be fought between 791/1389 and 851/1448. Urban populations often fled the approaching Turks creating manpower shortages in cities. Those cities taken by force obviously had more significant losses. As a result, there was an immediate decline in urban populations during the late-eighth/fourteenth and early-ninth/fifteenth centuries. In many respects, this provided the Ottomans with a blank canvas to remake urban centers. Because the Balkans constituted *Dar ül-Harb* (the "Abode of War"), the Ottomans were obligated to Islamicize these territories for productive use by the Muslim community. Lacking the legitimate Islamic institutional structures found in Arab cities, Balkan cities could effectively be reconstituted with greater central control and organizational symmetry. There was a strong degree of urban homogenization in the core areas of the Balkan territories—notably Bulgaria, Serbia, Bosnia, Albania, and northern Greece (Thrace/Thessaly)—that was lacking elsewhere in the empire.

Rural landholding was transferred to the provincial Turkish *sipahi* cavalry (the Turkish equivalent of a landed nobility) in the form of military fiefs (*timars*); Anatolian nomads (*yürüks*) were forcibly settled on uncultivated or dispossessed lands; itinerant sufis, auxiliary mercenary units, and *ghazi* raiders flowed into towns and cities. Muslim traders, Janissary regiments, and *kadis* to administer sultanic and Islamic law then took root so that urban institutions now reflected the political and cultural hegemony of the Turks. The Balkan urban milieu was rapidly altered. Muslim densities increased in cities and larger towns at an impressive rate; by the tenth/sixteenth century no major city had a non-Muslim majority, and several cities, such as Sarajevo and Tirana, were essentially Ottoman creations.

At the turn of the eleventh/seventeenth century, Balkan tax revenues outstripped those of all other regions, including the traditional granary of the eastern Mediterranean, Egypt. Grain, rice, cotton, wool, timber, gold, silver, and lead all flowed into the imperial city to sate the enormous needs of the capital. As a reservoir of goods and manpower, the Balkans drove the Ottoman economic system. However, despite the demographic transformation of the cities, the Balkans would remain overwhelmingly Christian over the course of five hundred years. The difficulties of securing stable and lasting rule among non-Muslim societies was considerable and, thus, why in this political context institutions such as the *devşirme* take on significant importance as a conduit of dynastic ideology, as will be discussed below.

Ultimately, the level of centralization achieved in the Balkans and the ability to remake the urban landscape by grafting a center-appointed synthetic ruling class onto new and existing towns gave the Ottomans sufficient flexibility to enforce the child levy. To have done so amongst Christian populations in Arab cities would have upset long-standing economic and social equilibriums the Ottomans had no hand in constructing. Unlike the Balkans, where the rural peasant population was almost wholly Orthodox even after Ottoman settlement, in Arab cities Muslims dominated the countryside and Christians (and Jews) were concentrated in the cities. Complex inter-religious networks among urban merchants in the region made non-Muslims an integral part of local economies. Confessional contacts with the West were also established here well before European missionary and economic penetration of the twelfth/eighteenth century that offered a measure of economic and political security. The Maronites of Syria, for example, were among the first Eastern-rite churches to foster closer ties to Rome, thus supplying an external "patriarch" beyond the reach of the Ottoman state. Unlike the Orthodox, who had lost their independent patriarch with the fall of Constantinople, Maronite communities exhibited a degree of autonomy unseen in the Ottoman Balkans. Eventually a similar linkage between the Orthodox and the Russian church will develop—but well after the period discussed here.

Generally speaking, the Christian/Muslim dynamic was different in Arab lands than in the Balkans, and despite periods of religious conflict not uncommon to urban settings, it could be argued that Christians to the south were in a more advantageous position. Over time, the forces of assimilation and population growth would reverse this trend—by the thirteenth/nineteenth century most Balkan cities held Orthodox majorities. Yet, during the first few centuries of

Ottoman rule in Europe this was not the case. In the Balkans, where Muslims were virtually non-existent prior to the Turks, cities exhibited a high level of confessional segregation. New Muslim quarters and markets were built apart from Christian neighborhoods. Cities grew in new directions, away from the historic urban center, and parallel public spaces that clearly delineated the separation of religious communities gave expression to the hierarchies of power within the new Ottoman system. Additionally, and according to the rights of conquering Muslim armies, post-conquest conversion and translation of Christian sacred sites into Muslim ones was permissible, and the first converted churches for military use were typically called *Fethiye Cami*, or the "Mosque of Victory."[13]

Once established, Ottoman military, political, and economic elites could operate virtually independent of the resident Christian population. Could it be that this overlapping, rather than interwoven, structure of urban and rural relations in the Balkans allowed the state to act with greater impunity against its own subjects? Southeastern Europe—as a land taken by *gaza* under the banner of Islam—was justification enough. However, to press this point a bit, it may well have been difficult for the Ottomans to utilize the manpower resources of other Christian communities without irreparable economic and social harm done to the urban fabric of Arab cities. There is an obscure reference attributed to an Arab *kadi* that argued Christian populations who had converted prior to the life of Muhammad were true "Peoples of the Book" and thus ineligible for the child levy—unlike the Orthodox Slavs, who were third/ninth-century converts. Perhaps both he and the Ottoman state realized what was at stake if they extended the collection here.

Formulation and Expression of Ottoman Legitimacy

Now that the geographic context for the child levy has been established, it might be instructive to highlight how the Ottomans formulated claims of legitimacy and then propagated these claims. In the Balkan setting this was doubly important, and closely links the *devşirme* as a transmitter of dynastic legitimacy. In this context we can see the rhetorical and symbolic linking of the center to the provinces; essentially the role of a punitive spectacle in bridging not only the overlapping structures of religious divide, but ultimately tying the remote Orthodox communities directly to the locus of dynastic power.

From the very beginning the Ottomans altered and modified their conception of legitimate rule to fit the needs of an expanding empire. The *Osmanlı* dynasty did not inherit a pedigree of acceptable legitimacy (i.e., descendants of the Mongol Khans or the Prophet Muhammad's family) and thus had to construct, at each stage of expansion, a proper legitimizing discourse. They happened to be quite adept at this, and this process of constant modification only ended with the empire's dissolution in 1922.

As the empire spread within Anatolia and the Balkans, and finally into the heartland of the Islamic world, the Ottomans culled legitimizing strategies from each regions' political traditions. They fused divine myths of dynastic origin, Turco-Mongol prophecies of world domination, Islamic religious and political rhetoric, as well as—after taking Constantinople in 857/1453—the adoption of Greek and Roman models of kingship and sovereignty. By the mid-tenth/sixteenth century, the Ottomans had constructed a matrix of legitimacy that was quite literally universal in scope. This was critical for the Ottomans, who ruled over vast populations for whom appeals as "Defenders of the Faith" or other Muslim-specific titles had no relevance. For instance, to co-opt the rhetoric of the sultan as Caesar made Ottoman claims to legitimacy over Christian populations perfectly understandable within the language of European political tradition. While rather transparent, the physical occupation of Constantine's Christian capital carried considerable weight; so much so that contemporary Europeans immediately viewed the Ottoman sultans as viable competitors to the papacy as the "inheritors" of Roman sovereignty in the Mediterranean.

Mimicking this process was the gradual evolution of the sultan's image. Early sultans had played a significant and visible role in the daily lives of their administrators and military personnel. The dynasty had earned its initial prestige in part through the personal leadership, accessibility, and munificence of the early Ottoman sultans. As expansion proceeded, the image of the sultan altered drastically to better reflect his new political stature. With Mehmed II's conquest of Constantinople, and the building of a new imperial capital, court rituals and court protocol became more sophisticated and regulated, eventually codified into imperial *kanun* law (based on the Byzantine models). By Süleyman I's reign (926-973/1520-1566) the Ottomans executed one of the most sophisticated courts in Islamic history. There were a few key elements worth noting. Ottoman claims of political legitimacy, court ritual, and the sultan's image adopted universal traits of sovereignty. The sultan became an increasingly exalted figure whose contact with the outside world, and even his own high-ranking officials, was considerably diminished. This was the mystification of his power.

Topkapı Sarayı, the sultan's palace, became the center from which imperial ideology was ritually expressed and radiated through elaborate ceremonies that elevated his person to near god-like status. Through the physical and spatial ordering of his administrators and slaves, court spectacles recreated the Ottoman hierarchy of social and political power to emphasize his dominion over all society. Naturally, in the pre-modern and early modern periods, political power was defined by proximity and access to the ruler's physical presence. Topkapı's layout is quite simple: three ceremonial courtyards were on-axis to increasingly restrict access to the sultan and his private quarters. It is not particularly impressive architecturally—there is nothing monumental about the palace. It merely provided the backdrop for the symbolic expression of power in the form of carefully orchestrated ceremony.[14]

Increasingly removed from the public eye, the sultan was gradually personified as a man apart and above normal social relations—theoretically he remained outside of the standard entanglements inescapable for the rest of society. Distance and seclusion within the palace affirmed this condition; his interpersonal relationships reinforced it. Those with private access to the sultan—mutes, pages, eunuchs—as well as the slave concubines who gave birth to the dynasty's heirs, were social non-entities, or in the case of eunuchs, physical non-entities. In essence, these were relationships that allowed the sultan to maintain his position outside the boundaries of Ottoman society. The point here is that, defined as such, the sultan embodied a man with the benefit of action without concern for reciprocity. As the exalted omnipotent force over his domains, the sultan could wield power over his subjects without fear of personal accountability or retaliatory retribution. He stood apart from the normative social and legal codes that circumscribed the actions of others.[15]

Punitive or coercive displays of power were integral to this process—the sultan, like the invisible hand of god, could arbitrarily seize and confiscate property, execute subjects, or in our case, take your children. The essence of unfettered power lies in the coercive and arbitrary acts of a ruler that may defy logic or reasoning, but equally defy censure from society-at-large. Real life was often much more complicated for Ottoman sultans, who, by the eleventh/seventeenth century, increasingly came under the sway of powerful court factions. But this was the ideological reality that had been refined over the years, and would continue to be propagated until the end of the dynasty.

If we approach the *devşirme* as a spectacle of coercive power, we can see how this ideology was reproduced for public consumption. What do we know about provincial spectacles in the Ottoman Empire, particularly in the Balkans? How did the state transmit its political worldview to Bulgarian or Serbian or Albanian peasants? Scholars have thus far failed to supply the answers, except to note that there was a dearth of instances in which the state displayed the rhetorical strategies of legitimacy and power frequently on display in Istanbul.

As the cornerstone of the Ottoman state, both fiscally and geographically, it was critical for the Balkans to remain stable and acquiescent to Ottoman rule. Power here could not be justified in Islamic terms; again, "defenders of the faith" had no resonance. This is why the collection of children became important in its own right—not merely as a conduit of manpower from the provinces to the center, but as a conduit of ideology from the center to the provinces. All Ottoman political spectacles transmitted ideology. As a coercive act against theoretically protected subjects, the *devşirme*, with devastating clarity, recreated the fundamental concepts of Ottoman court ritual and political ideology in a provincial Balkan setting.

In the *devşirme*, the invisible hand of the Ottoman sultan, almost external to this world, physically manipulated Christian subjects within the framework of public spectacle, and imparted his will in a coercive manner. All of this not only reinforced the conception of ruler as omnipotent power, but also helped define the political reality for many Balkan subjects. With the *devşirme*, this external "reality" of Ottoman rule became a fixed, rather than negotiable, component of the Balkan worldview, insofar as they understood relations with the state. It was in ritualized moments like this that the limits of their power as subject peoples versus the power of the sultan were clearly delineated.

Does this mean that the *devşirme* was designed solely to propagate imperial ideology? Certainly not, but as a public spectacle utilizing the rhetorical models of center-inspired ceremonial, it provided the additional function as an expression of state power. It should also be noted that the actual form of the *devşirme* seems to have evolved in step with the sophistication of Ottoman court ritual.

The earliest levies, undertaken in the fluid frontier marches of the Balkans, were generally ad hoc affairs conducted by military leadership on behalf of the sultan. By Süleyman I's mid-tenth/sixteenth-century reign (and perhaps earlier), the *devşirme* was far more regulated, systematized, and executed via palace decree alone. During this more formal period, there were specific protocols in the mechanics of the levy; with clarity such as who would administered the collection, which youth were eligible, and specific dress codes for the recruits. This declaration of the parameters of collection demonstrates at least a modicum of effort to regulate its public spectacle form.

The Punitive Spectacle

The physical setting for the *devşirme* recruitment was far more complex than historians typically describe. The Ottomans, for their part, thankfully left a wonderful image (*Figure 10.1*) of the levy as part of Süleyman I's illustrated *Süleymanname*, which dates 965/1558. Not only do Ottoman documents corroborate the accuracy of the illustration, but it also illuminates with unmistakable clarity that the *devşirme* was first and foremost a *spectacle* event.

Even a cursory glance makes this plain. Young boys, dressed in matching red robes and caps await departure, while parents (both mothers and fathers) and fellow villagers provide an audience in the courtyard of this Balkan town (Üskup/Skopje perhaps). The black robed men are Orthodox priests responsible for the baptismal records to ensure the youths were in fact Christian and not Muslim. Additionally, the officers of the Janissary corps (always recognizable in Ottoman illustrations by their tall white caps) are entering the recruits' names in a special register.[16] Not only was this a public spectacle, but the uniformity of the children's dress immediately suggest that the process had a ritual component as well; with a social or religious significance that needs to be addressed.

Treating the *devşirme* as a spectacle opens up all sorts of methodological and analytical options. The semiotics of the spectacle need to be properly "read"; ritual elements need to be discerned, and the entire event must be placed in its proper political and social context to fully understand its relationship to other Ottoman political displays; particular how it might have reflected or modified existing rhetorical strategies of power and legitimacy used elsewhere. To provide a methodological framework, the collection of children neatly conforms to Victor Turner's familiar but still viable theory of social transformation.[17] At its most elemental, the *devşirme* was a—one could say in fact the ultimate—*rite de passage* in the Ottoman world.

Collection as a recruit provided a youth the unprecedented opportunity to elevate social status from among the lowliest in Ottoman society to among the highest. Turner's tripartite division of ritual movement includes a "detachment" phase, a "liminal" phase, and a "reincorporation" phase, each representing, in structuralist conception, varying degrees of alienation from the original status group.

Within Turner's framework, this tenth/sixteenth-century Ottoman image captures the final stage of the "detachment" phase. Town criers had previously notified levied villages to bring their unmarried sons to the nearest district center or city—most likely a city square or courtyard of the *sancakbegi*'s mansion (*konak*).[18] Under full view of local Christians, several young boys had been selected after a cursory physical examination by Janissary officials, and are awaiting their transport to the capital.

Ritually symbolic acts demarcate the detachment phase. First, the boys are dressed in special cloaks that denote their persons as property of the sultan. The act of robing itself is significant in this context, and had historical importance throughout the Eurasian landmass.[19] In the Islamic world—including the Ottoman realm—the bestowal of ceremonial robes (*hilat*) recognized the wearer for a particular honor or meritorious act; it could also visually link the recipient to the giver as his personal client or servant. *Hilat* was a ubiquitous component of Ottoman court ceremony. Topkapı Sarayı even kept a special depository for robes of honor, and detailed registers (still extant) accounted inventories.

Additionally, the boys were shorn of their hair. Ottoman documents note that Christian villagers were responsible for both a clothing tax (to provide the red material to make their robes—contracted to wool makers in Plovdiv in modern Bulgaria) and a shave tax to cover the expenses of preparing the boys. In this respect, the levying of children was, from a fiscal perspective, implemented like an extraordinary tax. The visual effect, naturally, was to strip the youth of their former identities in favor of an undifferentiated appearance, somewhat akin to modern military boot camps. Upon departing for Istanbul, the boys—who marched bound, on foot, and under tight security—enter Turner's "liminal" state, which suggests liminal entities "have no status, property, insignia, secular clothing indicating rank or role, position in a kinship system—in short, nothing that may distinguish them from their fellow neophytes or initiates."[20]

As a procession viewable to spectators along the main trade and campaign arteries that linked the capital to the Balkans, the pitiful sight of bound, red-clad Christian youth must have left quite an impression. These boys however were neither Christian peasants nor Ottoman elites yet—they were suspended between two distinct social strata, collectively removed from the normative social structures of either Christian or Muslim. It would be left to another series of ceremonies once in the capital city to "reincorporate" the youth into their new roles. Rituals in fact book ended the entire process of social transition. Circumcision and the adoption of Muslim names superficially converted the boys to Islam; more rigorous examinations would dictate the career path of the recruit from that point onward.

The utility of this perspective is that the individual components of the physical process of selecting and removing these youths from their homes can be "read" as any other "text" or ritual event. Only a cursory example here may suffice: the use of the color red in this context. Red has no real symbolic importance in the Sunni Islamic world, unlike green, white, and black. The Ottoman dynasty used red liberally in sultan's kaftans as well as in Janissary battle flags and standards, yet the color was in no way universally recognized as the color of the sultan, and other colors were used with similar frequency on the sultan's person or in his court.[21] The Ottomans were certainly aware of red's symbolic link to Christian sacrifice and martyrdom, however, and passed sumptuary laws to prohibit its use by non-Muslims.[22] Perhaps more damning, red was very closely associated with the martyrology of messianic Shi'ism and the martyrdom of Husayn at Karbala (61/680), commemorated in the annual Shi'a Ashura (عاشوراء) day of mourning.[23] This may simply be a case of sultanic appropriation as a means to minimize or corrupt the powerful symbolic meaning the color red held with heterodox Sufi and Shi'a groups in society, as well as Christians.

Christian onlookers may or may not have been privy to these semiotic intricacies either, but they certainly could interpret meaning from their own cultural experience. The beauty of ritual is its inherent ambiguity. The depth and resonance of a ritual act is found within the multitude of possible meanings. Contemporary Christian writers almost exclusively used the very language of the Passion in lamenting the lost souls of the *devşirme* recruits. Surely the color red served to strengthen this connection: the martyred sons of the Christian faith, swept away by the unseen hand of a distant non-Christian ruler. Could the Christian's own interpretation of this act have reinforced the very ideology of omnipotent power the Ottomans conceived for their sultan?

This is the type of analysis that the *devşirme* has sorely lacked. As a spectacle event, the child levy became a locus of state-subject interaction with multiple layers of meaning and interpretation. Sultanic power and peasant obligation (and lack of political agency) were expressed through a ritualized process of social transition and personal sacrifice that embodies the ultimate form of coercive power. Because the *devşirme* was a commemorative spectacle, revisiting the same areas at intervals over the course of two centuries, the political utility of constant affirmation of the sultan's power was tremendous.[24] Repetitive displays are critical in solidifying a constructed reality of sovereign power. Over time, Christians subjected to the levy could not help but resign themselves to the collective fate of their existence under Ottoman rule. Opposition to the levy was rarely collective; there is only one significant revolt on record, in Albania in 1004/1596. Scholars often assume this is because many poor peasants actually welcomed the *devşirme* as a means to enhance the careers of their immediate and future family through incorporation into the ranks of the Muslim elite. However, there is a sizeable literature in Bulgaria and elsewhere that suggests otherwise, that instead many individual steps were taken to avoid the collection of one's son. Ottoman sources confirm that attempts to hide children were commonplace, as were attacks during transit in the hopes of freeing individual boys. Is there any way to qualify the efficacy of a ritual in disciplining and conditioning populations? Probably not; and a lack of organized resistance may simply reflect the Ottoman monopoly of martial and judicial power. But is it out of bounds to credit the *devşirme* a role in creating a perpetual state of fear or anxiety among Balkan peasants that contributed to their political acquiescence and lawful participation in the levy?

How this fits into the greater picture of the Balkan urban landscape needs to be addressed. One of the difficulties with this topic is that Ottoman documents do not reveal motivation or intent, but simply command or quantify. Part of the challenge is to illuminate the underlying logic of the *devşirme*'s implementation and especially to determine whether any political utility derived from its use was a conscious factor in the decision to levy a given area. There are several issues that need to be clarified beforehand.

The *Devşirme* as an Instrument of Negotiation

The *devşirme* was generally applied to areas that initially resisted the Ottoman advance (particularly Bulgaria, Serbia, Greece, and Albania), signaling its punitive intent. The state did, however, commonly issue exemptions from the levy within these regions. The politicization of the *devşirme* that transcended mere need for manpower is clearly evident; it was often used as a "carrot" in negotiations with individual cities and vassal states which promised exemption in return for submission to the Turks.[25] Groups who provided important services to the state could also secure exemptions from various levies. Exemptions could be extended to specific households, but were generally organized at the village level. These included *derbencis* (pass guards) who secured safe passage and performed sentry duties through rural mountainous terrain, and were armed as a local militia might be; *celepkeşan*, or sheep herders, who, located primarily in Bulgaria, helped provision Constantinople with mutton; Vlachs, the semi-nomadic tribesmen of Wallachia (but scattered throughout the Balkans) who provided auxiliary wartime services; and a variety of local Christian militias (*mortolos*, *voynuks*, etc.). These were the most common groups singled out by the state for exemption consideration. The Ottomans used this system of privileges carefully to secure services and goods, populate uninhabited areas, and increase taxable revenues to the state. An order to the *kadi* of Turnovo (Bulgaria) from 981/1574 shows the genesis of a town's founding:

> In a letter you informed us that the road over the mountain between the villages of Kilifar and Drianovo . . . is a dangerous and frightening road and a nest of robbers where nobody can pass through. For this reason the travellers make in all possible difficulties a detour over distant places. As this road is not safe scoundrels use it to drive stolen cattle from this side of the mountains to the other. There is, however, in the middle of the mountains a site known by the name of Triavna, which is suitable for founding a village there. So if it were ordered to have a village founded there, on condition of tax dispensation, in the manner of the Derbends, the travellers and all Muslim and Christian subjects, can pass in tranquility... after three years...report how many households are there . . . to have it registered as a Derbend, freed from the *avarız-ı divaniyye* and the *tekalif-i 'örfiyya* . . .[26]

Villages arranged as such enjoyed greater economic security and cultural autonomy. Taxes were considerably reduced and wartime levies, including the most the onerous—the costs of provisioning troops and billeting state officials (*nüzül*)—were generally waived. *Derbend* villages in particular were a ubiquitous part of the Balkan landscape, and were critical in the maintenance of a secure transportation network. This accounts for the sheer magnitude of their numbers: in the region of what today is modern Macedonia, there existed at least 175 such villages that enjoyed exemptions as *derbendcis*.[27] Not only did the state "create" new villages around *derbend* communities, existing villages could petition their local *kadi* for *derbend* status, in exchange for improving roads, providing security, and constructing bridges.[28] This was especially critical around larger towns and cities that relied on constant supplies from the surrounding hinterland.[29]

The possibility of having one's child protected via preferential tax status obviously made the state wary of people claiming exempt status as a ploy to remove their sons from consideration for the *devşirme*. Falsification of records, bribery, and misappropriation of the funds used to pay for the levy were not uncommon, as several Ottoman documents make clear.[30] Thus exemption status was carefully regulated as part of the overall effort to keep the system abuse-free; there were revocations of exempt status and, eventually, the privilege seems to have been contracted considerably. General edicts to Balkan *kadis* in 1031/1622 reflect this concern, and remind officials to take children regardless of what papers they may have claiming exemption.[31] By the eleventh/seventeenth century, the practice may have been largely abolished with the exception of *evkafs,* or lands classified as immutable Islamic trusts.[32]

In these instances the state used either exemption from, or the threat to renew the *devşirme* as a means to secure economic advantages. By granting privileges to certain groups for their meritorious service to the state, the Ottomans were able to divert resources better used elsewhere. In extending exemptions to specific industries (such as miners) they also ensured that sufficient pools of skilled workers would remain available. The division in Turkish society between *re'aya* (tax paying peasantry and merchants) class and *'askeri* (non-tax paying political, military, and religious elites) class is perhaps not as fixed as it appears. A large number of *mu'af ve müsellem* ("immune and exempt") occupied a fluid middle position that reflects the tensions of the ruling Ottomans in maintaining a balance between exhaustion of the peasantry and assuring state revenues and provisions.[33] This was an individual or a village that paid fewer taxes yet did not require a state subsistence (*dirlik*) in either land or cash. Viewed from this perspective, the *devşirme* indeed acted much like a fiscal burden enforced upon the subject population—one whose application was closely monitored to guarantee compliance of "extraordinary" service to the state.

But it also suggests that the Ottomans were well-aware of its power to favorably arrange local conditions through the threat of its use and that the utility of the levy extended into the day-to-day fabric of social and economic relations in the Balkans. With this in mind, it might be useful to construct a new conception of societal organization in the Ottoman Empire that softens the division between religion (Muslim/non-Muslim) and class (*re'aya* and *'askeri*) and instead groups members by gradation of fiscal exemption. Some urban Muslim merchants (part of the *re'aya*) paid taxes, tariffs, and customs dues that likely exceeded Christian peasants granted significant exemptions, which could even include at times freedom from the *cizye*, or non-Muslim poll-tax. In its continuing quest to offer incentives for the provisioning of the state, the Ottomans created a complex web of mutual dependence that transcended normative Islamic fiscal policies and blurred the traditional lines of confessional economic responsibility. More study of this phenomenon is necessary.

The *Devşirme* and the Creation of Patronage Networks

Perhaps the greatest mystery of the *devşirme* has been untangling the links between products of the child levy and their native families.[34] While Balkan administrators are typically thought to have cycled in and out of office to avoid the creation of local networks of power, the *devşirme* may have created circumstances that significantly impacted economic development, urban growth, and the incorporation of remote regions into the empire-wide economy. The rise of one's son to the highest levels of Ottoman governance could bring significant benefits. This line of thinking is not new, but certainly relevant when discussing center-periphery linkages of political and economic institutions.

Sokollu Mehmed Pasha, *vezir-i a'zam* under three successive sultans from 972-986/1565-1579, is an excellent example. Born in Bosnia and taken in the *devşirme* between ages sixteen and eighteen, Mehmed Pasha used his subsequent high office appointment to recruit family members into palace service, endow buildings in his native land, and even meddle in the affairs of the Orthodox Patriarchate of Peč in order to ensure his family's continued role in that office, all despite theoretical detachment from any native relations or institutions.[35] It is also known that he had an Orthodox church built for his brother (who was a village priest) in the Bosnian town of Ravanči—complete with a stained glass image of himself and his brother—despite the Ottoman prohibition of subject Christians constructing new churches.[36] Other family members, including his own two sons, achieved high office.[37] Mehmed Pasha is but one example of many prominent *devşirme* products who exhibited similar behavior, exposing rampant factionalism, nepotism, and continued association with their native land, with little regard for secrecy or concerns of punishment by the state.[38]

This was not a development over time, but rather a common feature of the *devşirme* class that likely existed from the beginning. A *vakıf* (pious foundation) register of 838/1435—one of the oldest extant Muslim documents from the former Yugoslav lands—details the founding of a *cami* (mosque), *zaviye* (*derviş* inn or lodge), and *medrese* (religious school) in Monastir by a *devşirme* recruit named Çavuş Bey, a commander under Sultan Murad II. Çavuş Bey did this upon return to his home following a campaign in Albania against Skanderbeğ. The document notes he built a *mescid* (small mosque) in the towns of Jedren and Vidin as well.[39]

Retaining links to family, home, and even faith among *devşirme* children would clearly facilitate a parallel development—the creation of geographic-specific factions of *kullars* within the Ottoman administration. Stanford Shaw has gone so far as to write that eventual Ottoman decline was a product of this very process, stating that:

> The devshirme class itself broke up into conflicting political factions, each group around one or several ambitious political leaders as determined by the dictates of *intisap*. With no single political group able to dominate very long, the Ruling Class fell into a maze of petty struggles, with the parties forming temporary coalitions and the revenue-producing positions of state becoming the rewards of victory.[40]

The very ties of patronage (*intisap*) the sultans were theoretically averting through the *devşirme* were simply recreated within the sultan's own bureaucracy. Bound by ethnic background, language, or religious affiliation, the *devşirme* then became a powerful tool of nepotism among former recruits to further the careers of friends, family, and political allies.[41] Hence there are periods in which certain Balkan segments dominate the highest offices of state, particularly among Bosnians and Albanians. The social bonds considered anathema to the sultan's efforts to centralize were now endemic within his very household.

In his 1991 article "On the Purity and Corruption of the Janissaries," Cemal Kafadar notes that "the fascinating realm of interrelations between the *kuls* [slaves] and family . . . awaits systematic study."[42] As of yet, no one has undertaken the enormous and difficult task of following career lines within the *devşirme* system to ascertain the frequency and quality of relations between these men and their native families and co-religionists, and to determine the practical impact such behavior may have had upon provincial society.[43]

Kafadar is interested primarily in the economic activities of Janissaries. As with marriage, the Janissaries were theoretically to abstain from engaging in economic activities that might foster the growth of personal interests and responsibilities outside of the sultan's control, thus undermining their capacity to act unreservedly as instruments of the sultan's will, as well as possibly lead to autonomous power bases that could in turn threaten the state. This condition of absolute servitude to the sultan was largely fictive, however, and the state was aware of widespread contradictions. Kafadar highlights a specific *kadi* register describing a business dispute involving a Janissary stationed in Macedonia and his natural brother, who happened to be his business partner. He also notes that an 895/1490 register for the Aya Sofya (Hagia Sophia) *cami* shows specifically that brethren and kin of palace slaves enjoyed special privileges within the imperial city denied to other residents. Clearly, once training was completed and official posts were taken, there was little proscription of *kullar* activities by the sultan and little attempt to maintain any theoretical standard of isolated behavior.[44]

Because the sultan alone ordered the *devşirme*, it is unlikely that these ties extended to the selection of boys, i.e., favoring one's own kin or village. However, powerful vezirs and provincial governors were expected to form their own household staff of slaves and retainers, and it was within these circles that nepotism could flourish. More importantly, what possible benefits could an Albanian or Serbian town receive as the birthplace of a high-ranking official? The establishment of *vakfs*, whose revenues could be earmarked for social services, construction of public works, or even as pensions for specific individuals and families, were probably the primary conduit of elite patronage. However, with so little known about the individual career arcs of *devşirme* children, more definitive conclusions will have to wait. Various studies have traced the development of local familial and patronage networks among Ottoman provincial notables (*'ayan*) beginning in the late-tenth/sixteenth century and the gradual breakdown of the centralized *timar* system. Historians point to this as the catalyst for the declining fortunes of the state. Yet, in our instance, it would be interesting to know how the *devşirme* was actually an instrument in the formation of patronage networks that extended from the center to the provinces among the various *devşirme* factions and their places of origin. As previously mentioned, historians often link the *devşirme* to the spread of centralization in the Balkans. They, however, interpret this to mean political agents loyal only to the sultan strengthened unilateral dynastic power. In this instance, it could be argued that centralization tendencies were bolstered by the child levy through the linkage of palace slaves and the economic and political windfalls absorbed at the local, provincial level. Regardless, the impact of the *devşirme* extended far beyond the number of children reluctantly surrendered to the Ottoman sultan, and likely played a significant role in shaping the political and economic structures of provincial towns and cities.

Conclusion

To consider the *devşirme* as merely a method of recruitment or as a tax, even a punitive tax, within the context of *zimmi* relations does not fully explain the variety of situations in which it was levied. Certainly it took on the functional appearance of the extraordinary *avarız* tax in Ottoman records, though its impact upon the *zimmi* population exceeded the typical discriminatory burdens placed upon subjected peoples. But the overall fluidity of application that transcended the traditional parameters of *zimmi* obligation, as well as the *devşirme*'s conscious utilization in diplomatic and labor negotiations, further reinforced its effectiveness as a uniquely powerful means by which the sultan could enforce his political will. This study has suggested that the patterns of *devşirme* application—which actually defy logic in many respects (i.e., it was not used extensively outside of the Balkans, it was punitive yet conditional, and it could be applied to Muslims in the case of Bosnians)—underscores its specific political value to the sultanate that was not always driven by the dictates of manpower needs.[45] The levy never provided more than a fraction of the palace slaves (most of whom were gifts or purchased in Aegean and Crimean slave markets), and when sons of Janissaries were allowed to inherit their father's *askeri* status among the military elite by the mid-tenth/sixteenth century, the military system reproduced itself.[46] The continuation of the *devşirme* for an additional 150 years (even at decreasing intervals) therefore served no real practical military or administrative function. All the while, its ritual form, applied or exempted at the sultan's behest, reflected the Ottoman conception of state power and the ability of the ruler to shape the external "reality" of his subjects.

The additional questions raised here may only relate tangentially to what traditionally constitutes "urban" history, but seem to be questions worth asking. As a spectacle within an urban setting, at the very least, the *devşirme* offers a unique moment in time that has no parallel in Ottoman society. While most Balkan subjects would never experience contact with the center in any meaningful fashion, in this case the center came to them and took their children. Surely this deserves a more thorough analysis. As the introductory quotation makes plain, it is highly unlikely that Bulgarian Christians took the time to sing about a mere tax.

Notes

1. Bulgarian folk song lyric, in Elena Grozdanova and St. Andreev, *Българите През XVI Век* (София: Отечествен фронт, 1986), 47. The following derives from Charles Argo, "Ottoman Political Spectacle: Reconsidering the Devşirme in the Ottoman Balkans, 1400-1700," Ph.D. dissertation (Little Rock: University of Arkansas, 2005).

2. The Ottomans also thought urban children to be soft and lacking the physical skills necessary for martial success. Janissary recruits were placed on Anatolian farms for several years doing hard labor and honing fighting skills before enrolling in their official barracks.

3. V.L. Mènage, "Devshirme," in *Encyclopedia of Islam*, ed. Clifford Edmund Bosworth (Leiden: E. J. Brill, 2004), 210-213. This is the second edition standard treatment on the *devşirme* in English. Henceforth this source will be abbreviated to *EI*[2].

4. As a matter of perspective, even a grand vezir's testimony was not admissible in *sheri'at* courts because of his slave status.

5. See Gabriel Piterburg, *An Ottoman Tragedy: History and Historiography at Play* (Berkeley: University of California Press, 2003), 6.

6. The Ottomans first crossed the Dardanelles into Thrace in the mid-eighth/fourteenth century.

7. Christian converts to Islam, whether voluntary or otherwise, were almost exclusively known as "renegades" to Europeans; *devşirme* products were considered the worst of this lot as zealous warriors of the sultan's faith.

8. For the Arab lands, see Bruce Masters, *Christians and Jews in the Ottoman Arab World: The Roots of Sectarianism* (Cambridge: Cambridge University Press, 2001).

9. I question this current trend to a point. It smacks of the proverbial "throwing the baby out with the bathwater." While the Ottoman world was not static, in their efforts to underscore economic, political, and social change, historians seem to lose sight of a single point—the conservative economic policies meant to maintain the provisioning of Istanbul were still in place well into the thirteenth/nineteenth century. Innovation and change were often undertaken *to keep the old system working*. Additionally, much of the manufacturing and market advances made by the state in the empire's later centuries were accomplished by non-Muslim subjects (under the protection and guidance of Western powers) who essentially acted independently of the Ottoman system. Part of this may stem from a desire to alter the "Orientalist" image of the Ottoman state as a despotic regime primarily organized around waging war. But this is exactly what they did, and more consistently than many comparable European state—largely because the Ottomans were frequently engaged on multiple fronts. The often overlooked wars with Safavid Iran (and later Russia) were incredibly draining on the empire's resources. Like all early modern European states, the Ottomans faced tremendous difficulties in provisioning gun-equipped standing armies in the face of sustained fighting; a condition that certainly hindered economic innovation.

Like most, I prefer not to think of the Ottoman state as one incapable of adapting to modern realities after the twelfth/eighteenth century (which *is* Orientalist), but rather as a state that was unable to overcome its own internal contradictions resulting from political/economic decentralization coupled with a continuing need to mobilize enormous human and material resources. But to suggest that the Ottomans vigorously embraced change (ultimately to be trumped by the imperialist West) just for the sake of correcting past prejudices only serves to undervalue the remarkable job the Ottomans did maintaining some semblance of sovereign independence into the twentieth century.

10. The resultant conclusions can be found in Edhem Eldem, Daniel Goffman, and Bruce Masters, *The Ottoman City Between East and West* (Cambridge: Cambridge University Press, 1999), especially 1-16.

11. Ibid., 4-5.

12. Halil Inalcık, "Ottoman Methods of Conquest," *Studia Islamica*, 3 (1954), 103-129, which is the classic and still relevant account of Ottoman policies of expansion.

13. The conversion of Christian churches—replete with public ceremonies of toppling church bells, burning the ropes, and melting the bronze down—proceeded in a rather puzzling fashion. Some areas were left almost wholly intact, others were not. It did not seem to matter if the city was taken by force. Salonica was captured by sultan Murad II in 833/1430 and contained fifty-three churches and nineteen monasteries; he converted only one of each. See Rossitsa Gradeva, "Ottoman Policy Towards Christian Church Buildings," *Institut d'études balkaniques*, 4 (Sophia: 1994), 14-36.

14. Gülrü Necıpoğlu's *Architecture, Ceremonial, and Power: The Topkapı Palace in the Fifteenth and Sixteenth Centuries* (Cambridge, MA: MIT Press, 1991), is the most comprehensive work on the sultans' palace complex. All spectacles in the imperial capital were conceived this way: the sultan's horseback ride to Friday prayers, circumcision festivals for dynasty princes, wedding ceremonies, etc. Every participant was carefully dressed and placed reflecting their social status. A guild procession in 1639 for instance, began with the highest Muslim religious dignitaries and ended with Jewish tavern owners—at the bottom of the social ladder as not only non-Muslims, but peddlers of a forbidden (*haram*) substance.

15. A good overview of this phenomenon can be found in Aziz Al-Azmeh's *Muslim Kingship: Power and the Sacred in Muslim, Christian and Pagan Polities* (London: I.B. Tauris, 1997).

16. The illustration is very accurate; alongside the *emini*, or Janissary *ağa* in harge of the collection, is a second register copy that Ottoman documents attest as a means of ensuring no children were switched along the way since each copy was sent separately to Istanbul and checked again once the children arrive. It was not uncommon for Muslims to attempt to bribe their children into the system, since they were technically ineligible.

17. Victor Turner, *The Ritual Process: Structure and Anti-Structure* (Chicago: University of Chicago Press, 1969).

18. In larger cities, the palace of the *beğlerbeği* could be the setting; the Ottoman Empire was divided into large *beğlerbeğiliks* (provinces) and smaller *sancaks* (districts).

19. See Stewart Gordon, "Robes, Kings and Semiotic Ambiguity," in *Robes and Honor: The Medieval World of Investiture*, ed. by Stewart Gordon (New York: Palgrave, 2001), 379-385.

20. Victor Turner, *The Ritual Process*, 94.

21. One of the few studies to look at this is Zdzislaw Zygulski, Jr., *Ottoman Art in the Service of the Empire* (New York: New York University Press, 1992).

22. Anonymous, *Kitab-u Mesalihi'l-Müslimin ve Menafi'i'l-Mü'minin*, in *Osmanlı Devlet Teşkilatına Daır Kaynaklar*, ed. Yaşar Yücel (Ankara: Türk Tarih Kurumu Basımevi, 1988), 49-141.

23. See Fred DeJong, "Pictorial Art of the Bektashi Order," in *The Dervish Lodge: Architecture, Art and Sufism in Ottoman Turkey*, ed. Raymond Lifchez (Berkeley: University of California Press, 1992), 228-241.

24. It is assumed that 200,000 children, or roughly 1,000 per year, were taken via the *devşirme* over the course of two centuries. This number is impossible to verify, though single levies taking as many as 7,000 youths are reported (though likely exaggerated) by European observers; see Hans Dernschwam's 961/1554 account of a levy in Anatolia that took 7,000 boys, in Hans Dernschwam's *Tagebuch Einer Reise Nach Konstantinopel und*

Kleinasien (1553-1555), ed. Franz Babinger, 1968 reprint (Berlin: Verlag von Duncker & Humblot, 1923), 61. The Ottomans typically ordered the levied districts to produce one male child per forty households, with no set quota regarding total numbers.

25. Oddly, in one case, the Ottomans offer this concession to Podolia (modern Ukraine) in 1082/1672 despite the fact that Christian borderlands conquered after the initial thrust into Europe (Hungary, Wallachia, Moldavia) were never subject to the *devşirme*; likewise, the institution was practically extinct by that point. Most likely, it had simply become a formulaic concession in Ottoman diplomatic language.

26. Machiel Kiel, *Art and Society in Bulgaria in the Turkish Period: A Sketch of the Economic, Juridicial, and Artistic Preconditions of Bulgarian Post-Byzantine Art and Its Place in the Development of the Art of the Christian Balkans, 1360/70-1700, A New Interpretation* (Maastricht: Van Gorcum, 1985), 101. *Avarız-ı divaniye* and *tekalif-i 'örfiyya* were "extraordinary" wartime taxes and "customary" taxes from the Balkan feudal past the Ottomans claimed rights to in order to finance military campaigns. Originally labor and in-kind taxes, they were eventually turned into cash taxes. Many contained a clause that specified exemption from the *devşirme* as well.

27. Ibid., 95.

28. Bridge-building was another critical need that warranted exemptions: Hungarian villagers who built and maintained bridges were given a reprieve of both the *tekalif-i 'örfiye* and the *avarız-ı divaniye*, as well as *kürekciden* ("oarsman duty"), *cerahor* ("fortress repair"), *nüzül* ("war-time provisioning"), and *gılman-ı acemıyandan* ("slave boys") for the Janissary corps. İsmail H. Uzunçarsılı, *Osmanlı Devlet Teşkilatından Kapukulu Ocakları. Volume I: Acemi Ocağı ve Yeniçeri Ocağı* (Ankara: Türk Tarih Kurumu Basımevi, 1943), 110. See also Machiel Kiel, *Art and Society in Bulgaria*, 97.

29. *Derbend*s along the route to Sofia (Sofya) and Samakov (Samakoya) in Bulgaria, for instance, were exempt from the levy to provide security; see İsmail H. Uzunçarsılı, *Kapakulu Ocakları*, I, 109-110.

30. As an example, see *Mühimme Defteri* 5, No. 791, 9 Cemaziyül'evvel, 973 (1 January, 1566) and the document (*Mühimme Defteri* 5, No. 304) reprinted in İsmail H. Uzunçarsılı, *Kapakulu Ocakları*, I, 101-102, for two decrees addressing the *kadi* of Semendire in Serbia (*Mühimme Defteri* No. 791 lists the town of Öziçe as well) about irregularities in the levy—the second such order within the year. Also see, regarding similar problems in Anatolia, *Mühimme Defteri* 3, Nos. 270 and 271, both dated 25 Zilkade, 966 (8 August, 1559) sent to the *Beğ* of Trabzon and to the *Beğlerbeği* of Erzurum respectively.

31. These orders (of which there are several) were "template" documents it seems. Some of them were not addressed to any particular region, and were apparently widely circulated to Rumeli ("Rome"—Balkan lands) *kadis* to ensure tighter regulation over the levy. One exists in most major archival centers in the Balkans, including Skopje and Sofia, and their primary aim was to warn of any "outside" influence, i.e., parents, family, gangs, etc., that may either try to illegally enter the levy, or conversely, may hinder the safe passage of the boys to Istanbul. See İsmail H. Uzunçarsılı, *Kapakulu Ocakları*, I, 97-100; *State Archives of SR Macedonia: Turkish Documents for the History of the Macedonian People*, ed. Metodii Sokolovski, Arif Ctarova, Vancho Boshkov and Fetah Ishac (Skopje: 1963), 105; and also Petar Petrov, *По Следите на Насилието: Документи и Материали за Налагане на Исляма* (София: Наука и Изкуство, 1987), 230.

32. Tsvetana Georgieva, *Еничарите в Българските Земм* (София: Наука и Изкуство, 1988), 55.

33. Halil Inalcık, *An Economic and Social History of the Ottoman Empire: Volume One 1300-1600* (Cambridge: Cambridge University Press, 1994), 16.

34. Two factors mitigate against this: the destruction of the Janissary Corps in 1281/1826 by the sultan Mahmud II and the subsequent dearth of Janissary records; as well as the fact that *devşirme* children were renamed, though they often carried a nickname that hinted at their origins. Career paths will likely have to be deduced through other means.

35. Gilles Veinstein, "Sokollu Mehmet Pasha," *EI*², 706-711. Sources differ on this point; the Patriarch, named Markariye [-ios?], was either Mehmet's cousin or his brother. Either way, his family dominated the office for the three decades after 964/1557.

36. Colin Heywood, "Bosnia Under Ottoman Rule, 1463-1800," in *The Muslims of Bosnia-Herzegovina: Their Historic Development from the Middle Ages to the Dissolution of Yugoslavia*, ed. Marc Pinson (Cambridge, MA: Harvard University Press, 1994), 32-50; 49, note 45. Heywood is quoting Franz Babinger in this instance.

37. Gilles Veinstein, "Sokollu Mehmet Pasha," *EI*², 708. A son of Mehmet Pasha's cousin Mustafa (himself a *beğlerbeği*, or governor, of Buda), renamed Lala Mehmed Pasha, eventually became grand vizier.

38. For more examples, see M. Tayyib Gökbilgin, "Ibrahim Pasha," *EI*², 998-999; V.L. Parry, "Ayas Pasha," *EI*², 779; and Christine Woodhead, "Rüstem Pasha," *EI*², 640-641. See also İ. Metin Kunt, "Ethnic-Regional *(Cins)* Solidarity in the Seventeenth-Century Ottoman Establishment," *International Journal of Middle Eastern Studies* (henceforth *IJMES*), 5, 3 (1974), 234-235. Hans Dernschwam noted in 961/1554 Rüstem Paşa, "once a Bosnian swine-herder," placed his brother Sınan in charge of Constantinople while he and the sultan were away fighting the Safavids. See his *Tagebuch Einer Reiser*, 78-79.

39. H.T. Norris, *Islam in the Balkans: Religion and Society between Europe and the Arab World* (Columbia, SC: University of South Carolina Press, 1993), 50. Monastir is synonymous with modern Bitola in Macedonia.

40. Stanford J. Shaw, *History of the Ottoman Empire and Modern Turkey. Volume 1: Empire of the Ghazis: The Rise and Decline of the Ottoman Empire 1280-1808* (Cambridge: University of Cambridge Press, 1976), 170. Shaw's book affirms the centrality of the "decline" paradigm common to this historiography.

41. For an important account of government patronage, see the specific career path of Ottoman historian and scribe Mustafa Âli in Cornell Fleischer's *Bureaucrat and Intellectual in the Ottoman Empire: The Historian Mustafa Âli (1541-1600)* (Princeton: Princeton University Press, 1986), especially 4-22.

42. Cemal Kafadar, "On the Purity and Corruption of the Janissaries," *Turkish Studies Association Bulletin*, 15 (1991), 273-280.

43. İ. Metin Kunt, "Ethnic Regional (*Cins*) Solidarity," 233-239. Kunt argues that among the palace staff, while distinct regional factions emerged, i.e. the Bosnians and Albanians, there was also a well-known "east" and "west" division between slaves of the Caucasus and those of the Balkans. Kunt cites Ottoman writers of the eleventh/seventeenth century who clearly saw this rivalry as a weakening factor in the empire.

44. Cemal Kafadar, "On the Purity and Corruption of the Janissaries," 276-280.

45. No one is certain why rapid Islamization took place in Bosnia, nor exactly why the Ottomans allowed these newly-converted Muslims to participate in the *devşirme*. Ottomans called them *Potur*, essentially creating a new class of subject, denoting Bosnians as distinct from other Muslims. Some suggest the presence of dualist Bogomils, considered heretical by the papacy, was a factor; or that the native Bosnian church had deteriorated to such a degree prior to the Ottoman arrival in 847/1463, that locals were starved for religious leadership. Whatever the cause, they were eventually favored by sultans for their fierceness and loyalty.

46. Perhaps prior or during Süleyman I's reign, Janissaries had successfully petitioned to marry while active; previously soldiers were not afforded this privilege until they retired and enrolled as pensioners.

11

A Tale of Three Cities: Burhanpur from 1400 to 1800

Stewart Gordon

Introduction: Big Cities/Big Questions

Any research on cities, however modest, theoretically places us in the presence of the largest questions that man has posed about his past.[1] From the earliest notions of "civitas" and "barbarian," whether in China, India, the Middle East, Greece, or Meso America, observers and proto-historians noted that cities were places of trade, courts, and religious ceremony. With their bureaucrats, priests, soldiers, and kings, they were just different from the countryside.

Big questions—they are largely the same today—arose as soon as writers realized that cities and kingdoms do not last forever. What caused the rise and decline of an empire or a great city? How did cities connect with each other? Did "civilization" flow outwards from urban centers to a less civilized periphery? Who was left out as not "civilized" or not possible to "civilize"? Did all people share common stages of "development," from no cities to cities, from smaller cities to larger cities? Or was the human experience fundamentally different from one part of the world to another? Right down to the present thinkers have focused almost exclusively on the great cities—Athens, Delhi, Beijing, Istanbul, Rome, London, Mumbai—and treated them, for better or worse, as places to which wealth and taxes flowed.

From Central Place to Networks

Though long discredited, the ghost of "central place theory" continues to haunt urban studies. There is the lingering assumption that a smaller city must somehow fit into a nested hierarchy at the top of which rests a connected big city. This structure, of course, sometimes happens. Appeals courts are generally located in big cities. Similarly, soft drink distribution plants and wholesale flower markets in a large city service a surrounding region. Often, however, "nested hierarchies" dramatically fails to describe the observed connections. For example, recent research shows direct connections between small Silicone Valley cities and Korea, China, and Japan without intervening connection to nearby San Francisco.[2]

To challenge the theory of central place and nested hierarchies, there is a need for alternate theory. The well-developed body of social network theory may be able to help.[3] Networks avoid the problems of defining centers and peripheries. The evidence for linkages is direct, person-to-person, not inferred. Following a network, one expects to cross political boundaries. The rise or decline of a network does not imply the rise or decline of a civilization. Social networks can be as productively studied in small cities as in large cities. And for those of us who see history as mainly the stories of actual people, rather than only impersonal trends, social networks are all about people and actual human connections across space.

In this spirit, this study will consider one small city in India, Burhanpur, particularly its networks, from about 1200 to about 1800. Informally, it will look at the following sorts of networks: intellectual, military recruiting, architecture and city planning, courtly protocol, political, long distance trade, local trade, religious, and educational. To what regions and specific places did these various networks connect the city? Did the networks fully overlap or were there significant differences in their spread and the important nodes? What sort of knowledge and information passed along these networks? How did it move? Let us begin, then, on the plains of North India in 1400.

North India c. 1400

What would urban India look like around 1400 CE? There are, of course, no direct census figures, but some inferences can be made. Research on the statistics of the Mughal Empire (two centuries later) suggests that the total population of India was about 150 million, with an urban population of about 25 million.[4] In 1400, the population was lower, perhaps 120 million, and the urban fraction was also likely lower. Based on these admittedly weak data, the urban population of India might have been 10 million in 1400.

We can be on slightly firmer ground on the distribution of India's cities at the time. Cities appear in dynastic narratives, biographies, travel literature, all kinds of fiction, and in their archaeological remains.[5] Note on *Map 11.1* the uneven distribution of India's early cities. There is an irregular "T" that runs down the plains south of the Himalayas, through the Malwa plateau and eastern Rajasthan and into Gujarat. Another batch of cities is located along the southwest coast and a third centers on the uplands and rivers of the southeast.

"Small cities" in India around 1400 were mainly capitals of not-particularly big or successful kingdoms. One example of this type of Indian city is named Burhanpur, located near the base of the irregular "T." Today, it is a dusty regional town of about 100,000 on the northern border of the state of Maharashtra, surrounded by tombs, fragments of walls, and ruins. This study's focus will be on the networks that connected this city, from about 1400 to about 1800, to its hinterland, other cities, and the larger world. How did such cities begin? How did small cities become great cities and the process reverse? Were there common spatial patterns among the early small cities in India?

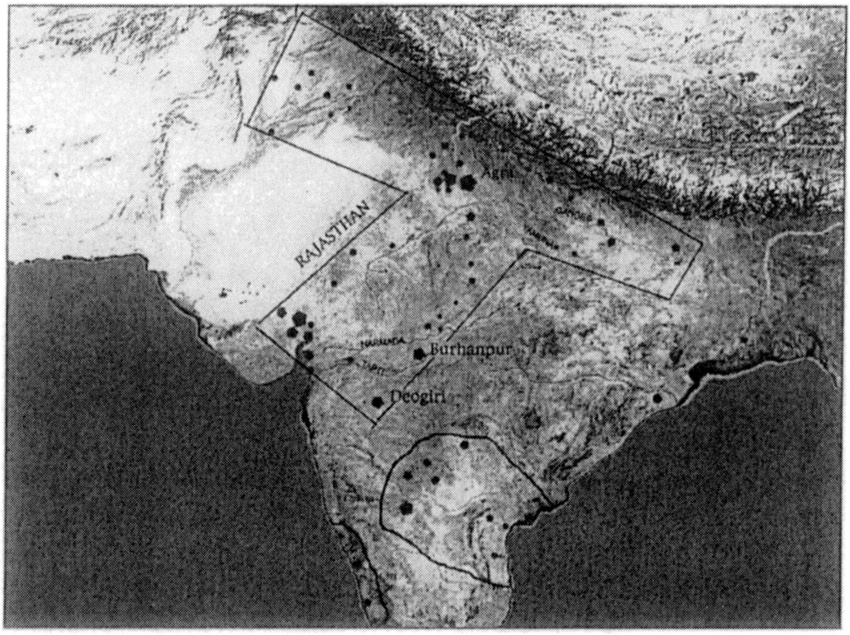

***Map 11.1.* Cities of India c. 1400**

Burhanpur under the Farukhi Dynasty

Mulik Raja, who founded the Farukhi dynasty and Burhanpur, descended from nobility at the Delhi court but started his career as only a horse soldier, leading no troops. In 1370, the Delhi Sultan assigned him a small force and posted him to Talner, a fort on the southern frontier of the kingdom in the Tapti river valley. After conquering some local chiefs, he sent the collected booty to Delhi and was appointed commander of Khandesh, coterminous with the Tapti Valley.[6]

By 1400, the geopolitics around Mulik Raja had completely changed. To the north, the general who controlled Malwa declared independence from Delhi and formed a large and powerful state. To the west of the Tapti Valley, so had the head of the Muslim forces in Gujarat. To the south, Berar went the same route.

With no help in sight from Delhi, Mulik Raja needed a powerful ally in the region. He chose Malwa and was promptly invaded by Gujarat. A few months later, Mulik Raja surrendered Nandurbar at the western end of the Tapti Valley, paid some tribute to Gujarat, and watched its army retreat before monsoon made the roads impassable. This was to be the pattern of the dynasty for the next two centuries—relatively weak independence crafted from careful diplomatic and military balancing between powerful neighbors. In this situation, there was no chance for expansion beyond the Tapti Valley, though several Farukhi rulers launched unsuccessful invasions of adjoining territory.[7] The Farukhi strategy of juggling alliances worked fairly well, as the kingdom was invaded only four times in two centuries.

There are unfortunately no travel accounts or remaining revenue documents from Burhanpur's Farukhi period and minimal research on the site. All that remains is a later history of the dynasty, later revenue documents, and the ruins themselves.

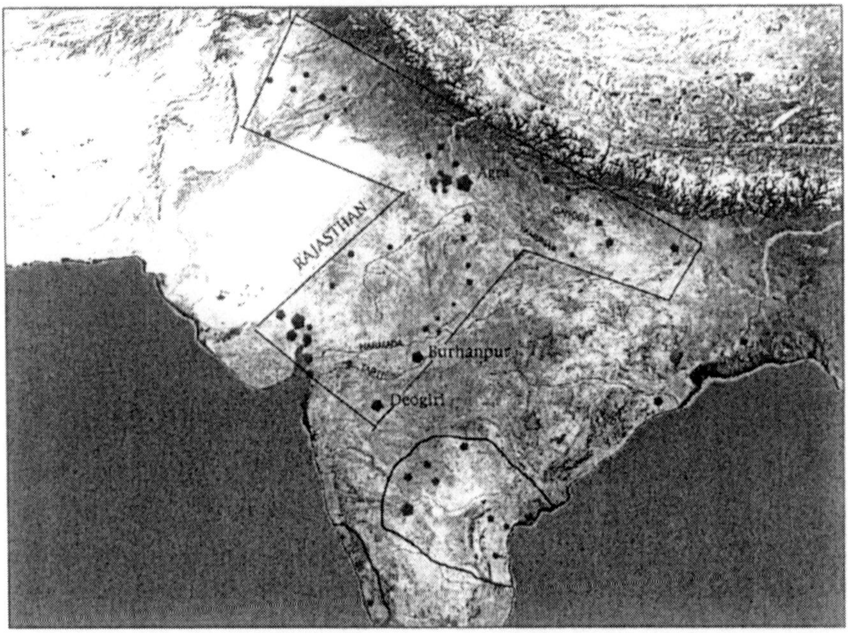

Map 11.2. **The Farukhi Sultanate**

Then, as now, as one approaches the city from the north the first feature—twelve miles north of Burhanpur—was the enormous fortress of Asir, situated on an isolated escarpment. Asir towers more than 900 feet above the road. Its garrison controlled the eastern Tapti Valley. Asir was taken only twice, once by subterfuge and once by bribery, before the British captured it with siege guns in 1818. It was the refuge of the city in its worst times. It did not take much of an opposing army to put the Farukhis into a retreat-to-fort mode. Gujarat did it with a force of about 8,000.[8]

Burhanpur's relation to Asir fort was typical of cities in India at this time. Cities were usually located on rivers—water was crucial—and in vulnerable valley settings, though usually walled. Serious fortifications were miles from the city on high hills.[9] Warfare of the time favored defense. Attacks were slow. Armies took weeks to muster and invade a neighboring kingdom. There was usually time for the city to move inside the nearby fort, which had a water supply and was typically stocked for a year.

In the fifteenth century any army attacking a fort lacked siege guns and explosives for blowing up walls. Typically, they beat away at fort doors with elephants. Defenders poured hot oil and dropped stones on them. The monsoon put an end to most hostilities as defenders had shelter from the rains. Attackers did not and usually went home.

On the way to Asir or in retreat, invaders typically sacked one or more of the kingdoms towns, each represented by a dot on *Map 11.2*, which administered a unit of 20-120 villages called a *pargana*. In each of these towns a bureaucrat of the Farukhi Dynasty collected taxes and forwarded them to the capital. Each town had a small fort. Later evidence suggests that locally powerful families staffed these garrisons rather than Farukhi troops. In the Mughal period, there were about 3,800 recorded villages in Khandesh.[10] Based on a designation of "original" and "later settled" in the Mughal record, there might have been about 3,000 villages in the Farukhi dominions, concentrated in the well-watered eastern half of the Tapti valley. This works out to a village every mile or two across the floor of the valley.

The immediate hinterland of Burhanpur was the pargana of Adilabad. It was fertile and had the best rainfall in the whole of the Tapti Valley, as well as several streams suitable for irrigation. Later Mughal documents show that the pargana's 120 villages grew grains, vegetables and large quantities of cotton.[11]

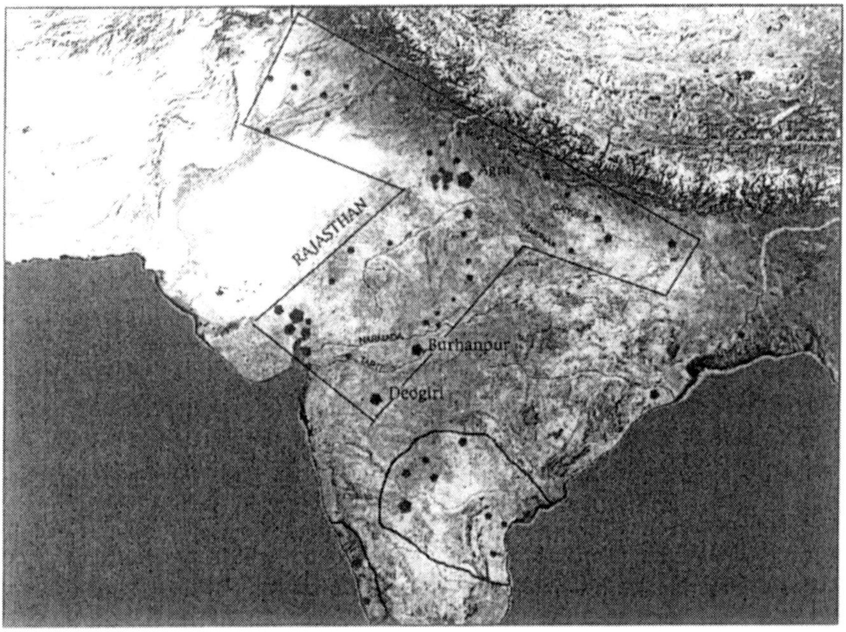

***Map 11.3.* Dynasties Patronizing the Sufi Shrines of Khuldabad**

We know only scattered information about the economic life of the city under the Farukhi Dynasty. Around 1600, prior to the Mughal conquest, the Tapti Valley yielded, by Mughal calculations, more than 100,000 ounces of silver every year.[12] Burhanpur is set in one of the premier cotton-growing regions of India that included eastern Malwa, the Tapti Valley, and eastern Gujarat. Cotton cloth was certainly loomed in the city. There would have been demand for basic textiles by the city's population, plus luxury textiles for the court and exports. The city was prosperous enough to have been attacked and looted in 1561, its inhabitants massacred and an immense booty carried off.[13] The city, however, quickly recovered.

The cultural networks of Burhanpur went beyond the Tapti Valley. In 1328, the Delhi Sultan forcibly moved large portions of the intellectual and administrative elite of the Delhi court to Deogiri, a newly captured capital on the southern borders of his domain. A few years later he relented and allowed the bureaucrats and scholars to return to Delhi. Many, however, stayed at Deogiri and a few Sufi teachers and their followers formed a community at nearby Khuldabad.[14] Several of the subsequent breakaway states of the south looked to the Khuldabad masters for spiritual blessing for their dynasties, as shown on *Map 11.3*. Khuldabad's closest tie was with the Farukhi dynasty, the founder of which named the new capital, Burhanpur, after the Khuldabad teacher Burhan al-din Gharib.[15] The Farukhis also granted the revenue of three villages for performance of ceremonies at Khuldabad. Two Sufi teachers, both claiming lineage from Burhan al-din Gharib, set up schools in the city of Burhanpur and had a numerous following in the city.[16]

Burhanpur was, even in the Farukhi period, connected to a far larger world than the 150 miles of the Tapti Valley from which it collected taxes or Khuldabad, from which it received spiritual blessing. Following the Delhi tradition, all the breakaway kingdoms of Central India and the Deccan welcomed soldiers from Afghanistan, Persia, and Central Asia. They also welcomed jurists and clerics from an even wider area that included Arabia, Egypt, North Africa, and Spain.

How was it possible to receive and integrate these men? Courts were multilingual. Persian was the language in widest use, but Arabic, various Turkic languages, and the local Indian language were all common.

Certain shared ceremonies and customs were found in many courts and served as an unspoken meta-language that made a newcomer suitable for courtly service. The central ceremony in this process was termed *khil'a* (in Arabic) or *saropa* (in Persian). With his nobles present, the king bestowed luxurious garments (often silk) on the newcomer. The basic gift was an outer robe, turban, mid-section wrap, belt, pants, and shoes (hence the Persian term *saropa*—"from head to foot"). The *khil'a* ceremony sometimes included gold, slaves, armor, decorated weapons or horse trappings. The newcomer donned the robes and thereby became a follower of the king and suitable for courtly attendance. The *khil'a* ceremony had a vast provenance, as documented by Ibn Battuta in his travels across Asia and Africa (1320–1350).[17]

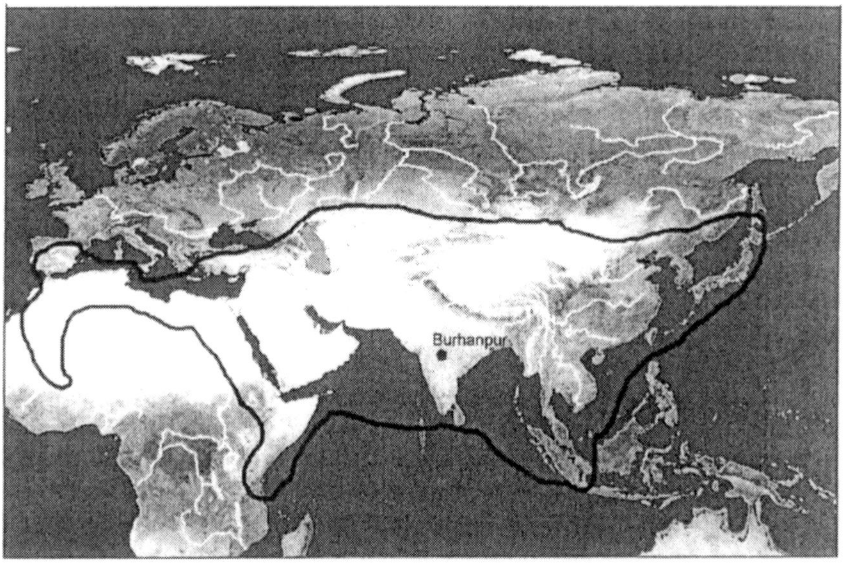

Map 11.4. **Regional Ceremonial Robing**

Burhanpur's Glory Days

The Mughal Empire conquered Burhanpur, Asir fort and the Farukhi kingdom in 1600. In the immediate aftermath, the city became the Mughal Empire's staging area in its push into the southern regions of India. In 1610, the English ambassador Thomas Roe found Burhanpur a bustling place with 6,000 troops attached to the garrison.

Nothing in Roe's account, however, suggests the amount of wealth that flowed into Burhanpur when it became a Mughal capital, around 1630. The Emperor built a palace, his nobles built large houses, and the military expanded the fort. A staggering amount of taxes flowed into the new Mughal court. About fifty percent of the entire collected revenue of the Mughal territories passed into the hands of the Emperor and less than 200 of his nobles. Even subtracting costs of administration, salaries for troops, and maintenance for horses, the Emperor spent about 70,000,000 ounces of silver on his establishment, and the nobles—as a group—spent about 200,000,000 ounces of silver on theirs.[18]

A good portion of this wealth was spent on craft luxuries central to the noble life style—luxury fabrics, horse trappings, weapons, jewelry, glassware, pan ("betel") boxes, palanquins, books, paintings—and all the necessities of a large household: pots, linen, wooden trunks, and tents for when the household moved. Consider just one example of the scale of consumption of the Mughal Emperor. At his death in 1606, the Emperor Akbar's library had 24,000 hand written books, many of them illustrated.

This sensationally strong centralized demand for craft luxury goods had two effects. It sustained distant small cities of specialized production. For example,

were in the midst of the Malwa cotton country. Later observers noted that each town produced at least one specialty, such as silk and very fine white cotton at Chanderi, coarse cloth at Sironj, coarse printed cotton at Ujjein, turbans at Sarungpur.[19]

If we look further afield, this pattern of cities and cotton specialty was also typical of the Ganges-Jumna valley in the Mughal period. Every city and town from the Indus River east to Oudh seemed to be famous for some particular cotton cloth. Agra produced a variety of cloth and carpets. Saharanpur was known for its chautars and khasa (whatever those might be). Historians have attributed this cotton boom to the relative safety of the roads during the Mughal Empire, the marketing skill of internal and overseas merchants, and the influx of silver from the Americas.[20]

Burhanpur itself experienced rapid growth. Nobles brought their large establishments. Armies were recruited. Artisans moved in to supply the demand for luxury goods. The agricultural areas around the developing city shifted to vegetables and grains for immediate sale in the city. With increased demand for leather horse trappings and armor, the market for hides and tanned leather expanded. Luxurious cooking demanded more spices and the spice market expanded. The market for pan leaves was almost insatiable.

The Spatial Layout

So, what did the place look like after several decades as a Mughal capital? A Mughal courtier named Bhimsen, born in Burhanpur, notes in his memoir (1663) that the city had expanded far beyond its walls. The Emperor and many nobles built pleasure gardens that also produced fruits for the table. The Emperor also maintained a large hunting preserve. Interspersed among the pleasure gardens were agricultural fields that produced at least a portion of the vast needs for vegetables and grains within the capital. Suburbs (termed *pura*) sprang up and Bhimsen names several, such as Ratanpura, Jaswantpura, and Bahadurpura.[21]

Let us pass through these suburbs and pleasure gardens with one Jean Thevenot, a French trader who arrived in 1663. Burhanpur lies on the north bank of the Tapti River but Thevenot would not have seen it as he approached. The city wall extended more than a mile and half upstream and downstream and encompassed somewhat over four square miles. The caravan he accompanied passed through one of nine gates to the city.[22] They sojourned at the large walled *caravanserai* for traders, which was equipped to maintain animals and travelers, store goods for traders and, for a fee, send them on subsequent caravans.

When the Frenchman walked out of the caravanserai he was on the central parade ground, called the *maidan*. It measured 500 paces long and 350 across and contained numerous stalls selling fruit and herbs. Several important buildings fronted on the *maidan*. A walled building, somewhat smaller than the *caravanserai* housed the government treasury, which received and stored taxes, paid government expenses, and minted money. A large fort, which housed 6,000 troops at the city's peak, occupied the space between the *maidan* and the river. It had round towers, thirty paces in diameter, flanking the gate and at intervals along the walls. The Emperor's palace occupied the top levels of the fort and overlooked the river.

Neither Thevenot nor Bhimsen commented on a large mosque and adjacent *madrasa* ("Quranic school") that adjoined the *maidan*. The present structure—a surrounding wall, two-storey entrance, two tall minarets, and a tree-planted courtyard—replaced that structure a half-century later. Likewise, the ruins of the several baths (*hamam*) exist but neither traveler commented on them. Mosque, *madrasa*, and *hamam* were, perhaps, such common features of Islamic cities at the time that they did not merit comment.

Immediately south of the fort ran the Tapti River, broad and shallow at the season Thevenot arrived. The residents knew that river water was muddy and unhealthy. Drinking water from a spring was piped to a large cistern in the *maidan*, storage facilities in the fort and palace, tanks in the *caravanserai* and the mosque, and various other outlets in the city. Across the river were (and still are) architecturally striking tombs which belong to members of the Farukhi dynasty and several learned Muslim teachers.[23] Thev walked the streets and noted the hills within the city walls. To him, the lower streets looked like ditches when viewed from the upper streets. The houses were stucco, with tile roofs. "The various colors of the roofs, mingling with the verdure of a great many trees of different kinds, planted on all hands, makes the prospect pleasant enough."

Bhimsen, the Mughal courtier, noted that the bazaar off the maidan consisted of large buildings owned by "nobles, traders, and merchants . . . rich men of industry dealing in all sorts of commodities and rare things of all places."[24] At least some of these rich merchants were Borah Muslims, a Shi'a sect originally from Persia but long settled in India. The head of the sect was based at Surat, the thriving port two hundred miles west of Burhanpur. The sect had branches in Ujjein, Bombay, Pune, and the cities of North India. They also had centers in Sind and Persia. Later, they would dominate the large opium trade from Malwa (the plateau north of the Tapti Valley). One large house, typical of the great merchants, survived into the nineteenth century and was drawn by a British artist (see the book jacket).[25]

In the narrow lanes behind these mansions, Bhimsen found "artisans of every type and craft" who have "settled thickly." Intermixed among the weavers were, as Bhimsen notes, Hindu temples and warehouses for grain: "The number of such places is quite large."[26]

Let us consider for a moment the spatial layout of a more familiar type of city, that is, small American cities built in the nineteenth century. Typically, they had a central public square (often with a band shell), a courthouse adjoining the square, a local restaurant or two, a hotel, the offices of the local paper, some law offices, shops crucial to the economy—a hardware store, yard goods, a bank or two, livery, post office, and churches. Off the square in one direction would be the local industries, such as grain mills, breweries, steelworks, or a rail yard. In the opposite direction off the square were the large houses of the successful owners of the industries, banks, newspaper, and the larger retail establishments. Even if the spatial layout varied, the common elements were there. The square might be off the main street or a rail line might bisect the city. Nevertheless, travelers to such American cities of the nineteenth century navigated them eas-

travelers to such American cities of the nineteenth century navigated them easily. They found a place to stay, something to eat, a place to stable their horse, local news, a new shirt, and, possibly, a job. For someone with basic knowledge, these small cities formed a network of information, services, and possibilities.

So it was for travelers to Burhanpur. Its spatial layout and functions would have been familiar to most local, regional, and long-distance travelers. It is not that all Muslim cities from Spain to India were the same. Rather, they had common elements. The Muslim cities' center included the main mosque. Friday prayers were the most heavily attended and the presiding cleric blessed the name of the ruling king, an act central to kingly legitimacy. The cleric might have been from Mecca or Baghdad. These two cities had the best religious training and clerics regularly traveled from them to outlying congregations across the Islamic world. Close by the mosque was the king's palace with guards and stables. Muslim cities generally included a broad open area near the palace that could be used for military practice, ceremony, and evening strolls. Muslim cities included one or more bathing building (*hamam*), training institutions (*madrassa*), and a central bazaar for both daily necessities and imported items. The city included one or more *caravanserais* where caravans stopped, traders stayed, and goods in transit were stored. The government buildings included a court and a mint. These cities generally had a legal structure that included professional, trained jurists who presided over courts of both civil and criminal Islamic law and a professional class of administrators who served the governor. For someone with basic knowledge—and he or she need not be Muslim—small Islamic cities formed a network of information, services, and opportunities.

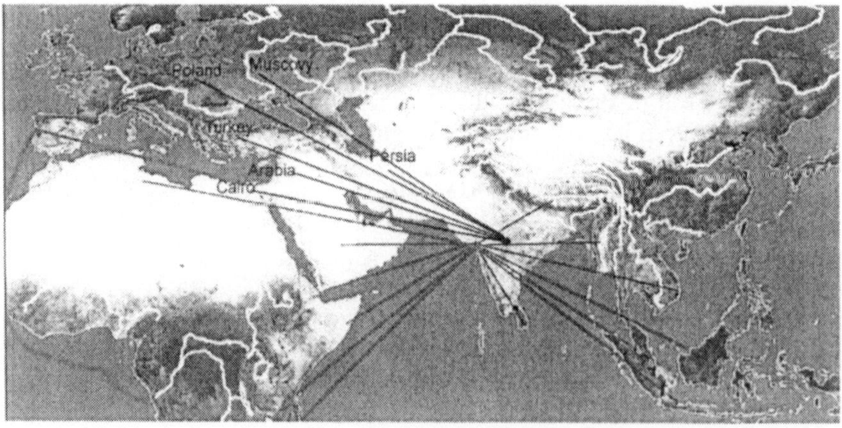

Map 11.5. **Cotton Exports of Burhanpur and Gujarat**

The Production Network

And what happened in these narrow lanes that lead off the *maidan*? Burhanpur hummed with the sound of looms. Another French trader named Tavernier spent several months in Burhanpur in the 1677 and described the basics of the local cotton industry. The city made "prodigious quantities" of calicuts, clear and white." Some were "painted with several colors, with flowers." Other firms produced a "sort of linen which they never dye, with a strip or two of gold or silver quite through the piece." This high-value cloth had gold and silk threads, often in floral patterns woven into a broad band at one end. The city also produced clothes called "*ornis*," the longer ones used for waist wraps and the shorter ones for women's veils.[27]

Tavernier noted that these specialized types of cloth went to Cairo, Arabia, Persia, Turkey, Muscovy, and Poland. Burhanpur's specialty cottons formed a complementary set of high-end cotton textiles to the many varieties loomed in the neighboring province of Gujarat and exported from west coast ports. Specialty cloth, mainly of lower quality, also came overland from Bihar and Oudh through Burhanpur, also for export. Gujarat cotton textiles were a major export to Europe at this time, especially for re-export to Africa in the slave trade.[28]

Cotton went out and information came back along the same trade networks. European observers noted that the Burhanpur weavers adjusted the length, width, and composition of their cloth to meet the desires of customers, whether Polish women for their veils or slave suppliers in Africa. We should not be surprised at this level of market-demand sophistication. Archaeological evidence from Cairo and Indonesia shows that Gujarat weavers were adjusting colors for distant markets as early as the twelfth century.[29]

Documents of the late Mughal period detail nine specialized wholesale markets within Burhanpur, as follows: cloth, cattle and horses, vegetables and fruits, pan and spices, gold and silver jewelry, tobacco, used metal and clothes, leather and hides, and carts and palanquins. There were also two retail markets for grains, oil, and general household supplies. The government made most of its local revenue from taxes on the sale of cloth, but it also taxed sales in all other city markets. Re-minting old silver currency, a ferry tax, and small charges at gates and doorways to the city generated additional local government revenue.[30]

The immediate supply hinterland for Burhanpur remained the Tapti Valley and especially Adilabad pargana. Non-irrigated crops included various millets, chickpeas, and wheat. Irrigated crops included ginger, turmeric, safflower, tobacco, perfume flowers, opium, sweet potatoes, and garden vegetables.

Actual networking of revenue flows was far more complicated than a simple movement from the countryside to Burhanpur. Careful research on the Mughal documents of the Tapti Valley shows that only about half of the taxes actually passed to Burhanpur. Another third was collected directly by Mughal nobles for personal maintenance and the maintenance of their troops. Larger nobles generally received taxes from several regions, often hundreds of miles from where they were stationed. Smaller nobles were often stationed within the area from which they collected taxes, though they would often be away on campaign. The third share of taxes, about twenty percent, was assigned to local men for maintenance of troops who helped keep the roads safe for trade. Retaining this large a percentage of taxes at the local level was enough to sustain smaller towns. The system connected their income to generally damping feuding and promotion of agriculture.[31]

The Eighteenth Century

As the Mughal Empire broke apart in the late seventeenth and early eighteenth centuries, Burhanpur went through a rough patch. Marathas, would be state-builders from the south, captured and sacked the city in 1685 and 1698. In 1711, a Dutch expedition, southbound from Delhi, carefully considered all the possible routes to the western coastal ports of Gujarat and opted for a more westerly route that bypassed Burhanpur.

From about 1700 to 1720, the Marathas were mainly occupied with their own succession struggles but soon thereafter retuned to raids on the Tapti Valley. They sacked the city again in 1728. In the 1730, the Mughal defenders built a new, larger city wall and a new mosque, but to no avail. The Marathas finally conquered the whole of the Tapti Valley and Burhanpur in the 1750s.

The city surely shrank some in the eighteenth century. It was no longer the recipient of vast tax revenues from the whole of the Mughal Empire and immensely wealthy Mughal nobles no longer resided there. In the Maratha dominions, Burhanpur was merely a regional capital, the hub of the Tapti Valley. Asir fort was stocked and garrisoned by the Marathas, though not on the scale of the Mughals. In the 1770s, there were only about 600 troops stationed at Asir. The administrative network also shifted. Following conquest by the Marathas, many administrative posts went to Brahmins from either Maharashtra or, further south, the Konkan coast.

Cotton weaving continued and the records mention several Burhanpur specialties—chintzes bound for Persia, byrames bound for Java, quilts to England, and gold threadwork for various courts of India. There were, however, no new tombs, walls, palaces, or mosques.

We have far fewer travelers and observers of Burhanpur in the eighteenth century than there were for the seventeenth century. A British military expedition lead by one Colonel Upton passed through the city in 1775 and noted the cultivated area outside the city and the walls. Upton thought that Burhanpur looked much like Banaras, which at the time had a population of about 100,000. He was clearly not very impressed with the place.[32] A second British expedition in 1899, under Colonel Goddard, found the area prosperous and supplies readily available. He estimated that there were about 300 shops in Burhanpur. Research on the revenue documents of the late eighteenth century suggest that tax collection in Khandesh had dropped by about one third from the high point early in the century.[33] Overall, through the second half of the eighteenth century Burhanpur seems to have reverted to a "small city." Weaving was still its specialty and it was the regional capital of the Tapti Valley.

The "Time of War"

Burhanpur's collapse came between 1803 and 1818, a time locally known as the "gardi-ki-wakt" or "time of war." Maratha control ceased. Various fragments of mercenary armies and raiding bands repeatedly attacked the city, pargana towns, and villages across the Tapti Valley. Local families built forts on every available hill (more than 400 up and down the valley) but they offered little protection.

The province emptied in response to these violent, perilous times. The British conquered the area in 1818. Their first survey, in the 1820s, found village after village deserted, the only evidence a few remaining buildings and fields among rapidly retuning forest growth. The survey statistics were shocking. On average only thirty-three people remained per square mile in the whole valley, and only eighty-three places had more than 800 remaining souls.[34]

Many weavers left Burhanpur. Some were given safe passage by the Bhonsles, Maratha princes of Nagpur (200 miles east of Burhanpur). Some weavers hung on and survived until the British conquest. All that was left in 1819 was one specialty, saris with threads of gold and silver.

The city never revived as the trans-shipping center it had been in the seventeenth and eighteenth centuries. The Bombay–Agra road, pushed through by the British for strategic reasons in the first half of the nineteenth century, bypassed the city, as did the railroad in the 1880s. Even in the late nineteenth century it was clear to observers that the city had neither the population nor the size it had had in earlier times.[35]

Conclusions

The analysis of the city of Burhanpur suggests a series of non–contiguous networks that shifted over time. Consider, for example, the network of military recruitment. In the thirteenth century, the conquering army came mainly from Delhi. With the formation of an independent kingdom, the Farukhis had to recruit locally and, in addition, welcomed fighters from the far reaches of Persia and Central Asia. When it was a Mughal capital, Burhanpur saw recruits from all over North India, especially from what is now Uttar Pradesh. In the eighteenth century, the Marathas recruited mainly from Maharashtra, to the south of Burhanpur. Later in the century, they hired Muslims from north India and Afghanistan. The British Army that conquered and occupied Burhanpur was mainly recruited from Bengal and the Ganges Valley.

The basic supply network was more stable. Throughout the period considered, the supply base of the city was the eastern Tapti Valley, especially the pargana of Adilabad. Vegetables, grains, meat, and leather regularly moved into the city's markets. At the city's height, noble families supplemented this supply base with productive gardens, hunting preserves, and orchards located in the Burhanpur's suburbs.

The network of Sufi shrines, once established, seems to have been stable throughout the period. Burhanpur's dynasty was one of several that looked to the sacred Khuldabad mosque near Aurangabad for spiritual and support and blessing.

Burhanpur's demand network rose and fell with its prosperity. Like any capital of a small Indian kingdom, Burhanpur, under the Farukhis, benefited from taxes that came to the king. Though its nobility was small, it was the center of demand for high-end craft skills and arts—weaving, ironwork, painting, book production, musical instrument making. The skilled craftsmen who serviced the court were part of a network that included such courts across much of India at the time. These small cities were the refuge from turbulent times for skilled craftsmen. A small city like Burhanpur was also the repository of courtly custom and knowledge. At every court there were professionals who knew how to organize a bureaucracy and arrange a robing ceremony. The network of such men went far beyond India and included jurists and clerics from Central Asia, Persia, Afghanistan, and the Middle East. With luck and military success, an empire might be crafted from the administrative skills found in any such small city.

In its glory days, Burhanpur was connected to astonishing, far-flung networks. A small number of specialized cotton fabrics multiplied to many varieties, all with specific local and distant markets. The stream of fabrics from Burhanpur joined those from the contemporary production centers of the Ganges Valley, Malwa, and Gujarat. This textile network was as much about information that flowed back as it was about production. India's exporters knew what sorts of cloth sold in Poland or Africa—length, fineness, uses, colors, and anticipated prices.

Maratha conquest in the middle decades of the eighteenth century brought great changes in Burhanpur's networks. Fewer varieties of cloth were produced though they still traveled far. The Marathas maintained patronage of Muslim shrines and mosques, so the religious networks remained. Military recruitment was less than under the Mughals but many Afghans and Central Asians remained in the regions and found opportunities for service. When governments collapsed in the late eighteenth century these troops became sub-regional armies, which looted and plundered. A few succeed in setting up small successor states.

Overall, during the pre-colonial era small cities like Burhanpur were—contrary to central place theory—not merely regional centers nor did they necessarily depend on or feed into large cities. Jurists and clerics came from as far away as Spain to these regional capitals. The local sultans also welcomed soldiers from as far away as Central Asia. Common customs and ceremonies made these newcomers feel welcome. If this process sounds surprisingly modern perhaps we have to adjust our notions of what is unique about our "globalized" world. A substantial amount of taxation was retained locally, funding small military forces, forts, and local officials. These small cities had the skills, information, and economic base to become—with a little luck—a great capital of a larger kingdom.

The rise and fall of Burhanpur suggests, however, a great deal of chance in whether a typical small city would become a "great city." Even its founder could only say that Burhanpur was where it was by the suggestion of a Sufi saint. Any number of towns along the main roads from Agra to the Indian Ocean might have similarly become a great city. Bhilsa, Shahabad, Chanderi, Sarungpur, and Ujjein all had similar access to water and were notable weaving cities with access to Malwa cotton. Each had a fort and family that had military skills. Each of these places had administrative and military talent and was a repository of courtly symbols and behavior. They were all surrounded by fertile hinterlands. Each could attract merchants and artisans if conditions were favorable.[36] That Burhanpur became, if briefly, a "great" city seems solely due to its selection as a southern capital by the Mughal emperor.

Burhanpur's experience also suggests that "great city" status was generally transitory. Serious long-term disruption meant that the administrative and craft talent fled. They rarely came back. For every enduring Delhi, there are a host of no-longer "great" cities: Vijayanagara, Agra, Ujjein, Srirangaptam, and Gulbarga. Sometimes the collapse was so complete that all that's left today are stones for archaeologists. Some formerly great cities, like Burhanpur, live on among the ruins.

Notes

1. It is sobering to contemplate even a few of the global thinkers who have considered cities—Lao Tzu, Confucius, Buddha, Christ, Muhammad, Tacitus, St. Augustine, al-Baruni, Durkhiem, Marx, Polyani.

2. Work on smaller cities and personal networks is challenging the dominant view of "meta-cities" in research on contemporary cities. See Anna Lee Saxenian, *Local and Global Networks of Immigration: Professionals in Silicon Valley* (San Francisco: Public Policy Institute of California, 2002). Also, "From Brain Drain to Brain Circulation: Transnational Communities and Regional Upgrading in India and China," *Studies in Comparative International Development*, 40, 2 (Sept. 2005).

3. Most contemporary research on social networks is confined to rigid quantitative data based on one-time interviews. See, for example, the journal *Social Network*. The original insights in the field, however, lend themselves to historical data that is not so easily quantifiable. See, for example, Everett M. Rogers and D. Lawrence Kincaid, *Communication Networks: Toward a New Paradigm for Research* (New York: Free Press, 1981) and Mark Granovetter's research on strong and weak ties, plus more recent research on networks of trust, degrees of separation, and dense connections, as in Mark Granovetter and Richard Swedberg, eds., *The Sociology of Economic Life* (Boulder, CO: Westview Press, 2001); Neil J. Smelser and Richard Swedberg, eds., *The Handbook of Economic Sociology* (Princeton: Princeton University Press, 1995); and Frank Dobbin, ed., *The New Economic Sociology: A Reader* (Princeton: Princeton University Press, 2004).

4. Shireen Moosvi, *The Economy of the Mughal Empire c. 1595: A Statistical Study* (Delhi: Oxford University Press, 1987), 395-406.

5. This map and others that follow are constructed from data from several sources, See Catherine B. Asher and Cynthia Talbot, *India Before Europe* (Cambridge: Cambridge University Press, 2006), 26, 36, 55, 90. See also Joseph Schwartzberg, ed., *Historical Atlas of South Asia* (New York: Oxford University Press, 1992); also, Irfan Habib, *An Atlas of the Mughal Empire* (Delhi: Oxford University Press, 1982).

6. Muhammad Qasim Firishtah, *Tarikh-I Ferishta* translated as *History of the Rise of the Mahomedan Power in India* by John Briggs, reprinted edition (New Delhi: Oriental Books, 1981), IV, 169-172.

7. Ibid., 172-194.

8. Stewart Gordon, *Marathas, Marauders, and State Formation in Eighteenth-Century India* (Delhi: Oxford University Press, 1994), 88-94.

9. Some of the larger pairings of fort and city include Pune-Singarh, Aurangabad-Daulatbad, and Hyderabad-Gulbarga.

10. *India Office Library*. Mackenzie Collection Vol. 44. "Hakeekut Hindostan of Letchmee Narain" [English translation], 47-54.

11. John Richards and Stewart Gordon, "Kinship and Pargana in Eighteenth-Century Khandesh," in Stewart Gordon, *Marathas, Marauders, and State Formation in Eighteenth-Century India* (Delhi: Oxford University Press, 1994), 125-150.

12. This amount comes from the first Mughal tax settlement in the Tapti Valley in 1605 and may be an overstatement but perhaps not by much. Neighboring Gujarat, which had been conquered earlier, yielded an actual tax collection of almost a third more than the settlement in the Tapti Valley. See Moosvi, *The Economy of the Mughal Empire*, 29-30. From the Farukhis until the twentieth century cotton was always the most heavily taxed non-irrigated crop in northern India. Taxes were often twice those of wheat and three times those of other grains or vegetables. Even with these high taxes, cotton was a profitable crop. Only irrigated crops, such as indigo, sugarcane, and opium had higher taxes. See Moosvi, 102-103.

13. Ferishta, *Rise of the Mahomedan Power,* 190.

14. Carl W. Ernst, *Eternal Garden: Mysticism, History, and Politics at a South Asian Sufi Center* (Albany: State University of New York Press, 1992) 107-117.

15. Ibid., 207-209.

16. Ibid., 206, 227-232.

17. See Stewart Gordon, ed., *Robes and Honor: The Medieval World of Investiture* (New York: Palgrave, 2002), Introduction.

18. Moosvi, 221-223, 287. See also, John Richards, "Official Revenues and Money Flows in a Mughal Province," in *The Imperial Monetary System of Mughal India,* ed. John F. Richards (Delhi: Oxford University Press, 1987), 193-231.

19. *India Office Library.* 114 MSS Eur, 1313, "Journal from Surat to Agra and Dehly by Way of Ugein by Captain Charles Reynolds, Surveyor, Begun 12th March, 1785," 74. See also William Hunter, "Narrative of a Journey from Agra to Oujein," *Asiatic Researches,* 6 (1801), 49-51.

20. Hameeda K. Naqvi, *Urban Centres and Industries in Upper India, 1556–1803* (Bombay: Asia Publishing House,1968), 138-143.

21. Bhimsen, *Tarikh-I-Dilkasha,* English trans. V. G. Khobrekar (Bombay: Department of Archives, 1972), 6.

22. Jean de Thevenot, *The Travels of Thevenot in Three Parts* (London: H. Clark, 1687), III, 71-72.

23. These tombs have never been adequately researched but I had the pleasure of touring them with a guide.

24. Bhimsen, 5.

25. Hand-colored engraving by J.E.Varrelle of a sketch by Meadows Taylor, c. 1820. From the collection of the author.

26. Bhimsen, 6.

27. John Baptiste Tavernier, *The Six Voyages . . . through Turkey into Persia and the East Indies Made into English* (London: Tollen, 1677), Part II, Book I, 31.

28. George Bryan Souza, "The Dimensions of Empire: The Portuguese Crown's Monopoly and Trade in Brazilian Tobacco and Afro-Asian Commodities in the Global Economy, c. 1674 to 1776," forthcoming.

29. Ruth Barnes, "Indian Trade Textiles: Sources and Transmission of Designs," paper presented at a "Communities and Commodities: Western India and the Indian Ocean, 11th–15th Centuries" conference, Kelsey Museum of Archaeology, Ann Arbor, MI: November 7-10, 2002.

30. Pune Daftar, Khandesh Bundles, #196. A Jhadti (Year-end summary) of the city of Burhanpur dated 1751. See also Bundle #118 for a detailed Jhadti of 1763-1764 (Marathi, Modi script).

31. Richards, "Official Revenues."

32. *British Museum*. add. 29 213. "A journal of the road traveled by Colonel Upton from Kalpi through Narwar to Bhopaul and Boorhaunpore [1775-1776]," Part 3.

33. Richards, "Official Revenues," 202-203.

34. *India Office Library*. Mss European D 148. "Sykes Report" [1828], 18-19.

35. *Gazetteer of the Bombay Presidency*, Vol. XII Khandesh (Bombay: Government Printing Office, 1880), 589-591.

36. I do not want to suggest that Burhanpur's experience was the only pattern for small cities in India. Several others would be equally relevant and interesting. For example, the port cities along the Malabar Coast were mainly connected to the Middle East through the export of their spices and had less contact with inner peninsular India. Large pilgrimage sites such as Madurai and Banaras had networks and flows of information quite different from Burhanpur. See James Heitzman's study that follows in this volume.

12

Secondary Cities and Spatial Templates in South India, 1300-1800[1]

James Heitzman

The history of urbanization in South Asia[2] encompasses a number of discourses that rest upon regional perspectives, but none is more influential than the view from Delhi, Lahore and Agra (*Map 12.1*). Their tale has its roots in hoary antiquity, of course, but becomes a powerful and continuous narrative when recounting the military conquests that emanated from Central Asia and led to the creation of the Delhi Sultanate (twelfth-sixteenth centuries) followed by the Mughal Empire (sixteenth-nineteenth centuries). The trio of cities that alternated as political capitals for over 700 years not only became at times the largest urban sites in South Asia,[3] but also stood at the pinnacle of a military-administrative apparatus that spun off regional capitals such as Ahmedabad in Gujarat or Gaur in Bengal, which also became very large cities.[4] Even the discussion of secondary cities in South Asia during the time of the Delhi Sultanate and the Mughal Empire must acknowledge their relationship to the three primary, metropolitan centers. The architecture of fortification, which reached its highest expression in the Mughal forts of Delhi, Lahore and Agra, influenced urban form within primary and secondary sites throughout South Asia. And military-administrative centralization within the fortified center expanded inexorably into the southern part of the subcontinent.

This study acknowledges the power of the discourse on Sultanate-Mughal urbanization but seeks to contextualize it with several alternative templates from South India.[5] One concerns the organization of cities just before the appearance of the Lahore-Delhi-Agra corridor, i.e., around the year 1000, when urbanization was alive and well, with specific architectural formats, polycentric settlement patterns and political-economic relationships that involved temples as important mediating institutions. This influenced the organization of cities well after the fourteenth century. A second template comes from commercial cities along the long coastline of peninsular India, where continuous contact with the Indian Ocean trading system always supported a string of secondary settlements that retained a polycentric character. After 1498 the coastal cities of South India came under the influence of European colonial ventures; the Europeans produced spaces that responded to indigenous settlement patterns including the military-administrative initiatives of interior powers, but also expressed imported features. During the period between the fourteenth and the nineteenth centuries, therefore, South India was an arena for the interaction of at least three significant templates defining the city. This study will look at these templates by concentrating on four cities that at different times exhibited the features of primary and secondary centers.

The argument of this study begins with a background discussion on the history of cities in South Asia during a two-thousand-year period before the fourteenth century, in order to outline the conditions that gave rise to an urbanization revolving around ritual relationships between regional kingdoms, temples, and commercial groups. The discussion leads into a more detailed examination of Kanchipuram, a "temple city" that enjoyed a long association with imperial powers but also served as a commercial node and a coordination point for processing and redistributing agrarian produce. There were probably several hundred sites resembling Kanchipuram throughout South India by the fourteenth century, a stratum of sub-regional central places upon which regional powers could build urban hierarchies. The unexpected growth of the city of Vijayanagara, one of the world's largest cities during the fifteenth and sixteenth centuries, transformed many of those central places into secondary urban sites within a multi-regional state apparatus that still rested on ritual interaction, but simultaneously applied the enhanced resources of a burgeoning commercial economy to military purposes. This paper will look at Vijayanagara, first as a study in the rise of a metropolis from a constellation of small villages and forts and its reversion back to small-scale settlements after a precipitous fall, and second as an example of anomalous hyper-centralization followed by a novel grouping of regional capitals in the seventeenth century.

The study then moves into a discussion of one of those successor sites, Bijapur, where the template of the fortified administrative center, already visible at Vijayanagara, allied with Islamic sovereignty. This template, which had become standardized during its expansion from the north, would dominate primary and secondary cities within the peninsular interior until the beginning of the nineteenth century. The final case presented in this study is the port of Pondicherry, the coordinating point for a French imperial presence that arrived late in South Asia, remained subordinate to Dutch and then British colonialism, and then enjoyed a meteoric rise followed by near-total collapse in the mid-eighteenth century. The fortified character of Pondicherry, in part a response to the military-administrative centralization exemplified at Bijapur and in part a manifestation of European colonial militarism, brings us to the final stages of the city-as-fort phase in South Asia's urban history and to the cusp of a city-and-cantonment phase typical of British colonialism.

This study looks at the spatial organization of cities in order to understand temporality. In this approach to urban forms the term "template" is used to highlight the purposeful and meaningful activities necessary to create these cities, which were the result, in whole and in part, of initiatives carried out over many decades or even centuries. Those who built these urban forms were cognizant of patterns, guides or models that existed partly in texts, partly in practice, and partly in living memory passed down over a long period. Having stated this, however, the reader must not consider this study an exercise in essentialism, as if we are scrutinizing here the application of ideal types lurking in terminology such as the *vastu* paradigm[6] or the "Islamic" or "Colonial" city. Whatever the utility of these concepts to scholars today, they express modes of analysis connected to more recent nationalist or communalist discourse and may be anachronisms when discussing the motivations of persons in the more distant past; in employing them one may run the risk of reducing the urbanization of South India (or South Asia as a whole) to a series of traditions, influences, or diffusions. A close reading of this study will indicate that the cities considered here were the material expression of goals and responses to problems that were embedded in the experience and practice of South Indian people. The results were South Indian cities—a unique range of human settlements. Thus, although this study will hopefully serve as the basis for comparative analysis, it is an excursion into the history of the South Asian city.

An Introduction to Early South Indian Cities

Early historical urbanization in South Asia originated in northern India and Pakistan perhaps as early as 800 BCE, and built up momentum that allowed its continuous expansion throughout the subcontinent at least until the fourth century of the Common Era. Three characteristics distinguish the cities constructed during this period. First, fortification walls delineated political and mercantile quarters from suburbs. Such fortifications were so commonplace that they now serve as the means for archaeologically identifying the presence of a city.[7] The walled city appears regularly in textual materials that discuss cities, including the *Arthasastra* or "Discourse on Power" originally composed by Kautilya in North India during the fourth century BCE, and the *Cilappatikkaram* or "Tale of the Ankle Bracelet" that describes the South Indian cities of Madurai and Pumpuhar around the third century CE.[8] Second, the surviving monumental architecture after the second century BCE consisted almost entirely of monastic institutions with their associated *stupas*, in many cases manifested within complexes located in the suburbs outside fortified zones. These complexes, associated with what we would call Buddhist or Jain religiosity, preserved and perpetuated imperial motifs expressed first under the Mauryan Empire during the time period of the early *Arthasastra*, and served also as devotional sites for commercial and artisan communities.[9] Third, this ubiquitous cultural orientation of cities was closely linked to a subcontinent-spanning trading system that stretched from the Mediterranean to Southeast Asia. Trade reached its peak between 100 BCE and 300 CE with the conjunction of political events that pacified the early Silk Road and brought South India into direct contact with Greco-

Roman shipping.[10] We may conceptualize the urban sites of this period as a series of nodes linked by trade routes, supporting a cosmopolitan bourgeois cultural ethos (*Map 12.1*).

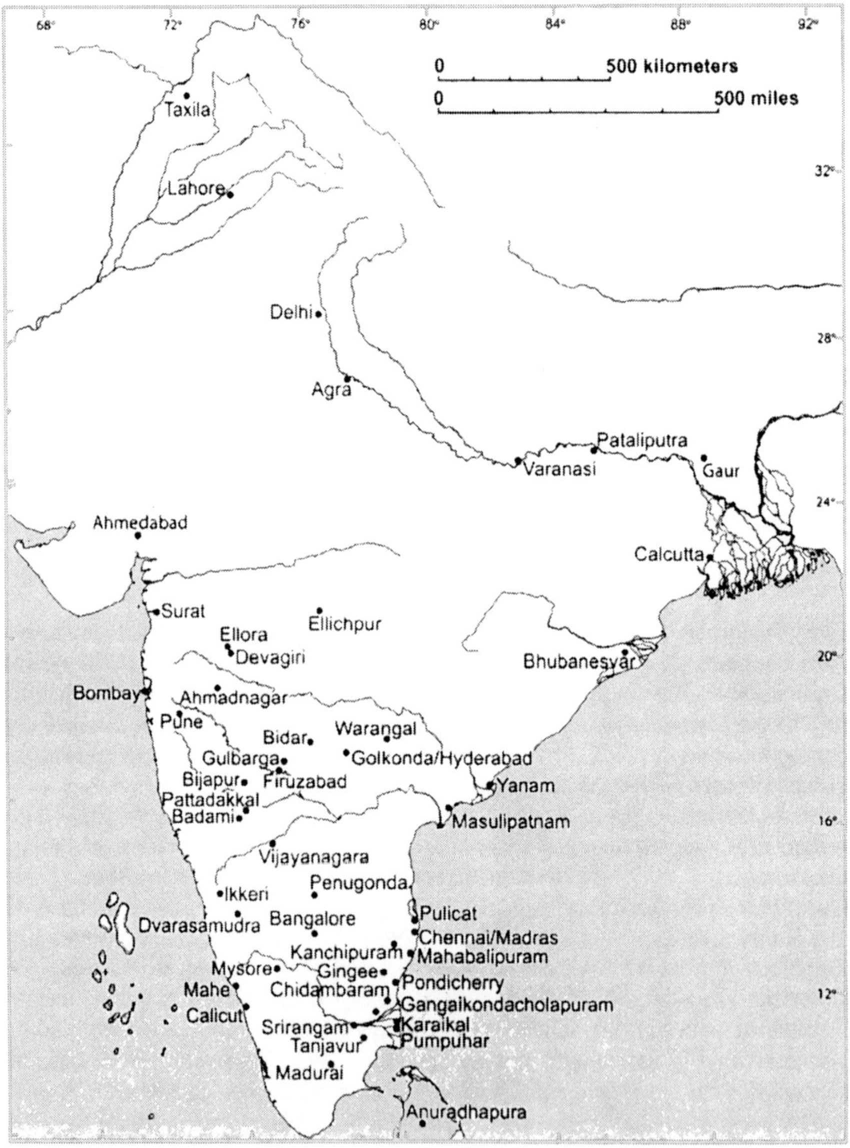

***Map 12.1.* Cities of South Asia, 1400-1800**

The cities of the north were centers of what early texts described as *janapada*, literally the "foot of the people," or what we now term a region.[11] The basis for the articulation of a hierarchy of secondary settlements around one or more regional central places rested, according to the *Arthasastra*, on the countryside, even if the activities within the city required occupational specialization, the activities of many types of merchants, and diversification of state offices. The subsequent spread of urbanization into peninsular India, through a combination of diffusion and independent socio-economic processes, also took place within geographical entities conceptualized as regions where agriculture and extractive industries were becoming the basis for population growth and occupational differentiation.[12] As this process reached its peak, a steadily expanding, hegemonic urban culture rested on class stratification and became independent from the agrarian organization of specific regions. In the *Kamasutra*, produced in Pataliputra, the largest city in South Asia, the "bourgeois" man-about-town (*nagarika*) moves within a completely urbanized milieu where laborers and service personnel, along with people of the countryside, are decidedly inferior.[13]

The radical changes occurring in Eurasian trade as a whole during the fourth-fifth centuries, influenced by migrations pushing outward from Central Asia, exerted pressure on the brittle urbanization of South Asia, and exposed what we may term the contradictions within an urban system that had created for itself a supra-regional base. Many sites of long standing in northern and central India suffered eclipse.[14] In southern India, the so-called Kalabhra interregnum, a period of several centuries for which scanty sources provide little insight into political organization, reflects the domino effect produced throughout the subcontinent.[15] Central places that survived operated within a reorganized economic system that found its roots again within regional agrarian regimes. At the political level, this process became manifest by the sixth century in the growth of several dozen major regional kingdoms, which based their power, as Hermann Kulke has described it, on their direct control over core territories and a primarily ritual sovereignty over peripheries where strictly local lordships developed.[16] The obvious importance of land grants within the inscriptional records that have survived points toward the grounding of these polities and their capital cities firmly within an agrarian economy. This process was particularly important in peninsular India, where powerful regional kingdoms were now capable of competing at the all-India level of imperial struggle. One must envision a continuing effort at agricultural growth and infrastructure construction occurring during the late first millennium—a deep, rather than expansive, economic development—that supported the more visible monumental projects of the regional polities. Suburban monasticism was supplanted by temple architecture and the incorporation of chthonic deities or the goddess within overarching Shaivite or Vaishnavite devotion.

What we often view as the classic settlement plan in South India, involving a quadrilateral space at the heart of a village dedicated to a shrine for the god and/or goddess, with different high-caste groups living along the surrounding street(s), is an artifact appearing in the historical record after the sixth century, when the decline of monastic institutions as the dominant architectural form allowed temples to serve as the linchpins of spatial organization. When a settlement grew in size, funding from political authorities or from mercantile groups supported the re-construction of originally wooden or thatch shrines in brick or stone, and the erection of a wall, with cardinally oriented entranceways, surrounding the shrine's campus. Donation inscriptions shifted almost entirely to temple compounds, and now give to the historian the most important source material providing spatial and temporal coordinates. This means that we understand settlement growth under the regional kingdoms primarily through the window provided by temple inscriptions. Urbanization appears as a process mediated by temple expansion.

One of the peculiarities of the early inscriptional sources, engraved either on the stone walls of temples or on copper plates, is their tendency to describe endowments (*brahmadeya*) aiming at the support of brahmana groups or gifts channeled through brahmana assemblies. A powerful argument developed by historian Burton Stein describes the alliance struck by regional kings and brahmanas that provided resources to support the ritual activities of the latter in return for the legitimacy accorded to donors by the performance of their rituals.[17] Many of the "place histories" (*sthala purana*) or "praise texts" (*mahatmya*) that purport to describe the origins of particular temples (even if they appear to be spurious or later compositions) hearken back to this process by describing the early site as the sylvan hermitage of holy brahmanas around a location where the deity became manifest. One may juxtapose this perspective to that provided by poetic texts praising the deities of specific locations, composed between the sixth and tenth century by Shaivite saints (*nayanmar*) and Vaishnava saints (*alvar*) in the Tamil country. The poem-songs present a social background featuring brahmanas and a hierarchical social order based on ritual purity, but often contrast it with the salvation offered to everyone by the deity endowed with attributes associated with a unique locale. There is no necessary connection between brahmanical rituals or administration and the site of the deity's manifestation on earth.[18]

By the tenth century, however, the assemblies of brahmanas (*sabha*) who received support from land grants were active in donations and management of temple endowments (*devadana*), and the state was creating spatially defined estates dedicated for the support of temple rituals, carried out by bodies of temple officials who included brahmanas. Separate assemblies of merchants (called *nagarattar*, or "people of the city," in Tamil records) were interacting with bodies of skilled artisans to manage the commercial economy that also served as a source of donations to temples.[19] The settlement assembly (*urar*), consisting mostly of leading members of local agricultural groups, provided probably the largest channel of resources to support religious institutions. The corporate bodies later gave way to private donors who often bore high honorific titles associated with the state and who controlled their own resource bases.[20] Support for the rituals occurring at the temples and for expanding groups of personnel came from grants of land (or, more commonly, re-directed tax income from land), money deposits lent at interest, and animals such as cows or goats that yielded products used directly for worship.

The regional states constructed big monuments at their capitals. Within the polity corresponding to the modern states of Maharashtra and Karnataka, the Chalukya rulers (sixth-eighth centuries) created artistic masterpieces at their dynastic centers of Badami and Pattadakkal, followed by the Rashtrakuta rulers (eighth-tenth centuries) who carved a huge, solid temple from a mountainside at

Ellora. At the beginning of the eleventh century, the Chola state (ninth-thirteenth centuries) of Tamil Nadu erected giant monuments at their seats, Tanjavur and Gangaikondacholapuram, while the Lingaraja Temple at Bhubanesvar in Orissa came up under the Somavamsa dynasty (tenth-twelfth centuries). In a later development, with expansions and artistic embellishments to the central shrine, establishments for other deities, pillared halls and administrative offices, and additional surrounding walls featuring a radical vertical extension of entrance towers, some temples attracting regular donations could grow to become effectively separate cities. This phenomenon is exemplified by sites of the later Chola period such as Chidambaram (sixteen hectares/forty acres) or Srirangam (78 hectares/192 acres). The prototvpical example of the embedding of this scheme within the larger urban fabric is Madurai. The sacred precincts of the city's main temple dedicated to Shiva as Sundaresvarar and his consort Minakshi, constructed in its current form under the later Pandya dynasty (thirteenth-fourteenth centuries), cover six hectares (fifteen acres). A series of quadrilateral streets surround the temple in a nested pattern, representing perhaps the most elaborate application of classical town planning around a sacred center.[21]

The state intervened locally to disburse funds for major projects such as big artificial reservoirs for irrigation, architectural renovation or expansion. The state periodically adjudicated disputes over resources. Sites attracting resources directly from the kings were, however, an exception during this period of intense temple construction. Central governments allowed considerable local autonomy in the regulation of religious affairs and governance. The edifice of state power rested in part on ritualized gift giving to religious institutions, which allowed local notables to establish their leadership credentials and their loyalty to the state through ostentatious display at subsidiary sacred centers. The multiplication of stone-built temples after the tenth century displays, therefore, the contours of a ritual polity, as the regional state incorporated local lords within a mode of public display at the heart of population clusters. By the fourteenth century, hundreds of small unfortified settlements clustered around temple sites in South India.

Do stone temples constructed between the tenth and fourteenth centuries, most of which today stand within places called villages, serve as markers of urbanization? In order to make this leap we must abandon population figures alone as determinants of urban status. Although historical source material provides no clue to the demographic characteristics of these early sites, one may safely guess that most of them housed just a few thousand people. They performed a wide range of artisanal and manufacturing occupations in addition to agriculture. They were well connected to ramified trading systems controlled by the "people of the city" at the local level and linked to associations or "guilds" of long-distance traders whose activities spanned peninsular India and extended to Southeast Asia.[22] Communication and transportation occurred through a dense network of roads.[23] Kenneth Hall initiated discussion of Chola-era urban networking by suggesting that the activities of the *nagarattar* in specific locales indicates the regular spacing of market centers, pointing toward an analysis of settlement patterns through application of central place theory. I have suggested that within "core" areas such as the densely-settled Kaveri River delta in Tamil

Nadu, the heart of the "circle of the Cholas" (*cholamandalam*), the close connections among dozens of sites created an economic and social dynamic that one might expect from the concentrated population clusters characteristic of early historical urbanization.[24] These many settlements, each without fortification walls but built around a walled central shrine, together could exhibit the population concentration and variegated economic activities that are characteristic of urbanization. South Indian cities, amalgams of many sites that we would today describe as villages, thus possessed a distinctively distributed, or multi-nucleated, quality.

Kanchipuram: The Temple City

Kanchipuram lies on a flat plain just north of the Palar River and a small parallel channel, the Vegavati River, about one hundred kilometers (sixty miles) from the coast of the Bay of Bengal. Since the first millennium the city has been the main settlement in a region called Tondaimandalam, where the slow and steady expansion of agriculture and village habitation has rested on the control of limited water resources, mostly through the creation of artificial reservoirs (often called tanks). Kanchipuram also has enjoyed a long reputation as a center of textile manufacture, with silk sarees a specialty today. This brief exploration of the city's history and geography will focus on the relationship between its economic roles as agrarian and commercial center and the activities of the state—both manifested in the support for religious institutions. It will note that the roots of the city in the early first millennium provide it with a compact spatial focus, but its subsequent growth exemplifies the type of polycentric urban form typical of the South Indian city in the fourteenth century.

Today Kanchipuram is the headquarters of a district which is home to three million people, located within the peri-urban sprawl surrounding the mega-city of Chennai (Madras), increasingly accessible from the metropolis through rapidly augmented road systems. The population of the city has been rising quite rapidly in recent years, from 145,000 in 1991 to about 156,000 in 2008, amid an urban agglomeration (including adjacent villages) with a total population of 211,000. The rapid growth of Kanchipuram is a relatively recent phenomenon, a response to the rise of Chennai and the general growth of middle cities throughout South Asia after Independence. In 1950 the city's population was about 85,000, and during the nineteenth century even lower.[25] When the British took control of the district in the eighteenth century, Kanchipuram was a hinterland town famous for its many religious institutions (its temples today attract lots of pilgrimage and tourist traffic).

The plan of Kanchipuram (*Map 12.2*) is a rough L-shape approximately four kilometers east-west and three kilometers north-south, lying amid a number of artificial lakes or tanks that provide, along with wells and some artificial ditches, water for irrigation and for daily life. The original settlement, dating back to the expansion of early historical urbanization in South India, was apparently restricted to the zone that today surrounds the temple of Kamakshi, the goddess with eyes of love, and the temple of Ulagalanda Perumal, or Vishnu who has measured the world—this latter site known 1,000 years ago as the home of "the lord who resides within the interior of the holy settlement" (*tiruvurakattu alvar*).[26] Archaeological excavations carried out around those sites have yielded a black and red ware and other objects associated with a time period around the beginning of the Common Era. It is likely that a fortification wall surrounded this original settlement, following a form typical of that time period, thus creating a "citadel" zone separate from its suburbs. Early literary references to a temple of the reclining Vishnu located in the suburbs have prompted identification with the site of the Yathotkarin Temple located to the southeast, which would mark the outer extent of the settlement about 2,000 years ago. Archeological work and literary sources indicate that Buddhist and Jain monastic communities occupied suburban locations; the survival of a Jain section called Jina Kanchi in the southwest suburbs around Tirupparuttikkunram is a reminder of this ancient connection.

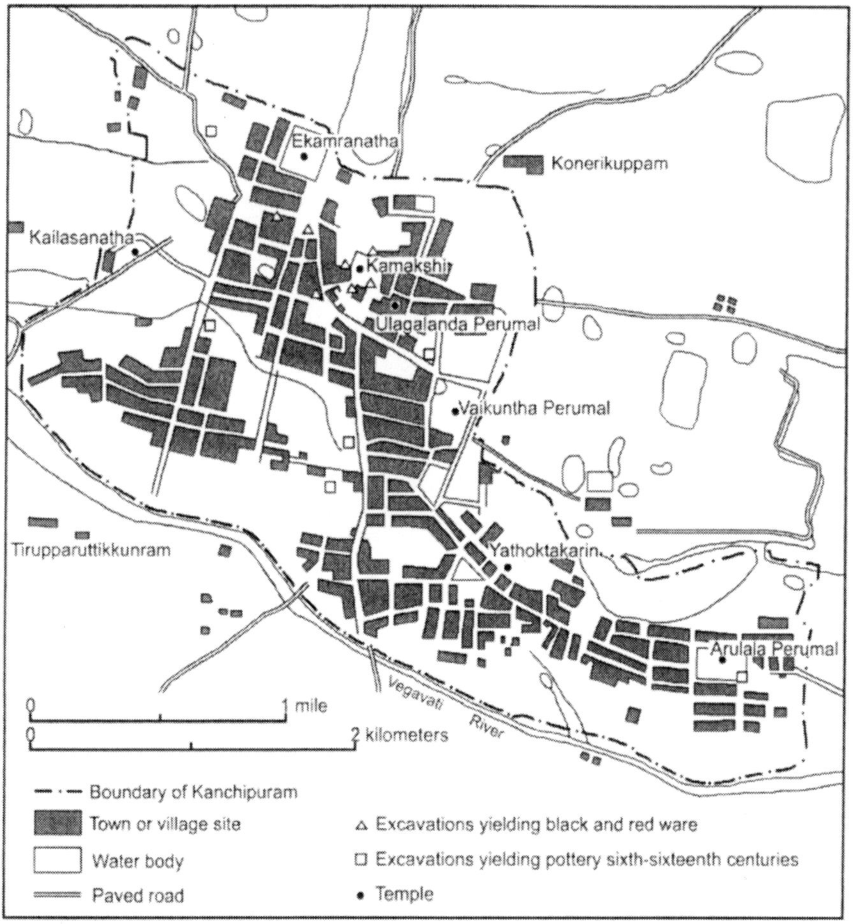

Map 12.2. **Plan of Twentieth-Century Kanchipuram (showing archeological excavations and major temples)**[27]

The hymns of the *alvars* and *nayanmars* referring to sacred sites in Kanchipuram point to a number of early temples located mostly on the outskirts of the early citadel or throughout the area covered by the modern city plan. Excavations outside the citadel have discovered remains associated with a period between the sixth and sixteenth centuries, indicating that the city expanded during that period to cover an area approximating the boundaries of the modern city. Work that I carried out with S. Rajagopal in the northeastern suburban village of Konerikuppam suggests that the boundaries of Kanchipuram and features of its suburban, mostly agrarian, geography remained relatively stable there after the eleventh century.[28] Extrapolating from this research, we may posit that the outline of the city as a whole was achieved around the beginning of the second millennium.

The locations of major temples support this basic chronology. The Pallava kings, who made Kanchipuram their capital, were responsible for the construction of significant monuments including the Vaikunta Perumal Temple on the east side and the Kailasanatha Temple on the west. The latter in the early eighth century was the largest free-standing temple in the Tamil country and an architectural challenge to the monuments being constructed under the Chalukya kings, the arch-enemies of the Pallavas. When the Chola kings took over in the tenth century, they retained Kanchipuram as the seat of their power in Tondaimandalam, which corresponded roughly to the heart of the old Pallava realm. The largest corpus of surviving inscriptions comes from the Arulala Perumal (also called Varadharaja Perumal) Temple in the southeast; this site attracted donations from a wide range of constituencies throughout South India during the last decades of Chola rule, as Tondaimandalam became the theater for struggles over political supremacy, and attracted extensive patronage from the rulers called Telugu Chodas who controlled the region during the late thirteenth century. The subsequent conquest of the region by Telugu-speaking warriors directed by the kings of Vijayanagara (see below) led to expansion of the Varadharaja Perumal complex and major architectural additions to the Ekamranatha Temple dedicated to Shiva on the northern edge of the city.

Kanchipuram owed much of its longevity as a regional capital to its commercial and manufacturing activities. At least by the Pallava period it was linked to Indian Ocean trade by land routes leading to the port that became known as Mahabalipuram (Mamallapuram) and to the port of Mayilai (Mylapore, now located in the southern part of Chennai). Within the "big city" (*managara*), the Kanchipuram *nagarattar* and sections of its trading or artisan communities including weavers (*caliyar*) featured prominently as donors and managers of endowments as well as taxpayers. It is likely that the city's access to cotton-growing districts of the interior gave it an early advantage in processing textiles consumed within the Tamil country and exported overseas. In addition, the city was the hub for a range of transactions providing agricultural resources for ritual activities and support for the staffs of religious institutions.[29] Roads emanating from the city included a route to the south linked to the major brahmana endowment of Uttaramerur, a settlement constellation controlled by a group of administrative committees and watered through a large artificial reservoir.[30]

Although there are references in the inscriptions of Kanchipuram to walls within the city, it remains unclear whether the citadel fortifications from the early first millennium still existed as viable defenses even as early as the Pallava period. The city as a whole by the early second millennium had no fortifications; habitation areas transitioned gradually into surrounding gardens and fields. Undoubtedly the Pallava kings maintained palaces, and Chola-period records also refer to royal residences, but (in a pattern typical of early South Asia as a whole) no traces of these have survived, since they were probably included large amounts of wood. Stone temples with their walled compounds stood amid habitations that probably did not rise above two stories, and in most cases were undoubtedly ground-level homes made of perishable materials such as wood and thatch—the standard housing for the urban poor who comprised the majority of the city population. Because clusters of residences and shops lay interspersed with urban gardens, Kanchipuram was a more concentrated version of the multinucleated urbanization typical of South India as a whole, but still retained the characteristics of many temple-centered settlements incorporated within a single plan. Although population figures are purely speculative, one could imagine a peak during the Pallava period between 50,000 and 100,000 inhabitants, and a plateau maintained during the Chola period and thereafter of 30,000 persons.[31] The demographic and spatial features of Kanchipuram remained generally stable right through the eighteenth century, and preserve for us the characteristics of old regional centers throughout South India.

Vijayanagara: Rise and Fall of the Metropolis

We now turn our attention to the Vijayanagara, the "City of Victory," which between the fourteenth and sixteenth centuries became the largest city South India had ever seen, and one of the largest cities in South Asia. Looking at the geography of this city at its peak allows us to contextualize it within the historical processes that changed a small ritual and commercial node into the head of the urban hierarchy, and then plunged it suddenly into obscurity. The unexpected fifteenth-century appearance of a giant city in the heart of South India relegated all other places such as Kanchipuram, which had long stood as a regional capital, to the level of secondary cities within an imperial-commercial hierarchy. The equally unexpected disappearance of the giant city in the late sixteenth century led to the re-shuffling of political-economic relationships and gave rise to a cohort of mid-level capitals that, like Vijayanagara, were magnets for consumption. During the several centuries of its predominance, Vijayanagara brought to its peak the model of ritual sovereignty manifested in the support of temples, but simultaneously stood as the most powerful fortified site in South India. In this sense the city stood as an intermediate form between two urban templates.

The main place associated with the beginnings of urbanization here is Hampi/Hampe, the site of a temple on the south bank of the Tungabhadra River set against a background of spectacular, rugged hills and bottomlands (*Map 12.3*). Archaic memory associated Hampi with the worship of the goddess Pampa, who later was said to marry Shiva in his form as Virupaksha at a temple that became a magnet for pilgrims. A Chalukya-period record referred to the settlement around the temple as Virupaksha *pattana*—the latter term signifying a commercial center. Roads linked Hampi toward Hosapete/Hospet (the "new market") in the west, a group of fortified villages including Kamalapuram in the south, the older fortified site of Anegundi/Anegondi in the northeast, and the old Chalukya center of Kampili eleven kilometers (6½ miles) to the east.

Political events cascading from northern India were responsible for the transformation of Hampi from market to imperial capital. Alauddin Khilji, ruler of the Delhi Sultanate (1296-1316), sent his general Malik Kafur on a campaign of conquest into peninsular India, resulting in the destruction of the main regional powers: the Seuna Yadava dynasty based at Devagiri (Deogir), the Kakatiya dynasty at Warangal (Orugallu), and the Pandya dynasty at Madurai. The Hoysala capital at Dvarasamudra (Halebidu, or the "Old Encampment"), was sacked in 1311 and again in 1327, leading to the elimination of the dynasty by 1343. The political dislocations caused by this annihilation of regional polities, and the inability of the Delhi Sultanate to control the conquests in the south, allowed a coalition of Telugu-speaking militarists under the Sangama dynasty (1336-1485) to set up a base at Anekundi and overrun much of the territory south of the Tungabhadra River. Under the Saluva (1485-1505) and Tuluva (1491-1570) dynasties the empire continued to expand and tightened its hold over conquered territories through the appointment of "leaders" (*nayaka*) controlling territorial divisions and based in a new stratum of secondary centers. The imperial capital shifted to a site on the south bank of the Tungabhadra River covering approximately twenty-five square kilometers (ten square miles) and its population grew to perhaps 500,000 people at its height in the sixteenth century. The growth came to a screeching halt in 1565, when a coalition of Deccani sultanates routed the Vijayanagara army at Talikota and proceeded to sack and dismantle the capital. Surviving officers of the empire shifted their operations to the humble site of Penukonda, but the northern divisions fell under the control of the sultanates and the southern divisions became independent under *nayaka* direction. Most of the ruined city was overrun with vegetation and was forgotten.

With the erasure of imperial pretensions, the site of Vijayanagara reverted to the grouping of villages that had been in existence at its inception and remained relatively unchanged for 400 years. Projects after Independence then altered the geography of the area and allowed the re-discovery of its architectural and urban heritage. The Tungabhadra River, which in the past may have been navigable for several months of the year, became un-navigable because of the construction of the Tungabhadra Dam during the 1950s at Hosapete, which created a lake encompassing 387 square kilometers (150 square miles). Archaeological excavations revealed or restored many of the excellent monuments surviving at the ruined metropolis, leading in 1986 to the naming of the "Group of Monuments at Hampi" as a World Heritage Site by the United Nations Educational, Scientific and Cultural Organization (UNESCO). In 2002, The Government of Karnataka created the Hampi World Heritage Area Management Authority that eventually covered twenty-nine villages and a town within an area of 236 square kilometers (ninety-one square miles) with a population of over 60,000 persons. The World Heritage Site and eight settlements lay within a "core zone" of forty-two square kilometers (sixteen square miles). The most important settlements within this zone were Hampi (population 2,134 in 2001), Anegundi (population 3,497), Kamalapuram (population 21,811) and Kaddiramapur (population 1,280).[32]

Map 12.3. **Plan of Vijayanagara (showing major fortifications, royal center, and major temples)**[33]

Looking now at the remains of the capital, we may follow the analysis of John M. Fritz et al.[34] and distinguish a tract stretching along the south bank of the river as a "sacred center" with four major temple complexes forming the nuclei of urban quarters (*pura*) with dedicated commercial malls. To the south, flanked on both sides by rocky ridges, lies an agrarian zone still irrigated by canals originating in the river several kilometers to the west; this zone seems to pre-date the metropolis, but became an integral part of the urban fabric. Farther to the south lies the residential and administrative heart of the city, the "urban core" protected by massive defensive walls and fortified gateways. Within this core, the "royal center" is a rough ellipse about one kilometer (½ mile) north-south and 1½ kilometers (one mile) east-west, consisting of thirty-one enclosures surrounding the Ramachandra Temple complex. Here we find some of the earliest palace structures surviving in South Asia, including the "great platform" and the base of a hundred-pillared hall forty meters square/431 square feet (which at one time supported multistoried wooden superstructures), and subsidiary buildings including massive elephant stables capped by some of the earliest true domes extant in South India. Residential neighborhoods surrounded the royal center on its north (e.g., the "noblemen's quarters") and east (e.g., the "Muslim quarter" marked by a series of stone tombs), and occupied the space on the southeast bounded by an outer defensive wall tied into the bund of the Kamalapuram Tank, which also features several bastions. By the sixteenth century, this large, man-made lake fed agricultural fields to its north and periodically provided water for the royal center through aqueducts and pipes that fed a number of pools, including the "great tank" measuring 67 by 22 meters (220 by 72 feet). The remainder of the city drew its water from canals, wells, and a number of tanks storing runoff water--the latter essential in one of the driest areas of southern India.[35] Archeological evidence of lime processing, stone working and ironworking aligns with travelers' accounts of peninsular India's largest commercial market to indicate a multifaceted economy surrounding a large military encampment.[36]

The Sangama dynasty was primarily Shaivite in orientation, and followed the practice long established for local lords in using donations for the Virupaksha temple and for shrines on nearby Hemakuta Hill as a means of legitimizing their authority.[37] They promoted a second level of sanctity by using their association with a mendicant preceptor, Vidyaranya, to create narratives of the city's foundation that confirmed its identity as an imperial capital. According to these narratives, Vidyaranya had traveled to the most sacred of all cities, Varanasi, where he achieved knowledge allowing him plan the urban core with its base on Matanga Hill. His actions, surrounded with miraculous events and governed by the ritual prescriptions of architectural treatises, led to the alternate naming of Vidyanagara, the "City of Knowledge." A third level of sanctity became salient under the Vijayanagara rulers after 1485, who were more Vaishnava in their orientation, and who tapped into older associations of the area with events occurring in the *Ramayana*. This led to the construction of the Ramachandra temple at the heart of the royal enclosure, which became the pivot of the city's architecture and transportation network. The annual Ramanavami Festival, described in detail around 1520-1522 by the Portuguese visitor Domingo Paes,[38] became the most important public event in the capital, an occasion when the leading personages of the empire assembled to link the king as representative of Vishnu with architectural gigantism, conspicuous consumption, artistic performance, and military review.

The result of these policies was the embellishment of Vijayanagara with religious architecture ranging from the large temples with royal connections to the many smaller shrines in the urban core apparently established by various occupational groups. A recent survey of surviving monuments has identified 350 temples, including ninety-one Shaiva and ninety-three Vaishnava sites.[39] The spatial alignment of various temple groupings toward each other and toward the movements of celestial bodies created relationships between the cosmos, the city, and the bodies of the ritual specialists and the royal family.[40] The concatenation of sacred associations with the city was so powerful that the later royal seats at Penukonda and (after the 1630s) Chandragiri—decidedly smaller and unimpressive centers—were called new Vijayanagaras.[41] The surviving sacred geography of the capital is, however, only the skeleton of what once must have been a densely inhabited landscape comprised mostly of single- or two-storey residences and commercial properties made of perishable materials. One may still see several markets in the stone frameworks of shops lining the malls in the northern sacred center, but one must assume the presence of additional bazaars scattered throughout the residential neighborhoods that filled much of the space up to the cyclopean walls on the south and east. And somewhere around the capital were the bivouacs of military personnel who numbered in the tens of thousands.

The urban gigantism manifested for 200 years at Vijayanagara was unprecedented and would not reappear on the Deccan plateau until the nineteenth-century growth of Bangalore, Pune, and Hyderabad. The immediate aftermath of Vijayanagara's fall was the re-emergence of smaller, regional polities throughout South India. The local reversion of the settlements at the capital to the tiny village-and-market configuration that antedated the construction of the royal and sacred centers suggests that the radical transformation of the site rested almost entirely in the unusual military-political transition of the fourteenth-fifteenth centuries, which allowed the incorporation of numerous regional cores within a single, militaristic polity that expressed legitimacy through old-fashioned support of religious institutions. One cannot, however, separate the phenomenon of the capital from profound economic changes. Agrarian expansion was manifested locally in the intensified utilization of water resources and the incorporation of multiple villages within the urban fabric; it was displayed throughout South India in an expansion of agricultural villages or horticulture linked to urban growth and to an increased capacity of state resource extraction. The multiplication of terms used to describe taxation during the Vijayanagara period[42] points to a diversification of artisanal and manufacturing capabilities coincident with the transformation of the Indian Ocean trading system, marked first by Chinese incursions and after 1498 by the Portuguese. The acceleration of commerce and the expansion of agriculture together provided the base upon which the emperors and their *nayaka* subordinates coordinated a new constellation of urban sites (e.g., Ikkeri, Ginji/Senji) that for some time revolved around the capital before embarking on independent courses within transformed regional contexts.[43]

Bijapur: Return of the Regional Kingdom

In northern Maharashtra, in the late twelfth century the Seuna Yadava dynasty established their capital at one of the great forts of South Asia, the "Mountain of the Gods" or Devagiri (Deogir). The final capture of this fort by the Delhi Sultanate in 1318 and improvements in its defenses elevated it to a position of great strategic importance for peninsular India. Muhammad bin Tughlaq (1325-1351) attempted to solve the problem of ruling a pan-South Asian empire by shifting his capital in 1328 from Delhi to Devagiri (renamed Daulatabad), but abandoned the scheme after seven years. The decision to return to Delhi betokened the infeasibility of ruling an empire stretching to Madurai (independent in 1336), and the need to maintain Delhi as the linchpin of a defensive and communication/trade system still oriented as much toward Afghanistan as the south. The divorce of the Delhi Sultanate from southern affairs became inevitable in 1347 when generalissimo Zafar Khan, taking the title Alauddin Bahman Shah, declared himself an independent sultan in Daulatabad. He quickly shifted his political seat to Gulbarga, a site poorly endowed with natural defenses, where he constructed a citadel enclosing a massive rectangular keep. At Gulbarga and also at the nearby palace-capital of Firuzabad (constructed between 1399 and 1406), the Bahmani rulers brought to peninsular India the standard sacred geography of the sultanate city, revolving around a central Friday Mosque and the peripheral shrines of Sufi saints, who according to popular notions bestowed temporal sovereignty and legitimacy on the sultans.[44] The capital of the Bahmani dynasty shifted in 1429 to the more centrally located Bidar, 96 kilometers to the northeast, positioned on a slope with the detached citadel at the upper end and the walled town below. The collapse of the dynasty resulted in the emergence of independent successor states identified with fortified capital cities—Bijapur (1489-1686), Ellichpur/Illichpur in Berar (1490-1572), Ahmadnagar (1494-1636), and Golkonda/Hyderabad (1507-1687)—built on centuries-old provincial administrative seats.[45]

The massive fortifications visible at Vijayanagara and standard at the capitals of the peninsular sultans were the consequences of a technological and organizational revolution accelerating after the year 1000 that made cavalry the most effective striking arm of the military. This revolution had underlain the successes or early Arab armies and the rapid expansion of Turkish empires in Central Asia beginning in the seventh century, affected Europe in the form of the mounted knight, and culminated in the unparalleled success of the Mongols (experts in the deployment of mounted archers) during the thirteenth and fourteenth centuries. The safety of permanent forts was a response to the mobility of mounted formations. The dissemination of gunpowder technology after the fourteenth century was a response to permanent forts, which in turn resulted in the strengthening of walls and the transfer of citadels to even more inaccessible locales. The consequence for military logistics in South Asia was the evolution of the siege train alongside massive cavalry and elephant formations. The corollary for central places was the increasing role of fortified enclosures—an amplified version of the role fortifications had played during early historical urbanization.[46]

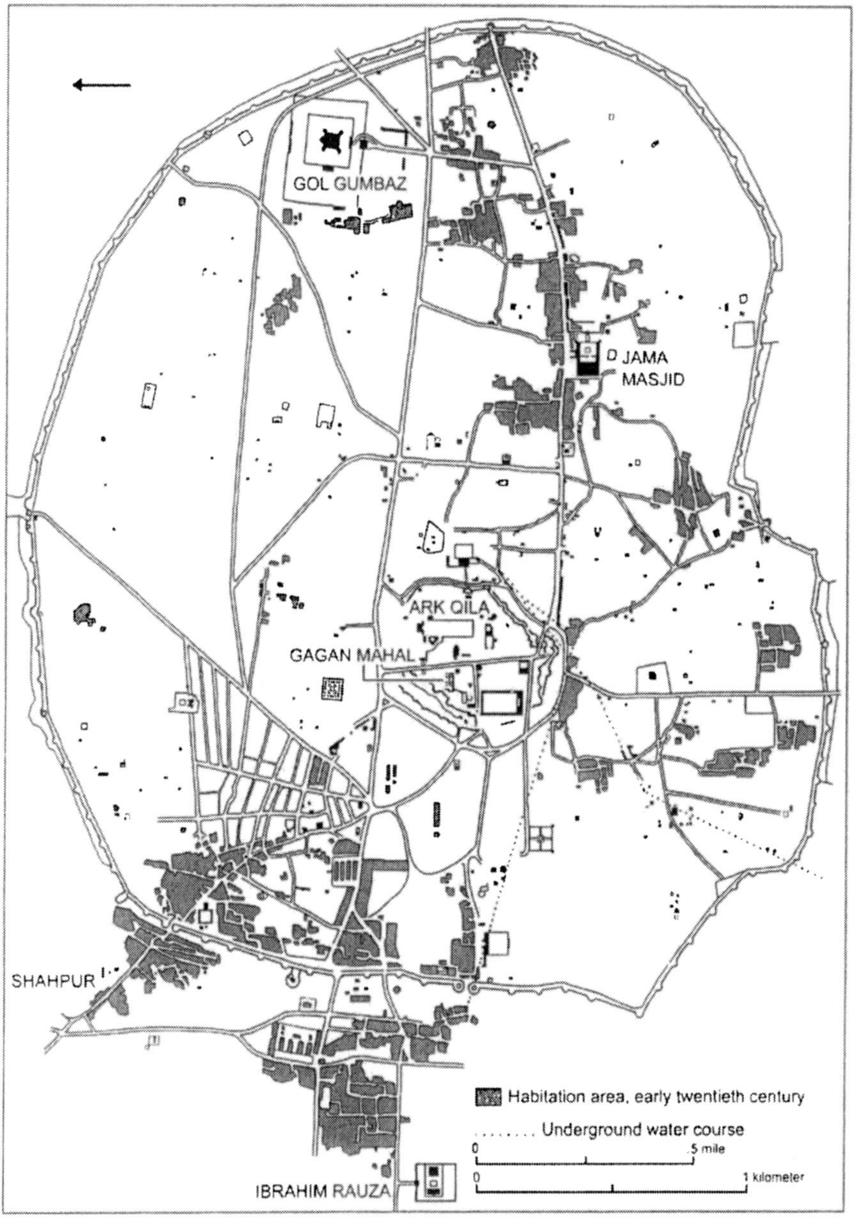

Map 12.4. **Plan of Bijapur (showing major archaeological remains, main roads, and habitation areas in early twentieth century)**[47]

The cavalry revolution came to South Asia in full force through the agency of Turkish polities established originally in Afghan cities. Central Asian military strategies pushed a steadily expanding wave of conquest that led to the progressive installation of Turkic or Afghan warrior elites at the head of well-entrenched regional polities. Because these conquerors found themselves a highly visible minority in a hostile land, and often fell out over the disposition of power, it was incumbent on them to appropriate and upgrade pre-existing fortified sites to serve as their bases of operation, or in some cases to found new fortified centers that served as secure administrative hubs and also magnets for service providers. The role of military adventurers and dynastic politics in city formation thus assumed greater importance in South Asia during the early second millennium. Installed at the head of their mostly inland regional states, the new warrior elites established relationships with indigenous administrative groups in order to appropriate sources of state revenue, including the major taxes on agrarian surplus.

Bijapur (earlier Vijayapura) exemplifies the organization of the Deccan fort-capitals (*Map 12.4*). It was the site of a Bahmani provincial governorship until Yusuf Adil Khan revolted and declared himself Adil Shah, an independent Sultan (r. 1489-1510). His son and successor, Ismael Adil Shah, attempting to consolidate the defensive posture of his capital, completed an almost circular citadel (Ark Qila) protected by a stone wall and moat, where a mud fort had stood earlier. Ismael's grandson, Ali Adil Shah (1557-1580), pulled together a coalition of all five Bahmani successor states that destroyed Vijayanagara in 1564. Buoyed by resources obtained through that victory, he embellished his new palace within the citadel (the Gagan Mahal) and constructed a new Friday Mosque, a nine-meter (thirty-foot) high fortification wall with ninety-six bastions and moat enclosing the entire city (encompassing in the process six independent villages), and the large suburb of Shahpur to the northwest of the city. In 1599 work began at Nauraspur, about six kilometers (3½ miles) west of Bijapur, to construct a new capital with better access to water and a more defensible position—a project abandoned after military defeats in 1624 resulted in the wrecking of the construction site.

The Sultans embellished Bijapur with monuments that brought to a peak the Deccani style of Indo-Islamic art: the tomb of Ibrahim II (d. 1627) or Ibrahim Rauza, which translated wooden architectural forms into stone; and the gigantic tomb of Muhammad (d. 1656) or Gol Gumbaz, which at a height of eighty-four meters (276 feet) displayed the largest domed space in the world. The Sultans of Bijapur and their nobles funded extensive hydraulic works designed to provide water to a constantly expanding population in an environment that remained arid during much of the year. Water facilities included a number of wells and step wells embellished with rest houses located near public thoroughfares and mosques; artificial lakes to the west that watered the city and its suburb, Shahpur; aqueducts supported on towers that served the citadel, Shahpur, and the neighborhoods around the Friday Mosque and the Gol Gumbaz; and a Persian-style underground tunnel (*qanat*) conducting water from the environs of Nauraspur to Bijapur. On the urban periphery lay the irrigated and cultivated properties of well-to-do citizens, where they raised tombs for their families and also funded tombs with attached endowments in memory of the lines of Sufi masters that made Bijapur their home.

One might guess that the population of Bijapur at its height during the seventeenth century was at least 100,000, but its prosperity was not fated to last. The military disadvantages of this prosperous regional capital, commanded by higher ground to the east and north, were minor when measured against the capabilities of fifteenth-century artillery. They became fatal flaws by the late seventeenth century, when ordnance was considerably more advanced.[48] The elimination of Bijapur's independence by the Mughal Empire and its reduction to a provincial capital in 1686 left behind a heritage of Sufi institutions associated with the Chishti, Qadiri, and Shattari orders in the form of tombs scattered within the city walls and in its suburbs, a rich literature in the composite Dahkni language originally developed at the court but popularized through Sufi folk literature, and a number of shrines (*dargah*) that remain important scenes of devotion today.[49] A steady decline in population resulted by the early twentieth century in pockets of habitation corresponding to the locations of older bazaars, preserving the pattern of main avenues and smaller side streets winding through residential quarters, amid a pattern of major monuments, smaller mosques and tombs that serve as a skeletal reminder of the formerly thriving capital. Population was about 65,000 in 1950. In the late twentieth century the city's position as a district capital within the state of Karnataka helped to stimulate substantial growth (population was 187,000 in 1991 and approximately 257,000 in 2008) that has refilled much of the space inside the sixteenth-century walls.

Bijapur represents another case of a small administrative center that owed its meteoric rise to the choice made by a newly independent political-military lineage to locate its base on a site utilized for local administration for at least 100 years previously. For almost seven decades the varying fortunes of that lineage allowed only the construction of a humble keep and the attraction of a relatively limited service population alongside a military garrison. Unprecedented success of the five-city coalition that brought down Vijayanagara was the stimulus not only for the embellishment of Bijapur, but also the realignment of state resource extraction and trade routes that stimulated demographic expansion during most of the seventeenth century. In this sense Bijapur as capital was a successor state to Vijayanagara, albeit of smaller size, and it even shifted to itself some of the trading capacity of the older capital such as connectivity with the port of Bhatkal on the west coast. It exemplifies a process whereby the gigantism of Vijayanagara, which retarded the growth of secondary sites, gave way after its disappearance to the vibrancy of smaller cities. Bijapur as the central place of a growing regional polity was only one of several dozen such cities in South India that enjoyed a century of expansiveness until their subordination to a Mughal-style order that temporarily encompassed almost all of South Asia. The erasure of such cities' imperial pretentions did not result in their annihilation, for they remained regional or sub-regional pinnacles of central-place hierarchies. In this role, they survived as provincial or district seats and were positioned for resurgence through the modern urban explosion.

Pondicherry: The Imperial Capital That Never Happened

Port cities, windows on trade of the Indian Ocean, developed for at least 2,500 years without any attempt by land-based administrations to regulate the port-based trade system as a whole. Until the sixteenth century, although piracy was a constant threat and ships required security personnel, the sea surrounding India was demilitarized. South Asia's ports were open to any ships ready to trade, assuming their captains and crews were willing to abide by local regulations and, most importantly, pay customs duties. The income from those duties was a crucial component in the budgets of the many independent kingdoms that grew up along the coasts of South Asia, and it was therefore in the interests of their petty kings to attract traders with reasonable customs rates and access to regional trading communities along with adequate hospitality. Even when coastal towns became parts of larger empires, port administration enjoyed considerable autonomy. The spatial configuration of South Asia's ports changed slowly over the centuries depending on the evolution of extractive and productive enterprises within the macro-region, the comparative advantages offered by littoral locations (which in some deltaic areas depended on rates of siltation), and alterations in the pattern of the Indian Ocean's long-distance routes. But the drive toward fortification that affected interior locations was slow to come to the coast.

A picture of the South Asian port comes from the experience of Vasco da Gama's 1498 expedition, which rounded Africa, sailed across the Arabian Sea, and reached Calicut (Kozhikode). After their ships anchored at the more protected inlet of Pantalayini-Kollam north of the city (where today one may randomly pick up fragments of fifteenth-century Chinese pottery), the Portuguese visited the coastal emporium of the Zamorin (i.e., the Samudri, or Lord of the Ocean). The city—still unfortified at that time—stretched for several kilometers along the coast, consisting mostly of walled compounds enclosing one-story houses, gardens and groves. Behind the beach were shops and warehouses, and beyond them the habitation-and-storage compounds of traders segregated by place of origin. Although he maintained a coastal domicile, the ruler's main palace was several kilometers distant from the coast, in close proximity to the main fonts of political power—Nambudiri brahmana and Nayar landowning elites and the sources of agrarian production. Access to spices or other trade goods would require the standard payment of customs duties to agents of the king's government, and interactions with local brokers and merchant princes who maintained contact with commercial intermediaries in the port's hinterland. Muslim trading communities were prominent competitors, including "foreigners" who controlled long-distance maritime commerce and native-born Mapillas who controlled coastal traffic. The entire complex presented all the functionalities of an urban site without dense habitation patterns, architectural concentration or monumentality.[50]

The Portuguese changed the rules by setting themselves as a colonial power with monopolies over seaborne trade, and they established fortified ports in order to mount a seaborne protection racket. They attempted a complete monopoly over the trade in spices to Europe. Their passport or *cartaz* system forced ships sailing in the Indian Ocean to purchase safe passage from Portuguese authorities; any ship intercepted at sea without a passport was subject to attack and confiscation. They also tried to force ships to sail in convoys (*khafila, cafila*) under the direction of their fleet, requiring stops in ports administered by Portuguese customs collectors. These attempts, partially successful at best, were foiled at the end of the sixteenth century,[51] when competing Dutch and English East India Companies were emulating the Portuguese in the construction of fortified warehouses or factories, while appropriating for themselves monopolies over trade. The newcomers learned what the Portuguese had already discovered: the necessary complements to transcontinental trade were the coastal "country trade" and intra-regional Asian trade. An important commodity of the latter was cloth produced within South Asia. The fortified trading posts of the East India Companies, which expressed spatially the increasingly racist European understandings of society, thus served as headquarters for the procurement of agricultural or mining products and also became the coordinating points for commissioning and trans-shipping manufactured goods, primarily textiles.[52] By the end of the seventeenth century, the coast called Coromandal (i.e., Cholamandalam, or the coast of what are today Tamil Nadu and Andhra Pradesh) had become a major source of exportable textiles, produced by caste-like weaving communities living in clusters of villages near the coast or within the interior—another example of the spatially distributed quality of South Indian urbanization.

During the seventeenth century the European trading companies were primarily interested in Surat, the main port of the Mughal Empire, home to a fleet of over 100 vessels, mostly of 200 or 300 tons, owned by indigenous entrepreneurs. Surat differed from most coastal emporiums because of its concentrated, fortified physical organization, more reminiscent of an interior administrative center, and its population was much larger, totaling somewhere between 150,000 and 200,000 people depending on the arrival cycles of shipping.[53] Along the Coromandal coast—a vital link for trade in Southeast Asia—the Europeans operated multiple bases but strove to maintain factories at Masulipatnam, which was the main harbor for the kingdom of Golkonda.[54] The Portuguese retained a presence at Saõ Tomé near Mayilai and the Dutch established their main base at Pulicat (Pazhaverkadu). English traders in Masulipatnam had discovered that desirable chintzes were procurable farther south, so in 1639 they persuaded a local ruler to grant them a beachfront at Chennaipattanam, which they called Madraspatnam or Madras. The Company's first exclusive possession in South Asia, it stretched only five kilometers (three miles) north from the mouth of the River Cooum, and about 1½ kilometers (one mile) inland, and lay about six kilometers (3½ miles) north of the older Portuguese settlement at Saõ Tomé. To command the completely unprotected beachfront-port, they immediately commenced construction of a castle called Fort St. George, originally a quadrilateral measuring roughly 100 by 80 meters (328 by 263 feet), with bastions at the corners and a factory house at its center, partially protected on the landward side by a portion of the river. They attracted 300 to 400 weaver families, and transferred the headquarters of all their east coast operations there, making Madras a Presidency (headed by a President-in-Council) in 1652; its population grew to about 50,000 in 1674.[55]

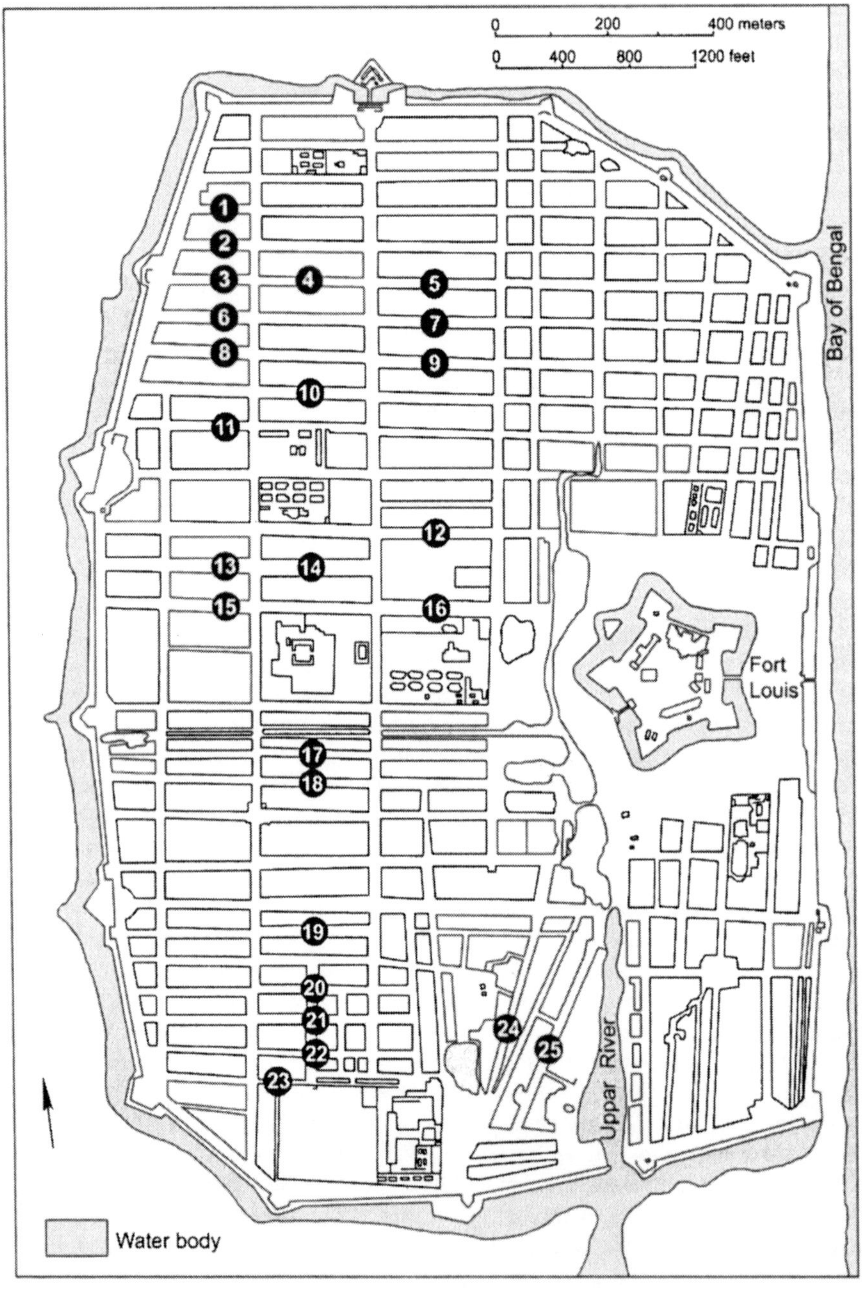

Map 12.5. **Plan of Pondicherry, 1755 (with names of major streets)**[56]

Key to Map 12.5

1. Street of the tile makers (*thuiliers*)
2. Street of the mendicants (*mendians*)
3. Street of the metal-workers (*chaudronniers*)
4. Street of the Malabars
5. Street of the Komatis
6. Street of the goldsmiths (*orfèvres*)
7. Street of the weavers (*tisserands*)
8. Street of the blacksmiths (*forgerons*)
9. Street of the Komatis
10. Street of the Chettis
11. Street of the Company merchants
12. Street of Nayanappa (Naynapa)
13. Street of the coral-workers (*corailleurs*)
14. Street of the villages
15. Street of the brahmana Mudali (Modély)
16. Street of the brahmanas (*brammes*)
17. New Street of the brahmanas
18. Street of Nayanapalli (Naynapouley)
19. Street of the *subedar* (*choubedar*)
20. Street of Chinnappayya (Chinapaya)
21. Street of Ayyatti (Ayoti)
22. Street of Timmu Chetti (Timouchetty)
23. Street of Mallappa (Malapa)
24. Street of the Moors (*maures*)
25. Street of the Chuliyas (*choulias*)

The French East India Company was a relative latecomer to Indian Ocean trade, obtaining state support and beginning operations only in 1664. They opened an office in Surat in 1668 and at Pondicherry (Puduchcheri/Puducherry, or the "New Village") on the Coromandal coast in 1674.[57] Governor François Martin at Pondicherry supervised construction of a roughly quadrilateral brick fort about 300 meters (984 feet) in length, with towers at the four corners, which enclosed their factory headquarters that was flanked on the north and south by stone buildings constructed for about 200 French employees. The remainder of the settlement, in a rough L-shape about one kilometer (½ mile) in length on each side following the course of the Uppar River, was the town of the "blacks," with separate neighborhoods in the north and west for weavers, artisans, and a brahmana community, and in the south for trading castes, a Muslim community, and (on the outskirts) despised service castes. Gardens and fields lay interspersed with habitation structures. An enclosure, part parapet and part hedge, encompassed the entire settlement, which may have had 50,000 people by 1690.

Military confrontation with the Netherlands led to the conquest of Pondicherry by the Dutch East India Company in 1693. The Dutch immediately negotiated a purchase of villages in a roughly semi-circular arc with a radius of about three kilometers (two miles) surrounding the original settlement. They also developed, as they had in their earlier settlements in South Asia, a plan for an orthogonal street grid surrounding the fort, and demonstrated an obsession with relegating different occupational/caste groups to exclusive neighborhoods. When, as part of a peace accord, Pondicherry and its surrounding villages reverted to French authority in 1699, the Company utilized the Dutch designs to plan a symmetrical fortress-town featuring the grid pattern that still forms the heart of the city (*Map 12.5*). At the center near the coast was Fort Louis, redesigned with five bastions and one *demilune* encompassing the old fort. By the time François Martin died in 1706, Pondicherry was a commercial center of 60,000 people with a garrison, a tax system, and a governing judicial and religious establishment.[58]

Reorganization of the French commercial operations under the new Compagnie Perpetuelle des Indes in 1723 rapidly led to its growth as a major competitor to the British and Dutch interests in South Asia, and Pondicherry emerged as the capital of an incipient French imperial presence in South India. Between 1724 and 1733 the entire settlement was surrounded by a masonry wall with projecting bastions. Buildings adjacent to the fort were eliminated to provide a free-fire zone around it. By 1740 the outer defenses of the town were supplemented with a moat, and a garrison of 700-800 men with 300 cannon protected the settlement. Governor Joseph François Dupleix (1742-1754), who took charge of a city with around 130,000 inhabitants, oversaw the construction of a magnificent palace within Fort Louis. He involved the French administration deeply in the affairs of the disintegrating Mughal Empire, while simultaneously fighting with the British East India Company based in Madras, a distant theater of what the Europeans called the War of Austrian Succession (1744-1748). The French were able to acquire control of more villages during the 1740s, creating a patchwork of holdings that survived for several centuries.

Around them lived the various artisan groups, including weavers (*Map 12.5 Key*, 7), who provided the goods and services required for an export-oriented commercial settlement. In the southeastern part of the city resided Tamil-speaking Muslim merchants called Chuliya and the "Moors," or Muslim merchants whose ancestry lay elsewhere in the Indian Ocean littoral (*Map 12.5 Key,* 24-25).

Hostilities during the Seven Years' War (1756-1763) led to the failure of French policy in India, the capture of Pondicherry, and its systematic demolition by the British in 1761. The city was restored to the French two years later, and reconstruction of the built environment and the commercial connections supporting the city brought the population back to about 60,000 by the end of the decade, Its role as a token in continuing French-British struggles led, however, to periodic occupation by the British and a decline of population (26,000 in 1777, 36,000 in 1791) until the final defeat of France after the Napoleonic Wars returned it to a stabilized French administration in 1816.[59] The site of Fort Louis became a park and the site for administrative offices. The path of the former fortification wall became a ring road around a compact town that preserved a French quarter and an indigenous business district to the west. Pondicherry adopted a very low profile, tolerated by the British Raj as the main city within a four-part French possession that included Karaikal further to the south, Yanam in Andhra Pradesh, and Mahé in Kerala. In 1950 the population was about

54,000. As the capital of a Union Territory with its own legislature and chief minister, Pondicherry expanded rapidly only at the end of the twentieth century, its population rising from 203,000 in 1991 to about 231,000 in 2008. The city center preserved the street pattern laid down 300 years earlier and the formal characteristics of urban planning informed by the rational principles of the European Enlightenment.

With the exception of Surat, and perhaps to a lesser extent Masulipatnam, the several dozen major ports that were always operating within South Asia until the eighteenth century attracted relatively limited populations; we might guess that they ranged from 10,000 to 50,000, depending on the time of year and their position within the macro-regional configuration of trade and empire. There is little indication that these ports were the venue for monumental constructions or public architecture aside from religious institutions, for the merchants based there or conducting business there did not sink their investments into fixed assets. The trend toward urban gigantism along the coast became apparent only at the end of the eighteenth century in the Presidency capitals of the British East India Company, which for the first time changed into city-states with imperial ambitions (the population of Madras was about 300,000, Bombay about 200,000, and Calcutta about 160,000).[60] In this context the rapid escalation of activity at Pondicherry was the harbinger of a new imperial style and associated commercial expansion that would fundamentally transform the urban pattern within South Asia, elevating coastal cities to the height of modern urban hierarchies. From another perspective, however, Pondicherry represents the final phase of an urban template based on fortified security that had enjoyed at least 700 years of increasing importance, and which was reaching its pinnacle in the designs associated with the Marquis de Vauban.[61] Although the British would apply contemporary European styles of fortification to its Presidency capitals for two generations after the fall of Pondicherry, and indigenous states would continue to use the more archaic style of fortified cities until the mid-nineteenth century, the future of urban form would lie in open cities with a radically altered security apparatus.

Conclusion

The urban history of South India over the long duration displays four distinct templates: the combination of fortified citadel and suburban monastic institution, which predominated between the second century BCE and the middle-late first millennium; a temple urbanism that placed the deity's shrine at the heart of the settlement that in turn was a component within an open, multiple-settlement complex, growing from the mid-first millennium until the mid-second millennium; the military-administrative center encompassed within fortifications, which became important while the Delhi Sultanate was being forged and achieved full development under its spinoffs and the Mughal Empire, predominant between 1200 and 1800; and the template of the colonial city-state borrowing elements of socio-spatial organization from earlier cities in South Asia but incorporating racial and security concepts from Europe. Obviously there is no clear-cut break indicating the moment when one form supplanted another, but instead a gradual process of laying one form above another like a palimpsest, or juxtaposing several within a single settlement. This study has concentrated on the last three templates during a period when South India was becoming a component within the early world system revolving around the Indian Ocean, as continental, interior forces expressed mostly on the Deccan plateau came into contact with shifts in the oceanic trading system. The result during a 500-year period was an alteration in the architecture and the lived environment of cities positioned within changing urban hierarchies.

The case studies examined here indicate that state policy was the crucial variable that allowed settlements to dominate urban hierarchies. Kanchipuram was the capital of the Pallava and Chola regional kings, Vijayanagara the royal center of the emperors, Bijapur the seat of the Adil Shahi dynasty, and Pondicherry the base of the imperial, colonial city-state. In these roles the cities achieved their largest pre-1800 spatial extent and demographic size, and became repositories of the high-quality architecture that expressed political ambition. Thus urban expansion until 1800 rested primarily on the state and its consumption patterns, in distinction to the dynamics of the capitalist world system wherein what we term economic activity became the prime motor for urban growth in most cities. But just as one cannot divorce more recent economic factors from state policy inputs, one cannot describe pre-1800 urbanization trends entirely as state-driven. Each of the settlements (or groups of settlements) described in this study existed in a smaller form prior to the expansionism of their states, and each continued to exist, again in reduced size, after the glory days had passed. Clearly these settlements were playing roles as regional or subregional coordinating nodes outside state intervention; it was, in fact, their prior existence as such nodes that attracted state intervention in the first place. We return, therefore, to the embedding of the city within its agrarian context, to a network of economic, non-economic, and multi-settlement transactions, and to a multi-factorial explanation for urbanization.

Notes

1. This study has emerged from research conducted during the last four years on sections within James Heitzman, *The City in South Asia* (London: Routledge, 2008). My thanks to Kenneth R. Hall and James Connolly, Director Center for Middletown Studies at Ball State University, for inviting me to their conference on Small Cities in March 2007 that led to the production of this article.

2. The part of the world termed herein the "macro-region" of South Asia includes the modern nations of Bangladesh, Bhutan, India, Nepal, the Maldives, Pakistan, and Sri Lanka.

3. For studies of the three cities under the Delhi Sultanate, see M. Athar Ali, "Capital of the Sultans: Delhi during the Thirteenth and Fourteenth Centuries," in *Delhi through the Ages: Selected Essays in Urban History, Culture, and Society*, ed. Robert E. Frykenberg (Delhi and New York: Oxford University Press, 1986), 21-31; Hamida Khatoon Naqvi, *Agricultural, Industrial and Urban Dynamism under the Sultans of Delhi 1206-1555* (New Delhi: Munshiram Manoharlal, 1986); Mehrdad Shokoohy and Natalie H. Shokoohy, "Tughluqabad, the Earliest Surviving Town of the Delhi Sultanate," *Bulletin of the School of Oriental and African Studies*, 57, 3 (1994), 516-50. For studies of the three cities under the Mughals, see Hamida Khatoon Naqvi, *Urbanisation and Urban*

Centres under the Great Mughals 1556-1707 (Simla: Indian Institute of Advanced Study, 1972); Ishwar Prakash Gupta, *Urban Glimpses of Mughal India: Agra, the Imperial Capital (16th & 17th Centuries)* (Delhi: Discovery Publishing House, 1985); Stephen P. Blake, *Shahjahanabad: The Sovereign City in Mughal India, 1639-1739* (Cambridge: Cambridge University Press, 1991); Shama Mitra Chenoy, *Shahjahanabad: A City of Delhi, 1638-1857* (New Delhi: Munshiram Manoharlal, 1998); Eckart Ehlers and Thomas Krafft, *Shahjahanabad/Old Delhi: Tradition and Colonial Change*, 2nd ed. (New Delhi: Manohar, 2003).

4. The extant archeological remains of Gaur (Lakhnauti), which was the capital of an independent Bengal Sultanate in the thirteenth and fifteenth-sixteenth centuries, cover an area about eleven by three kilometers (6½ by 1¾ miles) along the Bhagirathi River. This would have given it the largest footprint of any contemporary city in South Asia. See A. B. M., Husain, ed., *Gawr-Lakhnawti, A Survey of Historical Monuments and Sites in Bangladesh* SHMSB 002 (Dhaka: Asiatic Society of Bangladesh, 1997); Sutapa Sinha, "Archaeology of the Medieval City of Gaur," in *Archaeology of Eastern India: New Perspectives*, ed. Gautam Sengupta and Sheena Panja (Kolkata: Centre for Archaeological Studies and Training, Eastern India, 2002), 331-62. Ahmedabad, established in the early fifteenth century, had a population that peaked in the seventeenth century at between 250,000 and 500,000 persons. See Kenneth L. Gillion, *Ahmedabad: A Study in Indian Urban History* (Berkeley and Los Angeles: University of California Press, 1968), 25-29; R. N. Mehta, "Ahmedabad: A Topographical, Toponymical and Archaeological Perspective," in *Archaeology and History: Essays in Memory of Shri A. Ghosh*, ed. B. M. Pande and B. D. Chattopadhyaya (Delhi: Agam Kala Prakashan, 1987), 363-74; M. P. Singh, *Town, Market, Mint and Port in the Mughal Empire (1556-1707)* (New Delhi: Adam Publishers and Distributors, 1985).

5. "South India" refers here to the multiple regions encompassed within the modern Indian states of Andhra Pradesh, Goa, Karnataka, Kerala, and Tamil Nadu. This study places this more restricted term within a discussion of "peninsular India," which is synonymous with "southern India."

6. The Sanskrit term *vastu* refers to the site of a building, and *vastu-vidya* is the science of architecture, but as applied in a series of texts dating back to the early first millennium, the term also alludes to the proper alignment of spatial features with environmental attributes in order to maximize auspiciousness and the free flow of energy. For an example of these texts, see *Architecture of Manasara*, Prasanna Kumar Acharya, trans. (Reprint. New Delhi: Oriental Books Reprint Corporation, 1980). For a discussion of *vastu* principles applied in eighteenth-century Jaipur, see Vibhuti Sachdev and Giles Tillotson, *Building Jaipur: The Making of an Indian City* (London: Reaktion Books, 2002). For a discussion of these principles in Nepal, see Niels Gutschow, *Stadtraum und Ritual der newarischen Städte im Kathmandu-Tal: Eine architekturanthropologische Untersuchung* (Stuttgart: Verlag W. Kohlhammer, 1982), 15-27, 179-85.

7. Dilip K. Chakrabarti, *The Archaeology of Ancient Indian Cities* (Delhi: Oxford University Press, 1995); Monica L. Smith, "The Archaeology of South Asian Cities," *Journal of Archaeological Research* 14 (2006), 97-142.

8. R. Shamashastri, trans., *Kautilya's Arthasastra* (Mysore: Mysore Printing and Publishing House, 1915); L. N. Rangarajan, ed. and trans., *The Arthasastra* (New Delhi: Penguin Books, 1992); R. Parthasarathy, trans., *The Cilappatikaram of Ilanko Atikal: An Epic of South India* (New York: Penguin, 1993).

9. For general sources on the style and location of monastic institutions, see Debala Mitra, *Buddhist Monuments* (Calcutta: Sahitya Samsad, 1971); Vidya Dehejia, *Early Buddhist Rock Temples: A Chronological Study* (London: Thames and Hudson, 1972). The most well-preserved and studied cities for fortified center and suburban monasteries are Taxila in northern Pakistan and Anuradhapura in Sri Lanka. For Taxila, see Sir John

Marshall, *Taxila: An Illustrated Account of Archaeological Excavations*, 3 vols. (Cambridge: Cambridge University Press, 1951); Ahmad Hasan Dani, *The Historic City of Taxila* (Paris: United Nations Educational, Scientific and Cultural Organization; Tokyo: Centre for East Asian Cultural Studies, 1986); Saifur Rahman, "Dar, Dating the Monuments of Taxila," in *Urban Form and Meaning in South Asia: The Shaping of Cities from Prehistoric to Precolonial Times*, ed. Howard Spodek and Doris Meth Srinivasan (Washington, DC: National Gallery of Art; Hanover and London: University Press of New England, 1993), 103-122. For Anuradhapura, see Senaka Bandaranayake, *Sinhalese Monastic Architecture: The Viharas of Anuradhapura*, Studies in South Asian Culture 4 (Leiden: E. J. Brill, 1974); "Monastery Plan and Social Formation: The Spatial Organization of the Buddhist Monastery Complexes of Early and Middle Historical Period in Sri Lanka and Changing Patterns of Political Power," in *Domination and Resistance*, ed. Daniel Miller, Michael Rowlands and Christopher Tilley (London and Boston: Unwin Hyman, 1989): 179-193; Robin Coningham, *Anuradhapura: The British-Sri Lankan Excavations at Anuradhapura Salgaha Watta 2, Vol 1: The Site,* BAR International Series 824 (Oxford: Archaeopress, 1999); Anuradha Seneviratna, *Ancient Anuradhapura: The Monastic City* (Colombo: Archaeological Survey Department, 1994).

10. For the Silk Road, see Liu Xinru, *Ancient India and Ancient China: Trade and Religious Exchanges AD 1-600*, (Delhi: Oxford University Press, 1988). For early historical trade in the Indian Ocean and Southeast Asian connections, see Himanshu Prabha Ray, *Monastery and Guild: Commerce under the Satavahanas* (Delhi: Oxford University Press, 1986); *The Winds of Change: Buddhism and the Maritime Links of Early South Asia* (Delhi and New York: Oxford University Press, 1994).

11. Dilip K. Chakrabarti, "Mahajanapada States of Early Historic India," in *A Comparative Study of Thirty City-State Cultures*, Historisk-filosofiske Skrifter 21, ed. Mogens Herman Hansen (Copenhagen: Royal Danish Academy of Sciences and Letters, 2000), 375-91.

12. H. Sarkar, "Emergence of Urban Centres in Early Historical Andhradesa," in *Archaeology and History*, ed. B. M. Pande and B. D. Chattopadhyaya (Delhi: Agam Kala Prakashan, 1987), 631-42; Aloka Parasher, "Social Structure and Economy of Settlements in the Central Deccan (200 B.C.-A.D. 200)," in *The City in Indian History: Urban Demography, Society, and Politics*, ed. Indu Banga (Columbia, MO: South Asia Publications; New Delhi: Manohar, 1991), 19-46; Monica L. Smith, *The Archaeology of an Early Historic Town in Central India*, BAR International Series 1002 (Oxford: J. and E. Hedges, Archaeopress, 2001).

13. Vatsyayana Mallanaga, *Kamasutra*, trans. Wendy Doniger and Sudhir Kakar (Oxford: Oxford University Press, 2002).

14. Ram Sharan Sharma, *Urban Decay in India (c A.D. 300-c 1000)* (New Delhi: Munshiram Manoharlal, 1987); *Early Medieval Indian Society: A Study in Feudalisation* (Hyderabad: Orient Longman, 2001).

15. Natana Kacinatan, *Kalappirar* (Chennai: Tamilnatu Aracu Tolporul Ayvutturai, 1981).

16. Hermann Kulke, "The Early and the Imperial Kingdom: A Processural Model of Integrative State Formation in Early Medieval India," in *The State in India 1000-1700*, ed. Hermann Kulke (Delhi: Oxford University Press, 1995), 233-62.

17. Burton Stein, *Peasant State and Society in Medieval South India* (Delhi and New York: Oxford University Press, 1980).

18. For hymns of the Shaivite saints, see David Dean Shulman, *Songs of the Harsh Devotee: The Tēvāram of Cuntaramūrttināyanār* (Philadelphia: University of Pennsylvania, Department of South Asia Regional Studies, 1990); Indira Viswanathan Peterson, *Poems to Śiva: The Hymns of the Tamil Saints* (Princeton: Princeton University Press, 1989). For hymns of the Vaishnava saints, see A. K. Ramanujan, trans., *Hymns for the*

Drowning: Poems for Visnu (Princeton: Princeton University Press, 1981); John Carman and Vasudha Narayanan, *Piḷḷān's interpretation of the Tiruvāymoli* (Chicago: University of Chicago Press, 1989).

19. Kenneth R. Hall, *Trade and Statecraft in the Age of the Cōlas* (New Delhi: Abhinav Publications, 1980); Vijaya Ramaswamy, *Textiles and Weavers in Medieval South India* (Delhi and New York: Oxford University Press, 1985); "Craft Work & Wages in Medieval Tamilnadu (Based on Inscriptions from the 8th to 13th Century)," in *Craftsmen and Merchants: Essays in South Indian Urbanism,* ed. Narayani Gupta (Chandigarh: Urban History Association of India, 1993), 27-42.

20. Noboru Karashima, *South Indian History and Society: Studies from Inscriptions A.D. 850-1800* (Delhi: Oxford University Press, 1984).

21. Susan J. Lewandowski, "Changing Form and Function in the Ceremonial and the Colonial Port City in India: An Historical Analysis of Madurai and Madras," *Modern Asian Studies*, 11, 1 (1977), 183-212; George Michell and Bharath Ramamrutham, *Temple Towns of Tamil Nadu* (Bombay: Marg Publications: 1993).

22. Meera Abraham, *Two Medieval Merchant Guilds of South India* (New Delhi: Manohar, 1988); R. Champakalakshmi, *Trade, Ideology and Urbanization: South India 300 BC to AD 1300* (New Delhi: Oxford University Press, 1996).

23. The terminology appearing in Tamil inscriptions differentiates between small "paths" (*vati*) that traversed fields, "roads" (*vali*) that ranged from the often quadrilateral patterns of urban sites to routes connecting contiguous settlements, and "big roads" (*peruvali*) that served as highways between major sites. The latter categories were unpaved but often ran along causeways raised above surrounding agricultural tracts, and in some cases still serve as the roadbeds for contemporary paved roads. See Jean Deloche, *Transport and Communications in India Prior to Steam Locomotion. Volume 1: Land Transport*, trans. James Walker (Delhi: Oxford University Press, 1993), 79-81; James Heitzman, "Urbanization and Political Economy in Early South India: Kanchipuram during the Chola Period," in *Structure and Society in Early South India: Essays in Honour of Noboru Karashima*, ed. Kenneth R. Hall (Delhi: Oxford University Press, 2001), 117-156; James Heitzman and S. Rajagopal, "Urban Geography and Land Measurement in the Twelfth Century: The Case of Kanchipuram," *Indian Economic and Social History Review*, 41, 3 (2004), 237-68.

24. Kenneth R. Hall, *Trade and Statecraft in the Age of the Cōlas*; James Heitzman, *Gifts of Power: Lordship in an Early Indian State* (New Delhi: Oxford University Press, 1997).

25. Urban population figures after 1950 cited in this article come from *World Gazetteer* (http://www.world-gazetteer.com).

26. The name Ulagalanda Perumal refers to the story of Vishnu's incarnation as a dwarf (*vamana*) who received a boon from Bali, a world-dominating demon, promising that he would obtain all the land he could cover in three steps. The lord then expanded into his cosmic form and covered the entire universe in just two steps, placing his foot on Bali's head with the third.

27. Adapted from Survey of India sheet; R. Champakalakshmi, *Trade, Ideology and Urbanization: South India 300 BC to AD 1300* (New Delhi: Oxford University Press, 1996); P. Shanmugam, "A City in Transition: Early Medieval Kanchipuram," in *Tamilnadu: Archaeological Perspective*, ed. K. Damodaran (Chennai: Department of Archaeology, Government of Tamilnadu, 2000), 8-33.

28. P. Shanmugam, "A City in Transition"; James Heitzman and S. Rajagopal, "Urban Geography and Land Measurement in the Twelfth Century: The Case of Kanchipuram."

29. Kenneth R. Hall and George W. Spencer, "The Economy of Kanchipuram, A Sacred Center in Early South India," *Journal of Urban History*, 6, 2 (1980), 127-51; R. Champakalakshmi, *Trade, Ideology and Urbanization: South India 300 BC to AD 1300.*

30. K. A. Nilakantha Sastri, *Studies in Cōḷa History and Administration*, Madras University Historical Series 7 (Madras: University of Madras, 1932).

31. Guesses of Kanchipuram's population resemble those made for contemporary cities that served as political and commercial seats in Rajasthan. See Kailash Chand Jain, *Ancient Cities and Towns of Rajasthan: A Study of Culture and* Civilization (Delhi: Motilal Banarsidass, 1972).

32. Government of Karnataka, *Master Plan for Hampi Local Planning Area* (Hospet: Hampi World Heritage Management Authority, 2006) (http://www.bellarynic.in/HMP/Hampi-Master-Plan.html).

33. Adapted from Survey of India sheet; John M. Fritz, George Michell, and M. S. Nagaraja Rao, *Where Kings and Gods Meet: The Royal Centre at Vijayanagara, India* (Tucson: University of Arizona Press, 1984); Kathleen D. Morrison, *Fields of Victory: Vijayanagara and the Course of Intensification* (Berkeley: Archaeological Research Facility, University of California, 1995).

34. Fritz, Michell, and Rao, *Where Kings and Gods Meet.*

35. Dominic J. Davison-Jenkins, *The Irrigation and Water Supply Systems of Vijayanagara* (New Delhi: Manohar and American Institute of Indian Studies, 1997).

36. Kathleen D. Morrison, *Fields of Victory: Vijayanagara and the Course of Intensification* (Berkeley: Archaeological Research Facility, University of California, 1995), 64-66, 86-88.

37. Phillip B. Wagoner, "From 'Pampa's Crossing' to 'The Place of Lord Virupaksha,' Architecture, Cult, and Patronage at Hampi before the Founding of Vijayanagara," in *Vijayanagara: Progress of Research 1989-91*, ed. D. Devaraj and C. S. Pahl (Mysore: Directorate of Archaeology and Museums, 1996), 141-74; "Architecture and Royal Authority under the Early Sangamas," in *New Light on Hampi: Recent Research at Vijayanagara*, ed. John M. Fritz and George Michell (Mumbai: Marg Publications, 2001), 12-23.

38. Robert Sewell, *A Forgotten Empire: Vijayanagara*, (Reprint. New Delhi: National Book Trust, 1962), 253-69.

39. Anila Verghese, "Deities, Cults and Kings at Vijayanagara," *World Archaeology*, 36, 3 (2004), 416-31.

40. John McKim Malville, "Cosmic Landscape and Urban Layout," in *New Light on Hampi: Recent Research at Vijayanagara*, 112-25.

41. Philip B. Wagoner, *Tidings of the King: A Translation and Ethnohistorical Analysis of the Rayavacakamu* (Honolulu: University of Hawai'i Press, 1993), 33-50.

42. Noboru Karashima, *Towards a New Formation: South Indian Society Under Vijayanagara Rule* (Delhi: Oxford University Press, 1994).

43. Burton Stein, *Vijayanagara*, The New Cambridge History of India 1.2. (Cambridge:. Cambridge University Press, 1989), 21-27, 57-61, 72-76, 86-88; Jean Deloche, *Senji (Gingi): Ville fortifiée du pays tamoul* (Paris and Pondicherry: École française d'Extrême-Orient and Institut français de Pondichéry, 2000).

44. George Michell and Richard Eaton, *Firuzabad: Palace City of the Deccan* (Oxford and New York: Oxford University Press, 1992). See also Elizabeth Lambourn's study in this volume.

45. George Michell and Mark Zebrowski, *Architecture and Art of the Deccan Sultanates*, New Cambridge History of India 1: 7 (Cambridge: Cambridge University Press, 1999), 23-52; Bianca Maria Alfieri and Federico Borromeo, *Islamic Architecture of the Indian Subcontinent* (London: Laurence King, 2000), 144-73.

46. Jos J. L. Gommans and Dirk H.A. Kolff, *Warfare and Weaponry in South Asia 1000-1800* (New Delhi: Oxford University Press, 2001), 26-39.

47. Adapted from Henry Cousens, *Bijapur and Its Architectural Remains*. Archaeological Survey of India, Imperial Series 37 (Bombay: Government Central Press, 1916).

48. Henry Cousens, *Bijapur and Its Architectural Remains*. Archaeological Survey of India, Imperial Series 37 (Bombay: Government Central Press, 1916); Klaus Rotzer, Bijapur: Alimentation en eau d'une ville Musalmane du Dekkan aux XVIe-XVIIe siècles, *Bulletin de l'École française d'Extrême-Orient* 73 (1984), 125-96.

49. Richard M. Eaton, *The Sufis of Bijapur: Social Roles of Sufis in Medieval India* (Princeton: Princeton University Press, 1978).

50. Sinnappah Arasaratnam, *Maritime India in the Seventeenth Century* (Delhi: Oxford University Press, 1994); Geneviève Bouchon, "A Microcosm: Calicut in the Sixteenth Century," in *Asian Merchants and Businessmen in the Indian Ocean and the China Sea*, ed. Denys Lombard and Jean Aubin (New Delhi: Oxford University Press, 2000), 40-49.

51. M. N. Pearson, *The Portuguese in India*, New Cambridge History of India 1.1. (Cambridge: Cambridge University Press, 1987).

52. K. N. Chaudhuri, *Trade and Civilisation in the Indian Ocean: An Economic History from the Rise of Islam to 1750* (Cambridge: Cambridge University Press, 1985); Sinnappah Arasaratnam, *Merchants, Companies and Commerce on the Coromandel Coast 1650-1740* (Delhi: Oxford University Press, 1986), 39-63, 265-71; Om Prakash, *European Commercial Enterprise in Pre-colonial India*, New Cambridge History of India 2.5 (Cambridge: Cambridge University Press, 1998), 163-74.

53. Ashin Das Gupta, *Indian Merchants and the Decline of Surat 1700-1750*, Beiträge zur Südasienforschung, Südasien-Institut, Universität Heidelberg 40 (Wiesbaden: Franz Steiner Verlag, 1979); Balkrishna Govind Gokhale, *Surat in the Seventeenth Century: A Study in Urban History of Pre-modern India*, Scandinavian Institute of Asian Studies Monograph Series 28 (London and Malmo: Curzon Press, 1979); Sinnappah Arasaratnam, "India and the Indian Ocean in the Seventeenth Century," in *India and the Indian Ocean 1500-1800*, ed. Ashin Das Gupta and M. N. Pearson (Calcutta: Oxford University Press, 1987), 94-130.

54. Sinnappah Arasaratnam and Aniruddha Ray, *Masulipatnam and Cambay: A History of Two Port-towns 1500-1800* (New Delhi: Munshiram Manoharlal, 1994).

55. John E. Brush, "The Growth of the Presidency Towns," in *Urban India: Society, Space and Image*, Duke University Program in Comparative Studies on Southern Asia, Monograph and Occasional Papers Series 10, ed. Richard G. Fox (Durham NC: Duke University Press, 1970), 91-114.

56. Adapted from Jean Deloche, *Le vieux Pondichéry (1673-1824)*.

57. Unknown to the French, Pondicherry lay just a few kilometers north of a site called Arikamedu, known to the Greeks as Poduke and today also called Virampatnam, lying on the bank of the Ariyankuppam River where its final northward bend provides a safe anchorage just before it joins the Bay of Bengal. Several warehouse and production clusters survive in a mound stretching about 500 meters (1640 feet) along the river. Finds of Roman amphorae and other ceramics and artworks of Mediterranean origin indicate the direct import of wine, olive oil, and fish sauce peaking between 50 BCE and 50 CE. Scholars have traced the growth of a glass bead industry at Arikamedu that supplied a market reaching China and Japan by the third century at the latest. See Vimala Begley, ed., *The Ancient Port of Arikamedu: New Excavations and Researches 1989-1992* (Pondichéry: Centre d'Histoire et d'Archéologie, École Française d'Extrême-Orient, 1996); Peter Francis, *Asia's Maritime Bead Trade 300 B.C. to the Present* (Honolulu: University of Hawai'i Press, 2002), 27-50.

58. Om Prakash, *European Commercial Enterprise in Pre-colonial India*, 147; Jean Deloche, *Le vieux Pondichéry (1673-1824) revisité d'apres les plans anciens*, Collection indologie 99 (Pondicherry: Institut français de Pondichéry and École française d'Extrême-Orient, 2005).

59. Rose Vincent, ed., *Pondichéry, 1674-1761: L'échec d'un rêve d'empire*, Série Memoires 24 (Paris: Éditions Autrement, 1992); Jean Deloche, *Le vieux Pondichér.*

60. John E. Brush, "The Growth of the Presidency Towns"; Soumitra Sreemani, *Anatomy of a Colonial Town: Calcutta, 1756-1794* (Calcutta: Firma KLM Private Limited, 1994), 177-78.

61. Sébastien Le Prestre de Vauban, *A Manual of Siegecraft and Fortification*, trans. George A. Rothrock (Ann Arbor: University of Michigan Press, 1968).

Index

jun hu (military household), 129
Junagadh, 73
junces (junks), 187
Junior Ruler (Vietnam), 161
Jurchen, 11

Kachchh, 61-68
Kaddiramapur, 315
Kadi (Muslim "jurists"), 264, 268-269, 275-276, 278
Kafadar, 278
Kaifeng, 112, 142
Kailasantha Temple, 312
Kakatiya dynasty, 314
Kalabhra, 307
Kalah, 100
Kalimantan, 186
Kalyan, 68
Kalyani, 70
Kamakshi temple, 310
Kamalapuram, 314-316
Kamasutra, 307
Kampili, 314
Kanara, 64, 70, 72
Kanchipuram/Kancipuram, 13, 25, 303, 310, 328
Kangxi (Emperor), 221
kanun law, 270
kapukullar (slaves of the gate), 261
Karaikal, 326
Karaman, 267
karaweik (goose), 249
Karbala, 274
Karim, 61
Karnataka, 308, 314, 321
Kathaka (Gotama Siddhartha's horse), 245-246
katis (measurement), 185
Kautilya, 304
Kaveri, 309
Kedayan, 186
kehu (tenants), 104
Keling, 192
Kerala, 326
khafila (convoys), 323
khil^ca.(ritual gifting), 73
Khalji, 55-58, 63, 72, 81
Khandesh, 287, 289, 296
Khānfū, 60, 78
khaṭībs ("preachers"), 55, 61-63, 65-67, 69-71, 73, 75-76
Khazar, 59
khil'a (court ritual), 290
Khinmon, 236, 242-243, 245-246
Khmer, 205, 218
Khuldabad, 289-290, 297
khuṭba (sermon), 55-56, 61, 65, 73-74, 76, 77-83
Kilifar, 275
Kim Cang, 212
Kim Son, 212, 215
Kinbāya (Cambay), 59, 64-66, 72, 77, 80, 82
King-bac, 169
Kinh Ky Tu Phu (Four Pillars of the Capital), 163
Kinh-dong City (East of the Capital), 169
Kitāb futūḥ al-buldān, 68
Kitāb ṣūrat al-arḍ, 59
Kofuku Temple, 209
Kofuku-ji, 208
Kollam (Quilon), 73
konak ("city square"), 272-273
Kondanna, 250
Konkan, 58, 61, 64, 70, 296
Kota Baru, 186
Kota Batu, 185
kou (individuals), 103
Koxinga, 128, 209
Kozhikode (Calicut), 322
kraton (court), 192, 195
kruvnia danuk ("blood tribute"), 263
Kūdra (Godhra), 65-66
küffar(infidels), 265
Kugha, 59
Kullars (Janissary "factions"), 277-278
kuls (slaves), 278
Kundūr, 57-58
Kwangching Liu, 215
ky nam houng (Cochinchinese incense wood), 214
Kyaung U temple, 247
Kyushu, 116

Laguna, 188
Lahore, 303
Lalutan (Liloan), 190
Lamībāsūr (Barcelore), 64, 70
Lam-kinh, 158, 165, 169-170, 172
Lam-son, 158, 163-167, 170
Lao, 164, 167, 170
Laoe, 188
Lapulapu, 191
La-Thanh, 157
Laung U Hmaw, 247, 250
Lay Htat Kyuang U, 245
Le dynasty, 158, 164, 166-172, 221